# Teaching Secondary Mathematics

Solidly grounded in up-to-date research, theory and technology, *Teaching Secondary Mathematics* is a practical, student-friendly, and popular text for secondary mathematics methods courses. It provides clear and useful approaches for mathematics teachers, and shows how concepts typically found in a secondary mathematics curriculum can be taught in a positive and encouraging way. The thoroughly revised fourth edition combines this pragmatic approach with truly innovative and integrated technology content throughout. Synthesized content between the book and comprehensive companion website offers expanded discussion of chapter topics, additional examples, and technological tips.

Each chapter features tried-and-tested pedagogical techniques, problem-solving challenges, discussion points, activities, mathematical challenges, and student-life-based applications that will encourage students to think and do.

New to the fourth edition:

- A fully revised and updated chapter on technological advancements in the teaching of mathematics
- Connections to both the updated NCTM Focal Points as well as the new Common Core State Standards well-integrated throughout the text
- Problem-solving challenges and sticky questions featured in each chapter to encourage students to think through everyday issues and possible solutions
- A fresh interior design to better highlight pedagogical elements and key features
- A companion website with chapter-by-chapter video lessons, teacher tools, problem solving Q&As, helpful links and resources, and embedded graphing calculators.

**David Rock** is Dean of the School of Education at the University of Mississippi, USA.
**Douglas K. Brumbaugh** was Professor of Mathematics Education at the University of Central Florida, USA.

# Teaching Secondary Mathematics

## Fourth Edition

**David Rock**
**Douglas K. Brumbaugh**

 Routledge
Taylor & Francis Group

NEW YORK AND LONDON

First published 2013
by Routledge
711 Third Avenue, New York, NY 10017

Simultaneously published in the UK

by Routledge
2 Park Square, Milton Park, Abingdon, Oxon OX14 4RN

*Routledge is an imprint of the Taylor & Francis Group, an informa business*

*Library of Congress Cataloging-in-Publication Data*

Brumbaugh, Douglas K., 1939–
Teaching secondary mathematics. — 4th edition / by David Rock and Douglas K. Brumbaugh.
    pages cm
  Brumbaugh's name appears first on the earlier editions.
  Includes bibliographical references and index.
    ISBN 978-0-415-52049-2 (pbk.) — ISBN 978-0-203-12157-3 (e-book)
1. Mathematics—Study and teaching (Secondary)   I. Rock, David, 1964–   II. Title.
QA11.2.B854   2013
510.71'2—dc23       2012037601

ISBN: 978-0-415-52049-2 (pbk)
ISBN: 978-0-203-12157-3 (ebk)

Typeset in Times New Roman PS
by Apex Co Vantage, LLC

Printed and bound in the United States of America by Sheridan Books, Inc. (a Sheridan Group company)

# Dedication

Douglas Kent Brumbaugh (May 26, 1939–May 31, 2010)

This edition and all future editions are dedicated to Douglas Kent Brumbaugh, whose life influenced thousands of people across the globe! It was my true honor to have known Doug. He was more than a teacher; he was a mentor and true friend. Doug's passion and commitment to teaching and learning have shaped not only my professional and personal life, but also the lives of so many others.

In 1990, after three years as a systems analyst for two defense contractors, I walked into Doug's office for the first time. I told him that I wanted to change careers to become a math teacher. He asked me to sit down. He then asked why I wanted to become a teacher of mathematics. As I started to explain my past and why I had not become a teacher earlier in my life . . . he stopped me. He quickly said, "I am not here to judge your past but I am interested in your future and how I can help you become a teacher." And help me he truly did! His inspiration and guidance provided continual support for the past 22 years.

While you, the reader, may not have known Doug, his legacy and influence lives on through this book. Doug was a helper, a doer, a builder, and a powerful motivator. He believed in your potential as a human being. As you read this book, you can hear his voice guide you and challenge you to become the best possible teacher you can be. As you ask yourself questions, you are asking Doug, as well. No question was wasted as long as you understood that another question would come in return.

Doug was truly one of the most gifted and intelligent men I have ever known, but he always downplayed his own true gifts. There really was never a "stupid question," just a question that went unasked, which was unacceptable to Doug. This was who he was. When his phone rang, it was always answered. He never screened his calls. When a message was left for Doug, he returned the call as soon as he possibly could, regardless of what he was doing. No matter how many e-mails he received, he would spend the time to answer each and every e-mail, especially at 4:00 AM, his normal time to begin the day.

Doug, I miss you each day. From the bottom of my heart, thank you!

David

As Doug Brumbaugh always said, "Teach our students for their future, not our past."

Each student deserves your full attention. I can promise you that Doug believed and lived this every day.

# Contents

# Preface

This book is the result of the urging of former students, teachers, colleagues, and friends of Doug Brumbaugh to put his Secondary Mathematics Methods course at the University of Central Florida into print. It is designed to make you, a future teacher of mathematics, think. We have used an informal writing style in order to maintain a dialogue with you. We want to be talking with you, not to or at you.

We assume you will think about and do the problems, questions, and activities as you read through this book. Our intent is to have you begin thinking about your future or current classroom now. We do not expect you to accept all of our ideas, but we do anticipate that you will react to them and, in the process, begin formulating your own teaching style.

As this book was created, several undergraduate mathematics education students voluntarily read the manuscript. We incorporated their suggestions. They liked the style and practical approach. They appreciated the fact that they could see a variety of theoretical bases revealed throughout the text. We opted to take an eclectic approach to the learning theories as opposed to stressing any single one. Our assumption is that your teacher will emphasize an approach or preference. Between your teacher and this text, you should be more able to make an informed decision about how you will approach your professional teaching career.

We assume that you will have had some prior exposure to general learning theory and educational methods. This text is designed to build on those, coupled with experiences, specializations, and preferences of your teacher. We provide a collection of examples, activities, problems, challenges, and lessons using a variety of environments. They are designed to furnish you with a broad base of ideas that will stimulate the formative development of thoughts and models you will employ in your classroom.

The text is organized into three parts: General Fundamentals, Mathematics Education Fundamentals, and Content and Strategies. The General Fundamentals chapters (1–4) assume some formal background in courses designed to provide a broad overview of education, curriculum, learning theory, discipline, planning, and adolescent behavior. Our chapters are intended to refresh your memories, provide a basis for discussion that will lead into specifics related to the teaching of mathematics, and motivate you to begin thinking about how you can become an effective teacher of mathematics at the secondary level.

The Mathematics Education Fundamentals chapters (5–8) are designed to be more specific. Here we begin dealing more directly with topics within the mathematics education environment. Each chapter deals with a subject that will permeate your instruction. We encourage you to plan thoroughly long before you cover any topic with your class. As you plan, you need to think of how you will incorporate technology, problem solving, discovery, and proof into your lessons.

The Content and Strategies chapters (9–15) build on the General Fundamentals and Mathematics Education Fundamentals. We assume you will discuss these issues in the class using this text. This final section is designed to capitalize on those discussions and on the expertise and preferences of your teacher. It will provide you with models of how concepts typically found in a secondary mathematics curriculum can be delivered so all students develop a positive attitude about learning and using mathematics in their daily lives.

You are the major theme of this book. We try to talk with you. It is not our intent to provide you with the impression that we know all the answers. We do think that the dialogue between you, your teacher, and us can be beneficial as you grow and transition into a secondary teacher of mathematics. We want to motivate you to become a practicing professional who is a lifelong learner. We use a variety of approaches to stimulate your thinking (technology, reflective-thought questions, mathematical challenges, student-life-based applications, games, tricks, and group discussions). These approaches, coupled with the teaching styles you have seen in your pre-K to college career, study and readings in other classes, the interactions in and around the class using this text, and life in general, will all contribute to making you into the teacher you want to become.

As Doug Brumbaugh's coauthor, I am honored to bring you this fourth edition of *Teaching Secondary Mathematics*. Since the first edition, many things have changed in mathematics education as well as in this book;

- All chapters have been updated to incorporate current thinking.
- Technological advancements have resulted in a *significant* rewrite of chapter 5. I challenge you to carefully consider the major impact this chapter can have on your thoughts about the teaching and learning of mathematics.

- The Common Core State Standards Initiative was implemented by the National Governors Association Center for Best Practices and the Council of Chief School Officers (CCSSO), with mathematics becoming one of the first content areas to be adopted.
- Historical references for all mathematicians mentioned throughout the book have been added within the text and in the margins for easy reference.
- Updated Internet references and resources have been incorporated to enhance the use of the text.
- A course website has been developed to enhance the content of this book and includes:

  - Short videos to assist with strategies for teaching mathematics.
  - Additional exercises to stimulate thought and discussions.
  - A current list of technological resources as they are discovered.
  - Solutions to Problem-Solving Challenges at the end of each chapter.
  - Up-to-date information for the reader.

# Acknowledgments

Several people urged us to create this book. One major stimulus to getting it off the ground was Dr. Piyush Agrawal, who pushed it past thought and into writing. As was the case with the original manuscript, countless individuals helped us with the preparation of each revision. We acknowledge and thank all of them. There are a few that deserve special recognition.

Much of the outline and basic ideas contained in Chapter 15 Probability and Statistics are attributable to Dr. Marie Causey. Others who aided in the development of Chapter 15 include Peggy Moch, Melanie Miller, and Wendy Bush. After the chapter was finalized, longtime friend, colleague, and education statistics expert Dr. Chuck Dziuban looked through the material carefully. Thanx to one and all.

We offer a special thanks to the following undergraduate students who reacted to draft forms of the original manuscript: Rick Able, Ursula Fueerecker-Brogan, Katherine Harting, Roy Jones, Charity Martin, Peggy Moch, Glenn Oncay, Elizabeth Porter, Armando Royero, Frank Wargo, and Joe Woodward.

We are grateful to additional mathematics educators who took the time to review this manuscript to provide valuable feedback. Thank you for your time and effort.

My editor, Catherine Barnard, was an invaluable motivator to keep the project going. Without her, this book would not exist. I am also grateful to the staff at Taylor and Francis for their hard work and dedication.

People are factors that help mold who we are and what we become. Each person listed here is special. Our family and loved ones are obviously connected to us and have had a tremendous impact on us. Beyond that are all those we have met in the classroom, too countless to name, and yet each has exerted some level of influence on us. To all of you, we say—THANX!

# PART I
## General Fundamentals

**CHAPTER 1:** Introduction

**CHAPTER 2:** Learning Theory, Curriculum, and Assessment

**CHAPTER 3:** Planning

**CHAPTER 4:** Skills in Teaching Mathematics

# Introduction

**1**

What makes an effective teacher of mathematics? Who was your favorite teacher of mathematics? What qualities did that teacher possess, both inside and outside the classroom, that continue to keep the memory of that teacher with you? The effective teacher of mathematics exhibits many qualities. The "effective teacher of mathematics" must be an effective teacher as well as a competent mathematics instructor. Many studies have been conducted to identify those true qualities that all "good" teachers possess. The only two that are consistently identified are warmth and a sense of humor. Unfortunately, affective qualities are quite difficult to measure.

The effective teacher of mathematics should have competency in the mathematics being taught as well as its prerequisites. If the teacher is not competent and confident with the subject matter, difficulties will be encountered creating positive mathematical experiences best suited for the development of the learner. You must have the desire to learn mathematics. You must have the desire to learn how to educate the students. You must have the desire to learn how to supply the optimum mathematics environment for each student. An effective teacher continues to investigate new mathematical knowledge and effective teaching strategies. As you do, your thirst and excitement will easily be seen by your students. If you do not know an answer to a question asked of you by a student, hopefully your thirst for knowledge will drive you to pursue the situation until you do possess that information. At the same time, you can stimulate your students to make similar pursuits, as you travel the road to new knowledge together.

The effective teacher of mathematics must be devoted to the profession. A teacher must create a stimulating atmosphere conducive to learning. Whether in mathematics or in some other area, the teacher must possess the desire, passion, and patience to facilitate the learning of others. An effective teacher of mathematics wants to help erase the fear and anxiety that mathematics represents to so many students. A true teacher is always willing to learn new methods and strategies for introducing concepts to students.

As stated in the National Council of Teachers of Mathematics (NCTM) Curriculum and Evaluation Standards for School Mathematics (NCTM, 1989), an effective teacher of mathematics will be able to motivate all students to learn mathematics. Similar ideas are raised in NCTM's Principles and Standards for School Mathematics (NCTM, 2000). Mathematics is a key to many opportunities. It opens doors to careers, enables informed decisions, and helps us compete as a nation (Mathematical Sciences Education Board [MSEB], 1989). The only constant today's students will face in their working lives will be change. It is predicted that these students will change careers—not jobs—as many as five times. Changing a career implies major reeducation. If even a part of the statement about changing careers is accepted, teachers of mathematics have an awesome responsibility. We must teach our students to absorb new ideas, adapt to change, cope with ambiguity, perceive patterns, and solve unconventional problems (MSEB, 1989). Without these abilities, today's students will have a difficult time in their working future. A large segment of our society is willing and even eager to make statements like, "I hated math in school," "math, yuck," and "I am terrible in math." When people find out you are a teacher of mathematics, you are likely to hear many of these comments. How can the multitude of negative remarks continue to be acceptable in our society? Imagine if you were a teacher of English; would a person be eager to admit he or she is illiterate? If an individual said, "I cannot read," countless individuals would express sorrow, perhaps pity, and then skirmish to find ways to help that individual learn to read. Why is there not such a cry for the individual who confesses an inability to do mathematics? It is our commission to set the wheels in motion that will change this attitude. The time to change is now!

## WHAT IS MATHEMATICS?

What is mathematics? What kind of question is that? You might wonder why we would start with such a question. If we are going to be concerned about teaching mathematics to others, we need some idea of what it is we are teaching. Mathematics is "the study of quantity, form, arrangement, and magnitude; especially, the methods and processes for disclosing, by rigorous concepts and self-consistent symbols, the properties and relations of quantities and magnitudes, whether in the abstract, pure mathematics, or in their practical connections, applied mathematics" (Funk & Wagnalls, 1968, p. 835). Mathematics is "the systematic treatment of magnitude, relationships between figures and forms, and relations between quantities expressed symbolically ("Mathematics," 2005). Bertrand Russell said:

> Pure mathematics consists entirely of such associations as that, if such and such a proposition is true of anything, then such and such another proposition is true of that thing. It is essential not to discuss whether the first proposition is really true, and not to mention what the anything is of which it is supposed to be true. . . . If our hypothesis is about anything and not about some one or more particular things, then our deductions constitute mathematics. Thus mathematics may be defined as the subject in which we never know what we are talking about nor whether what we are saying is true. (Newman, 1956, p. 4)

After reading the three definitions of mathematics, are you comfortable with explaining these definitions to others? An eminent mathematician once said that he would not be "satisfied with his knowledge of mathematical theory until he could explain it to the next man he met on the street" (Newman, 1956, p. 4). This relates to the teaching of mathematics. As teachers of mathematics, we are responsible for providing effective learning environments that incorporate real-life mathematical activities. Students learn by making connections through a variety of experiences. Knowledge is gained through the context of meaningful activities. The teacher

must also emphasize student-centered instruction. The learning environment (cognitive, affective, and physical) should be conducive to the optimal learning of each individual.

The previous statements describe a constructivist's approach to teaching mathematics. The constructivist view relies on the premise that knowledge is constructed by learners as they attempt to make sense of their own experiences. Students must become active participants involved in the total learning environment. If either the teacher or student falls short of their given responsibility, the net result will be a less than satisfactory learning environment for mathematics.

We must be able to motivate all students to learn mathematics. No longer can we accept the idea that mathematics is only for the best and brightest. Too many basic mathematical concepts are an integral part of our daily lives to permit such a position. NCTM promotes significant mathematical learning for all students. Without such a goal, we, as a nation, risk creating a dichotomy in our society: those who can do mathematics and those who cannot.

To change our students and give them a willingness to accept mathematics, we need to understand the field. Some say mathematics is a way of thinking. That becomes evident to us as we do proofs, examine patterns, or organize our approaches to new and different problems. Others say mathematics is a language. We can understand that statement as we talk in our special language of Xs and Ys, graphs, patterns, and so on. However, if that language is one spoken only by a select few, what good is it? All students are capable of learning mathematics, and it is imperative that we include all of them in our inner circle of basic mathematical language. The inclusion should lead them to understand the world of mathematics and empower them to be more productive members of society.

Mathematics is often said to be an organized structure of knowledge. If one understands the structure, one is capable of surviving in the world of mathematics. Without the structural understanding, a student seems doomed to failure as far as being able to function mathematically. Too many students are willing to accept this risk, often out of ignorance. Many mathematics classes rarely experience applications of mathematics in real-world settings. Students assume that there will be no need for mathematics in their future world. It is our task to get students beyond this level of thinking.

The study of patterns is another method of defining mathematics. As we look at Fibonacci's sequence, it is obvious that patterns exist and we can use these to provide useful examples. Mathematics abounds with examples of the study of patterns. It seems natural and useful to us. How do we communicate that value to our students? The Fibonacci (Leonardo Pisano Fibonacci, http://www.gap-system.org/~history/Mathematicians/Fibonacci.html) sequence is 1, 1, 2, 3, 5, 8, . . . , where each new term is found by taking the sum of the two preceding terms; it supposedly grew out of the study of rabbit reproduction starting with two mature adults, one of each sex. This sequence of numbers appears in a variety of settings. For example, if the clockwise and counter-clockwise spirals of a sunflower are counted, the results will always be two successive terms in the Fibonacci sequence.

A generalized Lucas (Francois Edouardo Anatole Lucas, http://www.gap-system.org/~history/Mathematicians/Lucas.html) sequence is defined as a Fibonacci sequence that begins with any two integers (not 1 and 1), such as 2 and 5, for example, 2, 5, 7, 12, 19, 31, . . . , where each term is the sum of the two preceding terms. This can be used to develop an interesting number trick that has a variety of extensions. A student writes a 10-term Lucas sequence so everyone except the person doing the trick can see the sequence. The class has two responsibilities: assure the addition is correct, and be certain that the person doing the trick does not see the values of the sequence until the appropriate time. When the 10 terms are listed, the trickster looks at the sequence and announces the sum of all 10 terms.

This "sum of 10 terms in a Fibonacci-style sequence" can be used several places in the curriculum. Addition practice is not out of the question, because students can be convinced they need to be sure the trick worked (note the beginning of a "need" for proof). Proof can also be seen in the algebraic approach to the trick. Extend what is shown in this text by factoring (a skill found in several locations within the algebra curriculum) out an 11, giving $11(5x + 8y)$. The $(5x + 8y)$ is the seventh term down (or fourth one up) in the ten-term sequence. Stress this aspect of the trick and you see an application of the distributive property of multiplication over addition on the set of real numbers. Focusing on $11(5x + 8y)$ provides the opportunity to investigate the origin of the topics worked with earlier in the curriculum. Students have encountered concepts such as the distributive property of multiplication over addition in a given set, order of operations, and $2(l + w)$ at various points throughout the curriculum. This particular investigation can be used to amplify many mathematical concepts and provide bridges between various locations in the curriculum. It is important for the mathematical development of your students that you become aware of these connections.

### EXERCISE 1.1

1. If the first two terms of a Lucas sequence are 3 and 7, will the same sum be derived from a sequence starting with a 7, followed by a 3? Why or why not? Develop a series of questions you would use to assist a student in learning this result.

**Additional exercises can be found on the website.**

## WORKING AT TEACHING MATHEMATICS

Some people appear to be natural teachers. They possess that certain something that allows them to clearly deliver messages to others. Most people need to work at being effective teachers. The question becomes, how do we become proficient teachers of mathematics? How do we work at it?

There is no definitive list to becoming a competent teacher of mathematics. Certainly, attitude and enthusiasm must be considered. If we are not

| | Numeric Example | Algebraic Example |
|---|---|---|
| | 2 | $x$ |
| | 5 | $y$ |
| | 7 | $x + y$ |
| | 12 | $x + 2y$ |
| | 19 | $2x + 3y$ |
| | 31 | $3x + 5y$ |
| | 50 | $5x + 8y$ |
| | 81 | $8x + 13y$ |
| | 131 | $13x + 21y$ |
| | 212 | $21x + 34y$ |
| Sum | 550 | $55x + 88y$ |

excited about learning and doing mathematics, how can we expect our students to be? If we do not believe that all students can learn mathematics, then we will be hard-pressed to develop meaningful activities for our students.

In addition to attitude and enthusiasm, it is important to develop competency in mathematics. This sounds like a simple statement, and yet there is not complete agreement on how many mathematics courses must be taken to provide an adequate background for teaching the subject. Some college programs require a bachelor's degree in mathematics, with education courses offered as a part of a graduate degree, to meet state certification requirements. Others offer a certification program as a part of an undergraduate degree program in mathematics education. We are fortunate that NCTM and NCATE/CAEP (National Council for Accreditation of Teacher Education and the Council for the Accreditation of Educator Preparation) have provided guidelines for minimum standards for teacher certification in mathematics. Ultimately, each state has the final authority on minimum requirements for state certification and licensure in a specified teaching field.

If we are to be effective teachers of secondary mathematics, it is imperative that we understand the nature of our students. We need to investigate their interests and motivations. Once we know how students operate, it becomes our responsibility to take the knowledge we have and construct lessons that will attract their attention and stimulate learning. Specific examples of these and related issues are provided throughout this text.

Finally, there is a need to have effective lesson plans. Well-orchestrated lessons do not just happen. They require thought and organization. A daily lesson plan should focus on the important particulars regarding the organization and implementation that will make the learning activity successful for the student. A completed daily lesson plan should contain the following (Esler & Sciortino, 1991, pp. 43–44):

1. Topic
2. Goal statement(s): the purpose, concepts, or knowledge that the student will learn
3. Objective statement(s): activities used to assist the learner in achieving the goal(s)
   a. Concept objective(s) when appropriate
   b. Skill/attitude objective(s) when appropriate
4. Materials required (instructional and learning)

5. Procedures
   a. Set: how you introduce the lesson
   b. Instructional outline
   c. Examples (and nonexamples) of concepts
   d. Upper-level questions
   e. Review/closure/bridge to next lesson
   f. Assessment/evaluation procedures

Initially, there needs to be an objective for the lesson. Why is this topic being covered? As we rationalize why a topic is being taught, we must remember to look at it from the world of the students. We as adults might see applications of the topic in future mathematical arenas, but the students want to know where they can use it today. The lesson needs to connect the current topic with those from the past, while laying groundwork for those of the future. Ultimately, we must determine if the lessons were accomplished as designed. That is, we must evaluate ourselves as well as the students.

## GUIDELINES FOR TEACHING MATHEMATICS

Show sensitivity to the students. This cannot be superficial. Just like you can "read" your teachers, your students will be able to tell your sensitivity and sincerity levels. Students are human beings and, as such, are entitled to respect and concern for their personal growth.

"Cipher in the Snow" (Todhunter, 1975) is a story about a secondary student who dies on the way to school. He was a quiet boy, unnoticed by peers and teachers. The principal asks a teacher to relay the news of the boy's death to his family. The teacher was selected because, in the yearbook, the boy mentioned her as his favorite teacher. The teacher did not remember the boy! The story continues about the funeral and the struggle to find students to attend it as representatives of the school and his classmates. Ultimately, the teacher realized the need to be aware of each student and, in the process, to struggle to have a positive impact on each student in each class. An outgrowth of the experience was a vow by the teacher to assure that no student in future classes would remain unknown. She learned to be sensitive to the comments or actions of her students.

The preceding story illustrates the need to take students seriously. If a lesson does not go well, rather than assuming students were not paying attention, lacked adequate background, or were unmotivated, teacher reflection and self-evaluation should be performed. Did you strive to make the lesson interesting? Was your presentation clear? Were the examples similar to the problems in the homework assignment? Were the students involved in the lesson as it developed? Did the students have ample opportunity to seek clarification of the points presented? Answers to these questions will help you construct a more effective learning environment for all students.

A teacher of mathematics is often viewed as an answer machine. Rather than stimulating student thought by carefully steering inquiries so students can determine the answer for themselves, many teachers tell the answer. Refer to the algebraic development of the sum of 10 terms in a Lucas sequence. Would you have investigated why it worked if the algebraic approach had not been given? Would you have connected the factored sum with the seventh term down? Did you expect the answer in the upcoming text? Do you know how to apply Trachtenberg's multiplication by 11 rule (Cutler, 1960)? If self-motivated, lifelong learners are to be generated in our classrooms, we must learn to redirect the inquiries and motivate the students to accept responsibility for their own learning.

Redirecting a question is relatively easy to do. Consider a lesson in which the student is to discover the relationship between the length of the side of a square and the area when altering either the length or the area. Typically, a student is told that if the side length is doubled, the area is multiplied by four; if the side length is tripled, the area is increased by a factor of nine; and so forth. Use a dynamic geometry program. For this lesson, it will be assumed that you will be using a projection device and presenting the lesson to the entire class. Create a square in front of the class. One method is as follows:

1. Draw a segment.
2. Mark one end of the segment as rotation center.
3. Rotate the segment 90°.
4. Complete the triangle by joining segment endpoints.
5. Mark the hypotenuse as the mirror.
6. Reflect the two legs and third vertex.
7. Hide the diagonal "mirror" line segment.

(In the following dialogue, T refers to teacher and S to student)

T: How can the side length of the square be doubled?
S: Duplicate the square beside itself.

T: How can that be accomplished?
S: Use one side of the square as the mirror and then reflect the rest of the square over it. [Note that depending on the class, time, objectives for the day, and future lessons, it might be worthwhile to investigate other ways to accomplish this doubling with the class.]
T: What is the area now that the side has been doubled?
S: You need to double the other side, too.
T: How can I do that?
S: Mark one long side of the rectangle as the mirror. Then reflect the two squares over it.
T: What has doubling the side of the square done to the original area?
S: The new area is four times that of the original.
T: How do you know that?

This lesson could be extended to tripling the length of the side of the square, and more, as needed. The advantage here is that the students can see what is being discussed. By creating a mental image of the situation, they will better be able to formulate responses to similar problems in the future.

## EXERCISES 1.2

1. If the length of one side of a rectangle is doubled and the other tripled, what is the impact on the area of the rectangle? Does it matter if the roles are reversed as to which side is doubled and which is tripled? Why or why not?

2. If the base of a triangle is doubled and the height is quadrupled, what factor is the area multiplied by?

**Additional exercises can be found on the website.**

As an effective teacher of mathematics you must use different strategies in the classroom. One method would be direct instruction. Direct instruction is defined as the teacher placing the highest priority on the assignment and completion of academic activities. The teacher is responsible for selecting and directing the learning tasks for the student. One of the major goals for direct instruction is to maximize student learning time. Several studies have shown that a strong academic focus manifests greater student academic engagement and achievement

(Fisher et al., 1980; Madaus, Arasian, & Kellaghan, 1980; Rosenshine, 1985). You are probably all too familiar with the lecture mode, a common form of direct instruction. Still, lectures can make a positive contribution to the mathematics classroom, if they are dynamic, well planned, and organized. The use of the following guidelines can increase the effectiveness of your lecture:

1. Instructional objectives must be clearly stated. The teacher and the student must know exactly what they are trying to accomplish at all times.
2. Learning activities must match the desired objective. Inappropriate activities waste the time, cause confusion, and result in a lack of purpose and direction for both teachers and students.
3. Learning activities must be appropriate for each learner. The student must have a reasonably good chance of being successful. The curriculum should be success oriented.
4. The teacher should do everything possible to ensure maximizing "time on task," the time students are engaged in active learning during a class period.
5. The teacher should maintain an academic focus during learning activities.
6. The teacher should provide academic feedback of student work.
7. The teacher should handle discipline problems promptly (Esler & Sciortino, 1991, pp. 104–105).

Lecture, however, cannot be the only method of instruction in the classroom. It is the most efficient way for the teacher, but the focus should be on student learning, not convenience for the teacher. The use of indirect instruction also has advantages in the classroom. Indirect instruction promotes an increase in critical thinking and problem-solving skills. Students are encouraged to explore and discover information through the use of open-ended questions, group discussions and activities, experiments, and hands-on exercises. Indirect instruction has been shown to improve attitudes toward subject matter, especially for those students with a low success rate with direct instruction.

Consider discussing why it is necessary to know how to solve an equation like $2X = 6$ for $X$ by going through the detailed steps of the process. Groups of students have been assigned the task of establishing a speed trap. In a speed trap before the days of radar and VASCAR, two police cars were used. One was at the beginning of the trap and the other was at the end. A car would be timed through the distance, or trap. A more fundamental but similar approach is accomplished by drawing line segments on the road and timing vehicles through the distance from an airplane. If the car covered the distance in less than the computed legal time, the driver was speeding and, in the process, given an opportunity to have a discussion with one of the local department's finest officers. The formula $d = rt$ was being used to clock the cars through the trap. This is a generalized form of $2X = 6$. However, the numbers generated from the speed trap are not as easy to solve as those in $2X = 6$. Thus, the setting provides an opportunity to see the need to know the steps used in solving an equation like $2X = 6$.

The student groups are now ready to attack the problem. The teacher can adopt a variety of different roles in the setting. As a catalyst, the teacher can move between groups and prompt groups as necessary, providing them with just enough information to start them or keep them going. As an active participant, the teacher can accept a role in the group, being careful not to dominate and provide too many answers. Either as a group participant or as a catalyst, the teacher can serve as a resource person and experienced investigator. This cooperative group setting may be strange for the students, and they might need some help and direction acclimating to it.

## EXERCISES 1.3

1. Some schools do not permit students to go outside the classroom to do an activity like the speed trap described earlier. How could the activity be completed inside the classroom?
2. Describe at least two other variations of the speed trap activity that students could perform.

**Additional exercises can be found on the website.**

The phrase "teacher of mathematics" is used throughout this text, as opposed to "mathematics teacher." The reason is that the teacher of mathematics can be interpreted as being interested in teaching and doing mathematics. On the other hand, "mathematics teacher" can be thought of as someone who is into mathematics and happens to be teaching. An effective teacher of mathematics needs to be enthusiastic about teaching and mathematics. The two groups defined by these phrases cannot be thought of as mutually exclusive.

To exhibit enthusiasm about teaching, an individual needs to be knowledgeable about the age level of the student being taught. What are their basic characteristics? What makes the learner tick? These questions are dealt with in introductory or general education as well as in psychology courses, all of which are required in most education programs. We are assuming you have had some exposure to these ideas prior to using this text. The issues raised in class settings can be investigated as a part of the associated teaching assignments. Furthermore, observation, in and out of school, of individuals in the age category being taught will provide invaluable information on how to deal with them. You have lived through the age level you are observing, so remembering how things were for you then could provide some clues.

---

### EXERCISE 1.4

1. Think of your secondary teachers of mathematics. Hopefully at least one of them was a motivating factor in leading you to become a teacher of mathematics. List the characteristics of that teacher that helped you learn more about mathematics.

---

**Additional exercises can be found on the website.**

You are already showing enthusiasm for mathematics by selecting mathematics education as your area of concentration. There is so much more you can do. You need to continue to investigate the field. It has been said that the introduction of graphing and programmable calculators, along with symbol manipulating, function plotting, and dynamic geometry applications, has provided a multitude of opportunities for students to learn mathematics. Teachers who learn to use these applications, many of whom have strong mathematical backgrounds, have been known to make statements like, "I have learned a multitude of things about secondary mathematics that I did not know because of investigations done using technology." You have the wonderful opportunity to use technology to learn and teach mathematics as you go through the introductory stages of becoming a teacher of mathematics. What an exciting opportunity!

Another way you can continue to analyze the field is to keep investigating mathematics and ways to present it throughout your career. Regrettably, there are pressures in the education field that can deter this growth. These pressures come from all the demands placed on a teacher to do unrelated activities (attendance reports, school meetings, discipline problems, coaching, budgets, standardized tests, and school accountability and politics). You must guard against these pressures becoming convenient excuses not to continue your mathematical growth. Pursuing advanced course work and degrees is certainly one way to force yourself to stay current in the areas of teaching mathematics and its content.

Continuing your professional growth will provide you with a multitude of opportunities and examples of teaching mathematics. For example, the ability to conceptualize division by zero escapes many students. Investigating that topic can provide you with some new information that could be used with a class. Consider a "limit" approach to division by zero.

$$\frac{6}{n} = 1$$

$$\frac{6}{5} = 1.2$$

$$\frac{6}{4} = 1.5$$

$$\frac{6}{3} = 2$$

$$\frac{6}{2} = 3$$

$$\frac{6}{1} = 6$$

$$\frac{6}{0.5} = 12$$

$$\frac{6}{0.1} = 60$$

$$\frac{6}{0.000001} = 6,000,000$$

$$\frac{6}{0.00...001} = \text{approaches infinity}$$

The limit of $\frac{6}{n}$ as $n$ goes to zero is infinite.

The idea of limits can be used with the classic problem, "Fold a sheet of paper in half, in half again, in half again, etc., 50 times. How high will the stack be after the 50th fold?" Assume the paper is 0.003 inches thick and 1 square unit.

| Fold Number n | Stack Height (inches) (missing factor) | Stack Top Area (sq. unit) | Portion of Original Stack Top Area (factor) |
|---|---|---|---|
| Original | 0.003 | 1 | 1 |
| 1 | 0.006 | 0.5 | $\frac{1}{2}$ |
| 2 | 0.012 | 0.25 | $\frac{1}{4}$ |
| 3 | 0.024 | 0.125 | $\frac{1}{8}$ |
| 4 | 0.048 | 0.0625 | $\frac{1}{16}$ |
| ⋮ | | | |
| 10 | 3.072 | 0.0009766 | $\frac{1}{1024}$ |
| ⋮ | | | |

Considering only the stack top area, as the number of folds increases, the number being divided by approaches zero. As $n$ increases, the factor approaches zero (in division problems divisor, dividend, and quotient can be expressed as factor, product, and missing factor) and the missing factor (division answer) becomes infinitely large and undefined.

These last two examples of using limits to approach division by zero are not common. Thus, in your investigation of mathematics, you have learned new ways of looking at a standard topic. It may well be that this method could not be used with your classes, but your knowledge base has been expanded and, in the process, your interest and enthusiasm for mathematics piqued. Furthermore, there are several places within the curriculum where this example could be used. Early on, the idea of dividing a number by successively smaller numbers could be used as a skills development task. At the same time, groundwork is being laid for a later exposure that could extend the division to an algebraic notation of the problem. Still later, the idea of proof could be developed. Applying the concept to folding a paper in half many times allows the blending of the topic with exponents. These are only some of the places this topic could be inserted into the curriculum. There are others. Your responsibility becomes

twofold: learning about such things and deciding where each of them best fits into your curriculum.

## EXERCISE 1.5

1. Use a source like Newman's *The World of Mathematics* (1956), the *VNR Concise Encyclopedia of Mathematics* (Gellert, Kustner, Hellwich, & Kastner, 1977), Eves' *History of Mathematics* (1967), *Mathematics From the Birth of Numbers* (Gullberg, 1997) or the *MacTutor History of Mathematics Archive* (http://www.gap-system. org/~history/) to investigate a mathematical topic found in the secondary setting. You are to learn a new way of working with the topic. Present your conclusions in written form, giving appropriate bibliographic credit.

## ROLE OF MATHEMATICS IN THE WORLD

Students often struggle to see applications. For many, mathematics is a dead subject that has not changed over the years. The mathematics they see appears to have been chipped onto stone tablets and handed down from a mountain. It is the responsibility of all teachers of mathematics to change this impression.

Earlier in this chapter a speed trap was discussed. That application can be extended to drag racing, where a similar trap is used at the end of the quarter-mile run to determine the speed. The posted speeds are not the average speed of the run but, rather, the average speed over a short distance at the end of the run. Electronic equipment and computers are used to assure necessary accuracy and precision. The dragster can be used to show another application. Over the years, drag racing has migrated from a "shade tree mechanic" mentality to an extremely precise and professional multimillion-dollar atmosphere. With the increase in speed and power has come a tremendous expansion in the amount of information needed to maintain a competitive car. Drag racers often need to have several computers at their disposal (even to the extent of putting some in the car), because there is so much data gathered on each run. These results are compiled and used to guide alterations on the car for the next run.

In NASCAR (National Association for Stock Car Auto Racing), lap speeds are given to thousandths of a second. Tire temperatures are taken to help determine wear on the tires, and compound adjustments are made by the manufacturer to create a safer, longer-lasting product for consumers and race drivers. The volumes of data are compiled using computers and assorted spreadsheets, databases, and statistical packages. Richard Petty (the most successful stock-car racer of the 1980s) won 7 NASCAR Grand National championships, 7 Daytona 500 titles, and 200 races in his career. Petty commented that he had to change his operation because of the tremendous technological changes and complexities that entered the NASCAR arena. He stated that it is difficult for someone to compete, let alone win, without an understanding and use of the technology now available. Petty attributed part of the decrease in race wins in the latter years of his career to his reluctance to change from the old ways of running a race team to the technology-based patterns.

Another racing example shows an application of mathematics. During the 1993 NASCAR season, there were some spectacular scenes of cars getting airborne, flipping and rolling end-for-end. Rusty Wallace often got credit for having the wildest ride of 1993, as his car was shown flying several feet off the ground before rolling and tumbling to a stop several hundred feet from where it went airborne (http://www.youtube.com/watch?v=iLdvjpFYcIs). Show this video from YouTube to your class and you are likely catch the attention of your students. Engineering and wind tunnel tests led to conclusions that the car, when turned backward, acted like an airplane wing (foil). To stop cars from going airborne, flaps much like those found on airplane wings have been mandated on NASCAR cars. When a car spins backward and starts to lift, the flaps are automatically deployed, destroying the foil effect. Thus, rather than continuing to lift, the car is forced back to the ground. Replays of several incidents during the 1994 race season have shown the effectiveness of the flaps. Not only is this an application of mathematics, but it also shows how several different fields are brought together to solve a problem.

You might be thinking that the last few paragraphs are excessive, but it is important that you consider them from the vantage point of discussing the applications of mathematics. Students want to know where the things they are learning are used. That is not an unreasonable request, and it is something the NCTM Standards repeatedly call for to improve student learning. The difficulty is in obtaining information in areas that will allow you to build the background. Certainly all teachers of mathematics are not interested in racing and, thus, would not be inclined to use that topic as an example of the application of mathematics. Our experiences show that many students are interested in racing. If you accept that statement, along with the responsibility of viewing the world of applications through the eyes of students, it becomes imperative that you learn some basics about topics like racing.

One argument against the use of topics from the world of automotive racing is that it is a sport limited mainly to white males. Again, a little knowledge refutes that position. Willie T. Ribbs is an African American who received extensive publicity in the early 1990s for his driving at the Indianapolis 500 and NASCAR events. Shirley Muldowney achieved acclaim in the 1980s as a top driver in the fastest class of drag racing. In the late 1990s, a teenage girl achieved high acclaim as the driver of a top fuel dragster. Many of the world racing associations are of Hispanic heritage. In recent years, female driver Danica Patrick (http://www.danicaracing.com/) has made a huge name for herself on the Indy and NASCAR circuits. There are many more examples, but even these few can be used to attract the attention of some students.

We all have interests, hobbies, experiences, and imaginations. Combine those and you start to get suggestions of how you can begin to see some of the applications of mathematics. The difficulty is that we often take the mathematics we know for granted and do not realize the many different ways we use it. You are now being asked to look more carefully at the things you do and examine them for ideas of applications of mathematics. These topics can be inserted into your secondary curriculum with the intent of showing applications appealing to students, trying to intrigue them into a more careful and fruitful examination of the world of mathematics.

The history of mathematics, another area the NCTM Standards encourage us to insert into our classrooms, is rich with examples that show the creation of mathematics to solve problems. How does a spacecraft stay in orbit around the earth? Earth's gravity pulls on the craft, trying to get it back. At the same time, the craft is moving through space at a given velocity on a path that, for the sake of this discussion, will be assumed to be a circle around a sphere, the earth. A cutaway view would have

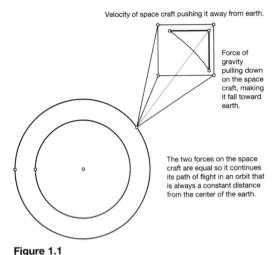

Velocity of space craft pushing it away from earth.

Force of gravity pulling down on the space craft, making it fall toward earth.

The two forces on the space craft are equal so it continues its path of flight in an orbit that is always a constant distance from the center of the earth.

**Figure 1.1**

the earth represented by a circle and the orbit as a concentric circle with a greater radius, as shown in Fig. 1.1.

Visualize a small segment of the craft's motion and suppose that during that time, the craft would fall 10 feet because of gravity. If the speed of the craft can be adjusted to move it forward 10 feet, then, since the earth "falls away because of its curvature," the distance between the craft and the earth is unchanged. Repetition of this scenario results in a circular orbit. As the radius of the orbit is increased, the speed of the craft can be decreased, because the pull of gravity decreases with distance from center of the earth.

Granted, this is a simplified description of how a craft stays in orbit, but the essentials are there. It certainly shows applications of mathematics. Another you might miss is an application of direct proportions (this concept alone can be placed in a wide variety of locations in the general mathematics and upper elementary curriculum); as the pull of gravity decreases, so does the required velocity of the craft to maintain orbit.

The space programs are wonderful examples of the need for development of mathematics. The initial suborbital flights were made when computers and calculators were in their formative stages. A simple analog computer was connected to switches and controllers so that when the little motors would run, the switches were turned on and off to control the flight. The computers did not do much data gathering or calculating. They looked at differences between voltages and also operated switches. The machines were on board the spacecraft but could

not measure or collect data the way they do now. Decisions were made on an electromechanical basis rather than from data gathering. Sequences were established to start at a given time and then run for a specified interval. If the craft was to head in a certain direction, the sequence would run so long and then a switch would activate another synchro motor to alter propulsion and change the movement or direction of the spacecraft.

At that time (1961), Control Data Corporation (CDC) had only a few engineers and technicians. CDC personnel visited the space operations in Florida. NASA engineers and their engineering subcontractors told CDC that machines (computers) capable of converting information from sensors were needed. All sorts of measurements needed to be converted into engineering units, so decisions could be made. These conversions gave a common language that could be interpreted. At the time, no system had the capability to do remote control. All of that technology had to be developed. Initial flights of the Mercury Program (http://www-pao.ksc.nasa.gov/history/mercury/mercury.htm) had no digital computers. There was one prototype that was used with the second flight. It had 8K (kilobytes) of memory! (It is difficult to find a USB drive with less than a gigabyte.) After the second flight, the memory was increased to 16K. CDC would design equipment to meet the specifications set forth by NASA. Eventually, the engineers asked for pictures of the fuel tanks and other parts of the spacecraft. Thus, the demand for computer drawing capabilities was born (R. Dorn, personal communication, 1995).

## EXERCISES 1.6

1. Describe mathematical applications or extensions related to a hobby or personal interest you have.

2. This text briefly shows examples from the worlds of racing and space, depicting how mathematics and applications grew out of need. Select some area that interests you and develop a written outline showing at least four areas where mathematics was developed or applied that you think could be used to appeal to secondary student curiosity.

**Additional exercises can be found on the website.**

## EXPAND CONCEPTS OR DEFINITIONS

Fractions provide a wealth of opportunity for discussion. In the discovery chapter, we discuss the use of the word "reduce." This term is quite common, particularly in the early grades. When a fraction is reduced, common factors are being divided out of both the numerator and denominator. We, in our infinite mathematical wisdom, know that the two fractions are equivalent. However, students are not that knowledgeable. How much verbiage and conceptualization can we expect of our students? The answer to that question has to influence us as we decide when to introduce concepts or expand them.

We would not expect a student to rationalize an algebraic expression if that student had not been exposed to fractions and many other prerequisite skills. That decision is clear. By the same token, it is fairly clear that we would not expect a student to do standard long division problems without the abilities in estimation, place value, multiplication, and subtraction.

In some areas, the decision is not as clear. Only recently has there been an effort to insert a great deal of probability and statistics into the K–12 curriculum. As topics are inserted, prerequisite skills must be defined. Elementary students are capable of arranging numbers in increasing or decreasing order. Does that mean it is appropriate to insert the concept of median into their curriculum? After learning to divide, students are asked to average their grades. Is it appropriate at that time to enter into discussions about mean?

## ANALYZE A PROBLEM IN MORE THAN ONE WAY

Traditionally, the teacher introduces a concept. Generally, a careful explanation of the concept is given, followed by appropriate examples. Throughout the explanation, questions prompt students for input, so there is some participation. When the teacher is satisfied that the idea has been adequately explained, seat work or homework problems are given. Often, the problems assigned are very similar. This is the standard direct teaching environment. An easy example would have a class finding the area of 20 different rectangles. Dimensions might be counting numbers, fractions, decimals, or a combination of elements of the rational numbers. Really, the problems are all the same; they just use different numbers.

There are alternative strategies that can be used to develop student comprehension when introducing new material. Suppose students are examining a triangle. Point D, which lies on one side of a triangle, is equidistant from all three vertices, A, B, and C. Prove triangle ABC is a right triangle, at least three different ways.

**Method 1** (usually the first one students see; Fig. 1.2):

AD = BD = CD

Segment AC is straight (side of given triangle)

Triangle CAD is isosceles

∠CAD and ∠ACD are congruent

Let ∠CAD and ∠ACD = $x$

Triangle BCD is isosceles

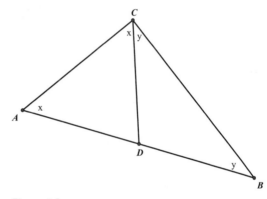

**Figure 1.2**

∠BCD and ∠CBD are congruent

Let ∠BCD and ∠CBD = $y$

∠ACB = ∠ACD + ∠BCD

∠ACD = $x$

∠BCD = $y$

So, ∠ACD + ∠BCD = $x + y$

∠BAC + ∠ACB + ∠ABC = 180°

$x + (x + y) + y = 180°$

$2(x + y) = 180°$

$(x + y) = 90°$

So, ∠ACB is a right angle

△ABC is a right triangle

**Method 2** (often takes a while for students to see; Fig 1.3):

AD = BD = CD

Let D be the center of a circle.

AC is straight because it is the side of a triangle.

∠ACB is right—it is inscribed in a semicircle

△ABC is a right triangle

**Method 3** (Fig 1.4):

AD = BD = CD

Extend CD through D to E so DE = CD

Construct quadrilateral ACBE

D bisects AB and D bisects CE

Therefore ACBE must be a parallelogram

But, CD and DE are congruent

So, the diagonals of the parallelogram are congruent

Thus, ACBE must be a rectangle

∠ABC is right—it is an angle of a rectangle

△ABC is a right triangle

The previous three methods demonstrated how the same problem is solved more than one way.

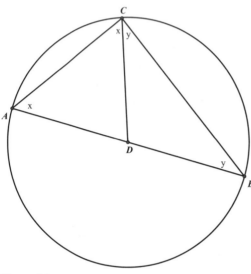

**Figure 1.3**

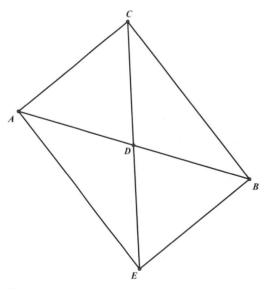

**Figure 1.4**

## EXERCISE 1.7

1. Do the "Point D, which lies on one side of a triangle, is equidistant from all three vertices, A, B, and C" problem a fourth way.

## USE AN IDEA IN MORE THAN ONE SETTING

A basic description of a computer often contains a parallel discussion dealing with the idea that a light switch is either on or off. This leads to base 2, with a description of how it is involved in computer development.

Base 2 is also an integral part of an interesting number trick. A student is asked to select a counting number less than a given value. For this example, we will use 16. The student is then shown a series of cards, one at a time, each of which will have some, but not all, of the values less than 16 on it. The student is to say "Yes" if the selected number is on the card and "No" if it is not. After a response is given for each card in the set, you can tell the student what the selected number was.

| Card A | Card B | Card C | Card D |
|--------|--------|--------|--------|
| 8 | 4 | 2 | 1 |
| 9 | 5 | 3 | 3 |
| 10 | 6 | 6 | 5 |
| 11 | 7 | 7 | 7 |

| Card A | Card B | Card C | Card D |
|--------|--------|--------|--------|
| 12 | 12 | 10 | 9 |
| 13 | 13 | 11 | 11 |
| 14 | 14 | 14 | 13 |
| 15 | 15 | 15 | 15 |

If the student selects 11, the answers for cards A, B, C, and D would be "Yes," "No," "Yes," and "Yes," respectively. The cards do not have to be shown in any given order, but all cards must be shown. The top value on each card is added if "Yes" is the response. Those values represent the powers of two: $8(2^3)$, $4(2^2)$, $2(2^1)$, and $1(2^0)$. Eleven is written in base 2 notation as:

| | $2^3$ | $2^2$ | $2^1$ | $2^0$ |
|----|----|----|----|----|
| 11 | 1 | 0 | 1 | 1 |

Notice that if there is a "1" in the respective column of the base 2 representation of 11, then 11 appears on that card. If the column has a 0 in it, 11 does not appear on that card. This is how the values for each card are determined. Adding a fifth card would extend the possible number candidates to 31; however, the concept of determining which cards would have which values less than 31 would be the same.

This same base 2 trick can be done with cards configured a different way. The values that go on each respective card are the same, but each card is a square. In addition, each card will have at least one rectangular (remember, squares are rectangles) hole in it. Each card will have "Yes" and "No" written on it once. The cards are arranged beneath a card containing all values with the "Yes" or "No" facing the ceiling as the student responds. After the final card is placed, the entire stack is shown to the student. The selected number will be the only one showing through a square hole.

**Additional exercises can be found on the website.**

## MODELS THAT ENHANCE UNDERSTANDING

Traditionally, students have been told that the square of the sum of two numbers is the square of the first term plus twice the product of the two terms plus the square of the second. The problem is that many students remember the words and even perform the operation, but have no understanding of what is being done. A sketch representation of the equation is found in many textbooks. Some students are not convinced that the model works for all similar equations. If the model is created using a dynamic piece of software, as in Fig. 1.5, the students can then change it, modeling Figs. 1.6 and

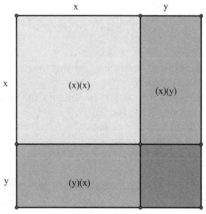

**Figure 1.5**

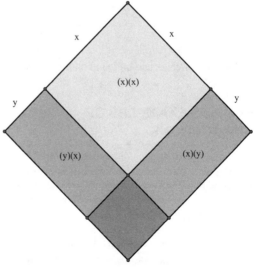

**Figure 1.6**

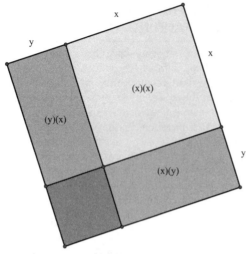

**Figure 1.7**

1.7. The students are able to see that the overall situation is still true.

Note that by rotating or dilating the original sketch, a student can see that $(x + y)^2 = x^2 + 2xy + y^2$ is true no matter how the initial figure is altered, as long as it is still a square.

---

**EXERCISE 1.9**

1. Use a dynamic geometry application or function plotting software to create a model of $(x + y)^2 = x^2 + 2xy + y^2$.

---

 **Additional exercises can be found on the website.**

## PROVIDE EXAMPLES OF APPLICATIONS

Students spend a considerable amount of time learning how to divide fractions. It is confusing to many of them, and some are unable to adequately master the concept. In the process of not fully understanding how to divide a fraction by a fraction, a student can be limited as far as what additional mathematics can be successfully completed. The question is, would examples help? We think the answer is yes. Rather than giving the students a process by which two fractions can be divided,

real-life applications can be used to stimulate the idea of what the process must be. For example, how many problems like $3 \div \frac{1}{2} = 6$ must be used before a student recognizes the connection between the 6, 3, and 2? The next task is to solidify the realization that $3 \div \frac{1}{2}$ has led to 3 × 2. What has transpired is that the second fraction was inverted and division was changed to multiplication. That is the rule! The difference is that rather than being told the rule, the students extrapolated the rule out of examples and experiences they generated. Now the problem is to come up with an example of a fraction divided by a fraction. We are opting to leave that to you as an exercise. Your willingness to investigate and think about this problem is a beginning of your professional development.

---

**EXERCISE 1.10**

1. Describe in writing a real-world example of a fraction divided by a fraction. For the sake of this example, $\frac{n}{1}$ where $n$ is a counting number and not considered a fraction.

---

**Additional exercises can be found on the website.**

## USE A MODEL MORE THAN ONE WAY

Often a given model can be used in more than one setting, depending on the precision or specifics needed for the situation. Consider finding the distance between points A and B on the ocean. Some factors that influence all the models include precision of locating A and B, distance between A and B, navigational accuracy, and ability of the students to deal with straight or curved distances.

If the distance is relatively short (note the ambiguity of that statement—who decides how short short is?), the ocean could be modeled as a flat surface. Given the location of A and B, say, in terms of longitude and latitude, the distance between them could be determined by using the Pythagorean theorem.

If the distance is too great to consider the earth as a flat surface, should the model be a sphere or an elliptical spheroid? Is the precision gained significant enough to matter? Several programs compute true distance and even work with great circles. What do you do if a student says the distance between the two points can be measured along a straight line and then that student suggests a submarine? Would the available computational resources influence the model selection?

As you can see, model selection can be varied, depending on the situation. There are other factors that could influence this and many other problems that are modeled. It becomes the responsibility of the teacher to facilitate learning, even through the use of models. Remember, the overall objective of teaching is to teach the students to think.

## AN EFFECTIVE TEACHER OF MATHEMATICS

If you are to be an effective teacher of mathematics, it is your responsibility to be a self-motivated lifelong learner. That means you need to be consistently reading professional journals, taking classes, attending in-service sessions, participating in workshops, and frequenting professional conferences. As you partake of these different opportunities, you need to report appropriate new information to your classes. It is imperative that each student be aware of the fact that mathematics is a dynamic, ever-changing, invaluable tool that can be used in a multitude of daily settings. Research findings reported to classes have the opportunity to enhance the learning of your students.

Countless pieces of research show us that not all students learn the same way, at the same time, at the same pace, and through the same modalities. It is your responsibility as a teacher of mathematics to be able to reach each of your students in a manner most appropriate for that student. You need to be aware of, and adept at using, different learning styles and then accommodate each student to the best of your ability.

We assume you are aware that a large part of mathematics instruction is board and lecture-based. NCTM has stated that this is not the most desirable way to conduct business. Many research findings indicate that even though it is known that lecture is often not the most effective method of instruction in certain settings, it is still a prevalent style used. As previously stated, the use of indirect instruction is an effective alternative to direct instruction in the mathematics classroom. You need to be

sure that your classroom will be a fitting learning environment for all students. This is an awesome responsibility and not easily accomplished. It will demand a significant amount of your time and energy. It will also provide you with the satisfaction of knowing that you have gone the extra distance to assure that your mathematics students can be all they can be.

The atmosphere of your mathematics classroom can be enhanced by the questions you ask. Like behavioral objectives, questions can be classified in the following levels: knowledge, comprehension, application, analysis, synthesis, and evaluation. We assume you have had some prior exposure to these classifications. It is generally accepted that any question above the knowledge level is an upper-level question. Upper-level questions are not easy to formulate and should be well planned.

Historically, the teacher has been almost like an answer machine. If a student got confused, needed additional explanation, or even needed assurance that the solution path being used was correct or acceptable, the teacher was viewed as the place to go for the needed information. That process did not foster student independence, something that is critical if self-motivated, lifelong learners are going to be cultivated in your classroom. Motivation for acquiring new information must go beyond teacher approval and guidelines. There needs to be a desire for more in each student, and it is your responsibility as the teacher to stimulate that yearning. The effective teacher stimulates students to investigate and seek self-assurance using the tools and skills available.

Finally, in this list of things an effective teacher of mathematics should do, there is evaluation. Where should the blame be placed when a lesson fails to live up to your expectations? You know you planned. You developed a rationale for the lesson. The lesson was related to prior learning. The students had the appropriate readiness skills. Examples were prepared. Questions were inserted throughout the lesson. Technology was used appropriately. Still, after all that, the lesson did not produce the results you desired or expected. It is so easy to blame the class. Surely there are times when the class is at fault for a failed lesson. They were not paying attention. They felt the information was too difficult. There were distractions taking away their concentration.

Remember, the first place to look when a lesson fails is in the mirror. Were your plans as good as you thought they were? Was your delivery as dynamic as it should have been? Could the presentation have been altered so it would have been more successful? After you have exhausted all the possible things you could have done to assure a successful lesson, then, and only then, should you look to the class as a reason. Thus, another segment of your evaluation program is a consistent and thorough assessment of your performance before, during, and after the class.

## CONCLUSION

What must an effective teacher of mathematics know and do? The list of items is probably endless, but the following collection of things should help you pursue your goal of becoming the best teacher of mathematics you can be. You should:

- Know more than the subject you are teaching.
- Motivate your students to want to learn the subject at hand.
- Convey your knowledge to students in words they can understand and that are meaningful to them in their world.
- Guide your students to new heights of thinking.
- Show your students paths that will lead them to greater insights in mathematics.
- Know what to teach when.
- Perceive when and why students are having difficulties.
- Determine how to make concepts meaningful.
- Decide when and how to practice skills.
- Figure out how to stimulate productive thinking.
- Read mathematics literature and insert it into class.
- Do more than just teach the subject.
- Select appropriate goals.
- Stimulate the learning of mathematics.
- Develop desirable attitudes and mathematics appreciation in yourself and in your students.
- Develop the ability to solve mathematical problems in yourself and in your students.
- Build understanding, accuracy, and efficiency.
- Provide opportunities for students at all development levels in your classes.

- Evaluate new curriculum proposals.
- Get, evaluate, and use multimedia aids.
- Get, evaluate, and use the latest technology as a teaching and learning tool.
- Diagnose.

That is a long list, but it is only a beginning. This book provides you with ideas you can add to that list and solutions to many of the questions you generate about teaching mathematics at the secondary level.

### STICKY QUESTIONS

1. Will you further your education if your school does not foot the bill?

2. Will you attend professional conferences if your school does not pay your expenses?

3. What will you do if your administration does not support the use of technology in the mathematics classroom (calculator or computer)?

4. What is the maximum number of students you can effectively teach in a secondary mathematics classroom?

### PROBLEM-SOLVING CHALLENGES

1. **Frog in the Pond.**
   There is a circular pond with a circumference of 400 meters. Dead in the center of the pond is a frog on a lily pad. If the average leap of a frog is 2.25 feet and there are plenty of other lily pads on which to jump, what is the minimum number of leaps it will take for the frog to jump completely out of the pond?

**Check out the website for the solution.**

2. **Cute Little Bookworm.**
   There is a three-volume set of books sitting on a bookshelf. The front and back covers of the books are each 1/8 inch thick. The page section inside each book is exactly 2 inches thick. A cute little bookworm starts eating at page one of volume one and eats, in a straight line, through to the last page of volume three. How far will the little worm travel?

**Check out the website for the solution.**

# LEARNING ACTIVITIES

## Handshake

An interesting problem-solving situation deals with a group of people in a room shaking hands. If persons A and B are the only ones in a room, and if they shake hands, there is only one handshake and it counts for both of them. If there are three people in the room, C, D, and E, there would be three handshakes: CD, CE, and DE. There would be no need to consider handshakes for DC, EC, and ED, because each handshake counts for both people. Thus, three people in a room generate three handshakes.

## Your Turn

1. Complete the following:

| Number of people in a room | Number of Handshakes |
|:---:|:---:|
| 2 | 1 |
| 3 | 3 |
| 4 | |
| 5 | |
| 6 | |
| 7 | |
| 8 | |
| 9 | |
| 10 | |
| 11 | |
| 12 | |

Figure 1.8 shows how the handshake problem could be shown geometrically. Each vertex stands for a person and each line segment connecting vertices represents one handshake between the two people.

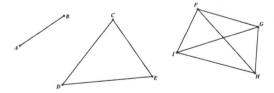

**Figure 1.8**

2. Show figures for five and six people shaking hands and show the total number of handshakes under the given rules.

A formula can be developed to show the number of handshakes needed for any number of people, given the stated rules. Some clues for finding the formula can be found by studying Table 1.1. Two people result in one handshake. That could mean, divide the number of people in half to get the number of shakes.

Test the idea with three people. The first conjecture fails. We could say that we just take the number of people as the number of handshakes, but we know that will not work with two people.

We need to take a look at more numbers and seek a pattern.

| People | Shakes |
|--------|--------|
| 2 | 1 |
| 3 | 3 |
| 4 | 6 |
| 5 | 10 |
| 6 | 15 |

The pattern in Table 1.1 doesn't seem obvious. What if we consider each handshake as counting for each individual? That is, A and B would generate two handshakes, one for A, and another one for B. Similarly, with C, D, and E, we would have six handshakes: CD, DC, CE, EC, DE, and ED.

Build a new table as shown in Table 1.2 by adding a column for this new rule:

| People | Shakes | Shake for Each |
|--------|--------|----------------|
| 2 | 1 | 2 |
| 3 | 3 | 6 |
| 4 | 6 | 12 |
| 5 | 10 | 20 |
| 6 | 15 | 30 |

There is a clue. Counting each handshake twice doubles the numbers in the second column. But look at the numbers in the first and third columns. The third column entry is the first column entry multiplied by one less than the first column entry. That is, 2 = (2)(1), 6 = (3)(2), 12 = (4)(3), and so on.

Now compare the third column entries with their respective second column entries. In each case, the third column entry is twice the second column entry.

 **Additional learning activities can be found on the website.**

# Learning Theory, Curriculum, and Assessment

**2**

## FOCAL POINTS IN THIS CHAPTER

- Specific mathematics education examples of concepts covered in general education courses
- Communicating with individuals teaching the same course, the next course in the sequence, the previous course in the sequence, and those in "feeder schools"
- Equity issues in the mathematics curriculum
- Error patterns
- Diagnostic teaching
- Evaluation of cooperative groups
- Assessment techniques
- Mathematics competitions available to secondary students
- Pressures on the secondary mathematics curriculum

Ed Begle said, "We have learned a lot about teaching better mathematics but not much about teaching mathematics better" (Crosswhite, 1986). When perusing the history of teaching mathematics, it appears as if we constantly look for a magic method or strategy that will serve all students. There is no enchanted formula that fits every learner. We need to realize that a variety of methods is necessary to meet the mathematical learning needs of all students. Our task, as teachers of mathematics, is to determine which method will be most beneficial to the mathematical learning of each student and when these strategies will be most effective. If a teacher uses a strategy with no positive result from the learner, at what point is that method abandoned in favor of another? The decision is most often influenced by our own background, training, experiences, bias, and current curriculum.

It is assumed you have had exposure to learning theories, curriculum, and assessment in foundational education classes. These are some of the topics to be discussed in this chapter. The intent here is not to provide an extensive discussion about these topics, but, rather, to briefly touch on many aspects of them. It is assumed you will investigate selected issues in greater depth as you see the need. The order in which the topics are presented is not to be construed as an indication of the value or importance of each topic.

## CONSTRUCTIVISM

Adherents of constructivism support the notion that children learn effectively through interactions with experiences in their natural environment. Steffe and Killion (1986) stated that, from a constructivist perspective, "mathematics teaching consists primarily of the mathematical interactions between a teacher and children" (p. 207). This indirect approach to instruction effectively allows the student to learn in the context of meaningful activities. Learning is an endless, lifelong process that results from interactions with a multitude of situations (Brown, Collins, & Duguid, 1989). The constructivist approach does not focus solely on the action of the teacher or the learner, but on the interactions between the two. The teacher should make a conscious effort to see personal actions as well as the student's from the student's point of view (Cobb & Steffe, 1983).

Constructivism has multiple roots in the psychology and philosophy of the twentieth century (Perkins, 1991). There is no single concrete definition of constructivism. Piaget is thought to be one of the first learning theorists to advocate a constructivist teaching approach, even though he did not identify himself as such. He believed in the importance of human interaction and physical manipulation in the gaining of knowledge. The emphasis of the constructivist classroom begins with the student! The constructivist educator demonstrates a respect for the student. The classroom should be a place that fosters and nurtures learning and development of knowledge.

The constructivist classroom creates an environment that encourages learning. The teacher should create surroundings where students can make sense of mathematics as it relates to the real world. Students are to be treated with respect and responsibility. The fear of failing must be erased, in order to foster the idea that students can learn from their mistakes. If we are to expect our students to comprehend and deal with complex problems, we need to establish an atmosphere rich with exposures. Students should become aware of their own thinking process, strategies, and critical-thinking abilities. Each student should become aware of the ability to invent and explore new ideas and concepts. The effective teacher of mathematics must be willing to capitalize on these natural thinking abilities.

Constructivism focuses on student-centered instruction, which is not new in education. The student plays a major role in the decision-making process as to what, when, and how learning is to occur. This is a bold approach, but students have great insight into themselves that teachers cannot always see! We need to show respect to each student by providing the opportunity to shape individual learning.

Other learning theorists stress that information students assimilate can be taught more effectively and efficiently by providing a structured approach. Providing a clear sequence of steps will allow the learner to incorporate a greater amount of knowledge, is the behaviorists' claim.

## BEHAVIORISM

The work of Edward Thorndike's connectionism paved the way for the behaviorist movement. Connectionism describes the link between stimuli and responses that can be initiated and fortified through reinforcements or repeated use of the stimuli. Thorndike's work led to B.F. Skinner's belief that only a small portion of learned behaviors were due to classical conditioning. Skinner proposed that operant conditioning played a significant role in learned behaviors. Operant conditioning is learning in which behavior is altered by events that precede and follow the behavior. Reinforcement is an example of operant conditioning. Positive reinforcement is used to strengthen a behavior by presenting a desired stimulus after an action. Rewarding a student for effort is an example of positive reinforcement. If a student will not stop distracting a neighboring student, the teacher can change the student's seat assignment. This is an example of negative reinforcement. The teacher is weakening the behavior by removing the adverse stimulus.

Thorndike's investigations, which looked at learning in terms of selected associations to related actions, strongly influenced the development of behaviorism. Behaviorism was introduced into American psychology by John B. Watson (Driscoll, 1994). Skinner, who followed Watson and became the major advocate of behaviorism, believed that a person's behavior is a function of environmental actions and results. Behaviorism centers on a direct approach and has been the dominant strategy for teaching mathematics in the United States for many years. The behaviorist approach essentially treats mathematics as a collection of skills. Learn all the skills and learn mathematics.

Robert Gagné used the idea that a sequence of tasks could be established for a desired learning outcome. If the student practiced each required task as it was learned and developed, then that student would then be able to move on to the next step in the continuum. When discussing addition of fractions, can a continuum for addition of fractions be established? Can a similar list be built for each concept in mathematics? Do you have adequate time and background to build a list for each concept you teach? Are you willing to trust someone else to build the list for you? (Essentially, this is what textbooks often do.) What happens if you do not agree with the established list? It appears that the emphasis has shifted from how students learn mathematics to what mathematics should be learned. Is this what we are after?

Within a department, suppose not everyone accepts the behaviorist approach to teaching. What is the impact on text selection? If departmental examinations are used, how are the different concepts tested? What impact will this have on students who move from a behaviorist-based class to a non-behaviorist-based class? What is the impact on students learning a procedure without conceptually grasping the reason for it?

The discussion about the learning theories becomes focused on whether it is wisest to provide an efficient learning environment that results primarily in the acquisition of academic knowledge, or to take an approach that provides a more in-depth, indirect process encompassing the whole learner. If a basic concept is not fully comprehended, should the student move on? If the student is taught how to mechanically do a problem but does not understand the process or application, is the knowledge useful to the learner? There is a need to consider the amount of time students are actively taught or supervised. In a direct instruction classroom, the teacher presents information and develops concepts through lecture and demonstration. As students question, respond to teacher queries, react to assignments, and do practice exercises, elaborations are given that are designed to clarify and strengthen understanding.

Behaviorism and constructivism generate a question about which is the best way to teach mathematics: Give the students the information, or encourage them to use the various curriculum materials and teacher support to actively discover the information in context through learning activities? Again, what is the best way, direct or indirect instruction?

Assuming the student understands each skill as it is presented and is capable of performing the defined tasks before moving on to the next, more complicated, concept, the need to preserve the current knowledge is present. How often should addition of fractions be reviewed and practiced? How many of each type of problem is necessary? Where do boredom and restlessness with the repetition begin? What do we do when we are confident that some students have mastered the task and others have not? When do we go on to a new concept that builds on the ability to add fractions? Is it mandatory that all students master the skill before you, as a teacher, proceed? None of these questions is easy to answer, but this last one is especially perplexing.

## MASTERY LEARNING

Mastery learning permits the teacher to go on as long as a student's learning pace is not hurried just to keep up with the rest of the class. This is based on the realization that we all learn at different rates. Mastery learning implies that each student will master a subordinate skill before proceeding to the next skill level. When using mastery learning with direct instruction, the teacher begins a unit of study by using techniques involving lecture, demonstrations, and review, along with drill and practice. At an appropriate interval (often about 3–5 days), the teacher deviates from the normal routine to administer some form of evaluation to assess student understanding. This evaluation is strictly for diagnostic purposes and not for assigning grades. Students meeting the standards set on the evaluation instrument will be given alternative assignments that might be considered enrichment activities (Esler & Sciortino, 1991). If half the class has mastered the task, what do we do with them while the other half is still working on it? Suppose only one student remains who has not mastered the task. Do we go on or do we persist until that one remaining

student exhibits the necessary competence at performing the task? Do "silly" arithmetic mistakes count against mastery? Should the class move on to new material, leaving that one student behind to master the concept? Will the one student continue to fall behind?

If only we could dissect each student's brain and somehow tell what has been learned, the processes that are most likely to succeed, and the propensities for learning. If that could be done, perhaps a better connection between theory and practice could be established. Then, learning theories could be more solid and identifiable. Alas, we cannot dissect a student's brain, so we are reduced to studying tendencies and creating theories. How many times have you heard, "There is a difference between theory and practice"? Many theories will "sound good" or "make sense" on paper. Often, theories are created out of observation, knowledge of student learning, thought, and discussion. The background is often built in a specific, sometimes controlled, setting or with a limited number of cases. The real world of the classroom often does not resemble the theory environment. Putting theory into practice is not that simple. Implementation of a learning theory also assumes the practitioner (teacher) is well-versed in the related ideas. That assumption is often unrealistic from the standpoint of a teacher who was exposed to the theory or strategy in a class or in-service session but is swamped with all the details related to classroom production.

We think back to our own learning environments, searching for clues about how we learned different skills and concepts. The assumption is that if we are "normal" and if we can figure out how we learned to perform a given task, we might gain some insight into what can be done to help students learn as they advance through the world of mathematics. Considering time and memory, the likelihood of our remembering minute details from our learning is not great. Besides, most of us who are involved in the teaching and learning of mathematics are not "typical" representatives of students found in secondary mathematics classes. Students and how they perceive or learn mathematics change from year to year.

We are talking about learning theories. Is it good, accepted, acceptable, or desirable to lock-step a class? Given that class sizes are close to 40 students in some areas, is it reasonable to think in terms of applying any of these theories? Would it be acceptable to create three groups within a class? Will all the students get the basics of the class?

Will average- and higher-ability groups be able to go beyond the basics with additional applications or extensions? This group of questions is purposely left unanswered. These are things you need to begin pondering as you enter the teaching profession.

---

### EXERCISES 2.1

1. What are the major characteristics you would ascribe to a positive mathematics classroom? Which of these would you control? Which would be dependent on your students? Which of these would be dependent on administration?
2. Was the mathematics learning environment you experienced in your secondary school years constructivist- or behaviorist-based? Describe your experiences to amplify your selection.

---

 **Additional exercises can be found on the website.**

## CHANGE

We no longer live in the industrial age. We live in the technological age. Times have changed. Yet much of the curriculum seems to have stayed in the industrial age. Over the years, many calls for change have been heard. One of the most famous, or infamous, is "modern math." More recently, various works have called for change. They include the following:

*The Underachieving Curriculum: Assessing U.S. School Mathematics from an International Perspective* (McKnight et al., 1987)

*Curriculum and Evaluation Standards for School Mathematics* (National Council of Teachers of Mathematics [NCTM], 1989)

*Everybody Counts: A Report to the Nation on the Future of Mathematics Education* (Mathematical Sciences Education Board, 1989)

*Mathematics Education: Wellspring of U.S. Industrial Strength* (1988)

*Reshaping School Mathematics: A Philosophy and Framework for Curriculum* (National Research Council, 1990)

*America 2000: An Education Strategy* (U.S. Department of Education, 1991)

*Professional Standards for Teaching Mathematics* (NCTM, 1991)

*The State of Mathematics Achievement: NAPE's 1990 Assessment of the Nation and the Trial Assessment of the States* (Mullis, Dossey, Owen, & Phillips, 1991)

*Handbook of Research on Mathematics Teaching and Learning* (Grouws, 1992)

*Principles and Standards for School Mathematics* (NCTM, 2000)

*Linking Research & Practice: The NCTM Research Agenda Conference Report* (NCTM, 2008)

*Report of the Joint Task Force on Common Core State Standards* (NCTM, 2011)

These publications discuss the status of school mathematics programs. They describe what has happened in mathematics classrooms of the past, what is happening now, and what should happen in the classrooms of the future. You might find some of these requests for change radical. Again, this becomes something for you to ponder. You need to arrive at an educated, informed, well-thought-out decision.

In the not-too-distant past, modern math was a change element. Many thought modern math was created because of the space race and the launching of Sputnik in 1957. In reality, the modern math movement had begun several years earlier. Educators and mathematicians realized that the mathematics being taught in the high schools in the early 1950s was not providing an effective background for individuals who would become future users of mathematics. They also were aware that the plug-and-chug, drill-and-practice approach was not creating the preparation for effective citizenry of that day. These modern math creators and developers were looking to the future. They realized that the system of teaching and learning mathematics of that time was not effective at building for the future. The system was broken and needed to be fixed.

There is debate as to whether or not modern math was effective. In the early 1960s, when modern math was beginning to be used in some schools, new texts were produced. Algebra II books were revised to be Modern Algebra II texts. Comparison of the Algebra II book with the Modern Algebra II book by the same publisher revealed some startling insights. The Modern Algebra II text might have had a few pages dealing with sets, subsets, set operations (union and intersection), and the field axioms (properties). Let us assume this information was covered in the first five pages of the new text. Page six of the new text was the same as page one of the old; new seven was the same as old two; new eight was old three; and so on. Rarely, if ever, were sets and field axioms directly referred to in the Modern Algebra II book. Frequently teachers skipped the first five pages of the Modern Algebra II text and taught the same old course. Many teachers of the early 1960s had not covered the set topics or field axioms per se in their college work. They received little, if any, instruction dealing with the changes called for in the modern math movement. Yet teachers were expected to insert the new ideas into their curriculum. It did not work. Curriculum proceeded as usual, and modern math rarely made it into the classrooms. Many people (experts, teachers, and citizens) and written commentaries presented modern math as a dismal failure.

Certainly there were exceptions to this. Individuals who developed and tested the School Mathematics Study Group materials delivered solid secondary mathematics courses. The same can be said for projects like the University of Illinois Committee on School Mathematics, the Ball State work, the Greater Cleveland Project, the Madison Project, and others. Each of these programs, and many like them, were well-founded and offered a strong mathematics program that would have moved our curriculum beyond the drill-and-practice stage. For a variety of reasons, those programs never made it into the mainstream curriculum. We now have publications, like those referred to earlier, calling for change in the way secondary mathematics is taught and learned. We now have the Common Core State Standards for Mathematics (http://www.corestandards.org/). This initiative was strongly supported by the National Governors Association Center for Best Practices (NGA Center) and the Council of Chief State School Officers (CCSSO). These curricular standards were developed by teachers, school administrators, and experts, with the goal to create a clear and consistent framework to prepare our children for college and the workforce. With state agreement on implementation of the Common Core Standards, will curricular change actually take place inside the classroom?

The motivation for these changes comes from a variety of representatives from industry. They list mathematical expectations from the perspective of an employer and say employers want people who:

Are capable of setting problems up, not just following formulas.

Know how to interpret the numbers or answers they get.

Are aware of a variety of approaches for solving problems.

Understand the mathematical features of a problem and can work in groups to reach solutions.

Recognize commonalities of mathematics in different problems.

Can deal with problems that are not in the format often presented in the learning environment.

Value mathematics as a useful learning and work tool.

This list of workplace desires is different from the student abilities produced in many secondary mathematics programs. It is time to change!

## THE STANDARDS

Some members of the mathematics community realized in the mid-1980s that "business as usual" would not be effective for future mathematics teaching and learning. NCTM took the lead and published *Curriculum and Evaluation Standards for School Mathematics* (referred to in this text as the Standards) in 1989. The guidelines presented in these Standards were formative ideas indicating mathematics learning that is desirable in school settings. The Standards focused on five general goals, which adopt the position that all students should:

Learn to value mathematics.

Develop confidence in their ability to use mathematics.

Become problem solvers, not answer finders.

Learn to communicate mathematically.

Know how to reason mathematically.

Problem solving, reasoning, communication, and mathematical connections were common strands through all levels, but there were other standards for various grade ranges. The additional standards for grades K–4 were:

Estimation

Number sense and numeration

Concepts of whole-number operations

Whole-number computation

Geometry and spatial sense

Measurement

Statistics and probability

Fractions and decimals

Patterns and relationships

For Grades 5–8:

Number and number relationships

Number systems and number theory

Computation and estimation

Patterns and functions

Algebra

Statistics

Probability

Geometry

Measurement

For grades 9–12:

Algebra

Functions

Geometry from a synthetic perspective

Geometry from an algebraic perspective

Trigonometry

Statistics

Probability

Discrete mathematics

Conceptual underpinnings of calculus

Mathematical structure

The final section of the Standards focused on evaluation. The basic premise was that evaluation is not a separate act within the classroom but, rather, a part of teaching. A test at the end of a section or chapter was no longer considered an adequate method of assessing a student's progress. There is a need for viewing more than an answer and whether it is right or wrong. A variety of assessment techniques need to be present in different formats.

## THE ADDENDA SERIES

As the Curriculum and Evaluation Standards for School Mathematics (NCTM, 1989) was being developed, it became apparent that supporting publications would be needed to aid in interpreting and implementing the Standards and the underlying instructional themes (Froelich, Bartkovich, & Forrester, 1991, p. iv.).

The Addenda to the Standards were to clarify the recommendations contained in some of the Standards and to give examples of how they could realistically be implemented in the school curriculum. The Addenda Series (Froelich et al., 1991) provides plenty of examples involving problem solving, reasoning, communicating, connections, technology, and assessment. It has been designed to reflect the "realities of today's classrooms and to make [the standards] 'teacher friendly'" (NCTM, 1991, p. iv).

The Standards showed mathematics as more than a body of knowledge. Mathematics is something we must do. Each student is expected to become an active, reflective participant as learning progresses. Students should recognize connections between topics, see applications of the material being learned, and appreciate the subject. In the process, the learning environment must change from teacher-centered to teacher-motivated. No longer can the teacher be the "sage on the stage." Rather, the effective teacher of mathematics is expected to function as a catalyst and facilitator of learning. This attitude is reflected in the Standards by the request for increased attention to:

- actively involving students in constructing and applying mathematical ideas;
- using problem solving as a means as well as a goal of instruction;
- promoting student interaction through the use of effective questioning techniques;
- using a variety of instructional formats—small cooperative groups, individual explorations, whole-class instruction, and projects;
- using calculators and computers as tools for learning and doing mathematics. (Froelich et al., 1991, p. vi)

The Addenda Series contains several features throughout the volume. "Try This" encourages students to do problems, exercises, and explorations related to the content. "Teaching Matters" contains suggestions and ideas that could prove helpful in introducing a topic, using technology, or understanding areas where students might generate misconceptions with the topic. Assessment is an integral part of the topics presented in the Addenda Series. "Sustainable change must occur first in the hearts, minds, and classrooms of teachers and then in their departments and school districts" (Froelich et al., 1991, p. viii). We cannot ask our students to change unless we first change how we teach mathematics.

## EXERCISE 2.2

1. Select an activity from one of the books in the Addenda Series. Critique the activity. Will it appeal to students? Why or why not? Would you change it before using it? Why or why not? Are the readiness expectations necessary for the activity clear? Will the students be able to connect the activity to something in their world? Why or why not?

 **Additional exercises can be found on the website.**

## PROFESSIONAL STANDARDS

The *Professional Standards for Teaching Mathematics* (NCTM, 1991; referred to in this text as the Professional Standards) also deal with how we should change the way we teach mathematics. The Professional Standards focus on teacher knowledge, beliefs, and strategies that will deliver the Standards into the classroom. The Professional Standards also include a discussion of methods of teacher support and evaluation necessary to promote reform. It is important to note that the Professional Standards, like the Standards, are broad frameworks designed to guide school mathematics reform.

To reach the goal of developing mathematical power for all students requires the creation of a curriculum and an environment, in which teaching and learning are to occur, that are very different from much of current practice. The image of mathematics teaching needed includes elementary and secondary teachers who are more proficient in:

- selecting mathematical tasks to engage students' interests and intellect;
- providing opportunities to deepen their understanding of the mathematics being studied and its applications;
- orchestrating classroom discourse in ways that promote the investigation and growth of mathematical ideas;
- using, and helping students use, technology and other tools to pursue mathematical investigations;
- seeking, and helping students seek, connections to previous and developing knowledge; and

- guiding individual, small-group, and whole class work. (NCTM, 1991, p. 1)

Change does not come easily. Barriers include student and teacher beliefs regarding how mathematics is taught, as well as learned blockages in mathematics education. To a large extent, these impressions are developed by prior experiences in mathematics. Here is a familiar scenario:

Attendance is taken.

Homework is reviewed with the teacher doing some problems.

Examples of "today's" problem types are worked, or students are told to read the book and see how to do the problems.

Seat work is assigned related to the assignment of the day.

This is how many students, and teachers, think mathematics is learned—the teacher models how to do the problem and the students mimic what they see. One thing organizations like the NCTM, Mathematical Sciences Education Board (MSEB), and Mathematical Association of America (MAA) have repeatedly asked for is that postsecondary teachers of mathematics model different behavior in their classrooms. If these educators take the lead, individuals studying to become teachers of mathematics will see a more modern teaching behavior modeled. The sad fact is, as you know, few postsecondary teachers of mathematics exhibit the desired behavior—most of the classes are lectures revolving around "here is how you do this kind of problem."

Student and teacher impressions are not the only obstacles to changing mathematics education. Administrators, parents, and society have strong ideas about how to educate our children, as well. The Professional Standards were built on two basic assumptions: "Teachers are key figures in changing the ways in which mathematics is taught and learned in schools. Such changes require that teachers have long-term support and adequate resources" (NCTM, 1991, p. 2). Because the Professional Standards ask for such a significant difference in how mathematics is taught and learned, they also implicitly expect ongoing professional development by each teacher of mathematics. It is unreasonable to expect a teacher to take one class, attend one workshop, or read and discuss a few articles and then be an effective agent of new ideas about teaching and learning mathematics. Teachers need to see classes taught that model the desired new behavior, and they need continued exposure to new strategies and methods of instruction.

The section on "Standards for Teaching Mathematics" develops a vision of what a teacher must know and be able to do if the curriculum goals outlined in the Standards are to be delivered. The assumption is that there are several important decisions teachers make in determining the learning environment:

- Select goals and mathematical tasks designed to assist students in achieving desirable mathematical growth.
- Establish a classroom environment that clarifies for both the students and the teacher what is being learned.
- Create a classroom atmosphere that is supportive of the teaching and learning of mathematics.
- Continually analyze student learning and the classroom environment in order to make ongoing instructional decisions.

The section on "Evaluation of the Teaching of Mathematics" presents the NCTM vision for how mathematics teaching should be evaluated. It is assumed that evaluation is present to assist in improving teaching. The section gives guidance to teachers who want to improve their professionalism and presentation skills. Vignettes are used to show a variety of assessment activities. Although they present a wide variety of examples, it is not an exhaustive supply.

The "Standards on Professional Development" indicate the NCTM vision of the "well-prepared" teacher of mathematics. The vision begins with the first postsecondary mathematics course taken and continues throughout the individual teacher's professional career. "These standards focus on what a teacher needs to know about mathematics, mathematics education, and pedagogy to be able to carry out the vision of teaching discussed in the first component of the document" (NCTM, 1991, p. 6).

These standards provide guidance to colleges, schools, and anyone involved in the development of teachers of mathematics. They stress the need for communication between individuals at all levels so that each is aware of the needs and actions of the other. Then, the mathematical community, as a whole, can grow toward the desired goals.

The "Standards for Support and Development" outline the responsibilities of decision makers.

Decisions of individuals from government, business, industry, schools, colleges, and professional organizations can either enable or hamper teachers of mathematics as we move toward the vision of teaching described in the Professional Standards. These decisions influence the environment in which the teaching and learning of mathematics is to take place.

The final section in the Professional Standards deals with issues on developing mathematical power for all students. The entirety of the Professional Standards is not intended to be a checklist. Instead, they are directions for moving toward a stronger, more meaningful mathematics education for all students at all levels: pre-K through postgraduate.

### EXERCISE 2.3

1. The Professional Standards (pp. 135–139) list courses that should be a part of the background for teachers of mathematics in grades pre-K–12. Focus on the courses for grades 5–8 or grades 9–12. Compare the coursework in your background with that listed. Elaborate on any differences and describe whether or not you feel they are significant.

**Additional exercises can be found on the website.**

## ASSESSMENT STANDARDS

The *Assessment Standards for Teaching Mathematics* (NCTM, 1995b; referred to as the Assessment Standards in this text) are based on research, experiences of the writing team, and developments related to national efforts to reform the teaching and learning of mathematics. The six standards presented in the document state that assessment should:

1. Reflect the mathematics that all students need to know and be able to do. This refers to providing examples from the real world of students as viewed by students, not adults.
2. Enhance mathematics learning. Due to some form of assessment, a student becomes aware of an inability to readily find the sum of rational expressions and realizes the deficiency is related to finding least common denominators. The student's choice should be to correct

the deficiency in order to enhance the ability to deal with the problem at hand and build appropriate background for future work.

3. Promote equity. Stereotyping is a well-documented problem. Everyone has the ability to succeed in mathematical settings. An effective assessment program should depict individuals of all races, creeds, and gender in environments showing true equity.

4. Be an open process. A teacher's assessment tool to measure statistical abilities should be open to colleagues for scrutiny. The more people viewing the assessment tool and process, the stronger the program becomes. This will enhance the program's ability to respond to the needs of each student.

5. Promote valid inferences about mathematics learning. The greater the number of assessments used to determine a student's understanding of a concept, the greater the likelihood that you have made a valid decision. These decisions come from your knowledge of students and how they learn, as well as from your professional judgment.

6. Be a coherent process. Not only should the student understand the assessment, but the assessment should reflect the overall program that is most beneficial for the lifelong learning goals of that individual.

We need to value the mathematical development of all students. Assessment should not be a tool used to deny access to mathematical learning. Assessment should be used to stimulate growth toward higher mathematical expectations. Demanding less than the best from each student is akin to wasting the potential of the respective individual. The Assessment Standards are designed to expand on the evaluation section of the Standards.

The Assessment Standards reiterate the call for systematic changes toward:

A richer variety of mathematical topics and away from just arithmetic.

Investigation of problems and away from memorizing and repeating.

Teacher questioning and listening and away from teacher telling.

Assessment that gathers evidence from several sources and away from a single test.

Using concepts and procedures in problem solving and away from mastering isolated pieces of information.

The Assessment Standards are designed to be a guideline as is the case with the other NCTM Standards publications, not a cookbook to be followed. Assessment is defined as:

The process of gathering evidence about a student's knowledge of, ability to use, and disposition toward, mathematics and of making inferences from that evidence for a variety of purposes. . . . Furthermore, by evaluation we mean the process of determining the worth of, or assigning a value to, something on the basis of careful examination and judgment. (NCTM, 1995b, p. 3)

Assessment is viewed as a process that describes what mathematics students know and what they can do with what they know. This outlook goes beyond the typical student interpretation reflected by the question, "Will this be on the test?"

The assessment process consists of four phases: planning the assessment, gathering evidence, interpreting the evidence, and using the results. Each part can be characterized through the following questions.

Planning the assessment:

What purpose does it serve?

What framework is used to give focus and balance to the activities?

What methods are used for gathering and interpreting evidence?

What criteria are used for judging performance on activities?

What formats are used for summarizing judgments and reporting results?

Gathering evidence:

How are activities and tasks created or selected?

How are procedures selected for engaging students in the activities?

How are methods for creating and preserving evidence of the performances to be judged?

Interpreting the evidence:

How is the quality of the evidence determined?

How is an understanding of the performances to be inferred from the evidence?

What specific criteria are applied to judge the performances?

Have the criteria been applied appropriately?

How will the judgments be summarized as results?

Using the results:

How will the results be reported?

How should inferences from the results be made?

What action will be taken based on the inferences?

How can it be ensured that these results will be incorporated in subsequent instruction and assessment?

---

**EXERCISE 2.4**

1. Read the "What's Next" section (pp. 81–83) of the Assessment Standards. What do you think? Are the descriptions accurate? Were there items that should be added to or deleted from the discussion? Do you think you could build this type of assessment program in your classes and school when you begin teaching? Why or why not?

---

 **Additional exercises can be found on the website.**

## STANDARDS 2000

The next installment to NCTM's Standards series was *Principles and Standards for School Mathematics* (NCTM, 2000; referred to as Standards 2000 in this text). NCTM's other standards served as guidelines for the establishment of standards, curriculum, assessment, professional development materials, better teaching efforts at all levels, and discussions among individuals interested in delivering mathematics to all students. The goal of Standards 2000 was to "build on the foundations of the original NCTM Standards documents and to consolidate the classroom aspects of all three documents" (NCTM, 2000). Standards 2000 has the benefit of being able to look back on years of stimulated change and the associated discussions and research. Building on this foundation of reflection, rethinking past ideas, and innovating for the future, NCTM presents ideas that will stimulate more thinking. But, isn't that what being a part of a learning community is all about? Shouldn't we all, as professional educators, examine what we say and do, and strive to become

better? We achieve that growth through in-service opportunities, classes, professional conferences, literature, research, and, of course, by discussing the efforts of others as expressed in publications like Standards 2000. NCTM is to be commended for continuing to lead the way in mathematics reform.

Standards 2000 is built around 10 standards. Within each standard you will find sets of focus areas that are elaborated within different grade band chapters. The 10 basic standards are:

Number and Operation

Algebra

Geometry

Measurement

Data Analysis and Probability

Problem Solving

Reasoning and Proof

Communication

Connections

Representation

To add to the breadth and depth of Standards 2000, NCTM developed the *Curriculum Focal Points for Grades Prekindergarten Through Grade 8* (NCTM, 2010). The focal points were designed to identify specific mathematical topics that should be emphasized at specific grade levels. According to NCTM:

Curriculum focal points are important mathematical topics for each grade level, pre-K–8. These areas of instructional emphasis can serve as organizing structures for curriculum design and instruction at and across grade levels. The topics are central to mathematics: they convey knowledge and skills that are essential to educated citizens, and they provide the foundations for further mathematical learning. Because the focal points are core structures that lay a conceptual foundation, they can serve to organize content, connecting and bringing coherence to multiple concepts and processes taught at and across grade levels. They are indispensable elements in developing problem solving, reasoning, and critical thinking skills, which are important to all mathematics learning. ("What Are Curriculum Focal Points?" n.d., para 1)

The focal points are designed to be an extension of Standards 2000, providing the development of mathematical topics across multiple grade levels. The focal points and Standards 2000 were designed to serve as a clear framework and resource to educators, state agencies, and the professional community.

**Additional exercises can be found on the website.**

## COMMON CORE STATE STANDARDS

In 2010, the National Governors Association Center for Best Practices (NGA Center) in collaboration with the Council of Chief State School Officers (CCSSO) prompted an initiative to raise the bar for the mathematical content being taught while creating a common set of standards. The Common Core Standards for Mathematics (http://www.corestandards. org/the-standards/mathematics) were developed by educators, school administrators, and the professional community with a goal to provide a common framework across the nation in specific content areas. The Common Core Standards define grade specific standards and describe the mathematics children should be able to comprehend and do.

These standards define the knowledge and skills students should have within their K–12 education careers so that they will graduate high school able to succeed in entry-level, credit-bearing academic college courses and in workforce training programs. The standards:

- Are aligned with college and work expectations;
- Are clear, understandable and consistent;
- Include rigorous content and application of knowledge through high-order skills; Build on strengths and lessons of current state standards;
- Are informed by other top performing countries, so that all students are prepared to succeed in our global economy and society; and

- Are evidence-based. ("About the Standards," n.d., para 4)

The Common Core Standards focus on kindergarten through high school mathematics. Content is specific at each grade level and identifies six specific areas for high school mathematics: Number & Quantity; Algebra; Functions; Modeling; Geometry; and Statistics & Probability (http://www.cores tandards.org/Math).

As of January 1, 2012, 45 U.S. states had adopted the Common Core Standards. Although states agreed on the adoption of these new standards, implementation timelines and transition dates significantly differ from state to state.

**Additional exercises can be found on the website.**

## PROFESSIONALISM

NCTM, MSEB, MAA, and many state and local groups deal specifically with teaching and learning mathematics. None of these organizations mandate how to operate your classroom. All of them provide a plethora of suggestions for you to select from. The formats of the information include publications, workshops, conferences, summer institutes, and evaluations of textbooks, technology, manipulatives, classroom aids, and so on. You are studying to become a professional educator and the information is available to you. As such, you should accept certain responsibilities. One of those is to be a member of your professional organizations. This means now, not when you start teaching. NCTM's phone number is 800-235-7566 or 703-620-9840, and you can visit http://www.nctm.org/membership to join NCTM instantly.

Student memberships are half-price for NCTM and many other professional organizations. Don't just join, become involved. Learn! Interact with colleagues. Volunteer for service and membership on professional committees. Seek out new and better ways to help yourself and your students use mathematical power.

Professional conferences dealing with the teaching of mathematics provide a multitude of opportunities. These meetings allow you the opportunity to hear and meet textbook authors, college faculty, colleagues, and suppliers of support products. Classroom scenarios from colleagues who have been successful in presenting information to their students are described in sessions and workshops. Others describe the latest research findings and developments dealing with the teaching of mathematics. Publishers maintain exhibits that show the latest texts, teaching aids, games, technology, and associated applications. Not only can you look at these items, but, in many instances, you have the opportunity to talk with a professional about how to use them in a classroom. Granted, the representative might be selling, but the example is still available to you. The final analysis is that, as a professional, you are obligated to maintain awareness in your chosen area of specialization. Otherwise, you continue in the same old rut as the sage on the stage, wondering why students are not absorbing what you tell them.

Many organizations provide publications ranging from one-page newsletters to books, with almost anything imaginable between those two ends. NCTM publishes newsletters, journals (one is included as a part of the student membership), research journals, and yearbooks on a regular basis. The newsletter (*NCTM News Bulletin*) contains information about recent curricular or commercial developments, news of federal legislative action that could impact the teaching of mathematics, activity ideas for students, discussions about developments within the organization, and so on. NCTM journals contain articles, activities, and resources authored by classroom teachers, textbook authors, professors, students, and professional authors. The journals include *Teaching Children Mathematics* (for elementary school educators and formerly called *Arithmetic Teacher*), *Mathematics Teaching in the Middle School* (for middle school educators), *Mathematics Teacher* (primarily for high school educators), and *Student Explorations in Mathematics* (formerly *Student Math Notes*). Often, the presentations in these publications describe a successful lesson from the classroom. The *Journal for Research in Mathematics Education* is a collection of studies dealing with how to teach mathematics more effectively. The NCTM

yearbooks cover a variety of topics, and usually the titles adequately describe the content of the book: *The Teaching of Secondary School Mathematics; Professional Development for Teachers of Mathematics; Assessment in the Mathematics Classroom; Calculators in Mathematics Education; Computers in Mathematics Education; Applications in School Mathematics; Understanding Geometry for a Changing World; Motivation and Disposition: Pathways to Learning Mathematics*; and so forth. Other national, state, and local organizations provide a variety of alternative publications as well.

Professionalism carries responsibilities with it. It is your obligation to keep the community and parents aware of recent developments in the field. They need to be educated and reminded about how things are different from when they learned mathematics in school. Otherwise, pressures to continue teaching mathematics as it has always been done will be so great that change will be difficult to accomplish. The broader and stronger your mathematics background and the more you know about how to teach it, the easier it will be for you to establish community trust. It is imperative that you become a self-motivated, lifelong professional who is involved in the field of teaching and learning mathematics.

## EQUITY

If we believe that all children can learn meaningful mathematics and science, there are significant educational structures and contextual conditions that must be changed to reflect a system that is equitable for all students. When equity is a fundamental principle of the reform movement, it serves as a template for designing and implementing programs, practices, and policies. The perspectives on equity vary, but the following statements provide guidance for thinking about this concept:

Equity has a variety of connotations, depending on who is using it. It is used to mean equal access of all children to instruction, inclusion of all in the classroom, capacity building, diversity, or the offering of special services. Some, however, fear equity in any form.

Equity is providing all that is needed to help students overcome the consequence of barriers, regardless of where we find them.

Equity as diversity or multiculturalism is not the addition of materials or ideas from under represented cultures; rather, it involves the integrated use of context and approaches of all cultural perspectives.

Equity means equal distribution of resources, particularly money, which implies that one school or district receives the same amount as another, usually in the same district or state.

The preceding statements illustrate how diverse the discussion on equity can be. However, some common language emerges: inclusion, access, fairness, enabling, diversity, multiculturalism, capacity building, special services, and learning. (Cummings, 1995, pp. 1–2)

Equity issues in education have been a focal point in the study of students learning mathematics. The NCTM Standards deal with the affective domain. A common theme focuses on students' self-confidence in their personal ability to learn and do mathematics. Society often presents views of mathematics that are not always conducive to good mathematics learning or instruction. Many times good performance in mathematics is viewed as the exception rather than the rule. Frequently, boys were expected to perform better than girls in mathematical settings. For years, there was an unstated position that "nice girls" did not do mathematics. Thankfully, that attitude has changed. There is still peer pressure in some segments of school society that places negative value on good performance in mathematics. Such perceptions can destroy the ambitions of some students.

As a teacher of mathematics, it is your responsibility to "sell" the subject to all students. As an effective representative of your product, what do you do to create an appealing atmosphere? How do you convince all students in your classes they can succeed? Can you demonstrate applications of the concepts being learned? When a student says, "When will I ever use this junk?" (perhaps not in those words, but the message will be that clear), what will you say? Students have become hardened to the learning of mathematics. Many of them are convinced there is no earthly value to the subject. We give them examples supposedly from everyday life. For some strange reason, the answers to our problems are almost always integers. Somehow the students are aware that, in the real world, the answers are not always integers. We give them real-world problems to work with, but often these situations are not from their world, and rarely are they aimed at girls. We must provide equity for all students, who must be encouraged in all mathematical settings.

---

## EXERCISE 2.7

1. Examine the problem sections of a secondary mathematics textbook. How many of the problems come from the world viewed by a student? Of all the problems, how many appear to be designed to appeal to girls?

---

**Additional exercises can be found on the website.**

Student perception is that we frequently make them learn mathematics as a means of torturing them and making their lives more miserable. Perhaps there is some truth to that last statement. Suppose we want to know the zeros of $f(x) = x^2 + 3x - 7$. The quadratic formula can be used to compute the values, but it could be easier to use a graphing calculator, software, or Internet application such as Desmos.com to plot the curve shown in Fig. 2.1. Then, either zoom as seen in Fig. 2.2 on the location where the curve crosses the $x$-axis, or use a table function as shown in Fig. 2.3 to approach the value.

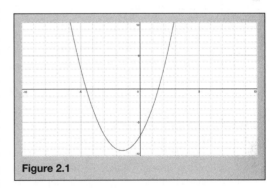

**Figure 2.1**

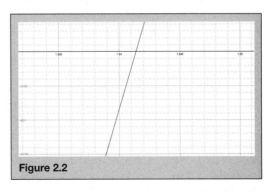

**Figure 2.2**

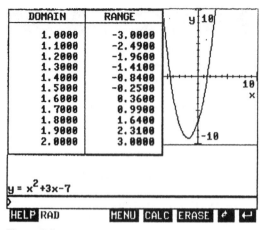

**Figure 2.3**

## CURRICULUM

The definitions of curriculum vary. Students often describe the mathematics curriculum in terms of some of the computations they learn in a given class. Students believe that the teacher has the power to teach whatever is appealing whenever desired. The students feel that the teacher is the ultimate controller of curricular power. They generally are not aware of the forces outside the classroom that drive the curriculum. Teachers would define curriculum as what they teach to the students. Administrators view curriculum as a body of course offerings including content in a specific course and all other planned school events. Members of the community view the school curriculum as a group of courses designed to produce what they want. A philosopher says the curriculum is the group of courses designed to expose the student to the necessary items that will develop an individual. Perhaps the best definition comes from the idea that curriculum is what happens in your classroom with your students. A multitude of forces affect the mathematics curriculum. Your task becomes one of determining which forces get emphasis, and how much.

## TEST-DRIVEN CURRICULUM

Some educators advocate a national test for different disciplines. Would this have a positive or negative impact on teaching and learning? Over recent years, many educators fear that future teacher success may be judged on the success of students on standardized tests. Some educators may feel that their success is currently viewed based on success of students on state standardized tests. The No Child Left Behind Act of 2001 (NCLB, http://www2.ed.gov/nclb) requires increased state and district accountability of student progress and learning. Increased pressure has been placed on standardized testing throughout the United States.

Increased pressure on standardized testing can put a teacher in an awkward position. As the impact of NCLB continues, the tests begin defining the curriculum. State tests are supposed to be based on state standards and curriculum frameworks based upon the NCTM Standards. Will Common Core Standards move the United States to a national assessment? Many state tests are already given a month prior to the end of school. If we use a national standardized test for all secondary grade levels and courses, we have shortened the curriculum by approximately one month. But some educators will begin reviewing for this examination at least 1–2 weeks prior to the test. Therefore, we have now shortened the curriculum by approximately 5–6 weeks. This supposition raises some interesting questions:

Can the essentials of Algebra I or Geometry be covered in this time frame?

Will some topics be de-emphasized?

Is it reasonable to teach to the test?

What weight is given to the national test score in placement?

If a student passes the course with an A but fails to achieve the basic proficiency score on the national test, what course is taken next year?

What do you do for the rest of the Algebra I or Geometry year?

But, you say, there is no national test—*yet*. At this point, that may be true. Does your state have a state Algebra I test? Did the high school you attended have such a test, just for the school? Did you have to pass the test to graduate?

---

### EXERCISE 2.8

1. Is it reasonable to have a test of major proportions (like the national Algebra I test that was discussed) at some point during the school year? Why or why not? Describe the impact on the curriculum.

---

**Additional exercises can be found on the website.**

## TEXT-DRIVEN CURRICULUM

Many educators say there is no nationally defined curriculum. If the Common Core Standards are implemented by each state, educators may see movement in the direction of a national curriculum. But will this significantly influence what is taught in the classroom? Regardless of the Common Core Standards, most textbooks are similar. The similarities are rather easy to understand. States have established learning outcomes that define a course. The lists of state objectives is given to publishers who, in turn, produce texts that cover the specified material. All the lists are similar, but if differences do occur, publisher decisions are made based on potential sales. The state offering the largest sales potential would appear to have the greatest influence. State textbook adoption lists are a significant factor here, too. Publishers cannot produce a book for each set of objectives. Instead, one text is produced. The expectation is that the material in this text will meet or exceed the objectives of each state and district. Generally, this is a safe assumption. If material is in the book that is not on the district or state list of objectives, the teacher can opt to omit it. If the text does not contain material the state or district wants included, supplemental information can be supplied by the respective teachers. Basically, the text covers most, if not all, of the topics required.

Because each publisher works from the same list of objectives, the texts become similar. The order of presentation may vary; colors are different; explanations are distinctive; problem sets change; and areas of emphasis or importance are not the same. The publishers use different frills to sell their books. Still, much of the content is the same.

---

### EXERCISES 2.9

1. Is a national curriculum or text-driven curriculum desirable? Why or why not?
2. If the curriculum framework requires a specific concept taught that is not addressed in the textbook assigned to the student, will you teach the concept? How will you supplement the text?

## TEACHER-DRIVEN CURRICULUM

A class consists of students, a teacher, boards, a projector device (possibly an overhead projector), books, calculators, a computer, and other technology. Similarities exist wherever you go. The boards are different colors; the books vary, depending on the publisher, but they are quite similar. The availability of technology ranges from some students having calculators (the use of which may or may not be permitted) to having powerful computers equipped with the latest and greatest in software offerings. The available technology is one thing that could be quite different. Some students may have laptops, others may have iPads (or other tablets), while some students may have limited use of any technology. While technology can differ, there is one more thing that is the same. In almost every classroom, the expertise and knowledge reside with the teacher. In many instances, the class becomes an exercise in giving the teacher the desired answers. Curricular decisions are influenced by what the teacher knows about mathematical content, how learners think about mathematical concepts, and what instructional materials are used to teach mathematics (Shulman, 1986).

The irony is that many students like an atmosphere where knowledge and expertise reside with the teacher. They know the rules. They are basically told what to do and how to do it, which is easier than having to think! It is less complicated for the teacher, too. Rather than having a varied set of answers, one stereotypical response is gathered. Grading—er, ah, assessment—is clear and simple. Either the student got the idea as presented, or not. Right or wrong. No shades of gray. No need for the teacher to reflect on responses that vary from the norm. Everyone is on the same wavelength. However, approaches like this are not conducive to student flexibility. The student must be encouraged to develop personal intellect. The student is not in the classroom for the sole purpose of repeating the words of the instructor. We want to develop critical-thinking skills, not robotic responses. If learners have latitudes in how they can approach a problem, the generated responses stimulate additional thought and insight on the part of everyone.

It is imperative that the current model used in many classrooms be abandoned if we are to have mathematical growth for all students. Teachers seem compelled to ask questions the students can answer. In the process, teachers ascertain that knowledge has been acquired. However, the knowledge indicators are dependent on what questions are answered by the students based on questions asked by the teacher. The teacher dictates what the student is learning. Teachers define specific behaviors as being important. What latitudes are afforded to the student? Where is the problem solving? Where are the open-ended opportunities for student growth? What are the applications seen by the students?

How much better it would be if all classrooms provided for and encouraged flexible thinking, creative approaches, a variety of ideas, an atmosphere of curiosity, and a compilation of prior knowledge to be applied to some new challenging situation. What a wonderful world that would be! Students must be taught and encouraged to think! Teachers are no longer the centers of attention. Rather, they are motivators, simulators, instigators, co-investigators, participants, and cheerleaders. They have to work much harder. Because teaching is already a demanding, time-consuming profession, perhaps it is unreasonable to ask for such changes in the classroom. Maybe the teacher should continue to be the "sage on the stage." Eventually, the good students will learn that the world of mathematics can be exciting and invigorating. After all, you did, didn't you?

## CURRICULUM AS USUAL

The preceding sections have dealt with test-, text-, and teacher-centered curriculums. Is it reasonable to continue in these manners? Leaders from NCTM, MSEB, MAA, and state and local groups almost universally answer that question, "No!" We essentially have a basic skills curriculum. "Over the long term, basic skills only give you the right to compete against the Third World for Third World wages" (MSEB, 1989, p. 84). Is that what we want or need? Absolutely not! It is time to change.

## EXTERNAL PRESSURES ON THE CURRICULUM

What drives curriculum: standardized tests, learning theories, textbooks, tradition? Certainly all these influence what is covered in the classroom, but there are other forces as well. Societal needs play a role in what is taught. The current value placed on advanced education, coupled with the belief that an educated populace needs adequate mathematical background, sways society's judgment about what is to be covered in the mathematics curriculum.

At times, specific community needs have an impact on what is delivered as a part of the mathematical curriculum. The Greater Cleveland Project of the 1960s was formulated to meet the industrial needs in the Cleveland, Ohio, area. Industries reported that high school graduates were unable to perform the desired mathematical tasks related to area employment. The curriculum was adjusted to include information that would resolve the dilemma. The project was successful in the Cleveland area, but it would not have been overly useful in Vail, Colorado. Why?

The discussion about the Greater Cleveland Project points out a curriculum-influencing factor. We, as educators, seem to consistently strive for the one way we can use to teach all students the mathematics they need. Each time some new idea surfaces, groups of believers endorse it, seemingly saying we have finally found the thing that will solve all of our teaching problems. The idea works well with some concepts but fails miserably with others. It is then discarded and the search for the way continues. When will we learn that there is not one way to teach and learn mathematics for all students?

Effective teaching and learning of mathematics demands a variety of instructional methods to meet the needs of individual students in the curriculum. Educators cannot permit pressures from parents, administrators, specific segments of society, or influential individuals to dictate how mathematics is taught. As a professional educator, it will be your responsibility to call on all possible resources: your secondary learning experiences, college mathematics education classes, college education classes, college mathematics classes, internship experiences, mathematical applications from your life, information gathered from reading professional journals and conference attendance, and so on. Compiling your experiences with conscious thought about what you are asking your students to learn will help you define the curriculum in your classroom. So many things available to you are merely guides. You are the qualified professional. You know the students in your class. You would be the most likely person to decide what their mathematical exposures under your tutelage ought to be. Outside pressures may influence your thoughts, but they should not exclusively dictate what happens with your classes.

The Virginia State School Board unanimously adopted standards for mathematics, science, English, and social studies. Many parent and teacher groups objected to the initial drafts of the standards. One source of argument was specific questions that the critics contended would stifle creative thinking by emphasizing rote memorization. Some of the questions were removed, but not all of them. The basic idea is that these standards will gauge student achievement from kindergarten through 12th grade. Early in 2000, there was a battle raging in Massachusetts pertaining to adoption of standards. Educators comprised a committee defined to create what mathematics should be taught in the K–12 settings. The report also dealt with how mathematics should be meaningfully taught. The report met resistance from state leaders, parents, and other educators, eventually causing the educators who had defined the standards to be adopted to resign from the committee. The rift was essentially over what and how mathematics should be taught. Similar situations are developing across the country. There are a lot of opinions on what should be done. For some reason, some of the opinions contradict established research and knowledge related to how students learn mathematics.

---

### EXERCISE 2.10

1.  Should you, the teacher, as the local authority on your class, solely determine the material to be covered in a given class? If yes, why? If you say no, how much outside influence should be acceptable and why?

## INTERNAL PRESSURES ON THE CURRICULUM

Parents, demands of society, tests, texts, and tradition are some of the external pressures on the mathematics curriculum. There are also internal pressures. Certainly the textbook can be an internal pressure. Usually a given text is purchased for a given class. Most parents assume a student should bring a book home to study from. If you elect not to use the purchased book, you will have to answer to the department, parents, and administration. Someone thought the text was a wise purchase for the class. In that context, the book becomes an internal pressure. Similar arguments can be made for the other elements mentioned in the first sentence of this paragraph or for topics discussed earlier in this chapter.

There are other internal pressures. As attempts are made to integrate mathematics with other disciplines, influences will be exerted to achieve

objectives from other subject areas. Some are easy to see. Can you imagine a physics class where students were unable to deal with variables? In this light, algebra becomes a prerequisite for physics. That influences when students take algebra—a pressure of sorts. Some students take Algebra II and trigonometry the same year they take physics. Can you teach concepts of sound waves without some exposure to the sine wave? This is a pressure on the timing of mathematical concepts being taught within a course. If you team teach with an ancient history teacher on a unit dealing with Egypt, students might be best served if they have had some exposure to finding surface area or volume of a square-based, right pyramid. Perhaps the general science teacher is doing a unit on the metric system and you have collaborated in the planning. If you teach the same students, it might work for you to teach part of the topic from a mathematical viewpoint and the science teacher to use a different perspective for the rest of the material. This is another example of internal pressure on what is taught when—influencing the curriculum you deliver to your students.

Examinations like the ACT and SAT are an even greater pressure on the secondary mathematics curriculum areas. Algebra and geometry topics are incorporated into these tests. Given this, shouldn't the secondary mathematics curriculum include algebra and geometry concepts that would enhance student performance? Examinations such as these are major factors in determining college admission. In addition, some states have set goals to increase the number of high school students taking these college admission tests.

## TANGENTIAL PRESSURES ON THE CURRICULUM

External and internal pressures to deliver a certain curriculum are relatively easy to identify. Some pressures are not as obvious and yet they are felt. Tradition can be a significant factor here. Things are done a certain way because they have always been that way. This is a form of pressure. Suppose you are not too excited about teaching the First-Outer-Inner-Last (F.O.I.L.) method for finding the product of two binomials. Assume that no one at the school has ever done anything other than F.O.I.L. Prior classes have scored well on the tests. Suppose the attitude is that there is no need to confuse students with extraneous information. This acronym and process is easy for the students to memorize and for the teachers to teach. Memorization does not demonstrate true conceptual understanding. Suppose you resist the temptation to use F.O.I.L. Not changing becomes a pressure—not a direct pressure necessarily, but still one you are fully aware of. In your realization of the situation, you know better than to try to change things. That is a tangential pressure on the curriculum.

Tradition is not the only potential source of tangential pressures. Administrators, texts, tests, parents, other subject areas, and business can also apply pressures in a tangential manner. The problem is that some of these are not recognizable. Suppose some influential member of the community, who is also a faculty member in the local university's mathematics department, says something to the school superintendent, who says something to your principal, who says something to your department chair, who says something to you about how mathematics should be taught. That is pressure; but it has passed through several filters on its way to you. Is the message you got the same as the one that was sent? Do you dare approach the source for clarification? Do you dare disagree with the suggestion of such a well-placed individual? Granted this example has been made up, but it is not as far-fetched as some might want to believe. This is one way tangential pressures grow.

## EXTRACURRICULAR MATHEMATICS

You should be familiar with the emphasis placed on sports in secondary schools. Athletes are touted as school leaders and role models. Trophies, scholarships, and accolades abound for them. Everyone in the school and community knows the star athletes. This is a wonderful experience for students (assuming it is kept within control). Recently, a splendid addition has been made to the list of school activities that generate pride, honor, and respect for leading students. Mathematics contests have become a serious business. Participants spend long hours practicing. They take road trips to contests. Students are in the stands cheering for contestants. Pride is evident in the participants, coaches, school officials, parents, and communities. Students who do not make the traveling team participate in club-level activities to build their mathematical knowledge and interest. What a wonderful opportunity for students! There are a variety of potential sources of mathematics competitions. Sponsorship for these events comes from a variety of sources. The American Mathematics Competitions (AMC; http://amc.maa.org/) are sponsored by the Mathematical Association of America (http://www.maa.org) and a host of other professional organizations that strive to promote and support the importance of mathematics in our society. The competitions are dedicated to strengthening the mathematical capabilities of our nation's youth through the participation in the following national contests:

- American Mathematics Contest 8 (AMC 8),
- American Mathematics Contest 10 (AMC 10),
- American Mathematics Contest 12 (AMC 12),
- American Invitational Mathematics Examination (AIME), and
- United States of America Mathematical Olympiad (USAMO).

The first MAA sponsor contest was given to approximately 238 schools and more than 6,000 students New York in 1950. In 2010–2011, more than 413,000 student from 5,100 schools participated in AMC contests (http://amc.maa.org/whatswhat.shtml).

Other competitions are available through:

MATHCOUNTS (http://mathcounts.org/)

Mu Alpha Theta (http://www.mualphatheta.org/)

Society of Engineers (http://www.nspe.org/)

This is not an all-inclusive list of competitions, but it will provide you with a starting point.

### EXERCISES 2.11

1. If you have been to a local, regional, or state mathematics contest, describe the emotion and general atmosphere of the setting. If you have not seen a competition, visit one as an observer and then describe what you noticed.

2. Locate a secondary student who is currently a member of a school mathematics team or who has participated in a mathematics competition in the past year. Describe that student's reactions and feelings about the associated experiences.

**Additional exercises can be found on the website.**

## VERTICAL COMMUNICATIONS

Items in the curriculum are influenced by a variety of people. There is a need for communication among individuals teaching the same course, those teaching the next course in the sequence, those teaching the previous course in the sequence, and even those in "feeder schools" for your school. A multitude of people can have an influence on the material taught. Formative background for the idea of variables can be approached in the early grades through using □, ?, or even __. The teacher needs to let the children know that the □, ?, or __ is taking the place of the desired answer. Once the appropriate response is determined, the □, ?, or __ will be replaced. The subliminal gains from such a reminder by the lower-grade teacher can ease some of the difficulties many students experience when encountering variables later. They are aware that the symbol □, ?, __ or even "x" is temporary in many situations. They should know it is waiting to be replaced by some value.

There is a need for vertical communication to make others aware of the mathematical background needs for your classes. Teachers from the lower grades have dealt with variables when they were taking mathematics classes in the pre-K–12 school environment and when they were in some college classes. In their curriculum, variables may not frequently be mentioned or stressed, so, even though they know the information, it becomes lost in the many other demands. Teachers who precede you in the curriculum want to help their students succeed, just like you will. It is imperative that you let them know what will make things easier for students in your classes. It is also important that you convey to these other teachers that these ideas are only suggestions that can assist student learning in the classes you teach. Remember, these teachers are professionals with educational knowledge as well. Few teachers like to have someone else mandate how to teach a class.

Some of the pressures that are placed on teachers have been briefly discussed in other sections. The following is taken from *Counting on You* (MSEB, 1991) and provides a different insight and, to some extent, a summary of the environment teachers face:

> The fact that teachers in the United States do not have the high level of professional status and respect afforded their counterparts in other countries has been a significant factor in our nation's inability to respond to the educational changes it faces. As each cycle of would-be reform comes around, we exhort teachers to do better, lament their poor preparation in college, search for additional ways to hold them accountable, and generally treat them as objects in need of repair.
>
> In the current cycle of reform, U.S. teachers of mathematics—more strongly and more effectively than any other group in the nation—have risen to the challenge presented by the President and the governors. Through their standards they have set the agenda for reform. Few teachers in today's schools have the authority or resources necessary to carry out this agenda. But as schools evolve from a model with teachers as hired hands to one in which teachers function as professional educators, they should welcome the challenge to implement national standards for mathematics education. (MSEB, 1991, p. 19)

NCTM and Common Core Standards are a beginning. They call for the vertical communication described here. Good conscience and common sense should dictate that we work toward this communication goal as rapidly as possible. But you should carefully read the remarks from MSEB and note the date of 1991. As we continue to reform education and raise standards, teachers of mathematics continue to rise to the occasion to meet the needs of students in an ever changing world.

## COOPERATIVE LEARNING

Cooperative learning is more than putting students into groups and giving them a task. You need to give careful thought to the tasks assigned to the groups, how the groups are formed, and the roles of members of each group. This can be shown through scored discussions (Leach, 1992). Four students form a group. In front of the class, they are required to solve a problem. Prior to getting in front of the group, they have no knowledge of the question they are to be asked. The teacher uses a checklist to evaluate the students' performance solving the problem. The emphasis is placed on the processes, strategies, and cooperativeness of the participants. For example, a student gets points for drawing a group member into the conversation. The check sheet is shown in Fig. 2.4 or you can download the rubric from the text website at www.routledge.com/cw/rock. The participants sit facing each other in front of the room. L1 refers to the student on the left side of the class, closest to the board. L2 indicates the other student on the left.

SCORED DISCUSSION

1. Determining a
possible strategy (3)
L1_____ R1_____
L2_____ R2_____

1. Inattention/
Distracting (–2)
L1_____ R1_____
L2_____ R2_____

2. Successfully
communicating a
strategy (3)
L1_____ R1_____
L2_____ R2_____

2. Interrupting (–2)
L1_____ R1_____
L2_____ R2_____

3. Correctly applying a
property (2)
L1_____ R1_____
L2_____ R2_____

3. Making an incorrect
application or Assumption (–1)

L1_____ R1_____
L2_____ R2_____

4. Recognizing
misused properties or
math errors (2)
LL1_____ R1_____
L2_____ R2_____

4. Monopolizing (–3)

LL1_____ R1_____
L2_____ R2_____

5. Drawing another
into discussion (2)
L1_____ R1_____
L2_____ R2_____

5. Making a personal
attack (–3)
L1_____ R1_____
L2_____ R2_____

6. Asking a clarifying
question (3)
L1_____ R1_____
L2_____ R2_____

**Figure 2.4**

Students are given 5 to 7 minutes in which to cooperatively formulate a solution to the given question. They are evaluated on their ability to work as a group, as they progress toward a ssolution. The teacher uses the checklist to evaluate the listed areas. Three points would be awarded to a student who develops a possible strategy for solving the problem. Three points are also awarded to a student who can successfully explain a possible solution.

A question that could be asked of the group is, Which costs more per pound?

(A)  M&Ms
(B)  Ice Breakers mints
(C)  Rib-eye steak
(D)  Toyota Corolla

A strategy might be to determine an approximate cost of each item. Another student might ask, "What does that have to do with anything?" That student would gain three points for asking a clarifying question. Another student would respond, "If you knew how much an 8-ounce bag of M&Ms

costs, you could find out how much they cost per pound." This student gets three points for successfully communicating a strategy. A silent group member might be asked how the cost per pound could be determined, and three points would be generated because a nonparticipant has been drawn into the discussion. As the exchange continues, students can be penalized for interrupting others or monopolizing time. Although the audience cannot receive positive points, they can earn negative points for their future discussion if they disrupt the class during this scored discussion. As students become more comfortable with scored discussions, the teacher can randomly ask students in the audience to also use the checklist to assess students participating in the scored discussion. This allows children to become active participants in the assessment process. Try a scored discussion once a week with four students each week in your classroom. You may be surprised at the generated enthusiasm for this weekly event.

The scored discussion is a method of leading students to the ability to work together as a group. One hurdle to group work in mathematics is the traditional view that mathematics learning is an individual activity. The prior mathematical experiences students possess may create anxieties that hinder the ability to function in a cooperative mathematics group. Some people resist the use of cooperative groups in mathematics because of their belief that only a few talented individuals are capable of learning mathematics. This is a clear contradiction of the approach that all students can learn meaningful mathematics.

Research results (Davidson, 1985) indicate that cooperative grouping generates positive results in areas of:

Academic achievement;

Self-esteem or self-confidence in learning;

Intergroup relations, including cross-race and cross-cultural friendships;

Social acceptance of mainstreamed children;

Ability to use social skills.

Additional findings about cooperative grouping in mathematics include the idea that each group member should have some accountability. There is lack of agreement about how to form groups. Some say groups should be homogeneous, while others say groups should be created to show a mix of race, ability, and gender. There seems to be agreement that forming groups comprised of all fast or slow students is not a good idea. Agreement about whether or not social skills should be modeled and taught as a part of the cooperative groups does not exist. Questions exist relating to how much interdependence is necessary within a cooperative group and whether or not there is a continuum of interdependencies (Johnson, 1981). A constructivist would say the classroom becomes an arena for the learning of the entire individual, social and academic.

## DIAGNOSTIC TEACHING

Students send messages to teachers that give clues about their levels of understanding in any class. Are those sent messages received by the teacher? Sometimes the signals have full impact and at other times they have none. If a teacher asks a class to perform some readiness task and none of the students can do it, the message should be clear—some background work is necessary before proceeding. Messages are usually more subtle and require careful examination and concentration. It is common for a student to attempt to conceal a lack of knowledge to avoid more work, embarrassment, or just admitting something is not clear.

You need to be aware of the "SOS" signals students send. These distress signals might be an obscure look of befuddlement. It might be done that way because the student "would never be caught" asking, staying after class for clarification, or showing interest. The message is sent, though. It is a cry for help. You need to receive the signal. At other times, the signal may be much easier to interpret. In the number trick "1089" a student selects a three-digit number without repeating any digits. The selected value is reversed and the smaller of the two three-digit numbers is subtracted from the larger. In the answer, the tens digit will always be 9. Asking for individuals who do not have a 9 in the tens digit of the answer provides some fast diagnostic information. If the hands of most of the class are raised, you need to examine your instructions. Typically, there is only a small number of students with raised hands. You can safely assume one of two things: The students did not understand or follow your instructions, or they have difficulty subtracting when regrouping is involved. There are other possible reasons for the error, but these are the dominant ones. You are now aware of the need to spend some extra time with selected individuals. You have diagnosed a difficulty and can now prescribe a remedy.

Diagnostic teaching is a lot like being a medical doctor. Individuals go to a doctor with symptoms of some illness. The doctor examines the person and compiles all symptoms. Based on the available information, education, and prior experiences, a diagnosis is made, corrective measures are prescribed, and the patient is told to call back in a given amount of time if the situation does not improve. The patient wants to get better and has volunteered information and asked for help. Teachers do not have that luxury. Students frequently try to conceal symptoms and rarely volunteer information. Still, teachers are expected to make these individuals better students of mathematics who are able to perform desired tasks based on their overall mathematical health. Ultimately, the teacher is expected to diagnose and prescribe for each student as needed.

Diagnostic teaching is not a simple task. Like the doctor, you must draw on a wide variety of training, experience, and understanding of the individual involved. You are expected to be aware of the basic psychological construct of all students. It is assumed you know the current social pressures as well. When you examine a mathematical illness, you must have a continuum of skills and conceptual developments that precede the problem area. If one, some, or all of those items are missing from the student's background, you are expected to be able to prescribe a series of remedies for the student that will correct all the deficiencies. Like the doctor, it is assumed your judgment is infallible and that you can resolve the situation quickly and effectively. Diagnostic errors and incorrect treatment in the medical arena can have dramatic consequences. Ineffective diagnosis and prescription in education can be equally tragic, because it can lead to the mathematical demise of a student. Diagnostic teaching is a serious endeavor and should be approached as such.

## ERROR PATTERNS

Sometimes, students use an incorrect method or algorithm for solving a problem. Error patterns can be generated from lack of understanding. There could be other reasons. Here the emphasis is on diagnosing what error has been made and how to correct it. Some errors are easy to determine.

If the subtraction problem 823–169 yields a response of 746, you are fairly safe in assuming the student subtracted the smaller digit from the larger in each place. Subtracting the smaller digit from the larger is a common error pattern. The motivation for such a move is often attributed to the student's being told at some time that a "big number cannot be subtracted from a little one." The genesis of this statement comes from the desire to have students realize the need for regrouping in the subtraction process.

Other error patterns are not as easy to determine. The following problems were submitted by a high school student. There was no scratch work. You see everything the student showed.

| 8431 | 9243 | 7152 | 8230 |
|------|------|------|------|
| −2576 | −1678 | −2649 | −4128 |
| 3965 | 5675 | 3513 | 3112 |

Here we are concerned with how to determine the error and a possible reason, so corrective measures to prevent the same situation can be taken. This is not always easy because the root of the problem might begin several grades prior to yours. Before reading on, you should have attempted to determine the error being made in the four subtraction problems given.

What was that student doing with these problems? How do we fix this? It appears as if subtraction facts are under control. Assuming that, the flaw must lie within the application of the algorithm. Regrouping is performed when necessary, so that is not the problem. The trouble is associated with the regrouping. Where is the regrouping performed? The student is going to the leftmost digit to regroup, skipping any places between the location of the desired regrouping and that digit. In the first problem, the necessary 11 is created in the units place and the 8 is decreased to 7 in the thousands place. The tens-place subtraction decreases that new 7 in the thousands place to a 6, creating the necessary 13 in the tens place. The hundreds changes the new 6 to a 5 and creates the necessary 14 in the hundreds place. Now, the problem becomes 5,000–3,000 and it is done. That error is not easy to determine.

Although we cannot be certain, some guesses can be made as to the cause of this error. In this particular case, the class had most recently reviewed subtraction problems of the type 4000−1235, which required initial regrouping from the thousands digit of the sum. It is assumed that the student was combining the two procedures and did some "creative mathematics." Discussions with the student did not reveal a clear picture of the cause.

Since part of the problem stems from place value, expressing each number in expanded notation form may help correct the misconception. For the first example,

| 8431 | expand | $8000 + 400 + 30 + 1$ |
|------|--------|------|
| − 2576 | expand | $− (2000 + 500 + 70 + 6)$ |

Using the student method, 8000 is changed to 7000 while the 1 is altered to become 11, because of the regroupings.

$7000 + 400 + 30 + 11$

$(2000 + 500 + 70 + 6)$

The key is that $8000 + 400 + 30 + 1 \neq 7000 + 400 + 30 + 11$ is understood by the student. Correctly regrouping to account for the units digit would yield

$8000 + 400 + 20 + 11$

$− (2000 + 500 + 70 + 6)$

where $8000 + 400 + 30 + 1 = 8000 + 400 + 20 + 11$. Continuing the procedure would yield

$8000 + 300 + 120 + 11$

$− (2000 + 500 + 70 + 6)$

$7000 + 1300 + 120 + 11$

$− (2000 + 500 + 70 + 6)$

The preceding discussion should give insight into how this particular error pattern was disclosed and remedied. Development of the skills necessary to perform such diagnosis and prescription is rooted in your understanding of the mathematics involved, time, and experience. Achieving the ability to determine error patterns is not an easy task, but it can reap large benefits for your students.

The following error pattern was submitted by a middle school student. What is the error involved?

| 36 | 45 | 92 | 68 |
|------|------|------|------|
| × 47 | × 68 | × 63 | × 98 |
| 492 | 640 | 276 | 964 |
| 204 | 420 | 602 | 1172 |
| 2532 | 4840 | 6296 | 12684 |

If you have not tried to define the error, now is the time! Otherwise you will read the solution, which will help you with this error type but will do little to build your diagnostic skills. It takes practice. Notice that, in the third problem from the left, the product of 92 and 3 is correct. This gives a partial clue. It appears as if the student has command of the multiplication facts but that the algorithm is confused. The error involves commuting steps, but it has a dramatic impact. The student is adding the regrouping and then multiplying, as opposed to multiplying first and then adding the regrouped value.

As your error pattern diagnostic skills increase, the problem areas are easier to detect. It does take conscious thought and practice. Each of the two error pattern types described in the text had four examples. Multiple examples are necessary to enable you to define patterns. You can easily convince yourself of the validity of that statement by attempting the following exercises, looking only at the first example in each problem set.

---

### EXERCISES 2.12

1. Determine the error pattern the student made in each of the following problems:

   $46.325 + 234.56 + 13.567 + 2.7964 = 111.312$

   $3.579 + 54.32 + 684.2 = 158.53$

   $35.234 + 67.531 = 102.765$

   $4.8 + 32 + 0.79 + 7.8 = 23.7$

   Describe the error the student is making. List the steps you would employ to assist the student in learning how to do the problem correctly and avoid repeating the same error. Could this error have been caused because the students are not accustomed to seeing addition problems written horizontally?

2. Determine the error pattern the student made in each of the following problems:

| 4567 | 389 | 2468 | 3421 |
|---|---|---|---|
| +7968 | +964 | +3517 | +2476 |
| 14635 | 1453 | 7085 | 5897 |

---

## ASSESSMENT

We in the mathematics community are fortunate to have the leadership provided by organizations like NCTM, MAA, American Mathematical Association of Two-Year Colleges, and MSEB. Their research and support have provided a solid background and set of guidelines we can use in the classroom. The Assessment Standards (NCTM, 1995b) provide a beginning point from which to work. The discussion in this section provides general comments about assessment. The Assessment Standards should be a part of your professional library. You should be familiar with the recommendations pro-

vided in the publication and work to install that direction in your curriculum.

Assessment is more than paper–pencil testing. You look at the work students do and determine their strengths and weaknesses. You examine your planning, presentation, and discussion methods to decide how they impact the learning styles of your students. You look at the curriculum on a day-to-day basis and from the vantage point of the big picture, considering a class as its own entity and also as it integrates into the sequence of courses available for students. You evaluate texts to determine which is most advantageous for your students, school objectives, and school curriculum.

You assess your mathematics program in order to determine:

The success of the overall program;

Whether students are learning;

How well the established mathematical goals are met;

If students are capable of applying the mathematical knowledge in other areas of the curriculum and life;

When students are enticed to study more mathematics;

The worthiness and usefulness of the content;

If the program is teachable and learnable.

As a teacher of mathematics, one of your basic goals is to help all students learn and enjoy mathematics to the fullest possible extent. Teachers assess achievement of students in the classroom because they must:

Determine the progress of each student;

Ascertain the status of each student;

Know the extent to which content and skills are mastered.

Knowing the extent to which content and skills are mastered involves diagnosing strengths and weaknesses for each student. This is necessary in order to:

Accurately place students in the curriculum continuum;

Assign grades;

Help you learn how to teach more effectively;

Gather specific rather than global information on individuals;

Analyze how an answer is determined;

Structure your teaching style.

---

Tests can be diagnostic instruments. If the information gathered is to be useful in your diagnosis, sufficient data must be taken. How many questions should be asked to assure adequate information about a concept? If one question is asked, you have little certainty about whether or not a student has mastered the material. Asking two questions dealing with the concept is better, but how sure can you be? If a student gets one of the two right, what do you know? You could give another test, assess other work the student has done, or talk with the student about the issue, but those each take time. Multiply the time required by the number of times you possibly will need to do something like this times the number of students you will be dealing with and you begin to see some constraints.

Maybe asking three questions would do it. If a student gets all three right or all three wrong, you would be fairly certain about the ability level pertaining to this concept. Perhaps five is a better number of questions to ask on a given concept. Your confidence level would be much greater if a student got all five correct. The problem is, the test becomes extremely long very quickly with five questions per concept.

Test length is particularly significant if concepts are closely and finely defined. Solving $X + 7 = 12$ involves a different set of skills from solving $3X + 7 = 12$. Realistically, even $X - 7 = 12$ is different from $X + 7 = 12$ in light of the fact that some students see these as entirely different, unrelated problem types. If you treat these as different problem types, and if you ask five questions per concept on a diagnostic test, the test will be very long. How much time can realistically be allocated to diagnostic testing?

Consider the following question that could be used to build part of a diagnostic test. Five possible methods to solve this multistep equation are shown. The first response is correct and each of the following responses is generated by an error pattern. There are other possible errors, but these will suffice for this discussion.

$3X + 5 = 17$
$\quad -5 = -5$     − constant from both sides
$\quad 3X = 12$     simplify
$\quad X = 4$     ÷ by coefficient

Another "solution"

$3X + 5 = 17$
$\quad 3X = 17 + 5$     + constant to both sides
$\quad 3X = 22$     simplify
$\quad X = 7$     ÷ by coefficient

Another "solution"

$3X + 5 = 17$
$\quad 3X = 17 - 5$     − constant from both sides
$\quad 3X = 12$     simplify
$\quad X = 36$     × by coefficient

Another "solution"

$3X + 5 = 17$
$3X + 5 - 5 = 17$     − constant from left side
$\quad 3X = 17$     simplify
$\quad X = 5.4$     ÷ by coefficient

Another "solution"

$3X + 5 = 17$
$3X + 5 - 5 = 17$     − constant from left side
$\quad 3X = 17$     simplify
$\quad X = 51$     × by coefficient

Good testing practices dictate that in multiple-choice tests, the same letter should not always represent the correct answer. For simplicity's sake, we will use A for the correct response in each question in Fig. 2.5; B for adding the constant to both sides (+ constant in Fig. 2.5); C for subtracting the constant from both sides but then multiplying by the coefficient (− constant/$X$ in Fig. 2.5); D for subtracting the constant from the left side only and then dividing both sides by the coefficient (− left/÷ in Fig. 2.5); and E for subtracting the constant from the left side of the equation and multiplying the right by the coefficient (− left/$X$ in Fig. 2.5). This will simplify the discussion for the example being built. There are five questions for the concept.

Figure 2.5 shows additional poor testing practices ($2T + 5 = 13$ having only one decimal answer; responses not arranged in ascending or descending order; inconsistent format by using mixed numbers, improper fractions, decimals). As was noted earlier, the emphasis in this case is on diagnostic matters, and other issues are ignored for the sake of this discussion. A student selecting answer A on all five questions in the test would adequately demonstrate mastery (assuming honesty). A student selecting A in four out of five of the questions would probably be considered as having mastered the concept. As the number of correct responses decreases, the confidence level in the student's ability to do that problem type also decreases.

Suppose a student selects B as the correct response for each of the problems in Fig. 2.5. Not only do you know the student missed them, but you also have a good idea about what was done to get

| Question | Correct | + con | -con/X | -left/÷ | -left/X |
|---|---|---|---|---|---|
| $3M + 5 = 17$ | A) M = 4 | B) $M = 7\frac{1}{3}$ | A) M = 36 | B) $M = 5\frac{2}{3}$ | E) M = 51 |
| $2N + 4 = 18$ | A) N = 7 | B) N = 11 | B) N = 28 | D) N = 9 | E) N = 36 |
| $4P + 6 = 32$ | A) P = 6.5 | B) P = 9.5 | C) P = 104 | D) P = 8 | E) P = 128 |
| $7R + 3 = 12$ | A) $R = \frac{9}{7}$ | A) $R = \frac{15}{7}$ | D) R = 63 | D) $R = \frac{12}{7}$ | E) R = 84 |
| $2T + 5 = 13$ | A) T = 4 | B) T = 9 | C) T = 16 | D) T = 6.5 | E) T = 26 |

**Figure 2.5**

those answers. This makes prescription easy and, in most cases, effective. A personal comment or note on the paper stating the error and what should have been done might correct the situation. This discussion would be the same for options C, D, or E. Only when a student responds randomly would there be a need for additional time invested to analyze the error pattern. In such a situation, an immediate question would be whether or not the student is interested in learning. If the answer is negative, there is an entirely different set of circumstances that need to be resolved before tackling the errors encountered in solving the equations.

One concept has been tested. $3X - 5 = 17$ is different because other skills are involved. This could lead to a very long test. Test length can be resolved by giving many short tests. The time required to create such questions is not an insignificant factor. Suppose you decide to ask five questions like the ones in Fig. 2.5 for each concept covered and that you teach the same course each year. A file of questions can be developed over a few years. In the first year, you create five questions. The second year, you create three more and use two of the initial five. In the third year, you create two more and select three from the pool of eight developed earlier. At this point, the amount of time required to create questions is drastically reduced, and you still have all the benefits of having a powerful diagnostic tool that provides information quickly.

One huge factor in teaching is finding time to do all the required tasks at a quality level. It can be done, though. One way is to have little life outside teaching. Another is through thoughtful organization of your assessment program. Using questions like those described in Fig. 2.5 is a start. Soon you have a pool of those questions and there is little need to add to the pool after a few years. Then you

have a battery of quality questions that provide extensive information for you. Little time is required to evaluate student responses. Not only can you tell if the answer is correct but, in the event a student answers incorrectly, you have sufficient information to quickly determine the errors being made in most instances. Other formats should be considered; however, using a multiple-choice diagnostic instrument as a mainstay of your assessment program does have advantages.

In addition to formats different from multiple choice, other assessment procedures help too. You need to listen, observe, reflect, interpret, and analyze your actions, as well as those of the students as individuals and as a collective whole.

Observation can be a valuable assessment tool. You can watch as you move around the room during group work. As students respond to your questions, notice facial expressions and body language. Be aware of the emotional climate in the room. When a particular student asks a question, is it sincere or an attempt to get some means of praise from you? Is the student a flexible thinker who is willing to try different approaches to the same question? Is the student asking merely as an attempt to lead you away from the objective at hand?

Observations sometimes lead to the need for additional information, perhaps coming from interviews with individual students. One advantage of the interview is the removal of writing skills. Students do exist who can talk through a proof when they cannot write it. Be careful that they do not look to you for visual clues as they go through it. This approach is in line with suggestions that students be able to communicate mathematically. Interviewing requires time and rapport with the student. You are attempting to determine what the student knows. Some students will attempt to tell you what they think you want to hear. You need to be able to discern the difference. Time is a major factor in this approach, but the idea should not be discarded as an option for some students, without careful consideration.

One answer to time as an assessment tool comes from a checklist. You are aware of what a student should know about a concept. A list of items related to that concept can prove useful. As you observe or reflect on what a student has done, you should be able to quickly establish a picture of what needs to be done to strengthen that student's understandings. A checklist can be an invaluable readiness tool. One specific checklist can be used to lay the foundation for attitudinal surveys. Does the student appear to like mathematics? Does the student work well with others? The scored discussion covered earlier is an example of how a checklist could be used as an assessment tool.

Other assessment tools include items you should be familiar with from education courses: criterion-referenced tests, norm-referenced tests, and standardized tests. Various versions of these tests are often supplied with the text or by the school system. Students are accustomed to this kind of test and, for the most part, comfortable with them. One significant drawback to these tests is that they often function at the knowledge level. It is imperative that we start asking students non-knowledge-level questions as a part of their assessment program if we truly want the student to learn in a constructivist environment. Only then will we begin to have insight into each student's true ability and understanding.

Another method of gathering information is the portfolio. A portfolio should contain examples of the best works of a student, as determined by the student. You can provide guidelines that suggest inclusion of an exemplary test paper, a proof, some homework problems, and so on. The portfolio should go beyond that type of information, though. Perhaps segments from a journal that indicate attitudes and feelings about the study of mathematics are appropriate. Certainly, examples of applications of topics covered would be acceptable. Demonstrations of the ability to use and interpret results generated through graphing calculators, spreadsheets, symbol-manipulating/function-plotting software, and dynamic geometry software would be appropriate. This is not an exhaustive list of elements that could be included in a student's portfolio, but it is a start. You need to consider the concept and build components into it that are appropriate for you and your students.

Not all assessment ideas are successful or accepted. This compounds the issue immensely. What methods should be adopted? Which ones are trends that will vanish? Will some of the new ideas have a lasting impact on the school mathematics curriculum? The curriculum and its associated tentacles are not easily altered.

Fourteen schools across the country that were considered pioneers in the use of performance assessment in evaluating their students' progress were studied for three years. The conclusion was that performance assessments are having little effect on what gets taught in the classroom. One part of the discussion was that multiple-choice and short-answer questions readily gauge what students know. On the other hand, performance assessments are aimed at evaluating what students can do with what they know. Researchers found that content taught in the classrooms had changed little. Teachers complained because the new assessment methods allowed them less time to cover all the material they had taught in the past. Students were writing more, but the writing was not necessarily better. The researchers concluded that the schools where changes in teaching and learning had taken a firmer hold were those in which teachers had been involved with the new assessment systems from the start.

Assessment is a continuing integral aspect of teaching mathematics. It helps you determine if the students are learning what you think they should. It helps the student know if the ideas garnered are those the teacher deems valuable. Assessment involves appraisal as well as measurement. No one form is appropriate for all aspects of assessment. You need to be aware of the multitude of avenues available to you and select those that will prove most beneficial to you in assisting your students to learn and appreciate as much mathematics as possible for each one of them.

## CONCLUSION

You have traveled from beginning foundations through the latest thinking of the mathematics education community as you looked at learning theory, curriculum, and assessment. The associated topics and ideas are intertwined to such a degree that it is difficult to discuss one without the other. You need to blend these discussions with those from your other classes into a position that is comfortable for you. You cannot include an item in your construct because we, or some authorities, say so. It should be there because it fits with your philosophy and beliefs about the teaching of mathematics. The only feasible way you can create your own view of teaching mathematics is to be familiar with all the facets of the arena. It takes time and energy to learn all the aspects, but the benefits you and your students will reap will be worth the effort.

## STICKY QUESTIONS

1. Read the NCTM *Professional Standards for Teaching Mathematics* (1991) that are appropriate for your proposed teaching level. Define areas of agreement and disagreement that you find. Search your thoughts and determine why you agree or disagree, whether or not you should, and if necessary why you should or should not alter your position.

2. Read the NCTM *Assessment Standards for Teaching Mathematics* (1995b) that are appropriate for your proposed teaching level. Define areas of agreement and disagreement that you find. Search your thoughts and determine why you agree or disagree, whether or not you should, and if necessary why you should or should not alter your position.

3. Read the NCTM *Principles and Standards for School Mathematics* (2000) that are appropriate for your proposed teaching level. Define areas of agreement and disagreement that you find. Search your thoughts and determine why you agree or disagree, whether or not you should, and if necessary why you should or should not alter your position.

4. Read the Common Core Standards for Mathematics (http://www.corestandards.org/the-standards/mathematics) that are appropriate for your proposed teaching level. Define areas of agreement and disagreement that you find. Search your thoughts and determine why you agree or disagree, whether or not you should, and if necessary why you should or should not alter your position.

5. Should you read the publications in Exercises 1–6? What will you do when you disagree with the "authorities" positions? Is this the gospel?

6. Select a secondary mathematics textbook. Discuss its strengths and weaknesses as a determining force in the curriculum for the selected class. How much emphasis should it receive as a curriculum for the class?

7. Select a secondary mathematics textbook. Discuss its strengths and weaknesses as a determining force in the assessment plan for the selected class. How much emphasis should it receive?

8. Select a secondary mathematics textbook's assessment resource supplement. Discuss its strengths and weaknesses. Would you select a text that has no resources? Why or why not?

## PROBLEM-SOLVING CHALLENGES

1. **Pyramid of Numbers**

   1
   11
   21
   1211
   111221
   312211

   What are the next two lines?

   **Check out the website for the solution.**

2. **The Letter Mania**

   Based on the following two groups of letters:

   Group 1: A, E, F, H

   Group 2: B, C, D, G

   Place each of the following letters in its appropriate group: I, J, K, L

   **Check out the website for the solution.**

## Why Are Manhole Covers Round?

For all discussions in this activity, it is assumed that the manhole and lid are similar shapes, with the lid being slightly larger, and that the ground is horizontal. In real life, manholes are round so the cover, or lid, cannot fall down the hole, no matter how the lid is held. If the requirement for the shape of a manhole is that the cover not be able to fall down the hole, what shapes other than circles, if any, could be used? Assume that when the manhole side length (for a square, for example) is 36 inches the side length of the lid (also a square) is 37 inches.

If we accept that the lid has to be similar to the hole, the lid can be made large enough so that it will not fall down the hole. As things are applied in real life, the manhole lid needs to be kept as small as practically possible to keep costs down, and be maneuverable. That is, a 10-ton lid probably would not fall down the manhole, but it would be rather difficult to move if access to the manhole was needed.

Given the side length of a square manhole to be 36 inches, the diagonal length, d, of the manhole for that lid would be d = $\sqrt{36^2+36^2}$ = $36\sqrt{2}$ ≈ 50.91 inches. Hold the manhole lid perpendicular to the ground so a side is horizontal and align that side with the diagonal of the hole. The lid will easily fall down the hole because the side length of 37 inches is much less that the diagonal length of almost 51 inches. In Fig. 2.6 the side length of the lid is represented by the thick section of the diagonal between the short segments perpendicular to the diagonal, showing that the lid could fall down the hole.

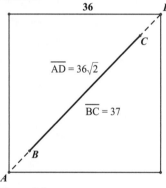

Figure 2.6

## Your Turn

1. Could a rectangle serve as a manhole cover? Experiment by creating a rectangle and comparing side lengths and diagonal lengths. Remember that the rectangle sides are an inch longer than the hole sides.
2. How much bigger does the lid have to be before it will not fall down the rectangular hole you created?
3. Could any triangle serve as a manhole? Experiment by creating some triangles and investigating the relation between the altitudes and side lengths of the hole and the lid. When you compute the altitudes, remember that the lid sides are an inch longer than the hole sides.
4. Could a regular pentagon serve as a manhole? Experiment by creating a regular pentagon and checking to see if there is some orientation of the lid so that the horizontal distance between any pair of points on the lid is shorter than some distance between a pair of points on the hole.

 **Visit the website for an extension of this learning activity.**

# Planning

## 3

**FOCAL POINTS IN THIS CHAPTER**

- Investigate basics of planning mathematics lessons
- Critique sample mathematics lesson plans
- Create mathematics lesson plans

Teaching is not simply standing in front of a group of kids and telling them how to do things. Teaching is not merely having students read information out of a book. Teaching mathematics is more than simply checking answers on tests or homework. We hope you are aware that becoming an effective teacher of mathematics involves much more. Teaching is not easy. It takes tremendous time, energy, dedication, and resilience. You need to:

Provide examples of where the information being covered will be used.

Motivate the students to want to learn.

Patiently explain again for those who did not comprehend the initial coverage of the topic.

Deal with a variety of learning modalities and capabilities.

Discipline.

Assess progress (both yours and the students').

Grow personally.

Be enthusiastic.

Keep up with new technology and strategies to effectively teach mathematics.

Teaching is selling. What would you think of a Ford salesperson who drove a Chevrolet? The teacher of mathematics must be an advocate of the field. Belief, excitement, and enthusiasm about what is being covered are mandatory. It the teacher does not seem interested in what is going on in class, why should the students be interested?

Good classes do not just happen. They are carefully planned and orchestrated. Certainly, there are deviations from the plan, depending on happenings during the class, but the framework is laid out well ahead of time. Here are three axioms a teacher of mathematics should consider (J.M. Anthony, personal communication, May 26, 1996):

1. Know the content being presented.
2. Know more than the content being presented.
3. Teach from the overflow of knowledge.

Knowing the content, and more, and teaching from the overflow of knowledge implies careful planning and organization. Prior to teaching, it is imperative that the topics covered be carefully contemplated and organized. This thinking and organizing needs to be done well in advance, to allow time for the ideas to germinate and blend in your subconscious. The advanced planning also provides the opportunity to connect topics from different lessons throughout the course.

## WHAT SHOULD BE PLANNED?

This is an easy question to answer, and yet the production of the answer is very difficult. Teachers generally have little input into the curriculum for a given course. The broad course objectives are dictated at the federal, state, district, school, and even department levels. Some schools and districts mandate that a given course be covered in lockstep fashion. Because of state testing and accountability issues, many districts mandate the objectives and time spent on the objectives for each mathematics class. All classes are given the same objective to be completed within a given time frame. Even with constraints such as these, there is opportunity for individualization by the teacher. Variation of presentation styles, relating the subject matter to background material, calling on student strengths established earlier in the curriculum, and use of technology can all provide extra time that permits some flexibility for teaching.

Individual teachers, unless they are in a lockstep setting that dictates the topic to be covered, can vary their curriculum in a manner that will best meet the needs of all students. This mandates that the teacher look at the full year and establish an outline that covers the topics and builds needed strengths that will enhance later learning, determine a sequence in which the concepts will be covered, and establish an evaluation plan. The goals and statements here will be broad and general, but they provide a basic skeleton from which to work. Often the textbook dictates this, which is not necessarily the best move. Textbooks are written to meet the needs of a wide variety of students. Your class may or may not be representative of the sample the authors had in mind. It may be the case that you will need to alter the sequence of topics for your students. There is nothing wrong with that, as long as appropriate readiness and background are considered.

Once the long-range plan has been established, more careful consideration should be given to smaller, but still sizable, chunks of information. Often, textbook chapters define these chunks. However, you need to reserve the right to delay sections of a chapter, or a whole chapter, until it is more suitable for your class. You may need to alter the sequence of the chapters and, perhaps, supplement the information in the text with material from other sources.

Certainly, each daily lesson must be carefully prepared and set forth. Pressures or time constraints often hinder the development of well-planned lessons. Consider the person who is about to discuss addition of fractions with a class. Suppose the specific objective is to cover how to add two non-unit fractions with denominators that are relatively prime. Consider a teacher who did not plan, but did skim the text for a few seconds prior to class thinking, "OK, I know how to do that." Class begins and the teacher says something like "Today we are going to add fractions; you know, something like $\frac{4}{7} + \frac{9}{13}$." while writing the two fractions on the board. Then there is a short pause and the teacher asks a series of questions like the following, with the class providing appropriate responses before going on to the next question.

"What is a fraction?"

"Define numerator."

"The denominator of a fraction tells . . . ?"

"In $\frac{4}{7}$, the numerator is . . . ?"

"And the denominator is . . . ?"

"When we add things, basically what do we do?"

And so on.

What is the teacher doing? These answers are all things the class should know. If they do not, how can the teacher justify dealing with the topic at hand? Ask a class of students what the teacher is doing and they will tell you the teacher is stalling. The teacher, for whatever reason, momentarily forgot how to add fractions. While each of those mundane questions was being asked, the teacher was probing memory banks, trying to recall how to do the problem, how to organize thoughts, and attempting to devise a coherent explanation. Most of us are very quick to say that would never happen to us. Many of us would be quick to say that we would not draw a blank on something as simple as that. Maybe, or maybe not. The real issue is not whether or not it will happen. The question is, when? The solution to the dilemma is so simple. Plan!

All planning requires time for ideas to germinate. Certainly the yearly plans need to be established at the beginning of the course. These may or may not be altered throughout the year. Units, more likely, will be changed some—perhaps not by interchanging one unit with another, but at least by increasing or decreasing emphasis on topics, or switching the order in which concepts are presented. Decisions that would influence such alterations would be based on information gleaned from students in the class: readiness, background knowledge, the need for a change of pace, and adjustment in the degree of difficulty of ideas, to name a few. Daily lesson plans need that germination time. Doing daily plans at least a week ahead allows time to adjust presentations and relate current information to prior or future work.

## DAILY LESSON PLANS

A rule of thumb for planning is to formulate ideas weeks before they are to be delivered, look the plan over a few times between development and delivery, and take time to review it the day before it happens. This procedure enhances the connections between different plans, stimulates thoughts, and amplifies needed changes. Even with all that, there will still be many times when changes will be made right before or during the class. The amount of time this takes is understood, but it is a part of being a professional in the beginning stages of your career. As time progresses, the preparations will take less time and you will find yourself struggling to select from among the many ideas you have, including the special one that is best for a given class.

Even if nothing happens that specifically causes you to be more cognizant of the plan, you should look at it periodically between the time it is prepared and when it is to be delivered. That is, two days after you prepare a lesson, skim through it, thinking about what you will be presenting. Do the same thing five days after you prepare it and then, finally, glance at it the day you will be teaching it. This process helps cement the overall scheme of presentation into your mind at a level that allows you to deliver a very natural presentation. That lesson has become a part of you. Because of your intimate understanding of the material to be covered, you should be able to adjust things quickly and naturally. However, this will not happen unless you organize your teaching so that you consistently prepare daily lesson plans at least a week before they are to be taught.

Many factors impact your plans:

Students;

Ability levels;

Administrative decisions;

Departmental procedures;

Personal bias;

Departmental policy;

Textbook;

Homework policies;

Testing practices;

Available class time.

Some of the items listed, along with others, are beyond your control. The teacher does have the power to influence some factors. Frequently, the textbook is handed to you for a class. You may or may not have participated in the selection. Either way, nothing mandates that the text sequence must be followed page by page.

Teachers, in general, tend to rely heavily on textbooks in their day-to-day teaching. Typically this is even more common with the teaching of mathematics. Most decisions about what to teach, how to teach it, when to teach it, and the associated exercises are based largely on what is in the textbook adopted for the course. Some people are concerned about the quality of textbooks, the way they are written, and the tremendous influence they have in determining what students learn. You can alter how things are done.

American education utilizes a spiral curriculum approach. It is not uncommon for a topic to be encountered more than once in a textbook. If encounters after the first add nothing new to the knowledge base, why bother with it? IF, and note that this is a big "if," the material is learned the first time, there should be no need for repetition. If these subsequent encounters with a topic do add to the knowledge base, how much time is necessary to review the prior material? Again, if the material was learned the first time, there is no need for the review, with the possible exception of a few minutes to relate the new topic to the earlier work and orient the student. Still, it is rather common for the text to provide more review than is necessary. Blindly following the text without consideration for the development and needs of students can lead to more repetition than is necessary.

Before dealing with the specifics of a daily lesson plan, one more issue needs to be visited. Homework is a part of the learning environment. Typically, a topic is covered in class, usually involving determination of how to do a problem type, and then an assignment is given in which the students practice the newly learned skill. Characteristically, a selection of odd- or even-numbered problems is then assigned. Some teachers like the students to have the answers available, whereas others do not; and because some texts list answers for only the odd- or even-numbered problems, the text again becomes a decision-making factor. More significant is consideration of the problem types assigned. Suppose the topic of the day deals with solving proportions for an unknown variable, which typically occurs at several places in the middle school curriculum and also in algebra.

That is, given $\frac{N}{6} = \frac{8}{24}$, the student is expected to solve the equation for a value of $N$ that will make a true proportion. Would it not be reasonable to anticipate that the homework problems would divide the location of the variable approximately equally among the four possible locations (i.e., $\frac{2}{N} = \frac{8}{24}; \frac{2}{6} = \frac{N}{24}; \frac{2}{6} = \frac{8}{N}$)?

Examination of assignment sections shows this is frequently not the case. The partitioning is not equal; in most cases, there are far fewer examples having the variable in locations other than top left. Furthermore, it sometimes happens that doing only the odd or even problems will eliminate one of the four possible settings where the variable could be located. How appropriate is this for the student learning process?

Saxon Publishing instituted a homework problem policy that is quite different from what was standard at the time. Since that time, some other publishers have adopted similar procedures. Assume there are 20 problems in the homework assignment. The first two are from today's lesson and often are exactly the same problems discussed in the example section of the lesson. If a student encounters difficulty recalling how to do the problem, the sample is available for review. Because only two problems in the homework assignment deal with today's lesson, the opportunity to seek additional clarification will also be available before more problems of this type are done. The second two problems in the homework assignment would relate to yesterday's lesson. They would be slightly different from the examples. Again, if the student needs help in working the problem, it might be available through the examples found with yesterday's lesson, because they are similar. Each problem pair increases in degree of difficulty and relates to lessons from prior days. As many as 10 different lessons could be encountered in an assignment. Spaced review, or incremental encounters and the opportunity for clarification, are strong arguments for such a homework policy. It provides time to learn the topic before inundating the students with problems based on knowledge they may not have.

One final note relating to homework is that an argument can be made for having you, the teacher, do the homework problems you assign before the assignment is made. This can be quite time consuming, but there are reasons for it. First, you are not asking the students to do something you have not done yourself. That is a minor point, but it is significant in the eyes of some students. Second, you become aware of any problem-type specializations or omissions, like the one noted when discussing solving proportions earlier. Third, as you work through the problems, you are strengthening your ability to reflexively deal with the topic at hand when it is covered in class. In a sense, you are reviewing the lesson plan you prepared. You might become aware of a better way for the students to learn the material or some useful shortcut that would help them. Finally, by doing the problems and recording your work in a manner similar to that expected of the students, you provide yourself with a teaching tool that can prove invaluable.

By the way, textbooks have been known to make a few mistakes. By doing the student assigned problems, you can quickly identify any potential errors in the text. This can greatly alleviate frustration for the students. For example, suppose you assign the odd-numbered problems for homework, knowing that the answers are in the back of the book. Your hope is that the students will work through the exercises and check their answers with the text. If a textbook answer is accidentally incorrect, imagine the frustration when the student repeatedly reworks the problem correctly, only to get a different answer from the book. Working the exercises ahead of time allows you to identify errors for the students before they begin their work.

Suppose, for the sake of this discussion, a class has three distinct ability groups within it: high, average, and low ability. Generally speaking, the high ability students understand the initial coverage of the content and do not need much help with homework assignments. Average students may need some help. If your solutions are available for student inspection, during seatwork time in class, many average students will be able to look at your solution and figure out what to do. Thus, you are free to deal with the lower-ability students who are most in need of your attention. Adopting such a practice demands some ground rules on how your notes are to be used, but that can be handled.

## WHAT CONSTITUTES A DAILY LESSON PLAN?

A completed daily lesson plan should contain the following (Esler & Sciortino, 1991):

1. Topic
2. Goal statement(s): the purpose, concepts, or knowledge that the student will learn
3. Objective statement(s): activities used to assist the learner in achieving the goal(s)
   a. Concept objective(s) when appropriate
   b. Skill/attitude objective(s) when appropriate

4. Materials required (instructional and learning)
5. Procedures
   a. Set: how you introduce the lesson
   b. Instructional outline
   c. Examples (and nonexamples) of concepts
   d. Upper-level questions
   e. Review/closure/bridge to next lesson
   f. Assessment/evaluation procedures

Initially, there needs to be an objective for the lesson. Why is this topic being covered? As you rationalize why a topic is being taught, you must remember to look at it from the world of the students. You, as an adult, might see applications of the topic in future mathematical arenas, but the students want to know where they can use it today.

Objectives are a must for any lesson plan. Some administrators may insist that objectives are stated in behavioral terms, with percentages included for how many students will perform at what level. For example, 80% of the students will correctly find the sum of 90% of two non-unit fractions with relatively prime denominators 95% of the time. There is a segment of the profession that takes issue with these percentages, claiming that they are fictitious numbers. You eventually will have to establish your own style for writing objectives. The important point is that objectives are necessary for a lesson plan.

There must be a reason you are requiring your class to learn this material. What is it? It is also assumed that the focus is on the students being able to perform tasks they could not do prior to the lesson. For example, suppose you are going to teach someone to bake banana nut muffins. This will be the first time the person will have done such a thing.

You say:

"Get the mix."

"Get a big bowl."

"Get a spoon."

"Get one egg."

"Get the milk."

"Get the measuring cup."

"Get the muffin pan."

"Put a paper baking cup in each hole in the pan."

At this point, you proceed to do the following:

Turn the oven on to preheat to 400°.

Empty the mix into the bowl.

Measure a third of a cup of milk.

Pour the milk into the bowl with the mix.

Break the egg and put it into the bowl. (Throw away the shells.)

Blend the ingredients.

Fill each muffin cup until it is half-full or half-empty, depending on your point of view.

Place the muffin pan in the oven.

Bake 13 to 15 minutes or until golden brown.

Remove the muffin pan from the oven.

Let the muffins cool.

Now, you say to the person:

"We baked muffins."

You did not let the person measure the milk because of potential spills or, perhaps, an inability to deal with a third of a cup. You did not let the learner break the egg because of the possibility of shells getting into the mix. Similar excuses can be made for other events that would occur during the making of the muffins.

Assessment of the muffin example shows that "we" did not make muffins. You did. You used the individual as a "gofer" by saying, "Go for this," or "Go for that." The objective in this case was to make muffins. Clearly, the objective was not that the learner would make the muffins. If the objective had been behaviorally stated and learner-oriented, the instructions would have had the learner doing each of the steps, or at least most of them. As lessons are considered in the context of this text and the mathematics classrooms described, it is assumed that they will be behaviorally oriented even if they are not so stated. It must be that way. Otherwise, you, the teacher, become a dispenser of information, paying no attention to whether or not it is received. More significantly, you run the risk of having a learning environment where the students are not active participants.

The ability to process information brings out the second of the five essential ingredients to a lesson plan: assessment. You need to determine how successfully you created an environment in which the students could learn the material, and you need to determine whether or not the class understood what was covered. Deciding how well you did is not always easy. Some of us tend to be supercritical of ourselves. Others are quite lenient when it comes to self-examination and decide that it had to be good because "I" did it. Somewhere between those two extremes is probably where most of us will lie. A few moments for reflection can be very revealing:

Were the examples clear and pertinent?

Did the students ask similar questions repeatedly?

How were the questions I asked answered?

Did the students show reflection and thought?

Were the students able to relate the topic to prior work?

Were the applications clear to the students?

Could the students see the relevance of the topic?

Did I act excited and interested as the lesson was taking place?

Where could the presentation be improved?

Would this lesson be effective with another class?

This is not an exhaustive list of questions to ask as you go over your self-evaluation, but it is a start. Video or audio recording a class can prove quite revealing.

Effectiveness can be defined by asking students to supply you with anonymous one- or two-word evaluations of the class. You could present this idea under the guise of the student writing to a friend who had asked for a one- or two-word description of how the class went. Another option would be to suggest to students that they have another person call and talk with you about your class. This third-party individual would be unknown to you. Alternatively, if a class seems to be totally off track, you could appoint a chair for the group and go outside for a few minutes. Clearly, this option could be used in some settings and not others—another place where you have to make a decision. The class would then have an open discussion about what was going on and how things could be reoriented. Finally, students could pair up and write thoughts about the lesson. That summary could be rewritten by a third person, so there is no way the submitting individuals can be identified. This would be a summary of what needs to be done to create a more productive learning environment.

Student assessment is more straightforward. You can give a homework assignment and then check it to see if the subject has been mastered. Quizzes, tests, portfolios, group work, reports, individual projects, and computer applications can all be used to provide insight into the progress of students. Each of these methods has strengths and weaknesses that you need to become aware of. A more detailed discussion of these topics can be found in Chapter 2, "Learning Theory, Curriculum, and Assessment." The NCTM *Assessment Standards for School Mathematics* (1995) lists six tenets about valid assessments:

Reflect the mathematics that all students need to know and be able to do.

Enhance mathematics learning.

Promote equity.

Be an open process.

Promote valid inferences about mathematics learning.

Be a coherent process. (NCTM, 1995, pp. 11–22)

This list is only a beginning, but it is something you need to study and integrate into your teaching process.

## EXERCISE 3.1

1. Create a list of advantages and disadvantages for each of the following evaluation techniques: quizzes, tests, portfolios, group work, reports, individual projects, and software programs. List any assessment techniques you feel are inappropriate for a secondary mathematics class and describe why you think they would not work for you.

Questions, lesson notes, and examples are major ingredients for any lesson plan. Each of these is equally significant to the overall development and delivery of the plan. The sample lessons used throughout this text portray manners in which these components can be blended to create effective lessons.

Questions and questioning techniques are crucial to a good lesson plan. Remember, you are trying to stimulate thought and learning in your students. Consider the level of questions you are asking. If your questions are all on the knowledge-level, there is little or no thought involved, because the student is merely regurgitating information previously encountered. The questions included in your lesson plans should be upper-level. Higher-order questions are generally defined as anything more complex than knowledge-level, using Bloom's taxonomy of knowledge, comprehension, application, analysis, synthesis, and evaluation. Upper-level questions typically are not generated "off the top of your head," although it does become easier and more reflexive as you mature within your career development. They require careful thought in advance of the class. Listing upper-level questions in your plans shows that you have given them appropriate consideration. Exact wording of the questions is not always necessary in your plans. You will be able to phrase the idea within the context of the class as long as you have the idea in the plans.

Questioning is not easy. Asking for an answer to a given problem is not the type of question to be considered as a part of the basic plan. A knowledge-level question, although still important, should be fairly reflexive. Similarly, when planning for questions, it is not necessary to state in the plans the name of the student who will be called on. It is assumed you will distribute participation throughout the class. Higher-order questions are designed to make students think and reflect about what they are learning. Upper-level questions strengthen students' reasoning ability and communication skills.

Usually questions requiring thought are not easy for students to answer. "How?" and "Why?" can be upper-level questions when connected to a response given by a student. Research shows that up to 80% of all questions asked in a classroom are lower-level (Fennema & Peterson, 1986; Hart, 1989; Koehler, 1986; Suydam, 1985). Probably the most likely reason for the preponderance of lower-level questions is that higher-order questions are difficult to create extemporaneously in front of a class. Planning becomes important for the development of upper-level questions.

Embarking on a course of designing upper-level questions is challenging. The questions themselves require careful thought and organization. As a question is asked, you have to decide if it is realistic for students to answer. Certainly, asking the right question can pique the interest of students. Suppose you prepare a lesson dealing with the impact of changing $A$ in the equation $y = A\sin(x)$. If your first question is "What happens if $A$ is changed in the equation $y = A\sin(x)$?" and students can answer it, you have fallen into a basic trap. The students' ability to answer that question indicates the information has been probably been covered before. Depending on the setting, you could be planning on covering information the students have already mastered. If the question is asked to establish a starting point for a new topic, then it is an acceptable question.

On the other hand, if students have never encountered this topic before, the question is impossible for them to answer at this point. Perhaps the question could provide motivation to investigate the situation. You have prodded the students to seek an answer. The prodding and investigation lead them along a path that ends with an possible solution.

| Lower Level? | Reworded to Upper Level |
|---|---|
| Find the area of a rectangle with dimensions 4 × 6 feet. | What is the maximum area of a 20' perimeter rectangle? |
| Round 3.87 to tenths. | What numbers round to 3.9? |
| How would you cut a pizza with 5 straight cuts to get 16 pieces? | What is the greatest number of pieces you can get if you cut a pizza with 5 straight cuts? |
| What is the sum of the measures of supplementary angles? | What are the possible measures of 2 supplementary angles? |

Often, questions that are lower-level can be restructured to become upper-level.

Jim Wilson created questions that could be used to provide some direction (Bloom, Hastings, & Madaus, 1971, pp. 643–698). The questions can be classified using Wilson's format. His work focused on providing possible responses for particular questions at each level of Bloom's taxonomy. Because we are concentrating on classroom discussion, the answers supplied by Wilson are omitted in most examples. Some examples are given here:

## KNOWLEDGE EXAMPLES

### Knowledge of Specific Facts

"Which of the following is not a whole number?" (Wilson, Cahen, & Begle, 1968, p. 665).

"The slope of a horizontal line is _____" (Wilson et al., 1968, p. 666).

### Knowledge of Terminology

"5! equals _____" (Wilson et al., 1968, p. 666).

"The absolute value of any number is written as _____" (Wilson et al., 1968, p. 666).

## COMPREHENSION EXAMPLES

### Knowledge of Concepts

"In what way does the set of whole numbers differ from the set of natural numbers?" (Wilson et al., 1968, p. 669).

"Suppose A and B are two acute angles of p° and q°, respectively. A and B are complementary angles if and only if _____" (Wilson et al., 1968, p. 670)

## Knowledge of Principles, Rules, and Generalizations

"If three fractions have denominators that are relatively prime, the least common denominator is equal to _____" (Wilson et al., 1968, p. 671).

"If the intersection of two different planes is not empty, then the intersection is _____" (Wilson et al., 1968, p. 671).

## Knowledge of Mathematical Structure

"If $(N + 68)^2 = 654,481$, then $(N + 58)(N + 78) =$ (?)" (Wilson et al., 1968, p. 672).

"If $a \cdot b = 0$, then _____" (Wilson et al., 1968, p. 672).

## APPLICATION EXAMPLES

### Ability to Solve Routine Problems

"Which of the following numbers, expressed in base 7 numeration, is both prime and odd?" (Wilson et al., 1968, p. 676).

"A piece of wire 36 inches long is bent into the form of a right triangle. If one of the legs is 12 inches long, find the length of the other leg" (Wilson et al., 1968, p. 677).

### Ability to Make Comparisons

"The difference in the circumference between the larger and smaller of two balls is 3 inches. Which of the following is the best estimate of the difference in their diameters?" (Wilson et al., 1968, p. 678).

"Ten objects are numbered from 1 through 10 and distributed into bags. If it is known that 1, 4, and 7 are in the same bag, the pair 2 and 10 are in the same bag, and similarly, for the pairs 3 and 6, 1 and 5, 3 and 8, 7 and 9, and 2 and 6, what is the largest number of bags that can contain at least one object?" (Wilson et al., 1968, p. 678).

## Ability to Analyze Data

"Five spelling tests are to be given to John's class. Each test has a value of 25 points. John's average for the first four tests is 15. What is the lowest score he can get on the fifth test to have an average of at least 16?" (Wilson et al., 1968, p. 678).

"On the same set of axes, sketch the graphs of $y = \sin x$ and $y = \cos \frac{x}{2}$ as $x$ varies from 0 to $2\pi$ radians. Determine from the graphs the quadrant in which $\sin x - \cos \frac{x}{2}$ is always positive" (Wilson et al., 1968, p. 679).

## Ability to Recognize Patterns, Isomorphisms, and Symmetries

"In an election, 356 people vote to choose one of five candidates. The candidate with most votes is the winner. What is the smallest number of votes the winner could receive?" (Wilson et al., 1968, p. 679).

"The last digit in $4^{10}$ is _____" (Wilson et al., 1968, p. 679). (This question should be altered to reflect the availability of technology.)

## ANALYSIS EXAMPLES

"Given the set $p = r^2 - t^2$, where $p$ is a prime number, find $t$ if (1) $r = 7$, (2) $r = 157$, (3) r = 58" (Wilson et al., 1968, p. 680).

"In Fig. 3.1 what is the shortest path from P to Q which touches both line XO and line OY?" (Wilson et al., 1968, p. 681).

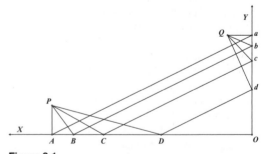

**Figure 3.1**

## Ability to Discover Relationships

"The length of a diagonal of a square is $x + y$. Find its area" (Wilson et al., 1968, p. 681).

"Find the number of diagonals in a convex polygon (1) with 5 sides (2) with 25 sides (3) with $n$ sides" (Wilson et al., 1968, p. 682).

## Ability to Construct Proofs

"Prove that for every positive integer $\frac{n^5}{5} + \frac{n^3}{3} + \frac{7n}{15}$ is an integer" (Wilson et al., 1968, p. 682).

"In Fig. 3.2, B is the midpoint of major arc AC. Chords BD and AC intersect at E. Chords AD and AB are drawn. PROVE: BD × BE = (AB)²" (Wilson et al., 1968, p. 683).

## Ability to Criticize Proofs

Let us attempt to prove the following remarkable proposition: *Any two numbers are equal.* Call the two numbers $a$ and $b$; call their sum $c$.

Thus we have the equation

$(1)\, a + b = c$

From (1) we obtain the equations:

$(2)\, c - b = a$

and

$(3)\, c - a = b$

Multiply each side of (2) by $-b$, and multiply each side of (3) by $-a$, to get

$(4)\, b^2 - bc = -ab$

and

$(5)\, a^2 - ac = -ab$

From (4) and (5) we have

$(6)\, b^2 - bc = a^2 - ac$

Add $\frac{c^2}{4}$ to each side of (6) to get

$(7)\, b^2 - bc + \frac{c^2}{4} = a^2 - ac + \frac{c^2}{4}$

Take the square root of both sides of (7) and get

$(8)\, b - \frac{c}{2} = a - \frac{c}{2}$

Then add $\frac{c}{2}$ to each side of (8) to get, finally:
$b = a$.
What's wrong? (Wilson et al., 1968, p. 684).

## Ability to Formulate and Validate Generalizations

"Without actually making the calculations, write out in detail a step-by-step procedure for determining (1) whether 12,087 is a prime number (2) the largest prime less than 5,000" (Wilson et al., 1968, p. 685).

This list of sample questions on the preceding pages is not exhaustive. It has been presented to give you samples of upper-level questions that could be used in a classroom setting. These examples should make you aware of the thought needed prior to attempting to use upper-level questions. Planning questions is essential.

Most students are curious about things and have questions. At times, they need to be trained to ask. One teacher used the following to stimulate questions. The students entered the classroom to find the teacher sitting on a chair that had been placed on the teacher's desk. The students asked each other what was going on. Some inquired of others whether or not they should call the principal or another teacher. The level of uncertainty and inquisitiveness was quite high. After a few minutes of this, the teacher hopped off the desk and removed the chair, saying to the class, "Isn't it interesting that you had several questions but no one asked me. Since I was the one sitting in the chair, wouldn't it be reasonable to ask me why?" The moral of the story: Know what to ask, and know whom to ask.

Examples are equally as important as questions. Specific examples must be carefully thought out as each lesson is planned. Investigation of specific examples helps many individuals learn. It is logical to assume that many students learn by observing specific examples. Each new problem type should

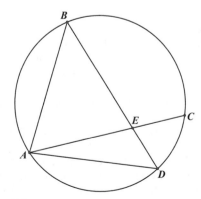

**Figure 3.2**

have one written example in your plans, solved in complete detail, just as you expect your students to do it. This should not be an example worked in the text. You will probably use more than one example in your lesson for each type of problem, but one should be sufficient for your planning. Inserting only one example of each problem type in your plans is adequate, particularly if you do the homework assignments before class.

Plan your examples carefully. If you are talking about factoring trinomials, $X^2 + 4X + 4$ is not a good example. First, there are two 4s in the example. As you discuss what you do with the third term, a student who may not be attending as well as desired might think you are talking about the 4 of $4X$. Furthermore, when factored, $X^2 + 4X + 4 = (X + 2)$ $(X + 2)$. Perhaps a student will get the wrong impression that the factors are always duplicates. A trinomial like $X^2 + 5X + 6$ is a better example. It is easy to spot what number is where, and the factors are different. Eventually, both types must be discussed, but care needs to be taken as to when. Saying something like "Forget it for now" will trigger some minds to venture in a different direction. The tangent those students take, wondering why they were to forget what was just seen, will cause some of them to get lost. In the factoring examples used earlier in this paragraph, it is assumed that concrete exposure that "shows" how factoring occurs would be part of the curricular sequence.

Your lesson notes should reflect the things you will say to students who are progressing from a point of not knowing something to a point of knowing. You should initially assume students do not know the material you are about to cover. If they know, why are you teaching it? The notes should be the major points that comprise your discussion or development of the topic. There is no need to give a word-by-word description of what will be said, just the major points. Some form of outline (not necessarily formal) is generally deemed most beneficial. You should be able to quickly skim the outline to determine if all the salient points have been covered. If you plan on discussing some issue, it is wise to elaborate in your outline. What essential points do you expect the students to see? What reactions do you expect them to have? Where is the discussion intended to lead? These matters should be a part of the notes about what is to be covered and the direction to be taken. Otherwise there is a risk that the discussion will become a random talk session with no apparent point or central theme.

## VARIETY OF APPROACHES

Not all students learn the same way. That is why learning modalities are discussed in education classes. You are responsible for knowing your students well enough to determine which is the best method for introducing a topic. Most instruction, even with all the options that are available today, is still done by the lecture method. The teacher tells the students how to do a problem type and the class mimics the model established by the teacher (cookie-cutter mathematics). Little student thought is required in this format. Thinking and flexibility are not highly valued. It basically becomes the teacher saying, "Here is how you do this. Trust me, I would not lie to you. Don't think about it, just do it." That is a sad commentary, but it is a lot closer to the truth than many teachers would like to admit.

You can be a catalyst for change in the secondary classroom. Use technology. Find applications. Create and use models. Insert activities. Establish expectations. You can take a student from an entrance or beginning level to much higher ground. You need to be able to reach that student, and every other student. That is why the variety of approaches is so important. Your college education has provided you the necessary tools. You know the mathematics. You know how students develop and how to teach them mathematics using different methods, at least at an intellectual level. You lack experience in two facets: teaching and creating lessons. Teaching experience comes with time. Your lesson-creating skills can be practiced and developed starting right now!

The basics have been discussed as far as establishing a lesson plan. There is another consideration. You have a strong mathematical background. You know more than what you will be teaching. However, your mathematical content is compartmentalized into classes and topics. You need to take the time to reflect on the breadth of mathematical knowledge you have and begin to devise ways to cross between the different compartments. That will create new and stimulating ideas for you. The "simple halving doubling" (Russian peasant) method for multiplication will show how you can begin taking knowledge out of compartments. Find the product of 47 and 78. One factor will be "halved" repeatedly until the result is 1. Each time the first factor is halved, the other is doubled. The row of any even value in the halving column is eliminated from consideration, including the original factors. The remaining values in the doubling column are added.

The sum will be the product of the two factors. Students tend to select 78 as the halving value because it is even. However, half of 78 is 39, an odd value. The object is to get the halving column reduced to 1. Logically, starting with the smaller value will achieve that objective faster. In the example following example 78 × 47, we will use 78 is the doubling column and 47 in the halving column.

| Problem Halving | | | |
|---|---|---|---|
| 78 | 47 | 23 remainder 1 | $1 \times 2^0$ |
| 156 | 23 | 11 remainder 1 | $1 \times 2^1$ |
| 312 | 11 | 5 remainder 1 | $1 \times 2^2$ |
| 624 | 5 | 2 remainder 1 | $1 \times 2^3$ |
| ~~1218~~ | ~~2~~ | 1 remainder 0 | $1 \times 2^4$ |
| 2496 | 1 | 0 remainder 1 | $1 \times 2^5$ |

Essentially, the halving factor has been expressed in base 2 numeration, and the problem is re-expressed as $78 \times 101111_2$. That is, $78 \times (32 + 8 + 4 + 2 + 1)$. Sixteen is not considered because there is a zero in the $2^4$ place. Therefore the row containing 2 and 1218 is eliminated. The product is the sum of $78 + 156 + 312 + 624 + 2496 = 3666$. The product of 78 and 47 is 3666.

Somewhere in your career you have worked with bases. Undoubtedly, you have investigated multiplication—perhaps not in the form of the "simple halving doubling" method. You are aware of the concept of multiplication. Surely, you have been exposed to the idea of proof. Yet, with all that background, each component seems to stay in its own compartment. It is unlikely you have seen this "proof" of why the "simple halving doubling" method of multiplication works. If you decompartmentalize and think about the process, however, the proof is fairly simple. It is impossible to show you all of these intricacies. You must capitalize on your background and develop the connections between the various mathematical exposures you have had.

## PERSONAL PROFESSIONAL GROWTH

Just as classroom management is up to you, your professional growth is also. Personal professional growth is critical for your classroom planning and organization. If you are stagnant, you will have difficulty becoming excited about what you are doing. You need to become professionally involved. Join NCTM and select the appropriate publications, being certain to read them. Think of ways the ideas can be applied in your classes. Join your state and local mathematics councils. Go to conferences dealing with the teaching of mathematics at local, state, regional, and national levels. Be willing to present new and innovative ideas to colleagues in your profession. Check the educational catalogs that focus on the teaching and learning of mathematics. Take classes. Participate in in-service opportunities. Grow. Learn. Stay excited about the teaching of mathematics, and let it show in your planning and actions.

## SAMPLE LESSON PLANS

These are presented in different formats on purpose. You need to select the style with which you are most comfortable. The samples are intended to provide you with ideas. It is assumed you will alter these to fit your style.

*Lesson A*. Suppose the objective is for students to become aware of and prove the theorem, "The segment joining the midpoint of two sides of a triangle is parallel to the third side and half the length of that third side." We will assume this is the first encounter these students have had with this idea. The conceptual development will be divided into two parts, which may be covered in one day, if the group moves rapidly enough, or on two successive days.

*Part 1—Informal Development*. (We assume the students have appropriate technology at their disposal.) The activity worksheet/lesson for the students follows. It is purposely open-ended and vague with the intent of having students discover items.

Create triangle ABC.

Determine midpoint D on AC and E on BC.

Place a line segment between D and E.

$m(\overline{AB}) = $ _____

$m(\overline{DE}) = $ _____

$m(\angle ABC) = $ _____

$m(\angle DEC) = $ _____

$m(\angle BAC) = $ _____

$m(\angle EDC) = $ _____

Describe relations that exist between the measurements (Fig. 3.3).

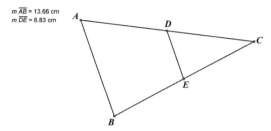

$m \overline{AB} = 13.66 \text{ cm}$
$m \overline{DE} = 6.83 \text{ cm}$

**Figure 3.3**

As the triangle is moved, selecting any vertex, what relations remain constant?

*Part 2.* This could be developed as a teacher-directed or student-centered lesson. The emphasis would necessarily shift one way or the other, depending on the lesson style selected. The students should have conjectured that "the segment joining the midpoint of two sides of a triangle is parallel to the third side and half the length of that third side" from Part 1. They would be asked to prove that $m(\overline{DE}) = 0.5m(\overline{AB})$ and that DE is parallel to AB. The students should suspect the statements are true because of the investigations from Part 1. The formal proof can be established in a variety of ways, one of which uses coordinate geometry. The triangle can be established so that one vertex, A, lies on the origin and one side lies on the positive x-axis with endpoint B $(r, 0)$. The third vertex, C $(s, 2t)$, would be located somewhere in the first quadrant. The plan for the proof would be:

> The midpoint formula can be used to define D and E.
>
> Use the distance formula to find $m(\overline{AB})$ and $m(\overline{DE})$.
>
> Use the slope formula for the slopes of $\overline{AB}$ and $\overline{DE}$.
>
> State conclusions.

Personal preference will determine whether the students develop the proof as individuals or as groups. It could be that you will discuss the plan with them, but you might elect to have them develop it on their own. If you do this proof in the format of a teacher-led discussion, perhaps because this is the first coordinate proof they have done, the preceding plan would be expanded to a more complete lesson plan by including calculations that show the distance and slope formulas. This is one of those places where you should know these formulas

but you do not want to risk forgetting. If you opt to do a teacher-centered lesson, a few logical extensions that would be student-centered lessons or assignments would be:

> Place the triangle anywhere on the axis system and prove that the segment joining the midpoints of any two sides is parallel to the third side and half its length.
>
> Show that a quadrilateral with opposite sides parallel has those respective opposite sides of equal length.
>
> Prove the length of the segment joining the midpoints of the two nonparallel sides of a trapezoid is the average of the lengths of the parallel sides and parallel to them.

***Lesson B.*** Suppose you have discussed translating word problems to equations to be solved with your class. The practice problems you give can impact their attitudes. One way this can be accomplished is to use nontraditional wording, like:

1. Jo Cool is 16. This is $\frac{1}{3}$ her dad's age. How old is Jo's pop?
2. Dum Diddy's salary is $12,000. This is 1.5 times as much as Q. Cumber's salary. How much does Dum Diddy make? How much does Q. Cumber make?
3. Izzi Zlow types 35 words per minute. This is 0.4 of Ty Pritter's speed. How fast does Ty type?
4. Walter Logged's body contains 57 kg of water. This is $\frac{2}{3}$ of his weight. How much does Logged weigh?
5. MT and ZT have a combined age of 68 years. If MT is 47, how old is ZT?

***Lesson C.*** Suppose you are trying to lead a class to the solution of the thousand-locker problem presented in the problem-solving chapter of this text. The problem states that 1,000 lockers are closed and 1,000 students are going to pass down the row. The first student opens every locker. The second student closes all multiples of 2. The third student changes (opens or closes) all multiples of 3. The fourth student changes all multiples of 4. And so on. Further assume they are not experienced at finding patterns. Have a number of students (it might be advisable to combine classes for this lesson, if possible) stand in front of the group. Suppose you use 18 students. Each student is given a card with a locker number on it and they stand in ascending order facing the class, holding their locker number in front of them.

In sequential order, starting with 1, each student does a 180° turn to indicate that locker has been opened. Then, starting with 2 and in successive order, all multiples of 2 do a 180° turn. Following that, all multiples of 3 do a 180° turn. And so on. After all students have done all their 180° turns, the ones left facing the group will be 1, 4, 9, 16, . . . This should help students recognize the pattern. (This particular adaptation was seen in a presentation by Steve Krulick and Jesse Rudnick at the Philadelphia NCTM Regional on December 1, 1995.) A slightly different variation of this problem asks for the number of lockers that are closed rather than the ones that are opened. An example of this problem can be viewed at the March 22, 2010, Problem of the Week at the Ole Miss Math Challenge (http://mathcontest.olemiss.edu).

This activity provides a solution for the problem in a concrete manner, as opposed to the two more abstract methods described in the chapter. Once the students know the result through this exposure, they can be led to a discussion about other solutions. They know what the answer is and now can investigate different manners of obtaining it.

*Lesson D*. Solving two equations in two unknowns by addition: Note that the format of this lesson does not include complete sentences. Eliminating complete sentences permits quick scanning of the lesson to determine if an item has been missed or what the next example or question should be. It is assumed that the students have already dealt with solving two equations by graphing and substitution.

Suppose

$x + y = 4$           (1)

$x - y = 6$           (2)

Could get either equation to "$y =$" and substitute. Recall—Can add same thing to both sides of equation.

Add (2) to (1) using "$x - y$" on the left and "6" on the right:

$(x + y) + (x - y) = 4 + 6$

The Vertical method is often easier:

$x + y = 4$

$\underline{x - y = 6}$

$2x = 10$

$x = 5$

In (1),

$5 + y = 4$

$y = -1$

Check in (2),

$5 - (-1) = ? = 6$

$5 + 1 = ? = 6$, OK

Summarize:

Wrote equations

Lined $x$ under $x$, $y$ under $y$, constant under constant

Added to eliminate one variable

Solved

Substituted

Checked

More examples or assignments as needed

## TRY THIS IN YOUR CLASSROOM

*Lesson E*. Suppose your goal is to have students learn the trick for squaring numbers ending in 5 and to prove why it works. This lesson deals with that topic but also extends the same idea into a very similar arena; and yet the students will probably not recognize it, even though they just did it with squaring numbers ending in 5. The cryptic style is used to show a "working" lesson plan.

$5^2 = 25$

$15^2 = 225$

$25^2 = 625$

$35^2 = 1225$

$45^2 = 2025$

$55^2 = 3025$

QQQ Talk to me

What do you see?

Products end in 25

QQQ Any patterns

QQQ Compare # to preceding one couple times

generally get difference increasing

25 to 225 up by 200

225 to 625 up by 400

625 to 1225 up by 600 etc.

Good generalization, BUT

QQQ $95^2 = ???$

curve ball
        previous pattern says need $85^2$
        could get $85^2$
        If do, ask $405^2$

—will take a while

implies another way

QQQ How get 25

comes from $5^2$

note 5 is last digit of each problem

QQQ Any way get rest of product?

in $45^2$, any way get 20 out of 4

in $35^2$, any way get 12 out of 3?

and so on.

CONCLUDE ($N$) ($N$–1) is first part

QQQ Now $95^2 =$

QQQ Limited to 2D numbers?

$125^2 = 15,625$

Could stop here or prove or extend
Proof:

$X5$ can be used to represent any number ending in 5 where $X$ is a counting number. (You would say it as "exty-five," much like twenty-five or one hundred-sixty-five.)

   $(X5)^2 = (10X + 5)^2$ using expanded notation and place value

Expanding gives $100X^2 + 100X + 25$

Focus on the first two terms getting $100(X^2 + X)$

But that says the product must end in two zeros

That explains how the last two digits are always 25

Focus on $(X^2 + X)$ and factor getting $X(X + 1)$ showing how the rest of the product is determined

Extension:
All do 4 problems starting at same time; include calculators if want.

$36 \times 34 = ???$

$23 \times 27 = ???$ $42 \times 48 = ???$

$51 \times 59 = ???$

Respective products are: 1224, 621, 2016, 3009

QQQ How so fast?

QQQ Similarities between this and square numbers ending in 5?

QQQ Patterns?

ones sum to 10

tens same

QQQ Extend beyond 2-digit factors?

QQQ Prove?

## CONCLUSION

We have dealt with planning. You should have discussed the merits of planning, objectives, goals, examples, and questioning in your education classes. We have extended those ideas into your world of mathematics education. There is no one best way to plan. You have to make various approaches and styles fit your personality and students. In your first few years of teaching, you will discover many things that work and some that do not. Help yourself out by keeping a journal or notebook of successful lessons, activities, problems, and questions. Try to update the journal daily so you do not forget these events. This may prove to be very informative the following year. The message of this chapter should be quite clear though. You MUST PLAN! Without those plans, you are doing a disservice to your students. It is your responsibility to help them learn. Planning is crucial as you strive to accomplish that goal.

### STICKY QUESTIONS

1.  The typical school year is approximately 180 days and a class period is about an hour long. Summer school classes or block scheduling environments offering a class "double timed" in a semester often contain about 120 to 150 hours of instruction. Is it reasonable to expect that average students can acquire the skills and conceptual development required in secondary mathematics classes? Why or why not?

2. Should your lessons follow the structure of the text? Should two individuals teaching the same subject to students of the same ability in the same school follow the same lesson plans? Will you follow the lessons of the senior teacher in your first school? Why or why not? What is the politically correct thing to do and what is the right thing to do? Are they the same?

3. If you can't finish the curriculum, how do you decide what to sacrifice? What are the ramifications of eliminating some topics? Is there a way this dilemma can be resolved?

4. Prove the extension of the "try this in your classroom" question found before the conclusion of this chapter.

## PROBLEM-SOLVING CHALLENGES

1. **Largest Number**

   What is the largest number you can write using three digits? You may use a digit more than once.

**Check out the website for the solution.**

2. **Handy Man**

   A man walks into a hardware store. He buys 1 for a dollar, 50 for two dollars, and 200 for three dollars. What is the man buying?

**Check out the website for the solution.**

# LEARNING ACTIVITIES

## GROUPS

A group is one of the simplest mathematical systems. With a group, there is a set and an operation that meets four stipulations.

Let $S = \{a, b, c, d, \ldots\}$ and realize $S$ may be finite or infinite. Define some operation $\nabla$ on the elements of the set. If $\nabla$ is closed, associates, and possesses both an identity element and an inverse element for each element in the set, then the set is said to be a group under that operation. That is:

for each $a \in S$ and $b \in S$, there is a $c \in S$ such that $a \nabla b = c$ (Closure),
for each $a \in S$, $b \in S$, and $c \in S$, $(a \in b) \nabla c = a \nabla (b \nabla c)$ (Associative property of $\nabla$ on S)
for each element $a \in S$, there is an element $y$ such that $a \nabla y = y \nabla a = a$ (Identity element $y$ for $\nabla$ on S), and for each element $a \in S$, there is an element $a'$ such that $a \nabla a' = a' \nabla a = y$ (Inverse element for $\nabla$ on S).

1. Do the integers form a group under addition? Explain your answer.
2. Do the integers form a group under multiplication? Explain your answer.

Consider the following equilateral triangle that rotates only about the incenter (intersection of the triangle's angle bisectors) so it is always in standard position (one side parallel to the bottom of the page). There are three possible configurations of the triangle as shown in Fig. 3.4.

**Figure 3.4**

"S" indicates that a figure is either rotated 0°, so it essentially stays in the same position, or that it rotates 360°, putting it back to its original position. "O" indicates that a triangle has been rotated One hundred twenty degrees (120°), and T means a triangle is rotated Two hundred forty degrees (240°).

Suppose the operation $\nabla$ is defined as "is followed by," meaning that one rotation is followed by another. For example O $\nabla$ T = S, meaning that a 120° rotation followed by a 240° rotation would result in a 360° rotation, or no change in the position of the triangle. Consider the table of all possible operations on triangle ABC, remembering that it must end up in standard position.

| $\nabla$ | S | O | T |
|---|---|---|---|
| S | S | O | T |
| O | O | T | S |
| T | T | S | O |

The set is closed since there are no results other than the listed elements of the set {S, O, T}. The operation $\nabla$ satisfies the associative property on the set, as can be determined by examination. S is its own inverse and O is the inverse of T and T is the inverse of O, so each element has an inverse element within the set. S is the identity element because S ∇ either O or T, or O or T ∇ S results in no change. Thus, the equilateral triangle ABC forms a group under the operation ∇, "is followed by."

3. Given the shape in Fig. 3.5, does the operation of rotating 60° form a group under the previously used definition of ∇ as "is followed by"?

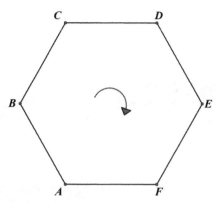

**Figure 3.5**

4. Consider the square in Fig. 3.6 where segments a, b, h, and v are fixed on the plane and DO NOT MOVE with the square as it is rotated or flipped. If the following moves are defined on the square onto itself along with the agreement that two movements are equivalent if they result in the same final configuration of the square, does the set {c, d, g, h, n, o, t, v} form a group with the operation ∇, "is followed by"?

c = identity, no rotation.
n = counterclockwise rotation about C through 90°.
o = counterclockwise rotation about C through 180°.
t = counterclockwise rotation about C through 270°.
h = 180° flip over segment y.
v = 180° flip over segment w.
d = 180° flip over segment x.
g = 180° flip over segment z.

It might prove helpful to make a square card and mark the segments w, x, y, and z on a different piece of paper and them move the square through the different possibilities.

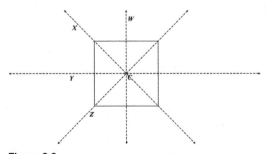

**Figure 3.6**

# Skills in Teaching Mathematics

**4**

How wonderful it would be if we knew everything about kids, teaching, mathematics, and the teaching of mathematics. We could bottle it, sell it, become rich, and solve a lot of problems for everyone in the process. We all know there is no magic formula for teaching mathematics. In the process of attempting to find keys, we often stumble and miss objectives, but we also learn a variety of things that can be catalogued and used at a later date in other settings. This chapter deals with a broad collection of ideas, concepts, and strategies that should be useful in a variety of teaching environments. As you work through your career and attempt these suggestions, you will compile a list of methods and activities that will help your students learn mathematics.

## THE BEGINNINGS

In order to teach mathematics, you need to know mathematics. Your undergraduate curriculum should provide you with that background. One thing you may need to insert is integration of topics. The content courses you take in college are specialized considerations of a particular segment of the world of mathematics. You need to blend those topics together and begin to see how they interact with each other. In geometry, we discuss the midpoint of a line segment. We can also discuss the midpoint in terms of coordinate geometry, which provides algebraic hints. Focusing on the coordinates of the points involved, we can shift the discussion to one of algebraic considerations, where we would give the equation of the line. This is an example of blending topics.

## EXERCISE 4.1

1. Describe how statistics and algebra could be related in a middle school setting.

**Additional exercises can be found on the website.**

Not only should you know mathematics, but you need to know about age-level characteristics of the students you will be facing. Your general education, educational foundation courses, and field experiences should begin to provide you with a background in those areas. That background should be a platform that continually grows and changes throughout your career.

Knowing mathematics and students provides you with an essential background. You need to put those ingredients together into a format that helps you present what you know to students who might not be interested in what you are trying to impart to them. This last sentence is very complex and should be reread and studied carefully. There is a lot of information in it, and it summarizes a plethora of positions, feelings, and opinions you will generate over the years. The essence of that sentence is the basis of this text and the course you are using it in. You have the tools to perform the task. Do you have the drive and desire?

## WHERE TO START

You will apply for and be interviewed for a teaching position. You should do some homework about the school and curricular objectives (school, district, and state); talk with experienced teachers about things they do; strive to understand secondary students and what makes them tick; create a background from which appropriate applications of the topics being taught can be derived; collect lessons, pictures, puzzles, games, and exhibits that could be associated with the topics you will present; have a sample lesson or two prepared to discuss during the interview; create a video of you teaching different groups of students that demonstrates your capabilities for the interviewer; and be prepared to discuss your ideas about the teaching of mathematics. This is not an exhaustive list, but it begins to give you a feel for the task before you.

## KIDS, MATHEMATICS, AND ITS TEACHING

Our society is too willing to accept a statement like, "I can't and don't like to do math." The typical response when that statement is made in polite society is, "Yeah, me too." That attitude extends to students as well. They say things like:

Getting As in math makes you a nerd or a geek.

Women who do well in math are masculine.

My mind goes blank when I see a math problem.

I won't use math when I get out of school.

No one in my family is good in math.

I do OK in everything but math.

My friends hate math because it is boring.

Facing a constant barrage of statements like these and the attitudes they represent presents a significant challenge to you as a teacher of mathematics. Somehow that perspective has been established and it becomes your responsibility not only to counteract it, but also to figure out ways to teach mathematics effectively in the face of these challenges.

Some other things you should be aware of relate to how teachers typically react in classrooms. These statements are made as a general position, not intended or related to any particular gender, age, or marital status. Typically,

Boys receive more attention in class from teachers.

Boys are called on more frequently.

Girls are asked simpler questions.

Boys are asked more complex, open-ended questions.

Girls are disciplined much less frequently.

Boys are praised more often for academic excellence.

Girls are complimented for behaving and following rules.

As an effective teacher of mathematics, you need to ascertain ways of avoiding such generalizations and stereotypical behavior. Even being aware of the situation, you will find often that you reflexively will react in manners similar to those stated.

Students come to you with a set of beliefs about mathematics. These positions may be incorrect, based on false information. The individual may be unclear as to why the convictions are held, but they are tenets to which many students adhere. Some of the more dominant ones are:

All mathematics problems can be solved by application of facts or rules, as demonstrated by the teacher or text.

Mathematics problems should be quickly solvable in a few steps.

Mathematics problems can be solved only by methods shown in texts.

The goal in mathematics is to get the right answer.

There is always one best way to do a mathematics problem.

The only mathematics worth knowing is what is tested.

Mathematics students are supposed to receive information and demonstrate that it has been obtained.

The job of a teacher of mathematics is to transmit information to students and check to see that students have gotten it.

Mathematics is created by very smart people. The rest of us just have to learn what they invent.

Learning mathematics is based on ability, not how hard you try.

Men are better in mathematics than women.

As you prepare lessons, you need to consider these positions, often held by a majority of students in your class.

## THINGS YOU WILL FACE IN TEACHING

The preceding listings of impressions students have about the learning of mathematics are a beginning. You are aware of them and that is the first step toward counteracting these negative impressions. That list is only a preliminary glimpse. There is much more you need to consider. The following list, although not exhaustive, should start you thinking about decisions you will have to make and hurdles you will face as you try to inspire mathematical learning in your students and as you consider your professional decisions:

> Most students think the only mathematics they will need after high school is arithmetic.
>
> Students get little exposure to problems that require thought before answering.
>
> Students do not acquire skills necessary for learning mathematics on their own.
>
> Students are not acquainted with how mathematics is used in jobs.
>
> Most students are not mathematically prepared for today's jobs, let alone those of tomorrow.
>
> Three out of four Americans stop studying mathematics before completing career prerequisites.
>
> Careers that are growing fastest are those requiring higher mathematics and reasoning capabilities.
>
> Employment opportunities that are not growing rapidly generally require less mathematics and reasoning capability.
>
> Our mathematics test scores are high. So is the failure rate.
>
> The demand for teachers of mathematics has exceeded the supply of qualified people.

This is only a small part of the challenges you will face. You will need to continue to grow professionally. You will regularly wrestle with how to effectively motivate students, present material, treat individual differences, find applications, and so on. Those topics will comprise the rest of this chapter. We will not cover everything, but the intent is to provide you with thought-generating background material you can amplify throughout your professional career.

## HOW DO WE MOTIVATE?

This is, at the same time, very easy to do, and most difficult. The challenge is to stimulate a student to want to learn something. You will be faced with students who defy you to try to teach them anything. You can see it in their body language, their eyes, and their reactions to your requests for them to perform some task. Part of this posturing is our fault and part of it is theirs. We cover the same topics using the same song and tune. There are differences, though. One teacher sings alto, another bass, and so forth. But, for the most part, the explanations are exactly the same. No wonder the students are not motivated to learn. It is not all our fault. The material is covered properly and well, most of the time. For whatever the reason, the students elect to ignore the coverage, not remember it, or forget it as soon as the test is completed. Even in the face of these statements, many students do want to learn. It becomes your responsibility as their teacher of mathematics to ascertain ways of teaching or strategies that appeal to all students.

Visualize a middle schooler who is not competent at multiplying. The easiest and often the most practical solution is to give the student a calculator and be done with it. For the sake of this discussion, we will assume the calculator is not an option (although that seems quite silly in this day and age). The claim that any student who can multiply by 2 and add is capable of doing any whole-number multiplication problem seems preposterous. Hopefully, that claim will attract the student's attention. Suppose we are doing $23 \times 436$. We will express 23 as a sum of powers of 2 by listing the powers of 2 below 23 until the next one will exceed 23. At the same time, we will successively double 436 to get from the first power of 2 to each ensuing one.

23 436
1  436
2  872
4  1744
8  3488
16 6976

Because $23 = 16 + 4 + 2 + 1$, then $6976 + 1744 + 872 + 436 = 10,028$, which is $23 \times 436$. After a few of these, a student will generally ask if there is an easier way to multiply. At this point, you have the opportunity to show the standard algorithm used for multiplication. The difference is, rather than you telling the student there is a need to learn the algorithm, you are being asked for it. The motivation is there. This is a simplistic example, but the message should be clear. This trick could also be used as a diversionary adventure for more capable students. The diversion could be to learn it or to research it and discover that this is the method used by Egyptians for multiplication as demonstrated in problem 48 of the Rhind papyrus (Eves, personal communication, 1995).

---

### EXERCISE 4.2

1. Find a number trick that could be used to motivate students to learn the standard addition algorithm.

---

**Additional exercises can be found on the website.**

Depending on the atmosphere and setting, you can "bet" or wager with a student. An answer is given. Your response is, "Wanna bet?" The response is so unusual that the student immediately assumes something is awry. The beauty is that the student begins thinking through the solution that leads to the response given. The student is often correct, but it is so atypical for the teacher to challenge a correct answer that the student is caught off guard. The significant thing is that the student thinks. Even after often arriving at the same conclusion, the student may not be willing to take the challenge. Certainly you should never take a student's money if the situation would come to that, but this variation stimulates many students to rethink and verify their conclusions.

Another motivating technique is to do things incorrectly. Students enjoy catching teachers in mistakes. A typical response from you can be, "I was just seeing if you were paying attention," in such a situation. Eventually, you will all laugh and at the same time, they will never be sure if you made the error intentionally or actually did do something wrong. Of course, this can be used to excess, and not everyone agrees that this is a good procedure to follow. Realistically, it is likely that some individuals would object to any method we list in this text. You may object. If you do, be certain that you are objecting because you have thought through the example and are making an informed decision, as opposed to responding to some bias you may hold.

Getting students to think is not always easy. Sometimes, well-planned traps can motivate them to do so. Have students show all the steps as they compute the square roots of each of the following fractions: $\sqrt{\frac{2}{3}}, \sqrt{\frac{3}{5}}, \sqrt{\frac{8}{7}}, \sqrt{\frac{4}{7}}, \sqrt{\frac{5}{8}}, \sqrt{\frac{3}{4}}$.

In the first example, they will multiply both the numerator and denominator of the fraction by $\sqrt{3}$, so the numerator would be $\sqrt{2}\sqrt{3}$ and the denominator would be $\sqrt{3}\sqrt{3}$. But the denominator becomes 3. This procedure would be used in each of the subsequent problems. However, the last one is much more easily solved by immediately taking the square root of 4. Getting caught in traps like this makes students much more conscious of the need to think as problems are done rather than blindly following a set pattern. In the process, you have maintained a level of unpredictability that is a valuable asset in keeping them thinking.

Students can be stimulated to action by weird statements. What is a Mobius strip? Investigations into the topic readily show what it is and some of the "magic" represented by it. Further probing could reveal applications like car fan belts, the cross section of which can be an equilateral triangle. When the belt is made, a one-third twist is put into it so that as it passes over a pulley the first time, sides A and B touch. The second pass has sides B and C touching, and the third revolution delivers C and A touching, as shown in Fig. 4.1. The cycle is repeated throughout the life of the belt. The result is that the belt wears longer because of its design based on the Mobius strip.

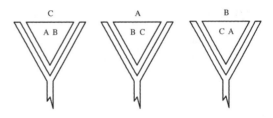

**Figure 4.1**

---

### EXERCISE 4.3

1. List five weird questions that could be used to stimulate students to learn mathematics. At least two should be appropriate for middle school and at least two for high school.

---

Questions requiring investigation provide opportunities for mathematical growth and learning. The "Tower of Hanoi" puzzle appears several places throughout the curriculum:

A puzzle to be solved;

Puzzle with a pattern;

Pattern extended to exponents;

Generalization;

Identification of which disk is to be moved next;

Where to move the disk (which pin).

A picture of this puzzle is shown in Fig. 4.2. The goal is to move the entire stack of rings from one post to another. The catch is that you cannot place a larger ring on a smaller one. You can place a smaller one on a larger one. The idea is to generalize the minimum number of moves as $2n - 1$, where $n$ is the number of disks being used. Predicting which disk to move can be determined by numbering the disks, with the smallest being 1. Write the counting numbers in base 2 notation. Count the number of zeros at the end of the successive counting numbers, beginning with 1. Three zeros means that is the disk number to move, as shown in Fig. 4.3.

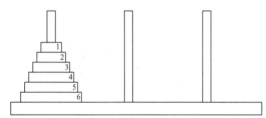

**Figure 4.2**

Fig. 4.3 solves the three-disk puzzle, showing the minimal moves to be accomplished in the order 1, 2, 1, 3, 1, 2, 1. An interesting question involves finding a method to predict where the respective disk should be moved. An interactive Internet-based version of the Tower of Hanoi can be found at the National Library of Virtual Mathematics sponsored by Utah State University (http://matti.usu.edu/nlvm/nav/frames_asid_118_g_2_t_2.html).

## EXERCISES 4.4

1. Do the tower puzzle for five disks and show the solution using base 2 numeration.
2. Can you define a process that will predict where to move a disk? That is, if the three pegs the disks are placed on are named A, B, and C, devise a system that would say where a specific disk in the sequence of moves would be placed.

**Additional exercises can be found on the website.**

Figure 4.4 shows how sets of numbers can be used to motivate students, because the environment stimulates the students to ask questions. Several connections can be made between the number sets as patterns are developed and investigated. Some examples of patterns that can be used are shown in Fig. 4.5. Students can be asked to identify patterns and establish generalizations like the ones shown in Fig. 4.6 ($n$ is a counting number).

| Base 10 | Base 2 | # zeros | Disk to move |
|---------|--------|---------|--------------|
| 1 | 1 | 0 | |
| 2 | 10 | 1 | 1 |
| 3 | 11 | 0 | |
| 4 | 100 | 2 | 2 |
| 5 | 101 | 0 | |
| 6 | 110 | 1 | 1 |
| 7 | 111 | 0 | |
| 8 | 1000 | 3 | 3 |
| 9 | 1001 | 0 | |
| 10 | 1010 | 1 | 1 |
| 11 | 1011 | 0 | |
| 12 | 1100 | 2 | 2 |
| 13 | 1101 | 0 | |
| 14 | 1110 | 1 | 1 |

**Figure 4.3**

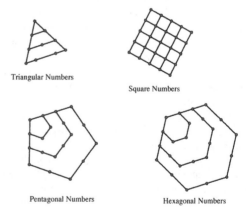

Triangular Numbers

Square Numbers

Pentagonal Numbers

Hexagonal Numbers

**Figure 4.4**

| Number Type | Numbers | | | | | | | | | |
|---|---|---|---|---|---|---|---|---|---|---|
| Counting | 1 | 2 | 3 | 4 | 5 | 6 | 7 | 8 | 9 | 10 |
| Triangle | 1 | 3 | 6 | 10 | 15 | 21 | 28 | 36 | 45 | 55 |
| Square | 1 | 4 | 9 | 16 | 25 | 36 | 49 | 64 | 81 | |
| Pentagonal | 1 | 5 | 12 | 22 | 35 | 51 | 70 | 92 | | |
| Hexagonal | 1 | 6 | 15 | 28 | 45 | 66 | 91 | | | |
| Column Difference | 0 | 1 | 3 | 6 | 10 | 15 | 21 | | | |

Column Difference refers to the difference between respective elements in any two rows.

**Figure 4.5**

| Triangular numbers | $\dfrac{n(n+1)}{2}$ |
|---|---|
| Square numbers | $n^2$ |
| Pentagonal numbers | $\dfrac{n^2 + n(n+1)}{2} = \dfrac{n(3n-1)}{2}$ |
| Hexagonal numbers | $\dfrac{n(3n-1)}{2} + \dfrac{n(n-1)}{2} = n(2n-1)$ |

**Figure 4.6**

Although the rest of this discussion involving Fig. 4.6 does not relate directly to the idea mentioned at the beginning of this paragraph, that of connecting problems more than one way, the numbers are so rich with generalization potentials that they are mentioned here. The intermediate steps are shown for pentagonal and hexagonal numbers in Fig. 4.6 to give you a hint on how to use respective $n$th column entries to generate the next number type. That is, there is a relation between the $n$th pentagonal and hexagonal number that can be used to establish the $n$th heptagonal number. The common difference row can be generalized. The table can be extended to include more rows beyond octagonal, and generalizations for each of them can be established. All hexagonal numbers are triangular numbers. Is there a pattern? Different rows can be compared similar to that for hexagonal and triangular numbers. What are they? Each of these questions could be a tool to motivate students to investigate patterns and connections between sets of numbers.

The numbers in Fig. 4.6 can be related in a variety of manners. Triangular numbers are seen in the lives of many—through bowling. The solution to the handshake problem involving each person in a room shaking hands with every other person is shown in the triangular numbers. As two people, A and B, shake, that process is counted as one shake. That is, it does not count as one shake for A and another shake for B. Given a number of points, the stipulation of joining them in all possible ways is solved with the triangular numbers too. These few examples involving triangular numbers show how a set of numbers can be associated in more than one way.

## EXERCISES 4.5

1. Define the generalized formula for the $n$th heptagonal and octagonal numbers.
2. Describe connections for pentagonal or hexagonal number sets like was done for triangular numbers, the handshake problem, and joining vertices of a convex $n$-gon with line segments.

**Additional exercises can be found on the website.**

## HOW DO WE TEACH SKILLS?

Basic skills are necessary for a student to function in the world of mathematics. None of us as mathematics educators agrees with drilling for the sake of it, with no regard for understanding, meaning, or connection with other topics in the curriculum. We all agree that a student needs to be minimally functional at adding, subtracting, multiplying, and dividing whole numbers, fractions, and decimals, for example. There is disagreement with how functional a student must be before a calculator or technology is permitted. At some point, the calculator becomes the mode of operation. Prior to that, and after that, there are skills that need to be learned.

As calculators are inserted into the curriculum, a dilemma is created, particularly as the ages of the students increase. In most instances, they have been exposed to explanations on how to perform algorithms. For some reason, the students are still not functional with the algorithms. It becomes our charge to get them functional. How do we accomplish that task? The students think they know it and, thus, are not anxious to pursue the topic again. This lack of enthusiasm can be attributed to the idea that drill exercises are often presented in sets that are alike. Drilling on a prior topic more than likely will involve doing problem sets quite similar to those used earlier and, in some instances, the same exercise sheets have been used. Little thought is required. A monotonous set of repetitious problems where the students do the same thing they have done before holds little appeal for them.

Why do students object to such treatment? Look at them in an athletic situation. The coach analyzes the game and foundational moves are practiced over and over again. The tennis backhand is hit repeatedly, in an attempt to groove the skill and get a consistent and controllable result. Skateboard skills like jumping a curb and doing a 360 are attempted time after time, striving for that perfect move. In these and so many settings like them, the participant willingly, and often voluntarily, joins in the drill. What are we doing to them in the mathematics class so that similar participation does not seem possible and, for the most part, is resisted? Don't they see the need for these drills? Don't they realize they will need these skills to be better at the more advanced levels?

You can be a factor in the success of the skill presentation. Like the coach, you need to analyze the smallest part of the overall picture. Get the skill clearly sequenced in your mind. Examine it from all angles, striving to be sure you consider every possible way a student could do it incorrectly. Then, make a concerted effort to cover those potential danger spots as a part of your presentation. Help students overcome the hurdles before they encounter them. Connect each skill with some final product. A world-class marathoner does not just get off the couch and run 26.2 miles. There are countless practice hours, many of which are spent developing basics that contribute to the overall picture.

One of the best ways to have students learn the required basic skills is to couch the necessary drill in a format that does not appear to focus on the task at hand. Suppose the desire is to provide drill in all four basic operations involving whole numbers. A problem could be presented where the students are

| Number | Way of expressing using four threes |
|--------|-------------------------------------|
| 1 | $\dfrac{33}{33}, \dfrac{(3+3)}{(3+3)}, \dfrac{(3+3-3)}{3}, \dfrac{3^3}{3^3}$ |
| 2 | $\dfrac{3}{3} + \dfrac{3}{3}$ |
| 3 | $(3^{3-3})(3)$ |
| 4 | $3^{3-3} + 3$ |
| 5 | $3 + \dfrac{(3+3)}{3}$ |
| 6 | $33 - 3^3$ |

**Figure 4.7**

asked to use four 3s and the four basic operations to express counting numbers. The challenge would be to see who gets to the greatest counting number, as displayed in Fig. 4.7. In the process, the student does a lot of practicing with the basic operations and will not realize it, particularly if encouraged to find each value in more than one way. The possibility does exist that the activity will not appeal to students. Other number tricks exist that will provide an enticing format. It becomes your task to locate and use them with your students.

Games are another option. Some games, like Concentration, provide some potential for drill. Another game would be like baseball, in which there are questions of different degrees of difficulty for singles, doubles, triples, and home runs. Students generally enjoy games like this, and they do provide an opportunity to work on skills that need practice. You are cautioned against using them too often. Typically, the format has a class divided into two teams. When it is Team A's turn, Team B players watch for errors. Team A players take turns answering questions. The problem is, when an individual on either team is not directly involved, it is possible that that person and several others will not be paying attention. The result is participation by a select few at any given time, when the intent was to have everyone practicing their skills.

Many computer and Internet-based applications involve drill and practice. Abandoning the questions about the sanity of using a computer to serve as a glorified copying machine, this option certainly holds potential. Students are attracted to technology. They quickly become aware of the limitations of drilling on the computer. Our position is that this scenario is not a wise use of equipment.

Consider middle schoolers who do not know their multiplication facts. Rather than drilling them with flash cards, worksheets, and the like, present them with an opportunity to sing along with a catchy tune or a rap song that repeats the facts in the music format. It provides an outlet, appeals to the students, and begins the necessary foundations that have been missing. Today's technology allows the student or teacher to easily record the audio or video of the class or student song using a variety of devices. One funny observation that comes out will be the opportunity to watch a student fast-forward through the song to get the necessary fact recalled. Those gyrations and antics are entertaining for all and can be used with many positive outcomes. You do need to take care not to single out a student who uses the fast-forwarding technique to give a number fact. One thing that cannot be forgotten with this— the student is asked for and produces the desired number fact. There should not be a stipulation that the fact must be recalled in a certain manner only.

## CONSIDER THE KIDS

Look at the people around you the next time you are in a crowd. We come in all sizes, shapes, and colors. These physical differences are easy to spot. Differences in mental capabilities, interests, aptitudes, and attitudes are not easy to ascertain. A study of mathematical achievement showed that a ninth-grade class exhibited a range from third-grade through college-level abilities (Educational Testing Service, 1970). There were students clustered across that continuum. How can a ninth-grade class meet the needs of such a wide variety of levels? Teachers seldom agree on who are strong and weak students. Teachers tend to teach in the same way, regardless of the ability level of the group. Teachers tend to classify well-behaved groups as more capable, even though IQ comparisons do not support this contention (Thelen, 1963). All of these factors, and many more, comprise the dynamics involved as we focus on considering the kids.

Several Algebra I textbooks were analyzed in 1990 for how they dealt with gender in assignments (Kysilka, 1990). Publishers have been trying to make texts more gender neutral to avoid stereotyping students. The basic assumption was, in addition to the shortcomings of stereotyping anything, that more females might be attracted to the study of mathematics if books were gender neutral. In the study, each word problem in the text was checked for the use of names. If names were used, they were classified as male or female. Because some names could be either male or female (Pat, Chris), those were classified as being both male and female. Similarly, occupations such as "clerk" and "shopkeeper" were classified as both. The rest of the problems were classified by name used as male or female. Once a problem was classified as male or female, it was checked to see if traditional roles were used:

Female—secretary, homemaker, beautician

Male—football player, farmer, barber

Neutral—pharmacist, artist, salesperson

The study concluded that most of the Algebra I texts studied are gender neutral. Some side issues surfaced in the study, however. The research showed that of the six texts examined, one contained 681 word problems and another contained 1,246. Many of the problems were found to be repetitious and boring. A natural question has to focus on how many times we can use money, speed, or time in a word problem before a student begins to desire other settings. Is there a value to investigating a situation involving the time required for eight people to paint a wall rather than seven? Finally, is there a connection between real-world problems and those typically found in texts?

Females and people of different ethnic backgrounds still need to be encouraged to study mathematics. Great strides have been made recently. Not too long ago, the dominant feeling was that "nice girls don't do mathematics." Some individuals openly discouraged girls from going into mathematics-related areas. Thankfully, the setting has changed. There is still room for improvement, and we all must struggle to continue the march away from stereotypical classifications and bias. We now have role models.

Sophie Germain (Marie-Sophie Germain, http://www-groups.dcs.st-and.ac.uk/~history/Biographies/Germain.html) wanted to study and learn, but her parents discouraged her. They removed light, heat, and even her clothes to dissuade her. When they found frozen ink she was trying to work with, they figured she was serious about studying. She focused on number theory and analysis and is often referred to as the Hypatia (http://www-history.mcs.st-andrews.ac.uk/Mathematicians/Hypatia.html) of the nineteenth century.

Ada Byron Lovelace, also known as Augusta Ada King, Countess of Lovelace (http://www-history.mcs.st-andrews.ac.uk/Mathematicians/

73

Lovelace.html) suffered from severe headaches and, at the age of 13, her legs became paralyzed. Over the next several years, she learned to walk normally. She is credited as being the person to detail the process we now call computer programming. She also provided a public account of Babbage's analytical engine.

Grace Brewster Murray Hopper (http://www-history.mcs.st-andrews.ac.uk/Mathematicians/Hopper.html) designed software over a three-decade span. She was only the third person to work on the Mark I, an $8 \times 8 \times 51$ foot digital computer. She was in the group that developed the world's first compiler in 1952 and was a pioneer in COBOL. In 1983, she was the oldest officer on active duty in the Navy, becoming the first female rear admiral in 1985.

Julia Bowman Robinson (http://www-history.mcs.st-andrews.ac.uk/Mathematicians/Robinson_Julia.html) overcame many hurdles in her life. She was slow to talk and pronounced words so poorly that only her older sister could understand her. When she was nine, the whole family was quarantined because she contracted scarlet fever, followed by rheumatic fever. She spent over a year in bed. Julia entered college with no intent of becoming a mathematician. She earned her doctorate at the University of California, Berkeley, and was the first female president of the American Mathematical Society. She said she preferred to be remembered not as the first woman who did something but, rather, as a mathematician who proved the theorems she did and solved problems.

Evelyn Boyd Granville (http://www-history.mcs.st-andrews.ac.uk/Mathematicians/Granville.html) attended Smith College and Yale. She is one of the first female African Americans to earn her doctorate in mathematics. She worked for industry and the government for over 15 years, and was a full professor at California State College in Los Angeles before retiring to Texas to teach mathematics and computer science.

Certainly, the list of contributions made by females could be extended. We conclude with some trivia that might prove useful to you. What do bulletproof vests, fire escapes, windshield wipers, and laser printers have in common? Women invented all of these products.

NCTM established some societal goals, one of which encompassed mathematics for all (NCTM, 1989). The reasoning behind this goal is that many employment doors are opened or closed based on an individual's knowledge of mathematics. Career advancement is frequently related to mathematical understanding. How can we, as mathematics educators, enhance the chances of all students learning more mathematics? First, be aware of how and why students avoid the study of mathematics. Know the research that discusses how teachers typically react to students of a given gender or race. Educate parents and colleagues about techniques that can be used to entice more students to study mathematics. List mathematical prerequisites for career choices. Show students how the study of mathematics or lack of it will impact the future. Be aware of sets of posters and fliers that discuss careers. Use materials that establish all races and both genders as role models.

Teachers can overcome the mathematical study barriers focused on by many students. Teachers can make the subject and topics come alive in the classroom. Teachers can stimulate inquisitiveness in all students. Teachers can avoid sexist language and examples. Teachers can assure equal representation of gender and race in example settings. If schools refused to purchase sexist or racially derogatory publications, things would change. "Generally though, studies that have dealt with change in teacher's beliefs have not provided the detailed analyses necessary to shed light on the question of why it is so difficult for teachers to accommodate their schemes and internalize new ideas" (Grouws, 1992, p.148). This is not an exhaustive treatment of the topic, but you should have an idea of the types of things to expect and do. Now it is up to you to effect the modifications necessary to make your classroom a better place for all students.

How do you consider the kids? Be available for them before school, after school, during school, and at lunchtime. Appropriate caution needs to be taken as far as propriety is concerned. Best practices dictate that it is most advisable to have more than one student present at all times, or to be in an open, public place. It is not wise to touch a student in any manner.

Listen to them. Treat them like real people. They have problems, desires, goals, and ambitions, too. They yearn to be heard. Some students feel alone and abandoned, even when they come from a "good" and "caring" home. Frequently, they just want a little attention. Show an interest in them as people. Show an interest in their problems.

Laugh with them: as they laugh at you, as they laugh at themselves. Help them see there are times when laughter can ease anxieties, pain, or frustration. We want them to learn mathematics. We want them to become contributing citizens. In the process, it becomes our responsibility to build our mathematics classroom into a productive learning environment where all is not drudgery.

What do you do with a talented student? A typical scenario has the capable student paired with a not-so-capable student. The thought is that the stronger one can help the weaker one. Surely, that can happen. Suppose the stronger one spends, over the course of a year, 100 hours helping the weaker one learn the material at hand. Certainly, the stronger one will better understand the concepts being covered and will learn how to impart knowledge to another, both of which are fine and desirable outcomes. Perhaps interpersonal skills will be enhanced, communication abilities will grow, and a lifelong friendship could be established. These, too, are good things. Is there an obligation to take some of those 100 hours and spend them on the stronger student? An outstanding tennis player once said that every competitor should play with people who are at higher, the same, and lower levels of the game. Play with the better ones to improve your game. Play with those as good as you to hone your skills. Play with those weaker than you for their game and for the sake of the game in general. The same could be applied to the mathematically talented student.

Talented students can be presented with situations that, although incorrect, provide opportunity for interesting investigations. Several famous comedy teams have used the problem $13 \times 7 = 28$ as a part of their acts. Suppose A and B are doing a presentation at a Mathematics Education Conference. The scene opens with A preparing to bake donuts for several influential individuals at the conference. B enters, asking A what is being done. A explains that donuts are being made for the important people, stating that each will receive a "baker's dozen," or 13. B comments on the large number of donuts. A says not really because $13 \times 7 = 28$. B asks how that can be and A shows:

13

$\times 7$

21 because $7 \times 3 = 21$

7  because $7 \times 1 = 7$

28 (should be $7 \times 10 = 70$)

B asks A how multiplication is checked and hears, "By division." A then shows the following:

$$\begin{array}{r} 13 \\ 7\overline{)28} \end{array}$$

$-21$  $28 \div 7 = 3$  $3 \times 7 = 21$  3 in ones place

7

$-7$  $7 \div 7 = 1$  $1 \times 7 = 7$  1 in tens place

0

B asks A what multiplication is, hearing, "short form of addition." B writes

13 B patiently points to 3, saying "3 + 3 is," pointing to the second 3.

13 A says, "6."

13 B says, "plus 3," and A says, "9."

13 B says, "plus 3," and A says, "12."

13 B says, "plus 3," and A says, "15."

13 B says, "plus 3," and A says, "18."

$+ 13$

At this point, A pushes B to the side, takes the writing tool, points to the bottom 3 saying, "21," and then points to the bottom 1, says, "22," and continues quickly up the column of 1s saying, "23, 24, 25, 26, 27, 28!"

This little role playing provides some rich opportunity for investigation. Only one thing is altered in each of the "standard algorithms" and yet the error made in the previous solution is supported or verified as correct. More capable students can be asked to explain how this can be.

There are other options available for the talented student. Provide that student with independent study activities (base -2 in the Discovery chapter would be an example) related to the concepts being covered. These activities would enhance and extend the basic information just learned. Ask stimulating questions (Why are manhole covers round? Will any other shape work?) that will motivate the student to investigate a topic. Expose the student to open-ended questions (see the eight-block problem in Chapter 6) that hold options for additional pursuit and investigation. Help the student build additional generalizations (see the discussion following Fig. 4.5). Have the student find an application of a topic covered (see the speed trap discussion in Chapter 10). Ask a student to do some historical research.

Some confidence can be built if students become aware that Gauss (http://www-history.mcs. st-andrews.ac.uk/Mathematicians/Gauss.html) was uneasy about the idea of infinity. Hamilton (http://www-history.mcs.st-andrews.ac.uk/Mathematicians/Hamilton.html) thought it was a big deal to develop the idea of ordered pairs, something almost all students take for granted. Descartes (http://www-history.mcs.st-andrews.ac.uk/Mathematicians/Descartes.html) called negative numbers false. Many schools offer dual enrollment opportunities to students in which they can take courses for community college or college credit while still enrolled in high school. Competitions provide a wonderful opportunity for student mathematical strengthening. Surely there are others, but these do provide ideas with which to begin.

---

### EXERCISES 4.6

1. Why do we teach the sequence Algebra I, Geometry, Algebra II?
2. What are the names of the women who invented the bulletproof vest, fire escapes, windshield wipers, and laser printers?

---

 **Additional exercises can be found on the website.**

What do we do with a student who does not want to learn? First, we probably need to find out about the student. What possibly got the student to a state of not wanting to learn? Encourage the student to see the value of mathematics. This will require energy, and perhaps research, on your part. Determine an interest area of the student and then find mathematical applications there, showing and discussing them with the student. Act excited about learning. Think about a favorite hobby. Remember, a person rarely is good at something if they do not enjoy it. Conversely, a person usually enjoys something they are good at. Therefore, as a teacher of mathematics, if you do not appear excited about the material you are working through with a class, how can you expect them to? Show students applications of the topic being covered. In the process, proceed with caution in some areas: redecoration of a bedroom, a middle schooler with a checking account, a middle schooler designing a house, and so forth may not captivate the interest of the student, because of lack of practicality in their minds. It could be that such topics will attract the interest of the students because it provides them an opportunity to act grown-up. Talk with a class about a mathless day—no mathematics can be done, and none exists in the world. That means clocks don't exist, cars cannot function, schedules cannot be met, food won't be prepared, and there is no music or video games.

At times, you need to pigeonhole a student. For whatever the reason, you do not have the time to focus on this one person when you have so many others to contend with. You mentally leave the needy student (who perhaps is capable but does not want to learn) for a while and hope, with all the compassion you can muster, that you will be able to return to that student. The hard truth is that you probably will not return to that student. There are so many other students that need your attention too. By the time you do get back to the student in question, the learning gap may be so great that it could require tremendous dedication and energy on the part of that student to catch up. Pigeonholing a student is not recommended. The consequences are too great.

What do we do for the less-capable student? Less-capable students are not unable to learn. Many who appear less capable are just not excited, and it becomes your responsibility to entice them into the world of mathematics. How is that done? You are a key. You need to believe in the advantages of knowing mathematics and show that to your students. Be excited in the classroom. Show them practical aspects of the things they are learning. Don't forget, these are practicalities from the world as viewed by students of the age you are working with, not from the world of the students as viewed by adults. There is a big difference between these two perceptions. Show them how information can be interpreted differently. For example, five incomes in a pool are $100,000, $10,000, $10,000, $10,000, and $10,000. The average income is $28,000, while the median income is $10,000. These two values are both true, but present a radically different picture of the situation. Students need to be aware of discrepancies like these. Have students show places or careers where they see mathematics used (this might take some prompting from you to give them some examples).

Less-capable students often just need an emotional push. Remember the work of people like Piaget, who says we all go through concrete, semiconcrete, semiabstract, and abstract stages of learning. Perhaps the less capable student needs to be taken to a more concrete stage of learning. This can be very difficult to sell to a student, because working with manipulatives might appear to be beneath the dignity of the student. Careful sales work by you as you begin the development can overcome most of the obstacles. Suppose the student in question is not able to divide using the standard algorithm. Excluding the calculator may not be the wisest route, but we will assume that is the mandate, whatever the excuse ("excuse" is used advisedly here). Showing the student how to do repeated-subtraction division might save the day. The standard algorithm demands that all estimations be exact. Repeated subtraction permits estimations below the value needed. Repeated subtraction is easier to visualize. Suppose we are doing 16,873 ÷ 47. Visualize 16,873 Popsicle sticks and the question is, how many bundles of 47 are contained in the group? Certainly, a bundle of 47 could be removed, leaving 16,826. Another group of 47 could be removed, leaving 16,779. This process could be repeated 357 more times, giving a total of 359 bundles of 47 contained in 16,873, as shown in Fig. 4.8.

Doing the repeated-subtraction example, one bundle at a time would take quite a while. Surely, there is a better way. At this stage of learning, the student should be aware of the impact of multiplying a number by a counting number power of 10 or multiples of 10. The student should realize that 100 bundles of 47 would take care of 4,700 sticks, leaving 12,079 sticks. The student may or may not notice that 200 bundles of 47 could still be removed, leaving 2,679 sticks. Another group of 100 bundles

of 47 cannot be removed because there are not 4,700 sticks left. Now, an approach similar to that of grouping by multiples of 100 bundles of 47 can be applied with multiples of 10. Fifty bundles of 47 would use 2,350 sticks, leaving 329, which can be taken care of by 7 bundles of 47. In total, 359 bundles of 47 sticks would have been removed. Certainly, this would not be done literally (but it could, if necessary), and yet the bundles of sticks help the student visualize what is being done. The process seems cumbersome, but if the student can be convinced to consider the workings, the basic ideas behind the standard division algorithm are revealed. You have the opportunity to show the student how this process collapses into the standard algorithm. The only difference between the two is the requirement in the standard algorithm that all estimates be exact, as opposed to being able to be low or exact in the repeated-subtraction process. If the pyramid approach as in Fig. 4.8 is used with repeated subtraction, a route for transition to the standard algorithm can be seen. If the largest values are done first, the transition procedure can become more obvious to some.

### EXERCISES 4.7

1. Do the problem 16,873 ÷ 47 using long division. List all the potential problem areas or places where a student might be expected to make errors.
2. Ask a group of students to write a personal answer the question, "What do you want to learn?" Allow 5–10 minutes to write an answer. Do not put restrictions on the question such as "in math class, what do you want to learn?" Review the student responses. What did you learn?

```
      7
     50
    200
    100    Total of 359 bundles of 47 in 16873
      1
      1
      1
47)16873
 -   47   1 bundle of 47 taken out
   16826
 -   47   1 bundle of 47 taken out
   16779
 - 4700   100 bundles of 47 taken out
   12079
 - 9400   200 bundles of 47 taken out
    2679
 - 2350   50 bundles of 47 taken out
     329
 -  329   7 bundles of 47 taken out
       0
```

**Figure 4.8**

What do we do with exceptional children? It was stated earlier that students differ. You knew that! However, exceptional children deserve some special attention. In today's approach to education, in which mainstreaming is practiced in many schools, you will encounter students who will have a variety of exceptionalities. You may encounter some students who are as much as three to two standard deviations below the mean, and frequently classified as mildly impaired. These students are limited in their capabilities, but they can learn. Concrete exposures through manipulatives would be mandatory with these students. Conversations with elementary or special education majors might prove enlightening in providing ideas for you. Certainly, the calculator as a working tool should be considered.

Some students will have speech impairments, many of which are noticeable and, once you are aware of them, can be worked with. These students might exhibit any of the following characteristics: omission of some speech sounds; inappropriate rate of speech characterized by repetitions, hesitations, broken words, or incomplete phrases; substitutions like "dat" for "that"; omissions like "ift" for "lift"; distortions like "shled" for "sled"; and additions like "puhlease" for "please." As you become aware of the additional challenges these students face, you can become a positive force in their mathematical learning world.

Hearing impairments can be determined and worked with easily in some instances. A student who does not respond when far from you might only be hard of hearing. Knowing that, move that individual closer to where the majority of the class activity is located. Be sure the speaker is in a well-lighted setting so it is easier for the student to watch lip movement. As you speak, face this student. Remember, if you talk to the board while you write, this student probably will not understand what is said. Clear writing style and the habit of not skipping steps can prove invaluable in working with a hearing-impaired student in a class.

Visual impairment can be particularly challenging. We depend so heavily on our sight, and take it for granted. More and more partially sighted and legally blind students are present in schools. Teaching them is easy if you learn to clearly explain each step you make, including things like saying that the particular digit is written in the ones column of the answer, for example. Many times, wide writing helps them see, or large letters, or even a magnifying glass.

Physically impaired students often are quite capable of handling the secondary mathematics curriculum, as are the visually and hearing-impaired students. They need special assistance and consideration, depending on their situation. They may have limited motor skills, inability to perform certain physical activities, or a lack of capacity to sit or stand for long periods of time. Again, being aware of the student's limitations, you can help the individual become well founded mathematically.

The following description relating to teaching about disabilities was written by Keri Upshaw,

who, at the time it was written, was a student at the University of Texas at Austin (K. Upshaw, personal communication, 1995). Put your hand, palm down, on a table. Make a tight fist with that hand. Put out your ring finger from the fist so it is the only finger not a part of the fist, while continuing to keep the fist tight and your hand on the table. Try to lift that ring finger off the table while leaving the fist on the table. It is physically impossible unless you are not making a tight fist. This is what it is like for quadriplegics, paraplegics, and others who have lost the use of a limb. You can look at your finger as long as you want and tell it to move, but it cannot. This should give you a little insight into how uncontrollable a disability can be. It should also help you understand how difficult it is for some students to perform some tasks.

Learning-disabled students can possess a variety of characteristics. No student will likely have all of these, but an individual could exhibit more than one. The list of characteristics includes being restless, fidgety, and in constant motion; talking without an audience; blurting out; speaking at the wrong time; acting impulsively; constantly touching and handling objects; not seeming to learn from experiences; showing aggressive tendencies; failing to observe classroom rules; having a short attention span; being unable to sort out important information; being distracted by irrelevancies; attending to every sound; being irritated or stimulated by visitors; being very rigid; fearing new situations; lacking self-esteem; having low emotional tolerance; being easily frustrated; retaliating; being unable to tolerate crowds; daydreaming a lot; laughing too loud too long; resisting change; performing with fluctuation from day to day; and being unable to organize. These are indicators. The presence of several of them is a sign that you might need to seek the advice of a professional on how to help a student exhibiting these tendencies learn mathematics. All of the material dealing with considering the student can probably be best summarized by "Cipher in the Snow" (Todhunter, 1975), which was discussed in the Introduction (Chapter 1).

Exceptional students certainly would include those who are extremely bright. Really, every student is exceptional, in that each is an individual.

## DISCIPLINE

As noted earlier, if we knew the key to discipline, we would bottle it and sell it. There is no royal road to discipline. Each of you must develop a strategy that is consistent and acceptable for you. No one can tell you what will or will not work with your students in your environment. That is something you will struggle with and discover as you grow. What works with one group may be a disaster with another. The following are some general directions you should consider:

Let the students know what is expected in your class.

Establish a healthy student–teacher relationship.

Help students feel they are a vital part of the school community.

Treating students as young men and women may help them try to live up to the associated expectations.

Aid the growth of self-discipline in each student by taking a personal interest in each of them, maintaining a pleasant manner as far as possible, adapting the level of requirements to the ability of individuals, and occasionally laughing with them.

Find special interests of students and talk about them.

Seek positive approaches to discipline instead of "No."

The best aid to discipline is not your strong right arm; it is your smile, your friendliness, your sense of humor, your lack of tension.

Good discipline does not come because you are older and the students respect you; it comes because you are warm and human.

Realize you are a part of any discipline problem in a classroom and determine if you are at fault or have aggravated a situation in any way.

Let students know they can approach you and discuss their needs.

Set the stage initially and you will eliminate many potential problems.

Planning is a powerful discipline tool.

Some "don'ts" associated with school discipline include:

Don't worry about superficial popularity.

Don't humiliate a student in front of peers.

Don't force an apology from a student—it might aggravate a situation.

Don't blame or discipline a whole class when an incident arises.

Don't discipline while you are angry.

Some "do's" for general discipline situations include:

Get all the facts before serving the consequences.

Defer consequences for a while—cool off. Offenders often see the error of their ways while awaiting sentence.

Convince offenders you like them but disapprove of their actions.

Other common characteristics of discipline and good teaching include:

Consistency.

Planning in advance for problem situations.

Willingness to blame self in some instances.

Thorough knowledge and understanding of class.

Training students in self-control.

There is no royal road to success. Similarly, there is no royal road to discipline. Discipline cannot be solved with a formula or a set of rules or regulations. Discipline begins with you, the teacher. Some teachers have that bearing, that poise, that grace, that attitude, that dignity, that certain indefinable something that commands the respect of students. That should be your discipline model.

In spite of preventative planning and measures, some discipline problems will occur. Insisting that problems should not happen is of little consequence. What is important is to identify what can be done about the problem and solve it. If there was a simple answer to all of this, it would be priceless. What can you do to promote discipline?

Remove privileges.

Have a private conference with the offenders on their time.

Allow students the opportunity to save face if possible.

Make the consequence fit the crime.

Call in parental help.

Seek administrative guidance.

Use personal experience as a guide.

Talk informally with students.

Begin lessons promptly.

Be enthusiastic.

Provide each student the opportunity for some success.

Admit your errors.

Make assignments reasonable and clear.

Be sure to learn your school, district, and state discipline procedures as soon as possible. By knowing these policies and procedures, you can save yourself, the administration, students, and parents much unneeded headache and embarrassment. These rules were put in place for a reason. You may not agree with all of them, but remember, you are working in this setting and agreed to abide by these rules.

You must build your own discipline framework out of the things mentioned in this text, your experiences, and the guidelines provided by your environment. This discipline is a difficult, ever-changing situation that will demand a lot of your time. As you are in a school over the years, your reputation will grow, and it becomes a valuable asset, or a curse—largely defined by how you reacted to prior students.

## READING AND WRITING IN MATHEMATICS

Reading is an essential tool in a mathematics classroom and every classroom. A nonreader is handicapped in mathematics, although familiarity with numbers and general formats can conceal many reading weaknesses. When reading formulas are applied to mathematics textbooks, typically they give false difficulty indexes because of the specialized vocabulary encountered. That does not resolve the issue, though, because the reading level of the students in a 10th-grade mathematics class could range from grade 4 through grade 16. If even a part of the reading range is accepted, you begin to see some of the problems associated with reading in the mathematics classroom. Reading is more than looking at a page and having a bunch of internalized words race by. Yet many mathematics students do not realize they cannot read their text like a novel. Reading a mathematics textbook is something like problem solving: Elements need to be selected; items should be placed in a right relation; proper weighting must be given to words; and not all words or statements are equal. A major part of reading is related to determining what is and is not important. Problem readers see all pages, paragraphs, and sentences as

equally important. We know that is not true. How do we convey that message to students?

One method used to help students read better is the keyword approach. We tell them that "sum" means "add." If they see "sum" in any word problem or environment, they know what to do. On the surface that sounds good, and it works for many students. You must remember that not all students read well, and not all students attend to words as closely as they should. Consider the question, "Some of the following are odd; which ones? 2, 3, 4, 5, 6, 7, 8, 9." A student who focuses on keywords sees "some." Spelling is not a big factor and "some" means add. The answer is 44. We know the difference. We are aware of the need to pay attention. But we are not talking about us. We are talking about students. Couple this reader with the attitude, "If all else fails, read the instructions," and you begin to have an idea of what you face with some students who are not good readers. It is extremely important that our students first comprehend the instructions to the problem they are attempting to solve. In the real world, understanding the situation to be solved is a significant part of the problem. The keyword approach should not be totally abandoned, but caution does need to be used as it is employed.

We hear of the three Rs. Typically, they are not thought of in the sense of complementing each other but, rather, from the standpoint of each standing independent of the other. Certainly each influences the other, and skills from one may be employed in the other. Reading is definitely required in mathematics work, as is writing. However, only recently has there been emphasis on using mathematics to teach and enhance writing skills.

For most students mathematics remains confined between the pages of a textbook or the walls of a classroom and ends with the ringing of the bell. Rarely do students consider mathematics a vital force in history, a part of their daily life, or an essential ingredient for their future. Writing assignments can build an awareness of the extended function of mathematics and its importance in the world.

The history of mathematics has countless individuals who led interesting and many times strange lives. Investigation and reports on one of them could prove interesting and informative, not only for the person doing the work, but also for peers who might be reading it. A historical example requiring writing could be:

You are the Roman general Marcellus, who, in 215 B.C., laid siege to the city of Syracuse. The city, home of one of the greatest mathematicians of all time, Archimedes, resisted for almost three years, largely because of the ingenuity of Archimedes (http://www-history.mcs.st-andrews. ac.uk/Mathematicians/Archimedes.html). Explain to your emperor how it came to pass that Syracuse could hold off the mighty Roman army for so long. Give specific descriptions of some of Archimedes' contrivances that foiled your attempts. Your explanation will be read to the full senate.

Assignments such as the one for Archimedes can be given for each student. You will need to allow some class time for initial research efforts and guidance. The Internet is an excellent place for students to begin their research. Try pointing your students to sites such as the MacTutor History of Mathematics Archive (http://www-history.mcs.st-andrews. ac.uk/index.html). Once drafts are written, students can work in groups, with the objective of helping each other create a better document. The collection of topics will expose each group participant to other ideas and provide hints of ways they can incorporate additional variety into their own work. Perhaps a group member, not the author, could read the paper to the group, while the author watches the group for reactions. This, too, could provide some additional information for strengthening the product. Listeners could have specific tasks to focus on during the trial report: organization, clarity, or content, for example. Comments could be made in writing and gathered, so the author has the ability to reflect and revise based on the impact of the work.

This group work and the critical listening associated with it will possibly provide additional insight for the individual's own paper. There should be some commonality of vocabulary that will allow for focus and assistance on spelling, punctuation, and mechanics.

There are parallels between mathematics work and writing. Understanding the problem is much like outlining a paper. Planning a solution for the problem is similar to organizing a writing project. Actually solving the problem is like writing. Finally, checking your work is parallel to revising a paper. Actual writing assignments can be incorporated into the mathematics classroom through story problems (creating new ones, rewording others), explanations (tell how or why you have arrived at a given answer or conclusion), paraphrasing (summarize an explanation for another person), or free writing (describe the emotions associated with a topic presented). Writing benefits include increased understanding, more flexible thinking, heightened awareness, better problem-solving skills, practice organizing thoughts, awareness of outside research requirements, information that can be used later, and communications on topics that are not clear.

## EXERCISES 4.8

1. Provide a paragraph-style summary of your last meeting of the class you are using this text with. Swap papers with another student from the class. How similar are the papers? What, if any, are the differences?
2. Locate a website other than MacTutor that can be used as an excellent resource or reference for the history of mathematics.

**Additional exercises can be found on the website.**

## WHY TEACH THE HISTORY OF MATHEMATICS?

Humanity has developed a systematic procedure for storing and passing on information from generation to generation—history. Much of what is passed on relates to mathematics. Beginning recordings are more mathematical than historical. People chronicled "how many" long before they recorded events. Even civilizations that developed at different rates and locations exhibit a wide variety of mathematical commonalties. Listing or keeping track of things precedes a system of naming numbers in almost every development. Once numbers are named, rules of operation develop.

The origination of numbers is difficult to pinpoint in history. Early documents from China, Egypt, India, and Mesopotamia all show questions dealing with "how many . . . ?" This implies that the idea of cardinality was around long before the ability to write. This, however, can easily lead to the conclusion that the idea of sets must be one of humanity's earliest fascinations. As time progressed, body parts and words were used to represent specific numbers. It appears as if it was clear that the emphasis was not on the order in which things were presented but, rather, on the total number. Developmentally, a giant stride forward occurred when it dawned on people that the last cardinal number named also gave a name for the total number of elements of a set. Even with this, it was not long before the number of objects exceeded the names for numbers. Body parts were limited. Another way was needed. This need prompted numeration systems. It must be remembered that spoken and written vocabulary limitations existed and, thus, formalization and extension of a numbering system was not an easy task. Look at the Roman numerals and you will see how it could have been cumbersome to write larger values. If nothing else, it should give an added appreciation for our Hindu Arabic place value system.

The Greeks and the Pythagorean Society did a lot to develop numbers. The Pythagorean Society was open only to aristocrats and all teaching was verbal. Written work would permit secrets to leak out more readily. The Pythagoreans spent a lot of their energy on geometry, but they did develop some good number structure. They developed tables and used the abacus to do computations. Although they would teach people how to do computations, they would not reveal how the tables were developed. They worked with a wide variety of topics seen today, including perfect squares, triangular numbers, perfect numbers, abundant numbers, deficient numbers, letters representing numbers, primes, and amicable numbers. These investigations involved computations, and that created a demand for some flexible, comprehensive, organized way to write numbers. This, in turn, led to place value.

Through the ages, different bases have been used for place value systems. Although base 10 has become the dominant base, the Duodecimal Society still pushes for base 12. Other bases that were used in the historical development include 20, 60, and 10,000. Imagine trying to get students to memorize operation facts in base 20! As the place value system got refined, computation demands increased.

Computational devices have been available for a long time. Society slowly adapts to new devices and, in the process, provides acceptability. The abacus was probably the first computational device. It is great for addition and subtraction, but the major drawback is that the previous step is consistently eliminated. In 1946, a competition was held between a desk calculator and an abacus. Both operators were equally good with their respective devices.

The problems included adding, subtracting, multiplying, and dividing three- to six-digit numbers. The abacus operator easily won the competition. Even today, we marvel at the abacus skills of speed and accuracy exhibited by some individuals. Other computational devices are Napier's bones, the slide rule, adding machines, handheld calculators, tablet computers, smartphones, and multitudes of computer software.

We take so much for granted. Arithmetic as we know it did not take form until close to the end of the fifteenth century. Fractions gave mathematicians of antiquity fits. Only in the past 500 or 600 years have fractions been relatively easy to deal with in a number system. Decimals did not appear until the sixteenth century. Think about it! How could they do some of the computations? It gives an even greater appreciation for the work of those individuals who developed so much of our mathematics. For example, Napier (http://www-history. mcs.st-andrews.ac.uk/Mathematicians/Napier. html) did not develop the concept of logarithms until the beginning of the seventeenth century. Formative slide rules are shown to have existed in about 1620 A.D. Newton (http://www-history. mcs.st-andrews.ac.uk/Mathematicians/Newton. html) suggested a "runner" for the slide rule in 1675, but it was not put into use until about 1775. Pascal (http://www-history.mcs.st-andrews.ac.uk/ Mathematicians/Pascal.html) introduced the first line of computers in 1642. Leibniz (http://www-history.mcs.st-andrews.ac.uk/Mathematicians/ Leibniz.html) completed a computing machine in 1694 and it had a moving carriage, wheels going in opposite directions for addition and subtraction, and latches to prevent over-rotation. Babbage (http://www-history.mcs.st-andrews.ac.uk/ Mathematicians/Babbage.html) created a "difference engine" in 1839, and his son completed the work and published results in 1906. Babbage had the idea, but the technology of the time was too limited to meet his dreams. He needed finer machining tools, electronic circuits, and better alloys. Given these, he would have had today's computer. Herman Hollerith (http://www-history. mcs.st-andrews.ac.uk/Mathematicians/Hollerith. html) developed the idea of holes in cards in 1880. Eventually, IBM adopted this process for use with early computers. William Burroughs (http://web. mit.edu/invent/iow/burroughs.html) in 1888 designed a machine that would print figures. Electronics entered the picture in 1944, transistors in

1948. By 1961, computers were taken over by transistors, and the rest is history.

Algebra was available in rudimentary stages from about 1700 B.C. through 1700 A.D. Symbolization developed slowly, and only minor improvements were made in algebra until the general cubic was solved. Modern symbolism began to emerge in the fourteenth century. Concepts such as negative numbers were unknown or denied by many mathematicians from antiquity. Realizing these limitations should give you new appreciation for how far we have come in recent years. It certainly gives new meaning to information explosion.

Mathematics as we know it started to be distinguishable only in the nineteenth century. Mathematics became known not as a tool, or as a descriptor of the world, but as a science. This development was a direct result of more and more people asking "why" something worked out the way it did. These developments brought higher levels of abstractions. Undefined terms were established and more rigorous definitions were devised. There was the understanding that, in response to the realization that as long as terms were loosely defined, varied interpretations would be available. The twentieth century found mathematics maturing on all fronts. It expanded in some areas and developed in others. Attraction was a unifying force.

The study of the history of mathematics can be summarized by the following paragraph, the author of which is unknown:

Many have wondered why we do things in mathematics as we do. Often there is the feeling that so much of what we teach just is, has always been, and will continue to be a ready-made conglomeration of rules and procedures that have come down to us from somewhere, to be used only by the select few that somehow seem to possess a talent for understanding how it all fits together. In short, there is no sense of history behind what we teach, no overview as to how it all began and evolved into the system of topics, concepts, and skills now taught in our courses. However, if topics from the history of mathematics are properly used, and are coupled with an up-to-date knowledge of mathematics and its uses, then it becomes an important tool in the hands of teachers who teach "why." Howard Eves said, "We should let the history of mathematics guide the order in which we present topics to students." (Eves, personal communication, 1995)

## EXERCISES 4.9

1. Describe some of the earliest uses of numbers and numerals.
2. Document the beginning of irrational numbers and how they were used in early computations.
3. Research at least one of the following topics and prepare a written summary of its development: Egyptian pyramids, golden section, golden ratio, Fibonacci numbers, networks, twisted surfaces, computational short cuts, percent, or measurement.

**Additional exercises can be found on the website.**

## TEACHING FOR GENERALIZATIONS

What is a generalization? What kinds of generalizations are there? How are generalizations used in mathematics? Are there advantages to a student learning generalizations? Generalizations are mentioned throughout this text: Gauss summing the first 100 counting numbers quickly, the doorbell/party problem, the locker problem, and the area of a triangle, for example.

Part of enticing students to generalize results is getting them to see a problem in a different light. A student is asked to find the length of a rectangle's diagonal given that one side length is 144 units and the other is 60 units. Certainly, the student could apply the Pythagorean theorem. More than likely, there would be a search for a calculator. By the time it is located and ready to go, the answer could have been derived longhand. However, a different view of the problem makes it even easier to solve. Notice that both 144 and 60 are multiples of 12. Divide out that common factor (12) and the legs of the right triangle are 12 and 5 units, respectively. Most students will have seen the 5, 12, 13 right triangle and frequently give the reflexive response of 13. All that remains is to multiply 13 by 12, something that many of them can do in their heads, to get the length of the diagonal of the rectangle to be 156.

Patterning and organization of information often lead to useful generalization skills. Figure 4.9 shows a series of cards. The task is to determine the numerical value and suit of XY, which has fallen face down. A hint could be given by putting

Figure 4.9

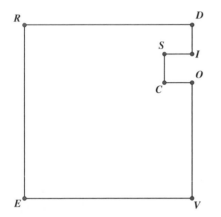

Figure 4.10

commas as shown: $1\spadesuit, 4\spadesuit, 9\blacklozenge, 1\heartsuit 6\heartsuit, 2\clubsuit 5\clubsuit, 3\blacklozenge$ XY, $4\spadesuit 9\spadesuit$. This should help emphasize the squares. Double digits are represented with the same suit, so the missing suit must be diamonds.

As we strive to have students generalize, care must be taken to keep an individual from revealing the "secret." Once the confidentiality is exposed, the thinking of others is thwarted. Furthermore, telling generalizations too soon in the investigation tends to lower performance levels on later tasks. Students become accustomed to you or another student eventually revealing the desired generalization. These people can become quite adept at patiently sitting and waiting, not thinking, until the time for revelation comes. Student generalizations warrant caution, because verbalization is not necessarily a reflection that there is associated knowledge and understanding.

The following problem is found in the *Thirty-Third Yearbook* (Rosskopf, 1970, p. 268). In the *Yearbook* chapter titled "Generalizations," Wills noted that problem solving benefits from generalization abilities. He discussed ways of "(1) telling whether a student has acquired a generalization, (2) motivating the need for generalizations, and (3) stating them" (Rosskopf, 1970, p. 268). Figure 4.10 shows the problem Wills used to stimulate initial discussion about generalizations. You should do this problem prior to reading the discussion about how to develop the generalization.

Refer to Fig. 4.10, which is not drawn to scale. Both RDVE and SIOC are "squares," so ER = DR = EV and CO = CS = IS. All side lengths are counting numbers. The area is 1,999 square units. The task is to find the perimeter of DISCOVER. The perimeter could be expressed as 3ER + 3C0 + OV + Dl. If segment CS is placed where I0 would be, DV is completed, giving another side the same length as ER and leaving two segments the length of CO, and the perimeter becomes 4ER + 2C0. If we can determine values for ER and CO, the perimeter will be determined. The area is known. It would seem that finding the side lengths would be easy, but that is not so. All we know is that $(ER)^2-(CO)^2 = 1,999$. If only we knew the length of one segment somewhere in the figure, maybe the task would be simpler. But we don't know any lengths.

The value 1,999 is so large that just plugging in numbers does not seem practical, but that certainly could be tried. Good luck. Would a generalization be helpful? We need to look at the problem from a different perspective. What do we know? We know the area. We know we can express that area as the difference of two squares. We know that the result is an odd counting number. Is there a way this information can be combined that would build to a generalization? Mathematicians often try to work with a similar problem involving smaller numbers. Applying that technique here, what is the smallest odd counting number? Use that to be the area. Then go to the next odd counting number and let that be the area. Continue this for a few steps and see if there is a pattern that can be generalized. The results of this approach are shown in Fig. 4.11. In general, from Fig. 4.11, we have two consecutive counting numbers giving the desired area. In other words, what two consecutive counting numbers sum to 1,999? Knowing that ER = 1,000 and CO = 999, the perimeter of DISCOVER is 4(1,000) − 2(999) or 2,002 units.

| ER | 1 | 2 | 3 | 4 | 5 | 6 | 7 | . . . N + 1 |
|---|---|---|---|---|---|---|---|---|
| OC | 0 | 1 | 2 | 3 | 4 | 5 | 6 | . . . N |
| $(ER)^2 - (OC)^2$ | 1 | 3 | 5 | 7 | 9 | 11 | 13 | . . . 1999 |

Figure 4.11

# CONCLUSION

This chapter has discussed some teaching skills. There are many more that you will develop throughout your career. Our intent is to start your thinking process toward developing a set of skills you will reflexively use in your classroom. The skills you use do not just happen. They are a result of conscious thought, effort, and professionalism. The more energy you devote to developing your teaching skills, the greater the benefit will be for your students.

## STICKY QUESTIONS

1. There is a generalization dealing with the sum of the interior angles of a polygon in relation to N, the number of sides. What is that generalization? Create a set of concrete models consisting of a triangle, a quadrilateral, a pentagon, and a hexagon, that could be used to help a student create the desired generalization.

2. Euler's line is defined by the intersection points from three of the following for any triangle: incenter, circumcenter, centroid, and orthocenter. Do the construction and determine which one is not on Euler's line. What kind of triangle yields all four of these points on the same line? What kind of triangle yields all four of these points as the same point?

3. Create triangle ABC and bisect angle B. Create an exterior angle of the triangle at B and bisect that exterior angle. State your conclusion.

4. The average of four fractions is 3. Three of the fractions are $[\frac{a}{b}, \frac{c}{d}, \frac{e}{f}]$, where all of $a$, $b$, $c$, $d$, $e$, and $f$ are nonzero. What is the fourth fraction?

5. The sum of two numbers is 4 and their product is 5. What is the sum of their reciprocals? (There is a hard way and an easy way to do this one.)

6. Visualize a checkerboard. Assuming you can travel only up or right, and only along sides of the little squares, turning or going straight through any small square's corner, how many different routes are available to go from the lower left corner of the board to the upper right corner of the board?

7. Fibonacci's triangle has nothing to do with the Fibonacci sequence, but it provides rich opportunities for generalizations.

$$1$$
$$3 \; 5$$
$$7 \; 9 \; 11$$
$$13 \; 15 \; 17 \; 19$$
$$21 \; 23 \; 25 \; 27 \; 29$$
$$31 \; 33 \; 35 \; 37 \; 39 \; 41$$
$$43 \; 45 \; 47 \; 49 \ldots$$

What is the sum of the terms of the $n$th row? What is the 69th term in the 75th row? How many terms are in the 48th row?

8. Would year-round school help solve the transition between Algebra I and Algebra II by reducing the amount of time for review? Why or why not?

## PROBLEM-SOLVING CHALLENGES

1. **Computational Madness**
   Simplify the following expression.

$$\frac{1234567890}{1234567891^2 - (1234567890)(1234567892)}$$

**Check out the website for the solution.**

2. **By arranging the digits 1, 2, 3, 4, 5, 6, 7, 8, and 9, it is possible to come up with a fraction equivalent to one-eighth. For example:**

$$\frac{1}{8} = \frac{3187}{25796}$$

Your task is to arrange the digits 1, 2, 3, 4, 5, 6, 7, 8, and 9 and come up with an equivalent fraction to one-fifth.

**Check out the website for the solution.**

# ■
# LEARNING ACTIVITIES

## One Size Fits All

The concept of "area" can be introduced by building squares on a number line where one side of each square is a segment between integers. Consider the following number line shown in Fig. 4.12.

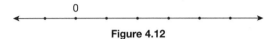

**Figure 4.12**

Squares can be added as shown in Fig. 4.13 to introduce the concept of area.

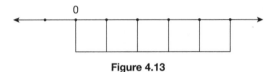

**Figure 4.13**

The total space covered by the squares is a rectangle with area 5 unit squares. Add a row of squares as shown in Fig. 4.14 and get a rectangle that is 5 units long and 2 units high and is covered by a total of 10 unit squares. The number of squares that cover the rectangle can be obtained by multiplying the number of rows by the number of columns, leading to the idea that the area of a rectangle is the product of the length of the base and the length of the height.

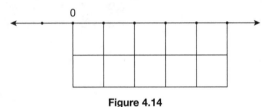

**Figure 4.14**

A parallelogram (Fig. 4.15) can be transformed into a rectangle. Since we know how to find the area of a rectangle, this transformation can be used to find a formula for the area of a parallelogram.

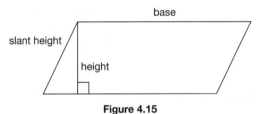

**Figure 4.15**

Translating the right triangle as shown in Fig. 4.16 produces the following rectangle. The area of the parallelogram is the same as the area of the rectangle, which is 10 square units.

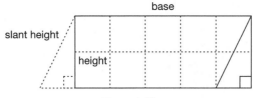

**Figure 4.16**

Notice though that the area could have been determined by finding the product of the base and height, even before the parallelogram was transformed.

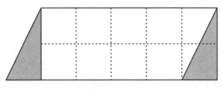

**Figure 4.17**

The shaded triangles shown in Fig. 4.17 are congruent and the rectangle has been transformed back to the original parallelogram, but the array of 10 unit squares would still cover it, no more and no less. So the area of a parallelogram is obtained by multiplying the length of the base and the height.

Trapezoids can be transformed into parallelograms, thus giving a means for finding their areas too. Starting with the trapezoid in Fig. 4.18,

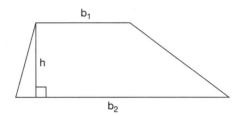

**Figure 4.18**

construct midpoints A and B on the nonparallel sides.

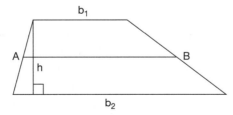

**Figure 4.19**

The figure is divided into two similar trapezoids by straight-line segment AB as shown in Fig. 4.19. Select either A or B and rotate the smaller trapezoid 180° as shown in Fig. 4.20.

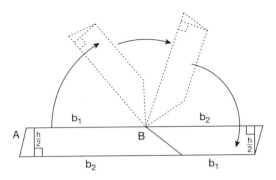

**Figure 4.20**

The transformed figure is a parallelogram, but the area is still the same as the area of the original trapezoid. The base of the parallelogram is $b_1 + b_2$ and the height is $\frac{h}{2}$. The area of the parallelogram (or trapezoid) can be expressed in the following ways: $\frac{h}{2}(b_1 + b_2)$, $\frac{h(b_1 + b_2)}{2}$, $\frac{1}{2}(h(b_1 + b_2))$, or $h\left(\frac{b_1 + b_2}{2}\right)$. Focus on $h\left(\frac{b_1 + b_2}{2}\right)$ to explore some familiar formulas for finding areas. Verbalizing the area formula $h\left(\frac{b_1 + b_2}{2}\right)$, one can say that the area of the trapezoid is found by multiplying the height times the average length of the bases.

Use the formula for the area of a trapezoid to calculate the area of a rectangle: $h\left(\frac{b_1 + b_2}{2}\right)$ becomes $\left(\frac{b + b}{2}\right)h$, which is $\left(\frac{2b}{2}\right)h$, or $bh$.

This same formula can be used to find the area of a parallelogram shown in Fig. 4.21.

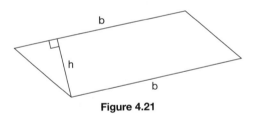

**Figure 4.21**

The average of the bases times the height is $h\left(\frac{b_1 + b_2}{2}\right)$, which becomes $\left(\frac{b + b}{2}\right)h$. That can be expressed as $\left(\frac{2b}{2}\right)h$, or $bh$.

### Your Turn

1. Find the area of a square using the average length of the bases times the height.
2. Describe how you could use the average length of the bases times the height to find the area of a triangle.
3. The ancient Egyptian, Hero of Alexandria (sometimes "Hero" is written "Heron") is credited with developing a formula to find the area of any triangle. "Hero's Formula" is $\sqrt{s(s-a)(s-b)(s-c)}$, where $a$, $b$, and $c$ are the side lengths of a triangle and $s$ is the sum of the three side lengths divided by 2, or $\frac{a + b + c}{2}$. Given a triangle with side lengths 5, 6, and 7, $s = \frac{5 + 6 + 7}{2}$ or 9.

The area of the triangle is $\sqrt{9(9-5)(9-6)(9-7)}$ or $\sqrt{9(4)(3)(2)} \approx 14.696938$. Use the average of the bases times the height to compute the area of this same triangle, using the 7 unit side as the base as shown in Fig. 4.22.

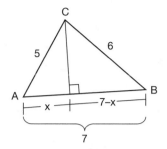

**Figure 4.22**

One way to understand the formula for the area of a circle involves dividing a circle into congruent sectors and rearranging them into an approximate parallelogram as shown in Fig. 4.23. The more segments, the closer the transformed circle will approximate a parallelogram. This approach relies on knowing that the circumference of a circle is $2\pi r$. The base of the "parallelogram" is $(\pi r)$, which is half the circumference $(2\pi r)$. The height is $r$ and the product of the base and height is $(\pi r)(r)$ or $\pi r^2$.

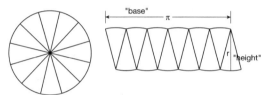

**Figure 4.23**

A more unique method for finding the area of a circle involves using the average of the lengths of the bases times the height. If the circle is divided into four congruent segments as shown in Fig. 4.23, the length of each "base" is $\frac{\pi r}{2}$ and the "height" is $2r$.

The average of the lengths of the "bases" times the "height" is $h\left(\frac{b_1 + b_2}{2}\right)$. This is $2r\left(\frac{\frac{\pi r}{2} + \frac{\pi r}{2}}{2}\right)$,

which is $2r\left(\frac{2\left(\frac{\pi r}{2}\right)}{2}\right)$, or $2r\left(\frac{\pi r}{2}\right)$. But $2r\left(\frac{\pi r}{2}\right)$ simplifies to $r(\pi r)$ or $\pi r^2$, the common formula used to find the area of a circle.

4. Will the "average of the bases times the height" work when trying to find the area of a regular hexagon?

# PART II
# Mathematics Education Fundamentals

# Technology

## 5

## FOCAL POINTS OF THIS CHAPTER

- Technological advancements in the teaching of mathematics
- Formulation of a personal plan for the use of technology in secondary mathematics education
- Determining what technology is appropriate throughout the mathematics curriculum
- Technology options inside and outside the classroom
- Handheld devices
- Technology as a discovery tool
- Software appropriate for the secondary mathematics classroom
- Apps for the teaching and learning of mathematics

We are living in a time when technology is changing almost faster than we can adapt to it, or afford it. New products and upgrades are marketed at a rapid pace. The level of complexity associated with some of the technology now available is so great that a product is not fully implemented and absorbed before its next generation is on the market. The third version of the iPad was out while people were still purchasing the iPad 2. The diversity and depth of technology available to us are increasing at a seemingly exponential rate. This is particularly true in mathematics. In the late nineties and early part of this century, many new programmable graphing calculators (Casio, Hewlett Packard, Sharp, and Texas Instruments) were introduced. Casio's development of the ClassPad 300 provided the power of a graphing calculator with an enlarged graphical display integrated with geometry software and a touch screen stylus. Texas Instruments introduced the TI-89 and TI-84 Plus graphing calculators as well as the TI Navigator, which allows students to contribute work to the learning environment by projecting calculator work in real time for the entire class. These new tools were powerful additions for the mathematics classroom. The potential to unlock powerful teaching and learning seemed to have arrived. Calculator wars began, not only with respect to which brand of calculator but when these new devices should be used. Every time a new calculator was unveiled, the debate continued. The irony is that most secondary mathematics classrooms did not fully utilize the power of the new handheld tools available to students. Why?

In the last two years, the powerful push of tablets, including the iPad, Xoom, and Tab, have created a drive for handheld computer technology in the classroom. By the time this book is in print, these entries will be several generations old, and the time between the release of those products and the printed copy of this text will be less than 18 months. In addition to the hardware, thousands of software (apps) will be created for a variety of handheld devices in all sorts of sizes.

In the relatively near future, if not now, mathematics and science study will be mandatory for all students because of the demands of our technological times. People in all walks of life will need a higher level of proficiency in mathematics and science. Mathematics is a key to the door of opportunity as students decide about careers, learn to make informed decisions, and function as self-motivated, lifelong learners. "Working smarter" is replacing "working harder" mathematically, particularly where more menial tasks (arithmetic would be included here) are concerned. In working smarter, individuals must be mentally fit to absorb new ideas, adapt to change, cope with ambiguity, perceive patterns, and solve unconventional problems (MSEB, 1989). This was an expectation in the late 1980s. Have we used technology to embrace the idea of "working smarter" or do we continue to debate what technology should be used in the teaching and learning mathematics?

It is imperative that students generate a greater command of all fundamental subjects in general, and mathematics in particular. This demand is evidenced by requirements of at least three mathematics credits for high school graduation in most states, and at least college algebra or its equivalent for graduation from most colleges. With this in mind, it is necessary that teachers of mathematics equip each student with the ability to use and comprehend the basics of mathematics.

What is truly stopping our mathematics classrooms from embracing new technology? If you graduated from high school in the past five years, what technology did you use in your high school mathematics classrooms? Did you use the latest graphing calculator technology (at that time), such as the TI-84 Plus Silver, TI-89, or the TI-Navigator? Did you use the Casio CFX-9850G Color graphing calculator or FX 2.0 Algebra Tutor? Did you use a computer as a learning tool in your mathematics curriculum? Did you use dynamic mathematics software such as Geometer's Sketchpad, Fathom or Mathematica? Were you allowed to use technology at all times in your high school mathematics classes? Did you use any technology in your middle school classes? All of this technology was available during middle and high school for you. Unfortunately, our mathematics classrooms have not fully embraced the current technology! Why not?

## THE LITERATURE

The computer has become an essential component of life in this age of technology. Computer technology is now integrated in almost everything we use. Technology has enabled previously difficult and even impossible tasks to become part of everyday life. Compound interest could formerly be determined only by specialists. Today, with the availability of many calculators and numerous apps, any interested layperson has the power to create an amortization schedule with the touch of a few keys. Computer technology has changed the way people live their lives through the use of automated teller machines, DVDs, handheld calculators, digital cameras, cell phones, handheld tablets, home appliances, automobiles, airplanes, state of the art audiovisual equipment, and even video games. In a span of four years, the television market has left behind large picture tubes (4:3 picture ratio) and converted to digital quality, flat screen monitors (16:9 picture ratio) with the capability of transmitting 3-D graphics and in high definition. Your television can now become a true home entertainment system, with full Internet access to replace your home computer screen. Items such as these are readily available, affordable, and accepted as desirable ingredients for living both today and in the future. You now have a computer in the palm of your hands. NCTM stresses the need for adaptation toward an ever-changing technological society. They suggest that today's mathematics curriculum needs to implement the use of computers and technology. In 2000, the Technology Principle of the NCTM standards stressed:

*Technology is essential in teaching and learning mathematics; it influences the mathematics that is taught and enhances students' learning.*

Electronic technologies—calculators and computers—are essential tools for teaching, learning, and doing mathematics. They furnish visual images of mathematical ideas, they facilitate organizing and analyzing data, and they compute efficiently and accurately. They can support investigation by students in every area of mathematics, including geometry, statistics, algebra, measurement, and number. When technological tools are available, students can focus on decision making, reflection, reasoning, and problem solving. (NCTM, 2000, p. 25)

If NCTM made these recommendations more than 10 years ago, why have we not fully embraced the use of technology throughout middle and high school mathematics classrooms? Do all of our teachers of mathematics support these recommendations? Did you know that handheld technology for the mathematics classroom was available more than 10 years ago, but schools did not readily adopt the devices? The Casio Cassiopeia was developed more than 10 years ago. This handheld pen-based device was loaded with Windows CE operating systems and could run Word and Excel. In addition, this revolutionary technology was Internet-ready and could run Geometer's Sketchpad and other mathematics software. The cost was under $300. The Cassiopeia A-10 and A-20 had the potential to change the teaching and learning of mathematics in the classroom. (http://en.wikipedia.org/wiki/Casio_Cassiopeia, http://www.pencomputing.com/WinCE/cassiopeia_a20.html)

Research shows the use of technology in the mathematics environment causes students to:

Become better problem solvers.

Better understand the concepts that are taught.

Demonstrate increased performance levels on standardized tests.

Achieve higher ACT and SAT scores.

Even with the endorsement of and successes described by NCTM, the introduction of computer technology into the educational setting has generated questions regarding its effectiveness on achievement in the mathematics classroom.

Using technology in the mathematics classroom still generates strong feelings in many mathematics educators. Some teachers believe student understanding of concepts must not be lessened by the use of technology. They do not want computers to become a "crutch" or "shortcut" method of learning. Others believe technology can be used as an instruction and teaching tool in the classroom, replacing much of the standard board or overhead tools of instruction. Still others indicate that computers can be used as a means of student self-discovery, learning, and development of their understanding of mathematical concepts. Technology, whether it is seen as a crutch or a tool in the classroom, is a component of today's world.

Kitabchi (1987) studied 30 fifth-grade inner-city students who were provided with a computer for home and school use. They showed significantly higher scores in mathematics comprehension and mathematics concepts/applications. Beyer and Dusewicz (1991) studied the effect of students receiving 30 minutes of daily computer exposure throughout the year. All grade levels and schools showed significant gains in mathematical achievement for the second and third years of the project. Ferrell (1985) found a small increase in achievement when computers were an integral part of instruction in mathematics.

Koscinski and Gast (1993) found computers to be effective tools when working with learning-disabled students in the area of multiplication. Mason (1994) examined the effectiveness of CAI (computer-assisted instruction) in improving mathematical skills of educable mentally handicapped students and students with learning disabilities. There was a significant increase in mathematics achievement for students at all grade levels. Nomeland and Harris (1976) studied the effects of a CAI laboratory with 111 deaf students. An analysis of Stanford Achievement Test scores demonstrated that students of all ages showed gain in their mathematical scores.

Johnson, Cox, and Watson (1994) studied the use of information technology in a variety of content areas including mathematics. They studied 2,300 students' achievement from 87 classrooms in England and Wales. The use of computers showed a positive result for ages 8–10, and highly positive result for ages 14–16. The results for ages 12–14 were inconclusive. Seever (1992) examined a four-year project involving the implementation of computers and CAI. When achievement was compared with the baseline from the beginning of the project, there were signs of higher achievement for those students. Yusuf (1991) studied the effects of LOGO-based instruction compared with instruction by teacher lecture accompanied by pencil-and-paper activities in informal geometry. The LOGO group scored significantly higher.

McCoy (1990) examined the achievement of students who used Geometry Supposers once every two weeks in a high school geometry class. The CAI class scored significantly higher on all except the lower-level items on the posttests. Funkhouser and Dennis (1992) found similar effects using CAI on problem-solving achievement. Wood (1991) studied the effect of two forms of computer-based education in second-year algebra. One form of computer-based instruction used a computer tutorial program, whereas the second form utilized the computer as an instruction tool in the classroom. The computer as an instruction tool led to the most significant gains in students' conceptual achievement.

Lang (1987) analyzed the effects of a computer-enhanced classroom on the achievement of 4,293 remedial high school mathematics students. The computer-enhanced classroom students showed significant gains in all areas and grades with the exception of 10th graders. Messerly (1986) found significant gains on the computation and overall score on the Stanford test after using CAI in mathematics for hearing-impaired students.

Palmitter (1991), Heid (1988), and Bitter (1970) examined the effects of student achievement when learning calculus using CAI. Palmitter studied the use of a computer algebra system rather than paper-and-pencil computations. The CAI group scored significantly higher on both a conceptual knowledge test and a calculus computational exam. Heid found that students using CAI showed a better understanding of concepts than those not using CAI. Bitter found computer assignments generated significantly higher scores on mathematical achievement for college calculus students.

O'Callaghan (1998) found students who use Computer-Intensive Algebra (CIA) achieved a better overall understanding of functions when compared with students who did not use computer technology in a traditional algebra curriculum. CIA is a mathematics program that places an emphasis on problem solving, conceptual knowledge, and extensive use of computer technology. The study also showed that CIA students were more proficient at modeling, interpreting, and translating mathematical concepts.

Research supports that "students can learn more mathematics more deeply with the appropriate use of technology" (NCTM, 2000, p. 25).

In a review of literature on the impact of dynamic geometry software (DGS), research shows that DGS can improve student comprehension of geometric shapes and figures (Clements, Sarama, Yelland, & Glass, 2008). Studies have also shown that dynamic geometric software can improve student Van Hiele levels to second and third levels during middle school.

The use of technology can improve achievement when teaching algebra as well. The extent of the impact on student learning can be a function of the specific use of the tool by the teacher and the student, as well as the particular learning activity selected. "It provides an environment that catalyzes changes in what students do in mathematics classrooms as well as how they do it" (Heid and Blume, 2008, p. 93). The teacher has the power to create a learning environment that stimulates learning beyond previous expectations. Technological tools, when properly designed, often can enable students to engage in ideas that are typically believed to be beyond the grasp of students and their particular grade level" (Blume and Heid 2008, p. 461).

This is not all the literature discussion relating to the use of technology in mathematics education. This review provides evidence prior to the beginning of the century. Even with what has been listed here, it is clear that technology can be an asset to student learning. Then why has it taken so long to change? Even today, we argue about whether a graphing calculator should be allowed in all mathematics environments. Should tablet computers be allowed in high school mathematics? Should a school allow handheld devices such as smartphones capable of utilizing apps such as WolframAlpha? Why has it been so difficult to change even after 30 years of literature supports the positive impact of using technology for teaching and learning mathematics? If you truly believe significant change has occurred with respect to embracing the power of

technology in teaching and learning, consider the following idea:

Do schools allow cell phone usage in schools?

Are you wondering why we ask such a strange question? Do you support the use of cell phones in the classroom? How could you possibly use texting in schools for positive learning? Would this be anarchy in the classroom?

Twelve years ago, schools were scrambling to enforce Internet usage policies. Educators were terrified of the dangers waiting for children on the Internet. Now, 12 years later, can you imagine students not using this powerful resource? Of course, the Internet is one thing, but not all students have smartphones capable of accessing the web. But can students use texting to creating a learning environment? If you are not sure, you need to visit www. polleverywhere. This interactive site is free to educators and allows teachers to create a dynamic poll to collect real-time data. The teacher creates a multiple-choice polling question. The website provides the poll with a number to text from your cell phone, and each response receives a different identifying number to record collect the response. For example,

## SHOULD ELEMENTARY CHILDREN USE DIGITAL BOOKS IN SCHOOL?

*Text a Code to 37607*

Yes. Children should absolutely use digital books. 33649

It is the teacher's decision in each classroom. 34099

No. We should never replace paper books. 34115

The student simply texts the code next to each of the three responses to 37607 from their cell phone as shown in Fig. 5.1.

The graph of the responses dynamically changes in seconds as texts are received at the site! Data

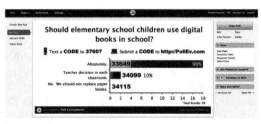

**Figure 5.1**

can be exported to a spreadsheet and you can even create a Wordle (www.wordle.net) to represent the data. You also have the option to share the poll on Facebook, publish to a blog, e-mail to a group, or create a PowerPoint slide for use in a presentation. This is just one use of cell phones in the classroom. Can you think of other educational uses? Remember, your goal is to increase interest and enthusiasm toward mathematics. Your students live in a world of social media and texting. How can you integrate their world with your classroom environment?

## IT IS TIME TO CHANGE!

"The teaching of mathematics is shifting from primary emphasis on paper-and-pencil calculations to full use of calculators and computers" (MSEB, 1989, p. 83).

Because technology is changing mathematics and its uses, we believe that: appropriate calculators should be available to all students at all times; a computer should be available in every classroom for demonstration purposes; every student should have access to a computer for individual and group work; students should learn to use the computer as a tool for processing information and performing calculations to investigate and solve problems (NCTM, 1989).

Mathematically proficient students consider the available tools when solving a mathematical problem. These tools might include pencil and paper, concrete models, a ruler, a protractor, a calculator, a spreadsheet, a computer algebra system, a statistical package, or dynamic geometry software. Proficient students are sufficiently familiar with tools appropriate for their grade or course to make sound decisions about when each of these tools might be helpful, recognizing both the insight to be gained and their limitations. For example, mathematically proficient high school students analyze graphs of functions and solutions generated using a graphing calculator. They detect possible errors by strategically using estimation and other mathematical knowledge. When making mathematical models, they know that technology can enable them to visualize the results of varying assumptions, explore consequences, and compare predictions with data. Mathematically proficient students at various grade levels are able to identify relevant external mathematical resources, such as digital content located on a website, and use them

to pose or solve problems. They are able to use technological tools to explore and deepen their understanding of concepts. (Common Core Standards—Mathematics, http://www.corestandards. org/Math, 2012)

With the quotes just given and the idea that teachers tend to teach as they have been taught, what will happen in your years in the profession? Will technology become an integral part of learning secondary mathematics? Will most teachers work smarter and harder in helping their students achieve mathematical power? It is up to you.

Maria Montessori (1967) pointed out the problem by saying, "Nothing is more difficult for a teacher than to give up her old habits and prejudices." The "modern math" movement of the 1960s was prompted for several reasons, but the main one was that the mathematics being taught was not meeting the needs of society. Graduates could not provide the level of mathematics needed to solve the complex problems of the day. It is now generally agreed that the recommended changes made in light of the modern mathematics movement, for all practical purposes, were not reflected in the school curriculum.

Are we facing the same predicament today? That is, are we in the midst of a technological revolution that is being written about and yet not making it into the K–12 setting? Much of the literature presented earlier in this chapter represented studies conducted in the late 1980s and early 1990s. This research supports the use of the computer in the mathematics classroom. Have we fully implemented the findings of these studies in the new century? The pocket-sized calculator has been available for 20 years. Research shows use of the calculator does not adversely affect students' learning of mathematics. Yet, how many teachers permit calculator use in ALL secondary math classes?

Part of the reason for a slow transition to the adoption of technology in the classroom is that we, as human beings, resist change. Some people hold the attitude that "if it was good enough for me, it is good enough for my children." It is almost as if people say things like, "I had to do my ciphering to get into the fraternity of life and so should the students of today," or "learning mathematics [there is a difference between mathematics and arithmetic] by doing hand calculations is part of the union dues of life." With cooperation from teachers, administrators, parents, and students, and an open-minded approach, the mathematics classroom can be adapted to changing technology. The issue is deeper than just the use of a calculator. Change breeds resistance to change. A body in motion remains in motion unless it is acted on by an equal and opposite force. As technological innovations become available for the mathematics classroom, they can be used to advance learning or hindered by resistance to adopt different approaches. Which way would you have it?

As would be expected, there is not agreement on the use of technology in mathematics classrooms. Should we use it? How should we use it? When should we use it? What skills should be present before implementing it? The graphing calculator has had a dramatic impact on the teaching and learning of mathematics, but it is dependent on the idea that each student can have one. With possession of a graphing calculator, each student is capable of doing more work alone, which is one of the prevalent models of instruction today (Bruder, 1993). If this is the case, why have some teachers resisted the use of the graphing calculator in all secondary mathematics classrooms?

A graphing calculator is now a minimum requirement for the SAT and AP mathematics exams. The testing services are informing parents, students, and educators that students will have a disadvantage unless the effective use of the graphing calculator is employed. Since these tests are so significant in college placement, is it correct to assume that educators have not only an educational obligation but an ethical obligation to integrate the use of the graphing calculator into the curriculum?

A choice looms. Should technology be integrated into the mathematics education curriculum or not? Two parallel stories are told about a man and a woman. The man learned his arithmetic by doing hand calculations. As advances were made either in the ways in which the calculations were done or the materials available to do them with, the man clung to "his" way of doing things—by hand, using paper and pencil only, no matter the size of the numbers. He persisted through the advent of the calculator, computer, and all other sorts of technological advancements that would have reduced the demand on his manual efforts. After all, he knew how to do it that way—why learn something new? At the same time, the woman, who was a master cook, learned on a wood stove but progressed through the innovative developments. Each new technological advancement was found in her kitchen during its time—gas stove, electric oven, convection oven, and a microwave oven. Certainly she could have

continued with the wood stove as her major cooking tool, but she opted to change with the times. Using the most efficient tools for the task, she can achieve the desired result in the least amount of expended effort. Remember, work smarter. Avoiding the use of technology, no matter what the "excuse," can limit the horizons of students. Technology can be used to deepen understanding, accelerate the pace at which students learn, and decrease the amount of time spent on review. Consider the following lesson about the area of a triangle, which was taught to a middle school class (Brumbaugh, 1994). When the class entered the room, they saw a multitude of triangles with fixed base and fixed altitude projected on the screen. The figure was created by animating point C along segment AB in Fig. 5.2. Scenes 1–3 show typical views of what the class saw, because the figure was moving.

The teacher made no comments as the class entered the room. Student discussion centered on the "neatness" and "coolness" of the projected images. As class began and the teacher still made no comment, student conversation began to focus on the idea that the triangles all had the same area, even though they were "different." While the teacher was still observing the interactions of the class, the students determined first as individuals and small groups and, finally, as a majority of the class, that the triangles must have the same area because the base and altitude were not changing. The teacher then entered the discussion. Using the dynamics of the software, the teacher changed the altitude and the students saw, in real time, the height and area change. The base was then dealt with in a similar manner.

In all, the lesson took between 15 and 20 minutes. The class had seen the area of a triangle formula before, but the dynamics of the projected images gave validity to the concept, particularly when confronted with so many "different-looking" triangles. As the discussion ensued, the true impact of the technology became obvious. Almost every student was convinced that as long as the base and height of a triangle are fixed, the area is unchanged, no matter what the triangle looks like. The students admitted having seen the formula for the area of a triangle in other mathematics classes. The software helped them accept the reality that all triangles with the same base and height will have the same area. They were no longer distracted by different appearances of the triangles.

When asked why this seemed so easy for them, they said it was because they could see so many

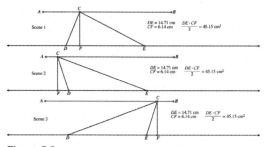

**Figure 5.2**

different-looking triangles all at the same time. When the height or base was changed and they could see the same idea with different triangles, they were convinced. For homework the class was given 10 problems. Each had the same base and height, but the pictures were different—Scenes 1–3 of Fig. 5.2 present three problems typical of the 10 given. The students were to compute each triangle's area. Almost every student completed the entire assignment within a few minutes. When asked how they had completed the 10 problems so quickly, the class explained that, because the base and height were the same for all triangles, all the computations would be the same, no matter how the picture looked. They did the first problem, checked their arithmetic carefully, and copied that answer for the remaining nine problems.

## CALCULATORS

Calculators have generated a significant increase in mathematical achievement versus paper-and-pencil computational skills. It appears that calculator use enhances understanding of concepts. Students have a more positive attitude when calculators are available. The Chicago public schools were among the first to encourage calculator use and, in the process, purchased almost 200,000 calculators for classroom use.

There still is a debate about where, and how, calculators should be used, if at all. How can this be? Calculators have been a discussion point since their introduction into the curriculum. One of the major criticisms has been that they will become an unremovable crutch:

I understand the principle—get them motivated. But I have yet to be convinced that handing them a machine and teaching them how to push the button is the right approach. What do they do when the battery runs out? I

see a lot of low-level math among college students who still don't understand multiplication and division. You take away their calculators and give them an exam in which they have to add 20 and 50, and they get it wrong. And I'm talking about business majors, the people who will soon be running my world. (McKinney, 1975)

Professor McKinney's comments were typical of those heard when the calculator was introduced into the curriculum. Research has shown results to the contrary of Professor McKinney's fears. The word "crutch" carries negative connotations with it. Why is it that paper and pencils are not classified as crutches? Typically, paper and pencil are used to assist with the computations and to record at least the major steps in the solution. For example, in solving some equation like $3.456X = 17.892$, the steps might be:

$$\frac{3.456X}{3.456} = \frac{17.892}{3.456}$$

$X = 5.177$.

If the problem is done without a calculator, the division of 17.892 by 3.456 would have most likely been done on scratch paper but not recorded with the problem. Why then could it not be the case that the division would be done on a calculator? The focus would become one of using the technology to work smarter.

Should we become purists about crutches and require students to do all computations mentally? After all, how can we say this "crutch" is acceptable but that one is not? Undoubtedly there was a time when individuals resisted the use of paper and pencil as aids to doing computations. Eventually, paper-and-pencil computations became acceptable. Some of the arguments for calculators in the classroom include:

Research shows no adverse affect as calculators are employed in the learning of mathematics.

Calculator use permits exposure to a larger and more useful mathematics curriculum.

Society uses electronic mediums to do arithmetic.

Your boss will not ask you to crunch numbers by hand if technology produces a quicker, more reliable result.

Ultimately, you are going to have to decide if students will be permitted to use calculators as they learn the mathematics curriculum you present them. It is imperative that you make an informed decision.

---

**EXERCISES 5.1**

1. Define "calculator" in today's society. Give four different examples of calculators. Compare your list to a peer. Were you both thinking of calculators in the same way?
2. Summarize and react to one article dealing with the use of calculators in a secondary mathematics classroom. Include all bibliographic information.

---

The first handheld calculator was an abacus. The Japanese model has one bead above and four below a crossbar. The Chinese abacus has two beads above and five below the bar, whereas the Russian *s'choty* has 10 beads per rod with no crossbar. Abaci similar to the s'choty have been used recently in Turkey and Armenia. The advantage of an abacus with a crossbar is there are fewer beads to move. One conjecture about the Greeks' emphasis on geometry and lack of algebraic skill was that the abacus made addition and subtraction so easy they saw no need to delve deeper into theoretical arithmetic (Newman, 1956).

Advocates for different calculator logics can be found, and they gladly extol the virtues of their particular selection. Assuredly, each group will adequately defend their respective tool. The calculator supplied by the school usually becomes the default tool of preference. The calculator used and how it works in comparison to others is not the issue. How to use it effectively as a teaching-and-learning tool is the issue.

Calculators on the market range from a basic four functions (+, −, ×, and ÷) through high-end programmable, graphing calculators and even computer algebra systems with built-in tutorials. Discussion can focus on issues about which calculator is most appropriate for what audience. Some see little value in basic calculators, arguing that the student will soon be using a scientific one. The premise is that the student should work with the scientific, programmable, or graphing calculator from the beginning, and just not use inappropriate keys. As the student progresses through the curriculum, additional capabilities of the calculator would be explored. Some authorities adopt the position that students will experiment with the other keys and discover some mathematics or at least pique their own curiosity.

Most people agree that the programmable, graphing calculator is inappropriate for elementary students. The school often dictates what calculator will be used, if any. Because Advanced Placement examinations as well as the ACT and SAT permit graphing calculators, students must become familiar with the tool. The level of complexity of some programmable or graphing calculators is such that students cannot become adequately familiar with the capabilities in a short period of time. Depending on prior experience with calculators, the time factor necessary for students to become adept at using the tool may vary. It appears logical that students be exposed to calculators early in their studies and progress to the more complex functions as needed. Learning to use a calculator and gaining confidence in it take time. No student should be expected to take a calculator-based test without extensive prior experience with the tool. Advanced Placement exams such as Calculus require the use of a graphing calculator to adequately succeed when taking the test. Since this is the case, teachers of mathematics must provide the students the necessary time and instruction using the technology needed for these exams.

Technology makes mathematics available to some students who would otherwise not have the opportunity to perform in those arenas. Many students are unable to carry out arithmetic computations and yet are quite capable of dealing with abstract concepts. These students are often excluded from subjects that permit them to use their talents, because ability to do arithmetic computations is a prerequisite to these classes. The calculator resolves that dilemma.

The calculator can open mathematical avenues for special education students. There are calculators with enlarged viewing windows or keyboards and those that talk. Depending on the situation, these tools can be motivating and stimulating to a student who, heretofore, has been prevented from the being an active participant in many mathematics classes.

## WHEN TO USE A CALCULATOR

Opponents of calculator usage argue for the need to have students possess basic arithmetic skills. Almost all authorities agree that a student should be able to do some mental computation. It seems silly to use a calculator to do a problem like $7 \times 8$. It is rather common for individuals to be confused between whether $7 \times 8$ is 54 or 56. Attempts to memorize the product often fail, because the confusion persists. A mnemonic like $56 = 7 \times 8$ (5, 6, 7, 8) or the realization that $9 \times 6 = 54$ can be used to resolve the situation. Calculator use avoids the dilemma, because the correct product is shown each time. Some efforts might be required, eventually, to convince a student it is more convenient to remember the product as opposed to using a calculator each time. It might be that the calculator will provide enough reinforcement for the correct product that the student will remember it, thereby removing the need to use the calculator to find the product of $7 \times 8$.

Like the product of $7 \times 8$, a problem involving division by an integral power of 10, a sum of several addends, or the difference between 4,000 and 357 may seem inappropriate for calculator use. If the alternative to an incorrect response to the problem is calculator use, then why not permit it? The calculator is a tool. Each individual possesses a variety of mathematical talents. The calculator can enhance one's mathematical performance.

When working with word problems, the objective is to understand the concept. Students are to sift through the words. In the process, students are expected to set up the arithmetic to be solved. When the words are sifted and the arithmetic set up, the purpose of the word problem has been accomplished. Students should be permitted to use calculators to perform the operations they deem necessary by their analysis of the problem. If the intent of the assignment is to have the students practice their arithmetic skills, then it would be wise to choose arithmetic problems. Appropriate word problems would be solved when the required arithmetic has been mastered. Replacing the drudgery of arithmetic in word problems with the emphasis on the conceptual setup of the problem removes some of the anxiety about word problems in general. Students become anxious when faced with word problems. These problems require setup and solution. Give students the tool (the calculator) to aid the arithmetic computations so their focus is on setting up the problem.

Ultimately, you must decide when to use the calculator. Prompting for the decision will come from the text series, the curriculum, parental attitudes, colleagues and, most of all, your background. You are the local authority in your classroom. You need to become a force that will lead your students into

---

## EXERCISES 5.2

1. Name a mathematical concept that you feel would be hindered by the use of calculators and one that would benefit from the use of calculators. Rationalize your position in both instances.
2. How would you convince a student that memorization of basic fact tables is a convenience?

---

their futures and prepare them to perform the mathematical skills required of them for the betterment of society.

## ORDER OF OPERATIONS ON A CALCULATOR

Students can begin to learn order-of-operation rules with a calculator. If they have not been told the rules, a selected series of problems can be given that will lead them to appropriate conclusions. A sequence of problem pairs like $2 \times 3 + 4$ and $2 + 3 \times 4$ can be used to guide students to the idea that multiplication is done before addition. The number of pairs necessary for students to arrive at the desired conclusion will vary with student ability and the amount of exposure they have had gleaning information from patterns. To use this procedure, the calculator being used must have the appropriate logic and follow order of operations. Most basic four-function calculators do not follow order of operations. It is critical that students test and understand order of operations before trusting the result of any newly used piece of technology.

Varying the problems and increasing the degree of difficulty to include other operations and parentheses could lead the students to the desired conclusions involving order of operations. The number of examples necessary to achieve mastery will vary with student ability, background, and the complexity of the concept being covered. As the degree of difficulty increases, it is likely that more than problem pairs will be necessary to cover all the potential results. In $8 + 7 (9 + 5 \times 6)$, all the discussion from $2 + 3 \times 4$ would be assumed. This new example is compounded by parentheses and the operations that preceded them. Parentheses within parentheses and operations following the last closing parentheses would need to be considered as well. It is critical that students test the order of operations on any calculator or calculator handheld/tablet application before trusting the answer on the screen. Computers, cell phones, tablets, etc., all come with some type of calculator application. Understanding order of operations is the key, and knowing to test the application is important in a student's development.

culators will express the missing factor as either a mixed number or an improper fraction.

Suppose the problem being considered is 17 divided by 3. If the problem is entered as $17 \div 3$, the answer is shown as 5.6666667. If the problem is entered as 17/3 on the TI followed by the "Ab/c" key, the response is 5 _ 2/3, which can be converted to 5.6666667 using the "FD" key. This can be an asset

---

## EXERCISES 5.3

1. Devise a set of problems that could be used as a basis to teach the order of operations for addition, subtraction, multiplication, and division on the set of counting numbers. What is the impact of considering the whole numbers, integers, and reals on your discussion?
2. Create a set of problems that could be used as a basis to teach the role of exponents and parentheses in the order of operations on the set of rational numbers.

---

## EXERCISE 5.4

1. Discuss the advantages or disadvantages of selecting a sequence of exposures that lead students from excess in division being expressed as remainders, then fractions, and finally decimals.

---

**Additional exercises can be found on the website.**

in teaching the relation between improper fractions, mixed numbers, and decimals. Many models can now convert fractions to decimals and decimals to fractions. Models such as the Casio fx-55 and fx-65 will display the fraction in true fraction display such as $\frac{17}{3}$ or $5\frac{2}{3}$.

## DIVISION OF A NUMBER BY A NONFACTOR

Typically, when students are first introduced to division, the problems involve a number being divided by one of its factors. As they progress, the division is shifted so a number is divided by a nonfactor. Once this happens, three stages occur: The excess is expressed first as a remainder, then as a fraction, and finally as a decimal. The concept of remainder is best shown by using sets of objects and discussing the number of elements left after the maximum number of sets have been set aside. That is, in $17 \div 3$, five sets of 3 would be set aside or removed from the 17 objects. Two objects would remain because there are not enough elements to form another set.

Casio's fx-55 or fx-65 permits a problem to be done showing the excesses as a whole-number remainder. Almost any calculator will show the missing factor as a decimal. Some calculators, like the Texas Instruments Math Explorer, permit the excess to be shown as a fraction or a decimal. Both cal-

## CALCULATORS AND EXPONENTS

Depending on the display capabilities, most calculators will have a limit on the size of the numbers they can deal with as factors, products, bases, or exponents. There will be variations on how exponents can be entered. Some calculators will have an "$x^2$" key and some will have a "$y^x$" key, whereas others might use the "^". Scientific and graphing calculators offer greater flexibility for entering numbers, the size of those numbers, and the results derived when operations are performed. Some of the graphing calculators provide wrapping capabilities(the answer continues to the next line), which permit more digits. In this section we assume the instrument available is limited to eight digits that can be held in its view window and is not a scientific or graphing calculator.

Enter "$9^8$" or $9 \times 9 \times 9 \times 9 \times 9 \times 9 \times 9 \times 9$ and the answer will be 43046721. If that product is multiplied by 9, calculator responses vary, giving things like "E 3.8742048" or "Error 0." What do these readings mean? As calculators are operated, knowledge of the window response and its meaning has to be a part of the user's repertoire of information.

There is a need for some number sense as well as awareness about how the calculator operates. Most of us would be comfortable saying that the answer to $9 \times 9 \times 9 \times 9 \times 9 \times 9 \times 9 \times 9 \times 9$ or "$9^9$" is not "Error 0" or "E 3.8742048." That knowledge still does not help us understand what the product is, or how to get it, in light of this calculator limitation. A calculator or software capable of performing the preceding operation could be acquired to handle the situation. But isn't it more important to have an idea about what is happening in the problem? Isn't there a need for some information beyond that provided by the calculator?

How does one go beyond these calculator limitations? Additional investigation into number theory or laws of exponents could be used. As the discussion is extended, is it important to know that $9^{15} = 205{,}891{,}132{,}094{,}649$, or is it sufficient to deal with $9^{15}$ and understand it is a sizeable answer? The answer to that question is going to be influenced by the problem situation, background, or knowledge of the students, and need. Most of the time $9^{15}$ is going to suffice. Learning about the impact of exponents may not be limited to the capabilities of the calculator.

Either 2,417,851,639,229,258,349,412,352 or 4,096 is the answer to $2^{3^4}$. Which one is correct? This is an order-of-operations problem that extends the standard rules beyond common knowledge. If $2^3$ becomes the base and 4 is the exponent, then the answer is 4,096. If 2 is the base and $3^4$ the exponent, the product is the much larger 2,417,851,639, 229,258,349,412,352. The question becomes one of determining the default mode of calculation if parentheses are not present. An additional question is whether the logic of the calculator follows accepted procedures. It happens to be that this problem is worked from the top down. That is, $3^4$ is determined first or is the exponent of the base 2. Most calculators, even those with "$y^x$" keys or "$^\wedge$" keys, will not be capable of doing this problem, because when the "$y^x$" key or "$^\wedge$" key is used a second time, the first $y^x$ is computed and then the new exponent is shown. Try this on your graphing calculator by entering 2 ^ 3 ^ 4 =. What did you get? Now repeat the process using a set of parentheses around the (3 ^ 4) as 2 ^(3 ^ 4) =. What is your new solution?

## EXERCISES 5.5

1. How does a calculator with a "$y^x$" key deal with $3^7 \div 3^5$? Describe how this information can be used to help students learn the laws of exponents. Does the calculator deal with $3^7 \div 3^5$ differently from $\frac{3^7}{3^5}$? If it does, what is the impact on its use as an instructional tool when having your students learn about the laws of exponents?

2. In Problem 1, describe your response to a student asking about the difference between $4^7 \div 4^5$ and an equation where the base is not a prime number. Is the answer in terms of 4 or 2?

**Additional exercises can be found on the website.**

## CALCULATORS AND DISCOVERY

Calculator usage to discover mathematics from patterns and problem pairs has been discussed earlier in general terms. Here we provide some specific ideas on how the calculator can be used as a discovery tool, and also how discoveries can eliminate the need for calculators in some situations. Divisibility rules are convenient substitutes for some operational procedures and calculators. If $\frac{234}{168}$ is to be simplified, a calculator that deals with fractions could be used. Knowledge of divisibility rules could substitute for the calculator in this situation. Both values are even, so they share a common factor of 2 that can be divided out, giving $\frac{117}{84}$. The digits of both numbers sum to a multiple of 3 ($1 + 1 + 7 = 9$ and $8 + 4 = 12$), another common factor that can be divided out, giving $\frac{39}{28}$. These two values, 39 and 28, are relatively prime and so all common factors have been removed. Some might say it is ironic that the calculator can be used to help students discover divisibility rules that would render the calculator less convenient. The advantage is that the mental capabilities of the learner will be enhanced.

How can a calculator be used to discover a divisibility rule for 3? One way would be to provide a three-column table that lists numbers to be considered, the missing factor when the number is divided by 3, and the sum of the digits in the considered number. The number of entries in the table necessary for student discovery of the divisibility rule for 3 will be influenced by that student's familiarity with discovery and prior exposure to patterning. The table, where the "number" is to be divided by 3 to get the "missing factor," could look something like Table 5.1. Some consideration might be given to supplying entries in either the "missing factor" or "sum of digits" columns and having the students generate the initial number.

A similar table could be created to assist students in discovering the divisibility rule for 9. Divisibility rules for 2 and 5 should be fairly easy for most students to develop using a calculator and an organized procedure for recording their results.

| Number | Missing Factor | Sum of Digits |
|--------|----------------|---------------|
| 23456 | 7818.667 | 20 |
| 1680 | 560 | 15 |
| 238791 | 79597 | 30 |
| 114 | 38 | 6 |
| 6042 | etc. | |

## EXERCISES 5.6

1. Suppose you decide to provide an entry in the "missing factor" column of Table 5.1. Can the entries in the "number" and "sum of digits" columns be uniquely determined? Why or why not?
2. Suppose you decide to provide an entry in the "sum of digits" column of Table 5.1. Can the entries in the "number" and "missing factor" column be uniquely determined? Why or why not?
3. Devise a calculator routine that can be used for discovering the divisibility rule for 2. Establish a table similar to Table 5.1.

 **Additional exercises can be found on the website.**

Calculators can be used as a discovery tool in algebra. One early activity involves students substituting for a variable and then simplifying. This becomes an extension of order-of-operations activities with the variable inserted in one or more locations. Many calculators have a memory storage key or ability to store a value for a variable within the device. Prior to this discovery activity, a value is stored in memory. In the process, equations can be built and conclusions drawn. Figures 5.3

and 5.4 provide examples. You place a 7 in memory as shown in Fig. 5.3 and then have a student investigate several expressions involving that variable. The goal is for the student to discover the value in memory. At this point, 7 is locked into memory and will automatically replace $X$ when $X$ is used in an expression followed by "Enter." Discussion could extend from expressions to equations at this point. This activity could just as easily have been done by hand, except for the "magic" of having the value automatically being recalled from storage. The discovery in this example should provide some indication of the different and valuable roles calculators can play.

| Key | Screen Result |
|-----|---------------|
| 7 | 7 |
| STO | 7 |
| X/T | 7 |
| Enter | 7 |

**Figure 5.3**

| Key | Screen Result |
|-----|---------------|
| 3 | 7 |
| X/T | 3X |
| Enter | 21 |
| | |
| 4 | 4 |
| X/T | 4X |
| + | 4X+ |
| 9 | 4X+9 |
| Enter | 37 |

**Figure 5.4**

The calculator can be useful in determining areas and perimeters of different shapes. It can also be helpful as an investigation tool. A classic problem involves finding the maximum area that can be enclosed by a given length of fence. Suppose for now that only rectangles will be considered for 240 units of fence. A useful table is shown in Fig. 5.5. It would take a long time to complete the table if the example were continued to fill all integral values. There might be some advantage to skipping around and looking for a different pattern. Using dimensions of 55 and 65 indicates there is little merit in pursuing situations with a large difference between the values for the length and width of the rectangle. The areas provided when the difference is large are small when compared with the area of values that are close to each other. The table, which could be generated by hand calculations but is much easier to create with a calculator, should provide a clue about a square providing the maximum area to be enclosed by the fence, if the shape is rectangular.

| Length | Width | 2L | 2W | Perimeter | Area |
|--------|-------|-----|-----|-----------|------|
| 119 | 1 | 238 | 2 | 240 | 119 |
| 118 | 2 | 236 | 4 | 240 | 236 |
| 117 | 3 | 234 | 6 | 240 | 351 |
| etc. | etc. | | | | |
| 110 | 10 | 220 | 20 | 240 | 1100 |
| 65 | 55 | 130 | 110 | 240 | 3575 |

**Figure 5.5**

## EXERCISES 5.7

1. Create a lesson that uses the calculator to discover the Pythagorean theorem.
2. Describe two unrelated situations in which a calculator would be a useful tool in assisting a student to learn a concept from geometry.

The calculator can be an effective tool that eases the difficulties in doing arithmetic on large numbers, such as those encountered in probability and statistics. Suppose a computer is assigning identification codes to users by selecting three letters randomly. The program does not permit repeated letters. The number of different codes would be 26 × 25 × 24 = 15,600. Suppose that two given letters are excluded from the code options. The codes allowed that would exclude those letters would be 24 × 23 × 22 = 12,144. The probability of having a code that excludes those two letters out of all the possible codes would be found by dividing 12,144 by 15,600, which is 0.778. Certainly, this example could have been done by hand, but it shows one advantage of the calculator as a tool for doing arithmetic, allowing the learner to focus on the concepts and processes involved in analyzing the data.

The mathematics of probability was born in France in the 1600s when gamblers turned to mathematicians for advice. Fermat (http://www-history. mcs.st-and.ac.uk/Mathematicians/Fermat.html) and Pascal (http://www-history.mcs.st-and.ac.uk/ Mathematicians/Pascal.html) brought the idea of

something for nothing, typically found in games of chance, into the mathematical realm. These two men are regarded as the founders of mathematical probability. Some states have a lottery and, generally speaking, the publicity focuses on the opportunity to win. Advertisements stress picking "your" winning number. What is rarely discussed is the point that if one set of numbers wins, there is a huge collection of sets of numbers that lose. Suppose the lottery offers customers a chance to pick any six numbers from a set of 49. This becomes a combination problem 49C6, which can be expressed as

$$\frac{49!}{(6!)(49-6)!}$$

Working that out gives

$$\frac{3(49)(48)(47)(46)(45)(44)(43)(42)\ldots(6)(5)(4)(3)(2)(1)}{(6)(5)(4)(3)(2)(1)(43)(42)\ldots(6)(5)(4)(3)(2)(1)}$$

or 13,983,816 sets of numbers, all but one of which is a loser for any given drawing. This figuring could be done by hand, but the calculator puts the computations, and perhaps even the conceptualization, within the potential reach of more students. Students may or may not realize that (49)(47)(46)(3)(44) represents a sizeable number. The calculator is a convenient tool to satisfy their curiosity about just how big it is.

## EXERCISES 5.8

1. Summarize the contribution to gambling theory made by a mathematician or technology from some decade.
2. Report on the role mathematicians played in the development of a topic. For example, how did the needs of surveyors impact the development of trigonometry?

## GRAPHING CALCULATORS

The Educational Testing Service (ETS) permits graphing calculators a variety of tests, including multiple tests for The Praxis Series (The Praxis Series™ tests are taken by individuals entering the teaching profession as part of the certification process required by many states and professional licensing organizations; http://www.ets.org/praxis). The policy can be found at http://www.ets.org/praxis/test_day/policies/calculators.

The College Board considers graphing calculators essential for AP examinations:

> The use of a graphing calculator is considered an integral part of the AP Calculus course, and is permissible on parts of the AP Calculus Exams. Students should use this technology on a regular basis so that they become adept at using their graphing calculators. Students should also have experience with the basic paper-and-pencil techniques of calculus and be able to apply them when technological tools are unavailable or inappropriate. ("Calculator Policy," n.d.)

There is even a list of approved graphing calculators for AP examinations (http://www.collegeboard.com/student/testing/ap/calculus_ab/calc.html#list). In addition, graphing calculator policies impact SAT and ACT examinations for high school students (http://sat.collegeboard.org/register/calculator-policy and http://www.actstudent.org/faq/calculator.html). This posture becomes a mandate to teachers of mathematics to begin use of the more complex calculators sooner in the curriculum. If an individual is going to be using a graphing calculator in an environment that will dramatically impact that student's future, it is your responsibility to provide continued and extensive exposure to the tool so the student will have every possible advantage on the examination. Without appropriate calculator experiences, the student will be handicapped and, thus, not perform to the highest potential.

A graphing calculator can be useful in helping students see the difference between linear and nonlinear equations. Give students a set of equations, asking for classification by some set of descriptors they define. Depending on the ability of the students and the examples given, two or more subsets may appear. Consider first the following set of equations:

$$y = 3x + 4 \qquad 3x^2 - 5 = y \qquad y = 4x^2 - 3x + 2$$
$$3x^2 - 8x - 9 = y \quad y = \frac{8}{3}x^2 - 1x + 2 \quad -7x + 3 = y$$
$$0.75x - 1.3 = y \quad \sqrt{5}x + 3 - y = 0 \quad y = 0.3x^2$$

Each equation would be entered and graphed. Perhaps a sketch of the graph could be made and the equation written with the appropriate sketch. At the conclusion of the activity, the student should see the graphs fall into two categories: straight and curved. At that point the discussion can be focused on the names for each of these sets of curves and the equations that generate them, along with associated characteristics and the impact the different changes made to the equations have on the associated graphs.

Stronger groups of students could be challenged by giving them equations involving exponents greater than 1 or with more than one variable possessing exponents greater than 1. What happens when fractional values are used as exponents? If $y = 4x^2$ is changed to $y = 4x^{-2}$, what is the impact on the graph? Given the power of a graphing calculator, such questions can be delivered to students sooner in their development. The student will be able to delve much more deeply into topics like this. Figure 5.6 shows a dynamic graphing feature. This can be used to help students discover the impact of changing the value of $A$ in $f(x) = Ax^2 + Bx + C$, for example. $B$ and $C$ would be fixed, whereas $A$ changes across a range in some predefined increment. As the value of $A$ changes, one of a set of graphs is highlighted. At the same time, the value of $A$ that is being substituted in $Ax^2 + Bx + C$ is displayed on the screen. Amazingly, some students will be surprised that one of the graphs will be a line (assuming the range includes zero). This description shows how the power of a graphing calculator can be used to stimulate thought, discussion, or discovery in the mathematics classroom. The addition of the TI-Nspire now provides the ability to not only graph in 3D but also share and present student work to the teacher computer in seconds.

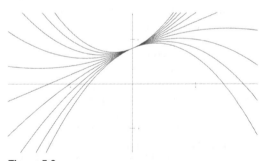

**Figure 5.6**

## EXERCISES 5.9

1. Create a lesson dependent on a graphing calculator. Do it on two different graphing calculators. Describe the advantages and disadvantages of each of the selected calculators. Does your bias show in the description?

2. Create a lesson dependent on dynamic geometry capabilities. Do it on a TI-Nspire, TI-89, Casio Classpad, or CFX-9850G. Describe your reactions and feelings.

**Additional exercises can be found on the website.**

This discussion of calculators has covered a wide variety of topics, but in limited detail. We would not presume to attempt to tell you which calculator to use or even when to use the one you select. Those decisions, along with many others associated with calculators, need to be made by you as you grow professionally. Some influence will be wielded by the environment in which you teach. We caution you to make informed decisions. Be sure you are aware of your bias and the impact it could have on your students' exposure to calculators.

## COMPUTER TECHNOLOGY USE

Computers are found throughout the K–12 setting. They have proliferated at all levels with staggering magnitude. Schools that had at least one computer in 1983 had at least three in 1985. By 1985, almost every secondary school and over 80% of the elementary schools had computers available for instructional use (Becker, 1986). Becker saw the increase in the number of computers in schools as reason for optimism. Even if the rate of increase kept that pace for another 10 years, growing threefold every two years, today there would be about 729 computers in each school. That translates to a machine for every three or four students in the larger high schools. On the surface, this sounds great, but consider the following:

1. Subtract the machines used solely for administrative purposes.
2. Discount the machines set aside for specialized laboratories available only to a select group.
3. Factor in that some of those machines are first generation and comparatively few possess the latest technology.
4. Subtract the machines in the media center, library, or career center that are not accessible to students in the classroom.

Given careful investigation of resources, there is still a collection of useful software that is appropriate for first-generation machines. The combination of first-generation equipment and old software

should not be overlooked, because it certainly still has worth.

Computer prices continue to drop dramatically. Calculator prices continue to plummet. Computers are becoming lighter, have longer lasting power supplies, and are more portable. Calculators are becoming more powerful. The differences have become difficult to distinguish. It was mentioned in the calculator section that most of the problems worked on calculators could be solved using some software. There are some problems that computers can deal with that calculators cannot. One such example relates to $2^{3^4}$, which was discussed earlier. Ask the students, "What is the largest number that can be written using three digits?" Depending on their experience, one of four answers occurs: 999, $99^9$, $9^{99}$, or $9^{9^9}$. The first, 999, is quickly eliminated from consideration by observation. Various approaches can be used to discuss $99^9$ and $9^{99}$. Many calculators have limitations here. Their screens are incapable of displaying such large numbers, for example. Because $9^{9^9}$ is more than 350,000,000 digits long, a display of the answer becomes cumbersome, even in a format that could do it. Notice that this discussion is not influenced by the age of technology or software.

---

### EXERCISES 5.10

1. Summarize and react to one article dealing with the use of computers in a secondary mathematics classroom. Include all bibliographic information.
2. Summarize and react to one article dealing with the use of technology other than calculators or computers in a secondary mathematics classroom. Include all bibliographic information.

---

**Additional exercises can be found on the website.**

Computers have become as portable as calculators, as the size and weight of notebook computers continue to decrease. The development of the tablet computers and handheld devices continues to progress dramatically. In early 1995, Digital announced a notebook computer that weighed 4 pounds. The cost differential still exists between computers and calculators. That can be an influencing factor. On the other hand, there is a difference in the power and capabilities of the two, with the computer being the more flexible and friendly for presentations and demonstrations, depending on the software. The distance between the two platforms is decreasing rapidly.

The Texas Instruments TI-92 calculator stirred expectation with its announcement and prototype demonstrations. This tool carries the power of a top-end graphing calculator, a very robust symbolic algebra package that seems similar in capability to Derive, interactive geometry that looks like Cabri, three-dimensional graphing, text editing, connectivity, and pretty print so that mathematical expressions appear as they would in a textbook. These features are added to the capabilities typically found in a graphing calculator. The price is greater than that of graphing calculators but less than that of a computer. Texas Instruments has succeeded in making the line between calculators and computers less distinct.

In 1999, Casio introduced the Casiopeia A-20 Computer Extender. This handheld device is a miniature laptop that fits in the palm of your hand. This technology comes with Geometer's Sketchpad, Maple V, a graphing calculator utility, Microsoft Word, Microsoft Excel, and is capable of connecting to the Internet. The Casiopeia is also touch-screen sensitive. This allows the user to touch the screen with a pen-sized stylus to operate software. The cost is under $450. All work done on this unit can be uploaded to a regular PC as well. Yes, this was available in 1999.

At the beginning of the twenty-first century, handheld computers/devices emerged to become widespread in the business world. Companies such as Palm, Casio, and TI explored the use of PDAs for the mathematics classroom more than 10 years ago. While the cost was in the $250–$350 range, limitations such as screen size, accessible software, and limited Internet capability have slowed their classroom use. Unfortunately, PC software did not necessarily run on PDAs. PDAs usually required a special version of the PC software with an additional cost. Also, limited Internet connection usually significantly increased the cost of the PDA for sustained classroom use.

Today, tablet devices such as the iPad, Galaxy Tab, Kindle Fire, and Motorola Xoom have become the powerful new gadget for business. These devices have become accepted across the globe. Schools across the world are looking at adopting these relatively new devices that are high-resolution, Internet ready, and touch-screen-operated for a cost between $199 and $600. With the cost of computers decreasing, why are tablets replacing computers?

To a large extent, computer use is determined by availability. How many computers are accessible? Are they in laboratory settings or equally distributed among all mathematics classrooms? How many teachers want to use them? What software is available? Assuming there are computers available, you become the deciding factor. Consider the setting where computers are in a laboratory, and all associated problems like availability and scheduling are such that you can use the lab whenever you want it. When should computers be used? It is a tool that can stimulate thought, individuality, problem-solving skills, and thinking. It is your responsibility to build those desirable traits into each of your lesson plans for each of your courses.

With so many educational questions about computers, it becomes easy to see why a portable 7- or 10-inch device becomes attractive inside the classroom. But what about outside the classroom? Tablets are portable, with the ability to house all texts, resources, applications, and more for student learning. With the addition of video cameras, students can connect with teachers and peers using video or audio at the click of a button. More and more educational applications are being created every day. It seems so logical to employ the use of this new technology. But what is best for student learning and engagement? Remember, you are a teacher of mathematics, and one of your goals is to increase interest and enthusiasm for mathematics. It seems reasonable that all students would want an iPad, right? Are you sure? Given the choice between an iPad and a 4.5" smartphone such as the iPhone or Galaxy Nexus, what would a student choose? Ask your students. The answer might surprise you. Our children want instant access to the world through texting, video chat, Internet access, social media, GPS applications, and instant searches of world databases, all in the palm of their hand with the capability of fitting in a pocket.

So, is a 10-inch device better than a smaller handheld device? It might be better for you, the adult, but may not be the choice of the user, the student. Check out a current smartphone with Internet access. Compare the size of the screen with a graphing calculator. Which is larger? With applications such as WolframAlpha available for smartphones, why have we not replaced graphing calculators? Is cost an issue? Graphing calculators cost $125. What if you could get the smartphone without cellular phone service? The smartphone is already Wi-Fi ready! The smartphone provides endless resources in the palm of the student's hand. It is their device of choice. Do we still want larger devices for the students or for the adults? Think about it!

## THE PLATFORM DEBATE

Years ago, the platform debate occurred inside and outside of education. Should we use Apple or Microsoft, Macintosh or PC? We were even forced to pick one or the other for an entire school because of software incompatibility. Who made the decisions, the users or the buyers? Did students have a choice? Was software really the driving factor?

Once again, we face the same type of decisions. Apple or Android, iTunes or Google Play? Does it matter? Remember to view this debate with an open mind. Be careful to push for a device simply because you have not used a different device. What is best for the students? What is best for student learning? Remember the calculator wars. Who made the choices and why? Students adapt and learn much more quickly than adults. Children can teach us if we let them. Marketing strategies are put in play to sway buyers, regardless of what is best for education. Be open and be careful. But most importantly, look at all of the amazing possibilities for the teaching and learning of mathematics. We do not have to pick one and only one device. Your students can text each other using 20 different brands of cellphones. They can video chat using multiple smartphones. They can access the Internet using five different browsers on five different brands of tablets. They can activate the same application regardless of the smartphone in a matter of seconds.

---

### EXERCISE 5.11

1.  Identify five applications for the mathematics classroom that can be installed on a handheld device such as an iPhone, Galaxy Nexus, iPad, Xoom, xyboard, Tab, or Kindle Fire. Rank order these applications for student learning value in the secondary mathematics curriculum. Justify your ranking.

---

## TEACHER EDUCATION IS CRUCIAL

Technology made a slower entrance into the secondary mathematics curriculum than in the working world. Many teachers were educated prior to the emergence of the Internet and cell phones. That means most teachers using technology as an integral part of the learning environment probably have done a considerable amount of self-guided investigation. Even if that statement is accepted, it seems as if there should be a broader use of technology in the secondary curriculum.

> With approximately 50 percent of school teachers leaving every seven years, it is feasible to make significant changes in the way school mathematics is taught simply by transforming undergraduate mathematics to reflect the new expectations for mathematics. (MSEB, 1989, p. 41)

This indicates that an important part of the current teaching population should have been educated during the Internet era. Why then is there such limited use of computers as a teaching/learning tool in secondary mathematics?

Surely, the undergraduate programs are beginning to require students to become technologically literate. At the University of Central Florida and the University of Mississippi, mathematics education majors are required to take a course dealing with the use of technology as a teaching and learning tool. Students also take an introductory course on computer programming. In addition, as a part of their mathematics education courses they are required to develop lesson plans that use available dynamic geometry, symbol manipulating/function plotting software, and programmable or graphing calculators. These lessons are designed to use technology to present concepts that cannot easily be presented by hand. Consider dealing with the impact of $A$ on $y = \sin(Ax)$. In a non-technologically-based classroom, the teacher could sketch the graph of $y = \sin(2x)$, $y = \sin(3x)$, and $y = \sin(4x)$ on the board and then discuss the differences with the class. In the discussion, the teacher would have to make a "hedge comment" about inaccuracies contained within the hand drawings. Students have learned to tolerate such comments. Perhaps the teacher would take the time to create a set of transparencies showing the differences between the three graphs, maybe even using different colors for each graph. Here the accuracy would be greater, but the ability to respond to a question about an unplanned equation involving $A\sin(Bx + C)$ where $B = 1$ and $C = 0$ would gravitate back to inaccurate board sketches. Graphing calculators and function-plotting software eliminate the shortcomings of the board or transparencies and give the teacher the power to respond to all related discussions. Figure 5.7 shows how $A\sin(x)$ can be dynamically graphed. In addition, DGS also allows

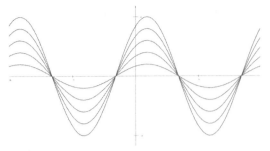

**Figure 5.7**

for a demonstration of seemingly infinite changes in magnitude with some creative lesson planning.

If we are going to convince our students to use technology as a teaching/learning tool, we should use it ourselves. While students in mathematics education courses tend to utilize technology in their education programs, how many of their college math courses require or allow the use of technology in the mathematics content classes? Is technology promoted, encouraged, and allowed? Many universities promote the use of graphing calculator technology and symbolic manipulation software such as Mathematica, Matlab, Maple, MathXpert, and WolframAlpha for the Calculus sequence. Some of these same universities will not allow the use of technology in a college algebra course. If technology promotes and increases interest in mathematics, how does the lack of technology in college algebra promote mathematics for non-mathematics majors?

A truly sad statement has to be made here, however. Even when students are allowed to use technology in some courses, the regrettable truth is that many teachers who graduate from programs that use technology may still revert to the board-and-marker presentations. There are many reasons (excuses?) for that:

The school does not have the equipment.

The objectives/frameworks I am required to meet do not permit the time needed to use technology.

The other department members do not use technology.

And so on.

The bottom line is that, even with teacher education in the preservice realm, many graduates are not implementing technology into their teaching. Certainly, in-service opportunities on a regular basis would help. The real issue, however, is that until teachers are willing to take the steps that force the change, things are not going to move in the direction that they need to be headed. You are the one who can make a difference. Will you?

## STARTING POINT

There is no need to discuss if technology will be inserted into the curriculum. That day is here! The question is, how? Technology is an integral part of our daily lives. Research shows that almost every household owns at least one calculator. Over two thirds of the students have access to a computer. Think about your home or apartment. Do you have more telephones or calculating devices in your home? Do you even still have a landline phone? Do you know anyone who does not have a cell phone? Actually, your cell phone probably has a calculator built in. Remember, any computer is a calculating device: desktop, laptop, tablet, smartphone, etc. Even in the beginning of the twenty-first century, the number of calculating devices usually outnumbered the quantity of telephones in home. When the telephone was invented, do you think people said that its use would stop people from visiting one another? The telephone would make people become lazy? It would be a crutch? Sound familiar? Can you imagine life without that technology? Where do cell phones fit into this picture? The invention of the telephone that enabled us to first have Internet access at home.

Before beginning any discussion about software, hardware has to be considered. The school will mandate, in most cases, what will be available to you as a teacher. One issue is whether or not a teacher should have a computer that is a personal possession. One discussion centers on the cost of maintaining computer laboratories for college students. That is, it would be less expensive for the college and better for the student if each student were required to purchase a notebook computer that could be used throughout the college years. What about a tablet such as and iPad, Xoom, or Galaxy Tab? If the purchase of a notebook computer or tablet were required of all college students, then each new teacher of mathematics would have a computer that could be used for demonstration purposes in a classroom. Because parallel software is available on the two major platforms (that is, PC and Mac—and all compatibles), the variety of computers in the classroom should be a benefit more than a detriment to the students who own and can share them. Does a school or college have to use only one platform?

That could settle at least part of the issue on getting hardware into the hands of the teachers of mathematics. There are still two remaining considerations: software and presentation capabilities. The presentation issue is, perhaps, the easier of the two to consider. Fifteen years ago, projection devices and large-screen monitors did not exist. Today there is an abundance of them at affordable prices. Computer projectors can be purchased for less than $600. Large-screen flat-panel monitors (HD televisions) are becoming more affordable each day. A recent advertisement when this edition was written offered an LCD 50" HD television for $499. In addition, the ability to wirelessly connect to large monitors allows a classroom to become a collaborative environment where students can take turns displaying their screen from their tablet, handheld device, or laptop. Therefore, you now have a variety of technology and display options for less than $1,800. Remember, this was the cost of a decent desktop computer five years ago.

That still leaves software. As was noted earlier, in most circumstances the teacher is limited by what the school has. If the new teacher of mathematics has a notebook computer, then it could be reasoned that some software would also be owned by the teacher. If the school or college had an extensive computer infrastructure, it could be the case that the student "plugged into the district server" and used available software. Even with that capability, the likelihood exists that the student would purchase a few "favorite" software titles. Issues that will have to be dealt with in the very near future are the cost of and availability of apps for tablets and handheld devices and how these apps will be purchased for student technology.

Assuming some software is owned by the teacher, a new issue surfaces. Should teachers demonstrate with software that is not available for student use? Yes! There are ways to get the software into the hands of the students. Some could purchase it (care must be taken to not create an elite group because of purchasing power). Some could be permitted to use the teacher's equipment in certain settings (assuming appropriate care). If the software is that useful, it should be available to all students and, thus, appropriate requests for purchase need to be pursued. It is unacceptable and illegal to distribute copies of single-user versions of software.

The list of available software continues to grow. Items are revised, updated, and extended so often that any printed offering is outdated. The following list is by no means an exhaustive treatment of the available resources. Most of the entries here are ones used throughout this text. They are reflections of our biases and preferences. Certainly other software could be used to accomplish the same tasks. In our opinion, none of these fit into the "plug-and-chug, choke-and-puke, drill-and-practice" category.

Symbol manipulator/function plotters:

Autograph (http://www.autograph-math.com/)

LiveMath (http://www.livemath.com/)

TI-Nspire (http://education.ti.com/calculators/products/US/home/)

Maple—Waterloo Maple Software (http://www.maplesoft.com)

Mathcad—MathSoft (http://www.ptc.com/product/mathcad/)

Mathematica—Wolfram (http://www.wolfram.com/mathematica/)

MathXpert (http://www.helpwithmath.com/)

Dynamic geometry:

Autograph (http://www.autograph-math.com/)

Cabri Geometry (http://www.cabri.com/)

Geometer's Sketchpad—Key Curriculum Press (http://www.keycurriculum.com/)

Dynamic statistics software:

Autograph (http://www.autograph-math.com/)

Fathom—Key Curriculum Press (http://www.keycurriculum.com/)

## EXERCISES 5.12

1. Do you think purchasing a notebook computer as a college requirement is a viable solution to getting computers into the mathematics classroom? Why or why not?

2. Do you think purchasing a tablet computer such as a iPad, Xoom, or Galaxy Tab as a college requirement is a viable solution to getting technology into the mathematics classroom? Why or why not?

**Additional exercises can be found on the website.**

## LEARNING TO USE TECHNOLOGY

Most of the time some form of technology could be used to enhance student learning of a concept. The important thing is that some form of technology is selected. Regardless, the teacher needs some level of familiarity if it is to be an effective tool. Time and energy need to be invested to learn at least the basics of the selected technology. This can be done in a variety of ways. Classes can be taken that may or may not offer college credit. Workshops in conjunction with private enterprises or professional meetings that are anywhere from an hour or two to a week in duration are another source of information. There are a multitude of online videos that explain the use of technology in various environments. Youtube.com has become a viable resource for education, but educators must carefully review these videos for appropriate use and reliability.

Some people resist using technology, no matter the format, until they possess a high degree of comfort and confidence. This is unreasonable. One way to learn is to simply start using the technology personally and in class. Some attempts will crash and burn, but you will learn and become more proficient with each attempt. When the slide rule was introduced, it was common to find users checking the result with hand calculations, because of uncertainties related to the use of the new tool. That does not appear to be the case with students and technology. They seem willing to trust it almost too much. The mentality seems to be one of, "If the calculator [or technology] says this is the answer, it must be correct." Teachers exhort students to use logic, common sense, or estimation. There can be some significant repercussions to such confidence, as demonstrated when evaluating $2\wedge3\wedge4$ on a graphing calculator where $2^{3^4}$ is evaluated prior to $3^4$.

Is there value to presenting students with such contradictions? Yes. The student is forced to think, reexamine the processes used to arrive at the conflicting conclusions, investigate thought patterns, consider alternative approaches, and reevaluate mental estimations. All of these are commendable habits to form in the learning of mathematics and should be encouraged.

## PROBES

Various sensory probes can be attached to calculators and computers. Through these instruments, data can be gathered. The information can be examined from a scientific or mathematical standpoint. The advantage of using data gathered from probes is that it is real-world information that lends itself well to mathematical investigations. The ThinkStation Probeware System (http://www.eyethinkcorp. com) (previously IBM's Personal Science Laboratory) connects motion, temperature, light, and pH probes to the computer. Using the temperature probe, students can accurately measure the temperature of the classroom. As this experiment is being conducted, slip a black balloon over the probe. The students will see the temperature rise as the data is recorded on the computer. Stretch the balloon and watch the temperature rise even more. Why does this occur? This is a real problem-solving problem in action.

Casio and Texas Instruments have data collection devices that collect and download data into a graphing calculator for further analysis. The TI CBR 2 and CBL 2 (http://education.ti.com) as well as the Casio EA-200 (http://www.casioeducation. com/products/Calculators_%26_Dictionaries/Software_&_Additional_Products/EA-200) are handheld tools that allow students to collect real-world data for instantaneous use in the classroom. Data can be downloaded to a graphing calculator for analysis. The TI-84 Plus and TI-Nspire graphing calculators even have the ability to automatically detect one of the following directly connected USB Vernier probes/sensors:

25-g Accelerometer

3-Axis Accelerometer

Low-g Accelerometer

Barometer

Biology Gas Pressure Sensor

Colorimeter

$CO_2$ Gas Sensor

Conductivity Probe

Current and Voltage Probe System

Direct-Connect Temperature Probe

Dissolved Oxygen Probe

Dual-Range Force Sensor

EKG Sensor

Exercise Heart Rate Monitor

Flow Rate Sensor

Heart Rate Monitor

Light Sensor

Magnetic Field Sensor

Microphone

Motion Detector

pH System

Pressure Sensor

Radiation Monitor

Relative Humidity Sensor

Respiration Monitor Belt

Student Force Sensor

Student Radiation Monitor

Thermocouple

Voltage Probe

(http://education.ti.com/educationportal/sites/US/productCategory/us_data_collection.html).

Statistical analysis can be conducted, as well as the construction of various graphs using the collected data.

## COMMUNICATION

The use of technology in the classroom has altered the way educators approach student instruction. It has also changed the way we communicate at home, school, and the workplace. How will you communicate with students outside the classroom? How will you communicate with parents during and after school? The advent of electronic mail (e-mail) and the Internet enabled teachers to incorporate previously unavailable material into the classroom and communicate with others outside the classroom. Parents, students, and teachers could send and receive messages 24 hours a day. Twelve years ago, most educators did not have an e-mail address or rarely checked e-mail. The Internet and e-mail have provided a means of communication other than the traditional parent phone call. The Internet has also allowed students and teachers to have an endless supply of resources at their fingertips.

E-mail is a means to send and receive messages from anyone in the world using computer technology. But is e-mail the only form of communication you can use as an educator? Google provides a variety of communication tools from chat between computers, texting between computers and phones, video chat between capable devices, and even Internet phone calling. Google Voice can even provide you with a free 10-digit telephone number that you can use in conjunction with your cell phone. In other words, your Google phone number can be forwarded to your permanent cell phone. When a parent calls your Google Voice number, the phone call is forwarded to your cell phone number and announces the incoming call from the parent. Therefore, the parent does not know your personal phone number, allowing you to use your Google Voice number as a business line. The feature is free! Many teachers are justifiably skeptical about giving a personal telephone number to students. These forms of communication can allow educators to freely communicate with students and parents.

When a student has a question or is having difficulty with a concept while at home, a reassuring word from a teacher might be all that is necessary. If the student e-mails a question, the teacher can reply with some words of advice or a comforting thought. Sometimes the teacher can give a quick hint or inform the student that the material will be covered in the next class. The student is reassured that the teacher knows that an effort was made.

There is one additional positive result when encouraging children to use e-mail for educational purposes. The use of e-mail promotes writing and mathematical communication. Children love to use computer technology. E-mail is now a workplace necessity and skill. Writing has always been a significant skill that has been part of the entire curriculum. The use of e-mail allows children to practice their writing skills. Since the use of computer technology increases student interest and the use of e-mail promotes writing, educators should promote the use of e-mail throughout the curriculum.

### EXERCISE 5.13

1. E-mail a challenging problem to a fellow educator or teacher-to-be. Make sure you request a response. Judge the answer and send back a reply explaining your reasoning.

## HANGING OUT

Google has recently added a new feature to its social network Google Plus (http://plus.google.com) called Google Hangouts. This application allows you and nine others to create a learning space using video. As the teacher, you can start a Hangout for your class at a specified time to assist with homework or to offer explanation of a mathematical topic. Students that are invited can join the Hangout. All 10 participants can be seen and heard via webcam. Hangouts comes with several excellent tools, such as an interactive whiteboard that allows all participants to write, draw, and illustrate on the screen for all viewers, as shown in Fig. 5.8. The teacher also has the ability to share any open

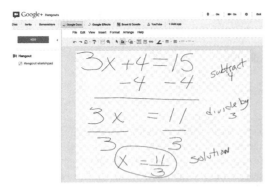

**Figure 5.8**

**Figure 5.9**

screen/window on her computer with all participants. In other words, if the teacher has Geometer's Sketchpad open in another window, she can allow all participants to see the sketch illustrating a concept, as shown in Fig. 5.9. In addition, the teacher can share documents with participants.

Think of the possibilities for collaborative learning. Think about how you can assist student learning. Think of the learning Hangouts you can create. You can provide lesson help to students. Your school can create tutoring Hangouts run by a different teacher each evening for students. Also, what about students who cannot come to school? Some students may be homebound for a variety of reasons. You can create a Hangout for your fourth period Algebra class. The homebound student can participate via video.

## THE INTERNET

You should now realize the tremendous usefulness of the Internet to students and teachers. Valuable Internet sites for mathematics education are being added daily. The Ole Miss Math Challenge is a website designed to encourage mathematical enthusiasm and develop problem-solving skills in students. Each week, a new problem-solving problem is displayed. Students are prompted to solve the problem and submit a solution. If the answer is correct, the student's name, school, city, state, and country (if outside the United States) are listed on the site. The most difficult problems are listed on the contest site under Challenge Mode. The percentage of correct responses indicates the difficulty of each problem offered over the past six years. Some of the problems might surprise you. Can you get your name listed on one of these sites?

## DO

Visit the interactive game site Plastelina at www. plastelina.net/examples/games. This amazing learning tool provides interactive online logic puzzles. You may recognize many of these puzzles as problems that have been posed to you in the past. The only difference is that you were given the problems on paper and asked to write a description of how to solve the problem. Computer technology and the Internet have provided a forum for children to explore by doing. The first three games on this site are free. You will recognize the first puzzle: the wolf, sheep, and cabbage. A farmer has to cross a river using his small rowboat. He must transport a sheep, his cabbage, and a wolf to the other side. He can load only one item in the boat besides himself. The catch is that if the sheep is left alone with the wolf, the sheep will be eaten when the farmer rows to the other side. If the cabbage is left alone with the sheep, the cabbage is consumed when the farmer leaves. Your task is to transport all of the items across the river. Notice that you will actually see the sheep or cabbage being eaten while playing this game. Good luck. When you have succeeded, try games 2 and 3 as well.

---

### EXERCISES 5.14

1. Find an Internet site that can be used for secondary mathematics. Develop a lesson plan using that site.
2. Locate the Ole Miss Math Challenge at http://mathcontest.olemiss.edu. Try the current week's problem for either the *Problem of the Week* or *Algebra in Action*. Your goal is to get your name added to the site. What number on the list did you achieve?

---

The Internet has prompted technology that will provide even novice computer users the ability to develop websites on the Internet. As with e-mail, the Internet allows students to utilize information from outside the classroom. Many teachers are posting their outlines and objectives for the school year on the Internet. This allows students and parents to view these documents any time. Teachers can also post important projects and assignments. This offers students access to this information in the event that the paper material or instructions are lost. It also enables parents to become more aware of and involved with student work.

Teacherweb.com is a user-friendly site that enables educators to create educational websites. Teacherweb is a text-based, easy-to-use website development tool for educators. Within minutes, you can have a working website up and running. Teachers can post assignments, create online newsletters, and post password-protected grades, class calendars, supply lists, educational links, online bulletin boards, and a multitude of additional information just by entering text and clicking. Graphics can be added as well. Educators are given a free 30-day membership.

With the increased bandwidth on the Internet has come the increased use of audio and video through the Internet. Our students are now part of the YouTube generation. Whether we like it or not, YouTube has made a significant impact on our society in many ways. As a teacher, it is your job to utilize resources to improve the teaching and learning of mathematics. With the development of the Internet came the phrase, "If it is on the Internet, it must be true." Part of our job as educators has been to teach our students to validate and verify their findings, whether seen on the Internet, read in a book, or heard on the street. Now we must also validate videos streaming across the globe. If the video is found on the Internet, it is not necessarily true or even real footage of an event. But video sites such as YouTube can play a vital role in teaching and learning as well.

Have you searched YouTube for videos that teach a particular math concept? Have you searched to find out how to utilize a particular piece of technology for teaching and learning such as the TI-Nspire or Casio Prizm? Some of these "how to" videos can be used for teacher training or student support. The key is for the teacher of mathematics to locate the valuable videos for teacher and student learning and provide these resources for colleagues and students. What can you find for your professional development? Can you create a video to teach a math concept and provide it to others on YouTube?

With the availability and use of video, educators now have the opportunity to *flip* the classroom teaching/learning environment. What would happen if you asked your students to watch a video teaching a new concept the night before introducing it in class? If the video is done well, a student could watch and rewatch the video if needed. A few short problems could be assigned with the video. When the students come to class the next day, you could facilitate learning activities to reinforce the concept. You would be able to assist the students that needed additional help. Students who were comfortable with the new topic would proceed to additional problems to show mastery of the concept. This allows you, the teacher, to work with students that need your specialized attention in class. Students would have questions as class begins. You could create small learning groups to foster collaborative learning. In other words, you have *flipped* the classroom—you are now the facilitator of learning, not simply the dispenser of knowledge.

### EXERCISE 5.15

1. Create a 5–8 minute video to teach a specific math concept. Show the video to a peer and ask for feedback. Show the video to a student and ask for additional feedback. Use the feedback from your peer and student to remake the video. Share the video on a site for the world to see. How do you feel about your product?

## HANDHELD TECHNOLOGY

The creation of the iPad, Xoom, Kindle Fire, Galaxy Tab, etc., has created the drive for powerful, handheld technology for business and education. Ten-inch and 7-inch tablets are becoming a common multimedia tool for video, audio, and communication via e-mail and social networks. In addition, these 10- and 7-inch devices have powerful counterparts that fit in the palm of your hand. Portability and accessibility have become driving tools for much of the newly developed devices. The hardware seems to go through new generations faster than the applicable software applications can keep pace. Hundreds of new applications are being created for these new devices. The question is, how can these new applications be used for teaching and learning mathematics?

Applications such as WolframAlpha (http://wolframalpha.com) provide the power of a symbolic manipulator and graphing calculator on any device. Examine the size of a smartphone screen. It is larger than the graphing calculator screen. If this is the case, why not allow student to use smartphones in class, using apps that promote the teaching and learning of mathematics? These devices can run full-motion video, allowing students to watch tutorials. These devices give students the ability to communicate and share information with teachers and students. Applications such as CloudOn (http://site.cloudon.com) allow users to create, share, and edit Microsoft Word, Excel, and PowerPoint documents. Do you need to use clicker systems in your classroom? Not if you use http://www.polleverywhere.com. This Internet-based application allows educators to create live, interactive polls in their classrooms. The teacher is provided texting codes allowing students to submit poll answers using cell phones to text responses directly to the site. Graphs are dynamically updated as responses are received.

Do you try to encourage your students to take notes in your class? Are students spending more time handwriting notes than absorbing the concepts you are teaching? Download the app Evernote for student and teacher use. This application allows the user to create online notebooks, take notes, and incorporate pictures, websites, and video within the notes. In other words, a student can take a picture of a problem the teacher is modeling on the board. This picture can be instantly uploaded to the Evernote (http://www.evernote.com) application and incorporated into the notes. Each user has their own space on the Evernote cloud so that all notes are available wherever you have Internet access. Teacher notes can be emailed out to the entire class.

The list of apps provided in this text is not comprehensive. We highly encourage you to check out these applications for use as a mathematical teaching and learning tool. Some may be used on the Internet in class, while others maybe a better tool on a 10-inch, 7-inch, or 5-inch device. After reviewing these applications, the choice will be yours.

Algebra Pro

Algebra Touch

CloudOn

iCrosss

Google Sky Map

Graphing Calculator HD

Math Algebra Solver

Mathination—Equation Solver

MathStudio

Polleverywhere

StatMate HD

Video Calculus

WolframAlpha

## SMARTPHONES

How many middle and high school students have cell phones? How common are cell phones in today's world? Are cell phones limited by socioeconomic status? The next time you are in a high school math class, poll the students: How many of the students have cell phones? How many of the students have smartphones (phones with the ability to access the Internet)? In less than two years, it will be very difficult to find a nonsmartphone cellular phone. Internet access will come standard with cell phones. If this is the case, how will you handle this in your class? What was the cell phone policy when you were in high school? Were cell phones allowed to be used in your school? If you are a student teacher or current educator, are cell phones allowed in the school where you teach? Should cell phones be allowed in class? Think about this for a moment. If all cell phones will be smartphones in two years, this means that all cell phones will have access to all of the educational applications available for handheld devices. Think of the power in the hand of the student. Will you need graphing calculators if a student has a smartphone with a full HD screen that is larger than the graphing calculator window? Students will have a portable device that can travel home and back to school. Videos will be available to assist with teaching and learning. Hangouts can be created to tutor students and create learning spaces.

With all of the possible teaching and learning opportunities for smartphone and handheld technology, how can we ban the use in our schools? If these applications can help improve teaching and learning, how will you react to cell phone policy in your school if smartphones are banned? Of course, proper rules for student use must be created. Please remember, 12 years ago, many schools were searching for reasons to use or ban the Internet in schools. Educators were fearful of the negative possibilities of using the Internet. How can we work together to provide effective training and guidelines for smartphone usage in schools? As a teacher of mathematics, you need to examine the teaching and learning tools for our students. The job is yours.

## TRY THIS IN YOUR CLASSROOM

*Topics*: Parabolas, best fit lines, estimation.

*Standards*: Problem solving, communication, reasoning and proof, connections, and algebra.

*Materials*: Graphing calculator or computer, and a stopwatch.

When Ray Evernham was Crew Chief for Jeff Gordon's Number 24 NASCAR stock car in late in 1997, Jeff was penalized for speeding while on the pit road. In a radio communication, Ray said he wondered how the officials could tell that Jeff was speeding.

NASCAR racing used to be a southern, rather localized sport. It has turned into a national sport that is big business. Jeff Gordon became only the second driver to earn an extra $1,000,000 for winning three of four predetermined races. Since then, several others have also won this extra $1,000,000. NASCAR teams use technology extensively. This is shown by the many notebook computers visible in the pits, sophisticated weather-tracking systems in some of the car haulers, and the many websites for the sport and drivers.

You can model this principle by establishing a speed trap of your own to check for speeders. Select a straight section of road where people are assumed to speed often. Measure 0.1 of a mile. Other distances could be used, but this is convenient and allows enough time to assure fairly accurate timing. Some methods for measuring 0.1 of a mile will be more accurate than others.

Describe the method you used for measuring your 0.1 of a mile.

You can use the distance formula, $d = rt$, to compute the time required for a car to pass through a distance at the legal rate. Suppose the speed limit for the 0.1 of a mile that you measured is 45 mph. Solving for $t$, you get $t = \frac{0.1 \text{ miles}}{45 \text{ miles/hour}} = 2\bar{2}(10)^3$ hours. The hours can be converted to seconds by multiplying by 3,600, which yields that the car traveling at the legal limit should take 8 seconds to cover 0.1 of a mile.

Suppose a car takes 9 seconds to travel 0.1 of a mile in a 45-mph speed zone. Is the driver speeding?

Suppose a car takes 6.5 seconds to travel 0.1 of a mile in a 45-mph speed zone. Is the driver speeding?

How fast is this driver going in the vehicle takes 6.5 seconds to go 0.1 of a mile?

Record times for 20 vehicles going through your speed trap. Enter the time required for each car to go through the trap in List 1 of the graphing calculator or column 1 in a spreadsheet.

List 2 or column 2 should be the vehicle's mph. Convert the vehicle's time to mph by dividing the trap distance by the time required to go through the trap (values in List 1 or column 1) and multiply that answer by 3,600.

How many vehicles were speeding when you obtained your times?

Is this a good place for a speed trap? Why or why not?

How much does a speeding ticket cost in your state?

$$\left( r = \frac{\text{trap distance}}{\text{time to cover the trap}} \times \frac{3600 \text{ seconds}}{1 \text{ hour}} \right)$$

You can check a speedometer by timing a vehicle through a measured distance. A mile is not a good distance, because small errors have a huge impact. For example, your timing could be inaccurate or the mile marker might be slightly off placement. It is best to take longer distance and drive at a given rate (according to the speedometer—cruise control is quite helpful). Runs of 10 miles or longer are good on an interstate highway because they generally have a marker at each mile. You will know the distance and time so you can compute the average speed.

Is the speedometer in your vehicle accurate? How do you know?

There is a 66-foot speed trap at the end of a drag strip with an electronic timing light at each end. The following information was taken from www.nhra.com. As of May 2005, Tony Schumacher held both the world elapsed time record and speed record for top fuel (TF) dragsters. While each record was established during different races, the world elapsed time record was set in 2003 by covering a quarter mile in 4.441 seconds. Tony Schumacher set the speed record in 2005 by traveling 335.32 mph in a quarter-mile drag race (www.nhra.com/stats/natrecord.html). Assuming the timing lights are 66 feet apart, and assuming this dragster was going 326.91 mph (335.32) across the trap, how long did it take this TF dragster to go through the speed trap?

Funny cars are high-performance dragsters that look somewhat like cars driven on the streets. Although the TF cars look like they should be much faster, the funny cars are amazingly close to the TF cars in performance. At the end of the 2004 season, John Force held both the elapsed time (4.665) and speed (333.58 mph) records for a funny car. Assuming Force's funny car was going 333.58 mph across the 66-foot speed trap at the end of the quarter mile, how long did it take him to go between the timing lights?

A high school girl campaigned a dragster during the 1999 season. She holds several records. Who is she and what are some of her records?

## CONCLUSION

How do we conclude a chapter dealing with technology? There is no end. Some technology mentioned in this text is cutting edge and exciting, now. By the time this is in your hands, it may be out of date. You are fortunate to be entering an age and profession where you will have the opportunity and responsibility to maintain an awareness of the latest developments. As a professional, you are obligated to make the learning of mathematics exciting and progressive for your students. Let your career begin!

### STICKY QUESTIONS

1. The two major microcomputer platforms are PC and Mac. Which one will you use in your classroom and why?
2. If your school's computer platform is different from the one you prefer, what will you do?
3. If you have a demonstration computer in your classroom, will you permit your students to use it? Why or why not?
4. Should a class be required to use the same brand and model calculator? Why or why not?
5. When should a calculator be permitted as a tool in all mathematics courses in high school?

6. Suppose your position is that a calculator should not be permitted in a class that precedes "$X + 1$." You are teaching class "$X$." Students are permitted to use calculators in class "$X - 1$." What do you say to the teacher of class "$X - 1$"?

7. Construct an ellipse using Geometer's Sketchpad (see Fig. 5.10).

Construct a circle centered at point A.

Construct point C within the circle.

Locate points equidistant from C and the circle.

Construct a segment from point C to any point D on the circle.

Construct the perpendicular bisector of CD.

Construct a line through points A and D.

Construct the intersection (F) of AD and the perpendicular bisector of CD.

Select points F and D, and choose Construct, Locus.

Move C around inside the circle.

Move C outside the circle (S. Steketee, 1996).

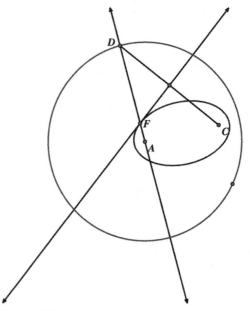

**Figure 5.10**

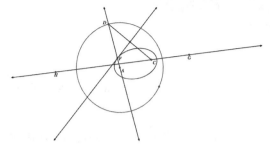

**Figure 5.11**

Make the preceding construction dynamic to illustrate and explore the changes to the ellipse as the point C moves across the inside of the circle and the effect of moving C outside the circle. Construct line segment GH outside the circle. Drag G outside the circle until point C lies on the segment GH (Fig. 5.11). Animate C bidirectionally along segment GH. What happens to the ellipse as the segment CD becomes collinear with line AD? What will happen to the ellipse as C moves farther from the circle?

8. Construct an ellipse using dynamic geometry software using a different procedure from that described in Sticky Question 7 of this chapter.

## PROBLEM-SOLVING CHALLENGES

1. How many rectangles of any size are on an 8 × 8 chessboard?

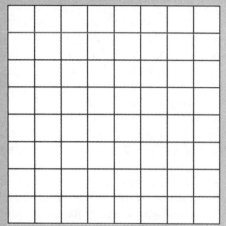

**Check out the website for the solution**

2. If it takes 10 sheep 10 minutes to jump over a fence one at a time, how many sheep could jump over the fence in one hour?

**Check out the website for the solution**

# LEARNING ACTIVITIES

## New York, New York

Investing money *early* is an important step toward financial independence in your future. That is the best advice anyone can ever give you. A small amount of money, invested early, can amass to a profitable sum in years to come.

In 1626, Peter Minuit is said to have purchased the island of Manhattan (in New York City) for $24 dollars worth of beads from the local Native Americans.

*Do you think Peter made a wise investment or did the Native Americans get the better end of that deal? Justify your reasoning.*

Suppose Peter invested the $24 dollars in a bank in England at an annual interest rate of 6%, compounded monthly. If he left the money in the bank until 2006, estimate how much money he would have accumulated. _____

To calculate the value in Peter's account in 2006, enter the Time-Value-Money (TVM) area of the calculator. Graphing calculators such as the TI-83 Plus, TI-84 Plus, TI-89, Casio 9850GB Plus, and Casio 9970 have financial applications built in, or they can be downloaded to the calculator. It is important to understand the typical variables being used:

n     number of compound periods
I     annual interest rate
PV    present value loan amount or initial investment
PMT payment of each installment
FV    future value principal including interest for investment or 0 for ending loan amount
P/Y   payments per year
C/Y   compounds per year

For this activity, enter the following values for each variable:

n     =   4560 (380 years x 12 months per year)
I%   =   6
PV   =   –24 (negative price of your investment or –24. This value is negative because you are giving the bank money)
PMT =   0 (your are not making any additional payments)
FV    =   0 (the future value or balance at the end the investment is not yet known), EXE
P/Y   =   12 (12 periods per year)
C/Y   =   12 (the bank will compound the interest on the investment 12 times per year or once a month)

Solve for the future value by highlighting FV and pressing Alpha-Solve on the TI or F5 on the Casio.

What is the amount of money in Peter's account in 2006? _____

How close was your estimate? _____ _____

How much money would be in Peter's account at the end of the following years?

| | |
|---|---|
| 1636 _____ | 1646 _____ |
| 1676 _____ | 1726 _____ |
| 1776 _____ | 1826 _____ |
| 1876 _____ | 1926 _____ |
| 1976 _____ | 1996 _____ |

What do you notice about the increase in value of Peter's account at the end of each year? When are the greatest increases in value to his account?

Suppose you invested 300 dollars right now in the stock market. A good investment would yield a 10% annual return per year.

How much money would your stock be worth in 60 years with no additional investment?

Is this a worthwhile investment on your money? Why or why not?

How much money would your stock be worth in 60 years if you added $50 per month for 60 years? Is this a good investment?

If you added $100 per month for 60 years, would the value of the stock be twice as much as the value when you only added $50 per month? Explain your reasoning.

Use your calculator to answer the previous question. What did you learn?

Is it worth investing at a young age?

# Problem Solving

Recent years have brought renewed emphasis on problem solving. Many claim that problem solving has been an essential ingredient since the beginning of formalized consideration of mathematics. History of mathematics textbooks frequently state that mathematical development should be in the context of problems. For example, Newman (1956) wrote that it is generally accepted that the ancient Egyptians invented geometry (*geo* meaning "Earth," *metry* meaning "measure") in order to restore land boundaries associated with landmarks swept away periodically by flooding of the Nile River.

The Rhind papyrus, dating back to 1650 B.C., is the basis for much of our knowledge of Egyptian geometry. Compiled by Ahmes, a scribe, the Rhind papyrus contains a collection of problems and their solutions. Problem 50 illustrates how the Egyptians calculated the area of a circle and the underlying estimation of $\pi$.

***Problem 50***. Example of a rounded field of a diameter 9 *khet*. What is its area? Take away $\frac{1}{9}$ of the diameter; namely 1; the remainder is 8. Multiply 8 times 8; it makes 64. Therefore it contains 64 *setat* of land.

$$\text{Area} = \left( d - \frac{d}{9} \right) = \left( \frac{8d}{9} \right)^2$$

$$\text{Area (as we define it)} = \pi \left( \frac{d}{2} \right)^2$$

Setting both formulas equal: $\pi \left( \frac{d}{2} \right)^2 = \left( \frac{8d}{9} \right)^2$

Here, we would solve for $\pi$, and the work of the Egyptians shows they had a good approximation with $4 = 3.1605 \ldots$ (Burton, 1995).

Effective problem solving requires open-minded approaches from teachers and students. This technique was demonstrated in another Egyptian problem, not found in the Rhind papyrus. Babylonians from 300 B.C. demonstrated a working knowledge of the Pythagorean theorem $a^2 + b^2 = c^2$ for right triangles.

Consider two rectangles, each having an area of 60 square cubits. One has a diagonal of 13 cubits and the other has a diagonal of 15 cubits. Find the dimensions of the rectangles.

You have a rectangle with a diagonal of 13 cubits (use x and y for the lengths of the sides): $x^2 + y^2 = 169$ ; Area $= xy = 60$ square cubits.

The scribe's method of solving:

Use the fact that $2xy = 120$

Add $2xy = 120$ to $x^2 + y^2 = 169$

Giving $x^2 + 2xy + y^2 = 169 + 120$

Subtract $2xy = 120$ from $x^2 + y^2 = 169$

Giving $x^2 - 2xy + y^2 = 169 - 120$

So, you have two solutions:

$$x^2 + 2xy + y^2 = 169 + 120$$
$$(x + y)^2 = 289$$
$$x + y = 17$$

And

$$x^2 - 2xy + y^2 = 169 - 120$$
$$(x - y)^2 = 49$$
$$x - y = 7$$

Solving yields x = 12 and y = 5.

Recall the initial system, $x^2 + y^2 = 169$, area $= xy = 60$ square cubits. Solving this problem as the Babylonians did makes it seem easy to do. However, notice that without doubling the area equation, the task is quite difficult.

---

**EXERCISE 6.1**

1. Solve this seemingly simplistic problem: $x^2 + y^2 = 169$; area $= xy = 60$ square cubits, without the doubling technique. Did you resort to more sophisticated methods than were used by the Babylonian scribe in 350 B.C.?

---

Mathematical history provides a wealth of information about problem solving and can be used as a rich source of ideas to attract the attention of students, integrate mathematics with history, provide connections between other disciplines, show applications, link concepts within the mathematical curriculum, and provide challenges for individuals. Historical examples come from Descartes (http://www-history.mcs.st-and.ac.uk/Mathematicians/Descartes.html) and Euler (http://www-history.mcs.st-and.ac.uk/Mathematicians/Euler.html), both of whom contributed to the development of topology. The "Seven Bridges of Konigsberg" (http://www-history.mcs.st-and.ac.uk/Extras/Konigsberg.html), which Euler proved impossible, is considered to be one of the foundation stones of topology, according to Newman (1956). Another example comes from Gauss (http://www-history.mcs.st-and.ac.uk/Math ematicians/Gauss.html), who is reported to have been presented with the task of finding the sum of the first 100 consecutive counting numbers. Gauss provided a quick solution to the problem, which is easily extended into algebra and number theory. This problem is discussed in detail in Chapter 7.

---

**EXERCISES 6.2**

1. Write a definition of topology that would be appropriate for middle school students.
2. Provide two different examples of topology that could be used in a secondary classroom to stimulate student curiosity about the subject.

---

Gauss provided the basis for another historical example.

Gauss studied ancient languages in college, but at the age of 17 he became interested in mathematics and attempted a solution of the classical problem of constructing a regular heptagon, or seven-sided figure, with ruler and compass. He not only succeeded in proving this construction impossible, but went on to give methods of constructing figures with 17, 257, and 65,537 sides. In so doing, he proved that the construction, with compass and ruler, of a regular polygon with an odd number of sides was possible only when the number of sides was a prime number of the series 3, 5, 17, 257, and 65,537, or was a multiple of two or more of these numbers. With this discovery, he gave up his intention to study languages and turned to mathematics (Microsoft Corporation, 1994).

The previous problem does not seem to have a practical application. Instead, it appears almost as if he solved the problem because it was there and attracted his attention. (Note that the quote says Gauss used a ruler and compass to do the construction. The classic Euclidean tools are a straightedge and a compass. A ruler was not an acceptable Euclidean tool.)

## WHAT IS PROBLEM SOLVING?

We are about to discuss problem solving, how to do it, and how to involve students in it. But what is problem solving? Before we can do it, talk about it, or teach it, we should discuss what problem solving is, and what it is not. Problem solving is a process that evolves through life. Problem solvers encounter situations that intrigue them enough to work through a mystery to arrive at a satisfactory solution. This is similar to the work of Gauss with the construction of a regular heptagon using only a straightedge and compass. Problem solving makes use of previously acquired knowledge, skills, and comprehension, which are then synthesized into a new format that provides avenues to resolve the question at hand. The expectation is that problem solving is going to require the student to use acquired facts and information to solve the mathematical mystery in which they are currently engaged. Most people think problem solving can be taught. Some people think problem solving evolves out of the practice of solving problems. There is more involved in defining problem solving, but this should suffice to get discussion, and thought, started.

It is easy to find people today who recognize the power of problem solving in the curriculum.

NCTM lists "Mathematics as Problem Solving" as Standard 1 in each of the K–4, 5–8, and 9–12 Curriculum Standards in *Curriculum and Evaluation Standards for School Mathematics* (NCTM, 1989b). The Grades 5–8 Standard 1: Mathematics as Problem Solving states:

> In grades 5–8, the mathematics curriculum should include numerous and varied experiences with problem solving as a method of inquiry and application so that students can—
>
> - Use problem solving approaches to investigate and understand mathematical content;
> - Formulate problems from situations within and outside mathematics;
> - Develop and apply a variety of strategies to solve problems, with emphasis on multi-step and non-routine problems;
> - Verify and interpret results with respect to the original problem situation;
> - Generalize solutions and strategies to new problem situations;
> - Acquire confidence in using mathematics meaningfully. (NCTM, 1989b, p. 75)

The Grades 9–12 Standard 1: Mathematics as Problem Solving states:

> In grades 9–12, the mathematics curriculum should include the refinement and extension of methods of mathematical problem solving so that all students can—
>
> - Use, with increasing confidence, problem solving approaches to investigate and understand mathematical content;
> - Apply integrated mathematical problem solving strategies to solve problems from within and outside mathematics;
> - Recognize and formulate problems from situations within and outside mathematics;
> - Apply the process of mathematical modeling to real-world problem situations. (NCTM, 1989b, p. 137)

Standards 2000 (*Principles and Standards for School Mathematics*, NCTM, 2000), NCTM's revision, consolidation, and extension of *Standards, Professional Standards, and Assessment Standards*, continues the emphasis on problem solving. It is listed as the sixth standard at each level. Close investigation reveals that problem solving is intertwined throughout the approaches to the curriculum NCTM is suggesting in Standards 2000.

> Problem solving means engaging in a task for which the solution method is not known in advance. In order to find a solution, students must draw on their knowledge, and through this process, they will often develop new mathematical understandings. Solving problems is not only a goal of learning mathematics but also a major means of doing so. Students should have frequent opportunities to formulate, grapple with, and solve complex problems that require a significant amount of effort and should then be encouraged to reflect on their thinking. (NCTM, 2000, p. 52)

In the Common Core State Standards for Mathematics (2011), the standards begin with eight standards for mathematical practice. The first standard is, "Make sense of problems and persevere in solving them." Problem solving continues to be a critical emphasis in the mathematics curriculum.

> Mathematically proficient students start by explaining to themselves the meaning of a problem and looking for entry points to its solution. They analyze givens, constraints, relationships, and goals. They make conjectures about the form and meaning of the solution and plan a solution pathway rather than simply jumping into a solution attempt. They consider analogous problems, and try special cases and simpler forms of the original problem in order to gain insight into its solution (NGA Center/CCSSO, 2011, http://www.corestandards.org/Math/Practice).

## REAL-WORLD PROBLEMS

Discussion within the NCTM Standards and the Common Core State Standards deals with the idea that mathematics students need problem-solving problems from the real world. It is common to find examples in a middle school setting that involve students "purchasing" stocks and tracking market movement. Is investigation into the workings of the stock market as interesting or relevant to a middle school student as creating a study of current fashion trends, comparing prices of in-line skates, or shopping for the best deal on MP3s, DVDs, or even cell phones? Certainly the stock investigation permits them an opportunity to act grown-up, but would other topics hold more interest for them?

**Additional exercises can be found on the website.**

## PROBLEM SOLVING TODAY

It is difficult to discuss problem solving without giving respect to George Polya. Many consider Polya to be the father of modern thought on problem solving. In 1945 Polya wrote *How to Solve It*, which provides a wealth of information and includes a list of four problem-solving steps, which are:

1. Understand the problem.
2. Make a *plan* for solving the problem based on data and ideas given.
3. *Carry out* the plan.
4. *Look back* at the solution. (Polya, 1973)

Comprehension, planning, implementation, and follow-up are basic steps involved in the business world. The similarities between these and Polya's list could be additional selling points for students. Investigation of the literature on problem solving will show a variety of lists of steps, but in almost every case, Polya's four steps form a basic framework. Those four steps are generic problem-solving skills that can be applied in a multitude of real-life settings.

## LEARNING PROBLEM SOLVING

How does one learn to solve problems? There is a limit to how long we should talk about a subject. At some point discussion should motivate us to take action. It will be difficult to convince students to become problem solvers if you are not a problem solver yourself. This does not mean that you must solve every problem you encounter. Some problems will appeal to you and some will not. You do need to model the desired behavior. As you solve problems, you should experience a joy and excitement that can be transmitted to your students. This enthusiasm helps students want to replicate your actions and acquire at least a part of the thrill you project about resolving a situation.

## ONLY ONE ANSWER

A good beginning point is investigating what constitutes a problem-solving problem. Consider the following: "Four DVDs are purchased at $17.98 each. How much money was spent?" For the time being, ignore sales tax, volume discounts, whether this is a store or buying club price, and so forth. In the real world there are many such factors, and they are frequently omitted from consideration. At some point, to add realism to the situation and to entice the students to become involved in the problem-solving process, we do need to insert such options into our discussions. Otherwise students will likely discount the whole process as unrealistic and unappealing because of the overlooked items. The whole point of problem solving could be missed because of our failure to attend to details that students might view as significant in real-world settings. Remember, we are attempting to convince students to become problem solvers. To that end, we must present situations and questions that will attract their interest. Once we have them focused on the process necessary to solve problems, we can shift their efforts to other areas that may not have real-world applications. The emphasis will eventually shift from the problem itself to the method and procedures needed to answer a question.

"Four DVDs are purchased at $17.98 each. How much was spent?" Is this a problem-solving problem? Certainly there are words involved and, to many, that indicates problem solving. Unquestionably, the words need to be translated into symbols, numbers, and expressed as an equation that will lead to the all-important answer. Many mathematics educators now think that, although the answer is important, it is not necessarily the "end all, be all" of the process.

In many instances, there is no right answer. For example, "How many squares do you see in Fig. 6.1?" Can the number of squares you see be incorrect? Will the number of squares you see be the same as the number of squares another individual sees? Outline each of them.

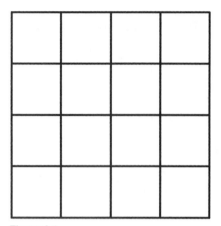

**Figure 6.1**

line segments on it, those segments should not be counted as sides of the rectangles.)

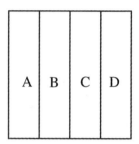

**Figure 6.2**

What happens if a student finds more squares than you do? We can present situations in which there is more than one correct answer.

Another example involving more than one right answer can be found in statistics. Statistical concepts can be inserted into the curriculum as needed to emphasize this point. Suppose a class completes a survey in which the birth month of each student is listed. The objective is to graph the data and discuss the mode. For this example, assume the number of births is equal in two different months. The graph would be bimodal, which can confuse some students. They are accustomed to seeing one right answer, especially when they think the mode will be the month with the greatest number of births. Even though they have learned that a bimodal result is acceptable, their prior conditioning for one and only one right answer may cause them to resist. "There is not one right answer?" will be the question of some students.

You need to do the following problem (this becomes part of the problem-solving learning process and will exemplify the point being made). The best way to proceed is to have several other people do this with you. Do not discuss the processes or the instructions. Just do what is requested. After the task is completed, analyze what has happened. Complete each instruction before reading the next.

Take a sheet of paper.

Fold the paper in half.

Fold the paper in half again.

How many rectangles have been formed? (Consider folds and edges only as you count rectangles. That is, if you are using paper with

Looking at Fig. 6.2, assume the request is to determine the maximum number of rectangles formed. The first answer probably will be 4. Other answers will be 7, 8, 9, 10, and perhaps as many as 24. Each of A, B, C, and D is easily seen. Generally, the rectangle formed by the outside edges of sections A and B (A + B) will be spotted early in the discussion, after which B + C and C + D readily follow. These usually lead to A + B + C and B + C + D. At this point, the total is 9 rectangles. Yet to be considered is the rectangle formed by the outside edges of the paper (remember, the paper itself forms a rectangular region—the rectangle is the edges only). At this point, it is possible that some student, particularly in a class that has some flexible thinkers in it, will say the total is 20 rectangles. Others who catch on to what has been done might say 19, prompting a discussion. The exchange will tell others that both sides of the paper are now being considered. The 19 or 20 debate centers on whether or not the rectangle formed by the edges of the paper is being counted twice. Some will focus on the thickness of the paper, which actually makes the sheet be a right, rectangular-based prism (box) and, thus, there is a top rectangle and a bottom rectangle. In this mode, some will want to count the edges themselves as rectangles, giving a total of 24. Others will argue that the thickness of the paper is negligible and should not be counted. Either way, a good discussion ensues and, in the process, some people on the fringe of becoming problem solvers are drawn closer to the inner circle of participants.

Figure 6.3 presents a different solution to the same problem, and those who have folded their paper this way will be involved in the class discussion but will be working from a different orientation. Often, each group will not realize the differences in folding at first, which makes for a livelier exchange

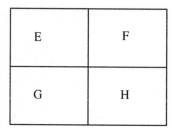

**Figure 6.3**

of ideas. As in Fig. 6.1, E, F, G, and H will be seen easily. Then students will describe E + F, G + H, E + G, and F + H. The rectangle formed by the outside edges of the paper cannot be overlooked. This collection gives a total of 9 rectangles. If two sides of the paper are considered, the total becomes 17 or 18, depending on how the outside edge rectangle is regarded. But don't forget, the edges could add 4 more to the total, depending on how they are considered.

Notice how different answers were derived for the same question, depending on the procedures followed. As the discussion progresses, decisions are made on whether or not the thickness of the paper allows for one or two outside edge rectangles, and whether or not the edges themselves should be counted. Even without that, the "right" answer is different, influenced by how the paper was folded. This becomes an exemplification of the idea that a problem may have more than one right answer.

Consider how a sheet of paper can be folded in half. Figures 6.2 and 6.3 show the two most common ways. As the initial fold is made, ask how it is known that the paper is folded into halves. Depending on the maturity of the students, you will hear the two pieces are the same size and the same shape, the two pieces are congruent, or the edges match. The matching edges response opens the door for another consideration. Fig. 6.4 shows that the matching edge approach does not always appear to give a correct answer. This leads to the need to cut the paper along the diagonal fold and then rotate one

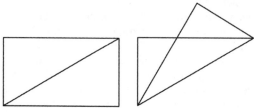

**Figure 6.4**

of the pieces to get matching edges. Do not be too quick to abandon the situation, however.

Figure. 6.5 opens the door to a multitude of other ways a paper can be divided in half. Granted, it may be difficult to do some of these by folding, but that is not the issue. The point is, we now are aware of an infinite number of ways to divide a piece of paper in half. This certainly exemplifies the idea that there is not always one right solution to a given problem. The processes followed to arrive at the answer opened a variety of avenues that could allow for additional discussions. This becomes one of the basic ingredients to good problem solving—there is not always one right answer. As different answers are discussed, additional opportunities for mathematical developments are encountered.

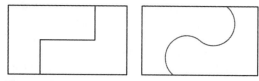

**Figure 6.5**

## EXERCISES 6.4

1. Describe at least one situation that does not have one right answer. Your discussion should include all the potentially correct responses. For example, what route do you travel to get to school? Many paths will lead to the same conclusion!
2. Show the construction steps needed to create the two examples in Fig. 6.5.

## WHAT IS A PROBLEM-SOLVING PROBLEM?

"Four DVDs are purchased at $17.98 each. How much was spent?" We have now determined that a problem may have more than one right answer, and that there is a multitude of acceptable methods for determining that answer. However, is this DVD question a problem-solving problem? Some perspectives and guidelines are needed to respond. Krulick and Rudnick (1987) gave a list of four essentials to determining if a situation is a problem-solving problem:

1. A nonroutine solution is necessary.
2. A challenge is presented.
3. An individual accepts the challenge.
4. A positive attitude about problem solving is being fostered.

"Four DVDs are purchased at $17.98 each. How much was spent?" The idea of a routine solution gives a clue about determining if this is a problem-solving problem. Undoubtedly, you have tackled similar problems where these numbers or descriptors were different, but essentially the idea was the same. This becomes a routine problem for you and would not be classified as a problem-solving activity.

On the other hand, the four-DVD problem would present a huge dilemma to many elementary students. A first- or second-grader might be dealing with buying three pencils at the school store when each one costs $0.15. Reflexively, we would probably multiply the $0.15 by three and determine we need $0.45 (sales tax?). The difficulty is, first- and second-graders typically do not know how to multiply. Some of the more resourceful ones will perhaps add, but that is not very likely, particularly with the first-graders. On top of the addition skills, it must be remembered that these children will not have encountered decimals at a level that would permit them to deal with this situation, although second-graders often deal with money using the cent symbol. The possibility does exist that coins could be used, particularly in the case of the second-grader, to arrive at the solution. Finally, the student could avoid the issue by going to the store, presenting a dollar bill, and hoping that it will cover the cost of the three pencils. If it will not, the clerk will inform the student of the shortage and the additional amount needed. Certainly at this level, the customer must have a significant amount of trust in the clerk.

"Four DVDs are purchased at $17.98 each. How much was spent?" It appears that this may or may not be a problem-solving problem. It depends on the mathematical maturity of the individual of whom the question is asked. The answer is also influenced by whether or not the person cares enough to pursue the solution—a challenge is offered and accepted. Finally, when the problem has been solved, the individual should feel good about the accomplishment, which begins to build a positive attitude about problem solving.

As problems are solved, ideas are bantered about either with others or in one's own mind. The discussion about folding a sheet of paper would be an example. The ability to generate ideas is important to the overall process of becoming a problem solver. Suppose a class is given the set of shapes shown in Fig. 6.6. The shapes are all comprised of congruent unit squares. The teacher is thinking of a particular question regarding the shapes, and the students' task is to determine the question the teacher has in mind. Several different questions will be generated, and each of them can be used to stimulate class discussion. We show some examples and possible associated discussions.

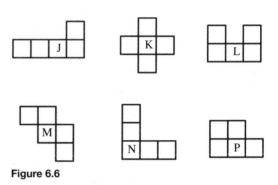

**Figure 6.6**

One question could be, "What is the area?" Because each figure is comprised of five unit squares, the realization that all areas are equal comes rather quickly. Area was not the question in mind when initially asked, yet that discussion provided the opportunity to investigate some mathematical concepts that may be valuable for the students. You would decide the depths to which you will pursue the discussion based on the background, abilities, and curriculum objectives of the class. The list of possible questions is not exhaustive. In reality, each class that considers the problem generates its own order influenced by ability level, familiarity with problem solving, exposure to flexible thinking, and so on.

Area is often associated with perimeter in the minds of students, so "What is the perimeter of each shape?" usually follows the area question, which opens the door to some interesting discussion. If the figures are considered in the order they are alphabetized, the perimeter is 12 units for each of J through N. The likelihood is that students will conclude that all six shapes will have the same perimeter. What a wonderful opportunity to discuss jumping to conclusions before adequate investigation is conducted. Perimeter was not the original question.

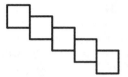

**Figure 6.8**

1.  Develop at least three additional questions a class could generate regarding the shapes in Fig. 6.6.

The perimeter idea presents an interesting consideration. "What is the minimum perimeter of a figure comprised of five unit squares?" Attempts to generate solutions that are less than 10 units will fail, and so it is usually concluded that 10 must be the minimum. This activity provides a superb opportunity to have students manipulate sets of unit squares. The process can stimulate concrete and abstract thoughts while offering a means of dealing with different ability levels. Ultimately, the point needs to be made that 10 units is the minimal perimeter for a plane figure comprised of five unit squares, because the least number of possible sides are exposed in configuration P of Fig. 6.6. While discussing the situation, some enterprising individual might suggest stacking one square on top of another, thus decreasing the perimeter. Good thinking (and that should be noted), but it is outside the rules of a plane figure. By the way, minimum perimeter was not the question either. ☺

The discussion focusing on a minimum perimeter can lead to another perimeter question. "What is the maximum perimeter of a figure comprised of five unit squares?"

## SELF-IMPOSED RESTRICTIONS

Figure. 6.7 shows one of many arrangements of the five unit squares that will yield a maximum perimeter of 20 units, because all edges are exposed.

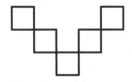

**Figure 6.7**

Discussion will frequently bring objections from students, because they thought sides had to be adjoining. This presents the opportunity to review self-imposed restrictions and assumptions. It also provides the opportunity to discuss situations shown in Fig. 6.8. Suppose that, in Fig. 6.8, half of

each adjoining edge is shared. That means the other half-length is exposed. What is the perimeter of the figure? What if the overlap takes three-fourths of a side length and the remaining one-fourth is exposed? Is this perimeter equivalent to the perimeter for a one-half overlap? Why or why not? And so on. However, that was not the question either.

One common response to, "What is the question?" associated with Fig. 6.6 is, "Can these pieces be put together to form a square?" If the group has worked with tessellations or tangrams, this response appears quickly. Once it is concluded that the pieces cannot be used to form a square, either physically or abstractly, "Why?" becomes a useful question to ask. The six shapes in Fig. 6.6 are made up of unit squares with a total area of 30 square units. The pieces, when put together, would have to give a square of a counting number side length, so a total of 36 unit squares would be necessary to even begin to perform the desired task. Note this solution is abstract. Students moving the shapes of Fig. 6.6 would be an example of a concrete approach to arriving at the solution.

1.  Create three higher order thinking questions from the shapes in Fig. 6.6. Discuss potential extension topics for each question.

**Additional exercises can be found on the website.**

Developing questions like those associated with Fig. 6.6 will help expand your ability to view a situation from different perspectives, a very important factor in problem solving. The intended question was, "Which of these shapes can be folded to form an open box?" This in itself is an extension of the flexible-thinking approach, or of self-imposed restriction, because typically, students will limit their considerations to the plane. A helpful hint to prompt the extension to the box would be to ask the students to "think 3-D." The explanation of which shapes can and cannot be folded to form the open box may provide you with clues about the abstract thinking abilities of individuals. Most students will be able to visualize some solutions. Other shapes are much more difficult to imagine being folded into an open box. The students may need to make models and actually perform the folding. This should be encouraged and is an excellent way to meet the needs of different ability levels or learning modalities. Remember, not all students are capable of abstract mathematical thought processes. The emphasis should be on arriving at the conclusion through some "legal" or acceptable manner, not whether or not the most abstract or efficient method was used.

Is there a real-world application for the generation of an open box from any of the shapes presented in Fig. 6.6? The investigation centered on the ability to take a flat pattern and fold it into an open box. There is a connection between that and the classic calculus question relating to cutting corners out of a rectangular sheet to create a box of maximum volume while considering minimum product consumption and waste. If the student is unable to visualize and think of the flat pattern being folded to form a box, there might be limitations on that student's ability to answer the question. In the calculus problem, once the box is formed, the student is expected to manipulate the dimensions to provide the desired response. We would assume that a student who is able to visualize the anticipated result should have a greater chance of understanding the total concept. In Fig. 6.9, the length of side $x$ changes to provide maximum volume of a box with no top.

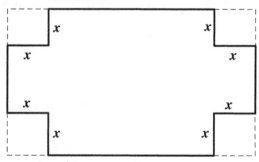

**Figure 6.9**

## ANSWER PROCESS

One of the basic objectives of teaching mathematics must be to go beyond the search for the right answer. The method of arriving at the solution can be more important than the result itself. That was discussed earlier when a sheet of paper was folded into fourths. Certainly the answer is important, but

the process used to arrive at the answer is equally, and perhaps more, important. As we strive to develop flexible thinking habits in students, emphasis on different approaches to a problem solution holds a multitude of advantages for all. Consider triangle ABC with point D on side AB so that AD = BD = CD. Prove that ACB is a right angle.

Recall that this problem was discussed in greater detail in chapter 1, but it is a good example of a problem being solved more than one way.

Figure 6.10 shows angle BCA to be a right angle by using two isosceles triangles and that the sum of the measures of the angles of a triangle is 180°.

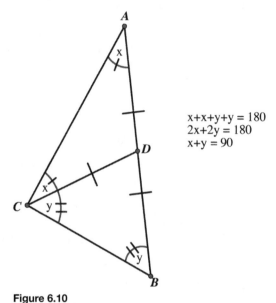

$$x+x+y+y = 180$$
$$2x+2y = 180$$
$$x+y = 90$$

**Figure 6.10**

Figure 6.11 shows BCA to be inscribed in a semicircle, making it a right angle. In Fig. 6.12, extend CD through D to E so that CD = DE, making ACBE a parallelogram, because the diagonals bisect each other. The diagonals are both diameters of the circle and therefore congruent, so the parallelogram must be a rectangle, and BCA is a right angle.

Consider the issue used to raise this approach—the answer to a problem is important, but the process(es) used to get the answer may be equally or more important. In showing BCA to be a right angle, different approaches were used: algebraic methods, geometric theorems, and geometric constructions. The focus should be on the idea that the question was answered satisfactorily in more than one way. This is important as you teach because you should not be insisting that students do a problem

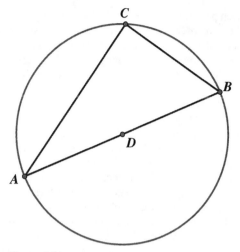

**Figure 6.11**

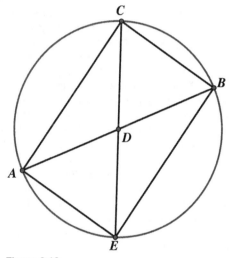

**Figure 6.12**

your way. Acceptance of a solution, as long as it is correct, needs to be a part of your professional life. This flexibility will be more demanding, because you will need to think through processes that vary from yours, but you will learn, and your students will benefit because they will have latitude in think-

---

**EXERCISE 6.7**

1. Construct Figs. 6.10 through 6.12 using a dynamic geometry program. Determine the measure of the angles, move your construction, and describe the results.

---

**Additional exercises can be found on the website.**

ing. Why should we try to channel students to think the same way we do?

## UNEXPECTED OPPORTUNITIES

Frequently, a problem-solving situation presents unexpected opportunities. The next problem appears frequently in the literature. It can be solved by students of multiple ability levels and can be pursued to greater depths. You are given a double-pan balance capable of holding as many objects on either side as desired. You are also given a set of eight blocks, and it is known that one of the blocks is lighter than the other seven, which all weigh the same. It is impossible to tell, by looking or lifting, which block is the light one. The balance must be used to determine the answer. What is the fewest possible number of weighings necessary to guarantee identification of the light block each time the problem is done?

Initial student attempts usually result in an answer of three weighings, which will work, but it is not the fewest possible number of weighings. A person could randomly select two blocks, placing one on each pan of the balance. If the pans do not balance, the lightweight would be identified, but that would be luck and could not be depended on time after time, which is one of the requirements of this problem.

Mathematicians frequently try to solve an easier problem and then apply the lessons learned to the more complex issue. Simplifying this problem, consider only two blocks and identify the lightweight. Placing a block on either side of the balance will show the desired result in one weighing. For some students, it might be necessary to switch sides with the blocks to demonstrate that the result is the same, no matter which side is occupied by the light block.

With three blocks, subtle revelations begin to surface. First, some students may not understand that placing two blocks on one pan and one on the other will always give an unbalanced result. That should be resolved. Blocks not currently in use should not be overlooked. Some students may not realize that with the light one identified, there is no need to weigh any blocks not in use. For example, suppose one block is on either side and the lightweight is on the right pan. That tells two things, one of which is not very obvious to some students. The block on the left pan is heavy and most students will grasp that idea. However, some students will ask to use the other block from the table because it might change the results. Remember that there is only one light block in the set. It has been identified. All the other blocks weigh the same. This is an important idea that is difficult for some students to conceptualize and must be considered throughout the solution of this problem. Therefore, it is imperative that you spend time resolving this issue for all students at this beginning level.

Another idea presented with three blocks is that of different cases, a common tool used by mathematicians. Case 1, the light block on one pan and a heavy one on the other, was just discussed. With this configuration, the lightweight is identifiable in one weighing. For Case 2, the blocks placed on each pan are the same weight. They balance. The conclusion is that the two blocks weigh the same and the lightweight would be the block left on the table. The concept that the light block remains on the table is difficult for some students to acquire, and it might be necessary to have the students do some additional weighings to assure them this is a true statement. Either way, the lightweight block is identified in one weighing.

Four blocks require how many weighings? Two are placed on each pan and one side will hold the lightweight. Once the lightweight is determined as being in one of the two pairs, the solution is complete because the information gathered with two blocks earlier in the problem can be used. The situation could also be solved with one block on each side. If the blocks do not balance, the lightweight is identified in one weighing, but that is luck. If the blocks do balance, weighing the second pair will identify the light block. The lightweight block is identified in two weighings. Students need to see the advantages of placing the optimal number of blocks on each side, so the idea of two on each side is more beneficial in the long run.

Five blocks can be solved just like four, leaving one block out. If the four balance (two on each side), the lightweight, which is the one not being used, is identified in one weighing, but that is luck. If the four do not balance, it is important that the students realize the excluded one is not light and would be exempt from the weighing process. Again, this abstraction is difficult for some students to comprehend, and care must be taken to assure their understanding. An additional weighing is needed to assure determination of the lightweight block, resulting in two weighings. It should be noted that this is another application like the cases considered when working with three blocks.

Six blocks can be done two different ways. Typically, students will want to place two blocks on each pan. If they balance, the lightweight is one of the two not being used. If the four on the scales do not balance, then the two not being used are heavy and only one more weighing is needed to identify the lightweight. Either way, the lightweight is identified with two weighings.

The second way of working with this problem has three blocks placed on each pan. The lightweight will be identified as one from a set of three. The three problem has already been done in one weighing. The problem is solved again in two weighings. The placing of three on each side extends the idea of optimal selection, an important consideration as the complexity of the problem increases.

Eight blocks, like six, can be done more than one way. However, the method selected impacts the final result. Students often want to select four blocks on each side of the balance. In this setting, the lightweight is identified as one of four, which can be resolved with two additional weighings. This approach gives a total of three weighings. Selecting three blocks for each side of the scale results in a case scenario like the one used with three blocks. If the three blocks on each side balance, the lightweight must be one of the two blocks not being used, because the six being considered all weigh the same. One more weighing will solve the problem and a total of two weighings is required. If the three on each side do not balance, the two not in use are now known to be heavy along with three on the heavy side of the scales. However, that means the lightweight is one of three blocks (on the light side), a situation that can be solved with one more weighing. Either way the problem can be solved with two weighings.

## EXERCISE 6.8

1. Describe how nine blocks, where eight are known to weigh the same and one is light, require two weighings to identify the lightweight. Can this be done more than one way?

Ten blocks are the first to require three weighings. The 10 blocks can be placed five on a side, and then the lightweight will be in one of two sets of five, a situation that requires two additional weighings to resolve. An initial setup of four on a side or three on a side will also lead to three needed weighings (excluding luck).

Certainly, this process could be continued using the pan balance and, for some students, that is appropriate. For other students, it is time to shift to a more abstract approach. Figure 6.13 shows the results discussed so far.

| Number of Blocks | Pattern of Weighings | Generalization Beginnings |
|---|---|---|
| 2 | 1 | |
| 3 | 1 | $3^1$ |
| 4 | 2 | |
| 5 | 2 | |
| 6 | 2 | |
| 7 | 2 | |
| 8 | 2 | |
| 9 | 2 | $3^2$ |
| 10 | 3 | |
| • | | |
| • | | |
| • | | |
| | | |

**Figure 6.13**

Prior to revealing the chart in Fig. 6.13, ask how many blocks can be done with three weighings. Once this answer is determined, along with an appropriate explanation (perhaps accompanied by some demonstrations) of why the given response is correct, ask how many blocks can be handled with four weighings. Usually, the better problem solvers will accept this as a clue that there must be a generalization, if they have not already started searching for it. The initial problem of weighing blocks to identify the lightweight has opened avenues for a variety of student abilities.

---

## EXERCISE 6.9

1. Explain, in writing, the steps required to show that 27 blocks would require only three weighings to identify the lightweight block, given that you have a double-pan balance capable of holding as many blocks as you desire on each side and that all the look-alike blocks weigh the same except for the one that is light.

## TEACHING PROBLEM SOLVING

If you have been working the problems in this chapter, you are progressing toward becoming a problem solver. If you are going to expect your students to be problem solvers, you must model appropriate behavior. Trying the problems presented is a great beginning. If you do not accept the challenges of these problems, how can you, in good conscience, expect your students to attempt the problems you pose for them? It becomes a matter of practicing what you preach. One beauty of becoming a problem solver is that your excitement about learning will spill over into other areas of teaching. Then, both you and your students will benefit.

Each teacher must do problem solving. In the process of doing, appropriate problem-solving behavior is modeled. How did we learn to solve problems? In most cases, the ability has taken years to evolve, and there was little, if any, conscious awareness of its development. Now the expectation is that you teach this ability to students. How can students be taught to become problem solvers without our modeling the desired result?

Do not be afraid to let yourself think out loud for the students. The examples done in class are prepared in advance to teach the concepts and skills we want students to acquire. As the lesson develops, student questions and responses the teacher did not anticipate can provide opportunities that might become part of their problem-solving skills. Do not be afraid to solve problems with the class. As this is done, describe each thought process, thus giving students insights into how the total picture is developed. Such an approach involves risk. A problem may be encountered for which no solution is immediately visible. Students are conditioned to believe that the teacher can immediately see the solution to a given problem. When they become aware that you are not functioning at that level, their confidence in you might be shaken. Do not panic. You are not the answer machine. They will learn to understand the thought process you are demonstrating to them. The value of your thinking in front of the class is too crucial to disregard. They need to become aware of how they should be examining problems to arrive at a satisfactory solution. This discussion about thinking in front of a class does not preclude the demand that lessons must be planned in advance. Thinking on your feet is not the same as not being prepared for a class. When a student works a problem out loud in class, others have the opportunity to observe their classmate's problem-solving process. At times, students can comprehend a peer's thought process better than the teacher's. We can learn from each other! Perhaps this is a good place to consider cooperative groups.

As problem-solving skills are developed, several issues warrant consideration. Most high school algebra students spend time doing specialized problem types: number problems, rate problems, age and coin problems, percent problems, mixture problems, and so on. The trouble is that if the first week is spent doing age problems and then percent problems are done the second week, at the end of the second week the students typically have forgotten how to do the age problems. This is a result of working with specialized problem types. It is easy to avoid this scenario by providing a wide variety of problems.

The problems presented must be appropriate for all ability levels, and yet fit into the curricular topics being covered. Presenting problems appropriate for students who have different ability levels is not overly difficult, thanks to the multitude of resources now available. However, using problems appropriate for the curriculum being presented is not always that easy; planning is crucial. One factor that should be considered is how frequently problem solving should be integrated into each lesson. The easy answer is "as often as possible." The thing is, that response does not provide much information. Problem solving can be frustrating, tedious, and tiring, as well as invigorating and stimulating. The frequency of presentation requires a delicate balance. Part of the question can be resolved by establishing a program whereby a problem-solving exercise is presented at least once a week. This problem may or may not be related to the curriculum being covered. As problems are offered, time must be allowed for discussion of solutions. A possible reaction of some students is not to accept the challenge of the problem and, therefore, they will not be interested in the solution. The discussion could be held during a time you have allotted for seatwork, for example. This allows those who are not interested to engage in other constructive objectives. Alternatively, discussing the solution during seatwork time can be viewed as punishment by those who accept the challenge. The allocated time could not be used to do the seatwork because of the problem-solving discussion, but the assignment is still due. These considerations are part of a delicate balance that must be maintained.

## DIFFERENT TYPES OF PROBLEMS

The idea of different problem types goes beyond nonspecialization. You need to incorporate problems appropriate for varying student ability levels, gathered from different subject areas, exemplifying a variety of real-world applications, and designed to reach a multitude of objectives. Many of these problems do not need to be invented. They do exist in a variety of resources mentioned throughout this book, including *Scratch Your Brain Where It Itches* (available through Amazon and Barnes and Noble, published by Critical Thinking Press) and websites such as the Ole Miss Math Challenge (http://math contest.olemiss.edu) and the MacTutor History of Mathematics archive (http://www-history.mcs.st-and.ac.uk). The major difficulty becomes one of being able to compile a set of problems appropriate for your classes. Because there is such a wealth of information available, time will be required to familiarize yourself with the resources and then make appropriate selections. It is necessary to go beyond the resources provided by your textbook if you are to have a stimulating problem-solving program in your classes.

One interesting source of problems is the students themselves. Have them create problems that appeal to them and offer those creations to their peers as a challenge. They are more likely to use topics that are interesting to their peers. You will also learn things about the world of the students and what they value. This source of problems must be approached with caution because of potential complications. The created problems could:

Be based on assumptions that are not stated;

Come from a topic unknown to other students;

Use topics or language that is socially inappropriate;

Not contain adequate information;

Be culturally or sexually biased.

Although student-generated problems can be extremely interesting, they do need to be viewed with appropriate caution.

As students conceptualize problems, evidence of creative thinking will surface. This will be especially evident in strong problem solvers. It also becomes an avenue that can be pursued as problem-solving skills are developed. Students need to be made aware of the value and rewards available for creative thinking. As groups begin to become problem solvers, their inventiveness can progress to extremely intricate levels. Encouragement of such developments, in turn, stimulates flexible thinking processes. As this is done, a spiral is started in which the problem-solving skills and excitement begin to fuel each other.

## THINKING GAMES AND PUZZLES

A method of stimulating creative growth that has shown promise for many years is the use of thinking games. This can be something as common as tic-tac-toe. "Standard" rules could be followed or the guidelines could be reversed so that three in a row, column, or diagonal would lose rather than win. This seemingly minor change creates a setting in which thought processes must be altered significantly if an individual is to win. This is a formative step in becoming a flexible thinker. Games like chess, checkers, Chinese checkers, card playing, billiards, and so forth, can be played with a premium placed on explanation of strategies used. The advantage of these games is that some students will be familiar with them and those individuals can help others learn how to play. A bonus of these games is that the teacher can become a participant, one of the roles that is assumed in group work. This can make a positive contribution to the overall dynamics of a class, as they come to the realization that the teacher adopts many roles.

Puzzles (Tower of Hanoi, Adam's Cube, Sneaky Squares, etc.) provide rich opportunities for the development of problem-solving skills. The Tower of Hanoi, shown in Fig. 6.14, offers the opportunity to develop thinking patterns, strategies, generalizations, and algorithms. The classic question asked involves determining the minimal number of moves required to get a stack of disks from one pin to another, moving only one disk at a time, and never placing a larger disk on a smaller one. The Tower of Hanoi can found as a manipulative in many educational catalogs as well as an interactive puzzle on the Internet. One version is located at the National Library of Virtual Manipulatives for Interactive Mathematics (http://nlvm.usu.edu/en/nav/ vlibrary.html). The web address for the Tower of

Hanoi puzzle is http://nlvm.usu.edu/en/nav/frames_ asid_118_g_2_t_2.html?from=topic_t_2.html

There is a folklore tale about a sect of monks who have a Tower puzzle consisting of three pins and 64 successively sized disks. They are able to correctly move a disk every second and work in shifts so the operation is nonstop. Their belief is that when they complete the task, the world will end. The question coming out of the tale is to determine how long it will take the monks to complete their task. Figure 6.15 shows a method leading to the desired generalization needed to answer this question.

| Number of Disks | Number of Moves | Rewriting Exponents | Generalization |
|---|---|---|---|
| 1 | 1 | 2 – 1 | $(2^1) - 1$ |
| 2 | 3 | 4 – 1 | $(2^2) - 1$ |
| 3 | 7 | 8 – 1 | $(2^3) - 1$ |
| 4 | 15 | 16 – 1 | $(2^4) - 1$ |
| | • | | |
| | • | | |
| n | • | | $(2^n) - 1$ |

**Figure 6.15**

The monks are going to need $(2^{64})$—1, or 18, 446,744,073,709,551,615 seconds. Dividing that number of seconds by 3,600 seconds in an hour, 24 hours in a day, and 365.25 days in a year gives $\frac{1,229,782,938,247,303,441}{2,103,840} \approx 5.845 \times 10^{11}$, or 584, 42,076,576 years. It will take a while for the monks to complete their task. Ultimately, what we want the students to do is develop a strategy, and extend their efforts enough to see the advantage of knowing and using mathematics to answer questions. If the student elects not to accept the challenge offered, there is no need for the generalization.

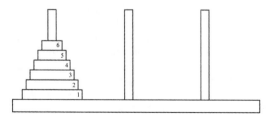

**Figure 6.14**

### EXERCISES 6.10

1. The Tower monk story makes a wonderful mathematics problem. Use a set of six disks or the following interactive website (http://nlvm.usu.edu/en/nav/frames_ asid_118_g_2_t_2.html?from=topic_t_2. html) at the National Library of Virtual Manipulatives for Interactive Mathematics to

solve the puzzle in 63 moves. Then try to do the puzzle in 63 or fewer seconds. How did you do?

2. Search the Internet and provide the web address for different interactive site that allows you to do the Tower of Hanoi puzzle.

As students generate creative or flexible thought patterns, posting them on a bulletin board can become very motivating to their classmates as well as others. The posting can be an unusual or exotic solution to a problem either you or another student has posed. As others view the work, discussion and interest are stimulated. The student whose work is posted receives recognition, and others begin to learn alternative methods of solving problems. Students who read the posted work might be stimulated to try the problem, thereby providing them another avenue for practicing their skills. There is a danger to posting work because of the negative connotations that could be attached to students who do not have work posted.

## DEVELOPING GOOD PROBLEM SOLVERS

There are several traits held by problem solvers. It is not necessarily the case that any problem solver will exhibit all these traits, and the list given here is not intended to be exhaustive, but it is indicative of the thinking process of many problem solvers. Some characteristics should be helpful as you attempt to develop good problem solvers. Reward any of the following:

Thinking

Reasoning

Hypothesizing

Educated guesses with follow-up

Idea getting

Patience

Persistence

Pattern searches

Generalization building

Flexible thought

Drawing on ideas from others

Inspiring others to begin thinking

Creative suggestions

Stating the obvious

Notice that many of these traits are identified when using scored discussions referred to in chapter 2. Scored discussions provide excellent opportunities to encourage and develop problem-solving skills for students.

Each of the items in the list provides some helpful insight as an individual seeks to solve problems. Do not overlook things like students who converse with themselves as they work through a problem. That person knows what questions to ask and answer. Most of us have had a conversation with ourselves and, in the process, determined some insights that lead to an appropriate conclusion. Often, a good problem solver will appear to skip steps. These steps may go unsaid because they are trivially obvious to the solver. The steps are being done mentally. The skipping is acceptable, as long as the solver can communicate the solution, including the skipped steps if they are necessary for another individual. The individual who skips steps is frequently identified as a good problem solver.

## DEVELOPING PROBLEM-SOLVING SKILLS

The most basic requirement to building problem-solving skills is to do problems. The following is a problem that has been used to entice many people into doing problem solving. At first it appears rather simple, and then the realization about its complexity hits. Individuals will insist that they need to know the house number, which is not the case. All the information needed to solve the problem is given.

*Problem.* Suppose you were attending a party. The person giving the party is asked to give the ages of their children. The following information is given to the requesting individual:

There are three children.

Each child has a counting-number age.

The product of their ages is 72.

The sum of their ages is the same as this house number.

The guest thinks about the information, goes outside, looks at the house number, goes back inside and says, "I need more information."

At that time, the guest is told, "The oldest likes strawberry ice cream."

On hearing the statement, the guest gives the correct ages of the children.

*What are the ages of all three children?*

If no challenge is accepted, the growth of a problem solver will not occur. In order to get students to do problems, the setting must be appropriate. The problem has to be presented in a manner that will motivate the student to accept the challenge. Only then will the problem be done. This section discusses doing problems. This section also contained a problem. Did you do it? Remember, if you are to effectively teach problem solving, you must be a problem solver. Now is the time to do "strawberry ice cream" if you did not. The "strawberry ice cream" problem can be altered in a variety of ways. For example, it could be stated as, "the three children's ages give a product of 252 and sum to my age." After thought, the guest would be told the youngest likes oatmeal.

Figure 6.16 provides a chart with possible solutions to the "strawberry ice cream" problem. After seeing the house number, the guest realizes there is a need for additional information. If the guest had seen a house number of 74, the ages had to be 72,1, and 1. Incidentally, this particular combination of ages bothers many students. It is important to point out that, although highly unlikely, the possibility does exist that an individual could have three children aged 72,1, and 1, if only through adoption. More significantly, however, we are dealing with a hypothetical situation that can be extended to include all possible mathematical combinations.

If the guest had seen a house number of 39, the ages would be known to be 36, 2, and 1. If the guest had seen a house number of 28, the children would be 24, 3, and 1. However, the guest did not see those house numbers. In fact, the only possible

house number that demands more information is 14. Because there are two sets of ages yielding a house number of 14, the guest needs to know the oldest. The children are counting number ages only, so twins are considered to be the same age. In the case of the ages 6, 6, and 2, there would be no clear oldest. With ages of 8, 3, and 3, the 8-year-old is clearly the oldest. Strawberry ice cream has nothing to do with the solution other than it provides the opportunity to have a statement about the oldest child. A nice serendipity related to this problem is that many people conclude the children must be 9, 8, and 1 because they count 18 letters in "strawberry ice cream."

The problem-solving skills should begin with easy problems and progress to more difficult ones. This statement might seem obvious, and yet, it must be considered carefully. Giving a problem of unrealistic difficulty or one that is beyond the capabilities of the students can create discouragement that is virtually impossible to overcome. If the problems are trivially simple, they hold no challenge, and the problem-solving process is never started. Again, the delicate importance of creating just the right problem-solving atmosphere is present. It takes time, careful planning, and energy.

Another easy way to build problem-solving skills is to post solutions. This has been mentioned before, but here the emphasis is on the ability to communicate. Students must build the powers of communication and reasoning.

Buffon's principle, developed by the Comte de Buffon in 1760 (Eves, 1967, p. 94), is a short class activity that assists in developing communication and reasoning skills. Each student needs a handful of toothpicks (20 to 30), a blank sheet of paper, a pencil, and a straight edge. Students should draw parallel line segments on the paper a toothpick's length apart. It is crucial that the segments are separated by the length of a toothpick. Next, have each student hold the toothpicks above the center of the paper and drop the toothpicks (the drop should be a minimum of 2 to 3 feet to create a valid spread). A toothpick crossing a drawn segment is an "ON" toothpick and one not crossing the line segment is an "OFF" toothpick. Any toothpick off the paper, or hanging over the edge, is not considered. The teacher should create a spreadsheet prior to class that will be used to record the data. The spreadsheet needs three columns: number ON, number OFF, and twice ON divided by OFF. The bottom of the spreadsheet shown in Fig. 6.17 displays the average of the third column.

| Child A's Age | Child A's Age | Child A's Age | Sum |
|---|---|---|---|
| 72 | 1 | 1 | 74 |
| 36 | 2 | 1 | 39 |
| 24 | 3 | 1 | 28 |
| 18 | 4 | 1 | 23 |
| 12 | 6 | 1 | 19 |
| 9 | 8 | 1 | 18 |
| 18 | 2 | 2 | 22 |
| 6 | 6 | 2 | 14 |
| 12 | 3 | 2 | 17 |
| 9 | 4 | 2 | 15 |
| 8 | 3 | 3 | 14 |
| 6 | 4 | 3 | 13 |

**Figure 6.16**

| Number On | Number Off | 2 Times on Divided by Off |
|---|---|---|
| 5 | 3 | 3.33333 |
| 11 | 5 | 4.40000 |
| 14 | 6 | 4.66667 |
| 12 | 8 | 3.00000 |
| 15 | 4 | 7.50000 |
| 10 | 3 | 6.66667 |
| 8 | 2 | 8.00000 |
| 6 | 11 | 1.09091 |
| 15 | 4 | 7.50000 |
| 15 | 7 | 4.28571 |
| 12 | 3 | 8.00000 |
| 11 | 5 | 4.40000 |
| 9 | 6 | 3.00000 |
| 11 | 10 | 2.20000 |
| 9 | 6 | 3.00000 |
| 9 | 5 | 3.60000 |
| 7 | 6 | 2.33333 |
| 13 | 5 | 5.20000 |
| 10 | 10 | 2.00000 |
| 13 | 11 | 2.36364 |
| 13 | 8 | 3.25000 |
| 4 | 7 | 1.14286 |
| 8 | 9 | 1.77778 |
| 8 | 10 | 1.60000 |
| 5 | 10 | 1.00000 |
| 13 | 12 | 2.16667 |
| 5 | 6 | 1.66667 |
| 9 | 7 | 2.57143 |
| 9 | 4 | 4.50000 |
| 8 | 7 | 2.28571 |
| 9 | 12 | 1.50000 |
| 10 | 5 | 4.00000 |
| 9 | 4 | 4.50000 |
| 6 | 7 | 1.71429 |
| 5 | 6 | 1.66667 |
| 10 | 7 | 2.85714 |
| 11 | 5 | 4.40000 |
| 11 | 5 | 4.40000 |
| 5 | 8 | 1.25000 |
| 14 | 10 | 2.80000 |
| 11 | 7 | 3.14286 |
| 6 | 11 | 1.09091 |
| 5 | 5 | 2.00000 |
| 6 | 9 | 1.33333 |
| 13 | 8 | 3.25000 |
| 9 | 10 | 1.80000 |
| 6 | 10 | 1.20000 |
| 6 | 8 | 1.50000 |
| 15 | 9 | 3.33333 |
| 6 | 11 | 1.09091 |

Average of 2 times on divided by off = 3.1466162

**Figure 6.17**

One by one, students call out their number of ONs and OFFs, which is recorded by a student on a computer. The screen should be projected for all to view as the data is being recorded. As the number of ONs and OFFs is entered, the third column is automatically calculated and its average is continually updated. The students discover an impressive development! As the number of trials increases, the average of twice the number of toothpicks ON divided by the number of toothpicks OFF approaches $\pi$. Try it! Similar activities using coat-hanger wire and a square tile floor can be developed. The seams would be the parallels and the coat wire would be cut equal to the length of the tile side (representing the toothpicks). This is another example of an activity that could be inserted at a variety of points throughout the curriculum, depending on the ability and background of the students.

Planning a problem-solving program is another essential ingredient in building problem-solving skills. This statement has been mentioned before but cannot be given enough emphasis. Good problem-solving programs do not just happen. They require a lot of reflective thinking on the part of the teacher. This thinking involves deciding which problems to use and where to insert them into the curriculum. Allowances must be made for alterations because of the discovery of a new problem or of differing student needs. The problem-solving program is a constantly evolving process. The textbook may have the framework of a plan you can work with, but you will undoubtedly need to expand it. Include problems not directly related to the curriculum that are designed to attract the attention of your students to problem solving.

## TRY THIS IN YOUR CLASSROOM

*NCTM Standards 2000*: Algebra, Problem Solving, Reasoning and Proof, and Communication.

*Materials*: Graphing calculator or algebraic software

*Introduction/Set*: Business decisions are influenced by factors designed to allocate resources so profits and productivity are maximized while costs are minimized. Linear programming is one method used to help the decision-making process by graphing a group of equations or inequalities. A polygon region bounded by equalities or inequalities is created. Mathematicians have proven that any point in the bounded region satisfies all the constraints and if there is a maximum or minimum value it will occur at one of the vertices of the polygon region.

Graph the following inequalities:

$$Y \geq 5 - X \qquad Y \geq 0$$
$$Y \leq -.08X + 7 \quad Y \leq X - 2$$

The graph should be similar to Fig. 6.18. Find the coordinates of the polygon constructed by the inequalities in Fig. 6.18. Observing the graph, the coordinates of the points of intersection could also be determined by solving systems of equations. This can be done on many graphing calculators or software (MathXpert Plus™).

First, have the students determine which lines intersect at a corner of the polygon. Have the students assign the corresponding inequality with each line.

You will be using only the equation form of the inequality to solve each the system. Have the students place each equation in standard form $Ax + By = C$ and solve each system. The solution will yield the coordinates of the corner of the polygon.

Do all of the answers here agree with the points of intersection found? Should they? Why or why not?

Industry is concerned with profit. Frequently, a company will use linear programming to determine the maxim profit given constraints that are real factors to the company. Suppose a manufacturer can produce a product one way (Method 1) using 3 hours of unskilled labor, 1 hour of machine time, and 2 hours of skilled labor. On the other hand, Method 2 takes 3 hours of unskilled labor, 2 hours of machine time, and 1 hour of skilled labor. Method 1 generates a profit of $45 per unit made while Method 2 generates a profit of $50 per unit. The immediate response would be to use Method 2 and be done with it. However, constraints have not been considered yet (X = items produced by Method 1 and Y = items produced by Method 2).

$3X + 3Y \leq 4200$ (up to 4200 hours of unskilled labor are available)

$X + 2Y \leq 2400$ (up to 2400 hours of machine time are available)

$2X + Y \leq 2400$ (up to 2400 hours of skilled labor are available)

$X \geq 0$ (not possible to produce a negative amount)

$Y \geq 0$ (not possible to produce a negative amount)

Sketch the graph that results from the preceding constraints.

Determine the coordinates of the vertices of the polygon determined by the constraints given for the manufacturing problem. Which of the vertices generates the greatest profit for the manufacturer under the given constraints? What is the maximum profit for the manufacturer?

## CONCLUSION—SOME POINTS TO CONSIDER—OR BEGINNING?

Evaluate different text series; decide if problem solving can be taught; plan a problem-solving program; teach problem-solving skills; and struggle to become a problem solver. The underlying premise is that you first must become a problem solver before you can teach it to others. A few problems are listed in Sticky Questions in the chapter and throughout the book to help get you started. The intention is that you will try these. Each has been the source of much learning and excitement for students of a variety of age and ability levels. The problems are not offered in any particular order of difficulty or from any curriculum section. They are just good, fun problems to try, and you should do them. As you do these problems, you should pay attention to the thought processes you use. You should also write your solution(s) so that your newly acquired knowledge can be communicated to others.

### STICKY QUESTIONS

1. How many squares are on a checkerboard? A standard checkerboard is a big square comprised of eight unit squares on a side. Once this question is answered, extend it to allow diagonal squares formed by joining selected vertices. Generalize the original question to an "N by N" checkerboard. What happens if the checkerboard is N by M where M ≠ N?

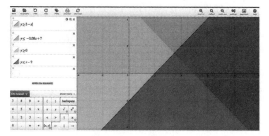

**Figure 6.18**

2. Suppose the earth is a sphere and the circumference at the equator is 25,000 miles. A band is placed around the earth, concentric with the equator. The circumference of the band is 25,000 miles + 10 feet. A standard sheet of 8.5-by-11-inch notebook paper is about 0.003 inches thick. Would that paper fit between the band and the equator in any of its three configurations (thickness, width, length)? What is the thickest thing that could fit between the band and the equator?

3. A mile-long, horizontal bridge is built with no expansion joints. Neither end will move. The bridge expands to a length of 1 mile + 2 feet due to temperature changes. The expansion causes the bridge to bow up in the middle. What is the distance between the center of the bridge in its normal and in its expanded state? The value of this question is suspect because, in the real world, bridge design must allow for expansion and contraction. However, the answer is so surprising that it is worthy of consideration.

4. Folklore describes a young man and a king's daughter who were very much in love and wanted to marry. The king did not want the wedding to occur because the young man was not of the appropriate breeding, and besides, the young man did not possess the wealth to provide the lifestyle to which the girl had become accustomed. The young man was a clever fellow and offered the king an opportunity that was too good to pass up. The boy offered to go away if the king would be willing to give him some grain. The king would place one kernel of grain on a square of a checkerboard. The second square would contain two kernels of grain, the third four, and so on, until all 64 unit squares on the checkerboard were used. The total of the kernels of grain would be the young man's wealth and with it, he would leave, unless the king deemed otherwise. The king accepted the challenge. Do you think the young man married the king's daughter?

6. A variation of Problem 5 involves building a stack of paper. A sheet of paper is folded in half, and then in half again, and again, and so on, until a total of 50 folds is made. The question is, "How high is the stack of paper?" The assumption here is that the 50 folds can be made.

7. A person was born in the 19th century. In the year $X^2$, the person's age was X. How old was the person in 1885?

8. Find the endless product $\left(\sqrt{2}\right)\left(\sqrt[4]{2}\right)\left(\sqrt[8]{2}\right)\left(\sqrt[16]{2}\right)\ldots$

9. You start at point A and walk 1 mile due south to point B. You rest for 10 minutes. Walk 1 mile due east to point C. Rest for 15 minutes. Walk 1 mile due north back to point A, where you see a bear that has eaten some of your lunch. What color is the bear?

10. The red stripe on a barber pole is one meter high and 16 cm in diameter and makes two complete revolutions around the pole. What angle does the stripe make with the pole?

11. A square of side 10 and a right triangle of sides 20, 21, and 29 overlap so the right angle of the triangle is at the center of the square. What is the area of the overlap? Do it more than one way.

12. In a 5-by-12 rectangle, one diagonal is drawn. A circle is inscribed in each of the formed triangles. Find the distance between the centers of the two circles. Do it more than one way.

13. A sphere is dropped into a right circular cone-shaped container that is 12 cm high having a 8-cm diameter at the opening. If the bottom of the sphere is 2 cm above the vertex of the cone, what is the radius of the sphere?

14. How many different routes can be taken to go from the bottom left corner of a checkerboard to the upper right corner, when you may move only up or to the right along the existing segments between the squares?

15. Suppose you want to install a mirror so you can see a full view of yourself. What is the minimum length mirror that will serve your needs, and how far above the floor should the bottom of the mirror be?

## PROBLEM-SOLVING CHALLENGES

1. Observe the five-column array of numbers. In what column will 1,000 appear and, more importantly, why?

|    | 2  | 3  | 4  | 5  |
|----|----|----|----|----|
| 9  | 8  | 7  | 6  |    |
|    | 10 | 11 | 12 | 13 |
| 17 | 16 | 15 | 14 |    |
|    | 18 | 19 | 20 | 21 |
| 25 | 24 | 23 | 22 |    |
|    | etc. |  |  |  |

**Check out the website for the solution**

2. A school has a hall with 1,000 lockers, all of which are closed. A thousand students start down the hall. The first student opens every locker. The second student closes all lockers that are multiples of two. The third student changes (closes an open locker or opens a closed one) all multiples of three. The fourth student changes all multiples of four. And so on. After all students have entered the school, how many lockers are open and which ones? This is a good problem to solve more than one way.

**Check out the website for the solution**

# LEARNING ACTIVITIES

## 8-4-2-1

### Background

Since this is a problem-solving chapter, we will provide you with a problem-solving challenge. As you read this activity, we encourage you to solve the problem as posed before reading the discussion. If you have bought into the discussion provided in the chapter, you should be willing to attempt this problem and give it your best effort, which is what you would expect of your students.

### The Problem

There are four boats numbered 8, 4, 2, and 1. The boat number indicates the amount of time in hours it takes that boat to go from New Bedford, MA, to Martha's Vineyard (an island off the coast of Massachusetts). All four boats are on docked in New Bedford and the task is to get all of the boats across Buzzards Bay in the smallest amount of time. One and only one faster boat can be carried in any slower boat. For example, the 8 boat could carry the 4 boat but the 4 boat could not carry the 8 boat. Therefore, it would take 8 hours to transport both boats across.

1. What is the minimum number of hours it will take to transport all boats across the bay from New Bedford to Martha's Vineyard?

**Assuming you have solved the problem, please read on. If you have not attempted the problem yet, now is the time!**

### Discussion

The typical response is 16 time hours. The reasoning is that the 1 is in the 8, taking 8 hours to go across. Return in the 1 boat, giving a total of 9 hours. The 1 boat is placed in the 4 and the return trip is made, giving a total of 13 hours. Return in the 1 boat, yielding a total of 14 hours. Finally the 1 boat is placed in the 2 and the bay is crossed, giving a grand total of 16 hours.

2. Is that how you did it?

Typically, the solver is surprised to hear that the crossings can be done in less time. Generally, the first thing the individual does is to repeat the process, again arriving at 16 hours for the total passage.

3. Determine some alternative ideas that might seem a bit more "creative" or "outside the box" for this problem.

Additional thought may generate ideas such as:

- Put the 4, 2, and 1 in the 8 boat and cross the bay. But that breaks the one and only one rule.
- Put the 4 in the 8 boat and tow the 1 and 2 behind. While that is not specifically mentioned in the problem, it is purposely left out. This allows the poser to say something like, "Good thinking, but the intent of the problem is that no boats are to be towed."
- Put the 4 in the 8 boat and cross the bay. Then swim back. Again, a neat idea but outside the intent of the problem especially if it takes one hour for a fast boat to cross. (By the way, Buzzards Bay has been known to contain a few great white sharks.)

- Put the 8 in the 4 and cross. This breaks the rules.
- Put the 4 in the 8 and cross, and then forget about the 1 and 2. This defeats the purpose of the problem.

You should notice that the open-ended statement of the problem invites creative solutions. As the teacher, you would respond in kind as modeled in the last paragraph. After several of the "creative solutions" are entertained, the focus needs to be shifted to thinking about solving the problem in a different manner—thinking "outside the box."

Some people link this problem with the Tower of Hanoi problem where 1 disk takes one move, 2 disks take 3 moves, 3 disks take 7 moves, and 4 disks take 15 moves and conclude that the correct response should be 15, but are unable to demonstrate how to shuttle the boats to come up with 15 hours. Ironically, 15 hours is correct, but the answer provides little value without the description of how to transport the boats.

The natural tendency is deal with the 8 boat first. Varying which boat is placed inside the 8 boat does not alter the final result from being 16. So, the clue has to be to start with a boat other than the 8.

Again, the desire to get the larger values out of consideration fast leads to using the 4 for the first trip. Alas, this too will end up with a total of 16 or more.

4. Describe the transportation of all four boats that will take 16 hours using the 4 boat on the first trip.

Often at this point in the process, the solver will declare that the problem cannot be done in fewer than 16 hours. Encourage more attempts.

Since starting with the 8 and 4 have proven fruitless, start with the 2, which mandates that only the 1 boat can be inside. Even now, often the result will be 16 hours, because the return in the 1 boat gives a total of 3 hours, but then the 1 is put in either the 4 or 8 and the process that has been being used appears again, just in a different order.

The true "outside the box" thinking happens after the 1 is put in the 2 and then the 1 boat is used for the return trip. Do not put the 1 in either of the 4 or the 8. Rather, put the 4 in the 8 and cross. At this point the total hours is 11 (2 + 1 + 8). Return in the 2 boat, giving a total of 13 hours. Finally place the 1 boat in the 2 and make the final crossing, resulting in a grand total of 15 hours.

5. Construct a pictorial representation for middle school students that demonstrates the 15 hours process.

We have elected to provide a more elaborate discussion of this solution to show you the value of thinking outside the box and also to provide examples of the creative thinking students can generate. We encourage you to integrate problem-solving situations into your curriculum as frequently as possible, keeping the challenges open-ended to entice your students to THINK!

# Discovery

**7**

## FOCAL POINTS OF THIS CHAPTER

- Participate in discovery learning activities
- Investigate how to establish an environment conducive to discovery learning
- Determine what types of discovery are most appropriate in different settings
- Analyze means of attracting student attention in a discovery atmosphere
- Learn how to integrate time for discovery learning into lessons
- Study how to ask intriguing questions designed to attract students' attention
- See examples of discovery-based lessons
- Participate in laboratory activities designed to lead students to mathematical discoveries

Discovery learning is a method of indirect instruction. The teacher structures the learning environment, enabling the learner to develop conclusions. The use of divergent questioning techniques often accompanies discovery learning. Divergent questions generally have more than one possible response and are usually associated with the development of critical-thinking or problem-solving skills.

There are various kinds of discovery learning. Pure discovery is defined as learning with no prompts, guidelines, or directions. Guided discovery occurs when specific questions are asked, intended to lead the learner in a particular direction toward a desired conclusion. Open-ended discovery begins with prompts to start the learner toward one of several possible conclusions. The learner selects the most desirable route and conclusion based on information, opinions, background, knowledge, and thought flexibility. Although there are other modifications of discovery learning, these examples are typical. Each discovery type has a place in education, depending

on the circumstances. The important thing is not discovery type identification, but that the opportunity to discover is available in the mathematics classroom. Discovery learning provides a multitude of learning settings for several learning styles.

Normally, when doing a discovery lesson, the students know the teacher will eventually "tell the big secret, formula, or conclusion." They quickly learn there is no need to work at discovering. Teachers need to provide learning time, appropriate tools and prompts, and expect the students to arrive at conclusions. This means teachers should not "tell" the answer.

Discovery learning is not a new concept. Discovery learning has been influenced by the works of Montessori (1870–1952), Piaget (1896–1980), Dienes (1916–), and through views such as self-paced instruction and individualized learning.

These prominent figures in education believed that the learner should be involved in and responsible for learning. Literature such as *Everybody Counts* (MSEB, 1989), *Curriculum and Evaluation Standards for School Mathematics* (NCTM, 1989), *Reshaping the Schools* (MSEB, 1990), and *Principles and Standards for School Mathematics* (NCTM, 2000) suggests that the student must become involved in the learning environment.

## EXERCISES 7.1

1. Summarize and react to at least three major points raised in one of these publications: *Everybody Counts, Curriculum and Evaluation Standards for School Mathematics, Professional Standards for Teaching Mathematics,* Assessment Standards, Standards 2000, or *Reshaping the Schools*. Are the suggestions practical? Do you think they could have been instituted in your high school? Why or why not?
2. Complete an annotated bibliography on all documents mentioned in Exercise 1.

If the teacher has never figured out a pattern or proved how a number trick works, it is difficult for that teacher to show, model, or motivate a student to complete such a task. Teachers tend to teach as they were taught. We have been teaching the same geometry as Euclid (Euclid of Alexandria, http://www-history.mcs.st-and.ac.uk/Mathematicians/Euclid.html) did when he compiled his famous "Elements."

The symbolism and order have been altered or refined, but the content is similar. Algebra is taught as it has been since its development in the eighteenth century. Again, the symbolism has changed, additional topics have been inserted, concepts may be developed earlier in the curriculum, but the approach to the subject has been virtually stagnant. With that in mind, it is relatively safe to assume that almost everyone teaching today has been taught algebra through a teacher-centered direct instruction setting:

"Here is the formula."

"Plug in these values for the variables and solve."

"Watch me do an example."

"Help me with this example."

"What step comes next?"

"Any questions?"

"Your homework is . . . "

The scenario changes, but this description is all too common in many classroom settings. Change will be difficult to accomplish, because most of us have not had the opportunity to discover mathematics in any of the pure, guided, or open-ended settings. We are being asked to model and present information in a format that is partially or totally foreign (for both the student and the teacher) to our conditioned way of thinking.

Even if you have discovered some mathematics, certain things need to happen before discovery can take place in or outside the classroom. Discovery learning does not just happen. There needs to be an atmosphere of inquisitiveness, which must be created and nurtured. Students need to be asked questions that will assist in developing discovery:

"I wonder what would happen if I changed to . . . ?"

"How was that developed?"

"Is there an easier way to do this?"

"Does this always work?"

"Is this the only possible solution?"

Technology provides wonderful opportunities for discovery. Suppose students investigate the exterior angles of polygons. In this example, we assume the definition has been covered and the thrust of the lesson is to have the learner become aware that the sum of the measures of the exterior angles of a polygon is 360°.

Figure 7.1 shows the exterior angles of a triangle summing to 360°. What you might not expect is the three individual angle measures of 136.589°, 77.768°, and 145.644°, adding to 360.000°.

It is important that students become aware that technology has a tendency to round values, depending on the level of precision selected. Students will also get this impression: If an angle measures 136.589°, that is its size exactly, no more and no less. We know that is not the case, but how do students become convinced of that? Technology is not necessarily an ally at this point. Figure 7.1 was purposely used here. Another example in which the actual values added to 360.000° could have been used, avoiding the issue. Often this is the case, either consciously or subconsciously.

You might be thinking, "How can I be expected to come up with all these strange concoctions?" Remember you are a professional. You are aware of your students, their basic knowledge, and thought patterns. You should know the area of mathematics. Putting all that together with some thought, you can think of special situations that might cause problems for your students or help clarify their conceptualizations. Also, these types of situation do accidentally arise during instruction when using technology. Embrace these opportunities and explore the situations with your class. Show the students that you are interested in these peculiar situations and they will become intrigued as well.

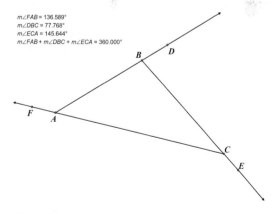

**Figure 7.1**

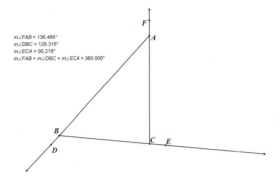

m∠FAB = 136.466°
m∠DBC = 128.316°
m∠ECA = 95.218°
m∠FAB + m∠DBC + m∠ECA = 360.000°

**Figure 7.2**

Figure 7.2 shows another triangle where the sum of the angles indicated is 360°. Notice the angles selected here sum to 360.000°. Students should have the opportunity to move the triangle to discover for themselves that the sum of the exterior angles of any triangle is 360°. If they cannot actually perform the motion on machines of their own, it is imperative that you provide a variety of dynamic examples.

Once students are comfortable that the sum of the measures of the exterior angles of a triangle is 360°, shift to quadrilaterals, as shown in Fig. 7.3. Depending on their background, you might ask them what they think the result will be before they actually do any investigation. At this point, a variety of answers could occur. For example, a student could reason that because a triangle has three sides and the sum of the measures of the exterior angle is 360°, each exterior angle is "worth" 120°. That means the sum of the exterior angles of a quadrilateral would be 4 times 120°, or 480°.

The reasoning is not correct, but perhaps logical. Figure 7.3 will dispel that assumption. Depending on background and experience in such situations, students should now quickly conclude the sum of

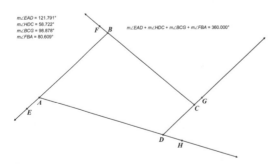

m∠EAD = 121.791°
m∠HDC = 58.722°
m∠BCG = 98.878°
m∠FBA = 80.609°

m∠EAD + m∠HDC + m∠BCG + m∠FBA = 360.000°

**Figure 7.3**

the measures of the exterior angles of an *n*-gon will always be 360°. Extending this physically to a setting where the number of sides is large with a regular polygon can lay some very useful groundwork for the idea that a circle contains 360°.

---

### EXERCISES 7.2

1. Use dynamic geometry software to construct a quadrilateral. Experiment by moving the vertices to show that the sum of the exterior angles will always be 360°.
2. If the quadrilateral from Exercise 1 is concave, what is the impact on the sum of the exterior angles? How do you rationalize this with students?

---

**Additional exercises can be found on the website.**

## CULTIVATING THE SETTING

The setting is established by the teacher. An approach is selected to develop the various topics. We should not be telling the student what to do next, what to expect, how to think, and how to do it. The thinking and developmental responsibility must be shifted to the student. How much does a student learn by modeling as we do a problem step by step? How much more would a student learn if we ask for each next step to be supplied as a situation is solved? This forces active participation by the learner and develops critical-thinking skills. In a teacher-centered lesson, students are asked to watch and memorize the steps or algorithm. Seldom is there much coverage about the how or the why. No longer should the student passively observe and agree with the presentation. The student should learn to create or project the next step(s) until an acceptable conclusion is reached. In the process, the student begins to formulate acceptable arguments that lead to mathematical independence.

All too often, students follow a teacher through a solution in a group setting, agreeing with each step put forward and explained. At the end, the students are convinced the procedure is understood and that it can be duplicated. When they later attempt to do a similar problem on their own, confusion points are found. Statements like, "I understood it when you were doing it, but when I tried to do my own, I got lost," are common.

## DETERMINING APPROPRIATE METHODS

A student must possess all the necessary readiness skills required to achieve the learning (discovery here) objectives established for a situation. An associated difficulty related to assuring a student has the necessary readiness skills is achieving some level of agreement on what prerequisite skills are necessary to perform a given mathematical task.

A student must want to discover things. This is not always easy to accomplish, because for years the student has been told when and how to do things. That student has become dependent on being told. It is a lot easier to be told what to do than it is to figure out what to do. Therefore, students resist discovery—it is too much work. Typically, teachers have been drill instructors. The students have been trained to expect the information to be handed to them. Even when the students are in a discovery setting, most of the time they are eventually told what should have been discovered. Strategies that could have been used to arrive at the correct solution are discussed after a time of working on the situation. The students are given so many hints that they don't have to discover anything. They know that if they wait, secrets will be revealed. The opportunities to exercise their thinking muscles and develop mathematics are removed when we supply all the answers.

Both preservice and practicing teachers of mathematics at all levels need experience in not revealing all the secrets. This requires much discipline from all segments of the mathematics education community. We all need to be strong-willed enough not to reveal answers to mathematical situations until we are certain a reasonable amount of effort has been expended by the learner. This is difficult because it is so foreign to how we typically have been taught to learn mathematics.

## ENTICEMENT

How reasonable is it for us to expect students to want to discover if they have never done it? The thrill of figuring out why or how something works generates a desire to discover more. A problem often given to students in a variety of settings (drill, number trick, application of algebra, demonstration of number property use) is shown in Fig. 7.4.

It is amazing to students that they all get the same answer in Number Trick 1 (assuming no arithmetic errors). It is not uncommon for them to ask how this works, indicating that their natural curiosity can be stimulated. An activity like this can be the beginning of discovery learning, part of which is being able to prove things, verify conjectures, or extend ideas into generalizations. (Did you do the problem? You should have!)

Doing problems like this could lead to the beginning of a change in your learning style. Most people select a small counting number. What happens if you pick zero? Will this trick work for integers? Fractions? Decimals? Complex numbers? Why or why not? Asking questions such as these and developing a willingness to use "unusual" numbers is a beginning indicator of your ability to become a more flexible thinker. In the process, your curiosity will lead you to make discoveries and, thus, begin your metamorphosis. That change is the beginning of your cultivation of a feeling for how to teach students to discover. Using "unusual" values in problems is facilitated by technology that can remove the drudgery experienced in working the arithmetic involved in such investigations.

| Number Trick 1 | Number Trick 2 | |
|---|---|---|
| Pick a number. Double it. Add four. | Pick a number. Triple it. Add twelve. | x 3x 3x + 12 |
| Divide by two. | Divide by three. | $\frac{3x + 12}{3} = x + 4$ |
| Subtract the original number. | Subtract four. | x + 4 − 4 = x |
| What do you have left? | What do you have left? | |

**Figure 7.4**

147

Indications about the general maturity of students show up in the values they select when you ask them to pick a number. If a student consistently selects zero or one, you might tend to think that student has discovered some things about the ease of operating with identity elements in the real numbers. It could be, however, that the student is just being lazy and uses either zero or one because those two values generally decrease the amount of required arithmetic. If it is suspected that a student is selecting out of laziness, a discussion of the value of seeking shortcuts or easy methods of arriving at conclusions, as long as those maneuvers are within the acceptable limits of work ethic, might be appropriate. A discussion about the advantages of using a calculator or computer to do the arithmetic could easily be appropriate as investigations into student motivation for the selection of a given topic are conducted.

If a student selects a negative value, fraction, or decimal value, don't be too quick to assume that student has no idea of the easy way to do example in Fig. 7.4. That student might be curious as to whether what is being done works for more unusual values. Such curiosity should be encouraged. The use of different values might be even more likely if calculators or computers are available to the students.

"Tricks" like "Pick a number" can stimulate students to look beyond the superficial and work with abstractions as opposed to specific values. When doing Number Trick 2 in Fig. 7.4 with students, particularly those who are more capable, purposely change the instructions as you do the "proof" example. Some will quickly see the similarity and others will not. Those who don't now have an additional problem to investigate. Some will accept the challenge and some will not. It is critical that all students have the opportunity to see why the problem works. Also, an occasion to introduce a basic application of algebra is now present. As the example is done with variables, students should discover that the problem works for any initial value.

---

## EXERCISES 7.3

1. Develop or find a number trick using at least four instructions (remember to give appropriate bibliographical credit). Have someone do the trick and record their reaction.
2. Will complex numbers work for your trick? What conditions must be placed on your trick?

**Additional exercises can be found on the website.**

## PROVIDING TIME

Time is an essential ingredient of discovery learning. If a student is somewhere along the discovery continuum for a concept and is told the answer because time is running out, the idea of "Just wait and the teacher will tell you" is reinforced, and the nondiscovery mode of operation continues. If a student is to discover, the necessary time for the thought process to develop must be available. We do not know how long it will take each individual to discover a given idea. Even with guided discovery, the time varies and, if the student is going to be a discovery learner, the necessary amount needs to be invested.

## MEETING CURRICULUM REQUIREMENTS

Critics of discovery learning say the mathematics curriculum does not lend itself well to discovery learning. The reasoning is that if the objectives are to be met within allocated time frames, the class must continue to move in its planned sequence. Teachers often rationalize that students should be told what to do and how to do it in order to accomplish the required tasks at the prescribed pace. Implementation of the No Child Left Behind Act of 2001 (http://www.ed.gov/nclb) has prompted many educators to focus on time on task for teaching mathematical content. This may cause many teachers to shift learning emphasis away from discovery learning because of time constraints. Telling might be more time-efficient, but it may not be more cost-effective for long-term learning.

Time is a factor as the curriculum is covered. So many topics are required and expected to be covered that insertion of anything that requires additional time is perceived negatively. Opponents to the use of discovery learning claim that the time required to learn how to discover is so great that it would demand elimination of segments of the required curriculum. Once again, the impact of NCLB and "high stakes" state standardized tests have alarmed educators to focus classroom instruction to mathematical content. Their solution is to eliminate discovery learning in order to save time. The reality is that by saving time now, we only lose time in the future. Frequent and early use of discovery learning will most likely save future mathematics curriculum time. Rather than discouraging the use of discovery, we should be encouraging it. We must stop telling before students will start discovering. Why should a student go through all the effort of discovering and thinking if someone is willing to tell the answer?

## TECHNOLOGY AS A TEACHING TOOL

Introducing discovery in the early middle grades can be extremely effective. The use of a dynamic geometry program and a simple paper fraction kit can lead to a discovery. In the following lesson, the teacher must be willing to let the students discover answers.

## Sample Lesson

*Lesson Objective*. Using a paper fraction kit (which the students have made previously) let the students discover different ways to cover one whole with eight eighths.

*Prior Lesson*. Students constructed color fraction kits from pieces of different colored 8.5 × 11" paper. One uncut piece of paper represents a whole. Fold a different color piece of paper (with original dimensions the same as those of the unit paper) in half with the fold being parallel to the shorter side (hamburger fold). Fold that piece in half again, making the second fold perpendicular to the first. Repeat this process with a third fold parallel to the first. You now have eight congruent parts that cover a whole. Cut the sheet on the folds so the eight congruent pieces can be manipulated.

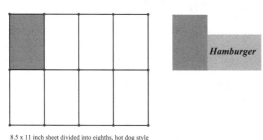

8.5 x 11 inch sheet divided into eighths, hot dog style

**Figure 7.5**

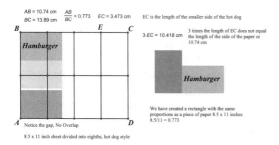

**Figure 7.6**

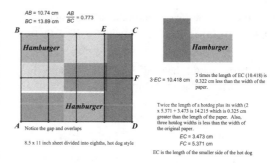

**Figure 7.7**

The students will be asked to cover the original sheet with the eighths pieces. The likelihood is that they will produce two different answers. One will have eight pieces arranged in hot-dog style as shown in Fig. 7.5, whereas another will have six hamburgers and two hotdogs covering the whole as shown in Fig. 7.6. The six and two look like they cover the original sheet.

*Question of the Lesson*. Does the six hamburger and two hot-dog arrangement cover the whole exactly? Closer examination with the use of technology shows that it does not, as demonstrated in Figs. 7.6 and 7.7.

## Sample Lesson

*Lesson Objective*. Students will discover the rules for adding and subtracting two equations with two unknowns.

*Prior Lesson*. The class learned to solve two equations in two unknowns by graphing. The students are familiar with the computer used as a teaching tool and are appropriately conversant with the software of choice. There is also a computer lab available for class use. Assume that the appropriate questions and situations that stimulate the students to think and discover are posed.

*Lesson*. In the last class, we solved two equations in two unknowns ("variables" could be used) by graphing. Review that procedure:

$y = x + 3$

Store $y = x + 3$ in "compartment" a

Graph $y = x + 3$

$y = -x + 7$

Store $y = -x + 7$ in "compartment" b

Graph $y = -x + 7$

The point of intersection is (_____,_____)

Assume the class comprehends the method. If the students do not, appropriate review would be necessary.

> What would happen if we tried something else, using the simplify capabilities of the software?

Call a + b out of storage.

Substitute equations for storage names.

> ($y = x + 3$ for a, $y = -x + 7$ for b)
> $y = x + 3 + y = -x + 7$

Simplify.

> $y + y = x + 3 - x + 7$

Simplify.

> $2y = 10$

We have one equation in one unknown.

Solve the equation and $y = 5$.

$y = 5$! [stated in a surprised manner]

That is what we got when graphing.

Maybe we have discovered another way to solve two equations in two unknowns.

What did we do?

We pulled two equations out of storage and added them.

Before class, store a variety of equations. These equations should all have coefficients of only +1 or −1. At this point in the lesson, the class would go to the lab with the instructions to add or subtract pairs of equations out of storage, as was done in class. The students should discover the rules for adding and subtracting two equations in two unknowns as a method of solving. More than likely, the students will also discover the concept of substitution as a means of solving two equations in two unknowns during this session. The examples would then be extended to include coefficients other than 1 for $x$ and $y$, leading to conclusions about when to multiply or divide to solve pairs of equations.

## FORMULATE CONJECTURES

Continuing with the preceding example, after a relatively short period of time (approximately 20 minutes), the students can tell when two equations can be solved by adding or subtracting, the advantages of each, how to tell which would be easier, when

their procedures would not work, and why. Responses will include:

> "If all the signs are the same, we get one equation in two unknowns."

> "If the coefficients of one variable are the same sign and the coefficients of the other have opposite signs, we can get the intersection point."

> "If both sets of coefficients have opposite signs, it won't work."

A discussion might follow that would summarize what had been said, and additional examples would be worked using the generalizations developed. Students should become aware that with two equations in two unknowns where all the variable coefficients are +1 or −1, the solution is relatively easy to determine, and it should not be necessary to use technology to solve those systems. This essentially accomplishes transferring the information to a paper–pencil setting. Technology was used to make a guided discovery. Included in the results of the investigation is the idea that sometimes paper–pencil work and thinking can accomplish tasks more easily and quickly than technology.

## EXTEND AN IDEA

The lesson dealing with solving two equations in two unknowns could continue in a similar manner but with a different objective.

> "Suppose one equation is $y = x + 4$."
> "The other equation is $2y = -3x + 8$."

Discussion about what would need to be done to determine the point of intersection (if it exists) of two lines should be developed. The students return to the computers with the intent of discovering how to solve the situation. The initial discussion can be used to establish a basis for the thought processes students will use. The discussion should generate comments like:

> "Adding or subtracting gives one equation in two unknowns."

> "We need one equation in one unknown."

> "If we had $3x$ or $-2y$ we could get one equation with only one variable."

(Note the use of "one unknown" and "one variable." Using different terms can aid the understanding of some students.)

"So, we need to multiply."

"But don't forget, multiply both sides of the equation."

"We need to multiply $y = x + 4$ by 3."

"We get $3y = 3x + 12$."

"Now we can add these two equations and get $4y = 20$."

"We can solve that."

A discovery lesson could be initiated with the questions just listed. When the students get to the "We can solve that" position, rather than continuing with the discussion and leading them to conclusions, the students should return to the computers. Procedures would be similar to those used when all coefficients were +1 or −1, only this time, no coefficients will be +1, −1, or 0, but they will all be integers. The students would use two equations from storage and determine what needs to be done to find the point of intersection. Ultimately, they are to determine a process they can use to solve these systems of equations. The result of their time with the technology will lead to conclusions typically generated in a traditional approach to this topic. The process could easily be repeated with situations where the coefficients of the variables are rational numbers.

## CONCEPTUALIZE A SOLUTION

While in the computer laboratory in the previous description of solving two equations in two unknowns, the objective is for students to generalize the situation. After a short period of time, they should be able to tell when to multiply an equation by a constant, what to multiply by, the advantage of working with opposite signs to eliminate a variable, the potential errors when subtracting one equation from another, and when to divide by a constant.

The time required to accomplish this set of discoveries is relatively short, because of using technology as a teaching tool. The time is certainly much less than the amount normally required to cover these topics. More important, the students, because they have discovered these generalizations as opposed to having been told, will:

Gain a deeper understanding of the learned concepts.

Have a greater retention level of the material.

Have a more positive outlook on their mathematical capabilities.

This development of the generalizations has encouraged students to conceptualize a more global picture of solving two equations in two unknowns. Typically, students are taken through the sequence of graphing, intersection, adding equations, subtracting equations, substitution, and multiplying or dividing by constants to allow addition or subtraction of equations. Rather than having each of the traditional steps as separate entities, often not recognized as related subjects by students, a level of understanding that recognizes the connections of the listed topics has been promoted. Not only is instruction time saved at this point, but there is less likelihood that the topics will need to be revisited at some later date. Higher levels of conceptualization and understanding have been achieved during the developmental stages.

In the formative stages of learning a concept, a different method of open discovery can also take place. The following algebra problem (no calculus skills available) assumes the student is familiar with, and has access to, technology. This activity can be done individually or in groups. The solution is quite difficult without the availability of technology.

By dividing through by $a$, the general cubic equation $aX^3 + bX^2 + cX + d = y$ changes to

$$X^3 + AX^2 + BX + C = Y$$

where $A$, $B$, and $C$ are real numbers. When this equation is graphed, one of three situations will appear as shown in Fig. 7.8. There is a relation between $A$ and $B$, the coefficients of $X^2$ and $X$, respectively, that can be used to determine which of the three

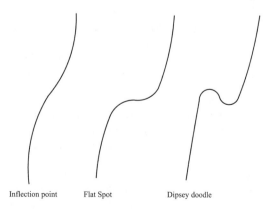

Inflection point     Flat Spot          Dipsey doodle

**Figure 7.8**

curves will appear. Using the available technology, the students would now discover the relation between $A$ and $B$ that would determine which of the three curves is generated.

Students need only the ability to plot curves to solve this problem. Doing the plotting by the typical "T" column chart listing $X$ and the corresponding values for $Y$ could prove extremely difficult. With technology, the degree of difficulty is reduced significantly and the option of working the problem is now opened to a much broader range of students. This reduction of difficulty is related to the elimination of hand computation and the ability to quickly see the graphed result of changed values. With this capability, conjecture alterations can be quickly made, and there is little concern about an increased workload involving tedious computations. Use of technology in this setting does not guarantee a reduction of failure but, given a teacher who poses the task appropriately and encourages students, the results of the lesson should be most encouraging.

As students discover and do mathematics, there are outcomes beyond the actual solution of the problem. Professional organizations, mathematics educators, and current publications consistently say students need to learn how mathematicians:

Think.

Solve problems.

Develop the ability to think.

Expand topics.

Formulate generalizations.

Apply learned skills.

The preceding problem dealing with the relationship between coefficients of variables encourages development of mathematical thinking skills. Mathematical organization and generalization skills are cultivated through the need to develop a pattern of keeping track of the effect of changes in values for $A$ and $B$ in the equation. The problem also shows the advantage of changing only the coefficient of $X^2$, while looking for sets of numbers that will give the three curves. Later, only the coefficient of $X$ would be changed, again working to get sets of the three curves. As the investigation progresses, results are recorded and, ultimately, a pattern is detected. Once a pattern is determined, the student will have "discovered" the solution, done some mathematics and, in the process, learned some procedures a mathematician would use to attack a problem.

Mathematics is often created out of a need for a practical solution to a real problem. Activities can be done in a classroom to stimulate discovery and, simultaneously, provide insights into how new mathematics can be invented. Pose a question, or a problem, or give an example that promotes more questions in the student's mind. For example, use technology to graph each of the following equations on the same axis system and have students generalize what is happening to each successive graph. Before plotting each new equation, formulate a conjecture about what the graph will be. Then graph it.

$$y = \cos(x)$$
$$y = \cos(\cos(x))$$
$$y = \cos(\cos(\cos(x)))$$
$$y = \cos(\cos(\cos(\cos(x))))$$

A multitude of intriguing questions can be generated by such a set of graphs shown in Figs. 7.9 and 7.10. Sample questions would be:

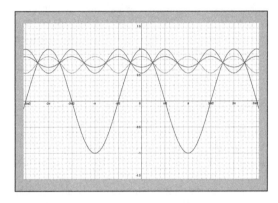

**Figure 7.9**

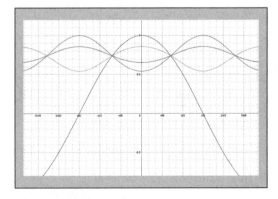

**Figure 7.10**

"How are the first two curves alike?"

"How are the first two curves different?"

"How do the first two curves compare with the second and third curves?"

"What limit is being approached as the number of cosines increases?"

"Does the curve ever flatten out?"

"What if the sine function is used instead of the cosine?" An immediate suspicion would be that the sine would act likes the cosine. Does it?

"What will the other trigonometric functions look like when treated this way?"

After students enter the questioning mode from an example like $y = \cos(\cos(\cos(x)))$, it is easy to extend their curiosity into other mathematical settings.

"What would a function like $f(f(f(f(X))))$ look like when $f(X) = X - 4$?"

"What if $f(X) = X^2 + 4X - 5$ and $g(X) = X^3 - 6X^2 + 7X + 8$ are given functions, and the student wants to know if $f(g(4)) = g(f(4))$?"

Typically, the student is told, either by the teacher or the textbook, that this is not true. That student has been deprived of an opportunity to apply many algebra skills and discover the answer to the question.

Expanding $g(f(4))$ and $f(g(4))$ when $f(X) = X^2 + 4X - 5$ and $g(X) = X^3 - 6X^2 + 7X + 8$ gives 15,506 and 27, respectively. It is now known that $f(g(4))$ does not equal $g(f(4))$. A natural follow-up question would be whether or not $g(f(5))$ and $f(g(5))$ would give values that are equal, further apart, or closer together (54,688 and 391, respectively). Many students, and teachers, would have no idea about the response to this question, but the technology permits substitution of another value (like 5) and determining the results for $g(f(5))$ and $f(g(5))$. Other students might conclude a smaller value is needed and use 1 for $X$, or perhaps 0. Would a decimal give a better approximation of the solution? Should negative values be used for $X$? If the student is willing to investigate, multiple opportunities exist for discovery. Because the technology eliminates most of the laborious tasks involved, most students are more willing to attempt such investigations.

Eventually, the student needs to investigate the general situation of $g(f(X))$ and $f(g(X))$. This can be done algebraically or by graphing. Use of a symbol manipulator capable of handling the manipulations could provide the answer. Looking at the solution graphically can heighten the insight of the situation, because it broadens the generalization. Furthermore, an algebraic question is being answered geometrically and the two topics become related. This is significant because traditionally algebra and geometry are presented as two unrelated topics, contrary to many discussions about the need to integrate mathematics within itself as well as with other fields of study.

## ASK LOADED QUESTIONS

The art of questioning is difficult to develop and yet plays a significant role in how topics are developed. It is easy to ask for the answer to a problem, what the next step would be, and for an explanation of what procedure was used. Upper-level questions are not as easy to ask. Upper-level questions carry with them the expectation that the students use higher-order thinking processes. Upper-level questions should become an integral part of any teacher's style.

Gauss intuitively "discovered" how to sum consecutive counting numbers while in his early school years (Beck, Bleicher, & Crowe, 1969). The teacher assigned Gauss the task of finding the sum of the first 100 consecutive counting numbers. Gauss quickly determined that sum to be 5,050 by using something similar to the following process.

Because there are 100 101s,

$$
\begin{array}{cccccccc}
1 & + & 2 & + & 3 & \cdots & + & 99 & + & 100 \\
100 & + & 99 & + & 98 & \cdots & + & 2 & + & 1 \\
\hline
101 & & 101 & & 101 & & & 101 & & 101
\end{array}
$$

the sum would be $(100)(101)$. But this sum is twice what it should be because each addend was used twice. The sum of the first one hundred consecutive counting numbers is $\frac{(100)(101)}{2}$. In general, the sum of the first $N$ consecutive counting numbers can be found by using $\frac{(N)(N+1)}{2}$, something many students can discover when given enough examples.

An additional topic can be pursued. At first, the connection may not be clear, which increases the opportunity to ask a "loaded" question. The sum of the first $N$ consecutive odd counting numbers can be determined via patterning. In general, the sum of the first $N$ consecutive odd counting numbers is $N^2$.

| Addends | Sum | Squares |
|---|---|---|
| 1 | 1 | $1^2$ |
| 1 + 3 | 4 | $2^2$ |
| 1 + 3 + 5 | 9 | $3^2$ |
| 1 + 3 + 5 + 7 | 16 | $4^2$ |

Beginning with 1, the consecutive counting numbers minus the consecutive odd counting numbers yields the consecutive even counting numbers. The loaded question is, "Is the formula for determining the sum of consecutive even counting numbers $\frac{(N)(N+1)}{2} - N$?" Simplifying or checking with a few numbers shows this is not a true statement. The loaded question that generated an incorrect supposition leads to a need to determine what is wrong.

## LESSONS RESULTING IN STUDENT DISCOVERY

Some students assume many mathematical things to be universally true. Because of this they are, at times, amazed to realize their assumptions have been false. For example, some students are not aware that the commutative property for addition operates in sets other than the counting numbers. A series of questions or problems like the following could help lead to the appropriate conclusions.

$$^-3 + {^+7} = \underline{\hspace{1cm}} \qquad \frac{1}{4} + \frac{2}{3} = \underline{\hspace{1cm}}$$

$$^+7 + {^-3} = \underline{\hspace{1cm}} \qquad \frac{2}{3} + \frac{1}{4} = \underline{\hspace{1cm}}$$

Two words often abundantly used by students are "always" and "never." Discoveries like the one described with the commutative property of addition on different sets of elements can lead them to become more sensitive about when to use those words in the world of mathematics. The discussion can be amplified with problems involving subtraction where commutativity does not generally hold, something that some students assume to be true.

$$^-5 - {^+8} = \underline{\hspace{1cm}}$$

$$^-8 - {^-5} = \underline{\hspace{1cm}}$$

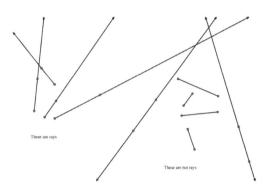

These are rays

These are not rays

**Figure 7.11**

It is important for students to determine what things are, as well as what they are not, if we are to help them avoid arriving at incorrect assumptions, conclusions, thought processes, and generalizations. In geometry, rather than defining a ray, examples could be given that show a ray and other figures classified as not being rays. After seeing Fig. 7.11, the student is asked to give an elaboration on what a ray is and what a ray is not. This leads to a broader understanding, a better feeling for the definition, and a generalization of the concept of a ray. The process may take a little longer, particularly at first. The student is actively involved in the learning situation and is much more likely to remember and understand because of the internalized thought processes involved. Certainly, if the student opts to wait, knowing that the teacher will eventually summarize what has occurred, or tell the generalization, the value of the lesson is significantly decreased. Remember, the goal is to develop student conceptual understanding as well as to enhance self-learning abilities. Memorization is not the answer.

## LABORATORY APPROACH

The laboratory approach can be an activity-based situation (either open-ended or guided, depending on class objectives) in which the students discover a concept, solve a problem, or develop a generalization. People shaking hands can lead to several discoveries for students. A number of people are in a room and each person shakes hands with every other person in the room. When A shakes with B that is also considered to be B shaking with A. How many handshakes are needed if there are eight people in the room?

One way to solve the problem is to allow the students to act out the problem. They may opt to begin with two students. Each student would shake hands. They repeat the process with three students, then four, and so on, recording each total number of handshakes, until a generalization is made. Students should determine that each Nth person will result in $N - 1$ more handshakes than the last sum.

An interesting revelation generally occurs when a new student is added. The students realize that there is no need to have the already standing students all shake hands again. The standing students need only shake hands with the new student. Four students create a total of 6 handshakes, and 5 students create a total of 10 handshakes. There is no need for the first 4 to reshake when the fifth student joins the group because those original 4 will still yield a total of 6 handshakes. The fifth person shaking hands with each of the original 4 will add four more handshakes to the total of 6, giving a grand total of 10 handshakes. Many student groups will go through several iterations of the process before this a discovery is made. The key here is that discovery is made by the students actively participating in their own learning.

Listing the derived information from the different groups in tabular form sometimes helps students see the "$N - 1$" pattern. The idea can be extended to convex polygons, because the results are the same if the number of line segments joining the vertices is counted. That is, 3 vertices use 3 segments for all possible joinings, 4 vertices use 6 segments, 5 vertices need 10 segments to make all possible connections, and so on.

With technology, a lesson involving the impact of changing $A$, a real number, in $y = \sin(Ax)$ can lead to an interesting problem and discovery.

Graph $y = \sin(1x)$ and $y = \sin(2x)$ as shown in Fig. 7.12.

Discuss similarities and differences between the equations and the graphs.

Add the graph $y = \sin(3x)$ to the figure as shown in Fig. 7.12.

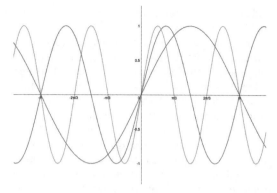

**Figure 7.12**

Discuss similarities and differences between the equations and the graphs.

Continue until students conclude that as $A$ increases, the curve becomes more condensed, the period shortens, there are more cycles than in the original span, and so on. Ask what will happen if $y = \sin(63x)$ is graphed. Typically, the students will say the graph would result in a "solid" coloring or they will indicate with their hands that the curve goes up and down very close together. The actual graph on a computer or graphing calculator might not show what the students expect, as seen in Fig. 7.13.

When the function $y = \sin(63x)$ does not behave as anticipated, an opportunity for investigation and discovery is created. The graph is not what was expected; the pattern does not seem to work. Most students will examine their thinking, because of the assumption that the computer would not make a mistake. Students assume something is wrong with the generalization they developed. This allows a discussion to ensue about the value of using one's inherent capabilities and critical-thinking skills,

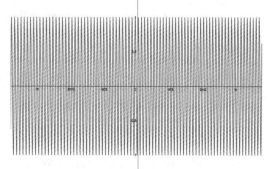

**Figure 7.13**

rather than blindly assuming the computer is always right.

With this discussion, a common objection to the use of technology in the classroom is refuted. Individuals who object to the use of calculators or computers in a mathematics class often cite that technology hampers learning "real" mathematics. Another argument is that the technology causes students to lose their ability to think. Such is not the case, particularly when questions like graphing $y = \sin(63x)$ are used. The intent is to convince the student of the value of questioning how reasonable an answer is and whether it is logical in light of the situation presented. One final intended use of such questions is to have students determine that there is virtue in using one's head to solve problems and that the response generated by technological assistance should not be accepted without thought.

## INTERESTING MATERIALS

Often, situations presented to students do not captivate their attention, because of the problem setting. Typical descriptions involve redecorating a room, working with a budget, and opening a checking account. Some adult situations, like buying a car, might have more appeal for the students. There is a need to ask more questions that have student appeal and develop problems around those ideas. Rather than dealing with redecorating the room, plan a skateboard ramp or compare the cost of in-line skates. To entice student interest, the problems posed for students should come from their view of the world rather than what we, as adults, think they might be interested in. We cannot continue to use the same old problems that have always been given to students. It is our obligation as teachers to diligently capture and maintain student interest by using mathematics as a tool to answer questions that occur in their world!

What is the range of a remote-control car? Is the range altered by the type of battery used, the age of the battery (what would you say to a student who used a dead battery and said the car had no range?), temperature conditions, or surrounding interference sources? The students who are familiar with using remote-control cars can inform the others about the general terminology. In some instances, the students doing the explaining may be taking a leadership role for the first time. Discussions such as these provide opportunities to integrate topics from other classes into the mathematics curriculum. Batteries are discussed in many elementary school science classes, for example.

## CAPITALIZE ON STUDENT RESPONSES

As lessons are presented, groups can discover why a particular situation seems to occur. In the early grades, students are told to reduce fractions. "Reduce" is not the best term to describe the situation, which can easily be shown by

$$\frac{4}{8} = \frac{2}{4}$$

"Simplify" is sometimes used rather than "reduce" when discussing fractions. That too can have some humorous outcomes. The fraction $\frac{16}{64}$ can be simplified by crossing out the two 6s. In this case, the result is correct because $\frac{16}{64} = \frac{1}{4}$. Situations such as these are called "howlers" and can provide discovery potential for some students. Use crossing out the two 6s to further the learning by asking the students to find other howlers. It is worth noting that while doing this investigation, students also practice the skill of developing equivalent fractions and all of the associated subskills that have been developed at various points earlier in the curriculum. Asking for a generalization about howlers can provide extension opportunities for more capable or interested students.

---

### EXERCISES 7.5

1. Research howlers. Provide at least two more examples similar to $\frac{16}{64}$.

2. Generalize your discussion of howlers from Exercise 1.

---

A third expression used in discussions about fractions is "divide out common factors." This would eliminate the first two error examples because of the more descriptive terminology and, at the same time, establish a background for the student's algebraic work. It can also help eliminate future errors. Some algebra students will simplify $\frac{x+4}{x}$ to $\frac{1+4}{1}$ or 5 by dividing out the $X$s. We explain that the $X$s are not common factors and cannot be divided out. If the terminology had been different earlier in the student's career, perhaps an error could have been avoided. A rebuttal to this idea is that there is a limit to the amount of verbiage a younger student can tolerate without confusion, a position that should be considered. This discussion does provide an example of how we can create problems for some students within a curriculum. A student entering algebra settings with a "reduce" mentality for fractions could be destined for difficulties in conceptualizing various aspects of the subject.

---

### EXERCISE 7.6

1. Another example similar to the development just done for "reduce" can be made for the expression, "Give me a number larger than 1." What would be encountered as this question is investigated? How could the pitfalls be avoided? Extended?

---

Capitalizing on errors can offer discoveries in seemingly unrelated areas. It is all too common for students to "add" two fractions by adding the numerators and adding the denominators so that $\frac{2}{3} + \frac{5}{9} = \frac{7}{12}$ (Spano, 1985). There are two approaches to handling this situation—correct the student, or discuss "twiddle." When appropriate, comment that the student did not add the fractions, but instead twiddled them. Given two fractions, $\frac{A}{B}$ and $\frac{C}{D}$, where $B$ and $D$ are nonzero, $\frac{A}{B} \oplus \frac{C}{D} = \frac{A+C}{B+D}$ defines twiddle.

Is twiddle closed?

Does twiddle commute?

$$\frac{A}{B} \oplus \frac{C}{D} = \frac{A+C}{B+D} \quad \text{dfn. twiddle}$$

$$= \frac{C+A}{D+B} \quad \text{comm. + on reals}$$

$$= \frac{C}{D} \oplus \frac{A}{B} \quad \text{dfn. twiddle}$$

Is there an identity element for twiddle?

Is there an additive inverse for twiddle?

Does twiddle associate? Initially the suspicion would be that twiddle is associative.

$$\left(\frac{2}{3} \oplus \frac{4}{5}\right) \oplus \frac{7}{9} = ? = \frac{2}{3} \oplus \left(\frac{4}{5} \oplus \frac{7}{9}\right)$$

$$\frac{6}{8} \oplus \frac{7}{9} = ? = \frac{2}{3} \oplus \frac{11}{14}$$

$$\frac{13}{17} = ? = \frac{13}{17}$$

This assumption appears naturally because students have rarely, if ever, seen a situation in which the associative property for some operation on some set has not held true. It appears as if twiddle associates. If the students first divide out all common factors in fractions, is twiddle still associative?

$$\left(\frac{2}{3} \oplus \frac{4}{5}\right) \oplus \frac{7}{9} = ? = \frac{2}{3} \oplus \left(\frac{4}{5} \oplus \frac{7}{9}\right)$$

$$\frac{6}{8} \oplus \frac{7}{9} = ? = \frac{2}{3} \oplus \frac{11}{14}$$

$$\frac{3}{4} \oplus \frac{7}{9} = ? = \frac{2}{3} \oplus \frac{11}{14}$$

$$\frac{10}{13} = ? = \frac{13}{17}$$

In this case, twiddle will not associate. Sometimes twiddle associates and sometimes it does not. It must be agreed that common factors will not be divided out if twiddle is to associate.

Twiddle appears to be a random, probably useless development, but is it? What is the general procedure for finding a fraction between two given fractions? Will twiddle accomplish that task? What if one of the fractions being twiddled is negative—will twiddle provide a fraction between two fractions? Can an impossible situation be generated? What if a negative fraction and a positive fraction are twiddled and the negative sign is written with the denominator?

---

### EXERCISES 7.7

1. Can twiddle be an arithmetic mean? ($B = D$ in the original definition.)
2. Can twiddle be a harmonic mean? ($A = C$ in the original definition.)

---

Are there any practical applications of twiddle? Suppose a ball player got two hits in five attempts in one game and was three for four in the next game. If that player's average is computed for those two games, the sum of the hits is divided by the sum of the attempts—twiddle! This example could provide an opportunity to expand on prior discussions about differences between fractions and ratios and their respective impacts on being used with various operations.

When is a half a half? It is not uncommon for young children to confuse half with two pieces. They will tear a piece of paper into two pieces and call one of the two a half, even if the two pieces are not the same size. As maturation occurs, that seems silly. However, many adults will break something into two pieces and ask another if their preference is for the "big half" or the "little half," a contradiction in terms, and an amplification of the incorrect conceptualization.

Ask students to fold a rectangular piece of paper in half and most of them will fold it so the fold line is parallel to the shorter of two sides. A few might fold it so the fold line is parallel to the longer side. In either case, discussion usually leads to an agreement that a paper is folded in half if the edges match. Rarely will anyone fold the paper along one of the major diagonals. Even if someone does happen to fold along the diagonal, the discussion about the edges lining up discourages that individual and raises doubts. Extending the discussion to cutting along the diagonal and rotating one of the pieces will convince most people that the paper has been folded in half, and the edges match under these conditions. The paper has been folded into two equal pieces and one of those two equal pieces represents a half. Subliminal groundwork has been laid for investigation of diagonals of rectangles in geometry.

Are the three folds discussed the only ways a rectangular piece of paper can be folded in half? Measuring down parallel sides an equal distance from diagonally opposite corners and joining those marks will give two congruent trapezoids. This divides the paper in half also. Students proving that these trapezoids are halves will employ some algebra skills in a geometric setting. It could be established that the fold passes through the center of the paper by folding the diagonals into a sheet of paper to locate the paper's center. Did you think of that? This is an example of open-ended questioning and a problem having more than one correct answer.

If the stipulation that a fold be made in the rectangular paper is removed, can other halves be created? An "S" curve passing through the center, made out of two semicircles of the appropriate radii and centers, should work.

Are there other curves? Are there any limitations? Can halves be established without going through the center?

The extensions of the original "fold the paper in half" idea involved several mathematical concepts: area of rectangles, triangles, and trapezoids to establish congruence, intuition, hypotheses, induction, rotation, axis of symmetry, and algebra. Responses to questions like those asked assist students in building a broader concept of ways of making the folds. The replies also enhance flexible thought patterns. Investigation of these activities might lead to some discoveries while raising student curiosity level.

## TRY THIS IN YOUR CLASSROOM

*NCTM Standards 2000*: Problem solving, communication, reasoning, connections, number relationships, estimation, patterns, and algebra

*Materials*: graphing calculator or software

"What is the largest number that can be written using 3 digits?" is a classic question found in the world of mathematics. Often, the answer is given as 999. Eventually someone will say $99^9$ or $9^{99}$. Generally, it is quickly agreed that either $99^9$ or $9^{99}$ is larger than 999, but which of the two is the larger?

$99^9 = $ _____

$9^{99} = $ _____

You know the order of operations to be:

| Please | (Parentheses) |
|--------|---------------|
| Excuse | (Exponents) |
| My | (Multiply) |
| Dear | (Divide) |
| Aunt | (Add) |
| Sally | (Subtract). |

There is another operation involving exponents that is not well known, called taking a power to a power, and the answer can get really big.

Consider $2^{3^4}$. There are two ways this problem can be done:

$(2^3)^4$ gives an answer of _____

Describe which part was done first to get this answer.

$2^{(3^4)}$ gives an answer of _____

Describe which part was done first to get this answer.

Enter 2^3^4 on your calculator and press ENTER, EXE, or = . What is the result? Describe which part was done first to get this answer.

In this type of problem, parentheses are necessary in order to get the desired response, which is $2^{(3^4)}$.

Enter 9^(9^9) and press ENTER, EXE, or = . What is the result?

You have encountered a situation where your calculator is unable to provide you with a response, because the answer is huge. Mathematicians encounter this type of dilemma frequently. Generally, a mathematician will look for patterns by working a similar problem with smaller numbers. A mathematician might approach the situation by doing the following on the calculator:

22^2 = _____
2^22 = _____
2^(2^2) = _____
33^3 = _____
3^33 = _____
3^(3^3) = _____
44^4 = _____
4^44 = _____
4^(4^4) = _____

Having done these problems, the mathematician would begin looking for patterns by comparing similar situations. A conclusion might be that 22^2 is 3 digits long; 33^3 is 5 digits long and 44^4 is 7 digits long, so the size of the answer seems to be increasing 2 digits at a time as the next digit is considered. Typically the mathematician would check a few more problems like that to see if the conjecture is correct. How do you know if the answers are continuing to increase 2 digits at a time?

Develop a conjecture for 2^(2^2), 3^(3^3), and 4^(4^4).

Since most calculators will not do 4^(4^4), you have to conclude that it is pretty big. In fact it is about 175 digits long, so you now see that the power to a power grows very rapidly.

Even though we cannot see the answer for 4^(4^4), an interesting question can be asked. What is the ones digit of the answer when 4^(4^4) is calculated? The question seems impossible, but it is not really that hard.

The base of 4^(4^4) is 4, so 4 is definitely a factor 4^4 times. Therefore, all factors are even. Will the last digit of 4^(4^4) be even or odd?

The ones digit has to be 0, 1, 2, 3, 4, 5, 6, 7, 8, or 9. Why?

Could the last digit be zero? Why or why not?

You should now know that the options available for the ones digit of $4^{4^4}$ is either 2, 4, 6, or 8, but which one? Patterning is a useful tool for determining the rest of the answer:

4^1 = 4
4^2 = 16
4^3 = 64
4^4 = 256

It appears as if the odd powers of 4 end in 4 and the even powers end in 6. Since 4^4 is the power, the ones digit must be _____.

## CONCLUSION

Some examples of how discovery can be used in a classroom have been shown. The thrill of teaching discovery is sometimes difficult to transmit to students, because of the necessary emotion, feeling, and conviction. This can be remedied: Do some mathematics. Take a graphing calculator or software and play "what if." The discoveries and realizations are amazing. Multitudes of things will be revealed. Learn to look for patterns and generalizations. Expect the unexpected! Discovery is a key to enthusiasm in the student as well as the teacher. Challenge your students and be amazed at what they produce.

### STICKY QUESTIONS

1. Two hundred logs are stacked. There are 20 logs in the bottom row, 19 on top of those, and so forth. How many rows are there? How many logs are in the top row? Devise a plan for explaining this solution to students.

2. At carnivals, county fairs, and such, a common game involves tossing a coin onto a large table subdivided into congruent squares. If the coin lands entirely within the boundaries of one of the small squares, the player wins. Otherwise, the player loses the coin tossed. Suppose the small squares are 25 mm on

a side (disregard the width of the segment). Find the probability that the player will win if the coin has a 5 mm radius. What if the coin has a 10 mm radius? How are the two probabilities related? Why?

3. In Problem 2, the coin can touch four segments by landing on a corner. It could touch one segment by being tangent to it. Describe a setting when the coin would touch two segments. Describe a setting in which the coin would touch three segments.

4. Nine playing cards from the same deck are placed so they form a rectangle. Five are placed side by side hot-dog fashion. Four are placed beneath them in a hamburg manner as seen in Fig. 7.14. The area of the rectangle is 180 square inches. What is the perimeter of the large rectangle?

5. Find the equation of a line parallel to $x + y = 4$ and 8 units from the line. (Be careful.)

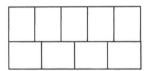

**Figure 7.14**

1. A camel merchant willed his 17 camels to his three sons. In the merchant's will, the camels were to be divided among them as follows:

   The eldest son was to receive half of the camels

   The middle son was to receive a third of the camels

   The youngest son was to receive a ninth of the camels.

   The executor of the merchant's estate was perplexed. Finally, he devised a method for dividing the camels without having to slaughter any of the animals. How many camels did each son receive? Explain his solution.

**Check out the website for the solution.**

2. Suppose the NCAA decided to have a single elimination tournament involving all Division 1A teams at the end of the basketball season. If there are 303 Division 1A teams, how many games will be played before a national champion is declared?

**Check out the website for the solution.**

# Proof

**8**

"Mathematics does not grow through a monotonous increase of the number of indubitably established theorems but through the incessant improvement of guesses by speculation and criticism, by the logic of proofs and refutations" (Lakatos, 1976, p. 5). We know there is a need to have proofs in the study of mathematics. Without them, we may arrive at incorrect conclusions. In geometry, it could be conjectured that Side, Side, Angle could be used to prove two triangles congruent. Initial considerations might generate the impression that this is a reasonable assumption, particularly if several other side and angle (ASA, SAS, etc.) combinations have been investigated and shown to be true. Figure 8.1 shows a construction that can be used to explain how two different triangles can be generated given sides AB and AC and angle BCA. Different locations of segment AB yield different lengths for side BC, contradicting congruency. The approach is flawed because the question becomes, which side AB is the one needed?

The Standards (NCTM, 1989) suggest a change in the role of proof in our mathematics curriculum. The call is for a decrease in attention given to Euclidean geometry as an axiomatic system and two-column proofs. At the same time, it is recommended that short sequences of theorems be developed and that deductive arguments be expressed orally and in paragraph or sentence form. Suppose the desire is to prove the base angles of an isosceles triangle are congruent using the typical two-column proof

as well as paragraph form. In Fig. 8.2 you are given triangle DEF with DE $\cong$ DF. Prove $\angle$DEF $\cong$ $\angle$DFE.

| | |
|---|---|
| DEF is a triangle | Given |
| DE $\cong$ DF | Given |
| $\angle$DG $\perp$ EF | Construction |
| $\Delta$DGF = rt.$\angle$ | Dfn.$\perp$ lines |
| $\Delta$DGF is rt. | Dfn. rt. $\Delta$ |
| $\angle$DGE = rt. $\angle$ | Dfn.$\perp$lines |
| $\Delta$DGE is rt. | Dfn. rt. $\Delta$ |
| $\angle$DGE $\cong$ $\angle$DGF | Trans. property of = |
| DG $\cong$ DG | Reflx. property of = |
| $\Delta$DGE $\cong$ DGF | Hypot., leg of rt. $\Delta$ |
| $\angle$DEF $\cong$ $\angle$DFE | Dfn. $\cong$ |

Other traditional two-column methods that could be used to arrive at $\angle$DEF $\cong$ $\angle$DFE include bisecting angle EDF or locating the midpoint of side EF. Another less common method can be used in the form of a paragraph proof:

You are given triangle DEF with sides DE and DF congruent. You are to prove angle DEF congruent to angle DFE. Construct triangle DEF. Imagine lifting the triangle, flipping it, and placing it back on top of itself so DE is on top of DF and DF is on top of DE. You now have triangle DEF on top of triangle DFE, with all points matching. This shows DE congruent to DF and DF congruent to DE. EF is congruent to itself. The two triangles are congruent by Side, Side, Side. This can be done via technology with software capable of dealing with transformations.

The change in emphasis on proof is based largely on information about learning patterns of students. Mathematical proof requires an understanding of definitions and logic, but also depends on insight into why and how they work and connect. This is a level of sophistication not available to many younger students. Asking them to complete formal proofs might exceed their developmental capabilities. Before we can expect students to effectively prove things, we must help them become independent thinkers, understanding the need for precision of language, definition, and expression.

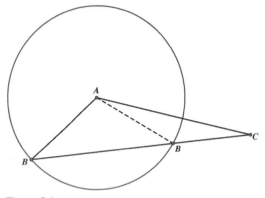

**Figure 8.1**

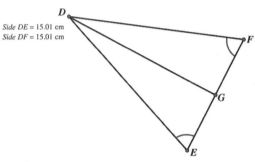

Side DE = 15.01 cm
Side DF = 15.01 cm

**Figure 8.2**

That is more work for us as teachers, but it will help students better appreciate the beauty of mathematics and the power of proof.

## WHAT IS PROOF?

Proof convinces one that a discourse and its associated conclusion are factual. Proven things could be replicated and do not contradict something else known to be true. Depending on the setting, the dialogue takes on a variety of approaches. A young child, talking with another, may attest to the proof of something being true because "someone said so." Here, the child yields to authority. Eventually, as the youngster gets a little older, the route to proof might turn to a less acceptable process: something like saying, "I am tougher than you are and will beat you up to prove it." The associated fisticuffs, although undesirable, do show an advancement in the development of proof. Students see lawyers convincing, beyond a reasonable doubt, that the position of their client should prevail in court—a proof of sorts.

Eventually the need for more exactness in proof develops. An immediate question becomes how to express the proof. The classic algebraic two-column demonstration is certainly one method. In middle-grade mathematics, pre-algebra, and algebra courses, the two-column proof does not appear very often. A structured approach to establishing the validity of an argument follows a clearly established sequence of steps leading to a result that is checked to assure the correctness of the answer. The paragraph proof, where the development of convincing evidence is put into words, can be the forte of some students. Really, the manner used for the proof is not critical. What is most important is the fact that a coherent, logically correct discussion is presented.

## CONVINCING STUDENTS PROOF IS NEEDED

The discussion involving Fig. 8.1 is a beginning point to establish the need for proof. Without investigation and verification or denial of ideas, we have no way of determining what is and is not acceptable thinking. Much of school mathematics is delivered in a manner that implies it was chipped in stone and handed down by some mathematical genius. We know that is not the case. We know mathematics is a creation of the human mind as attempts are made to describe, expand, and order our universe. The question is, how do we convince students of the need for proof?

One way would be to create situations that appear to be true but, in reality, are not. Lead the students to make false conjectures and then help them see the error of their ways. An example can come from the following pair of equations that are to be solved for the point of intersection. This example is particularly well placed when solution by substitution is being covered. The equations are:

(1)  $y - 3x = 10$

and

(2)  $x = \dfrac{(y+2)}{3}$

Substituting for $x$ in (1), $y - \dfrac{3(y+2)}{3} = 10$ or $y - y - 2 = 10$, which yields that $-2 = 10$.

Ridiculous! But, what went wrong? There is a need for further investigation in order to determine the error. Typically the first approach will be to redo the arithmetic. That provides no clue. A lesson

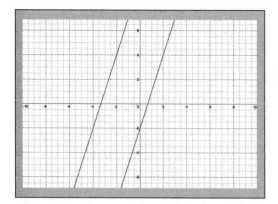

**Figure 8.3**

from problem solving where alternate avenues were suggested as a means of strengthening skills will be helpful. One replacement route would be to graph these two equations. Figure 8.3 shows that the lines are parallel, providing insight into why such a crazy response was generated with substitution. This is the beginning of a need for proof.

A classic problem involves asking a typically sized class if they think two people in the group will share a birthday (both month and day of month). The usual response is that such an event is highly unlikely. Common logic says it normally would take a large group before there would be at least one matching month and day. That idea can be stimulated through questions similar to those asked in the next paragraph.

Suppose each of 30 people knew the day of the week on which they were born. How many people would need to report their birthday before there would be a match? The first two could have both been born on Monday and thus match. However, that may not occur. Consider the worst-case scenario. Person 1 is born on Sunday, 2 on Monday, 3 on Tuesday, 4 on Wednesday, 5 on Thursday, 6 on Friday, and 7 on Saturday. Now what? The eighth person will match someone, unless there are more days in the week than we know of. That idea can be extended to consider a match for the month of the year, or even for which of the 52 weeks of the year.

Now look at the initial question—the probability of getting a match on month and day of the month in a group of 30. Logic seems to dictate that a very large number of people would be needed to have any level of assurance of a match and, certainly, it would appear to be highly unlikely in a group of 30 people. Use 365 for the number of days in a year. The month and day of birth for the first person is announced. There are then 364 days left that do not match. If a second person enters consideration, there would be 363 days left that would not match. The probability of a third person not matching means that this third person has 363 options left. At this stage of development, $\frac{(365)(364)(363)}{365^3}$ expresses the probability of having no match, which in this case happens to be 0.9917958. If 10 people are considered, the probability is 0.8830518 that none of their birth dates will be the same, and for 20, the probability is 0.5885616. Extending to 23 people, the probability is 0.4927027 that no two people will have a matching birthday. Another way of saying this is there is a 0.5072973 probability that, in a group of 23 people, at least two of them will share a birthday (only in terms of day of the month and the month itself).

Preposterous! That just does not seem right! In a group of 23 people, there is a fifty-fifty chance that two of them will share a birthday. Do the activity with a group and see what happens. Even if the group used does not have a match, the question still lingers for many, "How or why?" The question is generated even more quickly and emphatically if there are two people with the same birthday in the group of 30. When we were working on this part of the book, David Rock, one of the authors, asked some of his middle schoolers the problem. They started working on this problem, as did some of the advanced mathematics students in another class. They wanted to know how such a seemingly impossible answer could happen. They wanted to prove why it was right or wrong. The "right" environment was created, as was the need for a proof.

From previous discussions, Rachelle Yankelevitz, one of David's eighth-graders, knew that the probability of two people *not* having the same birthday out of only two people would be $\frac{365!}{(363!)365^2} = 0.9973$ (note this is a different expression of the earlier stated approach). Similarly, the probability of 3 people not having the same birthday is $\frac{365!}{(362!)365^3} = 0.9918$. Rachelle and her classmates developed a general formula for the probability of not having the same birthday $\frac{365!}{((362-n)!)(365^n)}$ where $n$ is the number of people. This would give the probability of $n$ people not having the same birthday. The difficulty was using a calculator to figure the probability of two people having the same birthday out of 23 people. Their calculators could not handle 365! Rachelle concluded that because she could calculate the probability with three people, the rest was quite trivial. To find four, you would multiply the result of 3 by 362 and divide by 365, which can be done on most calculators. Rachelle's reasoning is as follows:

$$\frac{365!}{(363!)(365^2)} = \frac{365 \times 364 \times 363 \times 362 \times 361 \ldots}{363 \times 362 \times 361 \times \ldots \times 3 \times 2 \times 1 \times 365 \times 365}$$

$$= \frac{365 \times 364}{365 \times 365}$$

$$= 0.9973$$

For three people,

$$\frac{365!}{(362!)(365^3)} = \frac{365 \times 364 \times 363 \times 362 \times 361 \ldots}{362 \times 361 \times \ldots \times 3 \times 2 \times 1 \times 365 \times 365 \times 365}$$

$$= \frac{365 \times 364 \times 363}{365 \times 365 \times 365}$$

$$= 0.9918$$

For four people,

$$= 0.9918 \times \frac{362}{365} = 0.9836$$

For five people,

$$= 0.9836 \times \frac{361}{365} = 0.9728$$

Rachelle realized her approach was effective but still tedious. Next, the class decided to use a spreadsheet to speed up the process. The first column became $n$ or the number of people. Using Rachelle's method for two people, the class used the spreadsheet to make the second column the probability of not having the same birthday and the third column the probability of having the same birthday. Figure 8.4 shows the class results.

| Number of people | Probability of 2 with different birthdays | Probability of 2 with same birthday |
|---|---|---|
| 2 | 0.9973 | 0.0027 |
| 3 | 0.9918 | 0.0082 |
| 4 | 0.9836 | 0.0164 |
| 5 | 0.9729 | 0.0271 |
| 6 | 0.9595 | 0.0405 |
| 7 | 0.9438 | 0.0562 |
| 8 | 0.9257 | 0.0743 |
| 9 | 0.9054 | 0.0946 |
| 10 | 0.8831 | 0.1169 |
| • | • | • |
| • | • | • |
| • | • | • |
| 20 | 0.5886 | 0.4114 |
| 21 | 0.5563 | 0.4437 |
| 22 | 0.5243 | 0.4757 |
| 23 | 0.4927 | 0.5073 |
| 24 | 0.4617 | 0.5383 |
| 25 | 0.4313 | 0.5687 |
| • | • | • |
| • | • | • |
| • | • | • |
| 30 | 0.2937 | 0.7063 |
| 40 | 0.1088 | 0.8912 |
| 50 | 0.0342 | 0.9658 |
| 60 | 0.0058 | 0.9942 |

Figure 8.4

Sometimes, a situation appears to prove something is true. The following description is of a scheme that is illegal, but it does show the need for an explanation (proof). A financial advisor sent out 64,000 letters to potential clients. Of those letters, 32,000 said the value of a stock would rise over a given period. The content of the other 32,000 letters said the value of that same stock would not rise (implying it would stay the same or fall) over the same period of time.

After a time, a second round of letters was sent, but only to individuals who had received an original letter containing a prediction that had been correct. The same stock, or a different one, could have been used in the second letter. The contents of the letter would be the same as the first one, with the possible exception of different stock. This time, of the letters sent, 16,000 predicted the stock would rise in value and 16,000 stated it would not. At the end of this second period of prediction, a quarter of the original 64,000 people, or 16,000, had received two letters with correct predictions. The scenario was repeated two more times and the original group of 64,000 was reduced to 4,000 individuals, each of whom had received four letters correctly predicting the movement of the stock market.

A fifth letter was sent, but this one did not contain a prognostication. Instead, it carried a simple explanation and reminder that the correct movement of the stock market had been demonstrated in the last four letters. That succession of correct forecasts "proved" to the individual that a successful system for foretelling the path stocks take was available. This letter carefully explained that the service would be made available only to a select few individuals for a modest annual fee. The implication was that no matter what amount was charged for the service, the client would easily recoup the expenses from profits.

Suppose, for the sake of this discussion, the letter, including letterhead, envelope, software, hardware, and postage required to produce it, was sent for $0.50. The payment for the producer's time (not jail time here, but the time spent bringing this scheme to fruition) will be computed later. The 128,000 (64,000 + 32,000 + 16,000 + 8,000 + 4,000) letters sent generated an expense of $64,000. Suppose each potential client was charged an annual fee of $500 for the services. If each of the 4000 individuals joined, $2,000,000 was generated over a short period of time. Delete the $64,000 cost and the "profit" is still rather significant. Even if only half of the potential clients signed up, after taking out the costs, the profit was close to $900,000. Only 128 people paying $500 cover the expenses. Anything above that is profit. Do you think there would be more than 128 takers on a scheme like this? Do you see why it is illegal? If you were to do it, you would be classified as doing business with the intent of defrauding people. This is one of the classic con games that has been used on unsuspecting victims who are duped into believing there are "foolproof" methods by which to get rich quick. Do you also see where "proof" can be a deceptive concept?

mind-over-matter routine sounds much more glamorous, and once again opens the door to opportunity for defrauding individuals. Seeing is not always believing, and if something seems too good to be true, it probably is. Investigation will yield a "proof."

The need for further investigation raises a significant point. Students need to be convinced of the need for proof, as opposed to accepting things because they "look" a certain way. Suppose a triangle and its three medians are constructed in a dynamic geometry program. As the triangle is moved, the medians appear to be concurrent. The demonstration convinces all but the most skeptical students that the conjecture is true. At some point, the students need to see the need to do a formal proof of this theorem. These individuals who ask for more than a visual verification are candidates to become the future mathematicians, scientists, and engineers.

## EXERCISES 8.2

1. Use a dynamic geometry program to create a setting like the medians of a triangle discussed in the chapter. Move the figure to confirm, visually, that an invariant has been created.
2. Graphing circles centered at (2, –5) and (5, –2), each with a radius of 2, and the line $y = -x$ yields a figure in which the line appears tangent to the circles. Zooming shows that is not the case. Create a similar environment using symbolic manipulating, function-plotting software.

## EXERCISE 8.1

1. 36 in. = 1 yd; 9 in. = 0.25 yd (divide both sides by 4); $\sqrt{9}$ in. = $\sqrt{0.25}$ yd; 3 in. = 0.5 yd (positive square root of both sides). Is it true that 3 inches equals a half a yard? What is wrong with this "proof"?

"Seeing is believing" is often accepted as proof. Paulos (1988) described firewalking on a bed of hot coals. When an individual performs this feat (pun intended), the discussion centers on the ability to control the mind and exclude the associated pain that should go with walking on hot coals. The walk is observed and spectators are convinced that the described process of mind over matter works, because of what they have seen. The event is based on a little-known fact that dehydrated wood has an extremely low heat content and is a very poor conductor of heat. A person walking quickly across the coals feels little of the apparent heat. Of course, the

## PROOFS IN THE HISTORY OF MATHEMATICS

Mathematics history grows on proofs. Singling out only a few examples here cannot do justice to all the developments. Perhaps that is one reason why the study of the history of mathematics and inserting it throughout the curriculum is encouraged.

James Abram Garfield, 26th President of the United States, is credited by some with one of the many proofs of the Pythagorean theorem. Figure 8.5 shows a sketch he used to develop his proof. Garfield created right triangle ABC. He duplicated it and had AC and B'C' both perpendicular to

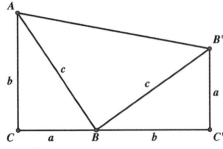

**Figure 8.5**

segment CC′, creating a trapezoid. He used the idea that the whole is the sum of the parts and expressed the area of the trapezoid in terms of the three triangles. He also used the formula for the area of a trapezoid to establish the equation:

$$\frac{ab}{2} + \frac{ab}{2} + \frac{c^2}{2} = \frac{(a+b)(a+b)}{2}$$

$$ab + \frac{c^2}{2} = \frac{(a+b)(a+b)}{2}$$

$$2ab + c^2 = (a+b)(a+b)$$

$$2ab + c^2 = a^2 + 2ab + b^2$$

$$c^2 = a^2 + b^2$$

This clever approach to "proving" the Pythagorean theorem has the added advantage of providing an avenue to connect the study of mathematics to social science.

**EXERCISES 8.3**

1. Create a lesson for an algebra class that includes a historical proof.
2. Create a lesson for a geometry class that includes a historical proof.

**Additional exercises can be found on the website.**

## PROOFS IN DIFFERENT ENVIRONMENTS

Algebra students are accustomed to using their basic skills to do problems. They need to be convinced that there may be acceptable alternative solutions to a problem. A typical algebra textbook problem could be: "I spend $\frac{1}{3}$ of my monthly income on housing, $\frac{1}{3}$ on transportation, $\frac{1}{4}$ on food, and have $100 left. How much do I make?" The implied so-

lution would be something like (where $M$ represents the income):

$$\frac{M}{3} + \frac{M}{3} + \frac{M}{4} = M - \$100$$

Simplifying yields

$$\frac{11M}{12} = M - \$100 \text{ and } M = \$1200.$$

There is another way to solve this problem that may be just as, if not more, effective.

Figure 8.6 depicts an approach devised by a student (Leiva, 1994). The initial rectangle is drawn and then divided into thirds with parallel line segments appropriately placed. One of the thirds represents the housing expenses. A second third shows the automotive costs. The remaining third is too much to stand for food, which is a fourth of the budget, but if that remaining little rectangle is divided into fourths with parallel line segments perpendicular to the "thirds" segments, a fourth could be indicated. This procedure leaves one small region to portray the remaining $100 in the budget. There are twelve of those small regions in the rectangle, and therefore the total income must be 12 ($100) or $1200. This shows another way to arrive at the answer. It represents a geometric solution of the situation and could be very helpful for student visualization, if the students are in formative stages of developing proof skills.

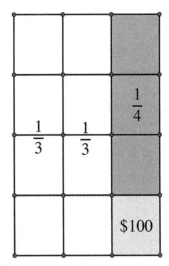

**Figure 8.6**

The classic trigonometry class deals with a variety of proofs of identities. Typically, the proof of something like

$$\frac{\sin A + \tan A}{1 + \cos A} = \tan A$$

would be done

$$\frac{\sin A + \dfrac{\sin A}{\cos A}}{1 + \cos A} = \tan A.$$

Simplifying the numerator gives

$$\frac{\dfrac{(\sin A)(\cos A) + \sin A}{\cos A}}{1 + \cos A} = \tan A.$$

Simplifying the left side gives

$$\frac{(\sin A)(\cos A) + \sin A}{(\cos A)(1 + \cos A)} = \tan A.$$

Factoring the numerator yields

$$\frac{(\sin A)(\cos A + 1)}{(\cos A)(1 + \cos A)} = \tan A.$$

Dividing common factors leaves

$$\frac{(\sin A)}{(\cos A)} = \tan A$$

and the proof is completed.

This is an acceptable way of establishing the identity. Technology provides an avenue that cannot be overlooked. Graph

$$y = \frac{\sin A + \tan A}{1 + \cos A}$$

and then, on the same axis system, but in a different color, graph tan A as shown in Figs. 8.7 and 8.8. The second graph will overlay the first and, because all points coincide, the two graphs appear to represent the same thing. The question becomes whether or not this is an acceptable proof. The answer is largely determined by the objectives that have been established for the class. If the intent is to have students manipulate identities via substitution and algebra, then the plotting solution would not be acceptable. If the intent is to provide verification that the two expressions say the same thing, perhaps the graphing solution would be acceptable.

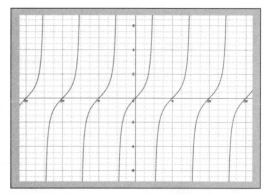

**Figure 8.7**

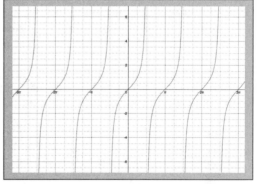

**Figure 8.8**

### EXERCISE 8.4

1. Show that $\sin^2 x + \cos^2 x = 1$ graphically. Describe how this development could be used in the secondary curriculum.

**Additional exercises can be found on the website.**

Proof is not always direct manipulation that verifies the issue in question. Mathematical induction occurs in a variety of settings throughout the curriculum. Mark Twain in *Life on the Mississippi* (as cited in Adler, 1972, pp. 56–58) described a series of events involving the Mississippi River abandoning a course and acquiring a new, shorter one when considering the distance traveled between Cairo, Illinois, and New Orleans, Louisiana:

The water cuts the alluvial banks of the "lower" river into deep horseshoe curves; so deep, indeed, that in some places if you were to get ashore at one extremity of the horseshoe and walk across the neck, half or three-quarters of a mile, you could sit down and rest a couple of hours while your steamer was coming around the long elbow at a speed of ten miles an hour to take you on board again. When the river is rising fast, some scoundrel whose plantation is back in the country, and therefore of inferior value, has only to watch his chance, cut a little gutter across the narrow neck of land some dark night, and turn the water into it, and in a wonderfully short time a miracle has happened: to wit, the whole Mississippi has taken possession of that little ditch, and placed the countryman's plantation on its bank (quadrupling its value), and that other party's formerly valuable plantation finds itself away out yonder on a big island; the old watercourse around it will soon shoal up, boats cannot approach within ten miles of it, and down goes its value to a fourth of its former worth. Watches are kept on those narrow necks at needful times, and if a man happens to be caught cutting a ditch across them, the chances are all against his ever having another opportunity to cut a ditch. . . . Since my own day on the Mississippi, cutoffs have been made at Hurricane Island, at Island 100, at Napoleon, Ark., at Walnut Bend, and at Council Bend. These shortened the river, in the aggregate, sixty-seven miles. In my own time a cut-off was made at American Bend, which shortened the river ten miles or more.

Therefore, the Mississippi between Cairo and New Orleans was twelve hundred and fifteen miles long one hundred and seventy-six years ago. It was eleven hundred and eighty after the cut-off of 1722. It was one thousand and forty after the American Bend cut-off. It has lost sixty-seven miles since. Consequently, its length is only nine hundred and seventy-three miles at present.

Now, if I wanted to be one of those ponderous scientific people, and "let on" to prove what had occurred in the remote past, by what had occurred in a given time in the recent past, or what will occur in the far future by what has occurred in late years, what an opportunity is here! Geology never had such a chance, nor such exact data to argue from! Nor "development of species," either! Glacial epochs are great things, but they are vague—vague. Please observe: In the space of one hundred and seventy-six years the Lower Mississippi has shortened itself two hundred and forty-two miles. That is an average of a trifle over one mile and a third per year. Therefore, any calm person, who is not blind or idiotic, can see that in the Old Oolitic Silurian Period, just a million years ago next November, the Lower Mississippi River was upward of one million three hundred thousand miles long, and stuck out over the Gulf of Mexico like a fishing-rod. And, by the same token any person can see that seven hundred and forty-two years from now the lower Mississippi will be only a mile and three-quarters long, and Cairo and New Orleans will have joined their streets together, and be plodding comfortably along under a single mayor and a mutual board of aldermen. There is something fascinating about science. One gets such wholesale returns of conjecture out of such a trifling investment of fact.

Mathematical induction can appear at a variety of locations within the curriculum, especially when number theory is considered. A typical exercise involves showing that $1 + 3 + 5 + \cdots + (2n - 1) = n^2$ for all counting numbers. It is known that $1 = 1^2$, so the theorem holds for 1. We can see that $1 + 3 = 4$ or $2^2$, so it holds for 2. Assume $n$ so $1 + 3 + 5 + \cdots + (2n - 1) = n^2$. Show that the theorem holds for "$n + 1$" and, by induction, the theorem is established. That is, prove that $1 + 3 + 5 + \cdots + (2n - 1) + (2n + 1) = (n + 1)^2$. The left side is $n^2 + (2n + 1)$ because $n^2 = 1 + 3 + 5 + \cdots + (2n - 1)$ and "$2n + 1$" is the next term. Because $n^2 + (2n + 1)$ does, in fact, equal $(n + 1)^2$, the induction theorem holds.

There is one point of potential difficulty for some students as they look at the preceding use of mathematical induction. Frequently, the statement, "It holds when $n = 1$" is taken to mean that 1 is substituted for $n$ and the associated algebra or arithmetic is done. That can lead to a silly situation. Consider the idea that $1 + 3 + 5 + \cdots + (2n - 1) = n^2$, and substitute 1 for $n$. The equation then becomes $1 + 3 + 5 + \cdots + [2(1) - 1] = 1^2$ or $1 + 3 + 5 + \cdots + 1 = 1$. The student needs to realize that $2n - 1 = 1$ when $n = 1$, 3 when $n = 2$, 5 when $n = 3$, and so forth. The problem with the example is that substituting 1 for $n$ means there is only one term to begin with, so $1 + 3 + \cdots$ does not make sense.

## EXERCISE 8.5

1.  Prove that $2 + 4 + 6 + \ldots + 2n = n(n + 1)$.

**Additional exercises can be found on the website.**

The foundations for proof can be established by examining divisibility rules. Most of the proofs for divisibility rules depend on an understanding of expanded notation. If a number is divisible by some factor, then any multiple of that number will also be divisible by that same factor. For example, show 27 as a sum of terms where each term shares a common factor. The number 27 can be rewritten as $3 + 9 + 15$. The common element can be factored out, which is 3, and the number written as the product of that factor and the sum of the residue of each of the terms, $3(1 + 3 + 5)$. This shows the original number is divisible by a common factor. The concepts in the preceding discussion are difficult for many students to comprehend, and it may take some time for them to be comfortable with the ideas. Once the realization occurs, students can easily understand, and produce, proofs for divisibility rules.

What is the rule for showing a number to be divisible by 2? Typically this question is answered with statements like, "The last digit is even," or, "The last digit is a 2, 4, 6, 8, or 0." Either one of those is acceptable, along with others, but the real question is, "How do you know that to be true?" or, "Can you prove it?" Extended investigation generally reveals that most people were given the rule and never paid any attention to how to prove it. One of the goals of the Standards is communication, which involves explaining why things work, or implies proof.

Discussion for proving divisibility by 2 often becomes cyclic, and students struggle for a way to begin. Consider any number $Xy$ where $X$ is any integer and $y$ is any digit. In 7,354 $X$ is 735 and $y$ is 4. $Xy$ can be written in expanded notation as $(X)(10) + y$. No matter what integer is used for $X$, $(X)(10)$ must be divisible by 2, because 10 is always divisible by 2. Any multiple of 10 will also be divisible by 2. One term of the expanded form is guaranteed to be divisible by 2. If the other term is also divisible by 2, a 2 can be factored out of the expanded form and the original number written as 2 times something. This verifies that the original number is divisible by 2. But, when can a 2 be factored out of both terms? Only when $y$ is even, or 0, 2, 4, 6, or 8, which gives the rule statement and the proof is completed.

The proof for divisibility by 5 and even 10 is similar to that for 2, except that the $y$ must be either 5 or 0 for divisibility by 5 and only 0 for divisibility by 10. It should not be too difficult for students to produce these proofs once they have seen the one for 2.

Divisibility by 4 is proven by applying the "2 rule" twice, or in a manner similar to that of 2, 5,

and 10, with one notable exception. The expanded expression of the number being considered cannot be $(X)(10) + y$ because 10 is not divisible by 4. The first counting number power of 10 that is divisible by 4 is $10^2$ or 100. So, the number being considered needs to be written as $Xyz$, where $X$ is any integer and $y$ and $z$ are any digits. The number is then written as $(X)(100) + yz$ (note $y$ and $z$ are not multiplied here—they represent the tens and ones digits of the number). Because 100 is divisible by 4, attention is turned to the last two digits, $yz$. If they are divisible by 4, the whole number is. If $yz$ is not divisible by 4, then the initial number is not, because 4 cannot be factored out of both terms. For example,

$$5,732 = 57(100) + 32$$
$$= 57(4)(25) + 4(8)$$
$$= 4[57(25) + 8].$$

If the initial number is 5,731, four cannot be factored out of 31. Thus, 5,731 is not a multiple of 4.

Once divisibility for 4 has been established, 8 can be considered in a similar manner. A rule for 16 can be established as well, but there is some question as to the value of it, due to the magnitude of the numbers involved. As the proofs of divisibility for 2, 4, 8, 16, are done, notice the parallel between the exponents of 2 and 10 ($2^1$ and $10^1$); $2^2$ and $10^2$ for divisibility by 4; $2^3$ and $10^3$ for divisibility by 8; $2^4$ and $10^4$ for divisibility by 16.

The proofs of divisibility by counting number powers of 3 are different from those dealing with counting number powers of 2. The idea of expanded notation is used along with that of having a common factor in each term, so the original number can be expressed as a multiple of a counting number power of 3. Suppose you want to know if the three-digit number $XYZ$, where $X$, $Y$, and $Z$ are all digits, is divisible by 3. The rule says to find the sum of the digits. If that sum is divisible by 3, then the original number is also. The "3 rule" could be repeated on the new sum, if desired, before determining divisibility.

Mathematicians often use the known answer as a clue for how to proceed with a proof. Rewrite $XYZ$ using expanded notation as $(X)(100) + (Y)(10) + Z$. This approach shows a useful proof technique. The answer is known; we want to have the sum of the digits as a part of expressing $XYZ$. Using that information, we have to rewrite $XYZ$ somehow so "$X + Y + Z$" are some of the terms (perhaps not grouped together as shown here). Focus on $(X)(100)$ in the expanded form of $XYZ$, because once it is seen how to rewrite this, the rest are similar. The challenge is to find a way to rewrite $(X)(100)$ so it is a sum of $X$ and something. Using the clue of knowing one term of the final answer needs to be $X$, we have to express 100 in a manner that will give us an $X$ when we are all done. If the 100 were rewritten so it contained a 100, when the entire renaming is multiplied by the $X$, the desired term appears as a part of the product. That is, $(X)(100)$ becomes $(X)(99 + 1)$ and distributing the $X$ yields $(X)(99) + (X)(1)$ or $99X + X$. The $X$ is now isolated. The 99 is a multiple of 3 and always divisible by 3. Using the same technique for $(Y)(10)$,

$$\begin{aligned} XYZ &= (X)(100) + (Y)(10) + Z \\ &= (X)(99 + 1) + (Y)(9 + 1) + Z \\ &= (X)(99) + (X)(1) + (Y)(9) + (Y)(1) + Z \\ &= 99X + 9Y + X + Y + Z. \end{aligned}$$

It is known that $99X$ and $9Y$ will always be divisible by 3, assuring the ability to factor 3 out of those two terms. The only thing left to consider is $X + Y + Z$, which is the sum of the digits. If the sum $X + Y + Z$ is divisible by 3, then the original number can be expressed as a multiple of 3, which would be factored out of $XYZ$. If the sum of the digits was not a multiple of 3, the original number cannot be expressed as a multiple of 3.

Divisibility by 9 works exactly like that of 3, except that the sum of the digits must be divisible by 9. Divisibility by 6 uses a combination of the 2 and 3 rules. The easiest way to explain the 6 rule to students is to have them check to see if the number in question is even. If it is not, the number cannot possibly be divisible by 6. If the number in question is even, then apply the 3 rule to determine if it is divisible by 6. The discussion about why divisibility for 6 uses the 2 and 3 rules should include items dealing with the prime factorization of 6.

Divisibility by 7 is a complex rule and yet provides exploration opportunities for more inquisitive students. The rule states, "Double the last digit in the number and subtract that product from the original number with the last original digit deleted. If the new number is divisible by 7, the original is. If the new number is not divisible by 7, the original is not. The process may be repeated." For example,

| 2 0 6 5 | Double last digit (5) |
| − 1 0 | Subtract $2 \times 5$ from rest after deleting 5 |
| 1 9 6 | Repeat the process—double 6 |
| − 1 2 | Subtract from rest after deleting 6 |
| 7 | Because 7 is divisible by 7, 2065 is also. |

---
## EXERCISES 8.6

1. Do a proof that shows how the divisibility rule for 9 would work with a four-digit number $WXYZ$.
2. Should students be required to prove a divisibility rule? Why or why not?

**Additional exercises can be found on the website.**

Divisibility by 11 seems complex at first glance. Closer investigation shows that the proof is relatively simple, revolving around renaming 10 as $11 - 1$ and using the concept of expanded notation. Consider $(11 - 1)^2$. Expanding yields $11^2 - 2(11)(1) + 1^2$. Because 11 is a factor of two of the terms in the expansion, that sum must be divisible by 11. Expanding $(11 - 1)^3$ gives all terms except $1^3$ as a multiple of 11. The situation is similar for all cases of $(11 - 1)^n$, where $n$ is any counting number—all terms except for $1^n$ will be multiples of 11. The sign of $1^n$ will be negative for odd values of $n$, and positive for even ones.

Using this information to check for divisibility by 11, on the number $UVWXYZ$ where $U$, $V$, $W$, $X$, $Y$, and $Z$ are any digits, $UVWXYZ$ would be rewritten as $U(10)^5 + V(10)^4 + W(10)^3 + X(10)^2 + Y(10)^1 + Z(10)^0$ or as $U(11 - 1)^5 + V(11 - 1)^4 + W(11 - 1)^3 + X(11 - 1)^2 + Y(11 - 1)^1 + Z(11 - 1)^0$.

From the earlier discussion, expansion of this polynomial will yield a set of terms that are multiples of 11 plus some residue. We know most terms are multiples of 11. The only terms in question are $-U, +V, -W, +X, -Y,$ and $+Z$. Inspection shows the rule to be the rightmost digit minus its left neighbor, plus the next left neighbor, and so on, until all digits are considered. In other words, the sum of every other digit is subtracted from the sum of the rest of the digits (for divisibility, the sign is not important). Only if that missing addend is a multiple of 11 will the original number be divisible by 11.

## PROOFS STUDENTS ASK FOR

A typical question is, "Why is anything to the zero power one?" Wording is important. As asked, the question is not reflective of what is true because, for example, $0^0 \neq 1$. Excluding situations that are not true, establishing the fact that $X^0 = 1$ is relatively easy if the student has experience with exponents and the idea that anything nonzero and noninfinite divided by itself is one. $\frac{X^n}{X^n} = 1$ where $n$ is any real nonzero, no-infinite value. But, $\frac{X^n}{X^n} = X^{n-n}$ or $X^0$. By the transitive property of equality, it must be the case that $X^0 = 1$. Another example that is extremely perplexing to students involves repeating decimals. For example, $0.\overline{999} = 1$ but demonstration, even through proof, is not convincing in many instances. Typically the problem is done as follows. Let $A = 0.\overline{999}$ so $10A = 9.\overline{999}$. Subtracting yields $9A = 9.000$. This can be accomplished because the right part of the decimal, in both cases, involves a repeating string of 9s. We are assured that no matter what place we select, the column will hold $9 - 9$, yielding a missing addend of zero. The final result becomes $9A = 9$. Dividing both sides by 9, $A = 1$. In other words, by the transitive property of equality, $0.\overline{999} = 1$. It just does not make sense that $0.\overline{999} = 1$ for many students. The difficulty is that they are thinking of a finite setting where the string of 9s terminates. Additional similar examples will typically be met with comparable disbelief.

When students resist $0.\overline{999} = 1$, have the class try $2.\overline{444} + 3.\overline{555}$. Find the equivalent fractions for each addend:

$$2.\overline{444} + 3.\overline{555} = 6$$

$$\frac{22}{9} + \frac{32}{9} = \frac{54}{9} = 6$$

$$(X - 1)\left(X - \frac{\pm\sqrt{5} - 1}{2}\right)$$

Let $n = 2.\overline{444}$ and then $10n = 24.\overline{444}$. Using the aforementioned procedure for $0.\overline{999} = 1$, $9n = 22$ and $n = \frac{22}{9}$. Similarly, let $m = 3.\overline{555}$ and then $10m = 35.\overline{555}$.

Subtracting as before gives $m = \frac{32}{9}$. Then $2.\overline{444} + 3.\overline{555}$ becomes $\frac{22}{9} + \frac{32}{9} = \frac{54}{9} = 6$ and so $2.\overline{444} + 3.\overline{555} = 6$. ☺

Number tricks provide opportunities for getting students to ask for a proof. A typical example would be, "We are going to add five two-digit numbers. You pick two addends, I pick three, and the sum will be 245." In addition to getting students to ask how it works, this is a marvelous chance to have them practice addition skills and ask for more, without even knowing they are practicing. Limitations, like not permitting students to select a value that has the same digits, can be established initially. Suppose 34 is one of their numbers and 75 is the other. You would select 65 to be paired with 34 and 24 to be paired with 75, without telling them what you are doing. Those two pairs have a sum of 99, each of which can be expressed as $100 - 1$. The four addends chosen so far have a sum of $200 - 2$. The remaining addend, or "magic number," is selected so that when 2 is subtracted from it, the missing addend will be, in this case, 45. This "magic number" is 47. This value will vary depending on the announced sum. Each "99" requires two addends. If the sum for this trick was 345, there would be a total of seven addends. Six of the addends would be for the three pairs of addends that would yield a total of $300 - 3$. The last addend would be the "magic number," which in this case would be 48, because 3 is to be subtracted from it. This trick can be extended to deal with addends having any number of digits in them. No matter what size the addends, a careful sequencing of problems can be used to lead students to conclude how the trick works.

## WHY PROVE?

Evelyne Barbin wrote, "The history of mathematics shows that the idea of mathematical proof has changed as time passed, and that to identify mathematical proof with deductive reasoning hides the questions, the doubts, and the process of invention" (Barbin, 1994, pp. 41–52). Sixth-century B.C. Greeks gave birth to "rational and geometrical" thought, which meant it was necessary to convince using speech based on reason.

Barbin continued, saying that the seventeenth-century mathematicians were dissatisfied with the ancient proofs. They were unhappy with:

Proving things that do not need proof. For instance, the sum of two sides of a triangle is greater than the third. (Barbin, 1994, pp. 41–52)

Proof by impossibility. Such proofs convince the mind without enlightening it, "because our mind is dissatisfied if it knows something is, but not why it is." (Barbin, 1994, pp. 41–52)

Proofs by ways that are distant from the original problem. "All Euclid is full of such proofs by extraneous ways." (Barbin, 1994, pp. 41–52)

Also, one of them said "Why prove irrational numbers? They do not exist" (Barbin, 1994, pp. 41–52). Amazingly, students today still echo similar statements about many of the proofs expected of them in secondary classes.

## TRY THIS IN YOUR CLASSROOM

*NCTM Standards 2000*: Problem solving, communication, reasoning, connections, algebra, and functions

*Materials*: Graphing calculator

Sometimes, graphing an equation holds the key to solving it. Sometimes, however, finding a solution by graphing will lead to a technological anomaly. One example of this is when sin(63X) is graphed.

Another situation can be investigated with $Y = X^3 - 2X + 1$. Enter the equation in the TABLE menu of the calculator. Set the range to go from $-5$ to $5$, with increments of 1. There is a root between $X = -2$ and $X = -1$, because of the sign change for the $Y$ values.

Furthermore, it appears as if there is a second root when $X = 1$. Since this is a third-degree equation, the possibility for 3 roots exists. Could it be that $X = 1$ is a double root? You could factor $X^3 - 2X + 1$ and determine the answer to the question, but that would not be an easy thing to do since the expression factors to $(X-1)\left(X - \frac{\pm\sqrt{5}-1}{2}\right)$.

Graphing might prove helpful, since factoring would be difficult without technology.

Graph the equation $Y = X^3 - 2X + 1$ after setting the $X$ and $Y$ ranges from $-10$ to $10$.

The graph appears to support the idea that $X = 1$ is a double root as shown in Fig. 8.9.

Zoom in on the region in question. Is $X = 1$ a double root? Why or why not?

Trace the curve and determine the $X$ value when $Y$ is zero. Your trace may not yield a value where $Y$ is zero. You might get something like $(0.61587301587, 1.85433938E-3)$. Moving one step to the right yields $(0.62222222222, -3.5445816E-3)$, indicating the curve has passed over the $x$-axis and thus, a root is present.

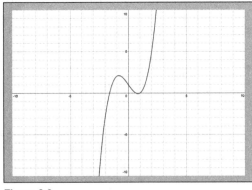

**Figure 8.9**

But, what is the $X$ value that makes $Y = 0$? Is this close enough?

Suppose this is not close enough. The value for $X$ can be substituted into the original equation $Y = X^3 - 2X + 1$ which will give a value close to $Y = 0$. Doing the substitution yields $Y = -3.5445816E-3$. How can that be?

Continue the trace and list the other root.

Return to the Graph Function window and enter a second equation, $Y = 0$. Graph again and use find the intersection between the horizontal line, $Y = 0$, and the curve. You now get $(0.61803398875, 0)$ and $(1, 0)$. The window could be reset to show all 3 roots, the third one being $(-1.6180339887, 0)$.

List another third-degree equation that appears to have only two roots when the table function is used but in reality has three. List the three roots to your equation and describe how you found, or created, your example.

Another interesting question comes out of a third-degree equation. Consider the general form of the equation

$$Y = RX^3 + SX^2 + TX + U$$

where $R$, $S$, $T$, and $U$ are real numbers. Without loss of generality, the equation can be divided through by $R$ leaving $Y = X^3 + AX^2 + BX + C$, where $A$, $B$, and $C$ are real numbers. Three distinctly different groups of curves will be generated by $Y = X^3 + AX^2 + BX + C$. There is a relation between $A$ and $B$ that tells which of the three curves will be generated. Substituting different values into the equation, graphing, and investigating the resultant tables will provide enough information to answer the question.

Set the View Window to $-10$, 10 for $X$ and $-10$, 10 for $Y$ and graph the following three equations:

$$Y = X^3 + 2X^2 + 5X + 6$$
$$Y = X^3 + 4X^2 + 5X + 6$$
$$Y = X^3 + 5X^2 + 5X + 6$$

What is the relation between $A$ and $B$ that indicates whether the curve will have an inflection point, a "flat" spot (not really flat, which can be seen with ZOOM), or a "backward, sideways S"?

## CONCLUSION

Should we continue proving? Is there room for or a need for proofs at all levels of mathematics? Can students be convinced of a need to prove things? What is the role of proof in the secondary mathematics curriculum today?

Our job, as teachers, is to entice our students to think. Their reasoning should not yield to authority, but rather reflect consideration about a given topic. They need to convince themselves of a position to be held, and they need to be able to support their position with reasons. Given that, this chapter is concluded with the questions in the preceding paragraph. Establish your position and be ready to implement it into your curriculum.

## STICKY QUESTIONS

1. More than 300 proofs of the Pythagorean theorem have been listed (Loomis, 1963). Describe two Pythagorean proofs that are new to you.

2. Is it possible to prove that $\sqrt{2}\sqrt{3} = \sqrt{6}$ when $\sqrt{2}$ represents the length of a rectangle and $\sqrt{3}$ stands for the width of that same rectangle? Explain why or why not.

3. A vehicle travels 30 miles in an hour. How fast will the vehicle have to travel a second 30 miles so the average speed for the total distance will be 60 miles an hour? Explain your answer.

4. A number trick asks students to write any three-digit number, repeating no digits. The selected number is then written in reverse order and the smaller three-digit number is subtracted from the larger. The missing addend is reversed and added to its reversal (if the missing addend is 99, it must be written 099). The sum will always be 1089. Why?

5. Prove that the segment joining the midpoint of a side of any triangle to its opposite vertex divides the area of the triangle in half. Watch out—there is a real slick, easy way to do this one but most people overlook it.

## PROBLEM-SOLVING CHALLENGES

1. Suppose that the surface of the earth is smooth and spherical and that the distance around the equator is 25,000 miles. A steel band is made to fit tightly around the earth at the equator, then the band is cut and a piece of band 18 feet long is inserted. Assuming the equator is a circle and the band is a concentric circle, to the nearest foot, what will be the gap, all the way around, between the band and the earth's surface? (Use 3.14 as an approximate value of pi.)

**Check out the website for the solution**

2. Two = One

Observe the following algebraic proof.
Given:

$A$ and $B$ are real numbers;
$A = B$

$$A = B$$
$$A^2 = AB$$
$$A^2 - B^2 = AB - B^2$$
$$(A + B)(A - B) = B(A - B)$$

Dividing both sides by $(A - B)$ yields
$$(A + B) = B$$
Since $A = B$, substituting $B$ for $A$ yields
$$B + B = B$$
$$2B = B$$
Dividing both sides by B yields

$2 = 1$

Since we know that 2 does not equal 1, clearly state the mistake made in the above algebraic proof.

**Check out the website for the solution**

# ■
# LEARNING ACTIVITIES

## Mathematical Induction

If the first statement in a list is true and every true statement in the list is immediately followed by a true statement, then it may be concluded that every statement in the list is true—the principle of mathematical induction (PMI).

Example 1. How could the PMI be used to prove the following—given the set of counting numbers, $\{1, 2, 3, \ldots\}$, is it the case that $1+2+3+ \ldots + n = \frac{n(n+1)}{2}$ where $n$ is a counting number? The logical approach to this would be to use a series of true statements. The first statement would have $n = 1$. Is the claim true when $n = 1$? That is easy enough to check. Stating it mathematically, we have an open statement.

$P(n) = 1+2+3+ \ldots + n = \frac{n(n+1)}{2}$. For $P(1)$, the question is whether $\frac{1(1+1)}{2} = 1$. Since this is true, the first statement is true. While it is not always necessary, check the next logical statement $P(2)$ that would be made. For $P(2)$, is it the case that $1+2 = \frac{2(2+1)}{2}$?

$$1+2 = \frac{2(2+1)}{2}$$
$$3 = \frac{2(3)}{2}$$
$$3 = \frac{6}{2}$$
$$3 = 3$$

This is true, so the second statement in the list is true.

Geometrically, we show the situation for $1 + 2 + 3 + 4$ in Fig. 8.10. The number of unit squares in it labels the column for each respective addend. Notice that the area of the entire figure is $n^2 + n$, or $n(n + 1)$. Another way of looking at it is that there are two staircase regions of the same area and an additional column that is one unit wide and the same height as the staircase. That is, the shaded region represents $n^2$ and there is still an $n$ besides that, giving an area of $n^2 + n$, or $n(n + 1)$.

While this process could certainly continue, it is not possible to do all examples. That is where PMI comes in. Assume it is the case that $P(k)$ is true. That is, assume that $1+2+3+\cdots+k = \frac{k(k+1)}{2}$.

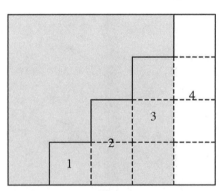

**Figure 8.10**

The next statement in the list would be $P(k + 1)$. If it can be shown that $P(k + 1)$ is true, knowing the one before it $(P(k))$ is true, then PMI is satisfied and the proof is complete (remember, it is critical that $P(k)$ is true when $k = 1$ as well).

$$1 + 2 + 3 + \ldots + (k + 1) = 1 + 2 + 3 + \ldots + k + (k + 1)$$

But we also know that for $P(k)$, $1 + 2 + 3 + \ldots + k = \dfrac{k(k + 1)}{2}$, so substituting

$$1 + 2 + 3 + \ldots + k + (k + 1) = \frac{k(k + 1)}{2} + k + 1$$

$$= \frac{k(k + 1)}{2} + \frac{2(k + 1)}{2}$$

$$= \frac{k^2 + k + 2k + 2}{2}$$

$$= \frac{k^2 + 3k + 2}{2}$$

$$= \frac{(k + 1)(k + 2)}{2}$$

Look at this closely. This is another way of saying $n$ and $n + 1$, so the statement is true for $P(n + 1)$ when it is assumed true for $P(n)$, where any counting number is used for $n$.

Example 2. Notice that $1 + 8 + 27 + 64 = 100$. Another way of saying that is to have $1^3 + 2^3 + 3^3 + 4^3 = 10^2$. Wow, a sum of consecutive cubes comes out to be a square. That should raise a question: How often does it happen that a sum of successive cubes is a square? For starters look at some specific cases:

| | | | |
|---|---|---|---|
| 1 | = | 1 = | $1^2$ |
| 1 + 8 | = | 9 = | $3^2$ |
| 1 + 8 + 27 | = | 36 = | $6^2$ |
| 1 + 8 + 27 + 64 | = | 100 = | $10^2$ |
| 1 + 8 + 27 + 64 + 125 | = | 225 = | $15^2$ |

This leads to the thought that the sum of consecutive cubes might always be a square, if the list starts with $1^3$. Look at the numbers that are squared at the end of each line in the last table:

$$3 - 1 = 2$$
$$6 - 3 = 3$$
$$10 - 6 = 4$$
$$15 - 10 = 5$$

But, that leads to:

| | | |
|---|---|---|
| 1 | = | 1 |
| 1 + 2 | = | 3 |
| 1 + 2 + 3 | = | 6 |
| 1 + 2 + 3 + 4 | = | 10 |
| 1 + 2 + 3 + 4 + 5 | = | 15 |

which is what was used in Exercise 1. More significantly, it appears as if $1^3 + 2^3 + 3^3 + \ldots + n^3 = (1 + 2 + 3 + \ldots + n)^2$, which could be expressed as $1^3 + 2^3 + 3^3 + \ldots + n^3 = \left(\dfrac{n(n + 1)}{2}\right)^2$. Before trying to prove this, test it for the first 10 consecutive cubes. Is it the case that $1^3 + 2^3 + 3^3 + 4^3 +$

$5^3 + 6^3 + 7^3 + 8^3 + 9^3 + 10^3 = \left(\frac{10(11)}{2}\right)^2$ ? $1 + 8 + 27 + 64 + 125 + 216 + 343 + 512 + 729 + 1000 =$ $3025 = 55^2$. It certainly works here and the indication is that it works all the time.

Check the situation for 1 and we get a true statement: $1^3 = 1^2$. Now assume it is true for $n^3$ and check for $(n + 1)^3$. That is, does

$$1^3 + 2^3 + 3^3 + \ldots + n^3 + (n + 1)^3 \quad \left(\frac{(n+1)(n+2)}{2}\right)^2 ?$$

$P(n)$ would be $1^3 + 2^3 + 3^3 + \ldots + n^3 = \left(\frac{n(n+1)}{2}\right)^2$ while

$P(n + 1)$ would be $1^3 + 2^3 + 3^3 + \ldots + n^3 + (n + 1)^3 = \left(\frac{(n+1)(n+2)}{2}\right)^2$

Subtracting $P(n)$ from $P(n + 1)$ yields

$$-(n+1)^3 = \left(\frac{n(n+1)}{2}\right)^2 - \left(\frac{(n+1)(n+2)}{2}\right)^2$$

or $(n + 1)^3 = \left(\frac{(n+1)(n+2)}{2}\right)^2 - \left(\frac{n(n+1)}{2}\right)^2$

The right side can be written $\left(\frac{(n+1)}{2}\right)^2 \left((n+2)^2 - n^2\right)$, which becomes

$$= \left(\frac{(n+1)}{2}\right)^2 (4n+4)$$

$$= \frac{(n+1)^2(4n+4)}{4}$$

$$= (n+1)^2(n+1)$$

$$= (n+1)^3$$

and the proof is done.

Not checking each of the two parts of the PMI can lead to false conclusions. Without that, you might end up making a claim that is not correct.

## EXERCISES 8.7

Note that in today's technological world, you can find each of these solved somewhere on the Internet. The challenge is to avoid doing that, and for YOU to do the proof. THAT is how you grow your own abilities.

1. Prove that $1^2 + 2^2 + 3^2 + \cdots + n^2 = \frac{n(n+1)(2n+1)}{6}$.
2. Prove that $r^m r^n = r^{m+n}$ for $r$, a real number, and $m$ and $n$ as counting numbers.
3. Prove that if n is a natural number, $a$ is a real number and $a > -1$, then $(1 + a)n > 1 + na$.
4. Find and prove a unique statement using PMI.

# Part III
# Content and Strategies

# General Mathematics

Knowing where to begin this chapter and what to include is difficult. There are so many topics to be covered. What is the best order? What background information will the students possess? Should topics be integrated in this discussion? You are expected to blend topics as you teach by relating one to the other. Perhaps this discussion should follow an integrated format. Still, if that is done, continuity will be next to impossible. This comment brings to mind the story about an individual wanting to borrow a chainsaw. The request was made and the response was "No." Rather stunned, the individual followed with "Why not?" "My dog is sick," was the reply. "What does your dog being sick have to do with my borrowing your chainsaw?" was the next question. The response was, "Nothing, but I don't want to lend it to you and one excuse is as good as another." The moral of that story is that no matter what order is selected, others could serve equally well.

## THE STANDARDS

The NCTM Standards (1989 & 2000) provide a listing of basic concepts and objectives that should be covered in P–12 school mathematics. The discussion in the Standards includes rationalization for shifting to a broader curriculum of mathematics, features that should be included in the curriculum, commentaries on technology, comments dealing with instruction, materials that should be present in every classroom, and learner characteristics. Suggested major changes in the curriculum both for mathematical content and instruction in the 1989 Standards for grades 5–8 mathematics (pp. 70–73) are as follows:

### Increased Attention

#### Problem Solving

- Pursuing open-ended problems and extended problem-solving projects
- Investigating and formulating questions from problem situations
- Representing situations verbally, numerically, graphically, geometrically, or symbolically

#### Communication

- Discussing, writing, reading, and listening to mathematical ideas

#### Reasoning

- Reasoning in spatial contexts
- Reasoning with proportions
- Reasoning from graphs
- Reasoning inductively and deductively

#### Connections

- Connecting mathematics to other subjects and to the world outside the classroom
- Connecting topics within mathematics
- Applying mathematics

#### Number/Operations/Computation

- Developing number sense
- Developing operation sense

- Creating algorithms and procedures
- Using estimation both in solving problems and in checking the reasonableness of results
- Exploring relationships among representations of and operations on whole numbers, fractions, decimals, integers, and rational numbers
- Developing an understanding of ratio, proportion, and percent

## Patterns and Functions

- Identifying and using functional relationships
- Developing and using tables, graphs, and rules to describe situations
- Interpreting among different mathematical representations

## Algebra

- Developing an understanding of variables, expressions, and equations
- Using a variety of methods to solve linear equations and informally investigate inequalities and nonlinear equations

## Statistics

- Using statistical methods to describe, analyze, evaluate, and make decisions

## Probability

- Creating experimental and theoretical models of situations including probabilities

## Geometry

- Developing an understanding of geometric objects and relationships
- Using geometry in solving problems

## Measurement

- Estimating and using measurement to solve problems

## Instructional Practice

- Actively involving students individually and in groups in exploring, conjecturing, analyzing, and applying mathematics in both a mathematical and a real-world context
- Using appropriate technology for computation and exploration
- Using concrete materials

- Being a facilitator of learning
- Assessing learning as an integral part of instruction

## Decreased Attention

### Problem Solving

- Practicing routine, one-step problems
- Practicing problems categorized by types (e.g., coin problems, age problems)

### Communication

- Doing fill-in-the-blank worksheets
- Answering questions that require only yes, no, or a number as responses

### Reasoning

- Relying on outside authority (teacher or an answer key)

### Connections

- Learning isolated topics
- Developing skills out of context

### Number/Operations/Computation

- Memorizing rules and algorithms
- Practicing tedious paper-and-pencil computations
- Finding exact forms of answers
- Memorizing procedures, such as cross-multiplication, without understanding
- Practicing rounding numbers out of context

### Patterns and Functions

- Topics seldom in the current curriculum

### Algebra

- Manipulating symbols
- Memorizing procedures and drilling on equation solving

### Statistics

- Memorizing formulas

### Geometry

- Memorizing geometric vocabulary
- Memorizing facts and relationships

## Measurement

- Memorizing and manipulating formulas
- Converting within and between measurement systems

## Instructional Practices

- Teaching computations out of context
- Drilling on paper-and-pencil algorithms
- Teaching topics in isolation
- Stressing memorization
- Being the dispenser of knowledge
- Testing for the sole purpose of assigning grades

Standards 2000 echoes these changes, although there is not a list such as the one above. Reading the guiding principles and the 10 standards presented for each grade section (five describing the mathematical processes that should be used to assist students as they learn the five standards of mathematical content) reveals a continuation of the thought set forward in the 1989 Standards publication. The Standards 2000 wording is different. The organization of the publication is different. But, the appeal to help all students learn more and better mathematics through better teaching and learning practices is still clear as embodied in "A Vision for School Mathematics":

*Imagine a classroom, a school, or a school district where all students have access to high-quality, engaging mathematics instruction. There are ambitious expectations for all, with accommodation for those who need it. Knowledgeable teachers have adequate resources to support their work and are continually growing as professionals. The curriculum is mathematically rich, offering students opportunities to learn important mathematical concepts and procedures with understanding. Technology is an essential component of the environment. Students confidently engage in complex mathematical tasks chosen carefully by teachers. They draw on knowledge from a wide variety of mathematical topics, sometimes approaching the same problem from different mathematical perspectives or representing the mathematics in different ways until they find methods that enable them to make progress. Teachers help students make, refine, and explore conjectures on the basis of evidence and use a variety of reasoning and proof techniques to confirm or disprove those conjectures. Students are flexible and resourceful problem solvers. Alone or in groups and with access to technology, they work productively and reflectively, with the skilled guidance of their teachers. Orally and in writing, students communicate their ideas and results effectively. They value mathematics and engage actively in learning it.* (NCTM, 2000, p. 3)

### EXERCISES 9.1

1. Reflect on your experiences with courses taken prior to Algebra I. Describe how the NCTM suggested changes would alter the mathematics education you received in grades 5–8.
2. After reading the introduction to "A Vision for School Mathematics" (NCTM, 2000, p. 3), select one (and only one) sentence that stands out to you. Why did you select that sentence?

## COMMON CORE STATE STANDARDS

In 2010, the National Governors Association Center for Best Practices (NGA Center) in collaboration with the Council of Chief State School Officers (CCSSO) prompted an initiative to raise the bar for the mathematical content being taught while creating a common set of standards. The Common Core Standards for Mathematics (http://www.corestandards.org/the-standards/mathematics) were developed by educators, school administrators, and the professional community with a goal to provide a common framework across the nation in specific content areas. The Common Core Standards define grade specific standards and describe the mathematics children should be able to comprehend and do.

These standards define the knowledge and skills students should have within their K-12 education careers so that they will graduate high school able to succeed in entry-level, credit-bearing academic college courses and in workforce training programs. The standards:

- Are aligned with college and work expectations;
- Are clear, understandable and consistent;
- Include rigorous content and application of knowledge through high-order skills;
- Build upon strengths and lessons of current state standards;

- Are informed by other top performing countries, so that all students are prepared to succeed in our global economy and society; and
- Are evidence-based.

("About the Standards," n.d., para 4)

The Common Core Standards focus on kindergarten through high school mathematics (http://www.corestandards.org/math). Content is specific at each grade level and identifies six specific areas for high school mathematics: Number & Quantity; Algebra; Functions; Modeling; Geometry; and Statistics & Probability.

The Common Core Standards provide eight standards for mathematical practice formulated from the "processes and proficiencies" of the NCTM standards and the National Research Council's report *Adding It Up: Helping Children Learn Mathematics* (2001). The expectation is that teachers will help children:

1. Make sense of problems and persevere in solving them.
2. Reason abstractly and quantitatively.
3. Construct viable arguments and critique the reasoning of others.
4. Model with mathematics.
5. Use appropriate tools strategically.
6. Attend to precision.
7. Look for and make use of structure.
8. Look for and express regularity in repeated reasoning.
   (http://www.corestandards.org/math/practice/)

## EXERCISES 9.2

1. Have the Common Core Standards for Mathematics been implemented in your state or country? If so, in which grades?
2. Rank the Standards for Mathematical Practice in order of importance to you. Should these standards be in a priority order for teachers?

 **Additional exercises can be found on the website.**

## INTEGRATING TOPICS WITHIN MATHEMATICS

You, as a teacher of mathematics, will regularly be asked to show applications of the material being covered. There is an increased emphasis on blending mathematics with the other subjects being taught. Science is rather easy to do this with, because of the many formulas used there. Geography can be done with relative simplicity as global locations are discussed through the use of a global positioning system (GPS) and the Internet. How about English? Chapter 8 of this text contains references to Mark Twain's *Life on the Mississippi*, specifically where the length alterations are discussed. "T. C. Mits" (The Celebrated Man in the Street) is a poetic rendition of a multitude of topics through and beyond calculus in which application is discussed. This is not an exhaustive listing of titles, but you can see there are literary presentations involving mathematics available.

You are being (or will be) asked to integrate mathematics with other subjects. There are examples of places where connections are relatively easy to make like those just mentioned. Still, even those are often not made or, if they are, it is only at some superficial level. Why is that? Part of the answer lies in the idea that many adoption committees work from a basis of personal knowledge and experience. The mathematics they learned and teach has always been pretty much self-contained. Each topic was treated at the necessary level and then the curriculum (or text) moved on to something else. At times, yesterday's topic was connected to today's, like prime and composite numbers being followed by GCF (greatest common factor) and LCM (least common multiple).

Students frequently have trouble finding the GCF and LCM and deciding which one they have after they have "shoved the numbers around." A group of seventh-graders were adamant about having the following method included in this text. Their position was that it is very easy to follow and remember. Suppose the problem is to find the LCM and GCF of 16 and 24.

What goes into both 16 and 24? 2 | 16 24

Two is a common factor of both 16 and 24. Other values could be selected, but 2 is a typical reflexive answer of students. They could say 8, or even 4, but often they do not see that (particularly middle school or pre-algebra students) and thus, the typical response is 2. You now are left with 8 and 12 from the original numbers and the process is repeated.

What goes into both 8 and 12? 4 | 8 12

Two could have been selected again, instead of 4. Regardless, eventually the final pair of numbers will be relatively prime (only common factor is one).

Two and 4 are factors of the GCF (8), and the factors of the LCM (48) are 2, 4, 2, and 3. This is much easier to see if the whole presentation is consolidated:

$$
\begin{array}{r|rr}
2 & 16 & 24 \\
4 & 8 & 12 \\
\hline
 & 2 & 3
\end{array}
$$

Notice how the 2, 4, 2, and 3 form an "L", indicating the factors of the least common multiple, which is $2 \times 4 \times 2 \times 3 = 48$. Notice also that the factors in the vertical part of the "L" comprise the GCF of 16 and 24 which is $2 \times 4 = 8$ (remember, you are not limited to two factors either vertically or horizontally in the "L"). You should also see how this process makes a very strong connection between GCF and LCM. There is a message here—connection of topics is possible.

More than likely the above process is new for you, so that generates another message—the way you learned to do things may not be the best one for your students. That, in turn, brings up another message for you—it is imperative that you be a life-long learner in the field of teaching mathematics. How do you accomplish that task? Read professional literature. Attend professional conferences that focus on the teaching of mathematics. Participate in in-service opportunities. Enroll in additional classes (both pedagogy and content). Watch and listen to your students learn. They will give you all sorts of clues about how to become a more effective teacher of mathematics. Finally, think about what you are doing. Please do not reflexively follow the book or do it the way you have always done it. Think about connections between topics and subjects.

Regretfully, topics often are not connected. How many times have you seen LCM related to LCD (least common denominator)? Or, as fractions are added, how often are equivalent fractions mentioned in that context? Have you ever wondered why equivalent fractions, which to some extent employ multiplication of fractions, are discussed before multiplication of fractions? The list goes on. We ask you to integrate topics, and yet the presentations given to you for reference to work from are not done in that manner. Is it fair to expect you to do that?

Why is topic integration so uncommon? Perhaps the writers and teachers think that students will not make the desired connections. Maybe the teachers never thought of making those bridges between topics. After all, today's classroom teachers had little opportunity to see this style of teaching in their school experiences. There could be a lack of exposure to areas in life where experiences provide the necessary background from which to build the requested associations. Look at the other individuals who are studying to become teachers of mathematics. The person who graduates from high school and goes directly to college, then into teaching, is not uncommon. The newly graduated teacher of mathematics could well be a 21- or 22-year-old who possesses volumes of book learning with limited life experience. How can that individual be expected to relate the learning of mathematics to a variety of world applications? In that context, how practical does the request to integrate subject areas seem?

Extend the 21- or 22-year-old newly graduated teacher of mathematics idea back to high school experiences. More than likely that person was in the top half of the graduating class. Probably that graduate was only in "college-bound" classes. There is a good chance that there was limited exposure to others who were in the "non-college-bound" set of classes. That is, presumably this person will not have experienced the classes they will be teaching. Certainly the mathematics will be within their realm of capabilities, but there are a few significant factors that must be considered. First, not knowing the audience and how they react to teaching in general can make matters difficult. Be assured, for the most part, the general mathematics students will not react as you and your classmates did when you were in high school. Second, even though you have experience with the topics covered, you probably will not have thought of them in the context of a beginning or introductory mathematics class. Thus, linking things together, finding applications, and knowing ways to make topics interesting (which is difficult for many teachers, even those who have years of experience) are expectations of the beginning teacher. This dilemma can be largely attributed to lack of exposure.

Integration of topics, although most desirable both within mathematics and between subjects, is not an easy task. It is going to require reflective thought. You will need to consider a topic and all the connection points for it, in the mathematics classroom, the school context, and the world in which the students live. This has to be the world as the students see it, not the world that we as adults think the students see. There is a difference! These thoughts will begin to reveal paths to follow that can make the subject you discuss more real, dynamic, and interesting to the students. That is your job as a teacher of mathematics!

**Additional exercises can be found on the website.**

## THE BIG 20

The Big 20 was developed by an individual with many years of experience teaching high school students who were not particularly motivated to learn, let alone to learn mathematics (G. Rule, personal communication, 2000). Initially, the collection consisted of about 50 problems, but items were gradually eliminated (duplication or not essential for daily survival). It now consists of 20 problems that use multiplying and dividing by powers of 10; adding, subtracting, multiplying, and dividing whole numbers, fractions, and decimals; percent; money; converting decimals to fractions or percent (and all other combinations of these three); and finding squares and square roots of numbers. The contention is that if the skills necessary to complete the Big 20 are mastered, students will have command of the basic ideas necessary for mathematical survival in daily life. The skills are ones encountered regularly, either directly as they are shown here, or as parts of other problems.

When the idea was first introduced, it seemed quite simple to students and teachers of "upper level" mathematics classes. Even claims that students in the non-college-bound mathematics classes could do the Big 20 in less than 2 minutes (without calculators) did not seem too preposterous. The Big 20 has been given to several college mathematics education classes and groups of teachers. Because mathematics students are required to be able to complete the set of problems in no more than 2 minutes, missing none, it seems reasonable that teachers or preservice teachers should be able to do the same. However, no one has been able to meet the challenge when the Big 20 has been presented to teachers or college students the first time. A sample Big 20 is shown in Fig. 9.1. Additional attempts

| Big 20 | |
|---|---|
| 1. $\$57 \div 10 =$ | 2. $\$627 \div 100 =$ |
| 3. $\$48 \div 1000 =$ | 4. $\$8.45 \times 10 =$ |
| 5. $\$0.28 \times 100 =$ | 6. $12.34 \times 1000 =$ |
| 7. $0.005 \times \$0.12 =$ | 8. $\$18 + \$0.22 =$ |
| 9. $\$15 - \$0.27$ | 10. $\left(\dfrac{5}{8}\right)^2 =$ |
| 11. Express 0.82 as a fraction | 12. $\$53.6249 =$ |
| 13. $3\dfrac{1}{2} + 5\dfrac{1}{2} =$ | 14. $5\dfrac{1}{4} - 3\dfrac{1}{2} =$ |
| 15. $7 + 1\dfrac{1}{4} =$ | 16. $\dfrac{1}{4} \times 3\dfrac{1}{2} =$ |
| 17. $5\dfrac{1}{2}\%$ of $\$60$ | 18. $8.65 \div 0.05 =$ |
| 19. Express $\dfrac{1}{4}$ as a decimal | 20. $(0.2)^2 =$ |

**Figure 9.1**

would find different problems, perhaps in an alternative order; but they would be similar to the ones shown here.

## A START

In your studies you have covered a wide variety of advanced mathematical topics, well beyond what you will be teaching. You will probably first teach middle school mathematics or Pre-Algebra/Algebra courses at the high school level. You have all this mathematical background and you will be teaching students how to add, subtract, multiply, and divide whole numbers, fractions, decimals, and integers. What a letdown. Most teachers of mathematics want to teach the "good" subjects—Algebra II, pre-calculus, and calculus. Those are the places where real mathematics is done.

Frequently, the beginning teacher is assigned lower level mathematics classes, and maybe an Algebra I class or two, if they are lucky. The rationale for this generally focuses on the idea that all teachers need to start at the bottom and work their way up to the better subjects—earn their stripes. In many schools, the department chair selects courses to be taught first, then the chair's best friend gets to pick, and so on down the line of existing faculty. Some individuals believe that upper-level courses are more difficult to teach and should be awarded to the "better" teachers. The thinking is, because the concepts are more difficult in the advanced classes, the best teachers should teach them. The belief seems to be that only the better teacher is capable of presenting the advanced classes effectively. The better teacher here is associated with the classes to be taught, not the mathematical teaching skills. Teachers have similar mathematical backgrounds and yet it seems to be assumed that those with experience will do a better job delivering the advanced courses. Now throw into the mix high stakes state testing. Because of outside pressures, some schools assign the course associated with the standardized test to more experienced teachers. For example, if the state requires students to pass a standardized Algebra I tests for graduation, the school may assign the more experienced teachers to Algebra I. That generally leaves the new teacher with lower level classes in high school such as Pre-Algebra and transitional mathematics courses. These courses are usually filled with the students who have repeatedly had difficulty in mathematics. They typically do not like math because of their lack of success in the past.

It is your job to stimulate your students to want to learn the mathematics placed before them. You must create in them the wisdom that these topics are needed. They have got to understand that these concepts establish a foundation on which they will build for the rest of their academic, work, and recreational lives. It is difficult to do this because in many instances, the topics being covered have been dealt with earlier in the curriculum. Why then, are they being treated again? There are two simplistic and yet very realistic reasons: tradition, and the students do not know the material well enough to go on. Tradition is difficult to change. It is almost like

paying one's dues—I had to go through it more than once to assure I had mastered it and so do you. As was said earlier, any excuse will do.

Students not knowing a particular topic is a more difficult area to discuss. How do we justify treating the same concept year after year? One reason is the spiral approach embedded in our curriculum. A topic is discussed to the depths students can handle it and then abandoned until a later date when additional background information and readiness have been established. At that time, the topic is treated in greater detail or depth, expanding the horizons of the students in a manner where they see that the new information has built on the prior experiences. The problem is, even though this sounds like a reasonable approach, often the coverage is the same as before. Why? Perhaps some of the students in the class have not mastered the background material well enough to permit advancement. What about those who have? Investigation of subsequent treatment of topics often reveals that the same tunes and words are used by teachers; only the voice, pace, and inflections change. The rest of this chapter deals with topics visited more than once in our mathematics curriculum.

## FRACTIONS

Formative concepts relating to fractions are introduced in the early school years. They are built on and expanded throughout the curriculum. More difficult fractions are encountered with rational expressions in algebra. The procedures are the same, but the complexities involved, because of the polynomials and associated necessary skills, are much greater. Still, topics like rational expressions are dependent on the basic skills of working with fractions. Consider addition of two fractions with denominators that are relatively prime. Students are told:

Find the LCD (least common denominator).

Divide the denominator of the first fraction into the LCD and multiply the numerator of that first fraction by the determined missing factor from the division.

Divide the denominator of the second fraction into the LCD and multiply the numerator of that second fraction by the determined missing factor from that division.

Add the two products in the numerators.

Put the answer over the LCD.

Simplify your answer.

Typically, students encounter this topic several times in their careers. Certainly the words might be different, but those alterations are only to meet local or personal preferences. The ideas are still the same. Students say, "I have heard this before. I know what to do," and they tune you out. Perhaps the students are correct as they say they know what to do. If so, why is the topic covered again? Then again, maybe the students do not know what to do, but they think they do. Often, this provides an opportunity for creative mathematics where students take bits and pieces of explanations and combine them to create some completed whole, disregarding whether or not the development is correct. The concern of many students is to do something so you will not focus on them or their behavior. The assumption seems to be, "As long as I act busy, I am safe." There is no concern for correct responses. Students are satisfied to have done something and gotten you "out of their face" for a while.

Student attitudes as described at the end of the last paragraph are devastating, and yet they are all too common. How can that mentality be combated? How does a teacher go about getting students to want to learn material, whatever it is? One idea is to sing a different tune and use different words. The addition-of-fractions example could be covered with a carefully prepared sequence of problems and egg cartons. Using only the bottom part of the egg cartons as shown in Fig. 9.2, assume that the 12-hole carton is the unit or whole.

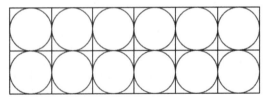

**Figure 9.2**

Prior discussion and exposure to egg cartons must ensure that students understand that for $\frac{1}{3}$ the unit is divided into three equal parts and only one part is selected. A variety of configurations can be used to indicate any fraction with egg cartons, but the ones shown in Fig. 9.3 for $\frac{1}{3}$ and $\frac{1}{4}$ are used in this example.

When addition has been discussed with the students previously, the basic idea was that things were put together to make a new whole. That idea can be used here. Assuming the students have no idea how to add fractions of any type, they at least

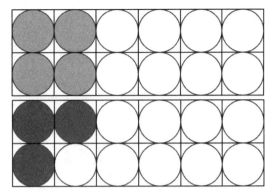

**Figure 9.3**

know that adding means to put together. Given that, they would represent the sum of $\frac{1}{3}$ and $\frac{1}{4}$ by placing representatives of those two pieces into the unit as shown in Fig. 9.4.

The discussion shifts to the number of holes in the unit that are filled out of the possible number of holes and the result is $\frac{7}{12}$, but that is the sum of $\frac{1}{3}$

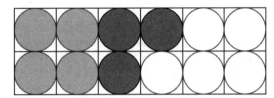

**Figure 9.4**

and $\frac{1}{4}$. The answer is determined and no discussion of LCD, dividing, multiplying, adding numerators, and placing sums over LCDs has taken place. This procedure will work for any fractions to be added. A method for determining the unit will be discussed later, but for now, consider the idea of carefully prepared sequences of problems that was mentioned earlier in this text.

Unit fractions with relatively prime denominators are selected for a reason. A number of them can lead students to a generalization that gives a large part of the rule discussed earlier for adding fractions with relatively prime denominators. The number of problems like $\frac{1}{3}+\frac{1}{4}=\frac{7}{12}$ that needs to be done before students notice some patterns will vary with the ability and patterning exposure of the class. However, given a collection like

$$\frac{1}{2}+\frac{1}{3}=\frac{5}{6}$$

$$\frac{1}{3}+\frac{1}{8}=\frac{11}{24}$$

$$\frac{1}{3}+\frac{1}{5}=\frac{8}{15}$$

$$\frac{1}{2}+\frac{1}{7}=\frac{9}{14}$$

it will not be long before some individual with an enterprising mind notices that the numerator of the answer is the sum of the denominators from the problem and the denominator of the answer is the product of the denominators from the problem. With that, the student has just announced that the LCD is found by multiplying the denominators. Also, although not quite as obvious, the student has laid the groundwork for stating that the numerator of each respective fraction is to be multiplied by something, in this case, the other denominator. You should notice that background work with equivalent fractions is quite handy here. At this point, there is a need to deal with non-unit fractions and again, a carefully prepared sequence comes into play.

Often texts do not deal with the fractions in such small breakdowns, but there are advantages if the consideration is to have students understand adding fractions. Treating each problem type with egg cartons provides the opportunity for students to build the appropriate partial generalizations that, when compiled, give the rule we all use when adding fractions. This would include fractions with the same denominator, related denominators (one is a multiple of the other, like 2 and 6), quasi-related denominators (they share a common factor other than the trivial case but one is not a multiple of the other, like 4 and 6), and relatively prime denominators (like 3 and 4). The only other consideration is to treat both unit and non-unit fractions. Mixed numbers react like those concepts already developed by separating the whole number parts off or by writing them as improper fractions and proceeding as if the fractions were just non-unit fractions.

Return now to determining the unit with egg cartons. A collection of egg cartons is desirable, and they should be cut into a variety of configurations from 1 hole through 12 holes. Suppose the task is to find $\frac{1}{2}+\frac{1}{3}$ using egg cartons. Determining the carton that can be used as the unit is the first objective. If students know that a "6-holer" is the unit, then one must question the sanity of using egg cartons. They already know how to find the LCD! For this discussion, we assume students do not know how to

find the LCD. Furthermore, we speculate that you can convince these secondary students that working with egg cartons as a learning tool is not too babyish (this might be a hard sell).

- Select a "1-holer" and ask if this can serve as the unit. There is no way to express a half or a third, so it cannot.
- With a "2-holer", a half can be expressed by filling one of the two holes, but not a third, so that cannot serve as the unit.
- A "3-holer" permits expressing a third by filling one of three holes, but not a half, so it cannot be the unit either.
- A "4-holer" shows a half but no third, so this cannot be the unit.
- The "5-holer" cannot be the unit because neither a half nor a third can be expressed.
- Finally, the "6-holer" provides the unit because 3 holes represent a half and 2 holes represent a third. Placing those two pieces in the unit yields a sum of $\frac{5}{6}$ for $\frac{1}{2}+\frac{1}{3}$. If, by chance, the "6-holer" is overlooked as a candidate for the unit, the procedure can continue to a "12-holer," which also would serve the purpose. However, the answer would be $\frac{10}{12}$, not in simplest terms. This might be contrary to some settings that demand that all fraction answers have all common factors divided out. More about that later.

Suppose, with the egg cartons, we discuss an LCD of 15. This exceeds the capacity of one egg carton (although some flats will accommodate this). That is no major hurdle. Place one carton beside another part of a carton or place one inside another to allow an overlap as is shown in Fig. 9.5. Then the fractional pieces are inserted and interpreted as needed.

One final issue with egg carton addition: Suppose the addends are $\frac{2}{3}$ and $\frac{3}{4}$. We assume that the students determined the "12-holer" is the unit. Placing the pieces inside the carton quickly shows that the pieces exceed the capacity of a carton. The question becomes, "By how much?" Place an additional

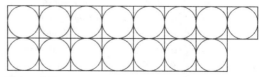

**Figure 9.5**

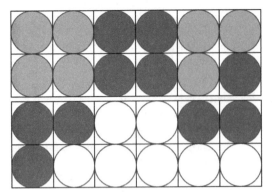

**Figure 9.6**

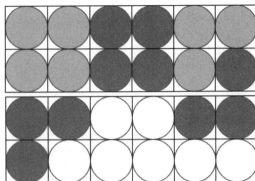

**Figure 9.7**

carton end to end with the initial unit as shown in Fig. 9.6. Continue filling until all the pieces are used. Then interpret the answer. There is one whole filled and part of another. The only remaining question is, how much of the next unit is filled? In this case, 5 more holes are filled and because a hole represents 1 of 12 equal-sized things, the extra is $\frac{5}{12}$. Thus, the response is $1\frac{5}{12}$ or $\frac{17}{12}$. Notice groundwork for the ability to discuss mixed numbers and improper fractions and converting between them has been laid. Many students gain the impression that $\frac{17}{12}$ is not simplified and that if it is simplified it must be expressed as $1\frac{5}{12}$.

Essentially, from here, any fraction addition problem can be done. Granted, the manipulation of cartons could be cumbersome. The intent would be that the students would understand what is going on with simpler problems and, thus, not need the cartons for complex ones. However, a very important factor is that if the student does need to see how the problem is done, the cartons can be used to demonstrate that information. Here again, the idea of a carefully laid sequence of problems mentioned earlier becomes extremely important. The student creates responses to some problems using the cartons and then conjectures the appropriate generalization, which essentially is the rule normally written in texts and told by teachers. This shows you an example of a different tune and words to teach a familiar concept.

Subtraction with egg cartons is similar. The unit is determined as in addition. The sum is placed in the unit and the known addend is inserted inside that sum. Any holes of the sum that are not filled become the missing addend. Figure 9.7 shows how $\frac{1}{3}-\frac{1}{4}$ would be computed using egg cartons. Again, the carefully defined sequence would be pursued and the students would use the egg carton examples

to provide the background for the necessary generalizations.

**Additional exercises can be found on the website.**

The egg cartons do not serve well as manipulatives for doing multiplication and division of fractions. Several other items can be used to model all four operations involving fractions: number line, paper folding, unifix cubes, Cuisenaire rods, fraction kits (either commercial or homemade), and so on. The essential problem is that of determining the LCD using any of these models. If the student knows how to find the LCD, there is little sense in working with the manipulatives, because with the LCD, associated abstractions become the necessary rules and generalizations that are established through the use of the manipulative. Students have already been told all the essential information. However, if they do not know the rules, the Cuisenaire rods are a wonderful tool to help them see how and why we do the fraction operations and why things come out the way they do.

It must be assumed there is appropriate background and familiarity with the rods. If not, it must be built prior to dealing with fractions. Figure 9.8 shows the basic set of Cuisenaire rods. The assumption is that initially White is the unit and all other rods are scaled to it. Red is the same length as two

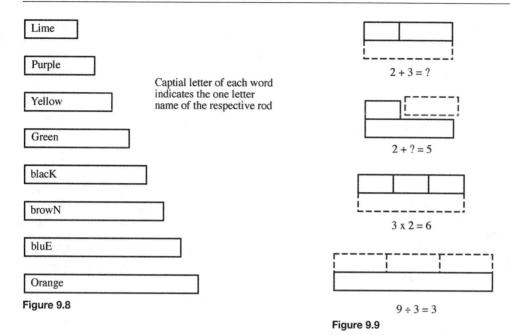

Captial letter of each word
indicates the one letter
name of the respective rod

Figure 9.8

$2 + 3 = ?$

$2 + ? = 5$

$3 \times 2 = 6$

$9 \div 3 = 3$

Figure 9.9

Whites, Lime is the same length as three Whites, and so forth. Shortened versions of notation soon appear like 5W = Y (5 Whites = 1 Yellow), and foundations for symbols representing objects are laid. This can be invaluable in settings such as the variable concept, which many students have so much difficulty with in beginning algebra.

It is now assumed that the student is aware of how to add, subtract, multiply, and divide using Cuisenaire rods. As was mentioned earlier, if this background is not present, it has to be established before dealing with fractions. Figure 9.9 shows an example of each operation with whole numbers. A series of foundational activities is important as beginning work for fractions. First, rods other than White have to be established as candidates for the unit. If Red is the unit, what is Green? Three, because it takes a "train" (two or more rods laid end to end in a straight line) to be the same length as the Green rod. If Red is the unit, what is Orange? Five. It is vital that a multitude of these activities be done, using various rods as the unit. Furthermore, at the beginning, fractional parts are not considered—only counting-number results.

The next activity type, also demanding a large number of exposures, involves statements like, "Can the browN rod be matched with a train of four cars where the rods are all the same length?" In this setting, the emphasis then focuses on the idea that there are four rods, all the same length, making up what will become the unit rod. Eventually the dis-

cussion will focus on a unit being divided into four equal-sized parts and a Red will be one of those four equal parts or $\frac{1}{4}$. This approach assists students in understanding the concept of fractions and that the unit is divided into equal pieces.

Only after extensive exposure to each of the preceding problem types do you proceed with problems like "If Red is the unit, what is White?" Now the student has an intuitive feel for what the response needs to be. You should reflexively say "one half," because you are familiar with all the related concepts. However, a student, no matter what the grade level, who is not fully aware will need to think. It can be shown that White is not the same as a full unit. The question becomes one of, "What part of the Red, or full unit, is the White?" Because it takes two Whites to make a Red, the White is one of two equal pieces necessary to make a Red; one out of two equal pieces: one out of two; one half. That verbal transition in the last sentence is extremely helpful to some students who struggle with understanding fractions and eventually operating on them. You should also note that the one out of two comments in the last sentence lays important groundwork for the concept of ratios. Problems like "If Red is the unit, what is Lime?" also need to be done. Selection of different rods as the unit and similar questions that yield fractional parts, both proper and improper, is appropriate here.

Only after all these examples and practice is the student ready to proceed to using the Cuisenaire rods to operate on fractions. If that background is not there, or if it is not established, use of the Cuisenaire rods as a manipulative is doomed to failure. The same is true with any manipulative in any situation. The appropriate background experience with the selected tool has to be present.

The key to adding, subtracting, and dividing fractions is to establish a unit rod, or common denominator, most frequently called the least common denominator.

Determination of the unit rod is the same for subtraction as it was for addition. Once that is accomplished, the focus shifts to the numerators and a procedure used for whole-number subtraction. Consider $9 - 4 = M$. The sum is 9 and the known addend is 4. The task is to determine the missing addend. That problem can be written in a different manner: $4 + M = 9$, or addend plus missing addend equals sum. Using the rods, the sum, 9, is known, as is the addend 4. The students need only find the rod that should be placed with the 4 rod to make a train the same length as the 9 rod. In this case, the 5 rod is the appropriate response. All others (except a train of 5 White rods, a train of 2 Reds and a White, etc.) will create a train that is either too long or too short. Transferring this procedure to fractions from the rods is now an easy task.

Division is easy to show with the Cuisenaire rods. Before proceeding, focus on any division problem, $8 \div 2$, for example. The real question in this problem is, "How many sets of 2 are contained in 8?" Accepting that and considering something like $\frac{1}{2} \div \frac{1}{6}$ the question is, "How many sixths are in one-half?" With the rods, the question becomes one of determining a rod that can be divided into halves and sixths at the same time. This procedure should be familiar to the students at this point. Assuming that, the students determine Green is the unit, Lime is a half and White is a sixth. Remember that the question is, "How many sixths are in one-half?" That can be translated to, "How many Whites are in a Lime?" Prior experience or a quick concrete manipulation should lead the student to the answer of "3." Thus, $\frac{1}{2} \div \frac{1}{6} = 3$. As before, a carefully developed series of problems like this should lead to a generalization. For example, using only the $\frac{1}{2} \div \frac{1}{6} = 3$, the discussion would focus on the ability to get an answer of 3 out of the numbers given. Students seem quite willing to focus on the 2, 6, and 3. So, the question really becomes one of, "How do you get a 3 out of

a 2 and a 6?" Almost all students will accept the idea of dividing 6 by 2 as trivially obvious, and now the task becomes one of determining how to convert $\frac{1}{2} \div \frac{1}{6}$ to a situation that yields 6 divided by 2. Invariably, some student quickly says that all you need to do is to have 6 over 1 rather than 1 over 6. That student has just said that we need to invert the second fraction and multiply; the rule has now been developed and verbalized. Certainly there is a need to consider non-unit fractions and all associated extensions involved in division of fractions, but do not miss the point that the basic rule has been established, and it is unlikely that it will be forgotten.

We now consider multiplication of fractions on the Cuisenaire rods. Continuance of the procedures already established for the other operations with fractions seems most logical at this point. However, it should be noted that there might be better, easier ways to model multiplication of fractions with the rods. Consider the product of $\frac{1}{2}$ and $\frac{1}{4}$. The problem can also be stated as finding $\frac{1}{2}$ of $\frac{1}{4}$. In terms of the rods, the task becomes one of finding a unit that can be divided into fourths and then take a half of one of those fourths. Purple is the first rod that can be divided into fourths. That fourth is represented by White. However, White cannot be divided in half. Two Purples would have 2 Whites representing a fourth and the 1 White would represent a half of a fourth. But 2 Purples is the same as a browN and thus, browN is the unit. With browN as the unit and White as the answer, the only task left is to interpret White in terms of browN. Because it takes 8 Whites to make a browN, White is $\frac{1}{8}$. Thus, $\frac{1}{2}$ of $\frac{1}{4}$ is $\frac{1}{8}$. Again, a sequence of carefully defined problems can be used to develop the desired generalization.

The significant thing to note here is that all four fraction operations can be modeled for the students using the same manipulative. Each respective model leads to the desired generalization and the students see the rules developed as opposed to being told. Again, the Cuisenaire rods are not the only model available for developing the operational rules for fractions. You should not forget that you have shown all four basic operations with the same manipulative.

Earlier it was mentioned that the Cuisenaire rods would be used to model multiplication of fractions to continue along the lines that had already been established. However, you need to consider one other model for multiplication of fractions before the issue is completed. Figure 9.10 shows a grid-type model for finding the product of $\frac{2}{3}$ and $\frac{4}{5}$.

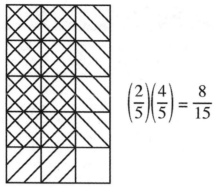

$$\left(\frac{2}{5}\right)\left(\frac{4}{5}\right) = \frac{8}{15}$$

**Figure 9.10**

A rectangle is divided into thirds in one direction and fifths in the other. The appropriate number of sections is marked to show the fractional parts. Vertically, $\frac{2}{3}$ is indicated with diagonal ("down to the left") segments. Horizontally, $\frac{4}{5}$ is indicated with diagonal "down to the right" segments. A smaller rectangular region indicates $\frac{4}{5}$ of $\frac{2}{3}$. This particular region indicates the number of small rectangular "criss-crossed" regions out of the total number of rectangles. This smaller number becomes the numerator of the final product and the total number becomes the denominator.

### EXERCISE 9.6

1.  Assume fractions with denominators of 3 and 5 are to be added. Describe a process to determine the unit rod that would permit expression of thirds and fifths at the same time that could be used with students.

**Additional exercises can be found on the website.**

Operations on fractions raise some issues that deserve mention here. Many discussions of fractions have students reducing fractions to lowest terms. Is that the most descriptive word that can be used? No. The idea of writing big and then little $\left(\frac{3}{6} = \frac{3}{6}\right)$ deals with a reduction in size—reducing. Certainly that is not the intent when a student is asked to reduce a fraction, but at the same time, it is literally correct. Another word that is often used is "simplify." Initially, that sounds better than reduce, but simplify can be interpreted as making things more useful. If that is the case, the idea of

simplifying $\frac{4}{8}$ to $\frac{1}{2}$ may not, in fact, be what is best. It could be that later $\frac{4}{8}$ is going to need to be expressed as $\frac{12}{24}$, and thus what was thought to be simplification actually turns out to be another potential source of error and takes the student in the wrong direction. Finally comes the phrase, "divide out common factors." Undoubtedly this is most beneficial when algebraic situations are considered. For example, it is relatively common for algebra students to "reduce" or "simplify" $\frac{n+3}{n}$ to 3, or maybe 4 if the 1s are shown for the division. Typically teachers explain that this is not an acceptable procedure because the situation requires that common factors be divided and, in the numerator, "$n$" is a term, not a factor. If the students had previously used "divide out common factors," perhaps this error could have been avoided. How soon is it reasonable to expect students to be able to grasp the meaning and say, "divide out common factors"?

Having fractions with all common factors divided out raises another question: "Why?" In problems sets sometimes students are given $\frac{4}{6}$ as a part of an exercise. Yet those same students are required to express their answers with all common factors divided out. Thus, a student would be required to express $\frac{4}{6}$ as $\frac{2}{3}$. If students are required to divide out all common factors, why then is it acceptable for textbooks and teachers to give them something like $\frac{4}{6}$ as a part of an assignment? Why don't we practice what we preach?

Finally, what is the presentation sequence for addition of fractions? Figure 9.11 shows a collection of types of addends that can be considered when doing addition of two fractions. "Related denominators" means that one denominator is a multiple of the other. "Quasi-related" means that one denominator is not a multiple of the other, and yet they are not relatively prime, either. "Unrelated" indicates that the denominators are relatively prime. Unit fractions have a numerator of 1, whereas non-unit fractions have numerators other than 1.

| Unit | $\frac{1}{5} + \frac{1}{5}$ | $\frac{1}{7} + \frac{1}{14}$ | $\frac{1}{4} + \frac{1}{6}$ | $\frac{1}{2} + \frac{1}{3}$ |
|---|---|---|---|---|
| Non-unit | $\frac{2}{7} + \frac{3}{7}$ | $\frac{2}{7} + \frac{5}{14}$ | $\frac{3}{8} + \frac{7}{10}$ | $\frac{4}{7} + \frac{2}{5}$ |
| Mixed | $4\frac{2}{7} + 5\frac{3}{7}$ | $3\frac{7}{7} + 6\frac{5}{14}$ | $4\frac{3}{8} + 5\frac{7}{10}$ | $6\frac{4}{7} + 3\frac{2}{5}$ |

**Figure 9.11**

Figure 9.11 is much more than a fraction addition chart. Notice that, in each example, dividing out common factors is not a consideration in either the problem or the answer. This is significant because, as students are beginning to deal with different types of addition problems, it is desirable for them to focus on the issue at hand. Including a problem that yields an answer of $\frac{4}{6}$ initially is not wise because a second skill is involved. At first, focus only on the one concept. Eventually situations involving dividing out common factors must be discussed, but not until a solid foundation has been built. Yes, the students should be familiar with equivalent fractions at this stage of their development, but even then, the possibility for confusion exists.

Figure 9.11 also contains a set of problems in which digits are not repeated within the problem (except for $\frac{1}{5}+\frac{1}{5}$ and numerators of unit fractions). Many people deepen their understanding of mathematics by looking at solved examples. During that examination period, they frequently trace the digits used from step to step. Duplication of digits needs to be considered, just not initially.

Figure 9.11 does not represent all possible problem types. Depending on the ability of the students, it may be necessary to insert an intermediate step between $\frac{1}{5}+\frac{1}{5}$ and $\frac{1}{7}+\frac{1}{14}$. A skill involved is to recognize the process for converting $\frac{1}{7}+\frac{1}{14}$ to $\frac{2}{14}+\frac{1}{14}$ so the addition can be completed. Students should have had prior exposure to prime numbers and equivalent fractions so getting $\frac{2}{14}$ should not be a major hurdle. If it is, why are you trying a task that depends on a skill that is not available to the students? If the only addition exposure the students have had involved adding unit fractions with the same denominator, those students, depending on capabilities, may not be able to alter their thought patterns to consider a non-unit fraction without some prompting from the teacher. This may seem like a trivial issue, and yet it is often the case that these innocent-looking little things are the major stumbling blocks for students. With just a little more care in the sequencing of the presentation, these obstacles can be avoided.

Notice that in Fig. 9.11 all sums are less than 1 prior to dealing with mixed numbers. Even with the mixed numbers, the fractional sums are all less than 1, thus avoiding the need to regroup. As noted earlier, this is a conscious decision to avoid making a confusing situation any more complex. Ultimately the topics will need to be encountered, just not in the initial explanation, examples, and problems.

## COMMON DENOMINATORS

When teaching addition and subtraction of fractions, students frequently hear that they need common denominators to perform the operation. When teaching multiplication and division of fractions, students are often told to forget that rule. Does that confuse some students? What would happen if common denominators were used when multiplying and dividing fractions? When doing $\frac{2}{3}\times\frac{4}{5}$, students would find equivalent fractions to get LCDs and multiply:

$$\frac{2}{3}\times\frac{4}{5}=\frac{10}{15}\times\frac{12}{15}=\frac{120}{225}=\frac{5\times24}{5\times45}=\frac{24}{45}=\frac{3\times8}{3\times15}=\frac{8}{15}$$

They should see that $\frac{8}{15}$ is the product of the original fractions, found by multiplying the numerators and denominators.

Dealing with division of fractions, students are traditionally asked to memorize a *new* rule. One such catchy rule is *keep it, switch it, flip it*. When doing $\frac{2}{3}\div\frac{4}{5}$, *keep it, switch it, flip it* means *keep* the first fraction $\frac{2}{3}$, *switch* the operation from division to multiplication, and *flip* the second fraction from $\frac{4}{5}$ to $\frac{5}{4}$. The resulting problem is $\frac{2}{3}\times\frac{5}{4}$, which yields a result of $\frac{10}{12}$ or $\frac{5}{6}$. What would happen if we found common denominators and then divided?

We know $8\div2=\frac{8}{2}=4$. In other words, 8 divided by 2 can be written as a fraction with 8 as the numerator and 2 as the denominator. This same problem could be expressed as $\frac{8}{1}\div\frac{2}{1}=\frac{8}{2}=4$.

Using other values, $12 \div 6 = \frac{12}{1} \div \frac{6}{1} = \frac{12}{6} = 2$. We could write 12 as $\frac{24}{2}$ and 6 as $\frac{12}{2}$ yielding $12 \div 6 = \frac{24}{2} \div \frac{12}{2} = \frac{24}{12} = 2$. The answer is the same. *Notice the use of common denominators.*

While the original problem, $\frac{2}{3} \div \frac{4}{5}$, divides fractions rather than whole numbers, it could be expressed as $\frac{10}{15} \div \frac{12}{15}$, using common denominators. As before, with equivalent fractions, we only need to divide the numerators. Therefore, the answer is 10 divided by 12 or $\frac{10}{12} = \frac{5}{6}$. Try a few and you just might like the process!

## DECIMALS

In today's technologically based world, why isn't there more emphasis on decimals and less on fractions? It seems as if decimals appear more consistently in real-world settings. Certainly in the world of students of all ages, decimals are present with money. Calculators are evident throughout the curriculum, and they work with decimals. Most calculators starting with the basic scientific models and up operate with fractions, but all calculators operate conveniently with decimals. Calculators are a part of the world in which the students live. One argument against permitting calculators in the school is that of expense. In an age where many students have cars, cell phones, tablets, hand-held devices, more than one video game, and part-time jobs, coupled with the low cost of basic calculators and calculators that are on cell phones, it seems incomprehensible that price would be raised as an excuse for disallowing calculators. Some districts have purchased a calculator for each student. Other districts buy classroom sets. In many communities individuals contact schools and commit to purchasing basic calculators for any student who cannot afford one. It seems fairly safe to assume that a calculator should be available for all students, something that is strongly recommended by NCTM. Calculators are inherent on almost all technological devices in today's world!

Accepting that calculators should exist in a school, how would the decimal curricular offering be altered? Certain readiness skills must be present before students can consider operating with decimals. These will be needed whether or not a calculator is available. If calculators are present, computation with decimals might be within the grasp of most students. Individuals opposed to the use of calculators rationalize that students should understand a concept prior to using the calculator. This could be used as an argument against the use of calculators early in the curriculum. We do not argue the value and necessity of understanding concepts. We totally agree. However, we must exercise caution that our zeal for "understanding a concept" is not an excuse to prevent the use of technology and teach as we always have. Remember, any excuse will do.

Calculator proponents contend that students have the opportunity to discover decimal operational procedures while they experiment with a calculator before formal instruction dealing with decimals. It should be noted that it is most desirable for students to have a good idea of what is going on as opposed to employing rote memorization of procedures and rules. For some reason, a vast majority of our population and colleagues seem much more ready to embrace memorizing rules with no understanding of the concepts involved than they are to embrace using technology where there is limited understanding of the concepts involved. We wonder why that is. Minimal readiness skills for operation with decimals include place value; ability to multiply by counting number powers of 10; ability to divide by counting number powers of 10; realization that $3.2 = 3.20 = 3.200 \ldots$; knowledge that decimals are fractions with denominators that are counting-number powers of 10; and facts for all basic operations.

As you undoubtedly know, not everyone is thrilled with the use of calculators. Close to the turn of the century, some state legislatures adopted the position that no calculators should be permitted in any school below seventh grade. The basic argument is that students need to know how to compute with the standard algorithms by hand. There is one huge flaw in this approach to the situation. It seems as if there is an assumption that if a student can perform an operation by hand, that student understands the workings of the algorithm. Nothing is further from the actuality in the classroom. Many students memorize how to do an algorithm and have absolutely no idea what is behind its function.

As a professional, you should visit the Mathematically Correct site (http://www.mathematical lycorrect.com). This is a part of helping you make an informed decision. If you are against new math in schools, this site presents plenty of fuel for your fire. It gives several articles on "the invasion of new math" in our schools. Plenty of enthusiasm is conveyed for their cause. There are articles on what is going on in teaching mathematics in the nation.

Many texts are reviewed in detail on this site. Mathematically Sane (http://mathematicallysane.com) presents an opposite position from Mathematically Correct. It is your professional responsibility to peruse that site as well.

Given the readiness skills, and assuming exposure to manipulatives (base 10 blocks, number line, century charts, etc.) in other areas of the mathematics curriculum, students can extend prior disclosures to deal with new topics. Base 10 blocks should have been a part of earlier curriculum discussions. Figure 9.12 shows the fundamental pieces of a base 10 block set as the students would have seen them in prior work with whole numbers. The transition to using the blocks with decimals is simple, if they have had exposure to some other manipulative where renaming of pieces was encountered. This renaming is an important background skill for working with decimals and also for the concept of a variable in algebra. If they have not been exposed to renaming pieces, that background must be established. Once students can rename pieces, concrete examples of addition and subtraction with decimals are similar to those that would have been done with whole numbers.

Let the large square (F for flat) be designated as the unit. The long thin rectangle (L for long) will then be 0.1 because it represents 1 of 10 equal parts, which can be written 0.1 or $\frac{1}{10}$. The small square (S for small) will be 0.01 or $\frac{1}{100}$ because it is one of 100 equal parts of the unit. Decimals up to hundredths can now be represented. This is beginning background for the special case of decimal fractions with denominators of 100, leading to percent. Developmentally, students would do problems concretely first, manipulating pieces to depict the operation. A significant step in the sequence would involve students drawing pictures of the blocks to show the work being done, followed by use of letters to represent the blocks being used. These letters provide more subliminal algebraic background. Ultimately, the students would achieve the desired goal of being able to perform the operation at the abstract level, without the blocks or representations of them. It is important to note that the blocks can be used for support when needed if the progress toward abstractions has been too rapid.

Consider 2.31 + 5.64. Figure 9.13 represents the sum with base 10 blocks. The addends can also be shown using F to represent the units, L for tenths, and S for hundredths.

```
FF        LLL         S
FFFFF     LLLLLL      SSSS
```

Their sum would be shown by joining the respective pieces together, giving

```
FFFFFFF   LLLLLLLLLL  SSSSS
```

or 7.95. Even with the duplication of digits the problem should not prove overly difficult for students to comprehend. Emphasis would be on the alignment of the ones digits (eliminating the need for the rule, "line up the decimal point"). Similar problems should prove relatively easy for most students. If necessary, the block set can be expanded to represent thousandths by using the flat to represent

## Base 10 Blocks

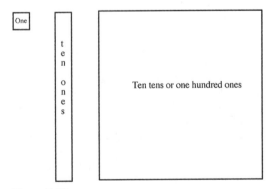

Figure 9.12

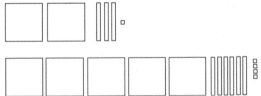

Figure 9.13

tenths. Note that the variable has changed (more algebra foundation). For many students who are functional with whole-number and decimal addition through hundredths, the transition to thousandths is natural. The blocks can be used with any student having difficulty.

Two potential problem areas exist with addition of decimals: regrouping and ragged decimals. Finding the sum of 3.4 + 5.27 is an example of a ragged decimal addition. If the student uses the blocks, interpretation is easy, as is the case with pictures or letters representing the blocks. The difficulty arises at the abstract level. Earlier it was noted that one readiness skill for students is the realization that 3.4 = 3.40. If that is in the students' background, 3.4 + 5.27 poses no particular obstacle. If that skill is not present, it is reasonable to ask why the student is being asked to perform this task without appropriate background capabilities.

A prerequisite skill when using the blocks provides the answer to regrouping situations. Students learn early in block use that 10 ones are equivalent to one 10 and the substitution can be made at any time—either way: one 10 for 10 ones, or 10 ones for one 10. Extend this background to include ideas like "one tenth is equivalent to ten hundredths," and most problem areas typically associated with regrouping in decimal addition and subtraction are eliminated. Consider 2.7 + 5.6 where L is the unit and S is a tenth. The problem shown with the blocks becomes

LL          SSSSSS
LLLLL       SSSSS

The sum expressed in terms of the blocks would be

LLLLLLL   SSSSSSSSS   SSS

The students know that ten Ss can be traded for one L, which leads to the idea that ten tenths are equivalent to one unit. Thus, the sum is LLLLLLLL SSS or 8.3. This exposure to the blocks greatly simplifies the dilemmas normally encountered by students, particularly those who have difficulty understanding new ideas presented at an abstract level. Using the blocks can take additional time to develop the concept, but the decrease in confusion provides justification for the time spent. In the long run, time will be saved, because the procedure will be understood in future encounters, avoiding the need for reteaching it.

Regrouping is a major hurdle for many students in subtraction. As in addition, the blocks eliminate much of the confusion for most students. Suppose the problem is 9.3 − 2.8. Using the blocks where

F represents the unit and the one-to-one correspondence model, the problem would be shown as:

FFFFFFFFF   LLL
FF          LLLLLLLL

The bottom row is to be matched with the top row using a one-to-one correspondence alignment. The top row does not have enough Ls to permit the one-to-one matching needed. A trade can be done in which one F is exchanged for 10 Ls, something that is easy because they are equivalent.

FFFFFFFF   LLLLLLLLLLLLL
FF         LLLLLLLL

Matching the Fs and Ls the problem becomes:

FF         FFFFF  LLLLLLLL  LLLLL
FF         LLLLLLLL

The top row of Ls and Fs is broken as shown to make it easier to see the one-to-one correspondence. At this point, the eight Ls can be paired off in the top and bottom rows and they eliminate each other, leaving five Ls. Similarly, two Fs are eliminated, leaving six Fs, and the final answer is FFFFFF LLLLL or 6.5. The transition to the abstract method for subtraction is much easier for students who possess this background. The 9.3 becomes $^{8}9.^{13}3$ and the subtraction can now be completed. Regrouping and its demonstration are important and, at the same time, a major source of confusion for many students.

In the take-away model, you start with the sum and take away an addend. To model this, begin with nine Fs and three Ls (FFFFFFFFF LLL). The problem is to take away two Fs and eight Ls. The dilemma arises when the students realize they can take away two Fs but they cannot take away eight Ls. Immediately the students come to the rationalization that one F is equivalent to ten Ls and make the exchange reflexively (we hope—FFFFFFFF LLL LLLLLLLLLL). Now the student can take away two Fs and eight Ls, leaving six Fs and five Ls, or 6.5.

All of the difficult areas that existed with whole-number subtraction involving regrouping still are present when considering decimals plus the complexities of ragged decimals. As mentioned in addition, if the students know that 7.4 = 7.40 = 7.400 . . . (readiness skill), many dilemmas are eliminated. One major hurdle still exists with decimal subtraction: 9 − 2.7. The student must be aware that there is a decimal point understood to be after the 9 in this case. Then the student must realize that 9 = 9.0, something that is even more difficult than 7.4 = 7.40. . . . Once those items are understood, most students are fairly adept at handling the rest of the related problems.

The problem 9 − 2.7 can be done another way, however, and it is often much easier for students. The 9 can be expressed in a multitude of ways. One very convenient name for 9 is 8.9 + 0.1. The subtraction can now be viewed as 8.9 − 2.7, which is 7.2. However, that 0.1 needs to be added back in to keep the numbers in balance so the answer is 7.3. You should note that this example has some duplication of digits. In other areas of the text, it is stated that this duplication can be confusing and should be avoided for the sake of student understanding. The mentality behind the statement is that students often track numbers as they learn a new procedure. With duplicated digits, they sometimes lose track of which digit went or came from where, lessening the likelihood that they will understand the process quickly.

---

### EXERCISE 9.9

1. Create an addition problem involving three addends with units, tenths, and hundredths in each of them so that each column requires regrouping. Show through a series of steps using F, L, and S how the regrouping from each place would be accomplished, being careful to adequately show the trades as they are made, doing one exchange at a time. Relate each step to an abstract representation of the same problem.

---

 **Additional exercises can be found on the website.**

One decimal setting appears impossible to students, as was mentioned in chapter 8. Even when they see a "proof" that $0.\overline{999} = 1$, they resist accepting it. The typical development would include a discussion that $0.\overline{999}$ is a repeating decimal that never ends. It would be distinguished from 0.9, 0.99, 0.999, and so on, each of which terminates and, thus, can be expressed as $\frac{9}{10}, \frac{99}{100}, \frac{999}{1000}$, and so on, respectively. We now assume the students possess some algebraic background and are able to subtract one equation from another.

Let

$X = 0.\overline{999}$ (1)

$10X = 9.\overline{999}$ (2) Multiply (1) by 10

$10X = 9.\overline{999}$

$X = 0.\overline{999}$ (3) Subtract (1) from (2)

$9X = 9.000$ (4) Collect like terms

$X = 1$ (5) Divide (4) by 9

But,

$X = 0.\overline{999}$ Given

$1 = 0.\overline{999}$ (6) Transitive prop. =

Assure students that the 9s repeat in $0.\overline{999}$ and in $9.\overline{999}$ as far as they want, and usually they will accept the subtracting of 9 from 9 in any place value to the right of the decimal, no matter how far to the right it is. This brings them to the conclusion that the missing addend for $9.\overline{999} - 0.\overline{999}$ is 9, which is generally accepted with little resistance. Only when the division is completed in Equation (5) and it is concluded that $1 = 0.\overline{999}$ does the resistance begin to build. You need to be extremely convincing in your discussion to get many students beyond this resistance. Then, you can tackle expressing the repeating decimal $3.\overline{273273273}$ as a fraction. The resistance to this will usually not be as great as that of $1 = 0.\overline{999}$. Finally, attempt to get a class to show the fractional value of $4.\overline{234234234}$. As these repeating decimal values are converted to fractions, a multitude of skills is practiced. With proper emphasis on your part, the students can begin to see the value of having a command of some of the skills we ask them to learn.

## AMUSEMENTS, FASCINATIONS, AND BEYOND

For a variety of reasons, students are not excited about the learning of mathematics. That is tragic, particularly in light of the idea that most children enter elementary school excited about learning mathematics. Still, for many children, when they leave elementary school, their attitudes and outlooks have changed to that of rejection. Why is it that so many students view mathematics as boring, having no useful value in their world, and being of little worth as they consider career options? Certainly, that impression merits investigation, but, for now, focus on ideas that might change the negative position about mathematics held by many middle schoolers.

The teacher, along with possessing excitement, enthusiasm, sincerity, an interest in students, adequate background knowledge, and stellar teaching skills, can have a tremendous positive impact on student learning. Assuming that, where does one begin to entice students back to being interested in learning mathematics? Games and tricks are a beginning. Examples are scattered throughout this text, and sources of them abound in the literature and support materials for teachers. One location of basic beginning information is NCTM publications, which have regular columns like "Technology Reviews," "Publications," and "Products." Each of these columns, but particularly "Publications," will give a basic description, along with an evaluation, of items submitted for review. Not everything that is appropriate as a resource is submitted, but the supply is adequate for a beginning. Another source of ideas is the Ole Miss Math Challenge maintained by one of the authors of this text and located at http://mathcontest.olemiss.edu. This interactive site provides fun challenging math puzzlers for all levels.

There are advantages to classifying games and tricks so they can be readily integrated into a curriculum. As you develop your collection, some will be your favorites. Those, you will probably be able to do reflexively and blend them into a class without much initial planning. For us, "1089" is an example of that. Students are asked to write any three-digit number, without repeating the digits. That number is to be reversed (358 becomes 853) and the smaller subtracted from the larger. At this point, two directions can be taken, both of which amaze students and each of which holds additional teaching value.

First, tell the students that the tens digit (note subtle use of place value) of their missing addend will be a nine. Careful observation on your part will reveal individuals who may not have that in their answer. You have just received a diagnostic clue. Those individuals may not have heard or followed the instructions. It might also be that these individuals have difficulty dealing with subtraction involving regrouping. Any student experiencing difficulty here often can be prompted and assisted quickly to get over the hurdle, at least temporarily.

The other direction can amaze students and lead them into discovering a pattern at the same time. Announce to them that if they tell you their ones digit, you will tell them the hundreds digit in their answer, or vice versa. They do not need to give the place, only the digit. Because the two digits have a sum of nine, determining the missing digit is quick and simple. The discovery part of this is valuable for the students. You do not want to tell the secret.

Instead, lead them through the process of figuring it out. One crucial word of caution here: Students who determine the pattern need to be kept from telling. Otherwise, the opportunity for discovery by others is squelched.

There are two clues to help students discover the pattern. First, when a student says a number, "three," for example, you say "un six." Repeat that with a few more students, supplying different numbers. Those who "know" the trick can be encouraged to play along to help others or to think of clues that will not tell the others the secret. Generally, this "un" will help more students past the barrier and they will know what is being done. Some, however, will probably need a little more help. For them, and this is the second clue that is to be used if the first one fails, if a student says "four" as the digit, you say "four un five." Most students will reflexively say nine because they often say "four un five" to represent the sum four plus five. Now almost everyone should know the secret. This discourse usually only takes a few minutes. Those who know the secret and play along will frequently give a reversal as a part of the examples; that is, if one student says two and you say "un seven," the knowledgeable student will say "seven" allowing you to say "un two." This too can be a very strong hint for those having difficulty.

There is one last thing that cannot be overlooked with the "1089" activity. If a student says the digit is nine, you say you know it is in the ones place. That statement is followed by instructions to write a zero in the hundreds place of the missing addend, even though that is not standard procedure. Having a zero in the hundreds place is necessary for the next stage of the trick.

Take the answer, whatever it is, and reverse it, adding the two values. Using the values listed earlier, $853 - 358 = 495$. Reversing gives 594. Adding 495 and 594 yields 1089. This will be the sum in all situations. A common question is whether or not this will work all the time. Resist the temptation to tell. Instead, have the students do another example and form a conjecture. More than likely, they will not think to consider the fact that each student selected different values initially. Because everyone got the same answer, it is probable that the procedure works for all examples. In the process of doing another example, the students are again practicing skills they need. If necessary, lead them to do still another example. Eventually they will conclude that the procedure works consistently, barring arithmetic errors.

The elaborate explanation was used with "1089" to give you insight into how to relate number tricks to a class. The rest of the number tricks discussed here are brief because it is assumed you will be able to insert the diversions, elaborations, and questions needed to attract student attentions. The examples given here are ones that are known to appeal to students. These are only a small part of attractions for students that are available. You should begin a collection of games, tricks, applications, and techniques you can refer to throughout your teaching career. Here are a few to start your collection. Remember, if you want your students to try these, *you should do them as well*! Enjoy.

1. Divide 30 by $\frac{1}{2}$ and add 10. What is the answer? Explain an error most students will make.
2. Use six 4s to make an equation that equals 3,748,107.
3. Given six congruent parallel line segments arranged so they are perpendicular to an imaginary horizontal line, add five more line segments to make nine.
4. 

| A | EF | HI | KLMNT | VWXY |
|---|----|----|-------|------|
| BCD | G | J | OPQRS | U |

Where does the "Z" go and why?
5. What value can be added to 1,000,000 so the result will be larger than if the 1,000,000 is multiplied by the same value? Is your answer unique? Why or why not?
6. Given a nine-stall-long horse barn, how can ten horses be housed such that no two horses occupy the same stall, none are running free, none are being ridden, and so on? (See Fig. 9.14.)
7. Pick a number. Triple it. Add 12. Divide by 3. Subtract 4. What do you get? Why does this work?
8. Select a three-digit number (374). Affix a duplicate of that number to either end, giving a six-digit number (374,374). Divide the six-digit number by 7. Divide the missing factor from that division by 11. Divide the missing factor from that second division by 13. What did you get? Why does this work?

9. Suppose a sheet of notebook paper could be folded in half fifty times. Assuming the paper is 0.003 inches thick, how high would the stack be? Do this problem on a spreadsheet.
10. Some movie scripts describe ransom situations where a million dollars in small unmarked bills is to be left at some remote location. The alleged culprit picks up the package and runs away. Suppose the payment was in $10 bills. How much would the $1,000,000 weigh? A bill in United States currency weighs approximately 1 gram. What is a reasonable denomination for the alleged culprit to request so the escape can be effected? What is the volume of the package for $10 bills?
11. A window was a square, a meter on a side. That window admitted too much light so half the area was covered. After that, the window was still a meter high and a meter wide. How can that be?
12. Use three line segments (straight, curved, open, or closed) to divide a circle into eight sections, each of which has the same area. Do this problem at least three ways: one using algebra, one using geometry, and a third using technology.
13. A bear was followed 3 miles south, 3 miles west, and then 3 miles north. At that point, the trail crossed the initial trail. What color was the bear?

This is but a small sample of the available elements that are viable candidates for your bag of tricks. It is your responsibility to begin now to build your bag of tricks. It should be a collection of ideas from classes, reading, conferences, texts, conversations with peers, and submissions by students. Once you start giving these to students as challenges, they will provide you with additional examples. A select few elements from your bag of tricks will become your favorites, and you will be able to do them reflexively. Others will mandate that you review as you plan to use them. This last statement implies the need for some organizational scheme that will permit you to find items appropriate for a given class or topic. A possible method of organizing could be by subject (algebra, geometry, etc.), topic (add fractions, divide decimals, etc.), or curricular issue (problem solving, patterning, etc.). It is important to develop some method of organization at the start of building your collection. It may be that the mode will be altered at a later date, but it is imperative that something be done early. Otherwise, the collection becomes too unwieldy and, as a re-

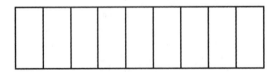

9 Stall Horse Barn

**Figure 9.14**

sult, is not used because items cannot be located. This would be an excellent place to let technology work for you by creating a database of your bag of tricks, readings, class examples, and so on.

## NUMBER THEORY

Number theory is one of those names that can mean different things to different people. Ideas dealing with prime, composite, perfect, abundant and deficient numbers, divisibility rules, greatest common factor (GCF), least common multiple (LCM), factors, multiples, basic proofs, and number oddities would all be included. For some, number theory is viewed as a tool that ties the various branches of mathematics together because of its broad-based appearance in most concepts. For others, number theory should be studied as a distinct topic. As is the case with so much of the teaching of mathematics, the decision is often made by what is contained in a text.

The terms *factor* and *multiple* are essential ingredients of number theory. Amazingly, they are difficult for many students to understand, even those who typically do well in mathematics. Many students are able to parrot the definitions, but there is limited comprehension of what is being said. When a task is to find the LCM of 10 and 12, students become confused because they do not know whether the multiples of 12 are 12, 24, 36, . . . or 1, 2, 3, 4, 6, 12. Furthermore, total agreement does not exist within the mathematical community on multiples. Some authorities say 0 is a multiple of 12 and others say it is not. Consider the dilemma this causes for students, especially if one text they use says 0 is a multiple of 12 and the next says it is not. A result of this confusion and inconsistency is students who are not certain of how to apply definitions. In that mode, their ability to deal with the task of finding the LCM is hampered.

Even with the potential for confusion, number theory holds a multitude of opportunities in the world of mathematics at all levels. Early number theory was dominated by arithmetic that emphasized geometric measurement and calculation. The Egyptians had a decimally based number system about 1800 B.C. They used unit fractions to express all fractions so $\frac{3}{14}$ was shown as $\frac{1}{7} + \frac{1}{14}$. The Greeks built on the work of the Egyptians and Babylonians. They added a level of abstraction to the known body of mathematics through a logical system based on definitions, axioms, and proofs. The Greek development began about 600 B.C. with Thales of Miletus (http:// http://www-history.mcs.st-and.ac.uk/ Mathematicians/Thales.html), the "father of Greek mathematics," and one of his students, Pythagoras of Samos (http:// http://www-history.mcs.st-and. ac.uk/Mathematicians/Pythagoras.html). Pythagoras was a religious leader who thought understanding of the world could be enhanced by the understanding of numbers.

Number theory lay dormant for centuries. Diophantus' *Arithmetica* (http:// http://www-history.mcs. st-and.ac.uk/Mathematicians/Diophantus.html) stimulated Fermat (http:// http://www-history.mcs. st-and.ac.uk/Mathematicians/Fermat.html) to advance the field of number theory. Fermat stated that the margin of his notes was too small to contain the "wonderful proof" he had found for where A, B, and C are whole numbers and $n > 2$. The idea of patterning, a common concept in geometry, was extended to numbers with Pascal's triangle. This was a very significant step in the development of mathematics. Gauss (http:// http://www-history. mcs.st-and.ac.uk/Mathematicians/Gauss.html) worked with prime numbers and investigated the classic question, "How often, or rare, is the appearance of a prime number, on average?" Others have made significant contributions to the study of number theory over the years, but even these few references should give you a flavor for the breadth and depth of the impact of this branch of mathematics.

In the school curriculum, counting numbers are classified as odd or even and also as one, primes, and composites. Primes and composites are encountered in their own right and extended as useful tools in simplification of fractions, LCM, GCF, multiples, and factorization of numbers. Perfect, abundant, and deficient numbers are also based on factoring. Six is a perfect number. The factors of 6 are 1, 2, 3, and 6. Excluding 6, the sum of the

### EXERCISE 9.10

1. Investigate perfect numbers. In the process, answer questions like the ones that follow. You should not limit your research to answering the listed questions. What are the next two perfect numbers after 28? How many perfect numbers have been found to date? Has it been established that all perfect numbers have been found?

**Additional exercises can be found on the website.**

remaining factors is 6. Twenty-eight is the next perfect number. Excluding 28, the sum of the other factors (1, 2, 4, 7, 14) is 28. From these two examples (even though it is a dangerous practice to base arguments on such a limited exposure) you should conclude that a perfect number equals the sum of its factors, excluding the number itself. In the same manner, 8, 11, 15, and 25 are deficient numbers whereas 12, 18, 24, and 36 are abundant numbers.

Investigation of prime numbers generally includes the sieve of Eratosthenes (http:// http:// www-history.mcs.st-and.ac.uk/Mathematicians/ Eratosthenes.html), typically shown in a 10 by 10 array listing the counting numbers beginning with 1 in the top left corner of the array. At times the 1 is omitted and the array shown in Fig. 9.15 is developed. In the sieve of Eratosthenes, students are encouraged to select a prime and then eliminate all multiples of it, knowing each multiple must be a composite because each is a product of the selected number and some counting number greater than 1. Once the multiples of that selected prime are exhausted in the chart, the next highest prime is chosen and the process duplicated until all numbers in the chart have been considered. It is not necessary to begin with the smallest prime, just as it is not mandatory that all multiples be exhausted before going to the next prime (not necessarily the next largest). However, mathematicians habitually begin with the smallest, exhaust those possibilities, and then proceed to the next largest. This is an organizational process that is common, and there are benefits to imparting that information to students. This description is a beginning groundwork for the thought process used in inductive proof (i.e., show a statement is true for 1, assume it is true for $N$, and prove it is true for $N + 1$).

The sieve contains several patterns, some of which might be obvious to you, but not necessarily to students. Care should be taken as lessons involving the sieve of Eratosthenes are developed so that these patterns are brought out to students. In the process, fascination with numbers can be cultivated. One generalization that can be made from the sieve is that primes can appear in, at most, four columns headed by 2, 3, 7, and 9. Explaining why this happens is an important component in students' development and should not be overlooked. The discussion can be prompted by asking, "What is the greatest number of primes that can occur in any one row of the sieve of Eratosthenes?" That could be followed by, "What is the greatest number of composites that can occur?" Using Fig. 9.15 appears to reveal the answers to these questions quickly. What if the sieve is extended using the same pattern?

## EXERCISES 9.11

1. It is possible to extend the sieve of Eratosthenes so there will be 100 consecutive composites. Where does that occur?
2. Excluding the first row, will there be another row in a 10-column sieve of Eratosthenes that will have four primes in it?

**Additional exercises can be found on the website.**

Thanks to technology, finding the square root of a number is not nearly the challenge it was in the past. Today, a student need only enter 746 into most calculators and press the "$\sqrt{\ }$" key to view the desired answer. Doing such a computation by hand is not an easy task, especially if you want it to the nearest thousandth. Some rationalize the need to continue doing such computations by hand so there is an understanding of the true meaning of the result. Do you think doing things manually provides insight we would call understanding? The process of finding a square root can be explained geometrically and algebraically, giving the students a much greater appreciation for the operation. When computing the square root, it must be realized that the answer is the length of the side of a square having an area equal to the number used to start the computation, 746 in this case.

12 out of 100
or 0.12

3 tenths of 4 tenths

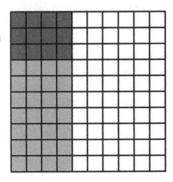

**Figure 9.15**

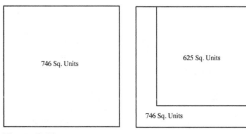

**Figure 9.16**

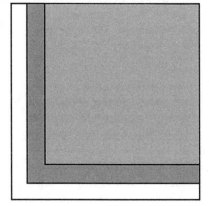

**Figure 9.18**

Figure 9.16 shows a square having area 746 on the left. The task is to determine the length of the side of that square. Assuming the same unit, a square of area 625 is known to be smaller than a square of area 746. The side length of a square with area of 625 would be 25. Inserting the smaller square inside the larger, as shown in the figure on the right in Fig. 9.16, shows the side length of the larger square is greater than 25 units. Similarly, Fig. 9.17 shows a larger square being placed inside the initial square of area 746. In each case, the length of the side of the square being inserted is known and is smaller than the length of the side of the initial square. This process can be repeated as many times as necessary, getting closer and closer to the desired value.

Figures 9.16 and 9.17 give a geometric interpretation of finding the square root of a number. Thinking algebraically and looking at Fig. 9.16, it is known that the total area is 746 square units and a square with side length 25 square units has been inserted in the top right corner. What is the area of the L-shaped region between the inserted square and the initial square?

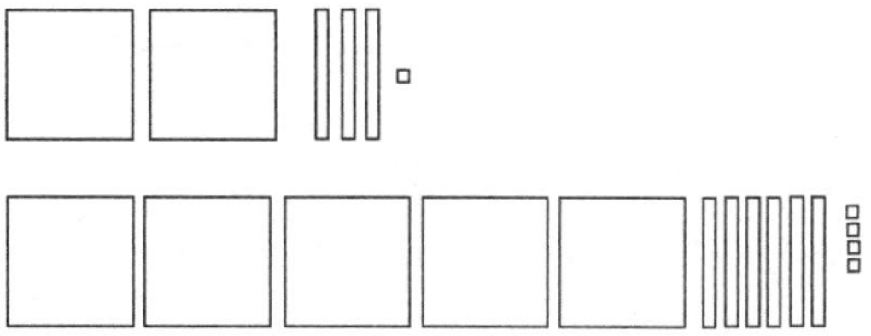

$$746 = (25 + X)(25 + X)$$
$$746 = 625 + 50X + X^2$$
$$746 - 625 = 50X + X^2$$
$$121 = 50X + X^2$$
$$121 = X(X + 50)$$

At this point, the student would be asked to approximate a value for $X$. Suppose the estimate is 2. An estimate of 2 units for the value of $X$ would mean that a new square is created, and its side length would be 27. This would be shown in Fig. 9.17. Algebraically, the new situation would be

$$746 = (27 + Y)(27 + Y)$$
$$746 = 729 + 54Y + Y^2$$
$$746 - 729 = 54Y + Y^2$$
$$17 = 54Y + Y^2$$
$$17 = Y(Y + 54)$$

The student would now be asked to approximate a value for $Y$. Figure 9.18 shows 0.3 being used as an approximation for $Y$. The process can be continued, approaching the value for the square root of 746 as closely as desired. Blending the pictures with the algebraic explanation clarifies the concept for most students.

## MATHEMATICS, ART, AND MUSIC

Vanishing-point and perspective drawings, scale, beat, and symmetry. Nearly everyone is aware of these connections, and mention of them is common throughout the curriculum. Most of the time the mentioning is about as far as it goes.

The Dutch graphic artist Maurits Corneille Escher (http://www-history.mcs.st-and.ac.uk/Math ematicians/Escher.html) explored the world of optical illusions in his work, which has become increasingly popular because of its unique combination of humor, logic, and meticulous precision with visual trickery. One aspect of his work involves covering a plane with the same object. Students, especially

**Figure 9.17**

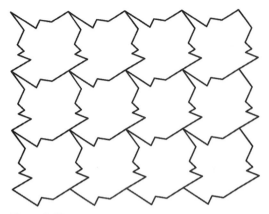

Figure 9.19

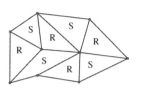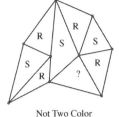

Two Color           Not Two Color

**Figure 9.20**

through technology, can readily create a work of tessellation along the lines of those made famous by Escher. Figure 9.19 is an example of student work. Additional tessellations produced by students can be viewed at http://www.worldofescher.com.

---

## EXERCISE 9.12

1. Write a summary of at least three instances where art could be inserted into the mathematics curriculum. For each of the examples, describe the mathematical application.

---

 **Additional exercises can be found on the website..**

Helaman Ferguson is a sculptor quoted as saying, "It is an experience to be able to touch mathematics," and "Mathematics is timeless and I like placing mathematical ideas into stone because it's been around for such a long time too" (Ferguson, 1994, p. 3). He generates his three-dimensional images via a computer-aided design (CAD) and uses a computer-guided system (computer-aided manufacturing, CAM) to build his images on a computer screen before starting on stone. The air drill used in cutting the stone is computer guided (CAD/CAM).

Map coloring has long been used as an exercise in art. There are mathematical map colorings as well, and the pursuit of them is not always trivial. A checkerboard can be colored with two colors in a manner such that each square is distinguishable because none of its edges touch the edge of another square that is the same color. That leads to a definition that a map is two-color if it can be filled so that

any two regions share an edge of different colors. Figure 9.20 shows two maps, one that can be colored with two colors and one that cannot. Investigation reveals that the map will be two-color only if an even number of segments emit from each internal vertex.

Map coloring has a practical application. Using the fewest possible number of colors on a map helps in keeping production costs and time to a minimum. On October 23, 1852, Francis Guthrie posed a question to his teacher, De Morgan, who wrote W. R. Hamilton:

A student of mine asked me today to give him a reason for a fact which I did not know was a fact, and do not yet. He says that if a figure be anyhow divided, and the compartments differently coloured, so that figures with any portion of common boundary line are differently coloured, four colors may be wanted, but no more. . . .

What do you say? And has it, if true, been noticed? My pupil says he guessed it in colouring a map of England. The more I think of it, the more evident it seems. (Stein, 1975, p. 346)

---

## EXERCISES 9.13

1. Consider Fig. 9.20 to be a body of water containing two islands. How many colors would be needed to color Fig. 9.20 with the restriction that no two edges share the same color?

2. Research four-color maps. Has the idea ever been clearly proven?

---

The Pythagoreans viewed music as a branch of mathematics. The octave is attributed to Pythagoras. Suppose that an octave is represented on the $y$-axis and beat on the $x$-axis of the first quadrant of a Cartesian plane. Graph $Y = X$ and $Y = -X + 8$. The intersection of these two linear equations is easily seen on the graph. Additional meaning can be given to the intersection if each equation's chromatic scale is played on some instrument (or MIDI) by students simultaneously. Suppose each equation is played on a clarinet. $Y = X$ will go from a low note to a high whereas $Y = -X + 8$ will go from high to low. The beat, which could be constant (e.g., all half notes) or varying, will be the same for both. As the equations are played, students will hear the intersection. Enhance this activity by having the equations displayed on an overhead while they are being played. The equations would be traced as they are played. The tracing pointers would be seen to intersect at the appropriate location and note. If MIDI were used, the sound and graphing intersection would be incorporated into the computer screen presentation.

> **MIDI** Musical Instrument Digital Interface: a standard means of sending digitally encoded information about music between electronic devices, as between synthesizers and computers. ("MIDI," 2012)

## INTEGERS

Students first formally encounter integers late in the elementary grades or in the beginning of their middle/junior high school years. In many instances, they have been proceeding through their mathematical careers totally unaware that there were any numbers other than wholes, fractions, and decimals. Integers seem so foreign at first. We discuss positive integers and elaborate on the need to express $2 + 3 = 5$ as $^+2 + {}^+3 = {}^+5$. In most instances it is difficult to rationalize this to the students, but usually, after enough insistence from us, they succumb. The negative integers along with the other operations are then introduced over a period of time. Somewhere along the developmental line, we abandon the demand that $^+2 + {}^+3$ be written as $^+5$ and permit them to revert back to writing it as $2 + 3 = 5$. We continue the rationalization by saying, "Everyone knows that if no sign is present, the direction is positive." Some students have to wonder why we made such a big deal of the situation if we are so willing to abandon it. Is it any wonder students question why we ask them to learn things at times?

With calculators, students may discover integers sooner than they are typically introduced in the cur-

riculum. Experimentation might lead to discovering that $7 - 3$ produces an answer different from $3 - 7$. Certainly this experimentation depends on observation skills of students because they need to notice the presence of the "−" associated with $3 - 7$. The calculator and patterning skills can be used to assist students in "discovering" the various rules of operation for integers. How many examples of the type $^+5 + (^-3) = {}^+2$ would need to be done on a calculator before a student determines that the second addend is actually subtracted from the first when the first addend is positive and the second is negative? Assistance is provided to the discovery process through a carefully developed set of problems that guide the student to appropriate responses. In this case, the problems would all have the first addend positive, the second negative, and the absolute value of the first greater than that of the second addend.

Patterning can lead a student to conclude that the product of two negative factors is positive. Appropriate readiness skills must be assumed. A sequence of problems would start:

$$(^+5)(^-4) = {}^-20$$
$$(^+4)(^-4) = {}^-16$$

After this second step, call attention to the following ideas:

> The first factor decreases by 1 when the second problem is compared with the first.
> The second factor stays the same in both problems.
> The product increases by 4 when comparing the two problems.

The sequence of problems will be continued, each time comparing the new problem with the last and amplifying the observation that the first factor is decreasing by 1, the second stays the same, while the product increases by 4.

$$(^+3)(^-4) = {}^-12$$
$$(^+2)(^-4) = {}^-8$$
$$(^+1)(^-4) = {}^-4$$
$$(0)(^-4) = {}^-0$$
$$(^-1)(^-4) = {}^+4$$

Plop! How can this be? If the pattern being followed to this point is true, it must be the case that a negative times a negative is a positive. The key to having the appropriate impact in this lesson is to make the sequence of problems long enough so the

203

students reflexively say with appropriate boredom for each new problem shown that:

"The first factor *decreases* by one."

"The second factor stays the same."

"The product *increases* by four."

If necessary start with a larger first factor to achieve the desired impact.

Another process can be used to provide indicators for students as to the outcomes of finding products of signed numbers. A video camera and large monitor are necessary for this activity. The students will be recorded while walking. In all environments of this activity, forward motion is defined as being positive and backward motion is defined as being negative. Students first are recorded walking forward, indicating they are walking forward by extending arms in front of them, wearing ball caps with peaks pointing to the front, and so on. They can walk in rows, columns, groups, and so on. Positive motion could be climbing up a tree (with appropriate consideration for risk). Playing the tape at this point by running it forward would contribute a second positive factor. The result on the screen would show students walking forward, a positive product produced by two positive factors.

Next, play the video in reverse. The students are indicating forward motion, but the result on the screen shows them walking backward. Thus, a positive factor (forward walk) and a negative factor (reverse tape play) yield a negative product.

Negative motion can be indicated by walking backwards, going up a sliding board, and so forth. Indication of the direction while being recorded is important, such as with hats pointing back. When the video is viewed, walking backwards with the tape running forward yields an image on the screen going backwards. Thus, a negative factor coupled with a positive factor yields a negative product.

All of the preceding activities are valuable in their own right, but they are background work for helping students conclude that two negative factors yield a positive product. This can be demonstrated by playing the video backward on a section where the students were walking backward when the video was made. The result on the screen will be forward motion. Thus, two negative factors yield a positive product!

The concept of using video can be extended to division as well. Students walk, but no indication of direction is given. When the video is played, if there is forward motion on the screen and if it is known

the projection unit is running forward, a positive product and one positive factor are present. The students then deduce the missing factor must be positive because the only way a positive product is generated is from either two positive factors or two negative factors. The rest of the division situations can be reasoned in a similar manner. This can be extended to a generalization that most students are not aware of. Dividing with like signs yields a positive result. Dividing with unlike signs yields negative results. Students are amazed to notice these generalizations are the same as those for multiplication.

Mnemonics are wonderful tools for helping students remember various material. When dealing with multiplication of signed numbers, one helpful statement is, "It takes two minus signs to draw a plus sign." Another helpful hint that students enjoy for remembering the rule for multiplying two signed numbers comes from the following story involving a "thing" (or happening), "person," and "moral." In this story, good is represented by "+" and bad by "−."

| Thing | Person | Moral | |
|---|---|---|---|
| + | + | + | (Good thing to good person is good) |
| + | − | − | (Good thing to bad person is not good) |
| − | + | − | (Bad thing to good person is not good) |
| − | − | + | (Bad thing to bad person is good) |

Stories, like the one about moral, have to fit within the tolerances of your personal construct as well as that of the school and community, but they are cute, and they do help many students remember rules. This can become another of those "delicate balance" issues you will have to face. Mnemonics are not overly necessary today in situations like finding the product of signed numbers. Use a calculator. They give the proper sign every time, assuming the information is entered correctly.

## GEOMETRY READINESS

Much of the information relating to this issue is found in the geometry chapter. It is important to insert as much geometry as reasonably possible into the general mathematics curriculum. For one thing, the subject offers practical applications in the real world of students: skateboards and curb jumping, in-line skates, balls for different sports, out-of-balance tires, and so forth. Technology that works with geometry brings in almost limitless opportunity for exploration. Students typically like the concept of geometry. We work against that in many instances by trying to formalize things. Let them investigate their curiosities. Show them where the things they intuitively know can be applied. Do not force them to proofs too fast. Let the natural and historical order of events take over wherein they see a situation, question it, convince themselves with sketches and pictures that it is or is not true, and then, after all that, begin to prove it.

There are a multitude of confusion points and contradictions in a student's world of geometry. We define line segment as having a definite beginning and end and then tell students to write the definition on "lined paper." A point has no length, width, or thickness and then we call little blobs, on the paper, board, overhead, or screen, points. They hear "pyramid" and think Egypt. Then we tell them about right and nonright pyramids as well as pyramids that do not have square bases. Area is a two-dimensional idea, but then they find the surface area of a solid. Oh yes, we know that each of those faces is on a plane and, thus, it really is a two-dimensional figure, for that part of the solid, but they do not always make the connection.

---

### EXERCISE 9.14

1. List at least three areas of geometry where you see possibilities for students to become confused. In each instance explain the source of confusion and describe how you would clarify it for students.

---

**Additional exercises can be found on the website.**

## ALGEBRA READINESS

Standard 5 of the NCTM Standards (1989) bears the title Algebra, as does Standard 2 in Standards 2000, and recently Algebra has been included as one of the mathematics Common Core Standards (http://www.corestandards.org/the-standards/mathematics). Each set of standards portrays algebra as a topic that is to be a part of the necessary curriculum taken by all students. The Standards introduction is very careful to explain that this is not necessarily the algebra course as described in prior years of school mathematics. Standards 2000 integrates algebra into the curriculum throughout the K–12 experience. The expectation is that all students will be competent with concepts like variable quantities, expressions, equations, inequalities, and matrices; use of tables and graphs; operations on expressions; matrices as a solution tool for linear systems; and performance of transformations based on the theory of equations. The Common Core Standards stress the importance of understanding, creating, and working with expressions, equations, inequalities, functions while integrating problem solving, abstract thinking and creativity. Students need to be able to:

Interpret the structure of expressions

Write expressions in equivalent forms to solve problems

Perform arithmetic operations on polynomials

Understand the relationship between zeros and factors of polynomials

Use polynomial identities to solve problems

Rewrite rational functions

Create equations that describe numbers or relationships

Understand solving equations as a process of reasoning and explain the reasoning

Solve equations and inequalities in one variable

Solve systems of equations

Represent and solve equations and inequalities graphically

Students are also expected to use a variety of mathematical practices including:

Make sense of problems and persevere in solving them.

Reason abstractly and quantitatively.

Construct viable arguments and critique the reasoning of others.

Model with mathematics.

Use appropriate tools strategically.

Attend to precision.

Look for and make use of structure.

Look for and express regularity in repeated reasoning. (http://www.corestandards.org/math)

This list represents a continuing study of algebra throughout the high school years, but demands for preparation are placed on the prior years as well.

Background for algebra begins with the study of arithmetic in the primary grades. Even with a problem like $7 - 4 = ?$, the ? becomes a representative of a variable. The Cuisenaire rods, with their letters representing the name of the rod, show another place where students will have formative background for the idea of variable. Still later, they encounter formulas for area and perimeter that have letters representing numbers. Again, variable is there, but not stressed. Why emphasize operations on fractions so heavily in the curriculum? One reason is for fractions in their own right, but another focuses on background skills for algebraic situations.

> Algebra is the language through which most of mathematics is communicated. It also provides a means of operating with concepts at an abstract level and then applying them, a process that often fosters generalizations and insights beyond the original context. (NCTM, 1989, p. 150)

The grades 9–12 Standards state they are extensions of algebraic concepts developed in the Standards for grades 6–8.

> The Standards for grades 6–8 (2000) include a significant emphasis on algebra, along with much more geometry than has normally been offered in the middle grades, and call for the integration of these two areas. The Standards for grades 9 - 12 (2000), assuming that this strong foundation in algebra will be in place by the end of eighth grade, describe an ambitious program in algebra, geometry, and data analysis and statistics and also call for the integration and connections among ideas. (NCTM, 2000, pp. 37–38)

The preceding description taken from the Standards speaks to courses taught before Algebra I. This is background information necessary for the study of algebra. Call it general mathematics, pre-algebra, informal algebra, or fundamental algebra, it is background work. These are the essential ingredients all students must possess prior to entering a formal study of algebra. A similar discussion could be developed for geometry, probability and statistics, number theory, problem solving, thinking skills, measurement, mathematics as communication, estimation, patterns, and number relationships. The bottom line is that all this background material must be developed for students prior to the more formal high school core curriculum. The Common Core Standards stress that:

> The K-5 standards provide students with a *solid foundation in whole numbers, addition, sub-traction, multiplication, division, fractions and decimals*—which help young students build the foundation to successfully apply more demanding math concepts and procedures, and move into applications. . . . Having built a strong foundation K-5, students can do hands on learning in geometry, algebra and probability and statistics. Students who have completed 7th grade and mastered the content and skills through the 7th grade will be *well-prepared for algebra* in grade 8. ("Key Points in Mathematics," n.d., para 1)

---

## EXERCISES 9.15

1. Should the curriculum of courses prior to Algebra I be changed to reflect items discussed in this text, NCTM publications, and the Common Core Standards? Why or why not?
2. Defend or take issue with the statement, "General mathematics is foundational work for future mathematical study. There is no need to connect general mathematics curriculum with the real world of students."

---

## MATHEMATICAL ILLITERACY

How is mathematics education viewed by society? Tell someone you are studying to be an engineer and they will say, "Wow." Tell that same person you are going to be a teacher of mathematics and you may hear something like, "Why?" The youth of our country are our future! Why not encourage our best and brightest students to enter the teaching profession? A second-semester college junior entered the office not long ago, wanting to transfer from engineering to mathematics education. The comment was, "I always wanted to be a teacher; but everyone told me I could do something better than that." The irony is, this student's teacher had been in that same office several years earlier and the same discussion had taken place. Did your high school teachers encourage you to go into teaching? Why or why not?

Society does not always seem to think very highly of the mathematics education received by students, as shown in the following excerpt.

> "U.S. PUPILS FARE POORLY IN MATH AND SCIENCE TESTS"

"POOR MATH SKILLS HURT U.S. ECONOMY"

"U.S. STUDENTS FAIL THE 4TH R—REASONING"

"AMERICA'S SCIENTIFIC FUTURE IS THREATENED BY THE DECLINE IN MATHEMATICS EDUCATION"

"RESEARCHERS FOCUS ON STUDENT DISINTEREST IN MATH, SCIENCE AND ENGINEERING"

| Number of Folds | Thickness of Stack (inches) |
|:---:|:---:|
| 0 | 0.0032 |
| 1 | ____ |
| 2 | ____ |
| 3 | ____ |
| 4 | ____ |
| 5 | ____ |
| 6 | ____ |

*Innumeracy* by John Paulos [1987, New York: Hill and Wang] describes the crisis in mathematics education as similar to the crisis in literacy for the American public—too many people know too little.

Are people aware of the consequences of mathematical illiteracy? No, and these headlines probably serve to educate very few. They play on the importance of keeping up with the rest of the world scientifically, which is important, but which most people see as someone else's responsibility. Unfortunately, the consequences of mathematical illiteracy reach well beyond our conquest of space, the development of new chips for computers, etc. (Cozzens, 1989, p. 2). After reading that you should say something like, "Somebody should do something about that." You're it! Notice the dates on these citations: 1987 and 1989. The century has changed but the comments from society have not! Reports continue to show that we are falling behind in mathematical understanding and interest in the topic. What can you do about it?

## TRY THIS IN YOUR CLASSROOM

*NCTM Standards 2000*: Problem solving, communication, reasoning, estimation, patterns, algebra, and measurement

*Materials*: Calculator that does lists and 1 piece of notebook paper

A piece of notebook paper is about 0.0032 inches thick. Fold a piece of notebook paper in half. Repeat this procedure four times. How thick is the stack? How would you calculate the thickness?

Fill in the table below for six such folds.

How fast is the stack's thickness increasing? Does color of the paper have anything to do with the paper's thickness? Is all paper the same thickness? Why or why not?

This type of increase is called exponential growth. The general formula is $y = a(C)x$, where $a$ is the initial amount you start with, $C$ is the change factor, and $x$ is the number of times the change occurs.

The initial amount is the thickness of the piece of paper before it is folded. The change factor is what is happening to the stack's thickness each time it is folded.

For the paper-folding experiment, what is the initial amount ($a$)? the change factor ($C$)? Write a formula by substituting your values for $a$ and $C$ into the general formula $y = a(C)x$. Find the thickness of your stack after ten folds by substituting 10 for $x$ and solving for $y$.

What is the thickness after 15 folds? Convert the 15-fold thickness to feet.

## Graphing Exponential Data

Enter the number of folds in column 1. Fill column 2 with the paper thickness after each fold by using the formula +0.0032*2^A1. Cell B1 will have the paper thickness for the fold number in cell A1. Copy the formulas in B1 to the remaining cells in column B. Highlight column A and B and create a scatter plot. Your list and scatter plot should look similar to the one in Fig. 9.21.

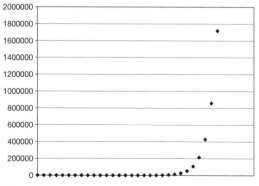

**Figure 9.21**

Examine your scatter plot. Would the equation for the data be linear? Is it exponential? Explain your response.

How thick would your stack be after 25 folds? What unit of measure is best used to express this thickness? Why?

What is the greatest number of folds you can actually make? Does the size or thickness of the paper used matter?

## CONCLUSION

This has been a long chapter. We have discussed many facets of mathematical foundation courses or course taught prior to Algebra I (or whatever you want to call it). There are many issues that have not been discussed. Still, you should be thinking about the general mathematics courses now and in the process you could probably generate a good list of items that should be included. Give yourself a pat on the back if you have already done that. As you think about the course, think about teaching it. Many teachers of mathematics view these courses as a punishment or something that beginning teachers should endure as they "pay their dues." *Au contraire!* This is a wonderful course to teach. The students often are not overly interested in taking it but that is OK. You can motivate them to want to learn. You can show them many wonderful applications of the concepts covered. You can do it! After all, you are a teacher, right?

### STICKY QUESTIONS

1. In 1994, it was announced that Fermat's last theorem was proved. Investigate the claim and summarize the reactions to, and the impact of, the statement.

2. Goldbach conjectured that any even number other than 2 can be expressed as the sum of two primes. Has a proof ever been established or a counterexample found? Summarize your findings on the subject.

3. This chapter began with a discussion about the difficulties related to calling "it" mathematical foundations or general mathematics. What should "it" have been called? What was "it" called in your school?

4. Should the typical "general math" student be allowed to use calculators? Why or why not?

5. Is the best technology of each school available to the "general math" student? Why or why not? Are these the students who need the use of technology the most? Why or why not?

6. Discuss the advantages or disadvantages of building a collection of games and tricks for your classes.

7. Did your high school teachers (family, friends, etc.) encourage you to go into teaching? Why or why not?

## PROBLEM-SOLVING CHALLENGES

1. You have a digital clock that shows only hours and minutes. How many different readings between 11:00 AM and 5:00 PM (of the same day) contain at least two 2s in the time?

**Check out the website for the solution.**

2. Start with a square piece of paper. Draw the largest circle possible inside the square, cut it out and discard the trimmings. Draw the largest square possible inside the circle, cut the square out and discard the trimmings. What fraction of the original square piece of paper has been cut off and thrown away?

**Check out the website for the solution.**

# LEARNING ACTIVITIES

## Paper Folding

An amazing array of creations come out of paper folding, an art practiced for years. In this activity, we will focus on some basic mathematical situations that involve paper folding. Waxed paper works well for these activities because a fold shows as a white crease on a translucent background, making some actions easier to perform and recognize.

We begin with 10 initial assumptions:

1. All folds are straight.
2. It is possible to pass a fold through one or two given points.
3. It is possible to place one point on top of another.
4. It is possible to cut along a fold to form the side of a polygon.
5. It is possible to fold the paper so a point can be placed on a line.
6. It is possible to place a fold on top of itself at some designated point.
7. It is possible to place a fold on top of another fold.
8. An angle reflected across a fold is congruent to its pre-image.
9. Line segments are congruent if their endpoints match.
10. Angles are congruent if one can be superimposed on another by folding.

Given a rectangular sheet of paper, fold on each major diagonal, as shown in Fig. 9.22.

Make a fold parallel to $\overline{AD}$, passing through E. With that, $\overline{AE}$ is on top of $\overline{BE}$ and $\overline{DE}$ is on top of $\overline{CE}$, making $\angle AEB \cong \angle DEC$. Thus, it is shown that vertical angles are congruent.

## Exercise 1: Sum of the Measures of the Angles of a Triangle.

Make triangle FGH similar to Fig. 9.23.
Fold to create altitude passing through point F creating altitude FK as shown in Fig. 9.24.

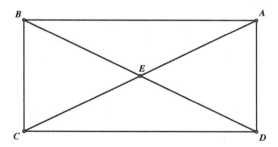

**Figure 9.22**

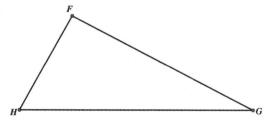

**Figure 9.23**

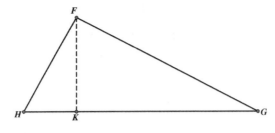

**Figure 9.24**

What is the measure of ∠GKH?

Fold so F is on top of K, creating fold $\overline{LM}$.

What is the measure of ∠LKM and how do you know that?

What angle is formed by ∠HKL ∠LKM ∠MKG?

What can be said about the sum of the measures of the angles of a triangle?

## Exercise 2: Area of a Triangle

Continue with the figure from Exercise 1 by folding H onto K, creating N (midpoint of HK).

What is known about ∠LNH and ∠LNK?

How does $\overline{LN}$ compare with $\overline{FK}$ and how do you know?

Fold G onto K, creating O (midpoint of GK).

What is known about ∠MOG and ∠MOK?

How does $\overline{NO}$ compare with $\overline{HG}$?

The area of rectangle LNOM is $(\overline{LN})(\overline{NO})$.

But, $\overline{LN}$ is $\frac{\overline{FK}}{2}$ and $\overline{NO}$ is $\frac{\overline{HG}}{2}$ so the area of LNOM $= \left(\frac{\overline{FK}}{2}\right)\left(\frac{\overline{HG}}{2}\right)$, and the area of triangle FGH can be stated as $\frac{(\overline{FK})(\overline{HG})}{2}$.

Restate that last fraction in terms of base and height and what do you get?

## Exercise 3: Radii of a Circle

Use a compass to create a circle, centered at point C.

While it might be advantageous to cut out the circle, it is not mandatory.

Make a fold that contains C, calling the intersections with the circle A and B.

What is $\overline{AB}$? How do you know?

Make a perpendicular bisector fold on AB, calling the circle intersection D.

What can be said of $\overline{AC}$, $\overline{BC}$, and $\overline{CD}$? How do you know this is true?

## Exercise 4: Altitudes of a Triangle

Create an obtuse triangle, ∠RST, by making three folds so is obtuse as shown in Fig. 9.25.

Making $\overline{RT}$ close to the long side of the paper and close to the center helps.

Fold an altitude through R.

Fold an altitude through T, creating U at the intersection of the altitudes.

Compare your exercise results with those of others. What is true of all the results?

## Exercise 5: Any Old Convex Quadrilateral

Create four folds to make Points A, B, C, and D, resulting in quadrilateral ABCD.

Create midpoints E, F, G, and H on the respective quadrilateral sides.

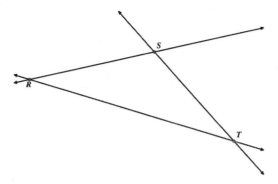

**Figure 9.25**

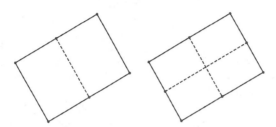

**Figure 9.26**

Make folds $\overline{EF}$, $\overline{FG}$, $\overline{GH}$, and $\overline{HE}$.
Use folding techniques to confirm that EFGH is a parallelogram.

## Exercise 6: Lotta Rectangles

Start with a rectangular piece of paper.
Fold it in half, making a fold parallel to one of the paper edges as shown in the left rectangle in Fig. 9.26.
Leaving the paper folded in half, fold it in half again with a fold perpendicular the initial fold as shown in the right rectangle in Fig. 9.26. You now have created four smaller, congruent rectangles. If the folding in half process continues 50 times, how many rectangles would you have?

## Exercise 7: Parabola

Make fold $\overline{JK}$ and point L, not on $\overline{JK}$.
Make a fold so L is on $\overline{JK}$.
Repeat the process at least a dozen times with L going to different locations on $\overline{JK}$.
Describe the figure formed by the collection of fold formed by putting L on $\overline{JK}$.

211

# Algebra I

The first records dealing with adding or subtracting the same magnitude on both sides of an equation are found in the Arabic writings of AI-Khowarizmi (http://www-history.mcs.st-and.ac.uk/Mathematicians/Al-Khwarizmi.html) (Mohammed ben Musa, which means Mahomet, the son of Moses) about 830 A.D.

This is an important work on which subsequent algebraic developments were based. The word "algorithm" is derived from the name of this ancient mathematician. "Algorithm" originally meant "the art of calculating." In England, mathematicians were called calculators. Now, algorithm means calculating by any method following a given set of rules. Just as the definition of algorithm evolved, so does the concept of algebra continue to evolve. Originally, algebra in AI-Khowarizmi's time contained no mathematical or numerical symbols. Its rules were proclaimed "as if they were divine revelations, which the reader was to accept and follow as a true believer" (Eves, 1990). Ironically, today's mathematics

student who does not fully absorb the concept being taught may feel there is a leap of faith involved in some algebraic calculations. There was a void created in the history of mathematics when the Greeks dropped algebraic proofs in favor of geometric language due to the Pythagoreans' inability to deal with irrational numbers. Algebraic reasoning was resurrected by AI-Khowarizmi, which eventually led to the proof of the existence of irrational numbers, allowing mathematicians to once again embrace algebraic reasoning and carry on from the point where the Greeks had abandoned it.

Fibonacci (http://www-history.mcs.st-and.ac.uk/Mathematicians/Fibonacci.html) introduced algebra to Italy about 1200 A.D., and Robert Recorde (http://www-history.mcs.st-and.ac.uk/Mathematicians/Recorde.html) introduced it to England in a 1557 A.D. publication. Algebraic methods and notations have been improved and revised. Unlike arithmetic, where $3 + 4 = 7$ (written that way for bases 8 and larger), algebraic notations like $x + y = z$ take on different meanings in different contexts. Thus, the subject of algebra provides challenges for some individuals because of their difficulty in dealing with the abstractions associated with unknowns.

The major contribution of Diophantus (http://www-history.mcs.st-and.ac.uk/Mathematicians/Diophantus.html) (circa 250 A.D.) was the syncopation of algebra. He used symbols as shorthand for often-used quantities and operations, that is,

K for cubed
A for squared
ι for subtraction
Ω for equals sign
M for units

Descartes (about 1637 A.D.) contributed to the development of algebraic symbolization. He used symbolic notation to express algebraic calculations. He also used letters at the beginning of the alphabet ($a$, $b$, $c$) to denote known quantities (Does this sound familiar from your high school days?)

and letters from the end of the alphabet $(x, y, z)$, particularly $x$, to indicate unknown quantities. He used numbers to indicate different powers of a quantity. We write $4x^3 - 6x^2 = 2x + 3$. Descartes would have written it $4xxx - 6xx = 2x + 3$ (Burton, 1985).

Some disagree about the timing and ability of students to adapt to comprehend the varying levels of abstractions. Not everyone accepts the philosophy of organizations such as NCTM that all students can learn mathematics. Individuals with skills limited to computational ability offer little to society mathematically. Technology can do the arithmetic. Society needs thinkers to employ technology. Still, discussion continues relating to what should be learned in mathematics and how it should be taught. In many algebra classrooms, students are not permitted to use technology until fact and operational mastery is evident. If a student cannot exhibit the skill of multiplying decimals at some satisfactory level, that student is prohibited from advancing algebraically until that computational ability can be mastered. How much better it would be to use a calculator and see what can be accomplished mathematically. There is a difference between arithmetic and mathematics, isn't there?

Traditionalists say, and many parents agree, something like, "The mathematics I learned and the way I learned it was good enough for me, so it is good enough for my child." Unfortunately, that statement is far from true. Yet the resistance to curricular and conceptual change is formidable. Today's world is much more mathematical than yesterday's, in that productivity in today's world requires greater mathematical abilities than did yesterday's. Even most common percents, ratios, and discounts are done with calculators instead of by hand. Tomorrow's world will be even more mathematical than today's. As technological advancements continue, some segments of mathematics will decrease in importance whereas others will grow. This can be seen in the continuing decrease of emphasis on computational skills involving large numbers because of the ready availability and low cost of calculators.

How do we rationalize the emphasis on factoring to determine the roots of an equation when it is so much faster to do the problem with a graphing calculator? Solutions can be derived in different manners. Roots can be found with graphing calculators, web applications, or apps such as Wolfram Alpha. Or, the equation can be graphed and solutions approximated. The results will sometimes be approximations, but the tolerance for error determines what is acceptable and what is not. Any approximate solution could be substituted into the original equation and simplified. If unacceptable, alterations can be made in the solution approximation and the substitution process repeated. This procedure of adjusting the approximation provides an opportunity for additional learning.

For example, suppose an approximation for one of the solutions for a third-degree equation is 2.5, and substitution shows it is not acceptable. The exercise now becomes one of knowing how to adjust 2.5 to get a better approximation. Is it 2.51 or 2.49? With technology, the decision is not a major hurdle. As the teacher, you must decide which skills you are trying to teach your students. Although some skills receive less emphasis, others attract greater attention because of the growth of technology. The use of technology in the mathematics classroom is essential for today's students to learn the necessary mathematics for tomorrow. The development of the NCTM Standards including the *Professional Standards for Teaching Mathematics* (NCTM, 1991) recommended an increase application of the use of technology as a teaching and learning tool and a decreased emphasis on algebraic topics such as the use of factoring to solve equations, operations with rational expressions, and paper-and-pencil graphing by plotting points.

## EXERCISES 10.1

1. You are teaching Algebra in your school. What will you do if another colleague teaching Algebra in your school disagrees with your teaching philosophy to use technology for a particular concept or skill? Should students be impacted by different teaching philosophies in school? Should all students use the same tools in the same classes?

2. As a professional mathematics educator, do you feel that these basic assumptions by NCTM are viable? Why or why not? Are these assumptions necessary for full development of algebraic skills during the middle grades?

**Additional exercises can be found on the website.**

## WHO SHOULD LEARN ALGEBRA?

Most of today's mathematics education world presents the position that algebra should be learned by all students if they are to be functional contributors to the world of the future. This is based on suppositions like:

The need for the development of a logical thought process.

The expected increase in the use of technology.

The need for employees to interpret professional literature.

Motivating a student to learn algebra is a challenge. There are avenues of pursuit that will help relieve this predicament. One remedy could be the chart from "When are we ever gonna have to use this?" (Saunders, 1993). Topics are grouped by the subject areas of basic math/pre-algebra, first-year algebra, geometry, second-year algebra/trigonometry, and other topics (calculus, calculator use, computer use, problem solving, mathematical modeling, and so on). First-year algebra topics listed are using formulas, linear equations, linear inequalities, operations with polynomials, factoring polynomials, rational expressions, coordinate graphing, linear systems, radicals, quadratic equations, and algebraic representation. Over 100 career options are listed on the chart. Career choices include all the mathematically obvious ones like engineer and scientist, but they also list trades like carpenter, electrician, mechanic, painter, and plumber. The medical professions are represented with categories like dentist, dietitian, doctor, nurse, physical therapist, veterinarian, and X-ray technician. Airline pilot, TV camera operator, museum curator, farmer, firefighter, golf pro, real estate agent, and waiter/waitress are also listed. As students ask for rationalizations about the need to learn algebraic concepts, the careers listed should convince them of the universal advantages of having a command of the subject. While this chart was produced almost 20 years ago, the need for mathematics in these fields has not changed! If anything, the need for mathematics has increased and the expectation of today's workforce to have appropriate algebraic skills is even greater.

One vision for including algebra in the curriculum of all students is the broad range of careers and subjects that depend on algebraic underpinnings. Another curricular point stems from the idea that so much of the curriculum prior to algebraic exposure is repetitious. About 75% of the time in a seventh-grade mathematics text is spent reviewing (Flanders, 1987, pp. 18–23). "Not much new material is introduced in

seventh or eighth grade, so the . . . mathematics experience is boring and counterproductive" (Usiskin, 1987). Indications are that a preponderance of new information is encompassed at the end of the book in sections frequently not covered. By introducing only small amounts of new material in courses preceding algebra, students are essentially lulled to sleep. Then when the student enters algebra, where so much of the information is new, difficulties are encountered.

## FIRST-YEAR ALGEBRA

What constitutes first-year algebra? Are Algebra I, first-year algebra, beginning algebra, introductory algebra, and pre-algebra all the same course? Will students entering an Algebra II course from each of these courses be adequately prepared for the expectations? Often the text drives the curriculum, which is a large portion of the dilemma. Challenging pre-algebra texts are similar to easy first-year algebra books. The quandary becomes more involved because different teachers, schools, districts, and states specify different topics to be included in the first-year algebra course. Some (teachers, texts, schools, districts, states) cover quadratics, some do not. Some focus on word problems, some do not. Some word problems show applications, some do not. Some include applications, some do not. Some teach for understanding, some do not. Some stress skills, some do not. And so on. A text-driven curriculum allows for the omission of many algebraic concepts. If quadratics are not introduced in the text, then this topic is often neglected in the curriculum. What should be taught in the first-year algebra course? Who should determine the concepts for a first-year algebra course?

The dilemma of what to include in first-year algebra is also encountered in second-year algebra. In addition, the second-year algebra curriculum is impacted by what is accomplished in the first year. Many school districts define an algebra course as the material covered in a year, usually consisting of 180 days, thereby implying that approximately 150 hours have been spent on algebra instruction (assuming 50-minute periods). In reality, teachers often hope for 120 hours of instruction, if they are lucky, because of time taken out of periods for announcements, getting settled, shortened days for assemblies, pep rallies, visits from guests, days off, and, of course, time for tests and quizzes. Extend the discussion by having more than one first-year algebra teacher doing the course. Second-year algebra teachers are faced with students who have had different teachers who emphasized a variety of first-year algebra concepts in a varied number of days. The one commonality these students have is credit in first-year algebra, even though the likelihood is great that there are extensive differences in what completion of that course means.

Usiskin (1987, p. 428) presented the following as a jumping-off point for his discussion on what should or should not be included in a first-year algebra course:

**Standard First-Year Algebra Content**

- Operations with positive and negative numbers; evaluation of expressions
- Solving of linear equations, linear inequalities, and proportions
- Age, digit, d = rt, work and mixture word problems
- Operations with polynomials and powers
- Factoring of trinomials, monomial factoring, special factors
- Simplification and operations with rational expressions
- Graphs and properties of graphs of lines
- Linear systems with two equations in two variables
- Simplification and operations with square roots
- Solving quadratic equations (by factoring and completing the square)

He then argued in favor of four alterations to the standard first-year algebra content to make a realistic first-year algebra course:

1. Use applications rather than contrived word problems.
2. Delete factoring trinomials (keep monomial factoring and special factored forms).
3. Delete rational expressions requiring factoring.
4. Use the quadratic formula to solve quadratic expressions.

The Ohio Department of Education (1984) published a content outline defining an average first-year algebra class. It did not include optional topics or ideas that could be used for enrichment, assuming rather that different texts, teachers, schools, districts, or states would include things deemed appropriate for the needs of their students. The Ohio outline is as follows:

1. Algebraic Expressions
   a. Variables and expressions
   b. Evaluating expressions
   c. Writing expressions
   d. Absolute value

2. Real Number System
   a. Computations
   b. Properties and structures
   c. Finite and infinite systems

3. Linear Equations and Inequalities
   a. Language and sets
   b. Number line and cartesian plane
   c. Open sentences in one variable
   d. Open sentences in two variables
   e. Problem solving

4. Polynomials
   a. Addition, subtraction
   b. Exponents, multiplication
   c. Factoring
   d. Division

5. Rational Expressions
   a. Ratio and proportion
   b. Simplifying, computing
   c. Fractional equations and inequalities
   d. Direct and indirect variation
   e. Problem solving

6. Relations, Functions, and Graphs
   a. Relations and functions
   b. Graphs

7. Systems of Linear Equations and Inequalities
   a. Equations in two variables
   b. Inequalities in two variables
   c. Problem Solving

8. Exponents and Radicals
   a. Radical exponents
   b. Radicals

9. Quadratic Equations
   a. Equations in one variable

Points of emphasis, or de-emphasis, become the option of the local authority (the teacher). However, it must be realized that those decisions have a dramatic impact on the first-year algebra learning of the students. This has a bearing on the offerings of the second-year algebra program, as was mentioned earlier.

Most states have made a concerted effort to develop curriculum frameworks for all levels of mathematics, especially first-year algebra. Because of NCLB, state standardized testing has forced school districts to correlate the concepts taught in class with the state frameworks. The idea was that if the standardized tests are representative of the frameworks and the teacher provides instruction that covers the concepts mapped to the frameworks, the students will succeed on the test. Is this logic flawed? Examples of state curriculum frameworks for Algebra I include Massachusetts and Mississippi as follows.

## MISSISSIPPI

### Algebra I

CONTENT STRANDS: Number and Operations; Geometry; Data Analysis & Probability; Algebra; Measurement

#### Number and Operations

1. Understand relationships between numbers and their properties and perform operations fluently.

   a. Apply properties of real numbers to simplify algebraic expressions, including polynomials. (DOK 1)
   b. Use matrices to solve mathematical situations and contextual problems. (DOK 2)

#### Algebra?

2. Understand, represent, and analyze patterns, relations, and functions.

   a. Solve, check, and graph multi-step linear equations and inequalities in one variable, including rational coefficients in mathematical and real-world situations. (DOK 2)
   b. Solve and graph absolute value equations and inequalities in one variable. (DOK 2)
   c. Analyze the relationship between $x$ and $y$ values, determine whether a relation is a function, and identify domain and range. (DOK 2)
   d. Explain and illustrate how a change in one variable may result in a change in another variable and apply to the relationships between independent and dependent variables. (DOK 2)
   e. Graph and analyze linear functions. (DOK 2)
   f. Use algebraic and graphical methods to solve systems of linear equations and inequalities in mathematical and real-world situations. (DOK 2)
   g. Add, subtract, multiply, and divide polynomial expressions. (DOK 1)
   h. Factor polynomials by using Greatest Common Factor (GCF) and factor quadratics that have only rational roots. (DOK 1)

   i. Determine the solutions to quadratic equations by using graphing, tables, completing the square, the Quadratic formula, and factoring. (DOK 1)
   j. Justify why some polynomials are prime over the rational number system. (DOK 2)
   k. Graph and analyze absolute value and quadratic functions. (DOK 2)
   l. Write, graph, and analyze inequalities in two variables. (DOK 2)

#### Geometry

3. Understand how algebra and geometric representations interconnect and build on one another.

   a. Apply the concept of slope to determine if lines in a plane are parallel or perpendicular. (DOK 2)
   b. Solve problems that involve interpreting slope as a rate of change. (DOK 2)

#### Measurement?

4. Demonstrate and apply various formulas in problem-solving situations.

   a. Solve real-world problems involving formulas for perimeter, area, distance, and rate. (DOK 2)
   b. Explain and apply the appropriate formula to determine length, midpoint, and slope of a segment in a coordinate plane. (i.e., distance formula, Pythagorean Theorem). (DOK 2)
   c. Represent polynomial operations with area models. (DOK 2)

#### Data Analysis & Probability

5. Represent, analyze and make inferences based on data with and without the use of technology.

   a. Draw conclusions and make predictions from scatter plots. (DOK 3)?
   b. Use linear regression to find the line-of-best fit from a given set of data. (DOK 3)

[2007 Mississippi Mathematics Frameworks Revised]

## MASSACHUSETTS

### Model Algebra I

#### Number and Quantity

*The Real Number System*

• Extend the properties of exponents to rational exponents.

- Use properties of rational and irrational numbers.

*Quantities*

- Reason quantitatively and use units to solve problems.

## Algebra

*Seeing Structure in Expressions*

- Interpret the structure of expressions.
- Write expressions in equivalent forms to solve problems.

*Arithmetic with Polynomials and Rational Expressions*

- Perform arithmetic operations on polynomials.

*Creating Equations*

- Create equations that describe numbers or relationships.

*Reasoning with Equations and Inequalities*

- Understand solving equations as a process of reasoning and explain the reasoning.
- Solve equations and inequalities in one variable.
- Solve systems of equations.
- Represent and solve equations and inequalities graphically.

## Functions

*Interpreting Functions*

- Understand the concept of a function and use function notation.
- Interpret functions that arise in applications in terms of the context.
- Analyze functions using different representations.

*Building Functions*

- Build a function that models a relationship between two quantities.
- Build new functions from existing functions.

*Linear, Quadratic, and Exponential Models*

- Construct and compare linear, quadratic, and exponential models and solve problems.

- Interpret expressions for functions in terms of the situation they model.

## Statistics and Probability

*Interpreting Categorical and Quantitative Data*

- Summarize, represent, and interpret data on a single count or measurement variable.
- Summarize, represent, and interpret data on two categorical and quantitative variables.
- Interpret linear models.

["Massachusetts Curriculum Frameworks," 2011]

If all states are developing curriculum frameworks such as Mississippi and Massachusetts, then wouldn't it make sense to identify one national curriculum for first-year algebra? Are the Common Core standards the national curriculum for the future?

The Common Core Standards provide the following framework for high school Algebra:

## HIGH SCHOOL ALGEBRA

### Seeing Structure in Expressions

*Interpret the Structure of Expressions.*

- A-SSE.1. Interpret expressions that represent a quantity in terms of its context.

  o Interpret parts of an expression, such as terms, factors, and coefficients.

  o Interpret complicated expressions by viewing one or more of their parts as a single entity. *For example, interpret $P(1+r)^n$ as the product of $P$ and a factor not depending on $P$.*

- A-SSE.2. Use the structure of an expression to identify ways to rewrite it. *For example, see $x^4 - y^4$ as $(x^2)^2 - (y^2)^2$, thus recognizing it as a difference of squares that can be factored as $(x^2 - y^2)(x + y^2)$.*

### Write Expressions in Equivalent Forms to Solve Problems.

- A-SSE.3. Choose and produce an equivalent form of an expression to reveal and explain properties of the quantity represented by the expression.★

  a. Factor a quadratic expression to reveal the zeros of the function it defines.

b. Complete the square in a quadratic expression to reveal the maximum or minimum value of the function it defines.

c. Use the properties of exponents to transform expressions for exponential functions. For example the expression $1.15^t$ can be rewritten as $(1.15^{1/12})^{12t} \approx 1.012^{12t}$ to reveal the approximate equivalent monthly interest rate if the annual rate is 15%.

• A-SSE.4. Derive the formula for the sum of a finite geometric series (when the common ratio is not 1), and use the formula to solve problems. *For example, calculate mortgage payments.*★

## Arithmetic with Polynomials & Rational Expressions

*Perform Arithmetic Operations on Polynomials.*

• A-APR.1. Understand that polynomials form a system analogous to the integers, namely, they are closed under the operations of addition, subtraction, and multiplication; add, subtract, and multiply polynomials.

*Understand the Relationship Between Zeros and Factors of Polynomials.*

• A-APR.2. Know and apply the Remainder Theorem: For a polynomial $p(x)$ and a number $a$, the remainder on division by $x - a$ is $p(a)$, so $p(a) = 0$ if and only if $(x - a)$ is a factor of $p(x)$.

• A-APR.3. Identify zeros of polynomials when suitable factorizations are available, and use the zeros to construct a rough graph of the function defined by the polynomial.

*Use Polynomial Identities to Solve Problems.*

• A-APR.4. Prove polynomial identities and use them to describe numerical relationships. *For example, the polynomial identity $(x^2 + y^2)^2 = (x^2 - y^2)^2 + (2xy)^2$ can be used to generate Pythagorean triples.*

• A-APR.5. (+) Know and apply the Binomial Theorem for the expansion of $(x + y)n$ in powers of $x$ and $y$ for a positive integer $n$, where $x$ and $y$ are any numbers, with coefficients determined for example by Pascal's Triangle.[1]

*Rewrite Rational Expressions.*

• A-APR.6. Rewrite simple rational expressions in different forms; write $a(x)/b(x)$ in the form $q(x) + r(x)/b(x)$, where $a(x)$, $b(x)$, $q(x)$, and $r(x)$ are polynomials with the degree of $r(x)$ less than the degree of $b(x)$, using inspection, long division, or, for the more complicated examples, a computer algebra system.

• A-APR.7. (+) Understand that rational expressions form a system analogous to the rational numbers, closed under addition, subtraction, multiplication, and division by a nonzero rational expression; add, subtract, multiply, and divide rational expressions.

## Creating Equations

*Create Equations that Describe Numbers or Relationships.*

• A-CED.1. Create equations and inequalities in one variable and use them to solve problems. *Include equations arising from linear and quadratic functions, and simple rational and exponential functions.*

• A-CED.2. Create equations in two or more variables to represent relationships between quantities; graph equations on coordinate axes with labels and scales.

• A-CED.3. Represent constraints by equations or inequalities, and by systems of equations and/or inequalities, and interpret solutions as viable or nonviable options in a modeling context. *For example, represent inequalities describing nutritional and cost constraints on combinations of different foods.*

• A-CED.4. Rearrange formulas to highlight a quantity of interest, using the same reasoning as in solving equations. *For example, rearrange Ohm's law $V = IR$ to highlight resistance $R$.*

## Reasoning with Equations and Inequalities

*Understand Solving Equations as a Process of Reasoning and Explain the Reasoning.*

• A-REI.1. Explain each step in solving a simple equation as following from the equality of numbers asserted at the previous step, starting from the assumption that the original equation has a solution. Construct a viable argument to justify a solution method.

- A-REI.2. Solve simple rational and radical equations in one variable, and give examples showing how extraneous solutions may arise.

*Solve Equations and Inequalities in One Variable.*

- A-REI.3. Solve linear equations and inequalities in one variable, including equations with coefficients represented by letters.
- A-REI.4. Solve quadratic equations in one variable.

  o Use the method of completing the square to transform any quadratic equation in $x$ into an equation of the form $(x - p)^2 = q$ that has the same solutions. Derive the quadratic formula from this form.

  o Solve quadratic equations by inspection (e.g., for $x^2 = 49$), taking square roots, completing the square, the quadratic formula and factoring, as appropriate to the initial form of the equation. Recognize when the quadratic formula gives complex solutions and write them as $a \pm bi$ for real numbers $a$ and $b$.

*Solve Systems of Equations.*

- A-REI.5. Prove that, given a system of two equations in two variables, replacing one equation by the sum of that equation and a multiple of the other produces a system with the same solutions.
- A-REI.6. Solve systems of linear equations exactly and approximately (e.g., with graphs), focusing on pairs of linear equations in two variables.
- A-REI.7. Solve a simple system consisting of a linear equation and a quadratic equation in two variables algebraically and graphically. For example, find the points of intersection between the line $y = -3x$ and the circle $x^2 + y^2 = 3$.
- A-REI.8. (+) Represent a system of linear equations as a single matrix equation in a vector variable.

- A-REI.9. (+) Find the inverse of a matrix if it exists and use it to solve systems of linear equations (using technology for matrices of dimension $3 \times 3$ or greater).

*Represent and Solve Equations and Inequalities Graphically.*

- A-REI.10. Understand that the graph of an equation in two variables is the set of all its solutions plotted in the coordinate plane, often forming a curve (which could be a line).
- A-REI.11. Explain why the $x$-coordinates of the points where the graphs of the equations $y = f(x)$ and $y = g(x)$ intersect are the solutions of the equation $f(x) = g(x)$; find the solutions approximately, e.g., using technology to graph the functions, make tables of values, or find successive approximations. Include cases where $f(x)$ and/or $g(x)$ are linear, polynomial, rational, absolute value, exponential, and logarithmic functions.★
- A-REI.12. Graph the solutions to a linear inequality in two variables as a half-plane (excluding the boundary in the case of a strict inequality), and graph the solution set to a system of linear inequalities in two variables as the intersection of the corresponding half-planes.

---

### EXERCISES 10.2

1. Have the Common Core Standards for High School been adopted in your state or region?
2. Is there a significant difference between the objectives for Algebra I for Mississippi, Massachusetts and the Common Core? Does this surprise you? Justify your response.

---

First-year algebra is new for students. Prior to this point in their mathematical development, generalizations played a relatively minor role in the scheme of mathematics. Now, generalizations and processes occupy center stage in their mathematical learning. Variables are introduced formally, and notions from their arithmetic background are extended to the set of real numbers. Language becomes more formalized, and symbolic manipulation and its associated skills begin to be central themes of each student's mathematical existence. Unification and blending of topics and subjects begins to occur. Problem solving occupies a more central location, and expectations about systematic reasoning increase.

First-year algebra begins to apply pressure to the mathematical framework of the student. For many, this is the initial exposure to mathematics beyond memorization, or a cookie-cutter-type curriculum. The course is a transition from the specifics of arithmetic into a confusing world where things are allowed to change. How these changes occur influences the final outcome. Before, students were told that division by zero was undefined. Now they are expected to be able to extend that to the realization that if a denominator of a fraction is "$X + 3.2$," then $X$ cannot be -3.2 because that would yield zero for the term. Such maneuvers are not easy for all students to see immediately.

A significant part of the first-year algebra work is highly dependent on the arithmetic processes covered earlier in the curricular development of the students. For the sake of this discussion, we assume individuals in a first-year algebra course have been exposed to finding a difference like $53^2 - 24^2$. We further assume that there was some discussion about solving this problem by taking $(53 + 24)$ $(53 - 24)$. Algebraically, there is a desire to extend this work to the generalization $a^2 - b^2 = (a + b)(a - b)$. Because the difference of two squares is so common in algebra, students have been encouraged to memorize this as one of the special factored forms, often with no relation to problems like $53^2 - 24^2$ or any concrete explanation about why the solution is as it is.

Certainly, $53^2 - 24^2$ could be presented to the students in the $a^2 - b^2 = (a + b)(a - b)$ form by lecture. On the other hand, if a clue is taken from the work of constructivists like Piaget, the presentation can be done concretely first. The thinking is that the physical manipulation establishes a stronger basis for understanding the process. At the same time, concrete manipulations can assist students in developing the capability to create mental images of the operation being performed. You should do this activity as you read these instructions. Perform each step before reading on.

1. Using any rectangularly shaped piece of paper, fold it so a square can be cut from it as in Fig. 10.1.

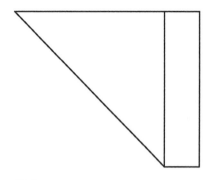

**Figure 10.1**

2. Cut the excess "tail" of paper as in Fig. 10.2.

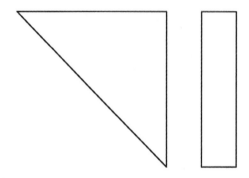

**Figure 10.2**

3. Express the side length of the square in terms of a variable. See Fig. 10.3. What is the area of the square?

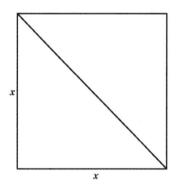

**Figure 10.3**

4. Fold the square along the previously established diagonal and name this new shape as seen in Fig. 10.4.

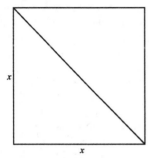

**Figure 10.4**

5. Make a fold in the triangle so it is parallel to one of the legs of the triangle. If the fold is done correctly as in Fig. 10.5, the possibility of a "sailboat" being created exists, although this is not the most common result.

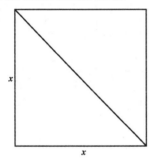

**Figure 10.5**

6. Cut along this new fold line and, for the time being, lay the resultant trapezoid to the side. Open the triangle and express the side length of the small square in terms of a variable as seen in Fig. 10.6.

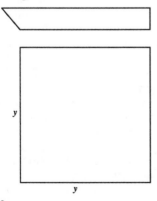

**Figure 10.6**

7. Open the folded trapezoid to show an L-shaped concave hexagon. Express the area of this paper in terms of the assigned variables. Label the dimensions of each segment of the "L" as shown in Fig. 10.7.

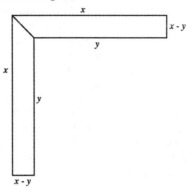

**Figure 10.7**

8. Cut the "L" along the established diagonal. Flip and rotate one of the two trapezoids, placing the two together at the common diagonal to form a rectangle, as shown in Fig. 10.8. Express the area as a product of the variable dimensions. But this new area is the same $a^2 - b^2$, determined earlier, so it must be the case that $a^2 - b^2 = (a + b)(a - b)$ and the special factored form has been developed concretely.

**Figure 10.8**

Doing activities like "Squares," described here, assists students with the ability to visualize a process. Similar benefits can be derived as factoring skills are developed (Brumbaugh, 1994, p. 18).

### EXERCISES 10.3

1. Describe or create an activity that could be used to show $(a + b)^2 = (a + b)(a + b)$.

2. Describe or create an activity that could be used to show $(a - b)^2 = (a - b)(a + b)$.

## VARIABLE

Logicians spend lots of time carefully defining open variables, closed variables, and so forth. Many mathematicians prefer to think of variable as a name for a number. Because they are not sure what the number is, they call it $x$. It is generally accepted that the concept of a variable is difficult for beginning algebra students to comprehend. They may have been exposed to the idea of a variable in a multitude of settings prior to coming to algebra class. They may or may not be aware of the times when they used a variable. Concretely, the situation could have evolved from combining a set of two trucks with a set of three dolls to yield a set containing five elements. As the scenes from their past changed to the semiconcrete stage developmentally, the objects gave way to pictures of the objects to represent the two trucks and three dolls.

That move involved a variable of sorts in that the pictures represented the actual trucks or dolls. Still later, as the students progressed to the semiabstract stage of their development, the pictures of trucks could have been depicted by a "$T$" and the dolls with a "$D$." This abstraction begins to show a more common algebraic use of a variable, again probably without any comment to that effect. Eventually, beginning in the early grades, they dealt with equations like $2 + 3 = \square$.

Most probably they were not aware of the idea that the $\square$ represented a variable, and yet it did. It stood for an answer they were looking for. Later, as students are exposed to word problems and formulas, variables appear in natural settings. For example, when they find the area of a rectangle, they use the formula $A = lw$, and it is accepted that "$A$" stands for "area," "$l$" represents the length of the rectangle, and "$w$" is the width. As they do word problems and translate them into equations to be solved, words give way to letters that represent the words and the concept of variable appears again. These informal exposures to variables give way to more formal approaches in the beginnings of algebra. Students like to make the correlation of a variable to a meaningful concept like $A = $ Area and $l = $ length. Why do we use "$x$" as the missing variable in most textbook equations more so than "$n$," which could stand for number, or "$m$" for missing number? Recall Descartes (http://www-history.mcs.st-and.ac.uk/Mathematicians/Descartes.html) and "$x$"; perhaps we are simply creatures of tradition when it comes to symbolic notation.

A very easy way to discuss a variable is through the use of a name. For example, my name is Douglas Kent. All my life, my father and grandfather called me Mike. Others addressed me as Doug, although at times at home if I was out of line, it was Douglas.

If I was way out of line, it was Douglas Kent, and then I knew I was in serious trouble. Different names were used for the same person in different settings. Students probably have experienced similar situations, and that example helps them begin to have a feeling about variables. Extend the name idea to include an example involving more than one student from the class having the same first name. They are familiar with this situation and realize the need for more explanation to be able to identify the appropriate individual. This is a situation showing a variable in the form of a name and that variable represents a set of individuals.

Often, variable is defined for students. The Standard College Dictionary defines variable as "Math. a. A quantity susceptible of fluctuating in value or magnitude under different conditions. b. A symbol representing one of a group of objects" (Funk & Wagnalls, 1968, p. 1482). Dictionary.com defines a variable as "a. a quantity or function that may assume any given value or *set* of values. b. a symbol that represents this." ("Math," 2012). Typical mathematics textbook definitions are:

> "A variable is a symbol used to represent one or more numbers" (Fair & Bragg, 1993).
> "A variable is any symbol, like $h$, $x$, or •, that may be replaced by numbers" (Shulte & Peterson, 1978, p. 5).
> "Letters or symbols like ?, •, and O used to take the place of numerals are called numerical variables, or simply variables" (Nichols, 1970, p. 245).
> "A letter used to represent an arbitrary element of a set (containing more than one element) is called a variable" (Allendoerfer & Oakley, 1955, p. 126).

Note that the definitions date from 1955 to 2012 and there is little difference in the wording. Unless you have a feel for the concept, the definitions add little to clarify the situation. It is almost like saying, "A rose is a rose is a rose." If you know what a rose is, you understand. If you do not, the definition does little to enlighten you.

Once a variable is defined, typically the texts go into how to write variables and how to operate with them. One significant technological issue is raised at this point. Most textbooks define five times a number $N$ to be either $5 \cdot N$ where the "dot" is elevated, $(5)(N)$, $5(N)$, or $5N$. Then the texts almost universally abandon all forms except for $5N$, which uses implicit multiplication. "Everyone knows that the multiplication symbol is there" expresses the common mentality on this issue. Students become accustomed to writing $5N$. The question is whether the student understands this notation to represent the product of "5" and "$N$." When technology is used, many software versions require insertion of the multiplication symbol. Thus, at least part of the world of technology is significantly different from the written text world. Is that difference acceptable? If the difference is accepted, how is it explained to the students? Because we are now well into the technological age, we need to be prepared to explain to students why mathematical notation is not universal.

The multiplication symbol is an excellent place to introduce this topic. The * operator is a common computer symbol for mathematics. We could not use a period, because of its many other uses in computer languages. Many students might ask, "What about the symbol $x$?" Computer languages are forced to recognized $x$ as the English letter.

---

### EXERCISES 10.4

1. Develop an alternative to * that is located on the keyboard. How could this be universally implemented?

2. Develop a new symbol for multiplication that is not currently on the keyboard. How will this key be universally accepted in the mathematics and computer community?

---

 **Additional exercises can be found on the website.**

Once the definition of variable is established, the work usually focuses on substituting some number for that variable and evaluating the expression. Extended exposure includes other variables that are added, subtracted, multiplied, and divided, but no exponents are used with the variables. Students are asked to convert word phrases into algebraic expressions using variables with problems like:

A number decreased by 4.
Some number $M$ is 5 greater than 13.
A value $M$ is tripled, then added to 86.7.

In the curricular continuum, exponents are generally one of the next places variables are encountered. In a setting like $x^n$, $x$ is defined as the base and $n$ is the exponent that "shows how many times $x$ is used as a factor." One question that should be asked eventually about the definition is, "What if the exponent is 0.5? How do we write $x$ as a

factor 0.5 times?" Consider that exponents are a shorthand notation for expressing the same factor. That is, $a^3$ is really $(a)(a)(a)$, which is now expressed in expanded form. This can lead into scientific notation and the use of exponent rules to deal with very large or very small numbers. Disregarding the question about how an exponent should be defined, the students are asked to evaluate expressions involving exponents. From there they move to the laws of exponents, which leads to another exposure to variables as factors.

## MULTIPLYING A MONOMIAL AND A POLYNOMIAL

After instruction on the laws of exponents, most first-year algebra texts introduce the product of a monomial and a polynomial. It is assumed that previous exposure has included collecting like terms. Frequently, there is some review and extension of the distributive property of multiplication over addition on the set of real numbers. Significant amounts of time are spent dealing with situations containing negative factors. The distributive property becomes an essential ingredient in the understanding of future explanations involving the product of two polynomials. Most of the time, the multiplication is expressed horizontally in forms like $5(2m^3 + 6m^3 - 7m - 8)$. The monomial eventually includes variables and exponents, and the polynomial may involve more than one variable. However, there are some advantages to showing the product in vertical format as well.

The idea of vertical multiplication is particularly advantageous if the students have had prior experience with expanded or partial product forms of multiplication. This can often be related back to concrete stages of multiplication learning with base 10 blocks. Base 10 block multiplication would show the product 3(21) as three sets of two longs (L) and a unit (U) block. Examples of the basic base 10 blocks are shown in Fig. 10.9. The pieces would be rearranged to show six Ls and three Us for a total of 63. Expanded notation would involve the distributive property of multiplication over addition on the set of counting numbers by showing $3(20 + 1) = 60 + 3$. That would be written in partial product format as:

21
× 3
3 from 3 times 1
60 from 3 times 20.

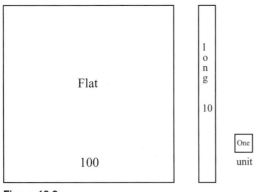

**Figure 10.9**

The 20 is significant in showing how place value is determined. The vertical writing is important in establishing format, because the partial products can be collapsed into the standard algorithm. It is meaningful to relate the current work to prior efforts as students are guided to a deeper level of understanding. Both formats are vital to helping students conceptualize different models of multiplication commonly used in algebra.

A set of manipulatives can be created that is similar to the base 10 blocks. These manipulatives are available commercially (Algebra Lab Gear [Creative]; Algeblocks [ETA]) but they can be made easily. Refer to the big square as $X^2$, the rectangle will be named $X$, and the little square will be a unit or 1. We are going to build some rectangles with these pieces. There are a few ground rules. It may appear that a number of units are the same length as an $X$ if they are placed edge to edge in a straight line segment like square bricks in a wall. (In the commercial sets the units will not add up to an $X$ or $Y$. They just don't fit that way. The creators made sure of that!) It is not permitted to make trades in such an instance. Trades such as this were permitted with base 10 blocks, and 10 ones could be traded for one 10 or 10 10s would be traded for one 100. The reason these trades cannot be done with the algebra manipulatives is that $X$ is a variable or unknown. If six units are traded for an $X$ when the value of the $X$ is really nine, errors would be produced. Thus, exchanges are not permitted between pieces in the set.

The set of algebra manipulatives can be used to express products in a manner very similar to that used with the base 10 blocks. $3(2X + 1)$ would be shown as three sets of two $X$s being added to a 1, giving a grand total of six $X$s and three 1s. The students would then interpret this product with a final expression of $6X + 3$. Note the similarities between

this and 63 expressed as $6(10^1) + 3(10^0)$ or $6(10) + 3$. The product needs careful association with the manipulatives to assist the students in creating a mental image of the product. As with young children in their early development of the concept of multiplication, care must be taken to not rush too quickly to the abstraction. Assure that appropriate intermediate steps are provided to assist the students in visualizing the overall operation. The students will want to shed the manipulatives as quickly as possible, which is fine, as long as they have had some time to understand the impact of the operation. The degree of difficulty of the problems can be expanded with manipulatives, but these examples can quickly become cumbersome.

Multiplication of a constant times a variable expression like $3(X^2 - 5X + 8)$ is easy to show. The size of the constant factor can make the setting overly complex because of the number of pieces needed to show the product. However, it is important to realize that even the large, cumbersome products can be shown—they just take time to create. The ideal is to work with small products, which are easy to show, and have the students understand what is happening. Then abandon the manipulatives as quickly as possible with the perception that they can be recalled if needed. Establishing a solid foundation with the small, simple problems is crucial to the students' ability to handle more complex issues. Discarding the manipulatives too quickly is akin to just telling the students the process. That method is not effective. Ultimately, if the manipulatives are not permitted to run their full course, it is better to not use them at all. Lecture on! Your students will not be as capable as they could be, but at least they will not have developed a negative attitude toward the use of the manipulative. Partial use of any teaching tool and then "telling the secret," for whatever reason, is more damaging than no use at all.

Exponents greater than squares can be shown with the manipulatives. Creation of the tools becomes cumbersome. $X^3$ can be built with a normal three-dimensional approach to building a cube that is $X$ units on an edge. These are represented in many of the commercial sets. Beyond that, representations become difficult. This amplifies the need to establish a solid foundation with the $X$, $X^2$, and perhaps the $X^3$. The hope is that the underpinnings will be sufficient for the students to visualize the processes necessary to complete the assigned tasks.

Similarly, multiplication by variables is possible in a limited format. For example, multiplying $(X + 2)$ by $X$ can be shown by building the appropriate pieces ($X^2$ and $2X$ in this case). However, the explanations necessary to build the appropriate manipulative results can become artificial. At that point, questions about the advantages of a model-replacing lecture, and when that model requires extensive lecture to explain it, need to be raised. Again, the hope is that appropriate formative background can be established with settings easy to represent. Then, once the conceptualizations are established, the manipulatives will be abandoned in favor of abstractions. Still, the possibility exists of returning to the concrete if necessary.

---

**EXERCISE 10.5**

1.  Create a paper set of manipulatives including units, $X$s, and $X^2$s. Do an example like $5(2X^2 + 3X + 4)$ using the manipulatives. Describe your thoughts and reactions to the manipulation in light of thinking about how this could help students understand the operation.

---

## THE PRODUCT OF TWO BINOMIALS

Most authorities agree there is value in having students understand the operations to be performed at some level beyond mechanical. Regrettably, there are some text series that still stress doing the process to get the answer, while overlooking a multitude of opportunities to connect the operation with previously covered topics and establishing groundwork for future study. Prior to working with the product of two binomials, students cover the products of two monomials and the product of a monomial and polynomials. F.O.I.L. (First, Outer, Inner, and Last) is a mnemonic used by many teachers to instruct students on how to find the product of two binomials. Let $(A + B)$ and $(C + D)$ be the two binomials to be multiplied.

Multiplying the *First* terms of each binomial gives $AC$.
Multiplying the *Outer* terms of each binomial gives $AD$.
Multiplying the *Inner* terms of each binomial gives $BC$.
Multiplying the *Last* terms of each binomial gives $BD$.

Although F.O.I.L. accomplishes the task of having students find products of two binomials, little

opportunity for understanding the process is evident. Use of the distributive property of multiplication over addition, even here, would give one rule that works for all polynomials. The major tragedy is that many students who learn to F.O.I.L. with limited understanding then proceed to apply this special case to polynomials, not just binomials.

If the idea of the distributive property of multiplication over addition on the set of real numbers was developed during exposures to the products of monomials with polynomials, then that idea can be extended to the product of two polynomials. Manipulatives can be used, but again, the complexities of being able to physically represent some products concretely arise; however, developmental work can be established. Furthermore, if the students grasped the abstractions involved when finding the product of a monomial and a polynomial, it is possible that they will not need additional concrete exposure at this point. If they do, careful selection of problems can provide limited concrete exposure that should lift students over the obstacles they are experiencing. Consider the product of two binomials $(X + 3)(2X + 4)$. It should be noted that all the signs are positive in this example. Negatives need to be considered, but because of the potential difficulties involved in multiplication of signed values, it is advisable to avoid them in initial explanations. Once the students begin to understand the situation, complexities like those involved with multiplying by negative values can be inserted. If the distributive property of multiplication over addition on the real numbers was used earlier, then the problem can be expressed as $X(2X + 4)$ and $+ 3(2X + 4)$ or $(X + 3)(2X)$ and $(X + 3)(4)$. Note that $+ 3(2X + 4)$ is purposely used here with the intent of showing continuity and laying groundwork for negative factors. Initially it is important to maintain order and use the commutative property of multiplication on the set of real numbers to change things if desired. Once this becomes a student's reflex behavior, the formality can be de-emphasized. When the problem $(X + 3)(2X + 4)$ is converted to $X(2X + 4)$ and $+ 3(2X + 4)$ or $(X + 3)(2X)$ and $(X + 3)(4)$, reference can be made to prior work and the results compiled accordingly. If this relation is clearly made, then factoring of trinomials becomes an easier concept to grasp. The concrete exposures can be inserted as necessary. However, the students should see the similarities and proceed, because a thorough understanding at this point will only increase conceptual development later. The distributive property approach to the product of two binomials explains why F.O.I.L. works and provides a vehicle to be used when dealing with the products of polynomials with more than two terms.

---

### EXERCISES 10.6

1. Create a paper set of manipulatives including units, $X$s, and $X^2$s. Do an example like $(X + 4)(2X + 3)$ using the manipulatives. Describe your thoughts and reactions to the manipulation in terms of how this could help students understand the operation.

2. Connect a product like $(3X + 4)(2X + 1)$ to a partial product approach used to multiply $(34)(21)$, which would look like:

   34
   ×21
   4 from 1 × 4
   30 from 1 × 30
   80 from 20 × 4
   600 from 20 × 30
   714

---

Describe your thoughts and reactions to the manipulation, focusing on how this could help students understand the operation.

## TOPICS TO HELP VISUALIZE FACTORING

Algebra students will have been exposed to factoring in previous classes. There is a good possibility that they will have forgotten, and the following lesson can help them overcome that memory lapse. At the same time, the lesson can be used to establish a basis for visualization of factoring. Anytime factoring is done, essentially the area of a rectangle is given and the task is to determine the dimensions. This can be established as a part of the introductory review. In the sample teacher questions that follow, it is assumed that the teacher would display appropriate enthusiasm and excitement as the described discussion develops. Furthermore, it is assumed that questions would be altered to meet the needs of a class and to probe for the desired responses. The major message is that phrasing the question is important to enhance student understanding. The following shows where the prior exposure occurred

and how to build on that information to deal with an algebraic setting.

| | |
|---|---|
| Question: | When multiplying, what names are given to the numbers? |
| Probable response: | Numbers. |
| Better question: | When multiplying, what are numbers called? |
| Probable response: | Factors and product. |
| Question: | Where is multiplication used in geometry? |
| Probable response: | Finding area. Each time two numbers are multiplied, you are finding the area of a rectangle. When dividing, you are given the area of a rectangle and one dimension. |
| Question: | What, then, is the task in division? |
| Student: | To find the other dimension of the rectangle. |
| Teacher: | What are other names for the length, width, and area? |
| Student: | Factor, factor, and product. |
| Teacher: | So if you have a product, what does it represent? |
| Student: | The area of some rectangle. |
| Teacher: | What else can you determine if you have the product or area of a rectangle? |
| Student: | Its dimensions. |
| Teacher: | Those ideas of dimensions and areas are used in algebra, too. We used that idea when we found the product of two binomials. Each factor was a dimension and the product was the "area" of a rectangle. |
| Teacher: | You each have a set of manipulatives. If I had an $X^2$, two $X$s, and a unit, can I build a rectangle? |
| Student: | I can build a square, but all squares are rectangles [see Fig. 10.10]. |

Note: At this point more examples would be given and the homework assignment should have the students using given sets of pieces to build rectangles. At this stage of their development, no mention is made of the rectangle's dimensions

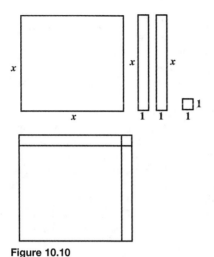

**Figure 10.10**

and all examples will result in a rectangle. For example, make a rectangle from two $X^2$s, three $X$s, and two units; two $X^2$s, five $X$s, and three 1s; and so on. Each time, the student is to sketch the solution using representations of the manipulatives.

The next lesson would begin by discussing the figures formed out of the given pictures, with students showing their sketches.

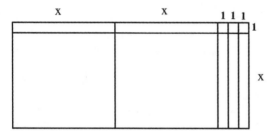

**Figure 10.11**

Teacher: Look at the picture made from two $X^2$s, five $X$s, and three ones [see Fig. 10.11]. What shape is the figure?
Student: Rectangle.
Teacher: What is the area of the rectangle?
Student: $2X^2 + 5X + 3$
Teacher: How did you determine $2X^2 + 5X + 3$ is the area?
Teacher: What are the dimensions of the rectangle?
Student: $2X + 3$ long and $X + 1$ high.

Note: Replicate as necessary. Emphasize the area that is derived by looking at the dimensions of the rectangle. Those dimensions become the factors of the product.

Teacher: Think back to your basic multiplication. Is there more than one set of dimensions for the area of a rectangle?
Student: Maybe. For prime numbers the answer is no, but for composite numbers the answer is yes. For example, if the area is 12, the dimensions could be 1 by 12, 2 by 6, or 3 by 4.
Teacher: So a product might have more than one set of factors?
Student: Yes.
Teacher: Do you suppose that would be true with the algebraic expressions we have been dealing with?

At this point the students would be assigned the task of determining if different sets of manipulatives could be arranged in more than one way, indicating whether or not there is more than one set of factors for a given product. The ensuing discussion would focus on the process and the algebraic name of factoring. The preceding vignette shows a series of questions, answers, and activities that can be constructed to assist students in creating mental images of the tasks they are asked to perform. One student who was very resistant to using the manipulatives because they were "baby stuff" responded at the end of this string of lessons, "Oh, I get it! Every time I factor something, I get a picture of the rectangle in my head and look for the dimensions. That's easy!" That reaction is exactly what is desired. From then on, factoring should take on a different meaning for the student.

## DRILL IN FIRST-YEAR ALGEBRA?

There is a need for some drill. The question becomes how much. The number of different answers to this question can be astounding. Some will insist on lists of problems to assure mastery of even the smallest nuances. Others will say that as long as the student "really understands" the concept, there is little need for drill, because the students have mastered the process. Many adopt the middle-of-the-road approach. One important factor is for you to arrive at your own conclusions about how much drill-and-practice is necessary. If you establish your position based on what someone else has said, the position presented in this text, the number of problems available in your textbook series, or what you had to do when you took first-year algebra, you are not doing what you need to do. You should listen to the authorities you come in contact with, read articles from the professional literature, discuss ideas with your peers and colleagues, and then reflect. Based on such exposures, you establish your position, which, by the way, should be open to change as influenced by your experiences. Do not forget, students will influence you and your decisions also.

Drill-and-practice can be made more enjoyable than it often is. Many number tricks have an algebraic base. For example, do the following problem and record the amount of time it takes you to get the answer.

$$\frac{1234567890}{(1234567891)^2 - (1234567890)(1234567892)}$$

If you did this by performing the operations, even with technology, there is a quicker way. Algebraically, the problem is

$$\frac{X}{(X+1)^2 - (X)(X+2)}$$

Simplifying the denominator gives $X^2 + 2X + 1 - X^2 - 2X$, which is 1. The solution is the numerator of the original problem, 1234567890 (Brumbaugh, 1994, p. 7). Certainly, there is nothing wrong with doing the problem via the arithmetic route. However, as students become accustomed to thinking algebraically, the potential increases that they will get used to using their newfound skills and knowledge as they approach different environments. Students can easily be convinced of the need to "think" algebra when confronted with problems like the one used here and other "pick a number" tricks.

Pick any counting number.
Add the next highest counting number.

Add 9 to the sum.
Divide this new sum by 2.
Subtract 5.
What did you get?
How does this work? Explain algebraically.

Drill can also be developed in the game format. A commercially available game, Winning Touch, provides a setting for practicing arithmetic facts. Winning Touch can be altered to entice algebraic practice. Make two game boards that are the same size and shape: One will be left blank and the other, as shown in Fig. 10.12, will be cut apart to form the playing pieces. The game board is rectangular, made up of a series of unit squares. For this example the operation will be multiplication, but that could be changed. The top row and left column show the factors for each row and column.

In the game, the products are placed on the respective cells of the game board. The playing pieces are the products cut from Fig. 10.12. The factors (top row and left column) are discarded. The playing pieces are placed facedown on the table. Each participant draws the same number of pieces (five, for example, so that not all the pieces are taken). The first person to correctly place all pieces under the rules of the game is the winner.

The first player puts a piece on its correct square of the board. No new piece is drawn to replace that one. The object of the game is to play all the pieces. Moving clockwise around the board, the next individual must place a piece so it touches an occupied square on one of its horizontal or vertical edges. Inability to place a piece results in a loss of turn, drawing an additional piece to play, or continuing to

| X | A | B | AB | $A^2B$ | $(AB)^2$ | $AB^2$ | $\frac{A}{B}$ | $\bullet \ \bullet \ \bullet$ |
|---|---|---|---|---|---|---|---|---|
| AB | $A^2B$ | $AB^2$ | $A^2B^2$ | $A^3B^2$ | $A^3B^3$ | $A^2B^3$ | $A^2$ | |
| A + B | $A^2 + AB$ | $AB + B^2$ | $A^2B + AB^2$ | $A^3B + A^2B^2$ | $A^3B^2 + A^2B^3$ | $A^2B^3 + AB^3$ | $\frac{(A^2 + AB)}{B}$ | |
| A | $A^2$ | AB | $A^2B$ | $A^3B$ | $A^3B^2$ | $(AB)^2$ | $\frac{A^2}{B}$ | |
| $\frac{A^2}{B}$ | $\bullet$ | $\bullet$ | $\bullet$ | | | | | |
| $\begin{matrix}\bullet\\\bullet\\\bullet\end{matrix}$ | $\bullet$ | | | | | | | |

**Figure 10.12**

draw pieces until a play can be made. The disadvantage of drawing additional pieces quickly becomes apparent. The decision to allow diagonal touches becomes yours.

Complexities can easily be added to the game. For example, rather than showing the product of $A$ and $B$ in the third row, second column of Fig. 10.12 as $AB$, it could be shown as $\frac{1}{(AB)^{-1}}, \frac{A}{B^{-1}}$, or $\frac{B}{A^{-1}}$. Each of these and the many possible variations for each of the responses can be used to make the game as challenging or simple as desired. Similarly, the degree of difficulty can be altered by the operation used and the terms or factors associated with it.

A card game can be created that could be used for drill or practice. A game deck has two parts: "statement cards" and "value cards." The same number of statement cards is dealt to each player. The value cards are placed facedown on the table. The top value card is turned up. Each player substitutes the number on the value card into each statement card held. Every person plays one statement card on a trick; the highest card using the given value wins that round. The next value card is revealed. Another round is played, substituting this new value into the remaining statement cards held. The winner of a trick plays first on the next round. It is not mandatory that the highest card be played from a hand on any given trick. The first person to win five tricks is the victor (statement and value cards may need to be reshuffled and dealt again). A set of statement cards could be:

$5z + (4 - z); z - (z - 1); 3z - (2 - 2z); z + (2z + 1);$
$3z - 5(z - 1) + 6; 4(z - 2) - 5(2z + 3); 5z - (2z + 4);$
　　$2z + (-z + 1); 10 - (5 + z);$
$(2z + 3) + (z - 5) - 2(2z - 7); 2z - 4 - (z + 4);$
　　$z(z + 1) - (z^2 - 5z); -z - (z - 3);$
$(z^2) - (z^2 + 6); 4(z^2 - 3(z^2 - 2z - 5); 4z - (2z^2 + 3z$
　　$+ 6) - (4z^2 - 5z);$
$z^2(z - 1) - z(z^2 + 2z - 4); 5z^2 - (3z - 2)2$
　　$- 7(4z - 6);$
$z^2(z - 3) - z(z - 3) + 4; z(z^2 + 4) + z(z - 5) + 6.$

Value cards could be: $z = 2.5$; -1; -3; 6; 3; -2; -5; 4 (Brumbaugh, 1994, p. 39). Different sets of cards can be used for different sections of a course. Experience has shown that students enjoy playing this game and do not realize they are practicing their skills. You have effectively inserted drill-and-practice with an enjoyable game.

Technology affords a multitude of opportunities for drill-and-practice. There is software available that essentially turns the computer into a glorified copy machine. In this mode, problem after problem is given to the student to work. For all practical purposes, the computer becomes an extension of the textbook in that a long list of problems is given to the student to practice. This appears to be a gross misuse of the power of the computer, and yet it is a popular mode because many students are enamored with the use of a computer. The Internet has a wealth of sites such as http://www.math.com that can be used to practice skills as well. The computer becomes an avenue in which the student wants to practice algebra skills.

## TECHNOLOGY IN FIRST-YEAR ALGEBRA

There are ways in which technology can be used for practice. A caution about technology first: Students must become aware of the fact that technology is only as good as the person using it. That is, an answer should not be accepted just because it was derived using technology. Estimation skills and reasonableness of the response are an integral part of the setting. Certainly, a graphing calculator or software could be available that would afford any student the opportunity to determine if an idea for the sketch of a graph is correct. However, it is possible that errors used to arrive at an answer can be carried into the technology. For example, suppose the task is to graph all values greater than $2x + 3$. Typically, the student is taught to graph the equation and then select a point to determine the region to fill. If the student does this problem on a graphing calculator, with most pieces of software, that same selection process could be used and thus the same region filled. If the student understands and uses the process correctly, all is well. If somehow the student fills the wrong side of the equation, all is not well. Some technology tools fill automatically as shown in Figs. 10.13 ($y > x^2 - 1$ and $y > x/2 + 1$) and, thus, avoid the potential shading error.

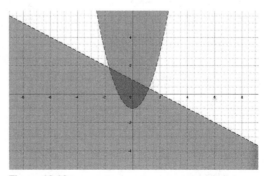

**Figure 10.13**

A skill that students should possess is estimation of values. Technology affords the opportunity to check the accuracy of those estimates. The use of a calculator to reinforce the concepts of exponents is an example. Does $3^2 = 2^3$? Students can test their hypothesis easily without the aid of a calculator, but does $8^9 = 9^8$? Are 9 factors of 8 equivalent to 8 factors of 9? The assistance of a calculator can help students develop a conceptual understanding of exponents quickly and easily.

Solving two equations in two unknowns is a typical activity found in first-year algebra courses. Most of the time, the first approach is graphing solutions, followed by substitution, addition/subtraction, and multiplication/division. Many text series devote an entire chapter, or at least several sections, to the treatment of these concepts, which means several days of instruction. Technology offers an alternative.

## EXERCISE 10.6

1.  Are there any hints that help tell how many points of intersection two linear equations will have? If so, what are they and how do you describe them to students? If not, what do we do to help students?

Symbolic manipulating, function-plotting software and Internet Applications (Derive, Desmos, Maple, Mathematics Exploration Toolkit, Mathcad, Mathematica, WolframAlpha), and graphing calculators (Casio CFX9800 series, Hewlett-Packard, Sharp, and TI-8X series) permit graphing two linear equations. The graphing window can be enlarged or zoomed in on to inspect the point of intersection more closely. For the sake of this discussion it is assumed that the two equations have a unique solution. It is further assumed that there is a projection device available for teacher demonstrations, a lab of computers with appropriate software for student use during the class, and that the students are familiar with the software so they can use it as an investigation/learning tool. For this discussion, assume the students did not have access to graphing calculators and, thus, equations were graphed either with the software or, for homework, with paper and pencil.

The following is a description of a few lessons dealing with solving two equations in two unknowns. The first demonstration dealt with graphing

two equations and determining the point of intersection by zooming, tracing, and inspection using software. For homework the students were to graph pairs of equations and determine the coordinates of the point of intersection. Their results were to be sketched on paper for the next class.

One frequent question about using software to teach mathematics is whether or not the material being covered transfers to paper–pencil tasks because they are still the dominant mode used in testing settings. The answer is a resounding "yes." In the class following the homework of sketching graphs of intersecting linear equations, the students were presented with the graphs of two intersecting lines ($y = x + 3$ and $y = -x + 7$) on the viewing screen and asked to determine the point of intersection. By inspection, they determined that the common point had coordinates (2, 5). The class was ready to proceed to the next topic.

The software used for this lesson permitted storage and recall of equations. The first equation, $y = x + 3$, had been stored in compartment $A$ and $y = -x + 7$ was placed in $B$. Investigating the impact of operating on the stored equations led to a discovery. We looked at $A + B$, which gave "$(y = x + 3) + (y = -x + 7)$." Simplifying gave "$y + y = x + 3 - x + 7$," leading to the observation that all the $y$s were on the left and all the $x$s and constants were on the right. Another simplification resulted in "$2y = 10$," and one student said that because that was one equation in one unknown, the $y$ value would be 5. As this statement was being made, several students vocalized that this was the same as the $y$ value obtained when graphing that pair of equations. A summary of what had transpired followed, and the class went to the computer lab to work with a group of equations (all coefficients of variables were positive or negative one) that had been stored. Their task was to experiment and arrive at some conclusions. They could add or subtract the stored equations, dealing with two at a time.

The ensuing discussion focused on realizations like:

Adding two equations where the respective signs of the variables were the same resulted in one equation in two unknowns.

Subtracting two equations where the respective signs of the variables were the same resulted in a nonsense situation like $0 = 6$.

When the signs of the respective variables were opposite and the equations were added, something like $0 = 6$ appeared.

If the signs of the respective variables were opposite and the two equations were subtracted, one equation in two unknowns appeared.

If one of the variables had the same sign and the other had opposite signs, either addition or subtraction would yield an equation in one unknown, which could then be solved.

Once the solution was determined, it could then be substituted into one of the original equations, and that situation solved for the value of the other unknown. After a short discussion of their perceptions, the class appeared to have a solid grasp of the general impact of adding and subtracting equations.

At this point, the students were asked how they would deal with a situation like "$y = x + 3$" and "$2y = 3x + 4$." Comments were quick and incisive, particularly considering that they had just done addition and subtraction. The basic statements made by the class were:

It won't do any good to add or subtract them because you will get one equation in two unknowns.

If we had $2y$ we could subtract.

That means we have to multiply that one equation.

Yes, but don't forget to multiply both sides.

Then we can subtract one equation from the other and get one equation in one unknown.

Maybe we should multiply by a negative 2 because we make fewer sign mistakes when adding as opposed to subtracting.

At this point, the class was sent back to stored equations on the computers. These equations had integral coefficients. In a short time the class defined most of the rules for multiplication, division, and substitution as a means for solving two equations in two unknowns.

All of the activities described since the review of solving two equations in two unknowns were completed in less than an hour. The students were able to transfer their computer work to paper-and-pencil assignments and complete them satisfactorily. Their retention was good. They were able to apply the knowledge throughout the rest of the class. Most important, what often takes several weeks to accomplish in a typical classroom setting that does not use technology as a teaching/learning tool was completed in a few hours, and the students' attitude about solving two equations was positive.

In the preceding discussion about solving two equations in two unknowns, technology was used as a discovery tool. There is ample opportunity for students to discover basic concepts with technology. Consider learning about the impact of changing the coefficient of $x$ in a linear equation written in slope intercept form. Traditionally, the teacher leads a discussion that guides students to the appropriate conclusions. During the course of that discussion, different equations will be sketched with varying degrees of precision. That same lesson delivered with technology can be much more dynamic, assuming the teacher is working with a projected image of a linear equation. For the sake of this discussion, it is assumed that the class is familiar with the use of technology by the teacher. Thus, it is safe to assume they will ask what happens if the 2 in $y = 2x + 3$ is changed to 4. Then, what happens if the 4 in $y = 4x + 3$ is changed to 5. And so forth. It does not take long for the students to conclude that as the coefficient of $x$ increases, the line gets steeper. They have just described the concept of slope and the definition could now easily be formalized. Certainly, this could be done without technology, but the speed, precision, spontaneity, and flexibility would be lacking.

It is possible that some student would want to change the constant. Careful discussion on the part of the teacher can lead to a delay of that idea until the slope exchange is completed. Eventually both the slope and the constant would be changed, but at that point the students should be adept at predicting the impact on the graph of the equation as either is altered. The advantage of technology is that it assists the students in creating mental images of what is happening. This, in turn, strengthens their understandings and provides stronger foundations for future work. Equally significant is that the students become willing to ask "what if" questions, something that will be invaluable in helping the student become self-motivated lifelong learners.

The Casio CFX-9850GB Plus has the ability to do dynamic graphing. An equation like $y = Ax + B$ can be used where $B$ remains constant and the value of $A$, which is the slope, can change across some defined range at some interval. When in operation, the calculator will display a collection of lines, one of which is highlighted. The equation for the highlighted line is displayed as shown in Fig. 10.14. The calculator will automatically step to the next line and equation, or it can be done manually. Desmos.com has the ability to create dynamic sliders for A and B as shown in Fig. 10.15. This feature allows you to alter A or B by a specified interval and a determined range. A few examples using this technology will benefit students as they attempt to understand the concept of slope.

An inequality such as $y < 2x + 3$ is typically graphed by shading the region below the graph of the linear equation $y = 2x + 3$, showing all values that satisfy the inequality. If more than one inequality is graphed on the same axis system, different shading routines are used for each, and the common solution area is shown as a combination of the different shadings. This is difficult to do with technology, because there is no way to show the different colors on top of each other. However, there is an easy and useful way around the dilemma. When graphing, color/shade the side that does not satisfy the inequality. When doing more than one inequality on the same axis system, the background screen color will show the region that satisfies all graphed inequalities. A natural extension and application of this idea is found in linear programming. By coloring the region that does not satisfy the inequalities, the resulting polygon of solutions will surround a region in the background color as seen in Fig. 10.16. We are moving into a more technological teaching world. We need to be able to deal with the graphing of inequalities. This linear programming discussion points out the need for an alteration of the curriculum as it is currently delivered—rather than texts and teachers emphasizing the shading of the regions that do satisfy an inequality, the accent should be on coloring nonsolution areas. This is merely another impact of technology on the secondary mathematics curriculum.

One advantage to integrating the mathematics curriculum with other subject areas is that students have the opportunity to see the information they are learning used in a different setting. It is possible that one of the subjects selected will be an area of interest for them, so the process might have a positive impact on their mathematics attitude. One excellent opportunity to integrate mathematics and science is through the use of probes that can be used to gather data (IBM Personal Science Laboratory, and probes for graphing calculators).

Using the distance sensor, a series of activities can be used to build the concept of the slope of a line. Students often deal in a world of absolutes. That is, they are confident they can stand perfectly still. Have a student stand in front of the distance probe assigned with the task of standing "perfectly" still for a few seconds while their distance from the probe is measured. As the experiment is conducted, a horizontal (or so it seems) line appears

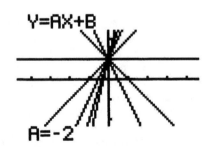

Figure 10.14

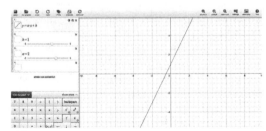

Figure 10.15

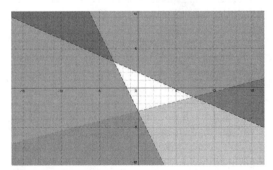

Figure 10.16

on the screen. Zooming in on (change to scale of the axis) the graph shows that it is not a horizontal line but may vary by as much as 5 centimeters. The students are amazed about this but soon come to realize that they do make small movements; their clothing will move because of breezes in the room, they will make slight reflexive body movements because of heartbeat or breathing, and so forth. After this discussion, the screen is rescaled so the small variations are not evident.

Next, a student is asked to walk at a constant rate away from the probe. It usually takes a few tries before a relatively straight line is established. This line will be used as a reference as another student is asked to walk, making a line parallel to the one on the screen. Even though they may not be able to formally express it, most middle school students know the meaning of parallel. As this is attempted, comments from the kibitzers in the class will encourage the walker to go faster or slower. The comments begin the understanding of slope. The term *slope* will probably not be used, but comparative statements like one line is steeper than the other will be common. This is the beginning, and the class can be guided to a formal definition of slope from here. This discussion can be extended to the difference between parallel lines. Proper calibration of the software can have the lines intersecting the $y$-axis at different points with the lines being parallel. Prior to this activity, the students learned about the slope intercept form of the line. Here, or at any point in the discussion, the mathematical characteristics could be discussed in the detail necessary to accomplish the objectives of the lesson.

## APPLICATIONS OF ALGEBRA

Research shows that activities can have a positive impact on the attitudes of students. Questions like, "When will I ever use this?" are common. A likely translation of questions is, "Where can I find an application of this concept in my world today?" It is imperative that the world be viewed from the perspective of a secondary student at this point, not from the perspective of an adult trying to convince the student to accept what is being given. There are situations that show algebra basics being used in the real world, as demonstrated by the following dialogue between a student and a tutor, which led to an activity called "Speed Trap" (Hynes & Brumbaugh, 1976, pp. 40–42).

Student: Why do I need to put in steps when solving something like $2x = 6$? Everybody knows the answer is 3.

Teacher: True, but you are learning a process. What if you had something like $14.5267y = 53.79825$? You wouldn't know the answer to that one. You learn the process in $2x = 6$ so you can solve things like this.

Student: OK, but where would you get something like that?

Teacher: Let's talk about law enforcement officers catching speeders. Modern technology allows a car to be timed as it travels a known distance. If the car goes through the distance too fast, the driver is exceeding the posted speed limit and, more than likely, that driver is going to have an opportunity to meet a representative of a police unit. We will go to a local road and establish a speed trap to see the equations that are generated.

A variety of other things will need to be done to complete this activity. They include:

Measure a reasonable distance, marking the beginning and end to establish the speed trap (100 yards provides enough time lapse to decrease the impact of many time measurement errors). Calculate the minimum legal time to cover the trap distance.

Establish the car part used to indicate entrance and exit of the trap (the front bumper does fine).

Determine how entrance and exit will be signaled to the timer (raising and lowering hands will work).

Station an individual at each end of the speed trap so the timer can see both of them.

Clock cars going through the trap.

Knowledge of speeders will be immediately evident from the recorded time. At this point, the students need to determine how much over the legal speed the car was traveling. In order to answer this question, the students need to compute the speed using the known time and distance. They are now solving equations that they will not reflexively know the answer to. In the process, they have also seen an application of the concept being discussed in class.

## EXERCISES 10.7

1. There are other applications of the principle used in the discussion of speed trap in this chapter. Find at least one more and describe how it could be used to answer the typical student question "When am I ever going to use this?" The example should be from the world as viewed by teenagers, not from your adult perspective.
2. Like adults, kids are often motivated by money. Find a real-world algebraic example that could be used during an algebra lesson that involves money.

## ALGEBRA IN PATTERNING SITUATIONS

In Chapter 7, Gauss's discovery of a fast way to find the sum of consecutive counting numbers was discussed. The description shows how Gauss (http://www-history.mcs.st-and.ac.uk/Mathematicians/Gauss.html) used a pattern to arrive at a solution and, ultimately, that pattern was extended to express a generalization. Most generalizations are going to require algebraic skills and notations in their final expressions. One such example involves the idea of being paid a penny on the first day, two cents on the second, and so forth, so that each subsequent day finds the pay to be double that of the preceding day, as follows:

| Day | Pay for Day | Total Pay |
|---|---|---|
| 1 | 1 | 1 |
| 2 | 2 | 3 |
| 3 | 4 | 7 |
| 4 | 8 | 15 |
| 5 | 16 | 31 |
| N | 2N-1 | 2N-1 |

Typically, the discussion focuses on how much money is earned on any given day, and that is often generalized because of the pattern. However, another generalization can be derived from the problem. If the pay was doubled for each of 30 days, starting with a penny on the first day, the pay for the 30th day would be \$5,638,709.12 and the total payment for all 30 days would be \$10,737,418.23. Without the assistance of patterning and algebraic skills, the solution to the question would be difficult to obtain (but not impossible). The idea of patterning and some basic algebra, coupled with the power of technology, puts a problem such as this within the reach of a wide selection of students.

Number theory relies on patterns that frequently can be generalized, calling on the use of algebra. Consider the following equations:

$$1 + 2 = 3$$
$$4 + 5 + 6 = 7 + 8$$
$$9 + 10 + 11 + 12 = 13 + 14 + 15$$
$$16 + 17 + 18 + 19 + 20 = 21 + 22 + 23 + 24$$

These equations offer a plethora of pattern and algebraic opportunities. The students need to have had experience investigating such information and to have learned the power of being able to generalize. There is a need to have an attitude of inquisitiveness about how and why numbers react to give patterns. This attitude comes essentially from exposure, and it largely becomes the responsibility of the teacher to ensure that activities or questions such as these are inserted into the curriculum as often as possible.

In this instance, several observations are possible. The first equation uses the first three counting numbers. The second equation uses the next five counting numbers, the next seven, and so on. Each equation begins with a perfect square, which makes sense if the students have been exposed to the task of finding the sum of consecutive odd counting numbers beginning with 1. ($1 + 3 = 4$; $4 + 5 = 9$ [where $4 = 1 + 3$]; $9 + 7 = 16$ [where $9 = 4 + 5$ and $4 = 1 + 3$]; and so on.) Even beginners to patterning will soon notice that the first addend in each

## EXERCISE 10.8

1. Given
   $$1 + 2 = 3$$
   $$4 + 5 + 6 = 7 + 8$$
   $$9 + 10 + 11 + 12 = 13 + 14 + 15$$
   $$16 + 17 + 18 + 19 + 20 = 21 + 22 + 23 + 24$$
   what is the first element of the 100th row? How many terms are in the row? What is the last element of that row? Describe the Nth row.

equation is a perfect square, algebraically expressed as $N^2$ where $N$ represents the row number. A little prompting should lead to the conclusion that there are $N$ addends on the left of the equal sign and $N - 1$ to the right. Given that information, a student should be able to describe any row from the four equations.

## THE ROLE OF ALGEBRA IN PROOF

Most nongeometric proofs rely heavily on algebraic skills. The concept has roots in beginning patterns, perhaps as simple as getting the next counting number. Young children often get to the next counting number in their exposures by adding one more object to a set of elements that comprise the number they just learned. That is, once a child masters "fourness" (four objects can be recognized in any configuration), five is presented. Often the presentation involves showing a set of five things, which is discussed and manipulated until "fiveness" becomes a part of the world of that child. The concept builds on the idea of one more than the last, and even though it is not expressed algebraically, the foundations are there. We would say that is just "$X + 1$" where $X$ represents the last number the child mastered.

As students progress through their learning exposures in mathematics, the complexities of the settings increase and the concept of proof begins to evolve. Young children see a set of three objects and a set of two objects placed together to form a set of five objects. They take the same sets of two and three and get five. The reversal of cardinalities is significant because eventually the setting is summarized into problem pairs of $2 + 3 = ?$ and $3 + 2 = ?$. At this point, the child gets an initial exposure to the commutative property of addition on the set of counting numbers. Eventually that becomes generalized to the commutative property of addition on some given set like the real numbers expressed as $A + B = B + A$. These formative abstractions are important proof building blocks.

Once the abstractions are started, more formalized expressions of proof become possible. The ability to represent things in algebraic terms is helpful at this stage of development. For example, students might conclude that the pattern in the following four equations

$$1 = 1$$
$$1 + 3 = 4$$
$$1 + 3 + 5 = 9$$
$$1 + 3 + 5 + 7 = 16$$

will generate a list of perfect squares, which could be generalized algebraically, leading to the need for algebraic capabilities. This then becomes the beginnings of proof. At the appropriate level, the information can be expressed by: "The sum of the first $N$ consecutive odd counting numbers is $N^2$." One nice advantage to this pattern is that it can be shown concretely, as in Fig. 10.17.

Pairing this generalization with that from the discussion about Gauss's generalization of the sum of the first $N$ consecutive counting numbers to be $\frac{N(N+1)}{2}$ leads to a wonderful opportunity for a generalization that turns out to be false. We have:

$\frac{N(N+1)}{2} =$ the sum of the first $N$ consecutive counting numbers

$N^2 =$ the sum of the first $N$ consecutive odd counting numbers

It would seem reasonable that $\frac{N(N+1)}{2} - N^2$ would yield the sum of the first $N$ consecutive even counting numbers. Assuming that and simplifying,

$$\frac{N(N+1)}{2} - N^2 = \frac{N^2 + N - 2N^2}{2}$$
$$= \frac{-N^2 + N}{2}$$

which is negative and cannot possibly represent the sum of the first $N$ even counting numbers.

Many algebra texts contain a "proof" that $2 = 1$. It is presented here to show you another example of the need to convince students to pay close attention to each step and detail in a proof.

Let $A = B$      $A$ and $B$ are any real numbers

$A^2 = AB$      Multiply both sides of equation by same value

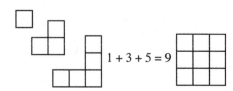

$$1 + 3 = 4$$

$$1 + 3 + 5 = 9$$

**Figure 10.17**

$A^2 - B^2 = AB - B^2$    Subtract same value from both sides of equation

$(A + B)(A - B) = (A - B)B$    Factor both sides of equation

$\dfrac{(A+B)(A-B)}{(A-B)} = \dfrac{(A-B)B}{(A-B)}$    Divide both sides of equation by same value

$A + B = B$    Result of division

$B + B = B$    Substituting B for A because A = B

$2B = B$    Addition

$2 = 1$    Divide both sides of equation by same value

This result contradicts what is known to be true and yet students often take a long time to recognize that because $A = B$, they cannot perform the step involving dividing by $A - B$.

---

### EXERCISES 10.9

1. What is wrong with determining the sum of the first $N$ even counting numbers to be $\frac{-N^2 + N}{2}$ in the text? Would the approach taken to arrive at this conclusion appear logical to a student? Why or why not?

2. Present another example of a "proof" that leads to an incorrect conclusion like 2 = 1.

---

Number tricks offer a wonderful opportunity to lead students into the world of algebraic proof. Suppose 9 and 5 are two of the three digits in a three-digit number. You are to find a third digit so that an addition equation can be formed where both addends and the sum are permutations of the same three-digit number comprised of 9, 5, and the third digit you find. This problem could be solved using guess-and-check routines, which some teachers use to generate the need for proof expressed at an abstract level. However, an algebraic approach shows some advantages. Let $N$ be the third digit used to make the three-digit numbers to solve this problem. The six possible combinations that can occur are $95N$, $9N5$, $59N$, $5N9$, $N95$, and $N59$. Neither of the numbers with 9 in the hundreds place can be an addend because that would force regrouping so the sum would be a four-digit number. Assume that the

sum must begin with 9. Assume one of the addends begins with 5. $9N5 - 59N$ is one possibility for the other addend. Expanding gives

$$900 + 10N + 5 - (500 + 90 + N) = 100N + 50 + 9$$
$$400 + 9N - 85 = 100N + 50 + 9$$
$$91N = 256$$
$$N = 2.813 \text{ (not digit)}$$

Another possibility would be $95N - N59 = N95$

$$900 + 50 + N - (100N + 50 + 9) = 100N + 90 + 5$$
$$950 - 99N - 59 = 100N + 90 + 5$$
$$796 = 199N$$
$$4 = N$$

Is this solution unique? This seems to be a reasonable question that the power of algebra can be used to answer.

Here is another demonstration of the power of algebra in determining why something works (or can be proved). Investigate a different algorithm for multiplication where the ones digits of the two factors sum to 10 and all other digits of the two factors are duplicated ($143 \times 147$ or $52 \times 58$). Find the product of the ones digits. That product becomes the ones and tens digit in the answer. In $52 \times 58$ it would be 16 because of $2 \times 8$. Call all of the digits to the left of the ones digit Z. Note that in each example, the value to the left of the ones digit is the same. Multiplying Z and (Z + 1) will provide the rest of the answer. In $143 \times 147$, that would become $14 \times 15$. This product is placed to the left of the product of the ones digits. To show why this works, let $10A + B$ be the first factor and $10A + (10 - B)$ be the second.

$$(10A + B)(10A + (10 - B)) = 100A^2 + 100A$$
$$- 10AB + 10AB + B(10 - B)$$
$$= 100(A^2 + A) + B(10 - B)$$

The number of opportunities to employ algebra as an investigation tool in proof is ample enough that, with a little energy on your part, each student can be shown the power of this branch of mathematics.

---

### EXERCISES 10.10

1. In the text, 4 was found to be a solution to the problem "Suppose 9 and 5 are two of the three digits in a three-digit number.

You are to find a third digit so that an addition equation can be formed so both addends and the sum are permutations of the same three-digit number comprised of 9,5, and the third digit you find." Is 4 the only answer?

2. Pick any prime number greater than 3. Square it. Add 15. Divide by 12. What is the remainder? Why? Will this always occur?

## TUTORIALS FOR LEARNING ALGEBRA

Statewide competency tests and algebra exams have entered the mathematics curriculum. Whether or not you are in favor of these tests is not an issue. They are here! The leaders in many states have mandated Algebra I as a high school graduation requirement. Several states require a high school competency exit exam before a high school diploma is awarded. Some states require students to pass a state algebra test before a student can be said to have passed Algebra I. This prevents the possibility of a student who receiving a passing grade but who cannot achieve all of the state competencies from receiving a high school diploma. This does allow the state to omit a diploma exit exam because the students cannot get a diploma without passing Algebra I, and they cannot pass Algebra I without passing the state algebra test. Agree or not, it is your ethical duty as a teacher of mathematics to do the best possible job to help students overcome these testing barriers.

One effective way to help students break the algebra barrier is the use of tutorials. Many schools have determined the importance of incorporating the graphing calculator and have found the funds to provide this technology for each student in the classroom in addition to software like MathXpert's Algebra Assistant. Graphing calculator technology such as Casio's fx-2.0 handheld computer algebra system has made algebraic tutorials affordable for each student to have in the mathematics classroom. In addition to software and calculators, the Internet provides a wide variety of tutorial assistance for Algebra.

The use of tutorials, software, and calculator assistants such as the fx-2.0 and MathXpert's Algebra Assistant can allow students to visually see the outcome of their mathematical procedures as they are performed on the tool. For example, when trying to solve the equation $\frac{3X+2}{4}=12$ students frequently decide that they should subtract 2 from both sides of the equation. Is this incorrect? Certainly not! This process may take the student longer to arrive at a solution though. The fx-2.0 and MathXpert allow the student to enter the equation and direct the application to perform an operation. If the student wants to subtract 2 from each side of the equation, the student enters the subtraction key followed by 2, which displays

$$\frac{3x+2}{4} - 2 = 12 - 2$$

Notice that the result shows the student that 2 is being subtracted from both sides of the equation. Now the student can simplify the right side of the equation to reveal

$$\frac{3X+2}{4} = 10$$

and find a common denominator for the left side of the equation and simplify to show

$$\frac{3(X-2)}{4} = 10$$

The student will quickly see that the performed process has not simplified the problem at all, as shown in Fig. 10.18. They might conclude they are not as well off as they were with the original problem statement. With the push of a button, the student can return to the original equation and multiply by four on each side of the equation to arrive at

$$\frac{3x+2}{4} \cdot 4 = 12 \cdot 4$$

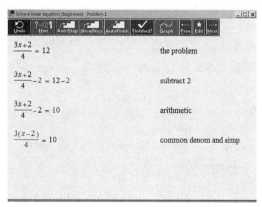

**Figure 10.18**

Simplifying the equation, subtracting 2 on both sides then dividing both sides of the equation by 3 yields $\frac{46}{3}$ as shown in Fig. 10.19.

Another powerful feature of some tutorials is the capability to provide tutorial assistance when solving equations. The student can press the "next" function and the tutorial will respond by displaying the next step for solving the equation. This allows the student to learn by observing a step-by-step solution process. Think of the power of seeing the device perform the steps for the students. Often students believe they have a clear understanding of the concept when watching the teacher demonstrate the concept in class. Later, when trying to complete an assignment at home, the concept

becomes foggy and uncertainty leads to confusion and frustration. Online applications such as Wolfram Alpha provide step-by-step process to solve equations such as $\frac{1}{4}(3x+2) = 12$, as shown in Fig. 10.20.

| | |
|---|---|
| $\frac{3x+2}{4} = 12$ | the problem |
| $3x + 2 = 48$ | multiply by 4 |
| $3x + 2 - 2 = 48 - 2$ | subtract 2 |
| $3x + 0 = 46$ | arithmetic |
| $3x = 46$ | $x + 0 = x$ |
| $x = \frac{46}{3}$ | divide by 3 |

**Figure 10.19**

Input interpretation:

solve $\quad \frac{1}{4}(3x + 2) = 12$

Results:

$x = \frac{46}{3}$

Possible intermediate steps:

$\frac{1}{4}(3x + 2) = 12$

Divide both sides by $\frac{1}{4}$:

$3x + 2 = 48$

Subtract 2 from both sides:

$3x = 46$

Divide both sides by 3:

$x = \frac{46}{3}$

**Figure 10.20**

### EXERCISES 10.11

1. Provide a list of five online Internet-based Algebra tutorials for students. How would you rate each of these applications?

2. Develop a lesson that would make use of an algebraic tutorial outside the classroom setting.

3. Is it possible that mathematics tutorials could replace the importance of classroom teachers? Justify your response.

## ALGEBRA IN THE K–14 CURRICULUM

"Algebra for all is the right goal at the right time. We just need to find the right algebra." This was the feeling generated at a conference in 1997 (Brumbaugh, 1997). The hope was to build a coherent vision of algebra for grades K–14, and then channel energies so the end product would be consistent.

Look at old algebra books. There has been little change in them over the past 150 years. Certainly, color and pictures have been added. There is a lot more white space on the page. Some have cartoons. Some contain historical notes. Some describe uses of the content in the real world. These are all good changes. But look beyond them to the guts of the text. You see a static system. You see things being taught the same way, year after year. Until the 1980s, the sequence was pretty much unaltered. A little bit of technology is inserted. There are some pedagogical changes. Still, most kids see little value to learning algebra, a subject that is often viewed as the gatekeeper of quantitative literature.

For sure, algebra needs to be livened up. We need to convince students that there is value in learning it. We need show them more examples of its use in their world. We need to think about how the whole subject should be structured, presented, applied, and sold to the students. Algebra needs to be approached from four different perspectives: graphical, tabular, symbolic, and verbal. The students need to have the ability to move between these different venues. They need to learn how to symbolize situations that have a numerical basis, structure that circumstance to show what is going on, and then model it. To help our students do this, we must think of how they transition from arithmetic to rate-based structures. Then we have to help them generalize things into abstract algebraic models. Finally we need to develop the idea of $x$ varying and its impact on f($x$), and how the two are hooked together.

Algebra is the ability to pull structure from a problem, then manipulate and interpret what we see. You know that is not easy to do. That is why we need to build a consistent K–14 algebra system. Students need to be involved with data and numbers early on. They need to learn to look for and describe patterns. Quantity needs to be recognized in what they discuss. Perhaps we should consider studying functions before equations. Evaluate what has been covered. Consider the meaning of the content. Then go to the abstract models.

Technology cannot be overlooked as we think of algebra. We must make some decisions on technology for doing algebra as opposed to technology for thinking algebra. Technology can be used as a sledgehammer/answer generator. Hopefully that is not the role it takes on. Rather we prefer to see it as a tool to remove computational distractions, reduce dependence on mechanical algorithms, provide alternative methods of approaching problems, and develop communication skills dealing with methods of solving problems. The focus is switched from getting answers to explaining processes used and interpretation of results.

Some say technology generates negative forces. They would say technology reduces exposure to proof, but we say it raises questions. Detractors of technology would say it creates dependence on machines rather than students' own minds, and we ask them to explain the graph of $y = \sin(63x)$. Antitechnologists claim motivation is lost in the time required to learn the technology or that it is cheating. We respond by asking them to graph a circle centered at (2, 3) with a radius of 4 and the line $y = -x + 10.8$. Then discuss whether the line is tangent to the circle, intersects it, or does not touch it based on the picture. Of course the ability of all students to own the technology is raised. While that objection does carry some weight, it is not sufficient to stop the technological momentum. There are too many ways available to supply the technology if it is truly desired. Technology does not reason for

the students. It is a tool. It can be used to force thought.

Algebra for all does not mean lowering expectations. It means raising expectations and expecting all students to meet them. It means rethinking the content and approaches to it. Each student must be able to access the important ideas of algebra. Each student needs to be able to experience algebraic concepts in a meaningful way. Each student has to make sense out of algebra. That is our responsibility as teachers of mathematics. We all have an obligation to deliver algebra in a way that will open doors for our students, not close them.

## TRY THIS IN YOUR CLASSROOM

*NCTM Standards 2000*: Problem solving, communication, reasoning, algebra, and functions

Using a graphing calculator or a dynamic algebra software system, enter $y = 2x + 12$ and graph it. The result should be something like Fig. 10.21, but you might have to adjust your window to effectively show the graph.

The trace function can be used to indicate the coordinates of a particular point as shown in Fig. 10.22.

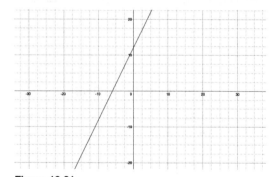

**Figure 10.21**

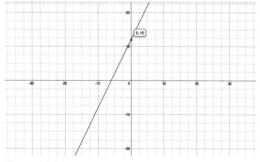

**Figure 10.22**

The place where the graph of the line crosses the x-axis is called the x-intercept. If you were to set the equation $y = 2x + 12$ equal to zero ($0 = 2x + 12$) and solve, what would you get? Do additional examples such as:

$$y = 5x - 30$$
$$y = 2x - 1$$
$$y = 4x + 12$$

Is there a relation between the solution and the x-intercept?

What does each graph have in common with all the others?

How many times does each graph cross the x-axis?

## CONCLUSION

Algebra is viewed as the gatekeeper. Success in algebra opens the doors to additional mathematical study and a wide variety of careers. Lack of success in algebra can inhibit the number of opportunities available for an individual to pursue. This is but another amplification of the need for your students to do well in algebra. We have given you but a few indicators of the many ways topics within algebra could be approached in your classroom.

### STICKY QUESTIONS

1. In a setting like $x^n$, $x$ is defined as the base and $n$ is the exponent that "shows how many times $x$ is used as a factor." One question that should be asked eventually about the definition is, "What if the exponent is 0.5? How do we write $x$ as a factor 0.5 times?" Describe how you would explain this to a beginning algebra class.

2. Is there a need to discuss implicit multiplication versus nonimplicit multiplication in beginning algebra? Why or why not?

3. Is there a need to discuss signs inside or outside parentheses, $(-4)$ or $-(4)$, in beginning algebra? Why or why not?

4. Is there a need to discuss the idea that $x$ really means $(1)(x)$ in beginning algebra? Why or why not?

5. Is there a need to discuss the idea that $x$ really means $\sqrt{mn}$ in beginning algebra? Why or why not?

6. Students are familiar with multiplication (we hope) by the time they enter an algebra class. Assuming that, they are ready to expand their horizons to include situations involving variables and exponents. Is that a safe assumption? Readiness—if they can't operate with common fractional numbers, how can we expect them to operate with rational expressions?

7. It is proper to say the distributive property (law) of multiplication over addition (subtraction) on the set of integers. Without the set and operation, we don't know much about what works and what does not. Yet we say distributive property and go on. How do we justify precision of language at some times and not at others?

8. Student ability to solve equations involving factoring skills is often weak. Couple that with the idea that students often do not understand the zeros of a function, the role of a graph of the equation, or why they are solving the equation. How should you deal with these problems in a beginning algebra class?

9. How much geometry should be presented in first-year algebra? Defend your response.

10. What logic should come out of a first-year algebra? Defend your response.

11. Do we do vectors in first-year algebra? Defend your response.

12. Should writing skills be covered in algebra? For example: Pretend you are an irrational number. You are about to see an old school friend you have not seen for many years. Write a letter describing yourself so you will be easy to spot.

13. Write a description of a linear equation, but you may not say it is a linear equation and you may not give the slope or y-intercept. Someone else has to be able to produce the correct graph from your description.

14. As an investigative reporter, you are to interview a quadratic equation. List five questions you would ask.

15. The calculator has brought to light that our emphasis has been on teaching rules and mechanics. Now we have tools to do the mechanics. So, the questions are, "Why do we teach algebra?" and, "What should we teach in algebra?" Should we focus on mechanics or concepts and applications? How would you answer those questions?

16. How does algebra quantify, control, predict, and prove?

17. How do we provide a basis for what algebra is?

## PROBLEM SOLVING CHALLNGES

1. Evaluate $\dfrac{1001! - 1000!}{999!}$.

**Check out the website for the solution**

2. If three hens lay four eggs in five days, how many days will it take a dozen hens to lay four dozen eggs? Please round your answers to the nearest egg!

**Check out the website for the solution**

# LEARNING ACTIVITIES

## Geometric Algebra

Long before algebraic notation was developed, the Greeks were able to represent numbers and values by length and algebraic operations geometrically. They could show algebraic identities by using scaled rectangles, much like the algebra tiles and blocks we use today. For example in Fig. 10.24, the Greeks showed $(a+b)^2 = a^2 + 2ab + b^2$ as:

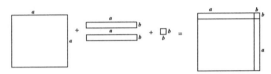

**Figure 10.23**

It should be noted that there is no assumption that $a$ is a multiple of $b$, as is done with base 10 blocks. Shading appropriate pieces showed negative values.

## Exercise 1: Algebraic Identities

Use scaled rectangles (algebra blocks like Fig. 10.23) to show:

a)  $(a-b)^2 = a^2 - 2ab + b^2$
b)  $(a-b)(a+b) = a^2 - b^2$

## Exercise 2: Adding and Subtracting

Use your own lengths $a$ and $b$ to show:

a)  $2a + 3b$
b)  $2a - 3b$

Establishing a unit length, two arbitrary lengths, $m$ and $n$, and using proportions can show multiplication via construction.

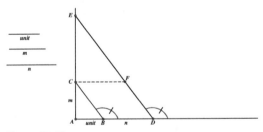

**Figure 10.24**

This construction shows the product of $m$ and $n$ as $\overline{CE}$. From similar triangles, $\dfrac{\overline{AC}}{\overline{AB}} = \dfrac{\overline{CE}}{\overline{CF}}$.

Substituting, $\dfrac{m}{1} = \dfrac{\overline{CE}}{n}$, or $\overline{CE} = (m)(n)$.

# Exercise 3: Constructed Division

Use your own unit, $m$, and $n$ to construct $\dfrac{m}{n}$.

Construction can also show square root by establishing a unit and some length $k$.

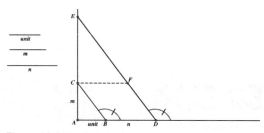

**Figure 10.25**

After establishing the unit $+$ $k$, which is $\overline{AC}$, midpoint D is established. The semicircle is established at D with radius $\overline{DC}$. $\overline{BE}$ is constructed perpendicular to $\overline{AC}$ at B, with E being the intersection of the perpendicular and the semicircle. The construction shows $\overline{BE}$ to be $\sqrt{k}$. This can be established algebraically because $\dfrac{k+1}{2} + \overline{DB} + 1 = k + 1$ and $\overline{DB} = k - \dfrac{k+1}{2}$, or $\dfrac{k-1}{2}$. From triangle DBE, $\overline{DE}$ is the radius of the semicircle, and $\left(\overline{DE}\right)^2 = \left(\overline{DB}\right)^2 + \left(\overline{BE}\right)^2$. Substituting,

$$\left(\frac{k-1}{2}\right)^2 = \frac{k-1}{2} + \left(\overline{BE}\right)^2$$

$$\frac{k^2 + 2k + 1}{4} = \frac{k^2 - 2k + 1}{4} + \left(\overline{BE}\right)^2$$

$$\frac{k^2 + 2k + 1}{4} - \frac{k^2 - 2k + 1}{4} = \left(\overline{BE}\right)^2$$

$$k = \left(\overline{BE}\right)^2$$

$$\sqrt{k} = \overline{BE}$$

# Exercise 4: Lotta Constructions

Establish a unit and lengths $m$ and $n$ and use them to construct:

a) $\sqrt{mn}$

b) $m\sqrt{n}$

c) $\dfrac{m^3 + n^3}{m^2 + n^2}$

(Eves, 1964).

# Geometry

It is not enough for a child to have mathematical knowledge. They must have *Mathematical Power* to succeed. *Mathematical Power* is the ability to feel comfortable in using mathematical knowledge to solve problems, to use mathematics in the real world, and to be willing to "try" and not feel afraid to fail. It is programs like Geometer's Sketchpad that help students transcend the gulf between mathematical knowledge and power.

Programs like this also give "teacher power." Teacher power is the ability for the teacher to provide opportunities for students to learn regardless of the student's stage of learning, the number of computers in the room, or teaching style. Adaptable to your teaching style, Geometer's Sketchpad can be used in a geometry lesson presented as teacher or student-centered, individually or as a group, or as a lecture or lab. Geometry can even be presented in an algebraic or axiomatic orientation. This latitude provides you, the teacher, the power to help students learn. (Ewing, 1996)

Where have we come in the past few years as far as the teaching of geometry? Consider teaching about the medians of a triangle and that they are all concurrent. Not too many years ago, teachers had only chalkboards, chalk, board compasses, and straightedges to work with. Usually, for the sake of time, figures were drawn freehand on the board and used as the focus of discussion. Often the productions were sufficient, but many times the sketches were inaccurate and statements to the class like, "Well, you know what I mean" were common. Figure 11.1 gives an example of how that statement was used.

In Fig. 11.1, triangle ABC on the left is constructed with side midpoints F, E, and D. In most instances the triangle itself and two of the three medians (AE and CF in this case) were rather quickly produced without much difficulty. In Fig. 11.1, AE and CF intersect at J. Often, when the teacher went to draw in median BD, inaccuracies developed when trying to align the three points B, J, and D on a straight segment. Frequently J would not lie on BD and so some maneuver like the one shown here, or a curve in the "median," was drawn to have it pass through J. It was at that point that the infamous, "Well, you know what I mean," was uttered. Surely, most students knew what was meant, but some did not and yet said nothing. It cannot be assumed that all students understand what is going on in the class. Is it reasonable to wonder whether, "Well, you know what I mean," had a negative impact on the understanding of geometry?

The dilemma could be resolved by taking care to construct the figure. Even then, however, minor details like chalk thickness could alter results enough that a little "fudging" might be necessary in order to have all three medians concurrent. Perhaps the "midpoint" determining the third "median" (Triangle ABC on the right in Fig. 11.2, point D on segment AC)

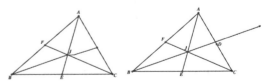

**Figure 11.1**

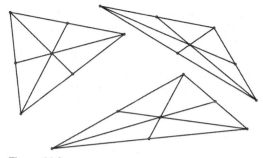

**Figure 11.2**

would be moved to accommodate getting all three "medians" passing through the same point. Once again, it was time for the infamous "Well, you know what I mean." And, for the most part, the students did.

More recently teachers began using the overhead projector. A sketch of the medians of the triangle could be prepared ahead of time and put up for the class when needed. That provided a more accurate figure to work with, but the possibility of problems because of pen width still existed. Usually these discrepancies were not as dramatic as the two shown in Fig. 11.1. Some students could not absorb all the information being presented by a picture that did not show the construction step by step. For them, seeing the setting constructed helped their understanding. When using overhead transparencies, a method of revealing information in a step-by-step process is to partially cover the transparency with a sheet of paper and expose the material as desired. That method works well with text, but it does not lend itself to constructing the medians of a triangle. That difficulty can be overcome by making a series of transparencies and then building the median figure one transparency at a time. Some people will tape them all together at the edges and then flip up the sheet as needed, which helps with alignment and, in the process, can avoid that "fudging" as shown in Fig. 11.1. Even at that, the class sees a picture that deals with only one triangle. Many students are not convinced that this will be true for any triangle constructed. Even when we tell them it is so, some doubt. Rather recently, that objection has been removed.

In the late 1980s two innovative products, Geo-Draw (IBM, Geometry Series) and Supposers (Sunburst), were introduced. Both of these pieces of software allowed for accurate median situations to be produced. With the advent of projection panels and large-screen monitors, a class could observe a

better representation of the sketch. These pieces of software permitted moving the triangle and, in the process, the medians stayed concurrent as is shown in Fig. 11.2.

In the early 1990s, Geometer's Sketchpad (Key Curriculum Press) and Cabri (Texas Instruments) were introduced. These newer generation pieces of software combine chalk, board, overhead, and beginning software advances while taking advantage of the growth within the computer and software industries. The triangle median construction is easily done with them, and the figures can be dynamically altered in real time. When the sketch is altered, measurements change accordingly, and things like the ratio of BG:GD (see Fig. 11.3) remain constant. Using this software shows a dynamic representation of the mathematics being developed. It is not possible to deliver the full impact of this situation in printed text. Seeing is believing. You should do this construction using a geometry computer application.

There is one problem with the description that has been presented in this chapter. Even with the technology that is available today, many teachers are still using the board to produce Figs. 11.1, 11.2, and 11.3. How can that be justified? Especially in light of positions presented by the Standards (NCTM, 1989) and Standards 2000 (NCTM, 2000), which state that every teacher should have a computer, large viewing capabilities for a class, and appropriate software available for all classes at all times? Only when these standards are met can Figs. 11.2 and 11.3 be available for students. After all, we do live in the technology age.

## RESEARCH IN GEOMETRY LEARNING

Diane van Hiele-Geldof and her husband Pierre van Hiele both did doctoral dissertations in 1984 that

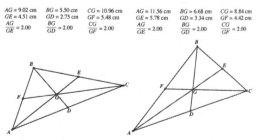

**Figure 11.3**

dealt with students learning geometry. Both dissertations dealt with the van Hiele assessment tool, which consists of five levels: visualization, analysis, informal deduction, formal deduction, and rigor. The van Hieles contended students can move from one category to another via appropriate experiences. Each of the five levels could be defined as follows, going from lowest to highest:

*Visualization (Level 0)*—Students are aware of space. Geometric shapes are recognized holistically by their appearance without paying attention to component parts. Students functioning at this level can recognize geometric shapes and can reproduce them upon request. These students recognize squares and rectangles, but do not realize the presence of right angles, opposite sides of the same length, and so forth.

*Analysis (Level 1)*—Students begin analysis of geometric concepts. Parts of geometric figures are recognized. Generally, definitions are repeated but not understood. Relations between properties are not explained. Students would be able to conclude that opposite angles of a parallelogram are congruent. They may not believe a figure can belong to more than one general class. For example, they might accept that a square is a quadrilateral, but they might resist the idea that that same square is also a parallelogram or rectangle, or both.

*Informal deduction (Level 2)*—Definitions now make sense. Informal arguments about why things are as they appear begin to be formulated. Students know there are relations between properties of a figure. For instance, if opposite sides of a quadrilateral are congruent and parallel, the figure must be a parallelogram. They also become aware of connections between groups of figures, like all squares are rectangles, but not all rectangles are squares. These students know there is a collection of rules and axioms, but they cannot put them together via deductive techniques yet. They can follow formal proofs, but the logic of connections is not fully understood. Changing the order of steps in a proof different ways confuses them. These students are essentially unable to construct an original proof when starting with different material.

*Formal deduction (Level 3)*—Students understand the role of axioms, rules, terms, theorems, definitions, and how they are interwoven. The ability to construct, not just memorize, proofs emerges. Doing a proof more than one way is within the sphere of these students. This means they are ready to study geometry as a formal mathematical system. As a part of that study, they will be able to write formal proofs using "if–then" type logic.

*Rigor (Level 4)*—Abstractions are comprehended. Students can investigate and compare different geometries. An example would be taxicab geometry in which it is assumed a city is organized with all blocks being unit squares. A cab is limited to driving on streets, assumed to have no width. As the taxi moves from point A to point B in Fig. 11.4 the distance covered is 2 units. If the cab could go off the roads, as is done in Euclidean geometry, the distance would be . In Euclidean geometry, the locus of all points equidistant from a given point is a circle. In taxicab geometry, the locus of all points equidistant from a given point is a "square." In Fig. 11.4, points B, C, D, E, F, G, H, and J are all 2 units from A. If we could put alleys between the streets at the half-unit mark, point K would also be 2 units from A (1.5, 0.5). Extending the alley idea one more level, point L is also 2 units from A (1.75, 0.25). Continuing this process in the same manner will result in a "square" when the points are joined. (van Hiele, 1986).

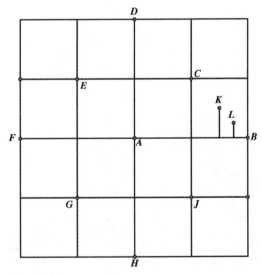

**Figure 11.4**

Piaget's research indicates a different outline of how geometric reasoning and proof develop. Piaget contended that logical operations develop in individuals independent of the content in which they are working. These operations, according to Piaget, can be applied in a variety of settings and are used to establish new mathematical knowledge. A student who knows that both squares and rectangles contain only right angles, and that their respective opposite sides are congruent and parallel, along with the idea that a square also has adjacent sides congruent, could deduce that all squares are rectangles. This would be an application of the Piaget idea in which known information is used to create new information.

The van Hiele and Piaget thinking represent two major positions on the learning of geometry. Research can be gathered to support either posture, as is the case in so many things. In reality, the situation is not one where either belief is totally correct. More than likely, there is some combination that adequately reflects how most students learn geometry.

## GEOMETRY IN THE ELEMENTARY SCHOOL

Before reading the next paragraph, please do the following. Take out a sheet of paper and draw a rectangle on it. After you have done that, read on. Remember, if you are going to be an effective teacher of mathematics, you need to walk the walk as well as talk the talk. Thus, you should do this!

The amount of geometry covered in the elementary curriculum is considerable. Children come into school having been exposed to a variety of shapes and related geometric concepts. They have a feel for geometry and a formalization process begins for them. Starting at an early age, the formalization begins to create areas of confusion for students, often in a very subtle, frequently unrealized manner. For example, "standard position" of a figure usually means that one side of the figure is drawn parallel to the bottom of the board or page. Consider a rectangle. Most of the rectangles students are exposed to are in standard position. Teachers draw them that way. Books show them that way. In other subjects, as well as in mathematics, pictures and special ideas are often presented in rectangular-shaped boxes that are in standard position. Now, observe Fig. 11.5. Students are asked to determine which figure is a rectangle. The number of students who select option E in this example is amazing. Do you have any idea why they might select E?

Before reading on, look at the rectangle you drew earlier. Was it in standard position? Color the rectangle. There is no need for you to get out your crayons; just mark the rectangle in some manner that indicates it is colored. When you colored your rectangle, did you fill the inside as is shown in Fig. 11.6? That is not the rectangle! That is the rectangular region. The rectangle is the set of line segments that comprise the border of the figure.

Compare the ratio of the long side length to the short for the rectangle you drew. Frequently the value is close to the golden section or golden ratio. This value can be described in the following manner. You are given line segment, AB, divided at

**Figure 11.5**

**Figure 11.6**

point C in a way such that $\frac{AC}{CB}=\frac{AB}{AC}$. The golden ratio is $\frac{AC}{CB}$ and can be derived by letting AB = 1, and AC = $x$. Then $\frac{x}{1}=\frac{1-x}{x}$ giving $x^2 + x - 1 = 0$. Solving for $x$ yields 0.6180339 . . . and the ratio $\frac{AC}{CB}$ is $\frac{AC}{CB}=\frac{0.6180339..}{1-0.6180339..}=1.6180339...$, which is the golden ratio, or golden section. Therefore, when you divide the larger side by the smaller side of your standard position rectangle, you will likely get a value close to the golden ratio. Try it! "The golden section is also known as the divine section after its Latin appellation *section divina*, which was first used by the Franciscan monk and mathematician Luca Pacioli (http://www-history.mcs.st-and. ac.uk/Mathematicians/Pacioli.html) in his work *De divina proportione*, published in 1509 in Venice." (Gullberg, 1997, p. 418)

> Some historians assert that the properties of the golden section aided the Pythagoreans in discovering irrational numbers, actually their geometric equivalents—incommensurable lines. It is certain, however, that since antiquity many philosophers, artists, and mathematicians have been intrigued by the golden section, which Renaissance writers called the divine proportion. It is widely accepted that a rectangle with sides in this ratio exhibits a special beauty. ("Golden section," 1993)

All the preceding information about rectangles is important but needs to be considered for another reason. It is common for the university mathematics faculty member to say to the community college mathematics faculty member (in a much more polite manner and phrasing), "If you had taught them correctly, I would be able to do what I want with them mathematically. However, because they did not learn from you, I have to redo what you covered." In turn, the community col-

lege mathematics faculty member says a similar thing to high school teachers of mathematics. The high school teacher makes a similar statement to the middle school teacher, who in turn puts the blame on the elementary teacher. In such a way, we absolve ourselves of ownership in the problem, placing all guilt at the feet of the elementary teacher. Secondary mathematics education majors would be well advised to take an elementary mathematics methods course. This course will provide insight into the teaching and learning of mathematics at a fundamental level while enhancing understanding of student learning processes. Students should learn the subject well. The best way to accomplish that is to teach it well and correctly the first time. Thus, an argument can be made to put the strongest teachers of mathematics in settings where students are learning the basics of the subject. Then much repetition could be deleted and students will have the readiness skills needed to learn the higher level mathematics concepts we want them to.

The reason you were asked to draw and color a rectangle is to emphasize the problem faced in the teaching of mathematics at all levels. You have the advantage of having had several college mathematics courses. Yet you probably drew your rectangle in standard position and colored the interior. In so, you indicate a tendency to not be mathematically precise. If we, as teachers of mathematics, are not accurate, how can we expect our students to be?

With that background, consider geometry in the elementary school. Current elementary education majors have a much broader exposure to mathematics than did their predecessors. They often take a mathematics content course and a mathematics methods course designed for the teaching of elementary mathematics as a part of their program. In addition, most colleges are requiring students to take a college algebra or finite mathematics course as a graduation requirement. Many states require at least three and possibly four mathematics courses for high school graduation. In the not too distant past, students were permitted to graduate from high school with only one mathematics credit, and college-level elementary education majors might not have even been required to take a mathematics methods course. Certainly, this had a negative impact on the mathematical learning of elementary students. With all the changes in our field over the past half century, it is unreasonable to expect elementary teachers with weak mathematical backgrounds to adequately prepare students mathematically to move on to the secondary level.

Even with all the changes in mathematical expectations for elementary education majors, the possibility of exposure to geometry is woefully lacking. Often, individuals intending to major in elementary education at the college level avoid mathematics classes in their secondary careers. Because they are required to generate a given number of credits, they often enroll in mathematics courses that are not as rigorous as those taken by some of their peers. In college, their mathematics course options, if required (college algebra or finite mathematics), generally do little with geometry. In their education courses, assuming both the elementary mathematics content and methods courses are required, geometry is a topic for discussion. However, it frequently is one of those things that appears late in the course. As such, there is a good chance that it will not be covered as extensively as would be desirable, or perhaps even at all. Thus, the opportunity exists for an elementary education major to be graduated and certified with little geometric exposure other than what they had in elementary school. Then they are asked to teach new geometric concepts for which they have not been as exposed to as other mathematical topics. How reasonable is this?

The Common Core Standards integrate geometry across all grade levels. It is the one consistent concept included at each grade level (K–8). This statement alone should provide you with the level of importance of geometry. The expectation is that teachers will teach geometry throughout a child's development of mathematics. Therefore, all teachers of mathematics should have significant exposure to geometry in their preparation for becoming a teacher!

Software exists that can be used to help students learn geometry. The beauty of software, particularly a piece that provides tutorials and the opportunity for "free play," is that the student has the opportunity to experiment and stimulate curiosity. Thankfully, producers like Key Curriculum Press (Geometer's Sketchpad), Texas Instruments (Cabri), and others have created collections of ideas and applications appropriate for elementary students. This certainly should help, but only if the materials get into the hands of the students. This all cycles back to the need for vertical communication so the elementary teachers have some idea of the expectations held for basic student knowledge of geometry by middle school teachers.

---

### EXERCISE 11.3

1. Compare and contrast the geometry expectations for elementary students in grades K–5 within the Common Core Standards and NCTM's Standards 2000. Are topics missing in the Common Core Standards that you feel should be in the elementary curriculum? Are there topics in the Common Core Standards you feel should be omitted?

---

**Additional exercises can be found on the website.**

## GEOMETRY TAUGHT IN THE MIDDLE SCHOOL

Of course, geometry is taught in the middle school! But what is taught and where or when? Geometry is scattered throughout the middle school curriculum. There is no specific course, and as the trend moves toward integrated topics, even if the course exists, it would be blended into a set of topics covered over the middle school years. Certainly, the topics broached in the elementary grades are revisited. Why? If the concepts were taught well, understood by the students, and so on, why would they be repeated in the middle school? One reason sometimes put forward is that we have always done it that way. That is not a good reason. If the students know the topic being covered, why go over it again? That only serves to stimulate their dislike of mathematics in general, and geometry in particular. At the same time, if the students do not know the necessary information, it is imperative that they be properly introduced to the topics. So, what can be done in the middle school geometry class?

The Common Core Standards (2012) clearly identify concepts of geometry for grades 6–8.

### Grade 6

*Solve real-world and mathematical problems involving area, surface area, and volume.*

- 6.G.1. Find the area of right triangles, other triangles, special quadrilaterals, and polygons by composing into rectangles or decomposing into triangles and other shapes; apply these techniques in the context of solving real-world and mathematical problems.

- 6.G.2. Find the volume of a right rectangular prism with fractional edge lengths by packing it with unit cubes of the appropriate unit fraction edge lengths, and show that the volume is the same as would be found by multiplying the edge lengths of the prism. Apply the formulas $V = l\,w\,h$ and $V = b\,h$ to find volumes of right rectangular prisms with fractional edge lengths in the context of solving real-world and mathematical problems.

- 6.G.3. Draw polygons in the coordinate plane given coordinates for the vertices; use coordinates to find the length of a side joining points with the same first coordinate or the same second coordinate. Apply these techniques in the context of solving real-world and mathematical problems.

- 6.G.4. Represent three-dimensional figures using nets made up of rectangles and triangles, and use the nets to find the surface area of these figures. Apply these techniques in the context of solving real-world and mathematical problems.

## Grade 7

*Draw construct, and describe geometrical figures and describe the relationships between them.*

- 7.G.1. Solve problems involving scale drawings of geometric figures, including computing actual lengths and areas from a scale drawing and reproducing a scale drawing at a different scale.

- 7.G.2. Draw (freehand, with ruler and protractor, and with technology) geometric shapes with given conditions. Focus on constructing triangles from three measures of angles or sides, noticing when the conditions determine a unique triangle, more than one triangle, or no triangle.

- 7.G.3. Describe the two-dimensional figures that result from slicing three-dimensional figures, as in plane sections of right rectangular prisms and right rectangular pyramids.

*Solve real-life and mathematical problems involving angle measure, area, surface area, and volume.*

- 7.G.4. Know the formulas for the area and circumference of a circle and use them to solve problems; give an informal derivation

of the relationship between the circumference and area of a circle.

- 7.G.5. Use facts about supplementary, complementary, vertical, and adjacent angles in a multi-step problem to write and solve simple equations for an unknown angle in a figure.

- 7.G.6. Solve real-world and mathematical problems involving area, volume and surface area of two- and three-dimensional objects composed of triangles, quadrilaterals, polygons, cubes, and right prisms.

## Grade 8

Understand congruence and similarity using physical models, transparencies, or geometry software.

- 8.G.1. Verify experimentally the properties of rotations, reflections, and translations:

  o  a. Lines are taken to lines, and line segments to line segments of the same length.

  o  b. Angles are taken to angles of the same measure.

  o  c. Parallel lines are taken to parallel lines.

- 8.G.2. Understand that a two-dimensional figure is congruent to another if the second can be obtained from the first by a sequence of rotations, reflections, and translations; given two congruent figures, describe a sequence that exhibits the congruence between them.

- 8.G.3. Describe the effect of dilations, translations, rotations, and reflections on two-dimensional figures using coordinates.

- 8.G.4. Understand that a two-dimensional figure is similar to another if the second can be obtained from the first by a sequence of rotations, reflections, translations, and dilations; given two similar two-dimensional figures, describe a sequence that exhibits the similarity between them.

- 8.G.5. Use informal arguments to establish facts about the angle sum and exterior angle of triangles, about the angles created when parallel lines are cut by a transversal, and the angle-angle criterion for similarity of triangles. *For example, arrange three copies of the same triangle so that the sum of the three angles appears to form a line, and give an argument in terms of transversals why this is so.*

*Understand and apply the Pythagorean Theorem.*

- 8.G.6. Explain a proof of the Pythagorean Theorem and its converse.
- 8.G.7. Apply the Pythagorean Theorem to determine unknown side lengths in right triangles in real-world and mathematical problems in two and three dimensions.
- 8.G.8. Apply the Pythagorean Theorem to find the distance between two points in a coordinate system.

*Solve real-world and mathematical problems involving volume of cylinders, cones, and spheres.*

- 8.G.9. Know the formulas for the volumes of cones, cylinders, and spheres and use them to solve real-world and mathematical problems.

(*http://www.corestandards.org/math*)
What happens if you do not have a text that covers each of these topics in detail in teaching mathematics in the 7th grade? Will you only teach the concepts in the text or find the supplemental material for you and your students to teach geometry in 7th grade? Remember, you help provide the foundation for high school mathematics for your students. How can you connect the geometry concepts addressed in the Common Core Standards with other topics in the curriculum? Does area and volume relate to algebraic expressions? Does angle measure integrate with solving equations and problem solving?

Intuitive backgrounds can be established for a variety of topics. Figure 11.7 shows a standard set of steps for showing that a parallelogram can be transformed to a rectangle, leading to the conclusion that the area of a parallelogram is base times height. This should, at the same time, establish a connection between two shapes and how to find area. It should also raise a question. Because the new figure looks like a rectangle, why don't we use length and width

as elements of the formula for the area of a parallelogram? Or, reverse the wording and use base times height for the area of the rectangle?

It may appear as no big concern for us because we know, but students now have two more vocabulary words to learn and are identifying the same thing by two different names, each of which is to be used in a given setting (length with rectangle and base with parallelogram). Does that make sense? Does it really matter? Could we be more consistent in our discussion with students?

Establishing a connection between two shapes and finding area should not be abandoned too quickly. The formula typically taught for finding the area of a trapezoid is $\left(\dfrac{b_1 + b_2}{2}\right)(h)$. This formula can be written in a variety of formats and, depending on the algebraic skills of the students, confusion can exist as teachers attempt to shift from one version of the formula to another. For this discussion, use the formula shown here and state it as the average of the bases, times the height. Using that, look at finding the area for a rectangle, parallelogram, square, trapezoid, triangle, and circle as shown in Fig. 11.8. Even though the figures are not in standard position, you can see that the area for each of them can be found by taking the average of the bases times the height.

The rectangle and parallelogram transformations are relatively straightforward. For squares, the area is usually given as $A = s^2$. Using that idea and the trapezoid formula of the average of the bases, the area of a square becomes $\left(\dfrac{\text{side} + \text{side}}{2}\right)(\text{side}) = \left(\dfrac{2\text{side}}{2}\right)(\text{side}) = (\text{side})^2 = s^2$. The triangle seems a little confusing at first, but the lower base is the side to which the altitude is drawn. The upper base is the vertex, which is the top of the altitude, and has a length of zero. So for the triangle area, using the average of the bases,

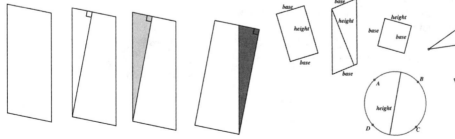

**Figure 11.7**

**Figure 11.8**

$$\left(\frac{\text{base} + \text{zero}}{2}\right)(\text{height}) = \left(\frac{\text{base}}{2}\right)(\text{height})$$

The circle area with this "one formula fits all" approach seems strange initially, and it does require some editorial liberty to discuss. We normally think of bases as being straight line segments. For this discussion, the base is a curved line segment, the length of which is one fourth of the circumference of the circle. That is, for this example, arc AB = arc CD = $0.5\pi r$. The diameter, or height in this case, will be $2r$. Using the average of the bases formula,

$$A = \left(\frac{0.5\pi r + 0.5\pi r}{2}\right)(2r) = \left(\frac{\pi r}{2}\right)(2r) = (\pi r)(r) = \pi r^2 .$$

You might be saying, "Why didn't someone show me this before?" "Why don't we teach this method in the schools?" Those are legitimate questions that can be partially answered, but not totally. The easy part of the answer involves preparation to get to the level where a student understands the average of the bases formula. Some students are confused by the algebra involved and are unable to readily relate average of the bases to

$$(b_1 + b_2)\left(\frac{h}{2}\right) \text{ or } \frac{1}{2}(b_1 + b_2)(h) .$$

Given that, it would be difficult for students to understand applying that formula to a variety of shapes. In addition, before applying the formula, areas of rectangles and parallelograms, at least, have to be considered. Once those are done, some would question the reasonableness of returning to them to give a different formula. The hard part of the question about why we do not teach this "one formula fits all" approach in the schools is not so readily answered. It seems that this approach would be a wonderful extension for those students who have mastered the formulas for area of the shapes mentioned. However, this average of the bases formula is rather obscure in the literature and, in so being, is not well known to secondary teachers of mathematics.

Most secondary mathematics education majors are aware that the middle school provides the setting for presenting a multitude of topics at an intuitive level that can be investigated in greater depth and more formally later in the secondary curriculum. Joining the midpoints of the sides of a triangle to form four smaller triangles, all of which are congruent and similar to the initial triangle, is one example as shown in Fig. 11.9. Here, triangles ADF, FEB, DCE, and EFD are congruent and all are similar to triangle ABC. Software now avail-

able will measure the area of each of the triangles, as well as slopes and lengths of sides. These tools provide students with the opportunity to investigate and develop insight into relations that exist in triangles. For example, they could conclude that the area of triangle ADF is 0.25 times the area of triangle ABC. They should also realize that segments AB and DE are parallel, and that the length of segment BC is twice that of segment DF. All of these intuitive feelings would spring from simple investigations and discoveries using the technology now available. Later, in a formal geometry class where such things are proven, the groundwork laid via the technology should establish valuable background information, and perhaps even a realization for the need for a more formal authentication of the intuitive feelings. Perhaps the Side Side Side congruence theorem would be used to establish that the four smaller triangles are, in fact, congruent.

Another interesting extension involving the initial triangle ABC in the preceding paragraph can be developed. Segment DE joins the midpoints of sides AC and BC, respectively. Rather than using the midpoint, establish D on AC somewhere. Construct a line parallel to AB through D and create E as the intersection of the new line and side BC. Measure the length of segments AC and CD and the area of triangles CDE and CAB. Establish a ratio between the long and short length and the large and small area. When the length ratio is 2:1, the area ratio will be 4:1. When the length ratio is 3:1, the area ratio will be 9:1. Before long, the students should be able to generalize the pattern. At the same time, many students will become aware of the differences between linear changes and those of areas. The informal setting leads to an extension that could provide stimulation and a desire for formalization for some students.

Another interesting topic available for investigation and extension in the middle school geometry program is the Pythagorean theorem. Different

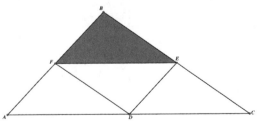

**Figure 11.9**

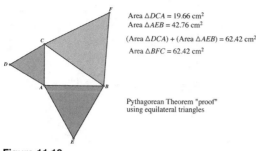

Area $\triangle DCA$ = 19.66 cm²
Area $\triangle AEB$ = 42.76 cm²

(Area $\triangle DCA$) + (Area $\triangle AEB$) = 62.42 cm²

Area $\triangle BFC$ = 62.42 cm²

Pythagorean Theorem "proof"
using equilateral triangles

**Figure 11.10**

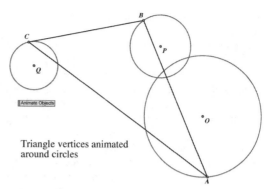

Triangle vertices animated
around circles

**Figure 11.11**

proofs can be examined, depending on the students' mathematical strengths. One example of proof shows how equilateral triangles can be used to establish the Pythagorean theorem as shown in Fig. 11.10.

---

### EXERCISES 11.4

1. Determine whether or not "proofs" like that shown in Fig. 11.10 are limited to regular polygons. Show an example to support your position.
2. One U.S. President did a couple proofs of the Pythagorean theorem. Name the President and show examples of his proofs.

---

**Additional exercises can be found on the website.**

The trace function of software permits an early approach to the topic of locus. At the same time, it can raise the curiosity level of students enough that they will investigate traces of a variety of things. Figure 11.11 shows a triangle that was constructed and shown to a group of seventh-graders. Each vertex was located on a circle of random radius length. After construction, each vertex was animated around its respective circle. An animation button was created and then the circles and their centers were hidden. As motion was started, the students were to determine how the construction was created. They were to create a similar situation to show the idea had been mastered. They did, and the objective was accomplished. However, one student traced the locus of a side of the triangle as the action was taking place. The idea spread and soon a multitude of traces was taking place. The variety of

designs created and the discussion about what could be done were invigorating. Several students created similar designs for other polygons and did traces with them as well. Given the tools, encouragement, and some latitude, students will investigate and discover many things. Perhaps more important, questions are raised and background is laid for the need for more formal proof, which could be approached at the time, or later, depending on student readiness as well as other factors.ww

Many middle school students are fascinated by scale drawings. Often, you will see grids drawn on a cartoon character and then a greater scale grid used to produce an enlarged version of the character. That method certainly works, but there is another, perhaps simpler way of accomplishing the objective. Tie a number of rubber bands together by looping one inside the end of another. Suppose you have three rubber bands connected in this manner as shown in Fig. 11.12. Fix one end of the string beyond one side of the figure to be enlarged so there is a slight stretching of the string of rubber bands to get the first knot to be over the closest point of the sketch. Place a pencil inside the other end of the rubber band chain. Visually trace the first knot of the rubber band chain along the figure. The pencil at the end of the chain will enlarge the figure.

Paper folding is a topic of interest. For years, students have been required to construct perpendic-

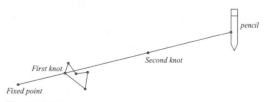

**Figure 11.12**

ular lines using a straightedge and compass. This has historical roots. It is a way to help students see and gain a "feel for" right angles. Another method of accomplishing the task of forming perpendicular line segments is to fold a piece of paper. Open the paper and then refold it so that part of the initial fold lies on top of itself. Opening reveals perpendicular line segments. Repeating the process of folding part of one segment onto itself at a different point will yield parallel line segments. The third segment, perpendicular to the other two, serves as a transversal. A fourth fold could be created to establish an oblique transversal. Folding with waxed paper is advantageous because its translucence permits easier multiple folds. Other classic folding activities involve bisecting an angle and constructing a parabola by folding a point onto a straight line segment. Patty Paper geometry (Serra, 1994) has come onto the scene as a distinct topic in the study of geometry.

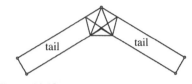

**Figure 11.13**

---

## EXERCISES 11.5

1. Describe the sequence of steps necessary to bisect an angle by folding it with paper. You should do this before you describe it. Give your instructions to a novice to determine if they are clear enough to produce the desired results.
2. Describe the sequence of steps necessary to produce a parabola using paper folding. You should do this before you describe it. Give your instructions to a novice to determine if they are clear enough to produce the desired results.

 **Additional exercises can be found on the website.**

One additional fascinating paper-folding activity is discussed here, but there is an abundance of other things that can be accomplished with this medium. An 11-inch-long strip of paper about an inch wide can be used to create what appears to be a regular pentagon. Tie a knot in the strip as shown in Fig. 11.13. Gently and carefully work the paper until the angles (formed by the top part of a loop and the disappearing end as that loop is doubled back) touch the width of the strip. Gently create each fold, taking care not to finalize the crease until the fold is as close to aligning with the edge of a hidden section of the strip of paper as reasonably

possible. The tails should then be folded so they are invisible from the "front" or torn off.

Finally comes the question of how we study informal geometry. In most instances, it is inserted into the middle school curriculum as separate features in the textbook. As the trend to integrate topics grows, the likelihood is that there will be more informal geometry. There is one text on the market carrying the title *Informal Geometry* (Keedy, Bittinger, Smith, & Nelson, 1986). This text covers most of a formal geometry course, except rather than proving theorems, they are basically given as fact and the students work exercises using the theorems given. At first glance this may not seem like a good thing to do. However, if the students gain insight and an intuitive feel for what the theorems project, that background can be used later when there is a need for more formal coverage of the topic. Of course technology applications such as Geometer's Sketchpad could also be used to generate this intuitive feel by manipulation of constructed figures.

---

## EXERCISES 11.6

1. Is the figure created in Fig. 11.12 an exact duplicate or distorted? Give a geometric defense of your response.
2. Is there a need for an informal geometry course in the curriculum that precedes the typical high school geometry course? Why or why not?

---

**Additional exercises can be found on the website.**

## GEOMETRY IN ALGEBRA

Peter Hilton stated that if you have algebra without geometry, you have answers to questions nobody would ask, and if you have geometry without algebra, you have questions you can't answer (cited by J. Anthony, personal communication, 1995). If Hilton's statement is accepted, then the separation of geometry and algebra is, perhaps, more tragic than one might think. If the two topics were treated together as needed, the curriculum would change. The amount of integration would increase. This flies in the face of tradition. Dare we do that?

Consider the example where a circle is centered at the point (2, 3) and has a radius of 4. One form of the equation of this circle would be $x^2 - 4x + y^2 - 6y - 3 = 0$. Graphing that circle and the line $y = -x + 10.8$ yields a situation in which the circle and line appear to be tangent, as shown in Fig. 11.14. Typically, we tell students to solve the situation by substituting $-x + 10.8$ for $y$ in the equation $x^2 - 4x + y^2 - 6y - 3 = 0$. The result is $x^2 - 19.6x + 48.84 = 0$. Solving for $x$ using software yields a message that there is no solution over the real numbers. Over the complex field, the solution is $\pm 0.1(\sqrt{41})i + 4.9$. With either solution, a large number of students do not comprehend the fact that the circle and line do not touch. To them, the answers are strange conglomerations of numbers that cannot be interpreted. However, zooming in on part of the graph as shown in Fig. 11.15 reveals that the two figures do not touch. In this case, geometry answers an algebraic question.

Heron's (Heron of Alexandria—http://www-history.mcs.st-and.ac.uk/Mathematicians/Heron.html) formula for the area of a triangle $A = \sqrt{s(s-a)(s-b)(s-c)}$ where $s = 0.5(a + b + c)$ can provide some interesting application opportunities. Many students are of the opinion that the only way to find the area of a triangle is to have the base and height. However, Heron's formula provides a method for finding the

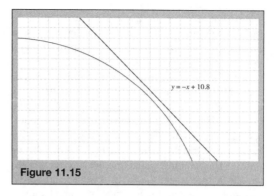

**Figure 11.15**

area of any triangle for which the lengths of the three sides are known. Suppose you are considering the purchase of a plot of ground that is 20 yards by 45 yards by 75 yards. The real estate agent is convinced the purchase price is very reasonable and is pushing for the sale. The property has not been surveyed, but that can be done once the nonrefundable deposit is submitted by you. Using Heron's formula,

$$A = \sqrt{70(70-20)(70-45)(70-75)}$$
$$= \sqrt{70(50)(25)(-5)}$$
$$= \sqrt{-437500}$$

Something is wrong! Algebra provided an answer to a geometry problem. There is not a triangle. The measurements must be incorrect.

### EXERCISE 11.7

1. Describe how you would deal with the problem described earlier that uses Heron's formula to find the area of a triangle in a class of appropriately ready students.

## ORDER OF COVERING TOPICS

As in most areas of the curriculum, geometry textbooks are similar. Certainly, there are differences, but examination reveals a long list of items that are comparable. This has to be, because of our system of establishing objectives that need to be met as a guide to completing a given course. Topics may be treated differently and some emphasized more than

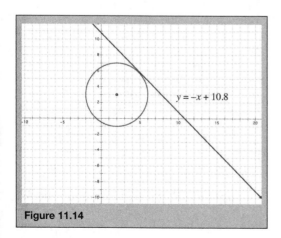

**Figure 11.14**

others, but still, the similarities are detectable. As is the case in most subjects, the geometry textbook often dictates the order in which topics are presented. That may or may not be ideal.

Two books deserve special mention here. The first, *Geometry: A Guided Inquiry* (Chakerian, Crabill, & Sherman, 1987), is available as a study, investigation, and learning tool. Activities are interspersed throughout the text and provide formative background preparing the student for more formal proofs. The thinking is that the intuitive feeling the student gathers from the investigations and activities will stimulate a higher level of understanding. Furthermore, as questions are raised during these research moments, students will begin to want to establish why things are true. In this way, the concept of and need for proof begins to emerge naturally.

The second book is *Discovering Geometry, An Investigative Approach* (Serra, 2002 & 2007). Examples that show what something is and is not are provided as a means of developing definitions. That way the students are actively involved in the learning environment as they are asked to define terms. Figure 11.16 provides an example of the type of presentations made for definitions in this text. The major part of the text has students doing a variety of activities and applications of geometry and there appears, at times, to be limited connection with either each other or with the ideas normally covered in a formal high school geometry course. However, the last part of the text asks the students to produce proofs. At this point, a wondrous thing happens— the students have a wide variety of intuitive feels for what needs to be done in the proof. It is at this point that the realization begins to surface that these inspirations are a result of the groundwork laid in the beginning parts of the text. Amazingly, a wide variety of proofs is covered quickly and, most im-

portant, the attitude about them is generally quite positive.

One final note on the order of teaching geometric topics. Howard Eves (personal communication, 1999) stated that it seems reasonable to let the history of mathematics be our guide as to the order in which topics are introduced. His thinking is that the development is following a natural order generated by need and expansion of known items. Following Eves's line of thought, many of the developmental topics can be motivated in the grade school or middle school environment. Then, as the curriculum becomes increasingly integrated, more extensive coverage can be offered as the students are developmentally ready. Until that time, we will need to rely on the formative work being done in more traditional time frames, but we can still look to the history of mathematics as a guide for order.

## FORMAL GEOMETRY

Is there a need for the formal high school geometry course? Absolutely. The format of the course may have changed and there might be less emphasis on proof than there was in previous years. However, the value of the course must not be overlooked. Some question the wisdom of changing the course from one of proofs essentially every day all year long. Others see that change as a breath of fresh air, citing that students did not like proofs, the course turns many students off from mathematics and, developmentally, students are not ready for the rigor demanded in the course. Recall the comments made earlier in this chapter about the work of the van Hieles and the idea that the current geometry courses might be being watered down so our students can tolerate them. Still others question the current situation in which the formal proof work is frequently done in the first part of the course. The less formal coverage of topics such as area, volumes, and applications is reserved for the second part of the course, citing again the developmental level of the students. The people questioning the current geometry course base their position on the premise that proofs of geometry require so much intricate thought, it would be better to do the less formal topics first and the proof section of the course last. That makes sense to many and seems to align itself with the thinking in Serra's text mentioned earlier.

Regardless of the philosophic position adopted, there is a place for the formal geometry class in the curriculum. Intuition is to be developed prior to

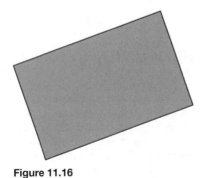

**Figure 11.16**

the course and then a more formal approach used in the course itself. For example, Fig. 11.17 shows an informal development that can be extended. The sketch and measurements taken indicate that the interior quadrilateral EFGH is a parallelogram. The student should realize that from looking at the figure and the fact that opposite sides are congruent and parallel. Experience has shown that the step to producing a proof is relatively simple if the students realize that each part of the original quadrilateral ABCD can be a triangle. Figure 11.18 shows line segment AC drawn into the figure, establishing the two triangles. When it is known that the midpoints of two sides of a triangle are joined by a segment that is half the length of, and parallel to, the third side, the establishment of a more formal proof that EFGH is a parallelogram is easier. Similar cases can be made for many theorems that would be covered in a formal geometry course.

Consider the theorem, "Tangent segments from a point outside a circle are congruent." Using dynamic software, two tangents can easily be created by constructing lines perpendicular to two radii. If the two tangent lines do not meet on the screen, one of the radii, or both, can be rotated so a convenient figure is available. The intersection of the two tangent lines can be constructed and then the lines hidden. Segments can be constructed between the radii

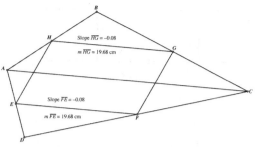

**Figure 11.19**

ends and the common point just constructed. The lengths of those segments can be measured, indicating congruence. Figure 11.19 shows the initial construction and that moving the figure will still provide congruent measurements, with both values changing as the figure is altered. These sketches create an intuitive feel for the theorem. We know it to be true in all cases. The dynamic software should help the students realize that too. The more formal proof will follow more easily when the student is aware of what the results should be, based on prior experiences and observation, as opposed to reading about it as the theorem is stated.

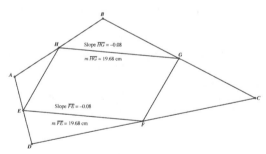

**Figure 11.17**

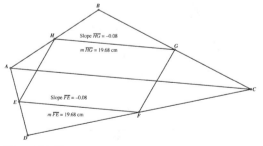

**Figure 11.18**

## EXERCISES 11.8

1. Create a lesson plan having the students complete a formal proof for the theorem shown in Fig. 11.19.
2. Select two theorems typically found in a formal geometry class and develop lessons designed to have students complete a formal proof of each theorem. In each lesson the selected theorem should be established intuitively with the students prior to the formal proof. The selected theorems should not be ones discussed in this text. The selected theorems do not have to be related.

## WHERE DOES GEOMETRY STOP?

Geometry study and learning do not stop. Geometry is a dynamic, ever-changing subject. Transformations. Tessellations. Vectors. Coordinate. Taxicab. Lobachevskian. Spherical. *Flatland* (Abbot, 1963).

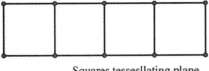

Squares tessesllating plane

Altered square

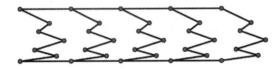

Altered squares tessesllating plane

**Figure 11.20**

*One, Two, Three . . . Infinity* (Gamow, 1961). *Donald Duck in Mathmagic Land* (Disney, 1959). Measurement. Projection. And so on.

Tessellations can be entertaining and thought provoking. The Dutch graphic artist Maurits Corneille Escher (http://www-history.mcs.st-and.ac.uk/Mathematicians/Escher.html) has been one agent in the popularizing of tessellations. "His work has become increasingly popular because of its unique combination of humor, logic, and meticulous precision with visual trickery" ("Escher," 1993). A square tessellates the plane, meaning that a set of squares of a given size can be arranged to cover the plane leaving no gaps. Escher and many others modify a shape like the square to present more interesting creations. Figure 11.20 shows how a square can be modified to make a different shape. The example given here is not particularly interesting, but the procedure is demonstrated.

The honeycomb is a practical application of the tessellation of the plane. It is important to show students applications as well as connections within geometry. For example, a proof in Euclidean, then coordinate, and finally vector geometry can show the power of going beyond standard Euclidean geometry. The study of geometry does not stop. We live in a geometric world. As we view surroundings, new questions are raised and the need for varied geometric understandings continues.

## TRY THIS IN YOUR CLASSROOM

*NCTM Standards 2000*: Problem solving, communication, reasoning, patterns, geometry, and measurement

An equilateral triangle has all sides and all angles the same size. What is the measure of each angle of any equilateral triangle?

Draw an equilateral triangle and cut out the triangle. Use your triangle to make 6 triangles that share one vertex as shown in Fig. 11.21.

If the length of a side = 1 unit, find the height of one triangle, the base of one triangle, the area of one triangle, the perimeter of the regular hexagon, and the area of the regular hexagon. Enter the information into the top row of Table 11.1.

Find the area and perimeter for the hexagon when the side length is 2, 3, and 4 units. Put your results in the appropriate area and perimeter cells in Table 11.1.

Use a technology tool and enter the unit side lengths (1, 2, 3, 4) in LIST 1 or Column 1. Place the collected data for the perimeter and area in LIST 2 and LIST 3 respectively.

Graph a scatter plot of the perimeters where the side lengths are in LIST I and the perimeters are in LIST 2

Graph a scatter plot of the areas where the side lengths are in LIST I and the areas are in LIST 3. What conclusions can you draw from the graphs of the two scatter plots?

Remove 1 of the 6 triangles as shown in Fig. 11.22. Put the perimeter and area of Fig. 11.22 for each of the 4 side lengths in Table 11.1 under the appropriate heading.

Remove 2 of the 6 triangles as shown in Fig. 11.23. Put the perimeter and area of Fig. 11.23

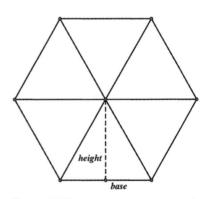

**Figure 11.21**

Table 11.1

| Side Length | Perimeter (P) | Area (A) | Remove 1 Triangle A \| P | Remove 2 Triangles A \| P | 2 Nonadjacent Triangles A \| P |
|---|---|---|---|---|---|
| 1 unit | | | \| | \| | \| |
| 2 units | | | \| | \| | \| |
| 3 units | | | \| | \| | \| |
| 4 units | | | \| | \| | \| |

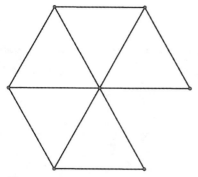

Figure 11.22

for each of the 4 side lengths in Table 11.1 under the appropriate heading.

Remove 2 of the 6 triangles as shown in Fig. 11.24. Put the perimeter and area of Fig. 11.24 for each of the 4 side lengths in Table 11.1 under the appropriate heading.

Enter the data for each of the new perimeters in LISTs 4, 5, and 6, and graph a scatter plot for each. Compare and contrast the scatter plots of the perimeters.

Enter the data for each of the new areas in LISTs 4, 5, and 6, and graph a scatter plot for each. Compare and contrast the scatter plots of the areas.

What aspects of the data caused variations in the plots for the perimeter? Area?

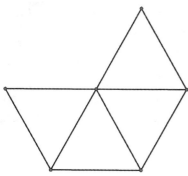

Figure 11.23

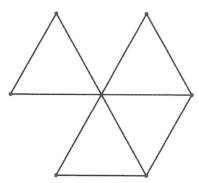

Figure 11.24

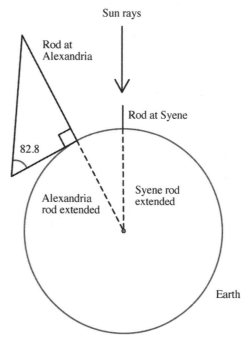

Figure 11.25

# CONCLUSION

Geometry! It is a wonderful topic. Regretfully, many secondary teachers of mathematics prefer to avoid teaching it. Perhaps it is related to the lack of background in the topic. Maybe it is because the proofs can take a long time to assess. Who knows why people prefer teaching other topics to geometry. However, looking at the technology that is available today, it seems as if geometry would be a fantastic topic to teach and entice students into the study of mathematics. Why not give it a try?

## STICKY QUESTIONS

1. Eratosthenes measured the earth's circumference to within 1% of what we now know it to be. He did it in the late part of the third century B.C. Eratosthenes knew that at summer solstice (about June 21) the sun would be directly over the city of Cyene in Egypt. He could tell this because the sun's rays were reflected from the water in a deep well with no well wall shadows. He put a vertical rod in the ground at Cyene and also at Alexandria. The Cyene stick cast no shadow at noon and the Alexandrea one did. From that, Eratosthenes calculated the angle of elevation of the sun to be 82.6°. He knew the distance between the two sticks was about 500 miles. He used the alternate interior angle theorem to conclude that the central angle between the two sticks was 7.2°. But, because 7.2° is $m\sqrt{n}$ of the circumference of a circle, he deduced that

the circumference was about 25,000 miles. Note: He computed in stadia (10 stadia = 1 mile; Rosskopf, 1970, p. 381). Figure 11.25 shows the idea behind what Eratosthenes did. Find an another example of measurement in the history of mathematics. Describe how the measurements were done and create a sketch using dynamic software that will show what was done.

2. Should we teach inductive, deductive, formal, or informal geometry in high school? Why or why not?

## PROBLEM-SOLVING CHALLENGES

1. The sum of the interior angles of two regular convex polygons is 21. The sum of the number of diagonals of each polygon is 85. How many sides does each polygon have?

   **Check out the website for the solution.**

2. A princess is in love with a dashing knight. Unfortunately, the king prefers another suitor for his daughter. The king has locked her in the castle tower. The castle is surrounded by a square moat that is 10 yards wide. The knight is attempting to cross the moat, but only has two 9.75 yard planks, and no way to fasten them together. How can the brave knight bridge the moat?

   **Check out the website for the solution.**

# LEARNING ACTIVITY

## Geometry Need Not Be Greek

Trisection of any angle was one focus of early Greek mathematics. Modern mathematics has shown that when using only a straightedge and compass, trisection of an angle can only be approximated. The classic straightedge was not a calibrated ruler like we use, and the compass could not be held in the same position after it was lifted. That is, after a compass was lifted, it collapsed, making it incapable of transferring distances. The classic Greek mathematics used Euclid's elements as the guiding influence or curriculum. In this activity, we will use two of Euclid's Elements:

The straightedge permits drawing an infinitely long straight line through two given points, and

The compass permits the drawing of any circle with a point given as its center and passing through any second given point.

## Exercise 1: Divide a Line Segment

Given the two Euclidean rules and a straightedge and compass, divide a line segment of given length into three congruent segments.

## Exercise 2: Bisect an Angle

Given the two Euclidean rules and a straightedge and compass, bisect a given acute angle.

## Exercise 3: The Tomahawk

A famous modern day mathematics historian, Howard Eves (1911–2004), discusses a tomahawk as an angle trisection tool, which was invented by persons unknown, but described in 1835. Follow these instructions to make a tomahawk:

Start with a trisected line segment so $\overline{AB} = \overline{BC} = \overline{CD}$.
Construct a semicircle centered at C and passing through B and D.
Construct $\overline{BE}$ perpendicular to $\overline{AD}$ at B.
Construct the remaining arcs for looks and functionality as shown in Fig. 11.26.

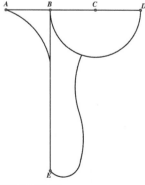

**Figure 11.26**

261

## Exercise 4: Trisecting with a Tomahawk

Given angle FGH, arrange the tomahawk so that A is on $\overline{GF}$ and the semicircle touches $\overline{GH}$ at J. Triangles ABG, CBG, and CJG are congruent with right angles at B, B, and J, respectively. Thus, ∠AGB, ∠CGB, and ∠CGJ are congruent and ∠FGH is trisected, as shown in Fig. 11.27.

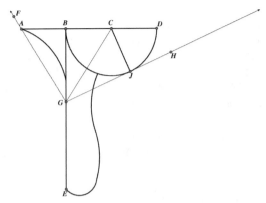

**Figure 11.27**

## Your Turn

1. Trisect an acute angle with your tomahawk.
2. Trisect an obtuse angle with your tomahawk.
3. Trisect a right angle with your tomahawk.

 **Additional exercises can be found on the website.**

# Advanced Algebra and Trigonometry

**12**

Topics in Advanced Algebra (previously titled Algebra II in many schools across the country) are dependent on developments from Algebra I. Even if the curriculum is integrated so the traditional topics covered in Algebra I, geometry, and Algebra II are blended together, developmentally, the Algebra I topics must precede those found in an Advanced Algebra course. All of the topics that were difficult to teach in Algebra I have the potential to create complications in Advanced Algebra. Whatever skills remain unmastered from foundational work will hamper student performance in future courses.

At the same time, new skills developed in Advanced Algebra will serve as foundations for future work. It is assumed that discussions like teaching factoring skills involved with second-degree equations or using the quadratic formula, both mentioned in the Algebra I chapter, have been resolved. As those issues were settled, it is assumed the students have the appropriate background to continue their study of algebra.

## PAST, PRESENT, AND FUTURE

For years, paper-and-pencil manipulations have been the focus of much of algebra. Technology has the ability to change that. Many traditionally difficult questions can now be answered with a few keystrokes, using the appropriate technology. Thought should be focused on how algebra needs to be changed in light of technological developments.

Should we continue with the emphasis on symbolic manipulation?

How do we integrate technology into the picture?

What is the impact of a more interdisciplinary and connected view of mathematics?

Will the complexities of the world that demand more flexible thinking, less manipulation of symbols, and more creative problem solving be strong enough to impact what algebra is taught and how it is delivered?

How much algebra should all students be expected to master?

When does/should algebraic instruction/learning/emphasis begin?

Today's students will be the workers and leaders of tomorrow. The world they will face is much more complex than the one in which we now live. These students will be expected to be flexible, creative thinkers who will deal with ever more complex issues and problems. As such, they need experience now in dealing with the type of thinking they will be asked to employ. Traditionally, teachers have told students how to do certain maneuvers and they mimicked the explanations through extensive practice until it was deemed they had, in fact, mastered the concept. At that point, students moved to the next agenda item or curricular issue.

How can we, in good conscience, expect students to be able to become flexible-thinking problem solvers, if we do not put them in an environment that demands that approach as a part of their learning process? Typical marathon runners train many miles for a race. They develop a mental and physical agility and toughness that will carry them through the stress and strains involved with participation. We have to provide students with the opportunity to train for their mathematical and algebraic demands by placing them in settings in which they will build strengths and thinking agility that can be called on in times of extreme necessity. The conclusion has to be that there is a need for a rethinking of the entire mathematics curriculum, particularly in algebra. We have to move from a standard of symbolic manipulation with little meaning or connection to anything other than more mathematical gymnastics. The time has come to embrace a different algebra: one where the tools are present with which students are able to solve problems.

Who is going to accomplish this switch in emphasis? *You!* You are going to be the leader of tomorrow. You are going to be the presence in the classroom. You will be determining the curriculum that will be covered. You are the one who will decide the examples, given in class, that will be designed to attract the attention of students and show them how algebra is applied in the real world. It will be your responsibility to know how algebra is used in other areas of your students' world and classes. You will be the salesperson responsible for convincing students of the value of becoming self-motivated, life-long learning, flexible-thinking, problem-solving members of society. That is an awesome responsibility, but one that cannot be shirked.

The NCTM Standards (NCTM, 2000) are not a set of rules. They are goals that were established some time ago. One objective of the NCTM Standards (although it is not written as such) could be to change each teacher of mathematics (present and future). As a change takes place in you, a vision will begin to grow. That vision will relate to how you see things happening in your classroom as you help your students learn mathematics. Not only will you see how to help the students learn, but you will also begin to formulate how to help them learn it better and what topics should be covered. That, then, begins to impact the curriculum.

Technology, your vision of mathematics learning, and knowledge about how students learn will influence what is emphasized in Advanced Algebra. It is imperative that we stop producing students who can mechanically do a problem but have no feeling for the answer once they get it. Industry and society have become much less tolerant of individuals who cannot move beyond the mechanical stages of symbol manipulation. If a person works a problem and, once an answer is determined, has no idea of the impact of that response, what good is the solution?

Consider the following situation that was discussed in chapter 11 from a different perspective. A student graphs a circle centered at the point (2, 3) with a radius of 4. The line $y = -x + 10.8$ is graphed

on the same axis system and the student is given a multiple-choice question: "Are the circle and line (A) tangent (B) intersecting (C) not touching?" The traditional teaching has been to have the student substitute $-x + 10.8$ for $y$ in the equation of the circle and then solve for $x$. The student is expected to realize there is now one equation in one unknown and there is a need to solve for that variable. Once that value is determined, it can be substituted into the linear equation and used to solve for $y$. Attempting to solve for $x$ leads students to a dead end in their computations, and many are unable to answer the original question. This inability to interpret results is prompting industry to become less satisfied with the mathematical capabilities of high school graduates. Industry and society are demanding changes.

Regrettably, technology is not a lot of help for some students on solving the circle, line problem in the last paragraph. Algebraically, students can manipulate the technology to yield one of two answers to the question: "Solution does not exist" or "$y = \pm 0.1i\sqrt{41} + 4.9$." The stronger algebra students realize either of these messages means the line and circle do not touch. However, there is a large segment of the algebra population that does not know what these messages mean. They are unable to interpret the solution and therefore answer the initial question of "tangent, intersecting or not touching." This inability to respond is what is causing frustration in industry and society about our algebra product. If they get an answer but don't know what it means, what good is the answer?

Technology does help those students who were unable to interpret the previously described results algebraically. The entire problem can be plotted on an axis system as shown in Fig. 12.1. It appears as if the line is tangent to the circle.

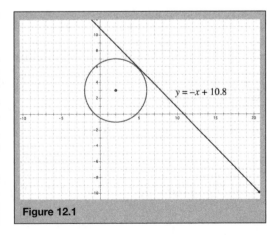

$y = -x + 10.8$

**Figure 12.1**

This picture is not supported by the algebra that has been done. If the line were tangent, the tangent point would have an $x$ and $y$ coordinate. Further investigation is necessary. Algebra has shown a point of impasse. Turn the inquiry to a geometric interpretation. Magnify or zoom in on the region around the apparent tangent point. Using multiple applications of technology, Fig. 12.2 and Fig. 12.3 show that the two graphs do not touch. The initial question is answered and the student is given a geometric interpretation of an algebraic stalemate. The student begins to gather some insight into the meaning of the messages received earlier: "Solution does not exist" or "$y = \pm 0.1i\sqrt{41} + 4.9$." In this one instance, technology created a dilemma and, at the same time, provided a solution that expanded the horizons of the students.

There is a need to rethink the algebra curriculum. Part of this was discussed in chapter 10. The Standards (NCTM, 1989) and Standards 2000 (NCTM, 2000) present the study of mathematics as one of problem solving, reasoning, communications, and making connections. The emphasis is for students to build conceptual understandings through activi-

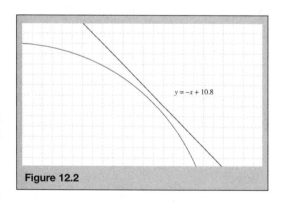

**Figure 12.2**

$y = -x + 10.8$

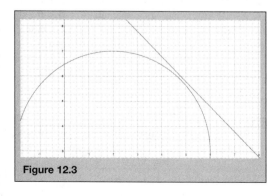

**Figure 12.3**

ties embedded in specific contextual environments. The context of the problem helps students connect with the world around them. Continuing with the linear programming idea mentioned in chapter 10, a contextual setting can be shown.

Thomas Cook, director of American Airlines, was interviewed in 1985 concerning his ideas on why optimal solutions are essential to his business: Finding an optimal solution means finding the best solution. Let's say you are trying to minimize a cost function of some kind. For example, we may want to minimize the excess costs related to scheduling crews, hotels, and other costs that are not associated with flight time. So we try to minimize that excess cost, subject to a lot of constraints, such as the amount of time a pilot can fly, how much rest time is needed, and so forth.

An optimal solution, then, is either a minimum-cost solution or a maximizing solution. For example, we might want to maximize the profit associated with assigning aircraft to the schedule; so we assign large aircraft to high-need segments and small aircraft to low-load segments. Whether it's a minimum or maximum solution depends on what function we are trying to optimize.

Finding fast solutions to linear programming problems is also essential. If we can get an algorithm that's 50 to 100 times faster, we could do a lot of things that we can't do today. For example, some applications could be real-time applications, as opposed to batch applications. So instead of running a job overnight and getting an answer the next morning, we could actually key in the data or access the data base, generate the matrix, and come up with a solution that could be implemented a few minutes after keying in the data.

A good example of this kind of application is what we call a major weather disruption. If we get a major weather disruption at one of the hubs, such as Dallas or Chicago, then a lot of flights may get cancelled, which means we have a lot of crews and airplanes in the wrong places. What we need is a way to put the whole operation back together again so that the crews and airplanes are in the right places. That way, we minimize the cost of the disruption and minimize passenger inconvenience. We're working on that problem today, but in order to solve it in an optimal fashion, we need something as fast as

Narendra Karmarkar's algorithm. In the absence of that, we'll have to come up with some heuristic ways of solving it that won't be optimal.

The simplex method, which was developed some 40 years ago by George Dantzig, has been very useful at American Airlines and, indeed, at a lot of large businesses. The difference between his solution and Karmarkar's is that if we can get his algorithm that comes up with basically the same optimal answer 50 to 100 times faster, then we can apply that technology to new problems, and even to problems that we wouldn't have tried using the simplex method. (Steen, 1994, p. 132)

Could this be a place where fuzzy logic or chaos theory could be applied?

The Thomas Cook discussion is rich with examples of mathematics being used in the real world. It holds the potential of attracting the attention of some students because they may be considering airline work as a career. Almost all students have an awareness of flying, and most who have flown have probably wondered how the complex issues of delayed flights are resolved. Cook's example points out the need for generalization, which is an essential ingredient of the algebra curriculum. There is a need for caution. If the student becomes so engrossed in the context of the problem, essential mathematical ingredients may be missed, particularly when a problem is encountered that uses all or part of the thinking process involved in the original setting. Because the student is so focused on the environment of the problem, the opportunity to recognize the similarities between the problems is diminished. Another delicate balance appears. How much context is too much?

One way to compensate for the potential loss of connectivity within algebra is to organize it around central themes. NCTM listed four general types of themes: functions and relations, modeling, structure, and language and representation (Phillips, 1995). Their discussion described functions and variables as a means of thinking about a large variety of mathematical settings. The contention is that issues arising naturally "can stimulate valuable mathematical activities for students in virtually all grade levels" (Phillips, 1995, p. 9). Modeling is seen as a tool that can be used to represent some complex phenomena, which is seen as an "effective way of giving life to them and bringing to the study of algebra the richness of experience all students carry with them" (Phillips, 1995, p. 10). Structure

is a useful organizational theme because it "implies thinking about how systems operate. . . . The search for primes by looking at the decomposition of whole numbers can be extended to the decomposition of polynomials, thus showing a connection between two different algebraic structures" (Phillips, 1995, p. 10). Algebra is a language with "various 'dialects' of literal symbols, graphs, and tables" (Phillips, 1995, p. 10). None of these central themes can stand alone as the way to organize algebra. The structure on which the content is built is evolving and will continue to change, molded by the impacts, needs, and impressions of society.

The Common Core Standards (2012) supports the use of modeling to link mathematics and statistics taught in school to real-world applications and experiences. The Common Core Standards for High School identify six high school standards: Number and Quantity; Algebra; Functions; Modeling; Geometry; Statistics & Probability. The standards emphasize a direct connection and integration of each standard at appropriate times in the curriculum.

Statements like "showing a connection between two different algebraic structures" are so easy to make. The difficulty is that carrying them into action is often not so easy. If these connections are to be seen, you, the teacher of mathematics, are going to have to reflect on the broad background of mathematics courses you have taken as a part of your preparation. The faculty under whom you have studied will not be able to tell you all the connections to be made. This text cannot list all of them. You have to look at the curriculum you are teaching, use your knowledge on student learning, think about your experiences, pull on the mathematics within your command, and build a connection that will be meaningful for your students. As you survey the terrain, you have to be constantly asking and answering questions like: "Where is the algebra?" "How does this work relate to what we are doing in class?" "Will my students associate this model with the topic at hand?" That is a tremendous responsibility and, done properly, it will take time. However, it is your obligation as a professional educator to provide the best possible learning environment for your students.

## READINESS

We would not think of giving a long-division problem to a typical first-grader. It seems laughable to even say such a thing. The student would need to have mastered a variety of skills that include subtraction, multiplication, estimation, place value, and unusual configuration for operations. Yet students often push on (or are pushed on) in algebra without the necessary background skills. Is it reasonable to expect a student to solve systems of equations in three variables if they are not adept at working with systems of equations involving two variables? That is a part of the readiness discussion. Readiness for each topic covered in Advanced Algebra cannot be overlooked.

The new topics covered in an Advanced Algebra course produce questions similar to those raised in the first algebraic exposures. Students want to see applications of the topics in their world. They are curious about how the skills will be employed in other mathematical areas. There are inquiries related to applications in other subject areas. At the same time, this new set of algebraic exposures provides them the opportunity to rise above mechanically following procedures and enter a fascinating world of extension and application.

The new topics to be covered, appropriate background skills, and need to show applications of the concepts from the world of the student are all essential ingredients of readiness. It is not sufficient to assume that because the student has completed first-year algebra, the background is strong enough to handle second-year algebra. After all, we are not sure what constitutes first-year algebra, so how can we step off from that endpoint? This is where readiness enters the picture. How can we justify simplifying rational expressions if the student is unable to factor effectively? Saying that the student should have learned how to factor in first-year algebra, although true, does not solve the dilemma. Can we assume that all teachers effectively cover the state prescribed frameworks and objectives for Algebra I? Can we assume that the students have mastered all of these objectives? Care needs to be taken to determine if the students have relevant information in their backgrounds that permits moving to the topic at hand. This is where discussions about diagnosis come into play. We can determine the framework available to each student. The problem is, it takes time and creativity on the part of the teacher. Are you willing to make that investment in your students? If you are to be an effective professional, you should be.

The Algebra standard for grades 9–12 in Standards 2000 lists the following expectations for students:

## Understand Patterns, Relations, and Functions

- Generalize patterns using explicitly defined and recursively defined functions;
- Understand relations and functions and select, convert flexibly among, and use various representations for them;
- Analyze functions of one variable by investigating rates of change, intercepts, zeros, asymptotes, and local and global behavior;
- Understand and perform transformations such as arithmetically combining, composing, and inverting commonly used functions, using technology to perform such operations on more-complicated symbolic expressions;
- Understand and compare the properties of classes of functions, including exponential, polynomial, rational, logarithmic, and periodic functions;
- Interpret representations of functions of two variables

*Represent and analyze mathematical situations and structures using algebraic symbols*

- Understand the meaning of equivalent forms of expressions, equations, inequalities, and relations;
- Write equivalent forms of equations, inequalities, and systems of equations and solve them with fluency—mentally or with paper and pencil in simple cases and using technology in all cases;
- Use symbolic algebra to represent and explain mathematical relationships;
- Use a variety of symbolic representations, including recursive and parametric equations, for functions and relations;
- Judge the meaning, utility, and reasonableness of the results of symbol manipulations, including those carried out by technology.

*Use Mathematical Models to represent and understand quantitative relationships*

- Identify essential quantitative relationships in a situation and determine the class or classes of functions that might model the relationships;
- Use symbolic expressions, including iterative and recursive forms, to represent relationships arising from various contexts;

- Draw reasonable conclusions about a situation being modeled.

*Analyze change in various context*

- Approximate and interpret rates of change from graphical and numerical data. (NCTM, 1989, p. 297)

The NCTM Standards continue that college-intending students should be able to "use matrices to solve linear systems; demonstrate technical facility with algebraic transformations, including techniques based on the theory of equations" (NCTM, 1989, p. 150). The Standards (Standards 2000; NCTM, 2000) point the way to the need for a strong foundation in algebraic skills. Providing anything less short-changes the student.

The Common Core Standards (2012) list the following expectations for high school students:

## Number and Quantity

- The Real Number System
- Quantities
- The Complex Number System
- Vector and Matrix Quantities

## Algebra

- Seeing Structure in Expressions
- Arithmetic with Polynomials & Rational Expressions
- Creating Equations
- Reasoning with Equations & Inequalities

## Functions

- Interpreting Functions
- Building Functions
- Linear, Quadratic, & Exponential Models
- Trigonometric Functions

---

### EXERCISE 12.1

1. Compare and contrast the expectations for students in high school between Standards 2000 and the Common Core Standards. Is there a significant different in the expectations? Justify your position.

---

## WHERE DOES ALGEBRA II BEGIN?

This is a difficult question to answer. Certainly, second-year algebra cannot begin at a point that skips material not covered in a first-year algebra course. It is said that the Algebra I, geometry, Algebra II order of the curriculum was determined by college entrance requirements. Some colleges began requiring evidence of basic algebra skills for entrance. That decision prompted the secondary schools to begin offering algebra as a part of their curriculum. The idea spread quickly and Algebra I came into existence "almost everywhere." Soon, the colleges decided evidence of basic geometry skills was needed and, before long, secondary schools incorporated a geometry course into their curriculum. The cycle was repeated again for more algebra, which was called Algebra II.

If the topics considered in secondary mathematics usually found under the headings of Algebra I, geometry, Algebra II, and trigonometry were integrated into a three-year coverage that stressed synthesizing ideas, the question about where Algebra II begins would be answered, perhaps. First, there would need to be some agreement about what is meant by abandoning the traditional manner of introducing the topics. Zalman Usiskin dealt with the topic when he listed five basic types of curriculum: simultaneous, braided, topical, unified, and interdisciplinary. The simultaneous integrated curricula has students taking two or more mathematics courses during the same time period. This is relatively common, particularly when a student wants to accelerate mathematical exposure in order to participate in advanced courses that are offered. One significant caution deals with prerequisite skills. That is, if one of the two courses requires knowledge from the other, the student may be compromised in the other.

The braided curriculum involves topics appearing over a series of years. This is quite common in many of our mathematical curricular areas, particularly at the elementary levels. Addition, for example, is considered over several years. The size of the addends increases along with expansion of place value, and this takes place over more than one grade. Fractions and decimals are added as those topics are developed in the curriculum. Certainly, addition is revisited in algebra as well.

Topical curriculum is much like braided. A variety of concepts are developed in a year and then those topics occur in greater depth in other years. It may be there are gaps between coverage of a given topic. That is, a topic might not be explored each year.

A unified curriculum focuses on topics. While in focus, a concept will be investigated to the extent permitted by the readiness and skills of the students. There is a difference between this and braided or topical in that the focus under consideration will be investigated in as much depth as possible prior to moving on to something else. It might be that the idea will not be revisited for some time after the consideration because there is not much related growth.

An interdisciplinary curriculum blends mathematics with other subjects. Reading in the content area is an example that has reading taught within all subjects. Mathematics is a good consideration because the reading of it is much different from that found in a literature course.

Given these descriptions, it seems as if an integrated curriculum would involve a blending of mathematical topics. Concepts would be treated as the students are ready for them. Bridges would be built between traditional areas, so it would be appropriate to cover them in some intertwined fashion, as opposed to the traditional manner. Just as applied and theoretical topics would be blended, so also would treatments of the topics in other curricular areas appropriate for the students. Not only would other subject areas be studied in the mathematics classes, but mathematics would be discussed, when appropriate, in those other courses. This is an easy statement to make but a difficult one to implement. How well, for example, will a typical teacher of literature or English be able to explain the idea of mathematical induction that is mentioned in Mark Twain's account of the shrinking of the Mississippi in his *Life on the Mississippi*? By the same token, how many typical teachers of mathematics will be aware of that particular segment taken from literature?

History holds a multitude of examples of an integrated curriculum. Many of the mathematicians of antiquity were specialists in other areas. Almost all the teachings they delivered were intertwined between the pure mathematics and applications from their fields of endeavor. The Egyptians were known to use mathematics as a practical tool to meet taxing and business needs. Thales (http://www-history. mcs.st-and.ac.uk/Mathematicians/Thales.html) was, among other things, a shrewd Greek businessman who brought the Egyptian methods back to Greece with him.

The Greeks embraced this knowledge and made it more useful by cultivating from it common mathematical principles, which set them on the road to discovery of new mathematical developments. Galileo (http://www-history.mcs.st-and. ac.uk/Mathematicians/Galileo.html) was a mathematician-physicist-astronomer who taught that mathematics was a tool that could be used to explain science. His teachings led to the idea that the observation and mathematical reasoning could be used to logically describe the behavior of the universe. Descartes (http://www-history.mcs.st-and. ac.uk/Mathematicians/Descartes.html) and Fermat (http://www-history.mcs.st-and.ac.uk/Mathematicians/Fermat.html) both had the insight to blend the concepts of algebra and geometry (at approximately the same time) into analytic geometry.

Grace Brewster Murray Hopper (http://www-history.mcs.st-and.ac.uk/Mathematicians/Hopper. html) was interested in how things worked as a youngster. She disassembled a clock because she wondered why it worked. Unable to figure out how to put it back together she took a second one apart, thinking she could use it as a model to put the first one back together. She was finishing her seventh clock when her mother discovered what Grace was doing. This woman was in her thirties when she joined the Navy at the outset of World War II. She pioneered much of the COBOL language and was promoted to the rank of Rear Admiral on November 8, 1985, making her the oldest commissioned officer on active duty in the Armed Services of the United States. She blended a variety of interests and activities into her career.

If we had a national curriculum that demanded that a given set of standards be met prior to a student satisfactorily completing first-year algebra, there would be no discussion here. There is debate on whether or not we have a national curriculum. Will the Common Core Standards become our national curriculum? At the time of the development of this edition, 45 states and three U.S. territories had adopted the Common Core Standards. While this is a majority, it is not a 100% adoption of these standards in the United States. Will this eventually occur? Some feel the NCTM Standards provide a framework that, for all practical purposes, stipulates what needs to comprise a first-year algebra course. Others will argue that most first-year algebra texts are similar enough to mandate a curriculum that shows a national set of objectives. These and several other related issues were discussed in the curriculum chapter. One nagging question persists: Should there be a national curriculum?

If a national curriculum existed, how long would it be until some sort of national examination is created to assure each student achieves the standards established for the national curriculum? What if a student passes a course with an A but does not pass the national examination? Does that student proceed to the next course in the national curriculum sequence? Does a national curriculum stifle the creativity of individual teachers? Will there be a movement to "teach to the test" with a national curriculum?

---

### EXERCISES 12.2

1. Establish a position on the question of a national curriculum for mathematics. Defend your position while considering questions like a national test and teaching to the test.
2. Determine if there is a mandatory mathematics test each student must pass to graduate from high school in your state. What happens if the student passes all required mathematics classes in high school put cannot pass the test? What happens if the student passes the necessary test but does not pass all of the required math courses to graduate? Is there an appeals process for the student?

---

There is another consideration. For the sake of this discussion, let us assume the school year under consideration is 180 days, which is fairly typical throughout the United States. Most secondary classes meet about 45 to 50 minutes a day, giving about 150 hours of potential instruction time in any given course. Of course, time is removed for testing, assemblies, pep rallies, and so forth. The remaining available time determines what is covered, and it is called first-year algebra. Different treatment depths of typical objectives cause a variety of student levels as second-year algebra is started. As a teacher, you will have to make critical curriculum decisions. More than likely, you will be given a curriculum framework and a book to follow. If you assume 150 hours to cover the concepts, you could list all of the essential topics and "backward engineer" the curriculum by fitting the list into the allocated time and strictly adhere to the schedule.

One last item needs consideration as a part of this available time discussion. Some students take Algebra I in summer school, which typically meets about 4 hours a day, 5 days a week, for 6 weeks.

That yields about 120 hours for instruction, not considering break time, testing time, endurance abilities of the students, and so on. Even at the consideration of gross hour level only, the Algebra I learning time is definitely less than a possible 180 or 150 hours some students will have had. How does this impact the Algebra II curriculum? How does it impact SAT or ACT scores? A dissertation study showed that students taking summer-school mathematics courses did not score as well on the SAT or ACT as those taking the same course during the academic year (Causey, 1995).

---

### EXERCISES 12.3

The questions in this section refer to points in the preceding paragraphs. For each of them, describe what you would use to influence your decisions and what those decisions would be.

1. What will you do when the students have difficulty on a particular concept? If you slow down to adequately cover foggy material, what algebra concepts will you choose to omit at the end of the year?
2. Will all algebra teachers omit the same concepts?

---

**Additional exercises can be found on the website.**

Students entering Algebra II have a variety of backgrounds from the course called Algebra I. These differences are often compensated for through a collection of review activities at the beginning of the year. For all practical purposes, the first three or four chapters of most Advanced Algebra texts are review. The review is needed by some of the students. Certainly not all of them need the review though. Providing so much repeat coverage of topics is not good use of the limited time available for instruction. Could we resolve this dilemma by striving to have the topics in first-year algebra covered at a more standard depth and quality so the second-year course can begin with new information? In other words, maybe we should apply the statement that the best way to teach any topic is to teach it right the first time the student encounters it, eliminating the need for in-depth repetition of so many concepts. When saying we should teach a topic right the first time, it must be assumed that the student is a willing learner. That is not a safe assumption. How do we change that?

If a concept is to be extended, perhaps a brief review to provide a common stepping-off place is in order. For example, in a second-year course, when systems of three equations in three variables are considered, a brief coverage of equations in two unknowns would be in order. This treatment would not involve extensive reteaching of the concepts. Perhaps an extension of the 3 by 3 system could include solutions by determinants or matrices, either of which could then be applied to the 2 by 2 systems, along with practicality questions. Topics typically reviewed in a second-year algebra course that should have been adequately covered in a first-year course include: real-number operations; variables; solving equations in one unknown; solution of inequalities; Cartesian coordinates; graphing equations; slope; parallel and perpendicular lines; equations of lines; solving systems of equations in two variables; operations on polynomials; factoring of quadratic trinomials; and the quadratic formula. Granted that treatment of these topics is extended in many sections of a second-year course, the question becomes, how much of the coverage is review?

## EXERCISES 12.4

1. Compare an Algebra I and Advanced Algebra text from the same publisher. List all topics that are repeated and to what extent.
2. Compare three Advanced Algebra texts. How does the material differ from chapter to chapter? Did any of the texts omit a chapter that you would not have? How many review chapters does each text have? Is the review too much, too little, or just right? Why?

A novel way of presenting three equations in three unknowns involves having the class function as the internal part of a computer. The focus can be on another way to solve a system, basic workings of a computer, row operations of a matrix, or as a beginning method for solving a system to motivate a desire within the students to see a different, easier way to accomplish the task at hand. This is a great idea for cooperative groups! It could be adapted to many algebra settings. Initially the students need to be aware of writing elements of a matrix in terms of $a_{ij}$ where $i$ represents the row and $j$ stands for the column where the element is located in an array of numbers. They also need to be aware that coefficients of the variables (assumed to already be arranged in alphabetic order) of the 3 by 3 system can be organized into a matrix. The matrix can be augmented by a column consisting of the constants found in each respective equation. That is,

$$2x + 3y + 5z = 12$$
$$4x + 2y + 4z = -2$$
$$5x + 4y + 7z = 7$$

becomes

$$\begin{bmatrix} 2 & 3 & 5 & 12 \\ 4 & 2 & 4 & -2 \\ 5 & 4 & 7 & 7 \end{bmatrix}$$

The process (Grady, 1970) involves a series of cards. Each card is numbered and has one command written on it. The cards are shuffled and distributed to class members. Card number one is read first. If the stipulations of the statement on a card are met, the instructions are followed. If the requirements of a statement on a card are not met, the card that is next in numerical order is used. As the statements are read, the mandated operations are performed on the board. The process generates some very unusual numbers and requires some arithmetic computations on the part of the students. After all the appropriate operations are performed, perhaps using technology, the resultant matrix will be

$$\begin{bmatrix} 1 & 0 & 0 & -4 \\ 0 & 1 & 0 & 5 \\ 0 & 0 & 1 & 1 \end{bmatrix}$$

which becomes

$$1x + 0y + 0z = -4$$
$$0x + 1y + 0z = 5$$
$$0x + 0y + 1z = 1$$

The commands for "Computer Solution" are presented in Table 12.1.

Computer solution is a wonderful activity. It takes time to prepare the cards but it is worth it. Students ask to do it again. They wonder about the wide variety of ideas it covers and are thrilled to see an activity that has the potential to deal with such a multitude of concepts. You should practice doing the solution using an erasable board. During the computations, you will be tempted to skip steps

**Table 12.1**

| Card Number | Command |
|---|---|
| 1 | Put a zero in the done box. |
| 2 | If there is 1 in a11, skip to 4. |
| 3 | Multiply row 1 by $\frac{1}{a_{11}}$ |
| 4 | If there is a 0 in a21, skip to 7. |
| 5 | Multiply row 2 by $\frac{-1}{a_{21}}$ |
| 6 | Add row 1 to row 2 and replace row 2. |
| 7 | If there is a 0 in a31, skip to 10 |
| 8 | Multiply row 3 by $\frac{-1}{a_{31}}$ |
| 9 | Add row 3 to row 1 and replace row 3. |
| 10 | If there is a 0 in a12, skip to 14. |
| 11 | Multiply row 1 by $\frac{-1}{a_{31}}$ |
| 12 | Multiply row 2 by $\frac{-1}{a_{22}}$ |
| 13 | Add row 1 to row 2 and replace row 1. |
| 14 | If there is a 0 in a32, skip to 17. |
| 15 | Multiply row 3 by $\frac{1}{a_{32}}$ |
| 16 | Add row 2 to row 3 and replace row 3. |
| 17 | If there is a 0 in a13, skip to 21. |
| 18 | Multiply row 1 by $\frac{1}{a_{13}}$ |
| 19 | Multiply row 3 by $\frac{-1}{a_{33}}$ |
| 20 | Add row 3 to row 1 and replace row 1. |
| 21 | If there is a 0 in a23, skip to 24. |
| 22 | Multiply row 4 by $\frac{1}{a_{23}}$ |
| 23 | Add row 3 to row 2 and replace row2. |
| 24 | If there is a 1 in a11, skip to 26. |
| 25 | Multiply row 1 by $\frac{1}{a_{11}}$ |
| 26 | If there is a 1 in a22, skip to 28. |
| 27 | Multiply row 2 by $\frac{1}{a_{22}}$ |
| 28 | If there is a 1 in a33, skip to 30. |
| 29 | Multiply row 3 by $\frac{1}{a_{33}}$ |
| 30 | If there is a 1 in the done box, skip to 33. |
| 31 | Put a 1 in the done box. |
| 32 | Skip to 2. |
| 33 | Stop. |

if you cannot erase your work and insert the new results. That will generate errors you will want to avoid. Practice is essential with this activity because of some of the unusual numbers that might be generated, depending on your starting set of equations.

# MATRICES AND DETERMINANTS

Technology becomes more valuable as the complexities of a course increase. Before the availability of technology, a 3 by 3 determinant would be solved in one of two basic ways: repetition of two columns to list all the possible diagonals shown (Sarruss rule) in Fig. 12.4 or expansion by minors. In a 3 × 3 matrix, you can repeat columns 1 and 2 to the right of the matrix as shown in Fig. 12.4, allowing the creation of 6 products (three diagonally from left to right and three diagonally from left to right). Using the variables in Fig.12.4 yields

$$afk + bgh + cdj - cfh - agj - bdk.$$

Using expansion by minors creates another possible strategy to compute the determinant.

$$\begin{bmatrix} a & b & c \\ d & f & g \\ h & j & k \end{bmatrix} = a\begin{bmatrix} f & g \\ j & k \end{bmatrix} - d\begin{bmatrix} b & c \\ j & k \end{bmatrix} + h\begin{bmatrix} b & c \\ f & g \end{bmatrix}$$

Allowing the student to test both strategies can help ensure conceptual understanding while examining the abstract processes.

Students in a second-year algebra course should be able to deal with these abstractions if time is allowed to determine that the final results for each method are equal. This is a typical abstraction encountered in a second-year course.

Technology permits rapid, accurate computation of determinants. This raises the question of the value of having students compute each of these. You need to investigate why such an assignment would be given. Giving the assignment so the student begins investigating partial expansions is an entirely different story. You need to decide what your objectives are in giving the assignment. Doing a Google search on matrix determinant provides results from more than four million sites, with the first 10 results providing step-by-step assistance on finding the determinant. The world has changed. Calculators, software, web apps, and a variety of Internet sites can also provide the solution to matrix calculations with the click of a button. You and

**Figure 12.4**

your students will even find videos that "teach" the topic. While you cannot search the entire Internet, as the teacher you need to take the time to locate and determine effective the applications and videos that can help your students learn the mathematics. WolframAlpha and Mathworld will provide you the step-by-step process with the accompanying application to find the numerical determinate using WolframAlpha (http://mathworld.wolfram.com/Determinant.html). Remember your goal: to help children learn mathematics. You cannot always be there but you can help provide the resources that will impact student learning. The choice is yours.

## HELPING STUDENTS VISUALIZE THINGS

Historically, if a student needed to "see" that a parabola is the locus of all points equidistant from a point and a line, a piece of paper was used to model the setting. You can do it too. On a piece of paper, make the point and segment dark to permit "seeing through" the paper. Place the point on the segment and fold the paper. Move the point to another location and repeat the process. After several folds, the form of the parabolic curve will begin to appear. Doing the same process with waxed paper makes the process much easier. You should do the process using both notebook paper and waxed paper to see the difference between the mediums.

There is a better way! Use a dynamic geometry software program that will trace loci. Construct a point A, a line segment BC, and point D on segment BC. Construct two circles, one with A as the center and D as the radius endpoint, and the other with D as the center and A as the radius endpoint. Construct the line joining the two points where the two circles intersect. Trace that line and move D along segment BC. The collection of traces will outline the parabola and show the concept more clearly because of the abundance of lines presented as shown in Fig. 12.5.

Ironically, the students probably have seen representations of all of the methods for outlining curves like the parabola described by folding paper or using software, but they may not realize it. String art applies the basic principle used to construct the curve. Granted, most of the string art they will have seen will not depict a parabola, and yet the concept of a multitude of line segments creating the illusion of a curve is present, and has been since they were in elementary school. This point should not go unnoticed or unmentioned.

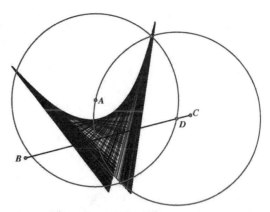

**Figure 12.5**

---

### EXERCISES 12.5

1. Create an ellipse on paper. The classic method is to establish two points, A and B, as foci and a third point, C, not on the segment between A and B. The sum of the distances AC and BC can be made constant by using a string. Put a pencil at point C, use tacks to anchor points A and B, and move the pencil, tracing the ellipse.

2. Create an ellipse using dynamic geometry software. Describe the steps necessary to create the ellipse.

---

Various techniques learned in second-year algebra have long-term carry-over potential as useful tools in future mathematics or science courses. Often, the techniques are introduced with little relation to prior experiences, but that does not have to be the case. Completing the square is a good example. Typically, the teacher begins the lesson by stating something like, "Today we are going to learn how to complete the square." This statement may or may not be followed by some rationalization about why the skill is valuable to learn. That is followed by a description of the things to be done that will accomplish the task of completing a square. How much better it would be to introduce completing the square in the context of prior experiences and, at the same time, create a need for knowing the skill.

The following is an example of another way to deliver a lesson that teaches the concept of completing the square. For each graph, focus the students' attention on the coordinates of the minimum point of the graph and relate them to the equation.

| Equation | Coordinates of Minimum |
|---|---|
| $y = x^2$ | (0,0) |
| $y = x^2 + 3$ | (0,3) |
| $y = x^2 - 4$ | (0,–4) |
| $y = (x - 5)^2$ | (5,0) |
| $y = (x + 6)^2$ | (–6,0) |
| $y = (x - 3)^2 + 4$ | (3,4) |
| $y = (x + 5)^2 - 6$ | (–5,–6) |

Enough examples need to be given so the students realize that if the generalized equation $y = (x - h)^2 + k$ is given, it will be known that the coordinates of the minimum point of the parabola will be $(h, k)$. Part of the discussion leading to the generalization would need to include the issue of signs of the coordinates and how they relate to signs in the equation. The final conclusion is that a parabola can always be expressed in the

$$y = (x - h)^2 + k$$

form, and the advantage is that the coordinates of the minimum will be immediately known.

At this point in the development, the student should be given an equation like

$$y = x^2 + 5x + 2$$

The assumption would be that somewhere in the development of things, the students would have realized that second-degree equations yield parabolas. Thus, they should know that $y = x^2 + 5x + 2$ is a parabola, too. They are not able to tell the coordinates of the minimum point, something they have been doing with parabolas. Is there any way to extrapolate that information out of this equation? Yes! Now the student has a need to learn how to complete the square. The difference between telling students they need to learn how to complete the square and showing them a need for the skill should not go unnoticed. From here, the discussion could focus on parabolas that open down, left, or right, the impact of multiplying the $x^2$ term by some value other than 1, and rotation of the axis of symmetry, as desired within the objectives of the course.

## SEQUENCES AND SERIES

Sequences become an integral part of many patterning situations. Students become accustomed to recognizing some of the more standard arithmetic ones like the odd counting numbers, which have a constant difference of two. A geometric sequence having a constant ratio of $\frac{2}{1}$ occurs regularly. Geometric ratios that are less than one are rather common. It is said that new cars lose value as soon as they are driven off the showroom floor. The amount of depreciation varies with the car, demand for it as a used product, and so on. The concept of decreasing value, and the assumption that the drop is somewhat regular, shows an application of geometric sequences. Suppose an annual depreciation ratio of 0.25 is used. That means a new vehicle with a purchase price of $30,000 would be worth $22,500 if it is sold after a year. Of course, this assumes the equipment has been maintained at a reasonable level, excessive wear and tear are not present, and so on, which is often a big assumption. Extending the value of the car into successive years provides the opportunity to use geometric ratios as a means of introducing the concept of limits, because the value of the car will continue decreasing.

The reality is that devaluation of things such as cars is not geometric, but it does provide the opportunity to discuss the concept. Ironically, once the car is old enough, it begins to increase in value, but the possibility is influenced by demand for the car, age, condition, acceptance by the public as a demand vehicle, and so forth. A few good examples are the 1957 Chevrolet, original Corvettes, two-seat Thunderbirds, three-window coupes from the 1930s, antique Packards, Auburns, or Cords, and street rods that have modern technology (engines, braking systems, transmissions, air conditioning, etc.) engineered into the classic bodies of cars produced years ago.

Several examples that use the geometric ratio that multiplies by 2 can be found. One asks how high a stack of paper would be if a sheet of 0.003-inch-thick notebook paper was folded in half 50 times. The result is mind-boggling in the eyes of many. Each fold has the "stack of paper" being twice as thick as the previous, even though there is a physical limit to the number of times this can actually be done. The problem is taking 0.003 and doubling it 50 times, or $(0.003)(2^{50})$, which is a geometric sequence with a common ratio of 2:1. Computation yields a stack of paper that is $\frac{422212465065984}{125}$ inches high. Dividing that by (12)(5280) converts the result and yields a stack that is $\frac{1095511627776}{20625}$ or approximately 53,310,000 miles high. The result is unexpected but dramatically shows the power of a geometric ratio of two (2:1), applied several times. This result could be approached through estimations by saying that the fifth fold yields a thickness of approximately

0.1 inch which, if doubled seven more times, gives a stack slightly more than a foot thick. Thus, 12 folds yield a pile about a foot high. Now the increase will appear to be much more rapid, and the final result a lot more obvious, although still quite unbelievable. However, the geometric sequence does not provide false information, just results that can be difficult to comprehend, particularly when starting with a sheet of notebook paper.

This concept of a geometric ratio occurs in the folklore of mathematics. The story is told of a young man who, although deemed unworthy, was seeking the hand of the daughter of a king. The king told the young man that sufficient wealth would be necessary. The suitor offered to work for the king for what appeared to be a nominal fee and the king consented, thinking this would eliminate the boy from contention for his daughter's hand. The young man proposed to work the first day for a single grain of wheat. It was agreed that the number of grains would be doubled daily until each square of a checkerboard had been used as a counter—that is, the boy would work for 64 days. Before the end of the agreement was reached, the king became so indebted to the young man that he relinquished his throne and all associated wealth to the suitor. The new king married the daughter of the former king.

The examples involving a geometric sequence having a common ratio of 2:1 are relatively common. Those, along with ones typically found in textbooks, investigate or explain how the standard presentations of arithmetic and geometric sequences form the foundational framework for most of the study of the topic. Regrettably, there is a multitude of other exposures that could be used to enhance student understanding. Students need to become aware of the differences between converging and diverging sequences and the impact generalizations based on them can have on the overall outcomes. For example, let

$$S = \frac{1}{2} + \frac{1}{4} + \frac{1}{8} + \frac{1}{16} + \dots$$

$$S = \frac{1}{2} + \frac{1}{2}\left(\frac{1}{2} + \frac{1}{4} + \frac{1}{8} + \frac{1}{16} + \dots\right)$$

$$S = \frac{1}{2} + \frac{1}{2}S$$

$$S - \frac{1}{2}S = \frac{1}{2}$$

$$\frac{1}{2}S = \frac{1}{2}$$

$$S = 1$$

This is a fairly common approach to showing the sum of the successive fractions where $n$ is a consecutive counting number starting with 1. There is a simple and powerful extension of the idea presented here that can help students realize generalizations must be made and used with caution. Let

$$R = 1 + 2 + 4 + 8 + 16 + \dots$$

$$R = 1 + 2(1 + 2 + 4 + 8 + 16 + \dots)$$

$$R = 1 + 2R$$

$$R - 2R = 1$$

$$R = 1$$

$$R = -1$$

which seems, and is, ridiculous. The student should realize this is not a reasonable answer to the sum of the terms. But what went wrong? The procedure worked in the first example.

## EXERCISE 12.6

1. Explain what went wrong in the example immediately preceding this question where the result was R = –1. Describe how you would have a class with the appropriate background become aware of the results.

Other extensions of sequences provide rich exploration ideas appropriate for the classroom. The Fibonacci sequence, 1, 1, 2, 3, 5, 8, 13, 21, 34, 55, . . . , is derived by finding the sum of two preceding terms to get the next. A method for quickly determining the sum of the first 10 terms was discussed in chapter 10. Other investigations can also center on the Fibonacci sequence. Pick any term, say 8, from the sequence and square it, in this case getting 64. The product of the term immediately before and the term immediately after 8 is 65. The product of the terms two places removed from 8 ($3 \times 21$) is 63. Both of these are one unit away from 64. The product of 2 and 34 (both three places away from 8 in the sequence) is 68, yielding a difference of 4 from 64. The values four places removed from 8, when multiplied, yield a product of 55, which is 9 away from 64. Is a pattern occurring?

It appears as if the absolute value of the difference between a squared term of the Fibonacci sequence and the respective products of values 1, 2, 3, and so on places removed from that squared term, are the squares of successive Fibonacci numbers beginning with the first one in the sequence. Alge-

| Term Number | Fibonacci Number |
|-------------|------------------|
| 1 | $A$ |
| 2 | $B$ |
| 3 | $A + B$ |
| 4 | $A + 2B$ |
| 5 | $2A + 3B$ |
| 6 | $3A + 5B$ |
| 7 | $5A + 8B$ |
| 8 | $8A + 13B$ |
| 9 | $13A + 21B$ |

braically the Fibonacci sequence can be represented with the first two terms being $A$ and $B$.

Suppose the fifth term $(2A + 3B)$ is squared (see Table 12.2).

Finding the sums of successive terms in the Fibonacci sequence gives:

Fibonacci term number   1 2 3 4 5 6 7 8 9 10 11

Fibonacci term   1 1 2 3 5 8 13 21 34 55 89

Sum of terms   1 2 4 7 12 20 33 54 88 143 232

Notice that the sum of the first three terms is one less than the fifth term. This generalization holds true throughout the sequence. In general, using $F_n$ to represent the $n$th Fibonacci number, $F_1 + F_2 + F_3 + F_4 + \ldots + F_n = F_{n+2} - 1$. The same process can be used to show that the sum of the even-numbered Fibonacci terms will be $F_2 + F_4 + F_6 + F_8 + \ldots + F_{2}n = F_{2}n_{+1} - 1$ and the sum of the odd-numbered Fibonacci terms is $F_1 + F_3 + F_5 + F_7 + \ldots + F_{2}n_{-1} = F_{2}n$ (Shaw, 1995).

## EXERCISES 12.7

1. Fold a standard sheet in half, then fold that in half again, and so on. What is the maximum number of folds you can make? Does the maximum number of folds change if you use a different size or kind of paper?

2. Assume that the thickness of a standard sheet of paper is 0.004 inches. How high would the stack be if that sheet could be folded 50 times? How does this result compare with the text description of the sheet of paper being 0.003 inches thick? Should you have anticipated that result? Why or why not?

## FUNCTIONS

As is the case with so many topics in second-year algebra, functions provide a wealth of opportunity for investigation. The students will have had some exposure to trigonometric functions. They are ready for a deeper understanding of them at this point. Often, creating a feel for what is going on in the classroom enhances a student's ability to grapple with the associated abstractions. The motion detection probe used in chapter 10 to investigate slope and intercept can be used again here. If the students are not familiar with the use of the probes, you might have them walk a few straight lines as was done in chapter 10. Then ask them to walk in a manner that would not yield a straight line. Lead them to the idea of more exotic walks and eventually to some sort of harmonic or repetitive motion. From there the discussion can be lead to walking a sine curve. Faster paced walks will yield a greater frequency, and longer lengths between direction reversals give larger amplitudes. At this point, the students should have a conceptual idea of the impact of changing different things and their influence on the sine curve. They should now be ready for a more formal investigation. Somewhere along the line, and not necessarily after all the discussion about sine has ended, the cosine should be walked and discussed.

Curve-graphing technology can easily be used to extend the investigation and intuition estab-

**Table 12.2**

| Squared Team | Product 1 | Product 2 | Product 3 | Product 4 |
|--------------|-----------|-----------|-----------|-----------|
| $4A^2 + 12AB + 9B^2$ | $3A^2 + 11AB + 10B^2$ | $5A^2 + 13AB + 8B^2$ | $8AB + 13B^2$ | $13A^2 + 21AB$ |
| Difference | $A^2 + AB - B^2$ | $-A - AB + B^2$ | $4A^2 + 4AB - 4B^2$ | $-9A^2 - 9AB - 9B^2$ |
| Difference when $A = B = 1$ | 1 | 1 | 4 | 9 |

lished by using the probes. The function $f(x) = A$ $\sin(Bx)$ can be investigated to determine the impacts of changing $A$ or $B$ or both. At first, either $A$ or $B$ should be changed while leaving the other remaining variable out of the problem. The decision will be influenced by the ability and adaptability of your students. Plotting $f(x) = \sin(Bx)$ as $B$ changes should provide insight for your students that $B$ impacts the frequency of the curve. They should generalize that as $B$ increases in value, the number of times the curve goes up and down over a fixed distance increases also. The statement was made here as it was to show you that the student may not always use conventional terminology. One of your tasks is to determine if the student is aware of the basic concept involved. You would also need to guide the students toward a more proper or appropriate way of expressing the concept of frequency increasing. A similar development would be used to describe amplitude and phase shift.

Part of the discussion on plotting $f(x) = A \sin(Bx)$ should include the specific problem $\sin(63x)$, because it can yield unusual and unexpected results. This is a wonderful opportunity to have students come to the realization that technology will not always provide the correct or expected answer. There is a need to assure a level of understanding that will provide enough background and intuition to realize whether or not the results are acceptable. Figures 12.6, 12.7, and 12.8 show results using different pieces of software to plot $y = \sin(63x)$.

Investigations of functions such as $\cos(\cos(\cos(\cos(x))))$ are possible with technology. Surely they could have been done prior to the insertion of the power of technology into our secondary curriculum, but something like $\cos(\cos(\cos(\cos(x))))$ would have been beyond the patience of most individuals, just because of the tediousness of the computations. Thus, even a hint of verification of the appearance of the graph would have been dif-

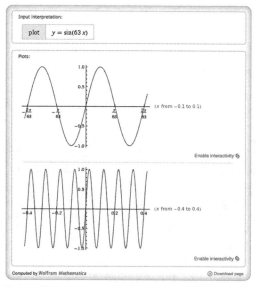

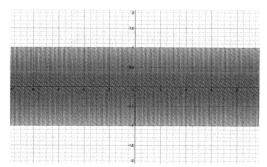

**Figure 12.8**

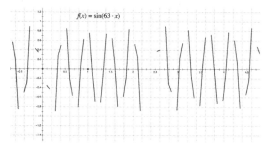

**Figure 12.6**

ficult. Granted, the more capable abstract thinkers may have arrived at the conclusion that because the cosine oscillates between -1 and 1, the graph of $\cos(\cos(x))$ would be forced to oscillate between y values of 1 and 0.54. Surely, there would have been a hesitance on the part of anyone investigating this question without the power of technology to even consider proceeding to $\cos(\cos(\cos(x)))$, let alone to the extremities of the limiting value. Here, even the better abstract thinkers would be limited until introduced to more advanced topics that would permit different approaches to the topic. The power of technology not only opens topics to individuals for investigation at earlier stages, but it also provides opportunities for formative intuition building through investigations that do not require the rigor or depth of understanding of many ad-

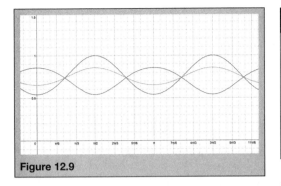

**Figure 12.9**

vanced topics. Later, when the explored concept is encountered, the individual will have an intuitive feel for what is happening, and a great advantage. The graphs of $\cos(\cos(\cos(\cos(x))))$, $\cos(\cos(\cos(x)))$, and $\cos(\cos(\cos(x)))$ can be found in Fig. 12.9. Can you determine which curve represents which function? How will you explain this discovery to your students? How will you allow your students to discover the relationship?

## DRILL IN EXTENDED ALGEBRA

Skills were developed in Algebra I. More skills are developed in Algebra II. There is a need for practice as the student grows. Again, a game format can provide avenues that make the necessary repetition more palatable. For example, another version of Winning Touch could be developed for multiplication of rational expressions. Figure 12.10 would need to be extended to make a viable game. The degree of difficulty might be so great here that

it is more trouble than it is worth. That is one of the many decisions you will have to make in your classroom, influenced by factors such as curriculum pressures, time, student ability, your time to create the game, student attitude, and peer pressure from other faculty members. The complexity of the game could be decreased by having more common factors. Increasing the degree of difficulty of the game is similarly easy, if only by expressing an answer like $\frac{64-32A}{A+5}$ as $\left(\frac{A+5}{-32(A-2)}\right)^{-1}$. Flexibility of thought is important in order to deal with such alterations of product, because they are not expressed in typical "standard" form.

## TRY THIS IN YOUR CLASSROOM

*NCTM Standards 2000:* Problem solving, communication, reasoning, algebra, functions, and geometry from an algebraic perspective.

One fancy name for a box is "right rectangular-based prism." The "right" is important because it

| X | $\dfrac{3A-6}{A^2-5A+6}$ | $\dfrac{4A^2-12A+9}{24-16A}$ | $\dfrac{2A+12}{A^2+3A-10}$ | ••• |
|---|---|---|---|---|
| $\dfrac{A^2-5A+6}{6-3A}$ | $-1$ | $\dfrac{2A^2-9A+9}{24}$ | $\dfrac{-A-6}{A+5}$ | ••• |
| $\dfrac{2A-6}{A^2+6A+9}$ | $\dfrac{6}{(A+3)(A+3)}$ | $\dfrac{(3-2A)(A-3)}{4(A+3)^2}$ | $\dfrac{4(A-3)(A+6)}{(A+2)(A+3)^2(A+5)}$ | ••• |
| $\dfrac{16(A^2-4A+4)(3-2A)}{2A^2+9A-18}$ | $\dfrac{48(A-2)^2}{(3-A)(A+6)}$ | $\dfrac{2(A-2)^2(2A-3)}{A+6}$ | $\dfrac{64-32A}{A+5}$ | ••• |
| • | • | • | • | |
| • | • | • | • | |
| • | • | • | • | |

**Figure 12.10**

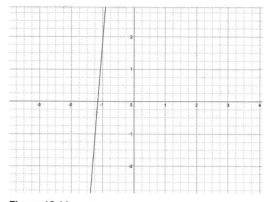

**Figure 12.11**

tells that all sides (faces) are perpendicular to the bases. "Rectangular-based" indicates that both bases are congruent rectangles. A right equilateral-triangle-based prism would have congruent equilateral triangles as bases and all faces would be congruent rectangles.

Figure 12.11 shows a right equilateral triangle based prism (referred to as a prism from here on in this activity). The base of the equilateral triangle and its sides are labeled "$s$," the altitude of the triangular base is "$a$," and the height of the prism is "$h$." Suppose we wanted to look at how the surface area of the prism changes. We could assign some value to the side length and then graph the surface area, letting $Y$ represent the total surface area and $X$ represent the height, $h$, in the equation [equation 12.12], which is the total surface area of the prism. We assigned a value of 4 to $s$ and graphed the equation, getting what is shown in Fig. 12.12. Does it make sense to have the graph as it appears in Fig. 12.12? Why or why not?

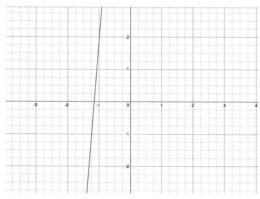

**Figure 12.12**

Suppose the total surface area of the prism is 20 square units. When you solve for $h(X)$, you will get two values. Do they both make sense? Why or why not?

What is the volume of the prism in Fig. 12.11? Suppose the side of the triangle is assigned some value and the height of the face is still expressed as a variable. What would the graph of the volume with this arrangement look like? Suppose the height of the prism is assigned some value and the side length of the triangle is still expressed as a variable. What would the graph of the volume with this arrangement look like? Suppose the volume is some fixed value. What will the graph of the resultant situation look like?

## CONCLUSION

How do we effectively conclude this discussion? You know there is no way we will have covered all the things that are in an Algebra II or Advanced Algebra course. Most certainly readiness is a huge factor as you contemplate what goes into your curriculum. Our good friend, technology, could show up in a multitude of locations now and when it does, you will have to shift from focusing on the answer to a problem to interpretations and applications. Technology makes a lot of the "standard" algebra questions obsolete. Once again, we leave you with a huge responsibility—that of being creative, energetic, resourceful, up-to-date, thoughtful, insightful, exciting as you present, excited about teaching mathematics, etc., etc., etc. Teaching—what wonderful opportunities exist for those who want to do it right. So, this is not a conclusion, it is a beginning!

### STICKY QUESTIONS

1. Describe the impact of graphing $f(x) = A\sin(Bx + C)$ as each of $A$, $B$, and $C$ changes. Compare those results with the graph of $g(x) = L\sin(Mx) + N$ as $L$, $M$, and $N$ change. Discuss the differences between the two function sets and where students could encounter difficulty. What error patterns could be expected? Is this idea worth extending to other trigonometric functions?

2. Tangent is often introduced as $\frac{\sin(x)}{\cos(x)}$. Assuming there is a value to having students consider the numerical values as $x$ changes from zero through 90°, describe a method for getting them to look at the numerical results.

What should they reasonably conclude and how will you guide them to those desired conclusions?

3. Describe how two different pieces of symbolic manipulator software accept the equation of a circle that can be graphed. Compare your results with those of your peers. What are the commonalties? What are the differences?

4. Describe how a graphing calculator accepts the equation of a circle. Compare your results with those of your peers. What are the commonalties? What are the differences?

5. Students have difficulty comprehending the impact of absolute value on various equations. For example, does $|y| = x$ differ from $y = |x|$; does $y = |x| + 2$ differ from $y = |x + 2|$; does $|y| = x^2$ differ from $y = |x^2|$; and so on. Investigate and describe conclusions for each of these as well as at least two significantly different absolute value problems of your choosing.

## PROBLEM-SOLVING CHALLENGES

1. Find a three-digit number $XYZ$ such that $X!$ + $Y!$ + $Z!$ = $XYZ$. For this problem, $X$ cannot equal 0 and $X$, $Y$, and $Z$ must all be whole numbers less than 10.

**Check out the website for the solution.**

2. In Pascal's triangle, how many odd numbers will there be in the 65th row?

$$1$$
$$1\ 1$$
$$1\ 2\ 1$$
$$1\ 3\ 3\ 1$$
$$1\ 4\ 6\ 4\ 1$$
$$1\ 5\ 10\ 10\ 5\ 1$$

**Check out the website for the solution.**

# ■
# LEARNING ACTIVITIES

## Vectors

Real numbers can be identified with the points on a number line. Adding real numbers geometrically is done by combining "directed" distances from the origin on the number line in a "tip to tail" procedure. A "directed" distance from the origin can be visualized as an arrow with the tail of the arrow at "zero" and the tip of the arrow at some fixed number. Technically such a directed distance is called a "vector." The "tip to tail" method of addition that will be illustrated is commonly taught in the elementary grades using Cuisenaire rods.

While our examples will involve only two addends and a sum, more addends could be handled by finding the sum of the first two, then adding that sum to the third addend, and so on until all addends are considered. When adding 2 and 3 on a number line, the first vector is 2 units long and the second vector is 3 units long. The tail of the vector for the number 3 is moved to the tip of the vector for the number 2. The resultant vector is the arrow going from the tail of the vector of length 2 to the tip of the vector of length 3 as shown in Fig. 12.13. This is the geometric way to see that $2 + 3 = 5$.

**Figure 12.13**

As mentioned earlier, this problem could be done with the Cuisenaire rods, a set of 10 related pieces, each with a defined color as shown in Fig. 12.14:

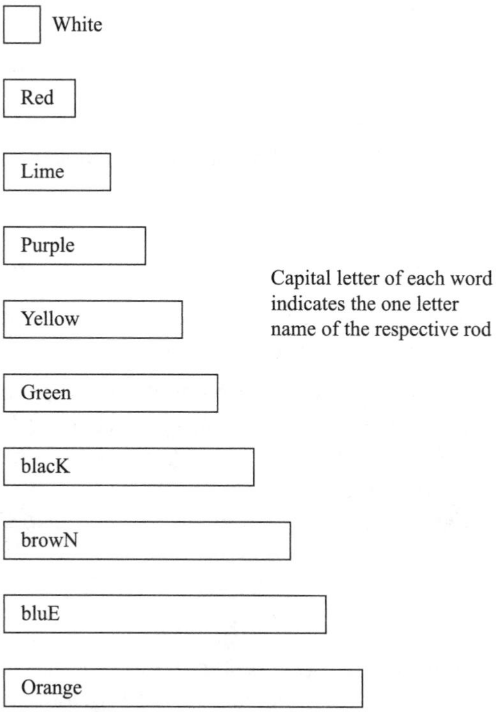

White

Red

Lime

Purple

Yellow

    Capital letter of each word
    indicates the one letter
    name of the respective rod

Green

blacK

browN

bluE

Orange

**Figure 12.14**

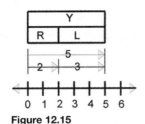

**Figure 12.15**

Examine the Fig 12.15 and notice the lead in to vector work provided by the Cuisenaire rods. We show this to amplify the need for concrete beginnings in the early years and to encourage vertical communication between teachers in the elementary, middle, and high schools. Even this basic example shows how backgrounds are established in the elementary school.

### Your Turn

1.  Show 3 + 4 on the number line using vectors for the addends and sum.

Notice that vectors for positive numbers point "to the right" and vectors for negative numbers point "to the left." We can add a negative number to a positive number with the "tip to tail" procedure. For example 6 – 4 is really 6 + (-4). This amplifies the very powerful vector concept of the "direction" for a number, and in the process, makes the problem a lot easier to understand as shown in Fig 12.16. Remember, the sum or resultant vector is from zero to the tip of the final addend.

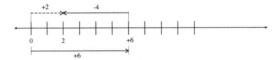

**Figure 12.16**

### Your Turn

2.  Show 8 – 5 on the number line using vectors.
3.  Draw vectors on a number line to show the geometric meaning of:
    10 + 3,
    10 – 3,
    –10 – 3, and
    –10 + 3.
4.  Use a vector diagram to show that 3 + 5 is the same as 5 + 3. (This is known as the "commutative" property of addition on the set of real numbers.)

We can think of points on a line as number. We can think of points in a coordinate plane as numbers. If a point in the plane has coordinates (a,b), we can use the "directed" distance (a vector) from the origin to (a,b) to represent that number. We can add these numbers in a coordinate plane. Adding (a,b) to (c,d) can be done with the same "tip to tail" procedure that was used on a number line. This vector addition is illustrated in Fig. 12.17 and also shows that (a, b) + (c, d) = (a + b, c + d).

### Your Turn

5.  Show the vector addition for the numbers in the plane identified with the points whose coordinates are (2,3) and (5,–1). Show that the resultant vector points from the origin to (7,2).

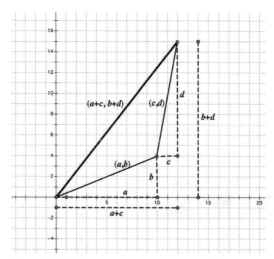

**Figure 12.17**

The numbers identified with points in the plane are usually called complex numbers to distinguish them from the points on a number line that are called real numbers. Be careful not to be misled by the ordinary meanings of the words real and complex. There is a tendency to think that if something is not real then it does not exist. And there is a tendency to think that something that is complex is complicated. But complex numbers certainly exist. Geometrically points on a number line are real numbers and points in a coordinate plane are complex numbers. In fact real numbers are just a special case of complex numbers that are on the $x$-axis.

## Your Turn

6. Show that the addition of complex numbers is commutative. If points on the $x$-axis in a coordinate plane are taken to be real numbers, show that adding them as complex numbers is the same as adding them as real numbers.
7. Is vector addition closed in the set of real numbers?
8. Is there an inverse element for vector addition in the set of real numbers?
9. Is there an identity element vector for addition of vectors in the set of real numbers?
10. Is vector addition commutative over the set of real numbers?
11. Is vector addition associative over the set of real numbers?

# Pre-Calculus

**13**

## FOCAL POINTS IN THIS CHAPTER

- Secondary pre-calculus concepts
- Appropriate proofs for secondary pre-calculus
- Extensions of previous topics

Pre-calculus can be considered an extension of Algebra II and trigonometry. It fills in the gaps and reviews students in preparation for calculus. It can be approached from a function and/or graphic perspective. Due to the advances in technology, a combined approach is a more feasible option when you consider the dynamics of the tools available.

The decision as to which approach should be selected is influenced by student backgrounds and desired outcomes. Technology can help the students visualize and understand the concepts with greater depth and clarity than could be realized when using a chalkboard or overhead. Technology is helpful with some of the more complex representations discussed in a pre-calculus setting. This is particularly true when three-dimensional representations are discussed (see Fig. 13.1, a sample from Geometer's Sketchpad called "Cabin").

Some question the use of a function approach to pre-calculus.

The Egyptians established the fundamentals of geometry around 3000 B.C., although it was not named geometry until around 460 B.C. by the Greeks. The Euclideans provided fundamental levels of formalization to the subject around 300 B.C. The Babylonians understood algebra and could solve quadratic equations as early as 1900 B.C. Around 1600 A.D., Fermat (http://www-history.mcs.st-and.ac.uk/Mathematicians/Fermat.html) and Descartes (http://www-history.mcs.st-and.ac.uk/Mathematicians/Descartes.html) translated algebra problems to geometry terms using rectangular coordinates. This was the beginning of analytic geometry. The work of these two could be called pre-calculus. That information led the way for Newton (http://www-history.mcs.st-and.ac.uk/Mathematicians/Newton.html), Leibniz (http://www-history.mcs.st-and.ac.uk/Mathematicians/Leibniz.html), and Jacob (http://www-history.mcs.st-and.ac.uk/Mathematicians/Bernoulli_Jacob.html) and Johann Bernoulli (http://www-history.mcs.st-and.ac.uk/Mathematicians/Bernoulli_Johann.html) to establish calculus as we know it. Their approach to calculus was based on knowledge of functions and graphs.

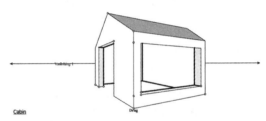

**Figure 13.1**

You have some historical background, but where do we start in pre-calculus and what perception depths should be expected? That depends on what students already know. Pre-calculus assumes they have had Algebra II and trigonometry. Algebra skills and comprehension of concepts must first be reviewed and tested. Student failure in college calculus is often related to weak algebra skills. A solid foundation will increase the likelihood of a successful transition to calculus.

One immediate question is how much review is enough. The impact of review and its resulting boredom have been discussed in other locations in this text. At the same time, trying to move on before students are ready is hazardous, at best. This too has been discussed. If you have had some of the students in prerequisite classes, you should have an idea of what to do with the situation. If not, you will need to talk with your colleagues. You will also need to assess the abilities of the individuals in your pre-calculus class, so you have some idea of their skills. This is a risky move, because it means you will be building a course while you are teaching it. Such a maneuver is not easy. It can be very exciting, rewarding, and exhausting. There is an additional payoff. Students who can move smoothly between algebra and trigonometry will have the confidence and competence to see an extensive collection of applications of mathematics.

## PRE-CALCULUS CONTENT

Most of the courses in the secondary mathematics curriculum are rather stringently defined. The latitudes applied to what is included in a pre-calculus course are often rather liberal. Teachers have opinions about what should and should not be included in pre-calculus. There is a relatively common core of concepts that are in the course. They include:

Advanced graphing

Calculus introduction

Circular and trigonometric functions

Complex numbers

Conic sections

Coordinate geometry

Determinants

Exponents

Field axioms

Functions

Identities

Inequalities

Limits

Logarithms

Mathematical induction

Polar coordinates

Polynomials

Probability

Proofs

Sequences and series

Sets

Space geometry

Statistics

Triangle trigonometry

Vectors

The amount of emphasis that should be placed on the concepts is where the differences begin to occur. Three major influencing factors exist: text, student background, and teacher bias.

Texts as a driving force in the curriculum have been discussed. Student background will influence what topics can be approached and at what depth. You should have some idea about their background as they walk into this pre-calculus classroom. Factors like Algebra II being defined as what is covered in 180 days (or fewer, because it too is sometimes taken in summer school) cannot be escaped, and different students from different Algebra II classes will have different backgrounds. The assumption has to be that the students taking pre-calculus are a little more serious about their mathematics and, because of that, you should be able to reach some common stepping-off points. Knowing where to start and assuming the students will be amenable to work at eliminating deficiencies, the major driving force for this pre-calculus course becomes your bias.

What topics will provide the essential background for calculus? As you answer this question, you will be thinking through your own experiences both before and during calculus. Try to remember any time in calculus where you said "I wish I had seen that in pre-calculus." That is a clue on what to include or emphasize in your course. Recall the concepts you viewed as vital in your calculus course. The pre-calculus course should provide adequate background so students succeed in calculus. It is your job to assure that happens. Talk with the calculus teacher and find out what is expected of students coming out of pre-calculus. Compile all this information and you will have an idea of what to emphasize in your course.

## PROOF

Pre-calculus students should value the concept of proof. This might take sales ability from you to convince some of them, but it can be done. As a part of emphasizing proof, time can be spent on expanding basic logic rules so students are able to recognize false assumptions, cyclic arguments, leaps of faith, and inconclusive arguments. Some authorities argue for delving into truth tables. That can be a beginning, but the value of logic does not stop there. Many pre-calculus texts do not go far beyond conjunctions, disjunctions, conditionals, negations, implications, combinations of some of these ideas, equivalences, and tautologies. Two problems exist with stopping at this point: There is so much more, and doing truth tables is not overly thrilling. Once a few have been done, the challenge is gone. Where to go for more becomes the difficulty. What is appropriate? How much time will it take you to become confident to begin to lead a class through the information?

1. It is said that you learn something best when you teach it. That is true—but does that give you license to use a class as guinea pigs? How much should you know about a topic before embarking into the study of it with a class?
2. You undoubtedly have had some logic as a part of your undergraduate program. Out of that information, what could be inserted into a pre-calculus course and why? If you have not had logic beyond basic truth tables, research the subject to determine what should be included in the pre-calculus class. As a part of your research, you should include a description of how much time it will take you to learn the material well enough to teach it.

 **Additional exercises can be found on the website.**

A direct proof begins with a hypothesis. The proof develops a position based on a succession of statements, each derived logically from definitions, axioms, or previously proved theorems. The last statement is the conclusion of the theorem. Most students will have worked through an abundance of direct proofs. Indirect proofs are not as common. Here, it is assumed that the conclusion of the theorem is false. Again, a logical sequence of valid steps is used, but this time they lead to a contradiction of some known position. Indirect proof is typically used to show that if $(a)(b) = 0$ where $a$ and $b$ are elements of the real numbers, then $a = 0$ or $b = 0$ (this is the inclusive "or" meaning they both could equal 0).

$a \in R, b \in R$

| | |
|---|---|
| and $(a)(b) = 0$ | Hypothesis |
| Suppose $a \neq 0$ | |
| and $b \neq 0$ | Neg. of conclusion |
| $\dfrac{1}{a} \in R$ and $\dfrac{1}{a}(a) = 1$ | $\exists$ Mult. inv. in $R$ |
| $\dfrac{1}{a} = \dfrac{1}{a}$ | Reflexive = in $R$ |
| $0 = \dfrac{1}{a}(0)$ | Mult. prop. of 0 in $R$ |

| | |
|---|---|
| $0 = \dfrac{1}{a}(ab)$ | Sub $(ab)$ for 0 |
| $\dfrac{1}{a}(ab) = \left[\dfrac{1}{a}(a)\right](b)$ | Assoc. x on $R$ |
| $\dfrac{1}{a}(ab) = [1](b)$ | Mult. inv. in $R$ |
| $\dfrac{1}{a}(ab) = (b)$ | Mult. iden. in $R$ |
| $0 = b$ | Subst. 0 for $\dfrac{1}{a}(ab)$ |

The equation $b = 0$ contradicts the hypothesis and assumption $a \neq 0$ and $b \neq 0$. The conclusion of the theorem being false when the hypothesis is true is a logical contradiction. The theorem must be true.

## COMPLEX NUMBERS

Throughout the curriculum, the number system is built slowly and carefully. New elements are added as the need arises. Throughout mathematical history, new kinds of numbers have been invented to fill deficiencies in the existing number system. Early times found only counting numbers. The Greeks developed rational numbers as a means of expressing the ratio of two integers or fractional parts of quantities. The Greeks became aware that some numbers were not rational as they tried to express the ratio of a diagonal of a square to its side length in terms of two integers (Fig. 13.2).

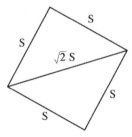

**Figure 13.2**

Zero appeared in India about 200 A.D. to represent an empty column in an abacus-like counting board. Negative numbers appeared in Renaissance Europe, perhaps as a means of indicating whether crates of goods weighed more or less than some standard amount. A basic property of the real numbers is that the square root of any negative real number cannot be a real number. The word "imaginary" was first used in the sixteenth and seventeenth centuries to describe numbers like $\sqrt{-13}$. It is generally accepted that the word "imaginary" reflects the initial uneasiness mathematicians had when dealing with them. Because this set of numbers is used in advanced mathematics, electrical circuitry, and mechanics, "imaginary" may be a poor term.

Any number of the form $a + bi$ where $a$ and $b$ are reals is called a complex number. A complex number can be either pure imaginary ($a = 0$) or real ($b = 0$). A whole set of operations is available to deal with complex numbers. In the quadratic formula, the material beneath the radical sign is called the discriminant because the sign of that section discriminates between whether the roots are real or imaginary.

The algebra of complex numbers is used in rotations in the plane. In typical mathematical fashion, attempts were made to do similar rotations in 3-space. Gauss (http://www-history.mcs.st-and.ac.uk/Mathematicians/Gauss.html), Cauchy (http://www-history.mcs.st-and.ac.uk/Mathematicians/Cauchy.html), and Hamilton (http://www-history.mcs.st-and.ac.uk/Biographies/Hamilton.html), along with many others, dabbled in the power of complex numbers and how to expand their usefulness. One of the extensions involved quaternions, which Gauss called mutations, probably because the commutative property of multiplication fails in quaternions. It is impossible to have an algebra of rotations in 3-space if commutativity is preserved. A complex number is written $a + bi$ and is a subfield of quaternions.

The algebra H of rank 4 with the basis elements 1, $i, j, k$ and the products $1^2 = 1, (1)(i) = i, (1)(j) = j, (1)(k) = k, i^2 = j^2 = k^2 = -1, (i)(j) = k, (j)(k) = i, (k)(i) = j$, and $(j)(i) = -k, (k)(j) = -i, (i)(k) = -j$ is called Hamilton's quaternion algebra. (Gellert, Kustner, Hellwich, & Kustner, 1977, p. 680)

Quaternions help reveal a part of Gauss's approach to life. He had done much of the formative work for complex variables before Cauchy and Hamilton started. Gauss did not compliment them on their developments because he had done similar work long before them. He had not published the work. He was content to have done it. That made Gauss seem cool and unresponsive. Yet he was quite cordial to many who sought him out as a professional. He showed a tremendous amount of respect and open-mindedness toward Mademoiselle Sophie Germain (http://www-history.mcs.st-and.ac.uk/Mathematicians/Germain.html), who was only a year older than Gauss. Germain corresponded with Gauss about some "arithmetical observations," but she used the name "Mr. Leblanc."

She eventually revealed her true identity and gender to Gauss. He said, "But how do I describe to you my admiration and astonishment at seeing my esteemed correspondent Mr. Leblanc metamorphose himself into this illustrious personage (Sophie Germain) who gives such a brilliant example of what I would find it difficult to believe" (Newman, 1956, p. 333).

## LIMITS

Some adopt the position that limits are one of the most, if not the most, important concept a student needs to have mastered prior to entering a serious study of the calculus. Exposure to limits actually begins in the primary grades, but many people do not realize it. A teacher wants to cover a bulletin board with construction paper. Each piece is to be adjacent to another and no piece is to be cut. Rarely is the bulletin board the "right size," so there is a part of the board, or border, left uncovered as shown in Fig. 13.3. The coverage reflects an area less than that of the bulletin board itself. Figure 13.4 shows coverage that is greater than that of the bulletin board, achieved by adding more sheets of paper to cover the exposed parts of the bulletin board. The two areas represent a beginning concept

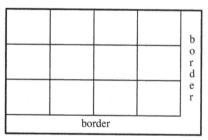

**Figure 13.3**

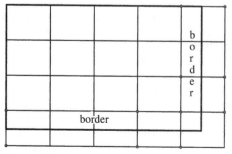

**Figure 13.4**

of limits. The actual area of the bulletin board is somewhere between the 12 and 16 sheets of construction paper used in this example. If the unit of paper was changed to half a sheet of construction paper, the upper and lower limits would change. At the same time, the deficient and excess coverage would be less, approaching the actual area of the bulletin board.

The bulletin board coverage can be made to more closely approximate the area by altering the size of unit paper used. A similar idea appears in the history of mathematics as a method for finding the area of a circle by inscribing and circumscribing regular polygons (Fig. 13.5). This approach is not uncommon in many classrooms today. It is important to let students know they are working with the beginning ideas of limits when they use these examples, something that is frequently overlooked.

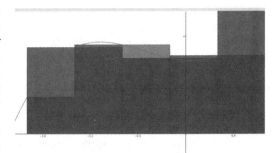

**Figure 13.6**

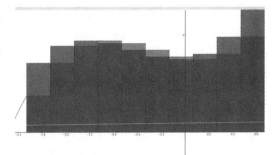

**Figure 13.7**

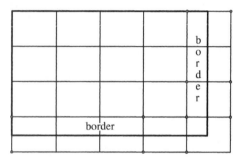

**Figure 13.5**

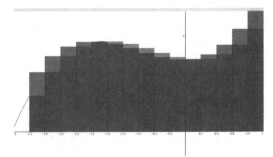

**Figure 13.8**

This enhances their ability to handle the abstractions associated with limits and areas under curves when they encounter them.

Software exists that dynamically shows this decreasing area approach to limits. Figures 13.6 through 13.15 show an example of limits applied through Riemann sums with 5 and then 10 and 15 partitions. The Riemann sums show how increasing the number of partitions closes in on the actual area under the curve. Maneuvers such as this can be done by hand or in print, but speed, accuracy, and drama are missing. Figures 13.6 through 13.8 show an extension of covering the bulletin board with construction paper. The "edge" is a curve and the border is created, and covered, by thin rectangles instead of construction paper. The development of the concept of limits from the primary grades through calculus is depicted in a similar manner.

Approaching the idea of limits in a manner similar to that discussed with the bulletin boards is unusual. But, you can see the similarities between that and the Riemann sums. Recall that limits were also discussed in the first chapter of this text as we discussed $\frac{6}{n}$ as $n$ decreased from 6 to 1 to 0.5, 0.1, and a continually smaller decimal value greater than zero. That was probably a new approach to division by zero for you. The other limit idea in the first chapter dealt with folding a sheet of paper in half over and over. That too was probably a new an unusual use of limits for you. The bottom line is that the idea of limits can show up in a multitude of places in the curriculum and some of the approaches can build phenomenal readiness skills for the formal study of limits.

## SEQUENCE AND SERIES

Foundation work for sequence and series is begun with patterns, again in the elementary school. Students are taught to skip count (2, 4, 6, 8, ... ) as a background activity to learn multiplication tables. Alter the description and emphasis and an arithmetic sequence with a constant difference of 2 appears. Problems like folding a 0.004-inch-thick sheet of paper in half several times in succession yields 0.004, 0.008, 0.016, 0.032... . Change the way the problem is discussed and you see a geometric sequence with a constant ratio of 2, as discussed in chapter 12. Students are exposed to sequences informally and formally throughout the curriculum. They see some sequence and series work in algebra, but pre-calculus provides the opportunity to review and extend the topics. One extension could involve the summation sign $\Sigma$. Students learn the advantages of being able to express concepts in condensed forms in algebra or geometry through the use of variables and formulas. As strings of numbers are expressed, needs for compact methods of writing continue to occur. The $\Sigma$ provides one such avenue by giving a lower and upper limit to the values to be applied to a variable. The variable increases in increments of one between the lower and upper limit. If the lower limit for $K$ is 1 and the upper limit is 5 in the expression $4K - 1$, it would be written $\sum_{1}^{5}(4k-1)$.

$$\sum_{1}^{5}(4k-1) = [4(1)-1]+[4(2)-1]+[4(3)-1]+[4(4)-1]+[4(5)-1]$$
$$=[4-1]+[8-1]+[12-1]+[16-1]+[20-1]$$
$$=3+7+11+15+19$$
$$=55$$

Notice how this extension brings in the idea of limit, too. This is another example of blending topics. As mentioned earlier, it becomes your responsibility to call students' attention to places within the curriculum where topics overlap. In the process, they need to be encouraged to look for such connections. This helps them become independent, self-motivated, lifelong learners of mathematics.

## FUNCTIONS

Euler (http://www-history.mcs.st-and.ac.uk/Mathematicians/Euler.html), the master in all according to Laplace (http://www.history.mcs.st-and.ac.uk/Mathematicians/Laplace.html), defined a *function* as "a variable quantity that is dependent upon another variable quantity." After the further development of mathematics, a more precise definition was needed. A function was treated as a mapping from one set into another such that to each element in one set there can be assigned a unique element in the other set.

The concept of function will have been discussed in earlier courses. The danger is that because the students have heard about functions, they acquire the impression that they know all about them. As you know, the topic grows and expands into a variety of complexities. Care needs to be taken to approach the topic in a manner that allows students to see the impact of a situation where functions exist, and what changes can be made to situations while still maintaining the function status. They will have dealt with the impact of something like changing $f(x) = x^2$ to $f(x) = -x^2$. They probably will have experienced a 90° rotation of some functions, making them become familiar with relations of functions. How much of that will they understand beyond the superficial level? The answer to that question can have a dramatic impact on the amount of review needed at the beginning of a pre-calculus course and the pace at which you will be able to move through the entire course.

---

### EXERCISES 13.2

Using a graphing calculator or software, do the following:

1. Graph one of each type of the functions:
   $f(x)$ = Constant
   $f(x)$ = Linear
   $f(x)$ = Quadratic
   $f(x)$ = Polynomial
   $f(x)$ = Rational
   $f(x)$ = Exponential
   $f(x)$ = Logarithmic

   Select any three of these functions and describe their similarities and differences. List the main points you would bring out to students if you were comparing and contrasting the selected three in a pre-calculus class.

2. Graph at least four trigonometric functions:
   $f(x) = \sin(x)$
   $f(x) = \cos(x)$

---

$f(x) = \tan(x)$
$f(x) = \csc(x)$
$f(x) = \sec(x)$
$f(x) = \cot(x)$

It is rather common to have an elaborate explanation of the development of sine using a unit circle. Use the unit circle to explain why one of the other trigonometric functions behaves as it does. Build your discussion in the form of a lesson plan. You should incorporate technology.

proaching this by using a graphing calculator or function plotting software.

2.  When $f(x) = x^2 + 5x - 6$ and $g(x) = x^2 + 7$, what is $f(g(x))$? What is $g(f(x))$? Does $f(g(x)) = g(f(x))$ in general? When does $g(f(x)) = f(g(x))$, if ever? Develop a lesson plan for this problem. It should include technology, and you should assume the students have the appropriate skills and background with the calculator or software selected.

 **Additional exercises can be found on the website.**

**Additional exercises can be found on the website.**

## ALGEBRA OF FUNCTIONS

Functions, like sets of numbers, have several properties that help form new functions. We can add, subtract, multiply, and divide functions. The commutative, associative, distributive, and identity properties hold for function operations as they do for the typical operations on real numbers.

Students will probably have seen some examples of combinations of functions by the time they take a pre-calculus course; however, perhaps that is not the case. We have to be careful about attributing skills to students that they may not have. Assume students have not seen $f(g(x))$ when $f(x) = 2x$ and $g(x) = 3x - 4$. The discussion to get them to understand how to deal with $f(g(x))$ is fairly straightforward. "Substitute $3x - 4$ for $x$ in $f(x)$ and see what you get" is what students are often told. Is that a sufficient explanation? What happens when a new set of functions like $h(x) = x^2 + 5x - 6$ and $k(x) = x^2 + 7$ are encountered? One could adopt the position that the only difference is that the largest exponent is now 2 as opposed to 1. How much of an impact could that have on the situation? For one thing, a lot of algebra skills that were subtle before come into play. They take on a much more dominant role at this point. Students frequently tend to gloss over such factors. It is your job to convince them of the need and value of being able to perform quickly and confidently with these situations.

### EXERCISES 13.3

1.  The text discusses dealing with $f(g(x))$ when $f(x) = 2x$ and $g(x) = 3x - 4$. Describe the advantages and disadvantages of ap-

## THE QUADRATIC FORMULA

Students will have encountered the quadratic formula previously in an Advanced Algebra course (Algebra II) for sure, and maybe in Algebra I. Those earlier encounters will have included working with it to solve second-degree equations and probably some derivation of the formula itself. Completing the square is a standard technique used in many secondary texts to show the derivation of the quadratic formula. Depending on the text, there might be some differences between what is presented here and another author's rendition of the derivation. You should be able to adjust your approach to what is seen.

Solving for $x$ to get the exact solutions involves:

Starting with

$$ax^2 + bx + c = 0$$

Subtracting c from both sides

$$ax^2 + bx = -c$$

Dividing both sides by $a$

$$x^2 + \frac{bx}{a} = \frac{-c}{a}$$

(For the expression to be quadratic, a ≠ 0.)

We want the left side of the equation to be the square of a binomial. Some value that will make the left side be the square of a binomial must be added. We know the middle term of a trinomial that is a binomial squared is twice the product of the square roots of the first and third terms of the trinomial. Then $x^2$ must be the first term and $\frac{bx}{a}$ must be the second. The third term can be built from the second. The $x$ can be removed from consideration because it is the square root of the first term. There is no 2 in the middle term. That means it had to have been divided out, which implies that the square root of the third term must have had a 2 in its denominator. We now know that the square of $\frac{b}{2a}$ or $\frac{b^2}{4a^2}$ is the missing term to be added to the left, and also to the right side of the equation. Now, you knew all that! Why would we write that and force you to read through it? One reason is for you to be aware of how complex mathematics can become. Another is to give some indication about the necessity for adequate algebra skills in a pre-calculus course. If a student has to stop and think about any of the maneuvers discussed so far in the development of the quadratic formula, that individual is likely to have a great deal of difficulty with the pre-calculus course. Just as it is expected that the basic arithmetic facts are reflexive as a student begins working with algorithms for addition, subtraction, multiplication, and division, students in a pre-calculus class must possess basic instinctive abilities. Without those skills, the student is destined to experience a long, hard struggle.

We continue with the development of the quadratic formula:

Adding $\left(\dfrac{b}{2a}\right)^2$ to both sides yields

$$x^2 + \frac{bx}{a} + \left(\frac{b}{2a}\right)^2 = \frac{-c}{a} + \left(\frac{b}{2a}\right)^2$$

Factoring the left side,

$$\left(x + \frac{b}{2a}\right)^2 = \frac{-c}{a} + \left(\frac{b}{2a}\right)^2$$

Adding right-side fractions,

$$\left(x + \frac{b}{2a}\right)^2 = \frac{b^2 - 4ac}{4a^2}$$

Taking the square root of both sides yields

$$x + \frac{b}{2a} = \frac{\sqrt{b^2 - 4ac}}{2a} \text{ or } x + \frac{b}{2a} = \frac{-\sqrt{b^2 - 4ac}}{2a}$$

Subtracting $\frac{b}{2a}$ from both sides to solve for x,

$$x = \frac{-b}{2a} + \frac{\sqrt{b^2 - 4ac}}{2a} \text{ or } x = \frac{-b}{2a} - \frac{\sqrt{b^2 - 4ac}}{2a}$$

Combining the two preceding equations gives

$$x = \frac{-b \pm \sqrt{b^2 - 4ac}}{2a}$$

more commonly known as the quadratic formula.

## EXERCISES 13.4

1. Find a different derivation of the quadratic formula. Compare and contrast it with the one presented here. Are the differences significant or mostly cosmetic and author preference? How should secondary students react to these different avenues to arrive at the same destination? Why?
2. Can the quadratic formula be introduced to students prior to the traditional algebra class? Defend your position.

What does the discriminant $b^2 - 4ac$ tell about the function? There are three possible cases:

Case 1. $b^2 - 4ac = 0$ has one $x$-intercept and its relative minimum or maximum is tangent to the $x$-axis.
Case 2. $b^2 - 4ac < 0$. The function has no $x$-intercept (no roots in the real plane).
Case 3. $b^2 - 4ac > 0$. This gives two distinct $x$-intercepts.

One might wonder why with graphing calculators or software available the derivation is even considered. After all, once derived, the only thing the quadratic formula is used for is to solve quadratics for roots. It is faster and a lot easier to avoid the quadratic formula, just graph the function, and look at it. That makes it very easy to see if there are 2, 1, or 0 roots in most instances. If numerical values are desired, zoom in on the location(s) where the curve crosses the $x$-axis. The precision of the response can be determined more accurately and rapidly than by hand. If the precision of the value is in question, substitute it into the original expression and check it. Alter it as needed to achieve the desired level of accuracy. Or, if more precision is needed, use the symbolic manipulation capabilities available in technology to solve the equation.

The answer to why with graphing calculators or software available the derivation of the quadratic formula is even considered is not that simple. There are tremendous advantages in being able to maneuver algebraic situations while deriving it. This is particularly true as more advanced mathematics is encountered. So the derivation becomes a good mental gymnastics exercise for the future. In addition, problems written in most books do not tap the capabilities of technology. For the most part, the answers are integers. That means that technology makes very easy work of finding most text solutions. If the problems are not overly complex, permitting technology radically simplifies the demands on the student. Once again, the emphasis has become one of getting the answer to the problem. There is a need for insertion of situations that demand thought on the part of the student. Students must be pushed beyond answers only, and into the mentality of analysis and reflective thought characteristics. That is why derivation of the quadratic formula becomes valuable.

You, as a teacher, must constantly be learning, reading, and working with mathematics and the tools of your chosen profession. You need to know the capabilities, advantages, and disadvantages of technology and when it is, and is not, appropriate to apply.

One of the easiest ways to ensure learning of concepts, and not "plug and chug" without understanding, is to "backward engineer" your problems. Looking at the vertex of a parabola, we know its coordinates are expressed by

$$\left(\frac{-b}{2a}, f\left(\frac{-b}{2a}\right)\right)$$

The axis of symmetry is the line $x = \frac{-b}{2a}$; remember a parabola has symmetry about the axis, where if $a > 0$ the parabola opens up and if $a < 0$ the parabola opens down. This gives us either the minimum value or maximum value, with $a > 0$ and $a < 0$, respectfully. Using rationals or primes for your $a$ and $b$ in the function most often is sufficient to evaluate

the learning curve of the students, when asking for exact values.

## TRY THIS IN YOUR CLASSROOM

*NCTM Standards 2000:* Problem solving, communication, reasoning, connections, algebra, functions, and trigonometry

Astronomers define black holes as regions in space where the force of gravity is so great that even light cannot escape the environment. In mathematics, some situations consistently collapse into a given number, creating a mathematical "black hole."

On the calculator:

Enter a whole number
Multiply by 2
Add 4
Divide by 2
Subtract the original number

What is your answer?

Repeat the process above using a different whole number. What is your answer?

Repeat the process with a fraction. What is your answer?

Repeat the answer using a decimal. What is your answer?

You have been dealing with a mathematical "black hole." Prove why you have been getting the same answer.

Create a mathematical "black hole" that will always yield 7. Give the algebraic steps to verify that any real number will result in 7 for the mathematical "black hole" you created.

Is there another mathematical "black hole" that will yield 7 besides the one you created? Explain your response.

Choose any 4 digits without repeating the digits. Subtract the smallest possible number formed by the 4 digits from the largest possible number formed by the 4 digits (for example, choose 2431; the smallest possible number formed is 1234 and the greatest is 4321). Repeat the process using the missing addend (answer) from the subtraction problem (note that digits might repeat now). Continue until something unusual happens. Describe what happened.

Take any counting number greater than one, square each digit, add the squares, and repeat the process until something unusual happens. Describe what happens.

---

### EXERCISES 13.5

1. Create a lesson designed to teach a class about a quadratic function (parabola) that is symmetric and opens downward.
2. Using Exercise 1, modify the lesson so the function shows the other two possible cases of roots. Do you think this is too much to cover in one day? Why or why not?

Select a counting number. Take the square root of the selected number and then take the square root of that answer. Now take the square root of the new answer, repeating the process until something unusual happens. Describe what happens.

Repeat the above process by taking the cube of each digit. Describe what happens.

Change your calculator to the degree mode. Find the sine of 57°. Now take the sine of the new answer, repeating the process until something unusual happens. Describe what happens.

What happens with the cosine and tangent when the repetitive procedure is applied to them?

What happens with sine, cosine, and tangent when the repetitive process is applied to them and the angle is expressed in terms of radians?

## CONCLUSION

This has been a brief glimpse into pre-calculus. Review is a part of the composition of the course. The difficult associated question focuses on what should be reviewed and to what extent. Extensions of familiar topics are necessary. Decisions about what to extend and how are not easy. There is a temptation to deal specifically with background skills that are needed in the study of calculus. Pre-calculus must go beyond that. Students need a breadth of background exposures from which to draw. It is your responsibility to open avenues of exploration for them. Areas of investigation should not be limited to preparing for specifics needed in the next course.

### STICKY QUESTIONS

1. The section "Pre-Calculus Content" contains a list of topics typically found in a pre-calculus course. Some of the listed topics were elaborated on as a part of this text. Most were not. Select one topic not discussed in this text and develop an argument for its inclusion.

2. The section "Pre-Calculus Content" contains a list of topics typically found in this course. Provide at least three areas of extension for two different items on the list.

3. The section "Pre-Calculus Content" contains a list of topics typically found in this course. Adopt a position for agreeing with the list provided or one for expecting the inclusion of additional topics. If you agree with the list, describe why you believe a course comprised of those elements would provide a student adequate background for studying calculus. If you feel items are missing from the list, provide a description of what needs to be added and why it should be included.

### PROBLEM-SOLVING CHALLENGES

1. What would be the units digit of $3^{9999}$?

**Check out the website for the solution.**

2. There is a hill that is two miles from the base to the top on the north side and one mile from the top to the bottom on the south side. Jack has an old car that can only go up the hill at an average speed of 40 miles per hour, but he can race down the hill as fast as he desires. What will Jack's average speed have to be going down the south side of the hill to average 60 miles per hour over the entire hill?

**Check out the website for the solution.**

# ■
# **LEARNING ACTIVITIES**

## **Border Target**

Mark the length of an altitude of an equilateral triangle on the two sides that form the vertex of the altitude. Join the two newly formed points with a segment as shown in Fig. 13.9.

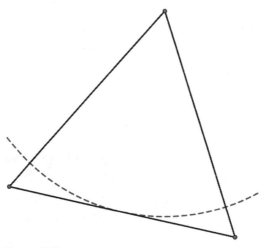

**Figure 13.9**

Repeat this procedure for the remaining two sides, producing a triangle similar to the one shown in Fig. 13.10.

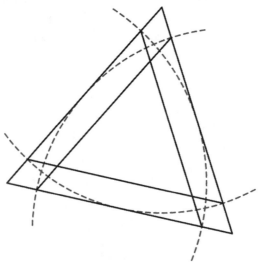

**Figure 13.10**

## Your Turn

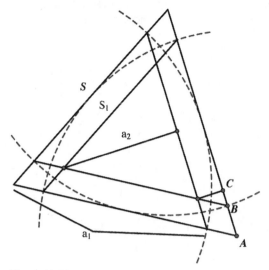

**Figure 13.11**

1. Consider the region between the two triangles as the border as shown in Fig. 13.11. Compute the area of the border.
2. Dilate the figure and determine the impact on the change in the border area.

   Suppose this triangle is divided into a number of congruent equilateral triangles and those little equilateral triangles are numbered 1 through $n$. Using a random number generator to select a region inside the triangle, what is the probability that the selected little triangle will be inside the border? If a partial triangle is selected, and if the majority of its area is within the border, it would be counted as being on the border. Compute the probability that the selected little triangle will be inside the border.

   If the length of one side of the exterior triangle is $s$, then the length of one side of the interior triangle is $\left(\frac{3\sqrt{3}}{2} - 2\right)s$. Both are equilateral triangles. The area of the exterior triangle is $A_o = \frac{\sqrt{3}}{4}s^2$ and the area of the interior triangle is $A_i = \left(\frac{43\sqrt{3} - 72}{16}\right)s^2$. The probability of hitting the shaded area between the triangles is $\frac{A_o - A_i}{A_o} \approx 0.64$.

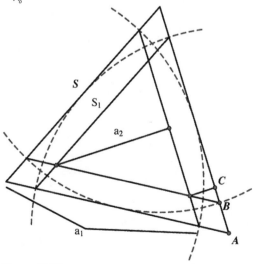

**Figure 13.12**

In Fig. 13.12, let $x$ be the length of segment $AB$. Segment $BC$ is $\frac{x}{2}$ since it is half of the side length of another triangle congruent to the one at the bottom right tip of the greatest triangle. Thus, the length of the side of the interior triangle is $s - 3x$.

$$a_1 = s - x \text{ and } a_1 = \frac{\sqrt{3}s}{2} \Rightarrow x = s - \frac{\sqrt{3}s}{2} \text{ or } s\left(\frac{2-\sqrt{3}}{2}\right)$$

$$A_o = \left(\frac{s}{2}\right)a_1 = \left(\frac{s}{2}\right)\left(\frac{\sqrt{3}s}{2}\right) = \frac{\sqrt{3}s^2}{4}$$

$$s' = s - 3x = s - 3\left(s\left(\frac{2-\sqrt{3}}{2}\right)\right) = s\left(1 - 3 + \frac{3\sqrt{3}}{2}\right) = \left(\frac{3\sqrt{3}}{2} - 2\right)s$$

$$a_2 = \left(\frac{\sqrt{3}}{2}\right)s' = \left(\frac{\sqrt{3}}{2}\right)\left(\frac{3\sqrt{3}}{2} - 2\right)s$$

$$A_i = \left(\frac{1}{2}\right)s'a_2$$

$$= \left(\frac{1}{2}\right)\left(\frac{3\sqrt{3}}{2} - 2\right)(s)\left(\frac{\sqrt{3}}{2}\right)\left(\frac{3\sqrt{3}}{2} - 2\right)(s)$$

$$= \left(\frac{3\sqrt{3}}{4} - 1\right)\left(\frac{9}{4} - \sqrt{3}\right)s^2$$

$$= \left(\frac{3\sqrt{3} - 4}{4}\right)\left(\frac{9 - 4\sqrt{3}}{4}\right)s^2$$

$$= \left(\frac{43\sqrt{3} - 72}{16}\right)s^2$$

## Your Turn

3. What does this last statement prove?

# Calculus

**14**

Beginning with a conference at Tulane University in January, 1986, there developed in the mathematics community a sense that calculus was not being taught in a way befitting a subject that was at once the culmination of the secondary mathematics curriculum and the gateway to collegiate science and mathematics. (Roberts, 1993, p. vii)

The sad truth is that calculus is not a realization of the secondary-school preparation and an exciting beginning to future mathematical study. Instead, calculus continues to serve as an exit from the study of mathematics and related subject areas for many students.

Much of the difficulty had to do with the delivery system: classes that were too large, senior faculty who had largely deserted the course, and teaching assistants whose time and interest were focused on their own graduate work. Other difficulties came from well intentioned efforts to pack into the course all the topics demanded by the increasing number of disciplines requiring calculus of their students. It was acknowledged, however, that if the course had indeed become a blur for students, it just might be because those choosing the topics to be presented and the methods for presenting them had not kept their goals in focus.

It was to these latter concerns that we responded in designing our project. We agreed that there ought to be an opportunity for students to discover instead of always being told. We agreed that the availability of calculators and computers

not only called for exercises that would not be rendered trivial by such technology, but would in fact direct attention more to ideas than to techniques. It seemed to us that there should be explanations of applications of calculus that were self-contained, and both accessible and relevant to students. We were persuaded that calculus students should, like students in any other college course, have some assignments that called for library work, some pondering, some imagination, and above all, a clearly reasoned and written conclusion. Finally, we came to believe that there should be available to students some collateral readings that would set calculus in an intellectual context. (Roberts, 1993, p. vii)

The preceding quotes were selected for two reasons. They describe the thinking of many individuals involved with the teaching of calculus in secondary, community college, college, and university environments. More important, those statements summarize the approach we have taken throughout this text. Technology is an integral part of our world and should be incorporated into our learning and teaching. Students cannot continue to be passive but must become actively involved in their learning. We cannot expect students to sit and listen as we tell them what they need to know. These individuals have to be convinced of the need to reflect on the mathematical world in which they are being nurtured. They have to see the value of pondering questions, applying their creative skills to topics, and determining where these subjects appear in the real world. Knowing or being aware of such things is wonderful, but it also carries with it the responsibility of being able to tell others what is known, learned, discovered, or created. Thus, the need for communication skills, both written and oral, is present not only in calculus, but throughout the mathematics curriculum.

The Mathematical Association of America (MAA) Resources for Calculus Collection, source of the earlier quotes in this chapter, was developed through a consortium of liberal arts colleges. One of the underlying premises to this work relates to the preparation of secondary teachers of mathematics. The writers developed the Calculus Collection from the vantage point that most secondary teachers seek the opportunity to teach calculus, much like graduate faculty members crave the opportunity to teach an advanced course in their area of specialization.

The MAA Calculus Collection is not the only work in this arena. The UC Davis Calculus Revitalization Project provides a similar description for the teaching of calculus.

> By the Fall of 1997, we hope to be enthusiastically teaching a Calculus sequence that builds students' understanding of the theory and application of the subject while incorporating the use of technology in a thoughtful way? . . . In our Revitalized Calculus Sequence, there is enough time for instructors to share their excitement about mathematics and to pursue digressions into such things as aspects of the field that are interesting to them, historical insights, alternative interpretations, different representations or sharing personal insights. (Hom & Silva, 1994, pp. i–ii)

The UC Davis and MAA works are indicative of some of the movements that have occurred in recent years in calculus. They are accompanied by work from groups across the country at locations like Harvard, the University of Michigan, and Duke. Mathematics departments were surveyed in the spring of 1994 by the MAA. Of the 1,048 schools responding, 22% reported major reform efforts taking place and another 46% indicated they were involved in moderate revision attempts. The data gathered from the survey indicate that about 150,000 students (about 32%) taking calculus during the spring 1994 semester were in reform-based classes (Tucker & Leitzel, 1995).

A major result of the study was that what was being taught in the calculus class has not changed much, but how it is taught has. A basic theme of the reform movement has been that students should have a stronger conceptual understanding of the subject. This comprehension is to be developed through interpretations based on numerical, graphic, algebraic, and modeling work. The reported changes include open-ended use of technology, writing, applications, cooperative groups, and projects.

The results of the new efforts are positive. Retention and passing rates are going up. Major re-

form themes like changes in the mode of instruction and use of technology are appearing in courses that precede and follow calculus. Enrollment in post-calculus courses appears to be increasing. Positive images of the study of mathematics are being generated by the extensive use of technology.

The reform calculus movement has generated some concerns. Faculty concerns have focused on time for preparation, assessing student projects, meeting with students, and dealing with technology. At the same time, the invested time results in faculty growth and professionalism. Faculty discussions have focused on teaching and learning how to teach as well as mathematics. These exchanges are resulting in an increase in research about how students learn mathematics. These beginnings are generating calls for more investigations into traditional and reform calculus teaching and learning. The appearance is that conversion to reform calculus is inevitable.

Much of the outline and basic ideas contained in this chapter are attributable to Dr. Joby Milo Anthony, associate professor of mathematics at the University of Central Florida. It is taken from personal discussions as well as a set of tapes he developed to accompany a calculus class.

## WHAT WE TEACH

Calculus is broken into three basic components: derivatives, integrals, and infinite series. The application of limits is a significant part of the study of calculus. Many times the idea of limits becomes obscure as the emphasis shifts to specific ideas or formulas. That is one reason why the study of limits is so important as foundation information.

Calculus grew out of Descartes's and Fermat's work with analytic geometry. They were the first to solve algebraic equations using geometry. They also developed geometric proofs involving algebra. This foundation spread to England and Germany where Newton and Leibniz, working separately yet almost simultaneously, developed most of the calculus we know today. By 1672, Leibniz (http://www-history.mcs.st-and.ac.uk/Mathematicians/Leibniz.html) had invented a calculating machine that added, subtracted, multiplied, and divided. Leibniz produced what we know as the fundamental theorem of calculus and many other theorems of calculus. He published his work in 1677, 11 years after Newton (http://www-history.mcs.st-and.ac.uk/Mathematicians/Newton.html) had developed many of his unpublished works on the subject. Newton often published information long after he had composed it. Who created calculus? Both of them. Leibniz was famous for logic. He created the elongated "S" that is our integral sign as a means of expressing the sum of a lot of related values.

Newton is credited with revealing secrets of motion and gravity. While contemplating motion, Newton created what we now think of as differential calculus. In his initial work, he visualized a curve as being generated by a moving point. He called those points "fluents," meaning "changing quantities." Newton looked at rates of change that we call derivatives. He was looking for a way to determine the equation of a line tangent to a point on a graph.

## EXERCISES 14.1

1. Summarize the situations in the lives of Newton and Leibniz that impacted their association with each other.
2. Find two historical texts on mathematics by different authors. Who is credited with the discovery of calculus in each text?

## TECHNOLOGY

Calculus, as a subject area, has not changed much in the past 200 years. The way we can teach calculus has changed recently. We are no longer bound to boards or overheads to graph a function. Calculators, computers, tablets including the iPad, Galaxy Tab, and Motorola Xoom and xyboard, internet applications such as WolframAlpha (http://www.wolframalpha.com), and dynamic software give us the power to visualize calculus graphically and to solve formulas symbolically. Casio and Texas Instruments all offer graphing calculators, many of which can take derivatives and do integration. Some graphing calculators incorporate a symbolic manipulator/function plotter and are capable of extensive and complex computations, much like that of many computer applications. WolframAlpha brings the power of graphing and symbolic manipulation to anyone with an Internet connection for free. You can also utilize the handheld WolframAlpha app on many devices for as little as $0.99. These technological devices can be used as stand-alone material or in conjunction with a specific textbook. There are several software programs that have be-

come a viable tool to solve the most complex calculus problems and much more. Where does all this technology leave the teaching of a calculus class? If we teach with the use of technology, do we alter our assessment methods of the students? How much do we teach, where does the technology fit in, and how much do we let students learn by discovery? Can we maintain situations at a level where all students have equal access to appropriate technology? If a student is not capable of acquiring the necessary technology for calculus, is that student eliminated from the opportunity to take the class? How much time will be needed to address the use of technology so students go beyond the basics and are able to use it as a learning tool? How much technological background should we expect from students? These are not easy questions to answer. Students must have an understanding of prerequisite concepts and theory as they begin the study of calculus. Will the benefits gained by using technology outweigh time that must be spent to help students become functional with it? High school graduates will be expected to be able to use technological approaches in many college courses and, ultimately, in the workplace. It becomes our responsibility to demand technological capabilities of them.

## EXERCISES 14.2

1. Describe how technology has been used as a part of your learning calculus. List strengths and weaknesses of your learning process in calculus. What would you suggest to make the course better through the use of technology?
2. Define your position on the use of technology in the calculus class at the secondary level. Advanced Placement (AP) exams are now written assuming technology is available for the student. How much emphasis should technology receive in the learning of calculus?

**Additional exercises can be found on the website.**

Technology, although a wonderful asset, does have its limitations. Many computations incorporate rounding automatically. Topics like fixing decimal points in a calculator, rounding, approximations, impact of range changes on graphs, and others have been discussed throughout this text. As you approach the study of calculus, it is important that your students be aware of the difference between two items being equal and two items being approximately equal. If they are of the opinion that a technologically based answer is exact, they might have some difficulties in calculus.

Calculus is a study of motion. There is a need for students to learn to visualize ideas as they investigate. We talk about the derivative being the slope of the tangent (if it exists) to a curve. The formulas for evaluating derivatives are really formulas for evaluating the limit without looking at the limit. In the process of developing the idea, we pick a second point close to the first on the curve. A secant line is drawn between the points. Then the second point is slowly moved toward the first. As that point moves, a new secant is created. As the distance between the two points decreases, or approaches the limit, the secant line becomes the tangent line. We depict this secant line through a series of presentations shown in Figs. 14.1 and 14.2. We can describe this to a class and even model it by drawing a curve, selecting two points, and then using a straightedge to show the new point and the secant it creates. Eventually the straightedge is representing the tangent,

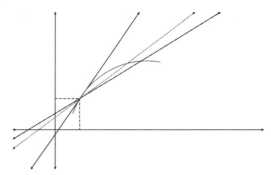

**Figure 14.3**

as shown in Fig. 14.3. This process could also be modeled by paper folding, much as is done to show the parabola as the locus of points equidistant from a point and a line.

<hr>

## EXERCISE 14.3

1. Draw a curve on a sheet of paper. Select two points on it. Let one point be fixed and let the other "move" along the curve toward the fixed one. Fold the paper several times between the fixed and moving points to depict the secant line approaching the tangent line.

**Additional exercises can be found on the website.**

Technology can be used to create an animation of the secant line getting closer to the tangent line. In Fig. 14.4, point P would move along the curve. As it moves, it can be seen to be getting closer and closer to the tangent line. You might elect to let the point animate bidirectionally to show how the motion of the point influences whether the secant line

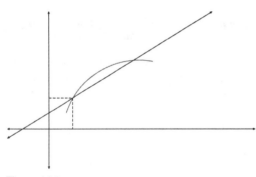

**Figure 14.1**

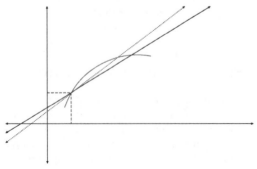

**Figure 14.2**

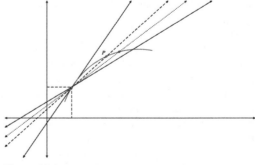

**Figure 14.4**

approaches or goes away from becoming the tangent line. The important thing to remember is that technology permits the viewing of this motion. The impact is much more powerful than anything you can do by hand, with transparencies, and so forth, and you can change the setup as necessary to meet the needs of your class.

### EXERCISE 14.4

1. Use software to create an animated representation of Fig. 14.4. Describe the benefits of your creation as contrasted with pictures like in Figs. 14.3 and 14.4.

The concept of approaching a limit is crucial to finding this tangent to a point on a curve. You let the point of the secant line move toward the point of tangency. Watch the secant line rotate. The moving point approaches the point of tangency. As it does, the secant line approaches the tangent line.

How can that rotating secant line be used to help find the tangent line? The tangent is known. We know a line cannot be determined by one point. What else can we find? Two points on the secant line, $x_0$ and $x$, are known. Those two points generate two function values or points on the $y$-axis, $f(x_0)$ and $f(x)$. The coordinates of two points on the secant line are known and can be used to find the equation of the line. The coordinates of the points on the secant curve will be $(x_0, f(x_0))$ and $(x, f(x))$. The rise becomes $f(x) - f(x_0)$ and the run is $x - x_0$. With this, the slope of the secant line can be computed (see Fig. 14.5). As $x$ goes to $x_0$ and as the secant line rotates to a limiting position of the tangent line, the slope of the secant line approaches slope of tangent line.

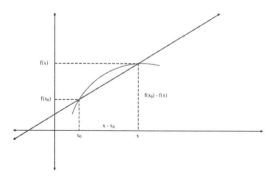

**Figure 14.5**

That information can be used to determine the equation of the tangent line. The limit of the slope of the secant line as the secant line approaches the tangent line is the slope of the tangent line. In other words, the slope is the limit as $x$ goes to $x_0$ in the rise over run formula or

$$\lim_{x \to x_0} \frac{f(x) - f(x_0)}{x - x_0}$$

Two things are now known about the tangent line: a point on it and its slope. With that, the equation is determined.

Notational changes are made with limits, as much for convenience as anything, when working in calculus. The $x_0$ becomes $x$ and the distance $x - x_0$, or run, in Fig. 14.5 becomes $h$ in Fig. 14.6. The slope of the secant is expressed as $\frac{f(x+h) - f(x)}{h}$.

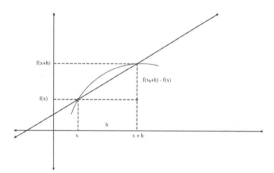

**Figure 14.6**

The slope of the tangent is the limit as $h$ goes to 0. These changes, as shown in Fig. 14.6, have no impact on the idea of the point moving along the curve. Either system could be used for computing the slope of the tangent line:

$$\lim_{x \to x_0} \frac{f(x) - f(x_0)}{x - x_0} \text{ becomes } \lim_{h \to 0} \frac{f(x+h) - f(x)}{h}$$

Looking at Fig. 14.6 gives a clue to a potential source of difficulty for some students. The coordinates of the point $((x + h), f(x + h))$ are used to compute the slope of the secant line. The coordinates are not written with the point but, rather, are written at their respective locations on the $x$- and $y$-axes. This becomes "intuitively obvious" at some point in time, but a brief comment at the time of development of these ideas might eliminate obstacles for some students.

## EXERCISE 14.5

1. Prepare a lesson plan designed to have students learn how the secant line approaches the tangent line.

## DERIVATIVE

The slope of the tangent line was gleaned from the limit of the slope of the secant line. The slope of the tangent line is important in its own right. Many times it has more significance. If we focus on the slope of the tangent line itself, the calculus language for that idea calls it the derivative. The derivative of a function at a point in its domain is geometrically the slope of the tangent line at that point. It is the limit of $\frac{f(x+h)-f(x)}{h}$ as $h$ goes to zero.

There are two standard notational systems to show the derivative. One uses $f'(x)$ to indicate the derivative of $f(x)$. The other is $\frac{dy}{dx}$.

The notational system selection is influenced by what is being solved as well as how the results are to be communicated. It is important at the beginning that students not think of $\frac{dy}{dx}$ as a ratio. They should think of it as a point on a graph. Later, they will learn of a way to think of $\frac{dy}{dx}$ as a ratio. Computing the slope of the secant line as $h$ goes to zero allows us to write an equation of the tangent line. The value of the derivative is influenced by how the two axes are identified.

Think in terms of an object moving in a straight line. We can graph its motion by identifying the horizontal axis as time measured from some fixed reference time. The vertical axis would be described as the distance related to some fixed reference. Motion then becomes a function where the time and direction are understood to have the defined meaning. The slope of the secant through two points on that graph will have physical meaning because it becomes the average velocity. The slope of the tangent line is not an average velocity; it is an instantaneous velocity. If you are driving in a straight line and look at the speedometer, that number is an approximation of the instantaneous velocity. It is like finding the derivative of a distance function. Realize that the derivative is an instantaneous rate of change. It represents the instantaneous rate at which the vertical variable is changing in relation to the horizontal one. If the horizontal is time and the vertical is distance, you have instantaneous velocity. If you have

time as the horizontal variable and a chemical as the vertical one, and the graph represents unused chemicals, the derivative or instantaneous reading is the rate of change of chemical to time.

Consider $\frac{1}{\sqrt{x}}$ and the point $(1,1)$. If you were looking at the original work Liebniz did, his notation would look like

$$\lim_{x \to x_0} \frac{f(x)-f(x_0)}{x-x_0} \text{ becomes } \lim_{h \to 0} \frac{f(x+h)-f(x)}{h}$$

That notation is necessary because the $\frac{dy}{dx}$ notation has no way of showing where the derivative is being taken. Using the limit notation the situation would be described as $\lim_{h \to 0} \frac{\frac{1}{\sqrt{1+h}}-\frac{1}{\sqrt{1}}}{h}$.

The question now becomes, what is this limit? There is a need for some algebra skills at this point. This can be another potential danger spot for some students who are algebraically not as strong as they should be. This can be dealt with through technology, but it also raises a question. In terms of readiness for the study of calculus, is there a minimal algebra skill level, or should we let technology resolve the dilemma? You need to proceed carefully to assure none of the students get lost, even though the algebra here is relatively simple for a student with adequate readiness. Finding the LCD in the numerator gives

$$\lim_{h \to 0} \frac{1-\sqrt{1+h}}{h\sqrt{1+h}}$$

At this point, a procedure similar to that used earlier with limits could work, but that is slow. It is more convenient to develop a set of formulas. Again, calculus is essentially a set of formulas that describes what happens as limits are taken. Fortunately, most of the functions we deal with have nice formulas for evaluating limits and for finding the rule for the derivative.

The task now becomes one of determining a formula for $\lim_{h \to 0} \frac{1-\sqrt{1+h}}{h\sqrt{1+h}}$.

Algebraic intuition here may not be overly obvious to some students. Rationalize the *numerator*:

$$\lim_{h \to 0} \frac{1-\sqrt{1+h}}{h\sqrt{1+h}} \left( \frac{1+\sqrt{1+h}}{1+\sqrt{1+h}} \right)$$

$$= \lim_{h \to 0} \frac{1^2 - \left(\sqrt{1+h}\right)^2}{h\left(\sqrt{1+h}\right)\left(1+\sqrt{1+h}\right)}$$

$$= \lim_{h \to 0} \frac{1-1-h}{h\left(\sqrt{1+h}\right)\left(1+\sqrt{1+h}\right)}$$

$$= \lim_{h \to 0} \frac{-h}{h\left(\sqrt{1+h}\right)\left(1+\sqrt{1+h}\right)}$$

$$= \lim_{h \to 0} \frac{-1}{1\left(\sqrt{1+h}\right)\left(1+\sqrt{1+h}\right)}$$

As $h \to 0$, $\sqrt{1+h} \to 1$ and $1+\sqrt{1+h} \to 2$ so,

$$\lim_{h \to 0} \frac{-1}{1\left(\sqrt{1+h}\right)\left(1+\sqrt{1+h}\right)} = -\frac{1}{2}$$

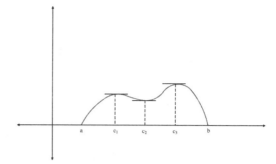

**Figure 14.7**

This is the derivative of $f\left(\frac{1}{2}\right)$ at the point when $x$ is 1. The potential for algebraic problems should not be too great if the students have the appropriate readiness skills, but caution and considerations should be exercised.

## ROLLE'S THEOREM

Every mathematical theorem is a statement that if one thing is true, then something else is true. It is often difficult for students to determine what part of the statement is the hypothesis and what part is the conclusion. They want to accept it all and continue. Mathematics tries to establish the truth of a relation between the hypothesis and conclusion, not the hypothesis or the conclusion. In Rolle's theorem, the hypothesis deals with a continuous function over some closed interval $[a, b]$. In the open interval $(a, b)$, there is a derivative at each point; $f(a) = 0$ and $f(b) = 0$. This is the hypothesis for Rolle's theorem. The conclusion of Rolle's theorem says there must be at least one horizontal tangent line somewhere in the open interval. Another way of saying this would be, "If we have a function whose graph crosses the $x$-axis at $a$ and $b$ respectively, and if the function is continuous on $[a, b]$ and differentiable on $(a, b)$, then there is some number $c$ between $a$ and $b$ such that $f(c) = 0$." The differences between the two statements of the theorem are slight, but it is important that you be able to express things in more than one way. (Recall the ideas from Chapter 6, relating to doing the same problem more than one way? Here is an application of that skill.) If a student does not seem to grasp one statement, the alternative expression might provide the necessary clarification.

The preceding statement of Rolle's theorem is shown geometrically in Fig. 14.7. Tangent segments are used to represent the tangent lines at each of points $c_1$, $c_2$, and $c_3$. The theorem does not stipulate how many points exist where the derivative is

zero; it only says there is at least one. Figure 14.8 provides another opportunity to demonstrate dynamically that there are horizontal lines at points $c_1$, $c_2$, and $c_3$. This would be done in a manner similar to that shown in Fig. 14.4.

**Additional exercises can be found on the website.**

## MEAN VALUE THEOREM FOR DERIVATIVES

The mean value theorem for derivatives is a generalization of Rolle's theorem, or Rolle's theorem is a special case of the mean value theorem for derivatives. The hypothesis for the mean value theorem for derivatives is almost the same as that for Rolle's theorem. The mean value theorem for derivatives does not require that the function has values of zero at its endpoints (see Fig. 14.8).

The mean value theorem for derivatives would be expected to say something about derivatives between $a$ and $b$. We look at the segment joining endpoints $(a, f(a))$ and $(b, f(b))$. The mean value theorem for derivatives says that somewhere there has to be a tangent line parallel to the secant line joining those endpoints. If you have a function that is continuous on the closed interval $[a, b]$ and differentiable on $(a, b)$, there has to be a tangent line

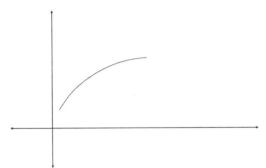

**Figure 14.8**

That means $f'(c) = \frac{f(b) - f(a)}{b - a}$. Often the equation is rewritten by multiplying both sides by $b - a$, giving $(b - a)f'(c) = f(b) - f(a)$. We know this point $c$ exists by the mean value theorem for derivatives, but we do no not know where. The mean value theorem for derivatives does not guarantee this will

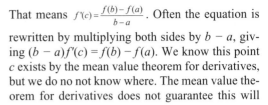

that is parallel to the secant line. That means the slope of the tangent line at some point equals the slope of the secant line. Figure 14.9 is a geometric interpretation of this discussion of the mean value theorem for derivatives.

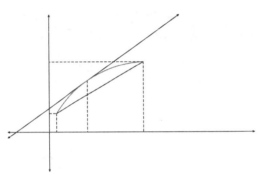

**Figure 14.10**

hold; it will hold only if we have certain kinds of functions.

One of the difficult things for students to grasp is the possibility that hypotheses of the theorem are not true. If they are not true, anything can happen. Students need to realize this. The mean value theorem for derivatives hypothesis fails for Fig. 14.10. The hypothesis is false and so is the conclusion. This thinking requires careful explanation to students. Figure 14.11 has one point of discontinuity, but it is possible to establish parallels to segment $ab$. Here, the hypothesis is false but the conclusion is true. We need to be careful to explain that the theorem is a study of the relation between the hypothesis and the conclusion. That is all the theorem establishes, and students need to know this and be fully aware of its impact.

**Figure 14.9**

As before, there is a desire to describe the geometric information in Fig. 14.9 analytically. The rise is expressed by $f(b) - f(a)$, and $b - a$ is the run. If the secant is parallel to the tangent line at some point $c$, the slope of the tangent line at $c$ is $f'(c)$.

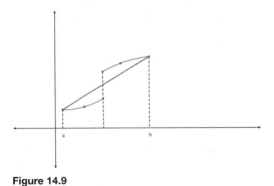

**Figure 14.9**

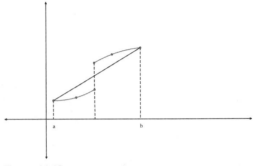

**Figure 14.11**

# AREA UNDER CURVES

Riemann (http://www-history.mcs.st-and.ac.uk/Mathematicians/Riemann.html) was shy and his health was not good. He had an unquenchable thirst for knowledge, earning a doctorate in mathematics at the age of 24. Gauss was his advisor. Gauss was not easily impressed, but Riemann managed to do it. Riemann studied geometry, functions of complex variables, and areas under a curve. He used the Greeks' exhaustive method of using several thin rectangles to approach the area under curves. Today we call that process "Riemann sums."

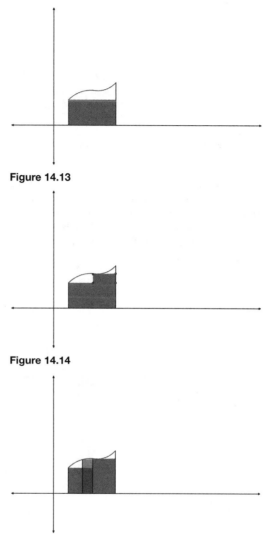

**Figure 14.13**

**Figure 14.14**

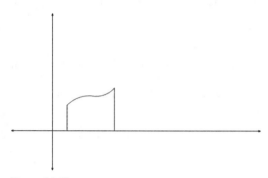

**Figure 14.12**

As the discussion shifts to area, we consider a particular kind of area where there is a nonnegative function over some interval on the $x$-axis, as shown in Fig. 14.12. We can approximate the area by using a rectangle, as shown in Fig. 14.13. We can get a better approximation to the area by subdividing the interval on the $x$-axis, as shown in Fig. 14.14, and even closer with Fig. 14.15. When subdividing, the width of the rectangle is controlled; eventually that width approaches a limit of zero. The height of each rectangle is the value of the function over the subinterval at the respective point. There are other ways to find the area under a curve, but this one is easy to see, potentially giving it special appeal to you as a teacher of mathematics. It is crucial that the students have a visual image of the issues you discuss. The limiting value of the approximations is the area we are seeking.

Any time an idea is encountered for the first time, it is beneficial to work through a specific example. The process amplifies understanding. Consider finding the area under the curve $x^2$ between 0 and 1. The approximation procedure would be to subdivide the interval between 0 and 1 in half; 0 to $\frac{1}{2}$ and $\frac{1}{2}$ to 1. Each subinterval has a width of $\frac{1}{2}$.

**Figure 14.15**

The left one has a height of 0, so its area is 0. The right subinterval has a height of $\left(\frac{1}{2}\right)^2$ and a base width of $\frac{1}{2}$. $A_1$, which is the first approximation of the area, is $\left(\frac{1}{2}\right)(0)+\left(\frac{1}{2}\right)\left(\frac{1}{2}\right)^2$, as shown in Fig. 14.16. This approximation is not too good. Factor out $\frac{1}{2^3}$ and write $A_1$ as $\frac{1}{2^3}(1)^2$. This may appear to be a strange way to write this product, but it is convenient in the long run. We are going to be looking for a pattern and $\frac{1}{8}$ is not serviceable for that objective. This may be difficult for some students to perceive. They have been "trained" to write fractions like this as $\frac{1}{8}$, not $\frac{1}{2^3}$.

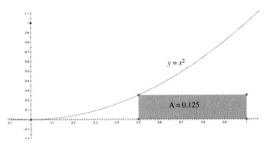

**Figure 14.16**

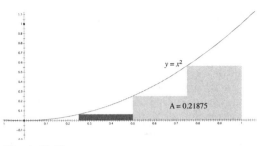

**Figure 14.18**

A few more approximations will make the decision more obvious for most students. Figure 14.17 shows the base subdivided into thirds, getting the approximation closer. Figure 14.18 subdivides the base into fourths, getting the approximate area even closer to what it actually is.

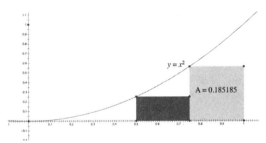

**Figure 14.17**

At this point we have

$$A_1 = \left(\frac{1}{2}\right)(0) + \left(\frac{1}{2}\right)\left(\frac{1}{2}\right)^2$$

$$= \left(\frac{1}{2^3}\right)(1^2)$$

$$A_2 = \left(\frac{1}{3}\right)(0) + \left(\frac{1}{3}\right)\left(\frac{1}{3}\right)^2 + \left(\frac{1}{3}\right)\left(\frac{2}{3}\right)^2$$

$$= \left(\frac{1}{3^3}\right)(1^2 + 2^2)$$

$$A_3 = \left(\frac{1}{4}\right)(0) + \left(\frac{1}{4}\right)\left(\frac{1}{4}\right)^2 + \left(\frac{1}{4}\right)\left(\frac{2}{4}\right)^2 + \left(\frac{1}{4}\right)\left(\frac{3}{4}\right)^2$$

$$= \left(\frac{1}{4^3}\right)(1^2 + 2^2 + 3^2)$$

We could continue in this manner, but precision and exhaustion enter the picture. This pattern should have emerged by now enabling you to proceed to $n$ subdivisions.

$A_n = \left(\dfrac{1}{(n+1)^3}\right)(1^2 + 2^2 + 3^3 + \ldots + n^2)$ gives a formula that works for this situation. This generalizes to $A_n = \left(\dfrac{1}{(n+1)^3}\right)\left(\dfrac{n(n+1)(2n+1)}{6}\right)$.

Logic dictates that as the number of subintervals increases, the width of each subinterval will decrease. The question now becomes, what is the limit of $A_n$ as $n$ approaches infinity? Some more algebra leads to the desired result.

$$\left(\frac{1}{(n+1)^3}\right)\left(\frac{n(n+1)(2n+1)}{6}\right)$$

$$= \left(\frac{1}{(n+1)^2}\right)\left(\frac{n(2n+1)}{6}\right)$$

$$= \left(\frac{2n^2 + n}{6n^2 + 12n + 6}\right)$$

This is close to a form where we can find the limit.

Divide both the numerator and denominator by $n^2$.

$$\frac{\dfrac{2n^2}{n^2} + \dfrac{n}{n^2}}{\dfrac{6n^2}{n^2} + \dfrac{12n}{n^2} + \dfrac{6}{n^2}} = \frac{2 + \dfrac{1}{n}}{6 + \dfrac{12}{n} + \dfrac{6}{n^2}}$$

In this form, as $n$ increases, the limit of approaches zero. The numerator becomes 2 and the denominator becomes 6, and the limit is $\frac{1}{3}$.

This area is not an approximation. It is an area. This is difficult for many students to comprehend. Earlier in the text we discussed the difficulty students have accepting the idea that the repeating decimal 0.999 equals 1. The emotions and quandary students feel are similar in these two situations. The area from Riemann sums is difficult to carry out at times. Patterns are often obscure, and even when they are determined it may be difficult to calculate the limit. Remember, calculation of area is an evaluation of a limit. Formulas are just a more efficient way of doing this. Every time an area is calculated, in actuality, a limit is being evaluated.

## TRY THIS IN YOUR CLASSROOM

*NCTM Standards 2000*: Problem solving, communication, representation, algebra, geometry. Note that we assume you are using a graphing calculator for this activity.

The world of mathematics contains a variety of cumulative knowledge issues where early work provides background for later encounters. The study of envelopes formally appears in the study of differential equations. However, it is possible to investigate them algebraically. An envelope in mathematics is the graph of an equation that contains, or forms a boundary for, the graph of another equation. In a very basic sense, it could be said that $Y = 1$ and $Y = -1$ form an envelope for $Y = \sin X$ as shown in Fig. 14.19.

The graph of the circle $X^2 + Y^2 = 25$ serves as an envelope for $Y1 = \left(\sqrt{-X^2 + 25}\right)\sin X$ and $Y2 = \left(-\sqrt{-X^2 + 25}\right)\sin X$. Resize the graph window to $X$ from $-12.6$ to $12.6$ and $Y$ from $-6.2$ to $6.2$.

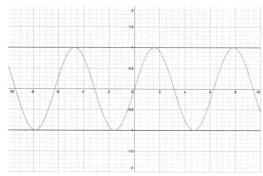

**Figure 14.19**

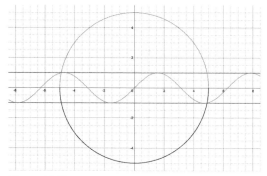

**Figure 14.20**

Graph $X^2 + Y^2 = 25$, $Y1$, and $Y2$ from above. It should look like Fig. 14.20. Describe what you think will happen inside the circle envelope in Fig. 14.20 if $\pm\left(\sqrt{-X + 25}\right)\sin(3X)$ is used rather than $\pm\left(\sqrt{-X + 25}\right)\sin(X)$ for $Y1$ and $Y2$. Graph the envelope using $\pm\left(\sqrt{-X + 25}\right)\sin(3X)$ for $Y3$ and $Y4$. Was your anticipated result correct? Why or why not?

If the circle is moved so the center is at $(2,0)$, maintaining the radius of 5, what is its equation? Solve the equation of the circle for $Y$. Place the positive expression in $Y1$ and the negative expression in $Y2$.

Make $Y3 = Y1(\sin(AX))$ and $Y4 = Y2\,(\sin(AX))$ and graph them. Describe the results.

Use a variety of values for $A$. Write your conclusions about the values $A$ can adopt.

If the circle is moved so the center is at $(0,2)$, maintaining the radius of 5, what would its equation be? Solve for $Y$ calling one part $Y1$ and the other $Y2$. Make $Y3 = Y1\,(\sin(AX))$ and $Y4 = Y2(\sin(AX))$ for some $A$. Describe your results. Explain why you got the results you did.

Describe what you think the following six equations will generate when they are all graphed on the same screen.

$$Y1 = (\cos(10X) + 2)\sin X + X$$
$$Y2 = -((\cos(10X) + 2)\sin X + X)$$
$$Y3 = \sin X + X$$
$$Y4 = -(\sin X + X)$$
$$Y5 = 3\sin X + X$$
$$Y6 = -(3\sin X + X)$$

Enter and graph the six equations above.
Describe your impression of the concept of envelopes.

## CONCLUSION

Calculus is a powerful tool. Many people in secondary mathematics departments crave the opportunity to teach calculus. The assumption is that this is where the best and most interested students are and, in most cases, that is true. A hard fact of life is that unless new teachers are extremely fortunate, the likelihood is great that instead of calculus they will be teaching lower level mathematics courses. There are bright students who, for whatever reason, elect to avoid advanced mathematics classes. Whatever level class you have, teach them well. The foundations for learning are provided in each mathematics class that precedes it. Remember, the best way to teach something is to teach it right the first time. Teaching it right means students learn it, understand it, and have a positive attitude about learning more mathematics.

## STICKY QUESTIONS

1. Assuming a student has successfully mastered Algebra II with trigonometry, should that student be enrolled in a pre-calculus class or a calculus class? Defend the position you take.

2. Different school districts offer different calculus programs: Advanced placement (AP) AB, AP BC, honors calculus, dual-enrollment calculus (with some community college, college, or university), or just calculus. Which program do you feel offers the greatest advantage for students, and why?

3. Should calculus be offered at a secondary school? Why or why not?

4. Assume you adopt the position that calculus should not be taught in the secondary environment. What alternative courses should be made available to students and why? In this discussion, assume the students are mathematically capable and desirous of learning additional mathematically based topics.

5. What is the role of technology in a calculus course? Describe the foundations of your position.

6. Create an ellipse with dynamic software using a procedure different from the one described in the preceding "sticky question." Provide a written description of the steps you followed to create the ellipse.

## PROBLEM-SOLVING CHALLENGES

1. You have three circles of radii 6, 7, and 8 units. Each is tangent to the other two. There is a circle inscribed in the central region created by the three larger circles. This little circle is tangent to the other three as well. What is the radius of this little inscribed circle?

**Check out the website for the solution.**

2. Observe the following 400-digit number:

1234567890123456789012345678901234567890123456789012345678901234567890123456789012345678901234567890123456789012345678901234567890123456789012345678901234567890123456789012345678901234567890123456789012345678901234567890123456789012345678901234567890123456789012345678901234567890123456789012345678901234567890123456789012345678901234567890123456789012345678901234567890123456789012345678901234567890123456789012345678901234567890

First eliminate all digits that are in odd-numbered places, starting at the left-most place. Repeat this process with the remaining 200-digit number. Continue this process until all digits are gone. What was the last number to be eliminated?

**Check out the website for the solution.**

# LEARNING ACTIVITY

## The Volume of a Box

A candy factory has a warehouse full of cardboard that have been cut into rectangular regions that measure 8.5 inches by 11 inches, which is the size of a standard sheet of paper as shown in Fig. 14.21. You have been asked to design a box (a bottom, four sides, and an open top as in Fig. 14.22) that will hold the most candy by removing a same-sized square from each corner of the cardboard (represented by red squares in Fig. 14.21), then folding and gluing or taping the sides. What should the size of the squares be so that the box will have the greatest volume?

Before reading on, think about possible ways to approach and solve the volume of a box problem. You have probably solved this or some other variation of it by:

1. Creating a model with construction paper and beans to approximate the volume of different boxes;
2. Constructing tables involving the values for different box sizes;
3. Sketching the course of the function for the volume as the box size changes;
4. Using formulas to calculate the volume of the boxes by substituting different values or finding the values of $x$ for which the first derivative is zero, and using the second derivative rule to find which values of $x$ are maximal and which are minimal.

Another way to demonstrate, discuss, and explore the volume problem is by using a dynamic geometry program. Some clarifications are important: This is a scale model of the real box, and all measures are approximated in inches for length, square inches for area, and cubic inches for volume based on transformations of the number of pixels given by the program. Notice that some situations are not practical or possible with the real-life model, and how these situations

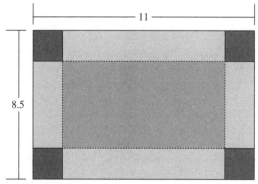

**Figure 14.21**

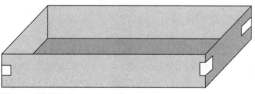

**Figure 14.22**

relate to the dynamic sketch. For example, squares to be cut out with sides close to, equal to, or larger than 4.25 inches are not practical or a possible alternative for making boxes. This could be represented by moving point K in the sketch and noticing that the volume approaches zero very quickly as the size of segment KB gets closer and closer to 4.25 inches (using a piece of cardboard measuring 8.5 by 11 inches). In the dynamic sketch, the size of line segment will roll over back to 4.25 and related calculations, but this is not a realistic alternative, or a proper representation of the live model. Notice that in the sketch the green rectangle representing the base of the box "disappears" as soon as the value of KB goes over 4.25.

## Exercise 1

Starting with an 8.5-by-11-inch rectangle and moving point K, what is the volume for the box if the sides of the squares to be cut from the corners are approximately equal to 1, 1.25, 1.5, 1.75, 2, 2.25, 2.5 2.75, or 3 inches long? Organize this information in a table, and represent it in a graph. What is the approximate maximum volume? Note: Use the information from the table and graph to approximate the maximum volume (maximum point in the graph) in cubic inches. When the graph is used, you should be looking for the extreme point of the graph (the point at which the graph changes from increasing to decreasing or vice versa, as you read the graph from left to right).

## Exercise 2

Starting with an 8.5-by-11-inch rectangle, move point K and observe how the values change. Using this method, what should the size of the squares be so that the box will have the greatest volume? How does this solution compare with your previous approach? Note: One way of solving this problem is by finding the first derivative of the volume formula (height = $a$ or measure of line segment KB, length = $11 - 2a$, and width = $8.5 - 2a$), and setting it to zero, then using the quadratic formula find the possible values of the line segment KB. Instead of substituting these values in the initial volume formula, you can use them within the applet by moving point K and evaluating their possibilities for maximum and minimum volumes. Notice that the second derivative rule could also be used to find which of these values is the maximum or minimum point.

## Exercise 3

Given the same dimensions (8.5 by 11 inches) for the cardboard pieces, the candy factory wants to have the same area of the base of the box (green rectangle GLOI) as the area of two sides of the box. Is this possible? If this were possible, what would be the approximate volume of this box?

## Exercise 4

What would happen if the factory wants the boxes to be in the form of a cube (without the top)? Is this possible with the 8.5-by-11-inch dimensions? If this were not possible, what would happen with other dimensions like 8.5 by 8.5 inches, 8.5 by 14 inches (legal-size paper) or 9 by 12 inches (construction paper)? Note: You should be looking for the extreme point of the graph (the point at which the graph changes from increasing to decreasing or vice versa, as you read the graph from left to right).

## Exercise 5

Assuming that you need a rectangular box with a square base, find the measures for line segments KB and LO such that the volume is 32 cubic inches and the amount of material needed to construct the box is minimal. Once you find the appropriate measures for the line segments, what is the amount of material needed (after cutting the squares from the corners)? Hint: Make the measures for line segments AB and AD the same length. In order to keep the length of these line segments the same, move point A in an out to change the dimensions of the rectangle, and point K to change the dimensions of the square to be cut from the corners.

*This activity was written by Dr. Enrique Ortiz, who is a mathematics education faculty member at the University of Central Florida, and his son, Enrique G., who, at the time of the writing, is an engineering student at the University of Central Florida.*

# Probability and Statistics

**15**

Probability and statistics are coming! Actually, they are already here. Selected topics have been incorporated and mandated into many state frameworks and mathematics curricula. The study of probability and statistics has been around for a long time. An important statistical test (*t* test) was developed by William Gossett of the Guinness Brewery at the turn of the century to keep hops and barley in the best condition. At the same time, John Dewey was using a "scientific method" that utilized no statistical processes. His well-accepted educational philosophies that were tested in his laboratory school were the result of a sample size of 10 nonrandomly chosen students. His scientific method used 80 years ago would not be accepted as valid research practices in master's or doctoral programs today. Maybe that says statistics is new. Statistics has received little to no emphasis in the secondary curriculum until relatively recently. That is changing, as evidenced by the number of texts that now include statistics and probability topics.

We live in an environment where we are inundated with data. We *must* learn how to interpret the information that passes before us. More important, it becomes our responsibility to help develop an educated populace that not only is able to sort and analyze data, but is also able to interpret and apply the answers in a practical and meaningful way. In addition, teachers are now required to analyze student data and make meaningful use of the data to improve student learning. Given that, the opening statement should be "Probability and statistics are here!" Now what?

## STATISTICS IN THE MATHEMATICS CURRICULUM

School mathematics education bears increasing responsibilities in a data-rich era. Mathematics instructional programs should provide individuals access to mathematical ideas and should promote students' abilities to reason analytically. In a society saturated with quantitative information ranging from global climate change data to political polls and consumer reports, such skills will help students to understand, make informed decisions about, and affect their world. School mathematics education should contribute to the development of a public aware of the contributions of mathematics to society and capable of determining the social and economic consequences of their own decisions as well as those made by elected representatives on their behalf. (NCTM, 2000, p. 15)

Probability and statistics topics show up throughout the curriculum. For example, many elementary and middle school classes will deal with flipping coins and determining the probability of getting a head or tail. Several current Algebra II texts contain sections dealing with sampling, standard deviation, data interpretation, and *z* scores. Standard deviation is a good topic in Algebra II since it answers the question, "When do we ever need to use summation symbols?" Stem and leaf plots along with bar graphs, box and whisker plots, all the measures of central tendency, and outcome probabilities are introduced in several current Algebra I textbooks.

Decisions or predictions are often based on data—numbers in context. These decisions or predictions would be easy if the data always sent a clear message, but the message is often obscured by variability. Statistics provides tools for describing variability in data and for making informed decisions that take it into account.

Data are gathered, displayed, summarized, examined, and interpreted to discover patterns and deviations from patterns. Quantitative data can be described in terms of key characteristics: measures of shape, center, and spread. The shape of a data distribution might be described as symmetric, skewed, flat, or bell shaped, and it might be summarized by a statistic measuring center (such as mean or median) and a statistic measuring spread (such as standard deviation or interquartile range). Different distributions can be compared numerically using these statistics or compared visually using plots. Knowledge of center and spread are not enough to describe a distribution. Which statistics to compare, which plots to use, and what the results of a comparison might mean, depend on the question to be investigated and the real-life actions to be taken.

Randomization has two important uses in drawing statistical conclusions. First, collecting data from a random sample of a population makes it possible to draw valid conclusions about the whole population, taking variability into account. Second, randomly assigning individuals to different treatments allows a fair comparison of the effectiveness of those treatments. A statistically significant outcome is one that is unlikely to be due to chance alone, and this can be evaluated only under the condition of randomness. The conditions under which data are collected are important in drawing conclusions from the data; in critically reviewing uses of statistics in public media and other reports, it is important to consider the study design, how the data were gathered, and the analyses employed as well as the data summaries and the conclusions drawn.

Random processes can be described mathematically by using a probability model: a list or description of the possible outcomes (the sample space), each of which is assigned a probability. In situations such as flipping a coin, rolling a number cube, or drawing a card, it might be reasonable to assume various outcomes are equally likely. In a probability model, sample points represent outcomes and combine to make up events; probabilities of events can be computed by applying the Addition and Multiplication Rules. Interpreting these probabilities relies on an understanding of independence and conditional probability, which can be approached through the analysis of two-way tables.

Technology plays an important role in statistics and probability by making it possible to generate plots, regression functions, and correlation coefficients, and to simulate many possible outcomes in a short amount of time.

(Common Core Standards, http://www.cores tandards.org/Math)

Incorporating statistical ideas into most mathematics classes requires in-services and textbook rewriting as a minimal start. Statistics is in many texts but is often skipped because the teacher is not familiar with the content, does not know how to integrate it into the curriculum, or does not have the time. We cannot ignore the fact that probability and statistics is included on state mandated assessments for our students. Teachers must be able to teacher these concepts and teach them well. Certainly additional coursework in probability and statistics, or workshops on how the topics could be blended through the curriculum, would be helpful. Many excellent teachers of mathematics have taken no probability and statistics courses or have had regrettable experiences with them. Often statistical topics meet extensive resistance in the K–12 environment. Administrators and colleagues might agree to support including probability and statistics topics provided they do not get "stuck" with doing any of it in their programs or courses. The approach seems to be, "Yeah, somebody should do something about that (but not me)." How about you; are you willing to do something about it?

Lest you think this is a passing fad, remember that the AP (Advanced Placement) Statistics course began in the 1995–1996 school year. Take a look at the data for the first six years, 1997–2002.

| Year | Number of Students taking the AP Statistics Exam |
|------|---------------------------------------------------|
| 1997 | 7,667 |
| 1998 | 15,486 |
| 1999 | 25,240 |
| 2000 | 34,118 |
| 2001 | 40,259 |
| 2002 | 49,824 |

Retrieved from the CollegeBoard AP Central Website (http://apcentral.collegeboard.com/article/ 0,3045,151-165-0-2151,00.html)

313

## LEARNING ABOUT PROBABILITY AND STATISTICS CAN BE FUN

Students love to learn about themselves. How do they compare with others? Are they as tall? Are they as strong? Are they as healthy? We can teach statistical concepts by gathering data that address these questions. Every concept in basic statistics can be taught and reinforced by gathering data about the students themselves. Teaching probability and statistics takes the idea of hands-on mathematics to new heights. What can be more intriguing to a secondary student than finding out peculiar information about themselves or their peers? What can be more fun than discovering amazing tidbits about your favorite foods?

Eating may be more fun than learning about yourself. Browse the candy aisle of a local store. Can you think of a statistical application as you look at the bags of candy? Picture this. At the end of the candy aisle is a display of a popular soft drink. You have seen the commercials that tell you about the national taste tests for the two major soft drinks. So you put a few of the two-liter containers in your shopping cart, knowing that you will teach the students about the design of experiments using the soft drinks. Do ninth-graders like Cola A significantly more than Cola B? Do you think soda companies care? How do companies make that kind of determination?

The first candy that you see is M&Ms. That is an experiment waiting to happen. As you load your cart with M&Ms, you accidentally pick up a bag of Skittles. Before you have time to put it back on the shelf, you realize that you could design a defective products lab using yellow Skittles as the defective parts. This will illustrate the sampling process in statistical process control (which is used routinely by major manufacturers). Are these the only candies in this aisle that could be used for a statistics lesson?

Certainly not! To the right of the Skittles you find gummy bears. As you read the package, you realize that many brands of gummy bears contain fruit juice, but no specific artificial flavor. But, many students think they are flavored. Add a few more bags of gummy bears to your cart. Another research question, "Do girls or guys have bigger mouths?" (defined by the quantity of marshmallow that fit in a mouth), could certainly be answered using statistics.

You now have enough candy to turn statistics students into diabetics, so look at the idea of gathering

data about the students. Displaying data is an important concept that seems trivial to students who are used to topics much more difficult than graphing. This is where student data enters the picture. Have students take their own heart rate for one minute (Fig. 15.1). Gather the data. Have students take the heart rate of a classmate (same gender, Fig. 15.2). This is your second list. Have students take the heart rate of another classmate (opposite gender, Fig 15.3). Compare the three lists of data by using your calculator or a web application such as Box-and-Whisker Plot Generator (http://math.andyou.com/tools/boxandwhisker.html) or Your Box and Whisker Graph (http://www.mathwarehouse.com/charts/box-and-whisker-plot-maker.php#boxwhiskergraph) to display three box and whisker plots as shown in Figs. 15.1, 15.2, and 15.3.

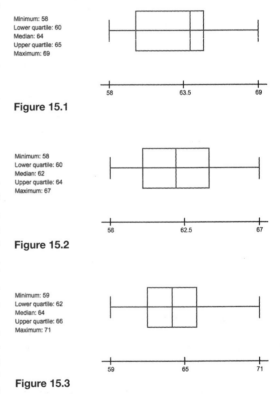

Minimum: 58
Lower quartile: 60
Median: 64
Upper quartile: 65
Maximum: 69

58    63.5    69

**Figure 15.1**

Minimum: 58
Lower quartile: 60
Median: 62
Upper quartile: 64
Maximum: 67

58    62.5    67

**Figure 15.2**

Minimum: 59
Lower quartile: 62
Median: 64
Upper quartile: 66
Maximum: 71

59    65    71

**Figure 15.3**

Histograms are another important way to display data, but they look too elementary to high school students. A hand strength lab will allow students to see histograms in a different perspective. Each student is asked to squeeze a bathroom scale with the dominant hand. The first squeeze is recorded and graphed, as is the second squeeze. You could create histograms on a poster (for future reference) by using sticky notes, and enter the data into a calculator or computer software. Once the data are entered, compare the resultant histogram with a box and whisker plot as both are displayed simultaneously. Save the data on first and second squeezes to use for linear regression and matched pairs $t$ test. These data are also helpful when illustrating the difference between a sample and a sampling distribution. Are any of your students outliers? How strong or weak do they have to be to be considered an outlier? Is the weightlifting coach at school significantly stronger than the students are? Is squeezing a bathroom scale a reasonable indicator of strength? If your statistics students truly were a simple random sample of teenagers, could we create a 95% confidence interval. Should we split the data by gender or age? Does this add much complexity to the process? We have taken one simple lab using student-generated data and illustrated many important statistics concepts that have strong student appeal: Each student is part of that data. Educational theorists believe that giving meaning to information provides a stronger foundation for students and ensures that the students are more likely to remember the concept at a later date.

Are there any cautions about student-generated data? Yes. We should remember to reinforce the idea that one of the basic assumptions of most tests of significance is that data are gathered by simple random sample (SRS). It is important for students to realize that by using themselves to illustrate the statistical concepts, we do not intend to use the data for inference about a larger population because we have violated an important rule (by not using an SRS).

Our confidence in statistics is in the process. When the process is properly applied, there is a level of confidence in the results. If the design is flawed, the results are not reliable. This basic understanding of the fundamental principles behind SRS data collection and the inherent pitfalls of samples of convenience (SC) is the message for all statistically literate consumers of research, namely all of us.

## WHY SHOULD STUDENTS STUDY STATISTICS?

Students of the future won't have a choice. In order to function in a technological society with overwhelming amounts of data, they must be well versed in the basic concepts of statistics. The increased use of statistics is everywhere. All one has to do is read a newspaper or news website, listen to the radio, or surf the Internet. Daily news regularly contains statistical information. Some of this knowledge should cause the educated viewer to question the validity of its presentation. Examples include:

How is information about unemployment generated and how accurate is it?

How can election results be predicted with only a small percentage of votes counted (especially after the 2004 presidential election)?

Who decides which television show ratings are good and which shows should be canceled?

How are real estate appraisals for tax purposes derived?

What guidelines are used for testing new drugs for human use and how are the appropriate numbers determined?

Topics such as these can be found every time you watch the news. The educated consumer must be numerically competent and aware of the ways that data can be convincingly misleading and/or irrelevant.

For example, does the following make sense to you? Is it statistically correct? Would it convince you to purchase the product? Would you take the time to read the box or label with all that "stuff" on it?

The following studies apply only to Cold-EEZE with Zigg (Zinc Gluconate Glycine) the only great tasting lozenge, proven effective in treating a common cold.

A randomized, double-blind placebo study with 23 mg of ionic zinc in a citrus favored lozenge, concluded that treatment of a cold with our Patented formula within 48 hours of the onset resulted in symptom relief and 42% reduction in the duration of the common cold.

Results were published in the Journal of International Medical Research, Godfrey et.al., Vol. 20, No. 3, June 1992.

A second, randomized, double-blind placebo study with only 13.3 mg of ionic zinc in a citrus flavored lozenge, concluded patients starting treatment with our Patented formula within 24 hours of the onset, taking an average of 6 lozenges per day, resulted in a 42% reduction in the duration of common cold symptoms. Results were published in the Annals Of Internal Medicine, Mossad et al., Vol. 125, No. 2, July 15, '96, pg. 81–88. (as cited by M. Causey, personal communication, 2000)

The preceding is from a cold medicine carton. It is stated in a statistically correct manner. Assuming that every consumer would take the time to read that information, what are the chances that the individual would understand what was read?

Because decisions are increasingly being based on statistical and probabilistic information, the new trend in mathematics education is responding to this changing need of society. Curriculum development recommendations in NCTM's Standards 2000 (NCTM, 2000) call for statistical literacy for everyone, not just those who perform surveys or experiments. NCTM has adopted the position that industry is requiring statistical knowledge of most employees. Furthermore, newspapers contain sophisticated presentations of data, advertisements to sway people with polls, amazing sports statistics, and convincing arguments that persuade people to buy lottery tickets. Paralleling this opinion, *The Curriculum and Evaluation Standards for School Mathematics* (NCTM, 1989) expressed the need for increased attention to statistics and probability in school mathematics using the applications of data and chance. The position is present in Standards 2000 as well. In the same vein, the most recent National Assessment of Educational Progress (NAEP) test has included an increased number of data analysis, statistics, and probability items. Survey results indicate that more attention is being given to these topics and that student performance on these test items is gradually improving.

However, in spite of these reported trends in the right direction, if you were to conduct a survey of current high school students, most of them would probably tell you they have had little or no exposure to probability or statistics in their mathematics curriculum. There is vast room for improvement. In particular, an educated consumer should have the ability to make inferences and decisions based on statistical or probabilistic information. These are the skills needed in the everyday roles of informed citizens and productive employees.

## WHAT SHOULD BE TAUGHT?

According to David S. Moore (1997), "The study of statistics is an essential part of a sound education." Through all the mathematical theory connected with statistics, the meat of the subject that we should be concerned with is the practice of statistics. The preliminary edition of statistics ad-

vanced placement course description states that "the purpose of the Advanced Placement course in statistics is to introduce students to the major concepts and tools for collecting, analyzing, and drawing conclusions from data." The four broad conceptual themes students should be exposed to are:

Exploring analysis of data

Planning a well-developed study

Anticipating models in advance

Using statistical inference to determine selection of the appropriate models

Exploring analysis of data involves organizing information, using graphical and numerical techniques, observing patterns, and interpreting departures from patterns. Upon examination of the distribution of data, students should be able to detect important characteristics such as shape, variability, and unusual values. After careful observation of the displayed data, students should be able to come up with conjectures about relationships between the variables involved. The relationship of variables is a common thread throughout statistics. An understanding of the difference between association and causation should accompany this concept as well.

Planning a well-developed study involves collecting data and making sure the information used to make conjectures is valid. Important variables must be identified and described with relation to the conjectures and how they will be measured. From the collected data and the method in which it is displayed, a model can be built and inferences made.

Anticipating models in advance that use probability and simulation will prove beneficial. Over time, with enough trials, an order emerges from any random phenomena that are described by a distribution. The probability required for statistical inference is primarily bent toward describing data distributions.

Statistical inference can be used to assist in the selection of appropriate models. There is a complicated relationship between data and models in statistics. Models can be used to draw conclusions from data. At the same time, data may criticize or contradict the model through inferential and diagnostic methods. Inference from data may be thought of as selecting a reasonable model and probability statement of confidence about the selection.

# HOW SHOULD STATISTICS BE TAUGHT?

*The College Board Advanced Placement Program Teachers Guide—AP Statistics* states, "Good statistics teaching is as much an attitude as a set of skills. Become a professional noticer of how data are collected and used in the world around you. You will find that teaching an AP Statistics course changes the way you look at the world" (Watkins, 1997). The AP statistics course covers a lot of material, and it is especially challenging when your students have no previous experience with the subject.

Inherently the study of statistics lends itself to collaborative, student-centered problem solving. The traditional study of mathematics consists of sequential sets of lessons that require manipulation, solving equations, practicing algorithms, and eventually learning problem solving, perhaps individually, and perhaps as a member of a group. This concept of mathematics learning is presented in all of the NCTM Standards publications, including Standards 2000. Students should be solving real-life problems, communicating useful mathematical reasoning, and actively participating in the learning environment.

A good statistics course requires the use of hands-on activities and insists that statistics be more than calculations, tables, and rehearsed responses to standard questions! It is the ideal class for a lab-centered environment, especially when integrated with a lab-centered science course. Special class scheduling may need to be arranged in order to accommodate the extra time needed for activities and collaborative planning.

The goal of statistics is to gain understanding from the data. The context of the data is what makes the numbers informative. More than manipulation of the numbers is required to help one understand what is present. Every student of statistics should quickly get into the habit of asking, "What information is hidden in the data?" A thorough understanding of the fundamental concepts of statistics needs to be developed. Thus you can see that statistical learning goes beyond mere memorization.

Because of the quantity of calculating and graphing involved, the availability of technology suitable for the interactive investigative aspects of data analysis is a very important component. The course should also include projects, labs, cooperative group problem solving, and journal or concept writing. These elements lend themselves quite nicely to interdisciplinary collaboration.

As you prepare to teach a statistics course, Education Testing Service suggests that you should:

Collect the materials you will need.

Assess your knowledge of statistics and fill in the gaps.

Investigate how to teach statistics and determine how students think about it.

Communicate with other teachers of statistics.

Get organized by collecting uses and misuses of data, filing them accordingly by topic. Start a data box with data that may interest your students. Start a collection of data reference books and websites that contain easily downloadable data sets and ideas. Take a course from an expert, read a book on elementary statistics, or use the World Wide Web to study examples of how great statisticians analyze data. The College Board is a good resource for teacher education. They sponsor regular workshops and institutes on AP statistics (http://www.collegeboard.org). Use other professional associations or journal resources too. Statistics teachers of the past were pretty much on their own. This is quickly changing. Collaboration is possible through the AP Statistics LISTSERV (majordomo@etc.bc.ca).

# THE PRACTICALITY OF PROBABILITY AND STATISTICS

People spend a lot of hard-earned cash on lotteries hoping to strike it rich. Oh, sure, a few actually hit the jackpot, but there is only one chance of that happening. At the same time, there are millions of chances of losing. In the Florida lottery, you are required to pick 6 of 54 numbers to win, and there are 25,827,164 chances of losing. The first big lottery jackpot game in Florida was a weekly game that required the player to pick 6 numbers out of 49, which offered about 14,000,000 chances of losing. (I reworded this to make it more current.) The providers of the current lottery sold it on the idea that players would have a chance to win twice a week rather than once. In Florida, the odds of getting struck by lightning are greater than the odds of winning the lottery. Yet Floridians will walk out in a rainstorm knowing that the odds don't apply to them, and they will buy a lottery ticket—because, you never know—confident once again that the laws don't apply to them. Would it be safe (although not very kind) to say that lotteries, games of chance, and so on, are a tax on the statistically ignorant?

Speaking of favorable odds, consider casinos. Gambling centers are popular and, as with lotteries, there are some people who win. Surprisingly, most people figure the house is markedly favored when in reality their chances of winning are close to being equal to those afforded the individual. However, the slight advantage of the house (often 2% or 3%) becomes a sizable amount when the millions of dollars that are bet are considered. Think about the casino hotels. Are they run-down dumps? How can they afford to give free, or almost free, meals and drinks? How can they afford to provide supercheap airfares and cruises?

## EXERCISES 15.1

1. View CNN (http://www.cnn.com) or ESPN (http://www.espn.com) on the Internet. Place your vote on one of their online polls. How are the results displayed? Do you feel this graphical representation is the best way to display the results? Can you enter your vote more than once? Should you be worried about skewed results?
2. What would you say to a student who comes from a limited-income environment who talks about spending money on the lottery?

 **Additional exercises can be found on the website.**

## WHERE DOES TECHNOLOGY FIT IN?

Suppose a teacher says, "I do not use technology to teach the process." Is that a reasonable statement? As we have said several times, technology is a teaching/learning tool, not a sledgehammer answer machine. Once students understand the process, they may use technology. In other chapters in this book, we have shown several instances where technology can be used to introduce concepts and learn processes. Surely that is possible with probability and statistics too. For example, suppose your students do not know what factorial is. Suppose, also, that the calculators they have possess the ability to compute factorials. You could have them do something like: $1! =$ _____, $2! =$ _____, $3! =$ _____, . . . , and record the results they get for each answer. Assuming that they are accustomed

to looking for patterns and developing conjectures and generalizations, it seems reasonable that they could formulate the meaning of factorial. Once the activity is completed, you might need to formalize the definition and provide the name "factorial," but they will have established the meaning ahead of you. Certainly they could do the activity by hand, if you tell them what "!" means, but that defeats the purpose because you have essentially defined factorial for them. The beauty of technology is that it removes the drudgery of the manipulation and affords the opportunity to look at the results. But, that is a main theme for the study of statistics.

The purpose of statistics is inference. Mean and standard deviation are not calculated solely to have a mean and standard deviation. They are needed to make inference about a population. Only after the students know the process may they use the technology to bypass the number crunching to reach the ultimate goal of statistics: inference. The question in statistics is not, "What did you get?" The question is, "What does that mean?" As you ponder the role of technology in statistics, consider the position of the College Board, which offers the AP Statistics Examination:

Each student is expected to bring to the exam a graphing calculator with statistical capabilities. The computational capabilities should include standard statistical univariate and bivariate summaries, through linear regression. The graphical capabilities should include common univariate and bivariate displays such as histograms, boxplots, and scatterplots.

- You can bring two calculators to the exam.
- The calculator memory will not be cleared but you may only use the memory to store programs, not notes.
- For the AP Statistics exam, you're not allowed to access any information in your graphing calculators or elsewhere if it's not directly related to upgrading the statistical functionality of older graphing calculators to make them comparable to statistical features found on newer models. The only acceptable upgrades are those that improve the computational functionalities and/or graphical functionalities for data you key into the calculator while taking the examination. Unacceptable enhancements include, but aren't limited to, keying or scanning text or response templates into the calculator.

- During the exam, you can't use minicomputers, pocket organizers, electronic writing pads, or calculators with QWERTY (i.e., typewriter) keyboards. ("Calculator Policy," n.d.)

## WHAT TO DEFINE?

We opt to leave the definitions to you. Are you interested enough to look up the things you have not had or have forgotten? That is part of becoming a self-motivated lifelong learner, you know.

As you insert statistical topics throughout the secondary curriculum, you will need to assure that your students have an understanding of the basic definitions and concepts you will be using. IF (note the big IF) your textbook contains statistical topics, you might get the direction and help you need. More than likely that option will be limited. Once again, the need for you to exhibit professionalism appears. You will need to develop your own statistical expertise, and then call upon that as you define appropriate topics, expectations, and activities for your students. As you do that, you may encounter the excuse that there is no room in the curriculum to insert statistical topics. Hopefully, your eyes are now open wide enough for you to discount this opinion as you strive to embed statistics topics in your curriculum.

### EXERCISES 15.2

1. Is it possible to insert statistical concepts into the secondary curriculum at multiple levels? Defend your position.
2. Where do the Common Core Standards expect you to integrate probability and statistics into the curriculum? What about the elementary curriculum?

**Additional exercises can be found on the website.**

## A RATIONALE FOR TEACHING STATISTICS

Have you ever heard the statement, "Let the buyer beware?" For years that has been the rationale used to convince people of the need for critical examination of sometimes outrageous claims made by manufacturers or salespeople. It was not until the advent of the consumer protection agencies that some high school basic mathematics classes taught young people to be wise consumers of products and services. Still, today information often is accepted at face value because of the inability to understand the methodology used to produce the data. Besides, the data are often interpreted for us, so why worry? Through the use of newspapers, magazines, computers, the Internet, television, and radio, we have the opportunity to access more information than ever before. The personal computer has dramatically increased the availability of information. Thus, we all need to learn to become better consumers of data and its interpretation. High school courses in statistics enable students to learn to be wise consumers of data and to examine research critically. Statistical literacy is the consumer watchdog for the age of scientific information.

As we continue to become more health conscious, we are bombarded with articles about health, exercise, and diet. How -rained is the average author to draw appropriate conclusions from data? How adept are you at interpreting the gist of these studies from the statistics? Suppose a new study claims to have found that people who eat more fiber are less likely to have heart attacks than those who do not eat as much fiber. Has a cause-and-effect relationship been established? Does this imply that everyone should eat more fiber? What evidence is necessary to help you conclude that you should increase your fiber intake?

Without an understanding of the importance of the proper design of an experiment and the inference that can be drawn from it, you, your colleagues, your future students, and our whole society are even more vulnerable today than we were just a few years ago. Claims backed by data sound trustworthy and can give readers the false impression that the interpretation of the data is accurate merely because the data itself exists. The study of data production and data analysis provides the opportunity to evaluate claims about the reliability of the information seen in everyday life. Because of the inundation of information now going on, statistical literacy must cease to be a luxury reserved for a few select individuals. Rather, statistical literacy must become part of the standard knowledge base of all members of society.

Until the recent past, precollege students studied little or no statistics. Even within the college ranks many students do not take a statistics course, hence statistical literacy is limited to a select group, of which you are a member. The first opportunity was made available to high school students to take an Advanced Placement statistics examination in the 1996–1997 school year. The popularity of the course has grown rapidly since its introduction. Advanced Placement Statistics is not only very practical; it is just plain fun. It is fun to learn and it is fun to teach.

## A RATIONALE FOR TEACHING PROBABILITY

Unlike statistics, probability does not have a "special" AP course. Most of the time the two topics are linked as "probability and statistics," so maybe the assumption is that when we say statistics, we are thinking probability is included. Check the course number and prefixes of college classes and you will see STA wxyz titled Statistical Methods 1. Read the description of the course and you will probably see something like "First methods course introducing probability and statistics . . ." How much of the course is probability and how much is statistics? Is it reasonable to split the two topics and treat them independently? How dependent is the study of probability on statistics, or vice versa?

Students certainly have exposure to some ideas of probability early in their lives. Flipping coins, rolling dice, and things like the lottery are part of their early exposure. There are other topics that need to be developed. First exposure is not enough. Second, they need to understand concepts such as bias, dishonesty, odds, false claims, and ideas like the lottery really having only one chance for a winner. Additionally, they need the opportunity to learn about probability.

Typically, the probability activities in a classroom involve flipping coins and rolling dice. The problem is that many students already know what to expect from these. The odds are that they do not know any of the mathematical reasoning behind why their answers are coming out as they are, but they "just know." Sometimes you will encounter a probability activity involving spinners on a board that has half of the region red and two regions that each occupy a quarter of the board that are blue and yellow respectively. The question asks about which region is going to have the greatest number of spinner landings. Here again, the students will know the answer, or if they do not, they will determine it very quickly. While there is value in working with coins, dice, spinners, cards, and other venues with which students are familiar, it is also important to expose them to new, different activities.

A paper cup, when flipped, is essentially able to land in one of three positions as shown in Fig. 15.4. Certainly it might be the case that it would land on one of the top or bottom edges as shown in Fig. 15.4, but that is a very delicate balance and highly unlikely. It is rather like trying to balance a salt shaker on one of its bottom edge points or sides, depending on the shape. Good luck.

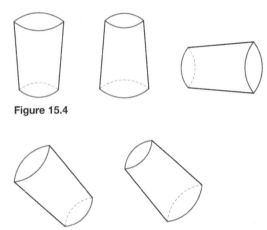

**Figure 15.4**

**Figure 15.5**

If you flip the paper cup many times, how many times will it land in each of the positions displayed in Fig. 15.4? Did you try this experiment? Could the cup be modified so it will land a given way every time? You would need to establish ground rules about what can and cannot be done as the cup is altered.

The paper cup activity described in the last paragraph is only one application that can be used to begin working with probability. Fold a sheet of paper in half. When you drop it, it normally will fall in one of the three positions as shown in Fig. 15.6. How could the probability for each position be established? How could the odds be adjusted?

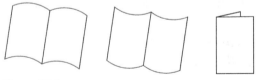

**Figure 15.6**

There are similar activities that could be done in your classroom to emphasize probability. It is your responsibility as a professional to become familiar with the related topics in probability and locate or develop methods for presenting them in an interesting and dynamic environment for your students. We have discussed the lottery in other places in this text. Topics such as that are essential as a part of developing a better understanding of probability in your students.

## REAL-WORLD DATA

The concepts relating to probability and statistics are usually presented to students through laboratory activities, a great thing to happen for the students. Experienced teachers are aware of the typical activities for these topics involving cards, dice, coins, spinners, population bar graphs, and circle graphs for budgets. Even though many activities for probability and statistics are available, the concerned teacher searches regularly for activities that appeal to students of both genders, varied backgrounds, different capabilities, and diverse interests. Girls and boys are often motivated to study mathematics through different activities. In the literature, boys frequently are associated with sport activities whereas girls align with cooking and grooming. Creative teachers struggle to devise gender-neutral activities that appeal to all students.

Traditionally, probability and statistics are joined, and yet there is ample opportunity to do one without the other. In society, the level of inability to deal with or understand topics relating to probability and statistics is much higher than it should be. Part of the reason lies in lack of exposure. Ironically, there are varied and interesting activities that can be done in a classroom that will attract students to probability or statistics, especially with the availability of technology. For example, have each student bring in at least 20 pennies for a class. These pennies should be gathered as change between the time the assignment is made and the time when the pennies are to be brought. Explain to the class that pennies are minted each year and ask them what they think the distribution of minting years student's collection will be. The general guess is that the mintings (dates) will be distributed over the past several years, with the possibility that as the difference between the current year and the minting year increases, the number of pennies will decrease in that category. Then, in class, have each student sort the pennies by minting year and record the results. Compile the totals. Usually, about two-thirds of the class total will have been minted in the last 2 years. Why is that? Piggy banks! A significant problem for our government stems from the fact that people tend to save pennies, taking them out of circulation for long periods of time. Thus, the supply needs to be replenished regularly and most of the pennies in circulation are relatively new. Believe it or not, there is a national organization called Penny Lovers of America [http://www.pennylovers.org] that provides articles and information on American's collection of and fascination with the U.S. penny. Your students will find some interesting information. Did you know that a pound of pennies contains $1.64?

The statistical potential using pennies is impressive. Students can be asked to do some, or all, of:

Gathering data
Formulating hypotheses
Organizing material
Classifying results
Compiling facts
Analyzing information
Presenting findings
Investigating reasons for the happenings

There are other extensions of this activity into the classroom environment, but the preceding list is a beginning. Consider the impact of using pennies in the classroom setting. The request is not typical. That in itself will generate discussion and some interest. The results are not what would normally be expected, which heightens awareness of the impact of personal activities. Most significantly is the affective influence. Students will generally laugh and be somewhat surprised by the results. Save the data. At some later date, when doing spreadsheets, for example, reproduce the data along with saying, "Remember when we gathered the pennies . . . ?" That question will generate the emotional highs that were produced in the class at the time the activity was done. You capitalize on prior positive experiences and use them to enter a new lesson with a positive attitude. (Credit for this idea goes to Jim Rubillo, NCTM Regional Conference, Boise, Idaho, October 8, 1994.)

Surveys are a typical statistical happening in schools as a part of the study of mathematics. Questions like the number of siblings, pets, CDs, TVs, pairs of tennis shoes, and so on are common. Traditionally the information is compiled using frequency distributions and graphs are produced. That in itself is a good activity if for no reason other than it makes a connection with the real world. Many publications contain graphs to represent data, probably the most notable of which is *USA Today* (http://www.usatoday.com). Incidentally, this paper provides a multitude of teacher help items, free, and they are on the Internet at http://usatodayeducation.com/k12. Regrettably, the emphasis almost always focuses on the graph production. The lack of connection comes from the idea that frequently, in the real world, the consumer interprets graphs and data as opposed to producing it. Thus, classroom consideration should be switched from production of graphs and data to interpretation of the information.

An additional topic often overlooked in surveying is sampling. Is it reasonable to assume discussions are held about samples representing a population and the need for samples because the total population cannot be contacted in most instances? Perhaps not. Even if those issues are raised with the class, there is still a need to consider how well the sample represents the population. The media often report results along with a statement about sampling error, so the result of a survey might be "67% of the population with a 5% sampling error." Will students, or the population, catch the significance of that statement? Clarification of the sampling impact can be delivered through an account of a blood test. In a poll, a number of random calls are made and, based on the answers to questions asked, predictions are made. If you do not believe sampling techniques adequately represent a situation, then the next time you have a blood test, you will need to give all your blood, not a sample (Rubillo, 1994).

Some sampling techniques are far from being random and yet the results are often presented in a manner that implies they represent the population. For example, suppose you conduct a survey where you interview a number of teenagers exiting an upscale clothing store. You ask the amount of their monthly allowance. Do you suppose that is going to be representative of the allowance of the students in your class? Ironically a reporter for a paper did interview students coming out of an upscale clothing store and then produced a featured article about student allowances being over $100 a week. Depending on where you start teaching, that means some of these teenagers were getting an allowance that is about 15% of your starting salary. Some random sample, isn't it?

One common activity for teaching statistics is achieved through the use of sports. A typical approach is to investigate the individual's salary and claim to fame. Suppose a baseball player is paid $4,000,000 a year and is famous for hitting home runs. Granted, the player does more than bat and runs. Granted, the player does more than bat and has hits other than home runs. However, if home-run hitting is the skill that merited the pay, and if the player is on the team to do that, how much is each home run worth? This idea could be extended to include all hits and pay per hit, or pay per base, catch, throw, and so forth. It can be projected to other activities as well. The point is, this is not a common approach to application of statistics within the salary consideration. Continuing with the hitting example, a person with career batting average of 0.300 is almost guaranteed a place in the Baseball Hall of Fame. Do you suppose the batting success rate is given as 0.300 rather than 30% for affective impact? But a 0.300 average means a 70% failure rate. What would be thought of a surgeon who was "batting 0.300"? When you intern, do you think your supervisor will be pleased if you have a 70% student failure rate? Do you suppose that would get you into the "Teaching Hall of Shame"?

## STATISTICS ON THE WEB

It is difficult to provide Internet sources throughout a text like this one because things are changing so rapidly. Therefore, we can offer no assurance that these sites offered will be active when you read this book. We are not saying these are the best sites available, but they should provide openings for you to begin a more thorough investigation of how to more effectively deliver probability and statistics education to your students. The following are a list of online tools/resources that should help you investigate the world of probability and statistics. Please note that there are hundreds of effective resources and apps available for many devices!

- **Shodor**—a national resource for computational science education. You will find a multitude of interactive mathematics activities that include multiple probability and statistics simulations and lessons. (http://www.shodor.org/interactivate/activities) Try the Simple and Advanced Monte Hall experiment! (http://www.shodor.org/interactivate/activities/AdvancedMontyHall)
- **Gametheory.net**—Interactive materials including Java applets, online simulations, and game theory demonstrations. (http://www.gametheory.net/applets/probability.html)
- **Virtual Laboratories in Probability and Statistics**—free, high quality, interactive, Web-based resources for students and teachers of

probability and statistics. (http://www.math. uah.edu/stat/)

**Illuminations**—Web links for data analysis and probability (http://illuminations.nctm.org/ WebResourceList.aspx)

**Easycalculation.com**—Online calculation for basic and advanced statistics (http://www. easycalculation.com/statistics/statistics.php)

You may also find the following publication useful as you explore how the integrate probability and statistics into the curriculum: *Journal of Statistics Education* provides resources for new and veteran statistics teachers. (http://www.amstat.org/ publications/jse/)

## TRY THIS IN YOUR CLASSROOM

CANDYGRAM LAB (Rock & Brumbaugh, 1997) *NCTM Standards 2000*: Number and operations, problem solving, measurement, statistics and probability

Purchase a bag of M&Ms for each student in the class. Ask each student to weigh their bag (before opening it) and compare the result with the weight listed on the package. Ask them to discuss what they observe.

Have each student open the package of M&Ms and weigh just the candy. Compare this result with the weight listed on the package. Ask them to explain the results.

Have the students sort the M&Ms by color. If a piece appears to be half or more, count it as a whole M&M. If a piece appears to be smaller than a half, discard (or eat) it. Record the number of each color in a table. Compile the results for the entire class. Find the percent of the total number of M&Ms that is represented by each color, rounding the result to the nearest whole number.

Before opening a package of M&Ms, predict which color will represent the greatest number of pieces. Explain why you made the choice you did.

CHANCES OF WINNING LAB (Brumbaugh & Rock, 1997)—Probability concept: Combinations.

Suppose you decide to guarantee that you will purchase the winning ticket for a weekly lottery that asks you to pick 6 numbers out of 49 possible options. How many of the tickets will be winners? How many will be losers? If the tickets cost a dollar each, how much will you have to invest before you can guarantee a winner?

Suppose the jackpot has rolled over a few times and is now worth $50,000,000. Could you still lose money if you bought one of each possible ticket?

Your desire to guarantee that you have a winning ticket means you have to purchase one of each possible combination available. The first one would be (1, 2, 3, 4, 5, 6), followed by (1, 2, 3, 4, 5, 7), then (1, 2, 3, 4, 5, 8) ... (1, 2, 3, 4, 5, 49), (1, 3, 4, 5, 6, 7), ... (1, 3, 4, 5, 6, 7, 49), (1, 4, 5, 6, 7, 8), ... (1, 4, 5, 6, 7, 49) ... (44, 45, 46, 47, 48, 49). Assuming that you can purchase a ticket every second, nonstop, for an entire week, you would not be able to buy all the tickets you need (one person can buy $60 \times 60 \times 24 \times 7 = 604,800$ tickets going one per second for a week). How many friends would you need to help you, assuming they each could work nonstop for an entire week, purchasing one ticket per second?

Given enough friends and the approximately $14,000,000 that would be needed to meet your goal of purchasing one of each of the possible combinations, a very challenging dilemma still faces you. You buy the first 604,800 tickets. What is the last number you get? Friend 1 will pick up with ticket number 604,801 and so on, through all the friends who participate. If, by some chance, someone messes up and misses one of their numbers, you know what the winner will be, don't you?

> GUMMY BEAR LAB—Statistical concepts: Two-sample *t* test, design of study, statistical significance.

This lab is designed to determine whether training received by students in the control group enables them to identify the flavor of gummy bears better than students who receive no training. Most brands of gummy bears come in five colors, and many do not actually have separate flavors. (Do not reveal the no-different-flavor information to the students.) Randomly divide the class into two groups: experimental and control. Each student in the experimental group will be given one of each of the five colors of gummy bears. The experimental group will be instructed to look at each color gummy bear before eating it, and make an effort to remember how that color gummy bear tasted.

Each member of both groups will then be given one of each of the five color gummy bears. Each student picks a partner within the group (control or experimental). With closed eyes, the student will taste one gummy bear at a time. Without giving any feedback, the nontasting partner will record the correct color and the color which the student identified. Use a two-sample $t$ test to determine whether the experimental group's training helped them to correctly identify significantly more gummy bears.

Because there is no real flavor associated with many gummy bears, the control group may outscore the experimental group. This poses an interesting dilemma for students: What do you do now? If students truly understand what "statistically significant" means, they will not do the two-sample $t$ test. Why? If you are trying to find out whether the experimental group can correctly identify significantly more gummy bears than the control group and you find that the experimental group has not identified more, than you automatically know that they have not identified *significantly* more. Many students will not be concerned that the control group did better and will still try to see if the results are significant. It may be worth creating this situation to test their understanding of the idea "statistically significant."

CANDY CANE LAB: Prepare a container of candy canes with twice as many candy canes as students in your group. Place four cherry candy canes in the container and use any other flavor for the rest. Prepare a worksheet that asks them to calculate the proportion of cherry candy canes using the sample proportion (p-hat) and find the standard deviation of the sample. Make sure to stress that they are to use procedures taught by the book and the instructor to find the p-hat and standard deviation and ask how useful the p-hat value is as a predictor of the population of candy canes in the bowl. The students should know to check to see if the population is at least 10 times as large as the sample. They should only use the standard deviation formula for proportions when this stipulation is satisfied. In this activity, you have made the sample size half the population. Additionally, the number of candy canes that have the characteristic you are looking for is less than 10. It is important that students learn to check the necessary assumptions. This is one tasteful way to remind them to do so.

CHUBBY BUNNY LAB—Statistical concept: Two-sample $t$ test, blocking.

The research question "Do males or females have bigger mouths?" is addressed in this lab. Mouth size is defined by the number of marshmallows that can be inserted in an individual's mouth whereby that person is still be able to articulate the phrase "Chubby Bunny." The number of marshmallows each individual can hold is recorded, along with the sex of the individual. A two-sample $t$ test is determined to see if males or females have significantly bigger mouths. Although you might get the impression that this lab would lack student appeal, experience shows that they actually look forward to the Chubby Bunny lab. Necessary precautions need to be taken to assure that participants do not choke as they attempt this activity.

STATISTICS OLYMPICS LAB—Statistical concepts: One-sample $t$ test, two-sample $t$ test, matched pairs $t$ test.

Students are occasionally confused about which $t$ test to use. This lab is will help them answer that question. As students come in the room, allow them to randomly select a piece of paper that tells them whether they are competing for Belarus or the United States in the Statistics Olympics. Each member of both teams will compete in two events (described next).

Balancing Event: With eyes closed, the left foot (bottom held parallel to the floor) of each member of the Olympic balancing team will be lifted six inches off the ground. Having done that, each individual will be timed on the established goal of staying balanced in that position for as long as possible. The time officially ends when the individual's eyes are opened, a person or object is touched for support, or the foot is returned to the floor. Record the balancing time for every team member. Note: Balancing with your eyes closed is not as easy as it sounds. Most students cannot do this as long as they think they can. This event will not take long.

Flexibility Event: Each contestant sits on the floor with the bottoms of both feet touching an immobile object (like an aerobics step or wide board). Both legs should be straight and together. The feet should be perpendicular to the "line of the leg." Contestants get two attempts in this event. Reaching the bottom of the toe of each shoe (hands together) is a zero. Reaching beyond the toe of each shoe is a positive value. Not reaching the toes is a negative value. Values are defined as the number of centimeters between the middle finger tips and the bottom of the toes of the shoes. The ruler should be held parallel to the floor when the distances are measured.

*Question #1*: Is there a significant difference (at 5% level) in the flexibility of Belarus and

United States Olympians? (A two-sample $t$ test should be used here.)

*Question #2*: The Olympic committee is considering doing away with the opportunity to have two tries, citing the second try as a waste of Olympic time. Determine whether there is a significant improvement between the first and second tries. A matched pairs $t$ test would be used. However, if there is not an improvement, students do not need to see if the results are "significant." The process would have List 1 (L1) be the first stretch. List 2 (L2) is the second stretch. To do matched pairs, create List 3, which is L2 − L1. A one-sample $t$ test by data or statistics can now be performed. When doing this by data, the technology will give you a $p$ value, which could mistakenly lead to the attempt to say whether or not the value is significant. If L3 is not positive, then it is not a viable consideration, since we were looking for improvement.

*Question #3*: Police departments are considering using the balancing test as a Field Sobriety Test for those drivers suspected to be under the influence of alcohol or drugs. In order to use this test, it must be determined what the average balancing time is for healthy (sober) people, such as Olympians. It is also important to see the range of scores of these healthy, sober athletes. (Use a one-sample $t$ test to determine the average and find a 95% and 99% confidence interval.)

A fun extension to this activity is to award medals for each event. Chocolate medallions are available and make great Olympic medals when taped to a couple feet of yarn. Gold, silver, and bronze medal winners in each event should be honored. It would be wise to have a participation award for individuals who do not "place."

DEFECTIVE PRODUCTS LAB—Statistical concepts: Sampling, statistical process control.

Sampling can be used to determine whether to reject or accept a shipment of a certain product. Create a container of Skittles with exactly 10% of the Skittles being yellow. Mix the contents of the container well. Tell the students to randomly select 100 Skittles from the container. Count the number of yellow Skittles in the sample. Record the number and replace the Skittles in the container and mix again. Repeat the process 50 or 100 times. Let them know that if they get 10 or more yellow Skittles, the shipment is to be rejected. Find a 90%, 95%, and 99% confidence interval. Explain why selecting one sample to accept or reject the shipment is the standard in industry (based on your lab results).

## CONCLUSION

So, where are we? It seems as if consideration of probability and statistics in our data-rich society is a reasonable thing to do. NCTM is asking for more coverage. Common sense dictates that if one is to make informed decisions there is a need to understand when the data and their interpretation are reasonable and correct. You have probably heard, "There is a sucker born every minute." Between general statistical ignorance and lottery fever, it would appear as if that is the case. You have the opportunity to turn the tide from ignorance to understanding. What are the chances you will actually do it?

Dr. Chuck Dziuban, longtime friend and outstanding teacher of statistics, said to one of his classes: "You can't get too serious about this stuff." With that in mind, and with the knowledge of how privileged some people are to study with a truly great teacher, we offer the following list of statements that could be applied to the study of statistics. By the way, are you going to be an outstanding teacher?

"IT HAS LONG BEEN KNOWN" . . . I didn't look up the original reference.

"A DEFINITE TREND IS EVIDENT" . . . These data are practically meaningless.

"WHILE IT HAS NOT BEEN POSSIBLE TO PROVIDE DEFINITE ANSWERS TO THE QUESTIONS" . . . An unsuccessful experiment, but I still hope to get it published.

"THREE OF THE SAMPLES WERE CHOSEN FOR DETAILED STUDY" . . . The other results didn't make any sense.

"TYPICAL RESULTS ARE SHOWN" . . . This is the prettiest graph.

"THESE RESULTS WILL BE IN A SUBSEQUENT REPORT" . . . I might get around to this sometime, if pushed/funded.

"IN MY EXPERIENCE" . . . Once

"IN CASE AFTER CASE" . . . Twice

"IN A SERIES OF CASES" . . . Thrice

"IT IS BELIEVED THAT" . . . I think.

"IT IS GENERALLY BELIEVED THAT" . . . A couple of others think so, too.

"CORRECT WITHIN AN ORDER OF MAGNITUDE" . . . Wrong.

"ACCORDING TO STATISTICAL ANALYSIS" . . . Rumor has it.

"A STATISTICALLY ORIENTED PROJECTION OF THE SIGNIFICANCE OF THESE FINDINGS" . . . A wild guess.

"A CAREFUL ANALYSIS OF OBTAINABLE DATA" . . . Three pages of notes were obliterated when I knocked over a glass of water.

"IT IS CLEAR THAT MUCH ADDITIONAL WORK WILL BE REQUIRED BEFORE A COMPLETE UNDERSTANDING OF THIS PHENOMENON OCCURS" . . . I don't understand it.

"AFTER ADDITIONAL STUDY BY MY COLLEAGUES" . . . They don't understand it either.

"THANKS ARE DUE TO JOE BLOTZ FOR ASSISTANCE WITH THE EXPERIMENT AND TO CINDY ADAMS FOR VALUABLE DISCUSSIONS" . . . Mr. Blotz did the work and Ms. Adams explained to me what it meant.

"A HIGHLY SIGNIFICANT AREA FOR EXPLORATORY STUDY" . . . A totally useless topic selected by my committee.

"IT IS HOPED THAT THIS STUDY WILL STIMULATE FURTHER INVESTIGATION IN THIS FIELD" . . . I quit.

## STICKY QUESTIONS

1. Should interactive polls from website such as ESPN.com and CNN.com be used in the classroom? Are the data and results valid? Justify your reasoning.

2. You have several "Try This in Your Classroom" suggestions in this chapter. Do you think activities such as these are reasonable approaches to teaching probability or statistics in a secondary school classroom? Why or why not?

3. Have your pulse rate measured by two males and two females. You record the gender of the taker and the result. With these data, the class could determine the average pulse of males as taken by females, females as taken by males, females as taken by females, and males as taken by males. Would you expect to get different results for each group? Why or why not? What other questions could be answered with these data?

4. Some people argue that calculators and software should not be permitted in the secondary classroom. Is this a reasonable position to adopt as one considers teaching probability or statistics beyond mean, median, and mode? What position would you adopt on this issue and how would you defend your stance to colleagues, administrators, students, and parents of your students?

5. The Advanced Placement Statistics course's popularity is growing each year. If we limit the statistics taught in the secondary school to the AP course, we will be creating an elite population of statistically knowledgeable people. We assume that is not acceptable to you, so when should statistics be introduced in the curriculum and what topics should be covered?

6. When should probability be introduced in the curriculum and what topics should be covered?

7. How do you rationalize inserting things into the curriculum wherever you say it should go as you answer the last two questions?

8. Find an article that discusses untruths generated with statistics. Assuming it is safe to say that most members of our society will not be reading (and understanding) articles such as this, how do you rationalize the need to help your students, their parents, your colleagues, and your administrators become aware of such tactics?

9. We have made several comments about your lack of background in probability and statistics. How, then, can it be justified that you be asked to teach these subjects? More significantly, how can the problem be fixed?

10. Ann Landers once asked her readers "If you had it to do over again, would you have children?" A few weeks later, her column was headlined "70% OF PARENTS SAY KIDS NOT WORTH IT." Indeed 70% of the nearly 10,000 parents who wrote in said they would not have children if they could make the choice again. These data are worthless as indictors of opinion among all American parents. The people who responded felt strongly enough to take the trouble to write Ann. It is not surprising that a statistically designed opinion poll on the same issue a few months later found that 91% of parents would have children. Ann Landers announced a 70% NO result when the truth was close to 90% YES. (Yates, 1999)

## PROBLEM-SOLVING CHALLANGES

1. Your teacher displays a monthly calendar in your math class indicating birthdays of you and your fellow students. Your math class contains 25 students. What is the probability that three or more students in your math class were born in the same month?

**Check out the website for the solution.**

2. The arithmetic mean of a set of nine different positive integers is 123456789. Each number in the set contains a different number of digits with the greatest value being a nine-digit number. Find the value of each of the nine numbers.

**Check out the website for the solution.**

# ■
# LEARNING ACTIVITY

Some of the earliest mathematics books were not written to teach mathematics, they were used for something much more important—making money. The books did not discuss agriculture, industry, retail, or science. Many of the earliest mathematics books dealt with *gambling*. Trying to make money by gambling has been around for centuries. Over the years, some people used their mathematical backgrounds to better their odds at winning money. For some people, mathematics became extremely useful because they could use this science to turn a potential profit. The mathematics used in gambling is the art of mastering the odds or *probability*.

Many areas have state run lottery systems that enable adults to purchase tickets that could possibly allow them to win a great deal of money. More than likely, students only hear about the glory of potentially winning lots of money. They rarely hear about all the money that is lost. Although gambling is a forbidden action in schools, teaching probability allows the teacher to demonstrate how unlikely winning when gambling is, especially with a lottery.

## Pick Three

*Materials*:     Paper, pencil, M&M's, and the Internet.

## Activity Procedure

Begin with a lottery game that allows the student/player to select a three-digit number. We will call this game *Pick Three*.

Have each one of your students take out a pencil and a piece of paper. You will need to use a random number generator from the Internet such as Custom Random Number Generator (http://www.mathgoodies.com/calculators/random_no_custom.html) or a calculator to produce a three-digit number for the entire class to view.

Pass out 20 M&M's to each student. The M&M's will be used as the lottery money for the activity. Ask each student to place one M&M at the top of the paper and then write a three-digit number on the first line. After that, the teacher will click use the random number generator to produce a three-digit number. A student can win M&M's in *Pick Three* in two ways. First, if their number matches the random number generated exactly (in the same order), the student wins 250 M&M's. We will call this match an "Exact" win. If the student has the same three-digits as produced by the random number generator, but in different places, the payout is 50 M&M's. We will call this match a "Box" win. If the student does not match for an "Exact" or "Box" win, the wagered M&M is taken up by the teacher. Repeat this activity 20 times. You will be amazed at the results. So will your students.

Have each student answer the following questions after 20 trials.

1. How many M&M's® did you begin with?
2. How many M&M's® did you lose?
3. How many M&M's® did you win?
4. How many M&M's® did the teacher win?

## The Following Day!

The next day, try the activity again. Give each student 20 M&M's. For the first 10 trials, all students must wager one M&M's® for each trial. After ten trials, tell the students they may choose to quit playing the game and eat their remaining M&M's.

Play the game for 20 trials and have the students answer the following questions.

1. How many M&M's did you begin with?
2. How many M&M's did you lose?
3. How many M&M's did you win?
4. How many M&M's did you eat?
5. If you stopped playing the game, explain why you did so.

Use the following questions to generate a class discussion. The object is for the students to see that gambling does not pay.

1. What is the probability of matching your three-digit number exactly with the one generated by the computer? How many M&M's do you win if you match the number exactly?
2. Are the chances of winning fair for the player? Explain your reasoning?
3. What is the probability of matching your three-digit number for a "Box" win? How many M&M's do you win for a "Box" win?
4. Are the chances of winning fair for the player for a "Box" win? Explain your reasoning.
5. If a state lottery system used the probability for a *Pick Three* game, would the state risk paying out more money than it received from wagers? Explain your reasoning.
6. Does gambling pay?

The probability is the number of actual outcomes compared to the possible number of outcomes. To match the *Pick Three* number exactly, the student picks one three-digit number. There are 1000 possible outcomes from 000 to 999. You have a one in one thousand or 0.001 or 0.1% chance of matching the *Pick Three* number exactly. Therefore, the odds are one in one thousand, yet you only win 250 M&M's for your wager.

To match the three digits in any order requires some additional thought. Suppose the *Pick Three* number is 257. A winning selection would consist of 257, 275, 527, 572, 725, or 752. There are only six possible winners out of a grand total of 1000 different possible three-digit numbers or a six in one thousand or 0.006 or 0.6% chance of a "Box" win. Not a likely chance of increasing your wealth of candy considering that you win only 50 M&M's. After discussing this activity, students should become more frugal with their M&M's. More important, hopefully they will begin to understand the slim chance of winning a lottery.

## Internet Resources for This Activity

Students might be intrigued to view the Florida State Lottery version of Pick Three titled Cash 3. The following link provides the reader with specific directions and odds for an "Exact" and "Box" win along with six additional winning possibilities. Hopefully, your students will carefully look at the odds and payouts.

http://www.flalottery.com/inet/games-cash3Main.do

Mega Millions is the eleven state mega-jackpot lottery game in the United States. You can play Mega Millions in Georgia, Illinois, Maryland, Massachusetts, Michigan, New Jersey, New York, Ohio, Texas, Virginia, and Washington. Jackpots begin at $10 million and can roll into hundreds of millions of dollars each week. In July 2004, a person in Massachusetts won and estimated $290 million dollars. The idea of winning millions of dollars excites everyone. By visiting the Mega Millions website, students can see that the chance of winning the jackpot is 1 in 175,711,536.

http://www.megamillions.com/howto/

# References

Abbot, E.A. (1963). *Flatland: A romance of many dimensions*. New York, NY: Barnes & Noble.

About the standards. (n.d.). Retrieved from http://www.corestandards.org/about-the-standards

Adler, I. (1972). *Readings in mathematics*. Lexington, MA: Ginn.

Allendoerfer, C.B., & Oakley, C.O. (1955). *Principles of mathematics*. New York, NY: McGraw-Hill.

American Mathematical Association of Two-Year Colleges. (1995). *Crossroads in mathematics: Standards for introductory college mathematics before calculus* (p. 15). Memphis, TN: Author.

Barbin, E. (1994). The meanings of mathematical proof: On relations between history and mathematical education. In J.M. Anthony (Ed.), *Eyes' circles* (pp. 41–52). Washington, DC: Mathematical Association of America, Notes Number 34.

Beck, A., Bleicher, M.N., & Crowe, D.W. (1969). *Excursions into mathematics*. New York, NY: Worth.

Becker, H.J. (1986). Instructional use of computers. *Reports from the 1985 National Survey, 1*, 1–9. Baltimore, MD: Johns Hopkins University, Center for Social Organization of Schools.

Begle, E.G. (1973). Some lessons learned by SMSG. *Mathematics Teacher, 66*, 207–214.

Bell, M.S. (1970). *Studies with respect to the uses of mathematics in secondary school curricula* (Doctoral dissertation). Dissertation Abstracts International, 30A, 3813–3814.

Beyer, F.S., & Dusewicz, R.A. (1991, March). *Impact of computer-managed instruction on small rural schools*. Paper presented at the annual meeting of the American Educational Research Association, Chicago, IL.

Bitter, G.G. (1970, August). *The effects of computer applications on achievement in a college introductory calculus course*. Paper presented at the annual meeting of the American Educational Research Association, New York, NY.

Bloom, B.S., Hastings, J.T., & Madaus, G.F. (1971). *Handbook on formative and summative evaluation of student learning*. New York, NY: McGraw-Hill.

Blume, G.W., & Heid, M.K. (2008). The role of research, theory, and practice in the integration of technology in mathematics teaching and learning. In *Research on Technology and the Teaching and Learning of Mathematics: Volume 2. Cases and Perspectives* (pp. 449–464), Reston, VA: National Council of Teachers of Mathematics.

Brown, J.S., Collins, A., & Duguid, R. (1989, January/February). Situated cognition and the culture of learning. *Educational Researcher, 18*(1), 32–42.

Bruder, I. (1993, March). Redefining science. *Electronic Learning, 12*(6), 20–29.

Brumbaugh, D. (1994, November). Moving triangles move students. *CONSORTIUM, The Newsletter of the Consortium for Mathematics and Its Applications*. Lexington, MA: Comap, Inc.

Brumbaugh, D. (1994). *Scratch your brain where it itches. Book D-1 Algebra: Math games, tricks & quick activities.* Pacific Grove, CA: Critical Thinking Press & Software.

Brumbaugh, D. (1997, May). *Algebra in the K–14 curriculum conference.* Washington, DC: Attendee.

Brumbaugh, D., & Rock, D. (1997). *Activities for the FX-7400 mini graph calculator.* Orlando, FL: Paragon Publications.

Brunbaum, B., & Shephard, G.C. (1993). Pick's theorem. *The Mathematical Monthly, 100*(2), 150–161.

Burton, D.M. (1985). *The history of mathematics: An introduction.* New York, NY: Allyn & Bacon.

Burton, D.M. (1995). *The history of mathematics: An introduction* (2nd ed.). Boston, MA: Allyn & Bacon.

Calculator policy. (n.d.). Retrieved from http://www.collegeboard.com/student/testing/ap/calculus_ab/calc.html.

Causey, M. (1995). *A study of the relationship between summer school courses and SAT-Mathematics scores* (Doctoral dissertation). University of Central Florida, Orlando, FL.

Chakerian, G.D., Crabill, C.D., & Sherman, K.S. (1987). *Geometry: A guided inquiry.* Pleasantville, NY: Sunburst Communications.

Clayton, M. (1999, November 9). The calculator effect. *Christian Science Monitor.*

Clements, D.H., Sarama, J., Yelland, N.J., & Glass, B. (2008). Learning and teaching geometry with computers in elementary and middle school. In M.K. Heid & G.W. Blume (Eds.), *Research on Technology and the Teaching and Learning of Mathematics: Volume 1. Research Syntheses* (pp. 109–154). New York: Information Age Publishing, Inc.

Cobb, R., & Steffe, L.P. (1983). The constructivist researcher as teacher and model builder. *Journal for Research in Mathematics Education, 14*(2), 82–94.

Coffin, G.C. (1987, February). *Computers as a tool in SAT preparation.* Paper presented at the annual Florida Instructional Computing Conference, Orlando, FL.

Cozzens, M. (1989). From the editor's desk. Lexington, MA: Consortium.

Crosswhite, J.F. (1986). Better teaching, better mathematics: Are they enough? *Arithmetic Teacher, 34*(2), 54–59.

Crouse, R.J., & Sloyer, C.W. (1977). *Mathematical questions from the classroom.* Boston, MA: Prindie, Webber & Schmidt.

Cummings, F. (1995). Equity in reforming mathematics and science education. *The Common Denominator, 1*(3), 1–2.

Cutler, A. (1960). *The Trachtenberg speed system of basic mathematics.* Garden City, NY: Doubleday.

Davidson, N. (1985). Small-group learning and teaching in mathematics: A selective review of the research. In R. Slavin, S. Sharan, S. Kagan, R. Lazarowitz, C. Webb, & R. Schmuck (Eds.), *Learning to cooperate, cooperating to learn* (pp. 211–230). New York, NY: Plenum.

DeTemple, D., & Robertson, J. (1974). The equivalence of Euler's and Pick's theorem. *The Mathematics Teacher, 67*(3), 222–226.

Disney, W. (1959). *Donald Duck in Mathmagic Land.* Hollywood, CA: Walt Disney Productions.

Driscoll, M.R. (1994). *Psychology of learning for instruction.* Needham Heights, MA: Allyn & Bacon.

Educational Testing Service. (1970). *ETS developments.* Princeton, NJ: Author.

Educational Testing Service, Cooperative Test Division. (1957). *Sequential tests of educational progress, Form 3A.* Princeton, NJ: Author.

Escher, M.C. (1993). *New Grolier Multimedia Encyclopedia.* Release 6.

Esler, W.K., & Sciortino, P. (1991). *Methods for teaching: An overview of current practices.* Raleigh, NC: Contemporary.

Eves, H. (1964). *An introduction to the history of mathematics* (Rev. ed.). New York, NY: Holt, Rinehart and Winston.

Eves, H. (1967). *An introduction to the history of mathematics* (Rev. ed.). New York, NY: Holt, Rinehart & Winston.

Eves, H. (1990). *An introduction to the history of mathematics.* New York, NY: Sanders College.

Ewing, D. E. (1996, February). *Demonstrating Sketchpad*. Oral presentation at NCTM Regional Conference, Rapid City, SD.

Fair, J., & Bragg, S. C. (1993). *Algebra 1*. Englewood Cliffs, NJ: Prentice-Hall.

Fennema, E., & Peterson, R. L. (1986). Teacher–student interactions and sex-related differences in learning mathematics. *Teaching and Teacher Education, 2*(1), 1–2.

Ferrell, B. G. (1985, March). *Computer immersion project: Evaluating the impact of computers on learning*. Paper presented at the annual meeting of the American Educational Research Association, Chicago, IL.

Fey, J. (1980). Mathematics education research on curriculum and instruction. In R. J. Shumway (Ed.), *Research in mathematics education* (pp. 388–432). Reston, VA: National Council of Teachers of Mathematics.

Fisher, C. W., Berliner, D. C., Filby, N. N., Marhave, R., Ghen, L. S., & Dishaw, M. M. (1980). Teaching behaviors, academic learning time, and student achievement: An overview. In C. Denham & A. Lieberman (Eds.), *Time to learn* (p. 176). Washington, DC: National Institute of Education.

Flanders, J. R. (1987, September). How much of the content in mathematics textbooks is new? *Arithmetic Teacher, 35*(1), 1–23.

Ferguson, H. (1994). *News bulletin*. Reston, VA: National Council of Teachers of Mathematics.

Froelich, G. W., Bartkovich, K. G., & Forrester, P. A. (1991). *Curriculum and evaluation standards for school mathematics*. Reston, VA: NCTM.

Funk & Wagnalls. (1968). *Standard college dictionary* (Text ed.). New York, NY: Harcourt Brace.

Funkhouser, C., & Dennis, J. R. (1992). The effects of problem-solving software on problem-solving ability. *Journal of Research on Computing in Education, 24*(3), 338–347.

Horn, C. L., & Silva, E. M. (Codirectors). (1994). *UC Davis Calculus Revitalization Project*. Davis, CA: Department of Mathematics, University of California.

Hynes, M. C., & Brumbaugh, D. K. (1976). *Mathematics activities handbook for grades 5–12*. West Nyack, NY: Parker.

Gamow, G. (1961). *One, two, three . . . infinity* (Rev. ed.). New York, NY: Viking.

Geliert, W., Kustner, H., Hellwich, M., & Kastner, H. (1977). *VNR concise encyclopedia of mathematics*. New York, NY: Van Nostrand Reinhold.

Gellert, W., Kustner, H., Heliwich, M., & Kustner, H. (1977). *The VNR concise encyclopedia of mathematics*. New York, NY: Van Nostrand Reinhold.

Gershman, J., & Sakamoto, E. (1981). Computer-assisted remediation and evaluation: A CAI project for Ontario secondary schools. *Educational Technology, 1*(3), 40–43.

"Golden section." (1993). In Microsoft Encarta. Funk & Wagnall's Corporation.

Grady, M. T. (1970). *Computer solution* (Unpublished undergraduate assignment). University of Central Florida (Florida Technological University at that time). Orlando, FL.

Grouws, D. A. (Ed.). (1992). *Handbook of research on mathematics teaching and learning*. New York, NY: Macmillan.

Gullberg, J. (1997). *Mathematics: From the birth of numbers*. New York, NY: Norton.

Hart, L. E. (1989). Classroom processes, sex of student, and confidence in learning mathematics. *Journal for Research in Mathematics Education, 20*(3), 242–260.

Hatfield, L. L. (1969). *Computer-assisted mathematics: An investigation of the effectiveness of the computer used as a tool to learn mathematics* (Doctoral dissertation). Available from Dissertation Abstracts International, 30(10), 4329A. (University Microfilm No. 7005569)

Heid, M. K. (1988). Resequencing skills and concepts in applied calculus using the computer as a tool. *Journal for Research in Mathematics Education, 19*(1), 3–25.

Heid, M. K. & Blume, G. W. (2008) Technology and the development of algebraic understanding. In *Research on Technology and the Teaching and Learning of Mathematics: Volume 1. Research Syntheses* (pp. 55–108). New York: Information Age Publishing, Inc.

Hollowell, K. A., & Duch, B. J. (1991, April). *Functions and statistics with computers at the college level*. Paper presented at the annual conference of the American Educational Research Association, Chicago, IL.

Hotard, S.R., & Cortez, M.J. (1983). *Computer assisted instruction as an enhancer of remediation*. Lafayette Parish, LA: The Title I Program.

Johnson, D.C., Cox, M.J., & Watson, D.M. (1994). Evaluating the impact of IT on pupil's achievement. *Journal of Computer Assisted Learning, 10*(3), 138–156.

Johnson, D.W. (1981). Effects of cooperative, competitive and individualistic goal structures on achievement: A meta-analysis. *Psychological Bulletin, 89*(1), 47–62.

Keedy, M.L., Bittinger, M.L., Smith, S.A., & Nelson, C.W. (1986). *Informal geometry*. Menlo Park, CA: Addison-Wesley.

Key points in mathematics. (n.d.). Retrieved from http://www.corestandards.org/about-the-standards/key-points-in-mathematics.

Kidd, K.P., Myers, S.S., & Cilley, D.M. (1970). *The laboratory approach to mathematics*. Chicago, IL: Science Research Associates.

Kitabchi, G. (1987, November). *Evaluation of the Apple classroom of tomorrow*. Paper presented at the annual meeting of the Mid-South Educational Research Association, Mobile, AL.

Koehler, M.S. (1986). *Effective mathematics teaching and sex-related differences in Algebra I classes* (Doctoral dissertation). Available from Dissertation Abstracts International, 46, 2953A.

Koscinski, S.T., & Gast, D.L. (1993). Computer-assisted instruction with constant time delay to teach multiplication facts to students with learning disabilities. *Learning Disabilities Research and Practice, 8*(3), 157–168.

Krulick, S., & Rudnick, J.A. (1987). *Problem solving: A handbook for teachers* (2nd ed.). Boston, MA: Allyn & Bacon.

Kysilka, M.L. (1990, November). *Gender assignments in Algebra I textbooks*. Paper presented at the International Conference on History and Gender in Education, Prague, Czechoslovakia.

Lakatos, I. (1976). *Proofs and refutations*. Cambridge, England: Cambridge University Press.

Lang, W.S. (1987, March). *Analysis of the effects of the computer enhanced classroom on the*

*achievement of remedial high school math students*. Paper presented at the annual meeting of the American Educational Research Association, Washington, DC.

Leach, E.L. (1992). An alternative form of evaluation that complies with NCTM Standards. *Mathematics Teacher, 85*(8), 628–632.

Leiva, M. (1994). *Mathematics examples from the classroom*. Paper presented at the NCTM Regional Conference, Charleston, WV.

Loomis, E.S. (1963). *The Pythagorean proposition*. Reston, VA: NCTM.

Madaus, G.F., Arasian, R W., & Kellaghan, T. (1980). *School effectiveness: A review of the evidence*. New York, NY: McGraw-Hill.

Mason, M.T. (1994). *A longitudinal study of the effects of computer assisted instruction on the mathematics achievement of the learning of disabled and educable mentally retarded* (Doctoral dissertation). Dissertation Abstracts International, 45(09), 2791A. (University Microfilms No. 8429270)

Massachusetts Curriculum Frameworks. (2011). Retrieved from http://www.doe.mass.edu/frameworks/current.html.

"Math." (2012). http://dictionary.reference.com/browse/mathematics

Mathematical Sciences Education Board. (1989). *Everybody counts: A report to the nation on the future of mathematics education*. Washington, DC: National Academy Press.

Mathematical Sciences Education Board. (1990). *Reshaping school mathematics: A philosophy and framework for curriculum*. Washington, DC: National Academy Press.

Mathematical Sciences Education Board. (1991). *Counting on you*. Washington, DC: National Academy Press.

Mathematical Sciences Education Board. (1993). *Measuring what counts: A conceptual guide for mathematics assessment*. Washington, DC: National Academy Press.

Mathematics. (2005). In *The American Heritage New Dictionary of Cultural Literacy* (3rd ed.). Retrieved from http://www.Dictionary.reference.com

*Mathematics education: Wellspring of U.S. industrial strength. Report of the Wellspring Symposium*. (1988, December 15–16). Irvine, CA:

ERIC Document Reproduction Service No. ED 338 498)

McConnell, B. B. (1983). *Evaluation of computer assisted instruction in math (final report).* Pasco, WA: Pasco School District.

McCoy, L. P. (1990, February). *Does the "Supposer" improve problem solving in geometry?* Paper presented at the annual meeting of the Eastern Educational Research Association, Clearwater, FL.

McKinney, J. R., professor of Mathematics, California Polytechnic State University of Pomona. (1975, January 5). As quoted in *The New York Times*, Section IV, p. 7.

McKnight, C. C., Crosswhite, J. F., Dossey, J. A., Kifer, E., Swafford, J. O., Travers, K. J., & Cooney, T. J. (1987). *The underachieving curriculum: Assessing U.S. school mathematics from an international perspective.* Champaign, IL: Stipes.

Messerly, C. (1986). The use of computer-assisted instruction in facilitating the acquisition of math skills with hearing-impaired high school students. *Volta Review, 88*(2), 66–77.

Microsoft Corporation. (1994). Encarta. Redmond, WA: Author.

"MIDI." (2012). Dictionary. com. http://dictionary. reference.com/browse/MIDI?s=t.

Montessori, M. (1967). *The discovery of the child.* New York, NY: Ballantine.

Moore, D. S. (1997). *The basic practice of statistics.* New York, NY: Freeman.

Mullis, I. V. S., Dossey, J. A., Owen, E. H., & Phillips, G. W. (1991). *The state of mathematics achievement: NAEP's 1990 assessment of the nation and the trial assessment of the states.* Washington, DC: U.S. Government Printing Office.

National Advisory Committee on Mathematical Education. (1975). *Overview and analysis of school mathematics in grades K–12.* Washington, DC: Conference Board of Mathematical Sciences.

National Council of Teachers of Mathematics. (1989). *Curriculum and evaluation standards for school mathematics.* Reston, VA: Author.

National Council of Teachers of Mathematics. (1991). *Professional standards for teaching mathematics.* Reston, VA: Author.

National Council of Teachers of Mathematics. (1995a). *Addenda series.* Reston, VA: Author.

National Council of Teachers of Mathematics. (1995b). *Assessment standards for teaching mathematics.* Reston, VA: Author.

National Council of Teachers of Mathematics. (1995c, January). *NCTM News Bulletin.* Reston, VA: Author.

National Center for Education Statistics. (1998, February). *Issue brief: Internet access in public schools (NCES 98–031).* Washington, DC: Author.

National Council of Teachers of Mathematics. (2000). *Principles and standards for school mathematics.* Reston, VA: Author.

National Council of Teachers of Mathematics. (2008). *Linking research & practice: The NCTM research agenda conference report.* Reston, VA: Author.

National Council of Teachers of Mathematics. (2010). *Curriculum focal points for grades prekindergarten through grade 8.* Reston, VA: Author.

National Council of Teachers of Mathematics. (2011). *Report of the joint task force on common core state standards.* Reston, VA: Author.

National Research Council. (1990). *Reshaping school mathematics: A philosophy and framework for curriculum.* Washington, DC: National Academy Press.

National Research Council. (2001). *Adding it up: Helping children learn mathematics.* Washington, DC: National Academy Press.

Newman, J. R. (1956). *The world of mathematics* (Vol. 1). New York, NY: Simon & Schuster.

Nichols, E. D. (1970). *Pre-algebra mathematics* (Rev ed.). New York, NY: Holt, Rinehart & Winston.

Nomeland, R. E., & Harris, R. (1976, August). *Computer assisted instruction at Kendell Demonstration Elementary School.* Paper presented at the Association for the Development of Computer Based Instructional Systems summer conference, Minneapolis, MN.

O'Callaghan, B. R. (1998). Computer-intensive algebra and students' conceptual knowledge of functions. *Journal for Research in Mathematics Education, 29*(1), 21–40.

Ohio Department of Education, Ohio Council of Teachers of Mathematics, and Ohio Section of the Mathematical Association of America. (1984). Secondary Math Monograph Series, 2, 5.

Ortiz, E. and Popovich, A. (2005). Solving a volume problem using the Geometer's Sketchpad. *ON-Math: Online Journal of School Mathematics, 3*(2).

Palmitter, J.R. (1991). Effects of computer algebra systems on concept and skill acquisition in calculus. *Journal for Research in Mathematics Education, 22*(2), 151–156.

Paulos, J.A. (1988). *Innumeracy: Mathematical illiteracy and its consequences.* New York, NY: Hill & Wang.

Perkins, D.N. (1991, September). What constructivism demands of the learner. *Educational Researcher, 58,* 19–21.

Petrella, G. (1999). Statistics knowledge baseline. *Mathematics Teacher, 92*(8), 657, 681.

Phillips, E. (Chair). (1995). *The algebra working group: A framework for constructing a vision of algebra* (working draft). Reston, VA: National Council of Teachers of Mathematics.

Polya, G. (1973). *How to solve it* (2nd ed.). Princeton, NJ: Princeton University Press.

Porter, A.C., Floden, R.F., Freeman, D.J., Schmidt, W.H., & Schwille, J.R. (1986). *Content determinants (with research instrumentation appendices).* East Lansing, MI: Michigan State University, Institute for Research on Teaching.

Rappaport, J. (1999, December). *The algebra times.* Retrieved from http://www.mathkits. com/news. html.

Roberts, A.W. (1993). Introduction resources for calculus collection. In A.E. Solow (Ed.), *Resources for calculus collection* (pp. vii–viii). Washington, DC: Mathematical Association of America.

Rock, D., & Brumbaugh, D. (1997). *Problem solving with the CFX-9850G/9850Ga PLUS color graphing calculator.* Goldenrod, FL: Paragon Publications.

Rosenshine, B. (1985). Direct instruction. In T. Husen & T.N. Postlethwaite (Eds.), *International Encyclopedia of Education* (Vol. 3, pp. 1395–1400). Oxford, England: Pergamon.

Rosskopf, M.F. (1970). *The teaching of secondary school mathematics: Thirty-third yearbook.* Reston, VA: National Council of Teachers of Mathematics.

Rubillo, J. (1994). Probability and statistics from life. Boise, ID: National Council of Teachers of Mathematics Regional Conference.

Rumsey, D. (1999). Cooperative teaching opportunities for introductory statistics teachers. *Mathematics Teacher, 92*(8), 734–737.

Salem, J.R. (1989). *Using LOGO and BASIC to teach mathematics to fifth and sixth-graders* (Doctoral dissertation). Dissertation Abstracts International, 50(05), 1242A. (University Microfilms No. 8914935)

Sasser, J.E. (1991). The effect of using computer tutorials as homework assignments on the mathematics achievement of elementary education majors. *Journal of Computers in Mathematics and Science Teaching, 10*(2), 95–102.

Saunders, H. (1991). *When are we ever gonna have to use this?* Palo Alto, CA: Dale Seymour.

Saunders, H. (1993). *When are we ever gonna have to use this?* Palo Alto, CA: Dale Seymour.

Saxon, J., & Hake, S. (1992). *Math 76: An incremental developmental.* Norman, OK: Author.

Scher, D. (1995). *Exploring conic sections with the Geometer's Sketchpad.* Berkeley, CA: Key Curriculum.

Seever, M. (1992). *Achievement and enrollment evaluation of the Central Computers Unlimited Magnet Middle School 1990–1991.* Kansas City, MO: Kansas City School District.

Serra, M. (1994). *Patty Paper geometry.* Berkeley, CA: Key Curriculum.

Serra, M. (1997). *Discovering geometry: An inductive approach* (2nd ed.). Berkeley, CA: Key Curriculum.

Shaughnessy, J., & Zawojewski, J. (1999). Secondary students' performance on data and chance in the 1996 NAEP. *Mathematics Teacher, 92*(8), 713–718.

Shaw, K.L. (1995, February). *Fibonacci numbers.* Birmingham, AL: NCTM Regional Conference.

Sigurdson, S.E., & Olson, A.T. (1983). *Utilization of microcomputers in elementary mathematics (final report).* Edmonton, Canada: Alberta Department of Education.

Shanker, A. (1995, July). A.F.T. decries lack of standards, "Gateway" exam. *Education Week, 7.*

Shulman, L. S. (1986). Those who understand: Knowledge growth in teaching. *Educational Researcher, 15*(2), 4–14.

Shulte, A. P., & Peterson, R. E. (1978). *Preparing to use algebra*. River Forest, IL: Laidlaw Brothers.

Spano, N. (1985, October). *Twiddle*. Paper presented at National Council of Teachers of Mathematics Regional Conference, Orlando, FL.

Steen, L. A. (Ed.). (1994). *For all practical purposes: Introduction to contemporary mathematics* (3rd ed.). New York, NY: Freeman.

Steen, L. A. (September 1989). *"Teaching Mathematics for Tomorrow's World." Educational Leadership* 47, 1: 18–22.

Steffe, L. P., & Killion, K. (1986, July). Mathematics teaching: A specification in a constructionist frame of reference. In L. Burton & C. Hoyles (Eds.), *Proceedings of the Tenth International Conference, Psychology of Mathematics Education* (pp. 207–216). London, England: University of London Institute of Education.

Stein, S. K. (1975). *Mathematics, the man made universe* (3rd ed.). San Francisco, CA: Freeman.

Suydam, M. (1985). Questions? *Arithmetic Teacher, 32*(6), 18.

Thorndike, E. L. (1924a). Mental discipline in high school studies. *Journal of Educational Psychology, 15*, 1–22.

Thorndike, E. L. (1924b). Mental discipline in high school studies. *Journal of Educational Psychology, 15*, 83–98.

Thelen, H. A. (1963). Grouping for teachability. *Theory Into Practice, 2*, 81–89.

Todhunter, J. M. (1975). Cipher in the snow. *Today's Education, 64*(2), 66–67.

Tucker, A. C., & Leitzel, J. R. (1995). *Assessing calculus reform efforts, A report to the community*. Washington, DC: Mathematical Association of America.

U.S. Department of Education. (1991). *America 2000: An education strategy*. Washington, DC: Author. (ERIC Document Reproduction Service No. ED 327 009)

Usiskin, Z. (1987). Why elementary algebra can, should, and must be an eighth-grade course for average students. *Mathematics Teacher, 80*(6), 42–38.

van Hiele, P. M. (1986). *Structure and insight: A theory of mathematics education*. Orlando, FL: Academic Press.

Varberg, D. E. (1985). Pick's theorem revisited. *The Mathematical Monthly, 92*(8) 584–587.

Watkins, A. (1997). *The College Board Advanced Placement Program Teacher's Guide—AP Statistics*. Northridge, CA: California State University.

Wetherbe, C. G. (1989). *The effectiveness of computer-assisted instruction integrated with a spreadsheet as an instructional tool for teaching quantitative concepts* (Doctoral dissertation). Dissertation Abstracts International, 50(11), 3455A. (University Microfilms No. 9008303)

What Are Curriculum Focal Points?" (n.d.). Retrieved from http://nctm.org/standards/content.aspx?id=264

Wilson, J. W., Cahen, L. S., & Begle, E. G. (Eds.). (1968). *Z-Population test batteries (NLSMA Rep. No. 3)*. Stanford, CA: School Mathematics Study Group.

Wood, J. B. (1991). *An investigation of the effects of tutorial and tool applications of computer-based education on achievement and attitude in secondary mathematics* (Doctoral dissertation). Dissertation Abstracts International, 52(06), 2118A. (University Microfilms No. 9132517)

Wright, P. A. (1983). *A study of computer assisted instruction for remediation in mathematics on the secondary level* (Doctoral dissertation). Dissertation Abstracts International, 45(04), 1063A. (University Microfilms No. 8412629)

Yates, D. S., Moore, D. S., & McCabe, G. P. (1999). *The practice of statistics: TI-83 graphing calculator enhanced*. New York, NY: Freeman.

Yusuf, M. M. (1991, October). *LOGO based instruction in geometry*. Paper presented at the annual meeting of the Mid-Western Educational Research Association, Chicago, IL.

# Index

# About the Authors

## DOUGLAS K. BRUMBAUGH
### (1939–2010)

Doug was the ultimate teacher. He taught college, in-service, or K–12 almost daily. He received his B.S. from Adrian College, and went on to the University of Georgia for his masters and doctorate. As he would talk with others about teaching and learning in the K–12 environment, his immersion in teaching was always beneficial and apparent. He spoke from real experiences. Students change, classroom environment changes, the curriculum changes—and Doug changed over the years. He adapted, improved, and continued to grow. The thoughts and examples in this book are based on his experiences as a teacher. As Doug stated, "Classroom-tested success stories are the ideas, materials, and situations you will read about and do. This text's problems and activities will stretch you while providing a beginning collection of classroom ideas. Learn, expand your horizons, and teach!"

## DAVID ROCK

I wake up every morning with the desire to go to work. The greatest feeling in the world is seeing the haze of math anxiety fade from a scared face, whether it is young or old. I teach kids the power of mathematics and grown-ups the excitement of mathematics education. Teachers must have an open mind and an eagerness to change. Students, classroom environments, curriculum, technology, and educational philosophy all change with every passing year. Teachers must also be willing to change. We must be reflective: What can I do to effectively teach the learners around me? Kids come to school at a young age, eager and excited about learning. We must foster and nurture this desire to learn at all ages, especially in the early years. I received my B.S. degree from Vanderbilt University and later received my master's and doctorate from the University of Central Florida; I am presently the dean of the School of Education at the University of Mississippi. I hope the real-life stores and activities, along with the infusion of technology in the book, build in you the excitement Doug and I share for mathematics and mathematics education.